Management Concepts and Canadian Practice

Frederick A. Starke
University of Manitoba

R. Wayne Mondy
Northeast Louisiana University

Robert E. Holmes
Southwest Texas State University

Edwin B. Flippo
The University of Arizona

Allyn and Bacon, Publishers
Toronto • Boston • London • Sydney

Managing Editor: Dennis Bockus

Editor: Susan Quirk

Designer: Pronk & Associates

Typesetter: Q Composition Inc.

Printer: John Deyell

Cover photo: © Gabe Palmer/The Image Bank Canada

Photos of John Evans, page 56; William Dimma, page 336; Michael Cowpland, page 416; and Robert White, page 584 courtesy of Canapress Photo Service

Photo of Edwin Mirvish, page 382, courtesy of The Globe and Mail, Toronto

Canadian Cataloguing in Publication Data

Main entry under title:
Management concepts and Canadian practice

Includes bibliographical references and index.
ISBN 0-205-08554-7

1. Management—Canada. I. Starke, Frederick A.

HD31.M36 1985   658.4   C85-098289-8

Printed in Canada

89 88 87 86 85   1 2 3 4 5 6 7

Preface

In developing *Management Concepts and Canadian Practice*, the author, Fred Starke, began with an excellent text written by R. Wayne Mondy, Robert Holmes, and Edwin Flippo and revised it for use by Canadian students. In some chapters dealing with such universally applicable concepts as planning, organizing, and controlling, it was possible to retain the theoretical ideas and to supplement them with Canadian illustrations. In other chapters — for example, the environment external to business, staffing, and management by objectives — it was necessary to make substantial revisions in order to capture the essence of the Canadian management scene. In all chapters, material is included which conveys to students how management is practiced in Canada.

This book is written for students who want management theory to be linked with practice. Although it is pragmatic in its approach, the text is balanced throughout with current management theory. The objective in this first Canadian edition is to convey to students the importance and the excitement of being a manager.

The text is organized into 6 major parts. Part I, Introduction, discusses the concept of management and introduces the idea of management functions. It describes the environment external to managers' organizations and how the uncertainty created by this environment affects managers. Part II, Planning and Decision Making, describes the first basic function of management. It also contains a detailed treatment of Management by Objectives at a large Canadian company. Part III, Organizing, introduces the concept and variations of organizational structure. It includes a discussion of the importance of the informal organization and organization politics. Part IV, Influencing, stresses the people aspect of the manager's job. Included in this section are chapters on motivation; leadership; communication and conflict; and organization culture, change, and development. Part V, Controlling, indicates the importance of ensuring that plans actually become reality. The basic controlling process is introduced and several controlling techniques that managers can use are presented. Part VI, Situational Applications, deals with circumstances that require particular managerial skills; included in this section are chapters on small business, international business, and corporate social responsibility and business ethics.

Each chapter contains a variety of features designed to stimulate student interest and understanding of the field of management. These features include:

Opening Incident   Each chapter begins with a realistic incident that deals with a specific management problem that relates directly to the material presented in the chapter. Students are encouraged to suggest a solution.

Opening Incident Revisited   At the end of each chapter the opening incident is reviewed and analyzed, using the material presented in the chapter. Students can compare their own solution formulated before reading the chapter.

Key Terms   The list of key terms identifies important terms in the chapter and helps to build the students' management vocabulary. Within each chapter, the key terms appear in boldface in the text and are defined in the glossary.

Learning Objectives   Each chapter outlines a set of objectives to help students anticipate the important points that will be made in the chapter. Once students have finished reading a chapter, they can return to the objectives to determine how well they have mastered the material in the chapter.

Talking to Managers   Each chapter contains an interview with a practicing manager. These managers, ranging from comapny presidents to first-line supervisors, are asked specific questions about how they carry out the functions of management.

Summary   The material in the chapter is briefly summarized. While not a substitute for reading the chapter, the summary does help to recall its main points.

Review Questions   The questions at the end of the chapter relate directly to the chapter's factual material. They encourage students to recall specific facts from the chapter and to analyze the issues that these facts may raise.

Exercises   Two or three exercises are presented at the end of each chapter. These exercises require students to talk to practicing managers or to put themselves in the position of a practicing manager and then conduct a small project that relates to the material in the chapter.

Case Studies   Each chapter contains two short case studies. These describe situations and problems that can be analyzed using the material in the chapter. At the end of each case, questions guide students in their analysis. The realistic orientation of the cases helps students to build their analytical skills.

Management in Practice Inserts   Each chapter contains several inserts that illustrate management in practice by describing a specific situation in an actual Canadian company.

Included at the end of the text are 9 comprehensive case studies. These cases are considerably more detailed than those found at the end of each chapter, and they generally raise several issues that are important to managers. These cases further build student analytical skills and they convey to the student the complicated nature of managerial work.

All these features are designed to enhance student interest and to provide students with an enjoyable learning experience. Numerous realistic situations are used as models in the text. We believe that certain managerial topics are easier to explain if the writers have had managerial experience; we hope the managerial experience of the authors has added a touch of realism to the book. Our sincere desire is that the reader is stimulated by the text and, therefore, will choose to go into one of the most challenging and rewarding careers possible — management.

Acknowledgements

I owe special thanks to the managing editor, Dennis Bockus, at Allyn and Bacon, to the editor, Susan Quirk, and to the proofreader, Judith Gulyas, for their dedicated efforts toward helping me complete this text. Special thanks go to Diana Sokolowski for her help in the preparation of the manuscript.

The following people helped by reviewing the text material. Their comments were gratefully received, carefully read, and implemented wherever possible.

Olga L. Crocker, University of Windsor
Lorne A. Fingarson, British Columbia Institute of Technology
Brian Harrocks, Algonquin College
Jim Mason, University of Regina
John Redston, Red River Community College
Elizabeth Reid, consultant
William J. Riddell, Seneca College
Garry E. Veak, Southern Alberta Institute of Technology
William C. Wedley, Simon Fraser University

Contents

PART I   INTRODUCTION   1

PART III   ORGANIZING   175

CHAPTER 7 | AUTHORITY, RESPONSIBILITY, AND ORGANIZATIONAL STRUCTURE 202

PART IV   INFLUENCING   311

PART V   CONTROLLING 467

Introduction

1

Management

Lawton Manufacturing Ltd.

Marshall Cizek graduated from high school 10 years ago and immediately went to work as a maintenance mechanic for Lawton Manufacturing Ltd. The maintenance department, comprised of 8 people, was responsible for routine maintenance and repairing factory machinery. Cizek liked his job, got along with his colleagues, and considered himself happy. In the past year, however, he had begun to think about a promotion. Graham Tonks, the plant superintendent often praised Cizek's work and his cooperative attitudes. This spring, when the head of the maintenance department left Lawton for another position, Tonks appointed Cizek to replace him.

Cizek energetically threw himself into this new job. He wanted to make his department the most efficient in the entire plant. He came to work early, stayed late, and became a dominating presence in the maintenance area. He continued his technical interests in the machinery, often doing repairs himself. He disliked paperwork, so he spent most of his time in the plant, dealing with what he called "problems on the firing line."

After several months as head of maintenance, Cizek was called into the plant superintendent's office for a talk. Tonks began by asking Cizek why his reports were always late and often incomplete. Tonks went on to state that he was concerned about growing inefficiency in the maintenance area. In Tonks's opinion, Cizek was not giving proper leadership either to maintenance and repair or to the people in his department. Tonks noted that several maintenance workers had complained about Cizek's meddling in the technical details of their work. The superintendent was sympathetic, saying that he had high regard for Cizek's technical skills; but Tonks reminded Cizek that he was now a manager and, unless Cizek could begin to manage the maintenance department more productively, he would have to be replaced.

Cizek left work that day feeling dispirited. That evening he played softball with some friends; after the game, he talked over his problem with Jim, one of his close friends. After listening to Cizek for about half an hour, Jim said: "You know, Marshall, a baseball player can't play every position on the team."

KEY TERMS

business firm
profit
sole proprietorship
partnership
corporation
shareholder
common stock
preferred stock
board of directors
corporation bylaws
not-for-profit
  organization
management
planning

organizing
influencing or
  directing
controlling
lower-level managers
middle managers
top management
coordination
interpersonal role
informational role
decisional role
technical skill
communication
  skills

people skills
analytical skills
decision-making skill
conceptual skills
classical school of
  management
scientific
  management
behavioral school of
  management
Hawthorne effect
behavioral
  management
science

LEARNING OBJECTIVES

After completing this chapter you should be able to
1. Define and describe management and explain the work of managers.
2. Relate the importance of service industries in the economy.
3. Identify the forms of business ownership.
4. Identify and describe the management functions of planning, organizing, influencing, and controlling.
5. Explain the managerial roles — interpersonal, informational, and decisional — and the important managerial skills — technical, communications, people, analytical, decision-making, and conceptual.
6. Describe the classical and behavioral schools of management.
7. Identify and describe the various schools or approaches to the study of management.

Did you know that almost half of all new Canadian businesses fail in the first 4 years of operation and that over 60 percent fail within the first 6 years of operation?[1] In over 75 percent of these cases, managerial incompetence and inexperience are the cause of the failure. The costs of poor management to individuals and to Canada's economic stability are great. Not only are financial and physical resources wasted when businesses fail, but individuals often suffer psychological damage. Clearly, business failure can be avoided through good management practices: a reason why management is a subject of increasing importance.

The Canadian economy comprises both large and small organizations. In these organizations, people work together to accomplish goals that are too complex or large in number to be achieved by a single individual. Throughout life, Canadians have contact with a variety of organizations — such as hospitals, schools, churches, businesses, colleges, universities, and many government agencies. The most significant factor in determining the quality of performance and success of such organizations — and the quality of life in Canada — is the success of its management.

Why are some managers successful, while others are not? This question requires a complicated answer; in this book we examine a variety of factors that influence managerial success. For now, we will simply say that successful managers are those who are able to carry out effectively the basic functions of management — planning, organizing, influencing, and controlling. We should also note that successful managers foster the cooperation and goodwill of others inside and outside the organization. Managers must work through others to achieve success.

In this book, we provide you with knowledge about the fundamental concepts and techniques used by effective managers in all types of organizations. The material is presented from the standpoint that there is no one best way to manage. In order to illustrate the concepts, examples of how management is actually practiced are presented. While our primary focus is on the management of profit-oriented business firms, most concepts and principles will also apply to not-for-profit organizations such as schools, churches, government, and charitable organizations.

MANAGEMENT IN VARIOUS SETTINGS

In Canada, there are many different kinds of organizations. Consider this list:

Falconbridge Nickel	Eldorado Nuclear	Winnipeg Blue
Ron's Hairstyling	Ltd.	Bombers
Shop	Algonquin College	Scott Mission

Canadian National Railways
Eaton's
Revenue Canada
Shopsy's
Imperial Oil
The Canadian Mint
Canadian Broadcasting Corporation
Mienke and Mienke Meat Market
Canadian Wildlife Federation
Canada Post
The YMCA/YWCA
Canadian Kidney Foundation
Creditel
Imperial Bank of Commerce
Inuit Tapirisat
Atomic Energy of Canada
Shoppers Drug Mart
Perth's
Women's College Hospital
Air Canada
Jim's Taxi
Loto Canada
Underground Gourmet
Safeway
The United Way
Cashway Lumber

Some of these organizations operate in the private sector and pursue a profit, for example, Falconbridge Nickel, Shoppers Drug Mart, Jim's Taxi, Perth's, and Cashway Lumber. Some of these private sector firms produce a physical product (for example, Imperial Oil), some produce intangible services (for example, Winnipeg Blue Bombers), and others produce both physical goods and intangible services (for example, Underground Gourmet).

Some of these organizations operate in the public sector and do not pursue a profit, for example, The YMCA/YWCA, The United Way, the Canadian Broadcasting Corporation, and the Canadian Kidney Foundation. Some of these public-sector firms produce a physical product (for example, Eldorado Nuclear Ltd.), some produce intangible services (for example, Canada Post), and others produce both physical goods and intangible services (for example, The Canadian Mint).

All of the privately owned firms are profit-oriented; some of the government-owned organizations are also profit-oriented (for example, Air Canada), but many others are not (for example, The Canadian Mint, Canada Post, Atomic Energy of Canada).

All organizations — whether they are profit-oriented or not-for-profit, whether they produce a physical product or an intangible service, whether they are private sector or public sector — need managers in order to function effectively. The general work that managers do (making decisions and allocating resources) is similar in all organizations. However, the specific jobs that need to be done vary depending on whether the organization is profit-oriented or not-for-profit. We now consider the difference between profit and not-for-profit organizations, and between manufacturing and service organizations in more detail so that the role of managers is clearer.

The Profit-Oriented Business Firm

Business firms play an integral role in the Canadian economic system. A **business firm** is an entity that seeks to make a profit by gathering and allocating productive resources to satisfy demand. This demand may be for either goods or services.

Although some people think that business firms are found only in the private sector, a government organization which pursues a profit is also a business firm. Like any private-sector firm, it tries to gather and allocate resources in such a way that a profit is made.

The business firm is the basic building block for the making of economic decisions in Canada. Through it, resources are organized for production. Land, labor, and capital are assembled and converted into products and services that can be sold. This activity is directed and guided by managers. (See Exhibit 1-1.)

Business activity, regardless of whether the firm conducting it is publicly or privately owned, requires decision making to produce and sell goods and services at a profit. It requires buying as well as selling. Thus, the market plays a role. How resources are used depends mainly on choices made by firms and consumers. Both are primarily guided by market prices. The firm is the key to the market's operation because it guides the flow of resources through the marketplace. The firm is an input-output system. The inputs are productive resources the firm buys in the market. The outputs are the goods it makes and sells in the market. Both input and output depend on market prices. In some instances, decisions will be guided by social and political considerations in addition to economic ones.

Resources and the goods made from them are both scarce. Therefore, they command prices. The firm's costs of doing business (converting resources from one form to another) must be less than its revenues if it is to earn a profit. To determine how profitable it is, a firm must keep records of its costs and sales. Accounting traces the effects of resource flows on its profits. **Profit** is the difference between the cost of inputs and the revenue from outputs. People form business firms to produce and sell consumer-demanded goods and services so that they can make a profit. Profit, however, does not appear until it is earned. In this system there is no guarantee that a firm will make a profit. The hope for profit leads people to start and operate businesses. By providing products and services that satisfy customers, a firm may make a profit.

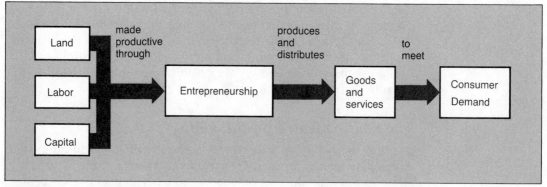

EXHIBIT 1-1   Basic business activity

If revenues are greater than costs, a profit is earned. Profit may be increased by raising prices, lowering costs, or selling more units. But most firms cannot raise prices much without reducing sales. Most of them try to increase profit by cutting costs and/or increasing the number of units sold. If a firm's revenues and costs are equal, it earns no profit. It only breaks even. Few people, however, go into business to break even. This is especially true if there is no "owner's salary" included in the firm's list of expenses. Firms that just break even give their owners no economic return from being in business.

Any after-tax profit earned by a firm is reinvested in the firm and/or is distributed to its owners. For many firms, reinvested profit is the major source of funds to finance their growth. The owners, in effect, are willing to reinvest their profit in the firm rather than taking it out and spending it on consumption.

Governments also have profitability in mind when they form business firms. However, they also take into account other social and political factors. It is an accepted fact in capitalist economies that all types and sizes of business firms seek profit. There is some argument, however, whether profit should be their only objective. Later, we discuss the concept of the social responsibility of business. At any rate, it's one thing to seek profit and another to make it.

Forms of Business Ownership

Business firms vary in size from single-owner firms to giant corporations owned by thousands of people. A business firm may be a sole proprietorship, a partnership, or a corporation.

The sole proprietorship is the oldest and still the most common form of legal ownership in Canada. A **sole proprietorship** is a business owned and managed by one person. That person, however, may have help from others in running the business. The sole proprietor is the classic case of the entrepreneur. Only a sole proprietor can say: "I am the company" or "This is my business." Ron's Hairstyling Shop and Jim's Taxi are sole proprietorships.

A second form of business firm, a **partnership** comes into being when two or more individuals agree to combine their financial, managerial, and technical abilities for the purpose of operating a company for profit. Mienke and Mienke Meat Market is a partnership. Many law firms and accounting firms are run as partnerships.

The third form of business ownership, the **corporation**, can be defined as "an artificial being, invisible, intangible, and existing only in contemplation of law." Unlike a sole proprietorship or partnership, the corporation has a legal existence apart from its owners. It can buy, hold, and sell property in its own name, and it can sue and be sued. Originally, the corporate form of ownership was used most frequently for charitable, educational, or public purposes. In order to incorporate, a charter was required from the federal government. That is why the corporation is legally separate from its owners. It is a creation of government authority. Eaton's, Imperial Oil, Shopsy's, Safeway, Falconbridge Nickel, Creditel, and Shoppers Drug Mart are corporations.

Shareholders are persons who own the common and preferred shares of a corporation. The number of votes a shareholder has depends on the number of shares he or she owns. It is not a case of "one person, one vote," and explains why many small shareholders do not vote their shares in large corporations. For example, a person who owns 10 shares of INCO may choose not to vote. Control of such a corporation can be effective if a group of shareholders pools its votes to get a voting majority. In some cases, a person with 10 percent or even less of a corporation's stock can exercise much control over its affairs. Most corporations have thousands of shares and hundreds of shareholders. Some, however, remain quite small in terms of number of owners and the number and market value of shares outstanding.

A shareholder need not, and generally does not, participate in managing the corporation. Ownership and management are separate. Most of the shareholders in Canada do not participate in managing the corporations of which they are part owners. The shareholders come from many backgrounds — for example, schoolteachers, plumbers, or salaried executives.

Shareholders are the direct owners of a corporation. There are, however, millions of other people who have an indirect ownership in many corporations. For example, the members of many labor unions make payments to their union pension funds. Some of this money is used to buy shares in corporations. Thus, the union members are indirect owners of stock.

A shareholder owns a partial interest in the whole corporation. Suppose you own one share of stock in Norcen Energy Resources. You are not entitled to walk into the corporation's headquarters and demand to see the "property" you own. The property is owned by the corporation. What you own is a small part of the entire corporation. The value of that part varies with changes in the value of the shares of stock which you own. This is determined by the supply of, and demand for, the shares on the market.

The two basic types of stock are common stock and preferred stock. **Common stock** shows ownership in a corporation. It is voting stock and all common shareholders enjoy the same rights. Common shareholders have a right to earnings that remain (residual earnings) after the corporation has met the prior claims of bondholders and preferred shareholders. The actual payment of a common stock dividend from these residual earnings does not occur until the board of directors declares a common stock dividend. If the corporation goes bankrupt, the common shareholders are the last to receive any proceeds from the sale of the corporation's property. Creditors, bondholders, and preferred shareholders share in the proceeds before the common shareholders. Thus, common shareholders are the residual owners of a corporation.

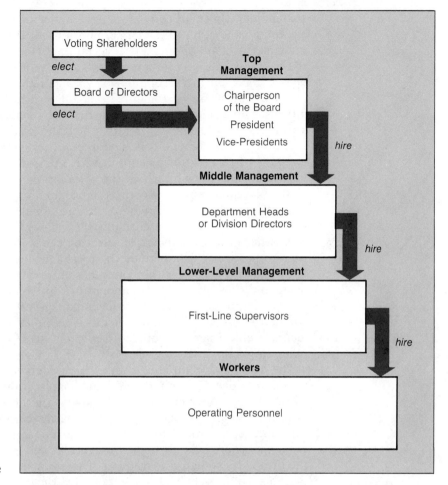

EXHIBIT 1-2
Corporate structure

Preferred stock also shows ownership in a corporation. Preferred shareholders usually cannot vote their shares, but they do enjoy certain preferences with respect to dividends and assets. As we have seen, they have a right to receive the dividend indicated on their share certificates before common shareholders receive any dividends. This dividend also is not owed until declared by the corporation's board of directors. If the corporation goes out of business and pays off its debts, preferred shareholders have the right to receive their share of any remaining assets before the common shareholders receive anything.

The number of votes a shareholder has in elections of board members and other business voted on at shareholders meetings depends on the number of shares he or she owns. Each share of common stock carries one vote; thus, a person with 20 shares has 20 votes.

A corporation's board of directors is elected by its shareholders. (See Exhibit 1-2.) The **board of directors** is a group of people who are given the power to govern the corporation's affairs and to make general policy. This power comes from the corporate charter and the corporation's shareholders. In small corporations the major shareholders often manage the business. But in larger corporations, with thousands of shareholders, the board of directors is accountable for guiding the affairs of the business. It's easy for a board to keep itself in power as long as it does a good job in the opinion of voting shareholders. Unseating a board member can be tough. The board of directors elects its own officers. These board officers usually include a chairperson of the board, a vice-chairperson, and a secretary. The board holds periodic meetings.

Although the shareholders have the authority to draw up the corporation's bylaws, they usually leave it up to the board. **Corporation bylaws** are the rules by which the corporation will operate. They include: place and time of meetings, procedure for calling meetings, directors' pay, duties of corporate officers, regulations for new stock issues, and procedures for changing the bylaws.

Another task of the board is selecting the corporation's officers, or its top managers, who include the president, vice-president(s), secretary, and treasurer. The corporation's officers are employees of the board and they also are the corporation's top management. These officers, in turn, hire other, lower-level managers to help in running the corporation. In actual practice boards sometimes select only the president, or chief executive officer (CEO), and he or she then selects the other corporate officers.

The board is accountable to the shareholders for the actions of the corporate officers. In other words, the board performs the function of a "watchdog." As such, the board usually has the authority to accept or reject the officers' actions in managing the corporation.

In some corporations the board plays a very active role in managing the corporation. It holds frequent meetings and has a lot of say about the firm's day-to-day management. This is especially likely to be the case in small, closely held corporations. On the other hand, some boards are content to select the company president. The president then selects other corporate officers and the board merely acts as a "review board" for the president and the other officers' decisions. In this case, the president pretty much runs the entire corporation subject to "rubber stamp" approval by the board.

The distinctions between the board and the corporate officers often are blurred. In some corporations the chairperson of the board is also the company's president. The corporation's other top managers also may be on the board. In such a case the board members who are not corporate officers are called outside directors.

Board members have certain legal obligations. They must act in the best interest of the shareholders and be reasonable and prudent in doing their jobs. They must be as careful in managing the corporation's affairs as they are in managing their personal affairs. In the past, board members have been held liable for illegal acts and fraud, but not for poor judgment. More recently, however, some courts have held directors liable for using what the courts consider to be poor judgment.

Not-for-Profit Organizations

Many organizations in Canada do not have profit as their objective; in fact, business firms are the only profit-oriented organizations in Canadian society. Examples of not-for-profit organizations include the Scott Mission, The United Way, the Canadian Wildlife Federation, the Canadian Red Cross, The YMCA/YWCA, the Canadian Kidney Foundation, and Inuit Tapirisat — to name just a few.

Not-for-profit organizations usually stress service objectives instead of profit. The Canadian Union of Public Employees, for example, provides, expert service for its members regarding grievance and wage negotiations. The Fort Richmond Community Club provides services to people in its local area. The YMCA/YWCA provides a variety of social services.

In spite of the differences between profit-oriented and not-for-profit organizations, two crucial similarities make management important to both of them. First, all organizations have objectives that must be reached if the organization is to remain in existence. Second, in both types of organizations, people must be directed and motivated toward the organization's goals. Since managers direct the efforts of other people in accomplishing organization goals, it is clear that both kinds of organizations need managers.

The importance of these similarities can be shown by analyzing the activities of two organizations that appear very different — the Canadian Wildlife Federation and Imperial Oil. Although it is a not-for-profit organization, the CWF needs managers to ensure that it reaches its objectives of protecting and managing wildlife in Canada. To reach these objectives, individuals in the CWF must be motivated to make the public aware of its goals and to act in ways consistent with preserving wildlife. Imperial Oil also needs managers to reach its goals of providing oil products to Canadian consumers so that it can make a profit. Managers at Imperial Oil must also motivate their employees so that these goals can be reached. Thus, even though these two organizations have markedly different goals, they both need managers to help them reach their goals.

Manufacturing versus Service Organizations

In the past, when business management was discussed, most people thought of the operation of buildings with smokestacks, assembly lines, and workers with lunch pails. While the factory system is still important in Canada's economic system, working conditions for Canada's workers have changed drastically in the past few decades.

Most business organizations in Canada are involved in providing services rather than physical products. Service organizations do not produce tangible products; rather, they create intangible services. Banks, insurance companies, transportation, real estate, schools, government, and personal grooming businesses are all service organizations that do seek to make a profit. Service organizations employ about 2 of every 3 Canadians. Service industries also account for a substantial part of the expenditures of Canadian households.

A complicating factor in dealing with the manufacturing versus service issue is the fact that many organizations are involved in both. IBM, for example, manufactures computers, but its after-sales service and its advice to customers on how best to use the computer are clearly service activities. IBM is not an isolated example; many large manufacturing firms are both service and manufacturing organizations.

Regardless of whether a firm is involved in service or manufacturing, or both, management is important. Resources must be properly allocated so that organization goals can be reached. This is the job of managers.

WHAT IS MANAGEMENT?

Likely, you will be employed by some type of organization and, as a result, be working with managers. Understanding what is involved in managing is important even though you probably will not start out as a manager. Therefore, knowledge of basic management concepts will be beneficial to you either as a worker or as a manager. If you have plans for a management career, you should gain a full understanding of what managers do and what management is all about.

There are almost as many definitions of management as there are books on the subject. Most definitions of management do share a common idea — **management** is concerned with the accomplishment of organization objectives through the efforts of other people. Objectives, or goals, are the final results expected. For example, your immediate objective may be to pass this course, while your long-term goals may be to complete your schooling and obtain a good job. The objective of business firms is to make a profit by providing goods and/or services to customers. In order for a business firm to achieve this goal, the managers in the firm must perform four main functions:

- Determine what is to be achieved (**planning**).
- Allocate resources and establish the means to accomplish the plans (**organizing**).
- Motivate and lead personnel (**influencing** or **directing**).
- Compare results achieved to the planned goals (**controlling**).

Thus, management may be defined as the process of planning, organizing, influencing, and controlling to accomplish organization objectives through the coordinated use of human and material resources.

WHO ARE MANAGERS AND WHAT DO MANAGERS DO?

In a sense, everyone is a manager. People manage their lives by planning, organizing, directing, and controlling their skills, talents, time, and activities. Parents manage their jobs, households, and children; children manage their allowances; and students manage their time if they expect to succeed in various subjects in school.

Take the example of Laurie Steen, an accounting major at a university. Her objective is to pursue a career as a chartered accountant. In order to accomplish her goal, she must first complete her B.Comm. degree. Next, she must find a job articling in one of the CA firms. While she is working in the profession, she will be taking further specialized accounting courses toward the Uniform Final Examination, which must be passed by all people who wish to become a CA. In order to accomplish her goal, Laurie must be a good manager of her time. She must plan her schedule, organize her time and financial resources, and evaluate or control her own performance to maintain her grades. Laurie uses management concepts to achieve her objectives.

Managers in business and in not-for-profit organizations also pursue objectives — but, those of the organization, not their own. Pursuit of a common goal can lead to the grouping of managers. For instance, the term *management* is sometimes used to refer collectively to all the managers in a firm. This usage is most often heard in connection with negotiations between workers or unions and their supervisors. The uppermost managers in an organization — usually called executives — may also be referred to collectively as *management*.

Because *management* so frequently refers to a firm's top executives, people sometimes forget that managers occupy other positions within large organizations. Actually managers operate at most levels within every type of organization — large or small, private sector or public sector, business or not-for-profit. As shown earlier in Exhibit 1-2, there are 3 basic levels of managers.

Lower-level managers, often referred to as supervisors or first-line supervisors, are responsible for managing employees in daily operations. In a manufacturing firm, a factory supervisor is responsible for ensuring that the assembly line runs properly and that the right type of product is produced. In a government office, the supervisor of clerical staff ensures that paperwork is processed correctly and on time.

Middle managers, such as department heads, are concerned primarily with the coordination of programs and activities that are necessary to achieve the overall organization goals, as identified by top management. In a manufacturing company, sales managers and production superintendents are middle managers. In government organizations, department heads are middle managers.

TALKING TO MANAGERS

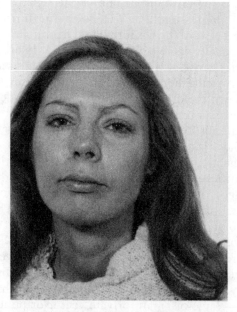

Wendy Currie-Mills
Campbell, Albo, Low Limited

Wendy Currie-Mills, a Certified General Accountant with additional training in business evaluation, has been a consultant for a Toronto firm for the past 4 years. The firm, Campbell, Albo, Low Limited, provides business evaluations to establish the worth of a company, primarily for purposes of buying and selling. Previously, Currie-Mills worked for CKOC radio station in Hamilton, Ontario and later was the controller of the editorial department at Maclean's Magazine. Currie-Mills is a graduate of Mohawk Community College.

Q: How have courses in management helped you in your career?
Currie-Mills: They gave me an awareness of how organizations are structured and of the various management styles that exist and their effects on any given organization.

Q: What sort of impression of the business world did you get from your education?
Currie-Mills: One somewhat different from what I've been exposed to since. I thought that the business world was very impersonal, very structured, with people's positions well defined. However, I discovered that wasn't necessarily the case. I can't recall any textbooks telling me how important interpersonal relationships were; I have found since that they are as important as professional skills, particularly in a smaller organization. Managers' attitudes and interpersonal skills can have a substantial impact on the morale of employees, affecting their level of productivity. The ability to work well with another person, to be flexible enough to absorb the next person's thoughts and methods of working, and to work within a wider scope are extremely important, especially in a creative atmosphere where several people's ideas and efforts must be combined to produce results. I have witnessed instances of people coming into an organization, having already thought themselves into their function as they perceived it, only to be disillusioned when they discover that they must expand their scope in order to function effectively. Prior to my postsecondary education I had worked for 6 years; but, primarily because of the types of work I had done — clerical positions — I was not as concerned about or aware of how an organization is run.

Q: When doing a business evaluation, what sort of information do you compile about a company?
Currie-Mills: We interview top management to discuss the company's present and future op-

erations. We obtain information on the company's products or services and its position in the marketplace. We discuss management style and employee relations. A tour of the company's facilities is conducted so that we can better understand the manufacturing process and assist in assessing the state of the company's assets. We acquire all pertinent financial information and research the industry in which the company operates in order to appraise the company's future potential more effectively. The value we place on a company is based on its future performance.

Where we find a company relying on any key individual, we are concerned that the value of the company could decrease dramatically if that person were to leave. For instance, an individual who has personal contacts with international markets, in terms of negotiating contracts, can be irreplaceable. People who are strictly managers tend to be more dispensable. We look at the effectiveness of a person. If an individual is in charge of one department, how profitable is that department? Will it continue to be profitable? A high turnover of staff can be indicative of poor management.

Q: What differences have you observed in management of smaller versus larger businesses?

Currie-Mills: The attitudes, decisions, and management style of managers tends to have more of an impact on the operations of a small organization. Commonly, only one aspect of the operations and only a certain group of people are affected by a particular manager's style or decisions in a large organization. Larger organizations tend to be more structured and to have better defined job descriptions; on the other hand, they are likely to be less flexible and are inclined to be far more formal in their management style than smaller organizations. Managers in larger organizations often are more expendable than in smaller organizations where much reliance is placed on certain key managers.

Q: What differences exist between manufacturing and service industries?

Currie-Mills: Service industries tend to be more elusive and more flexible. People's attitudes and interpersonal skills are critical. Peer goal-setting becomes more prominent. Manufacturing is much more structured. Communication between employees is not as crucial; however, efficiency is of the essence as products must be produced in a predetermined timeframe. Manufacturing industries must have very explicit, well-defined job descriptions to which the employees must adhere in order to accomplish their objectives.

Q: How have you observed boards of directors influencing companies?

Currie-Mills: The determining factor is whether the company is tightly controlled by a few individuals, or widely controlled by a larger number of people. In the former situation, the board of directors is more likely to make decisions, whereas in the latter they tend to act more on an advisory basis. For instance, in a tightly controlled company where a family owns 51 percent or more of the shares, the board tends to make all the everyday operating decisions, as opposed to acting on an advisory level.

Q: How would you summarize the effects of management on an organization?

Currie-Mills: Managers give direction and make decisions. For the most part, I perceive them influencing the culture of an organization, the attitudes of people within the organization and their behavioral patterns. Interpersonal skills are important and can have a major impact on people's performance and, hence, the success of a business.

Top management includes the chief executive officer, the chairperson of the board, the president, as well as vice-president(s). In not-for-profit organizations, the top manager is sometimes called the executive director. These individuals are responsible for providing the overall direction of the organization.

In the final analysis, a manager is anyone, at any level of the organization, who directs the efforts of other people in accomplishing organization goals. Wherever a group of people work together to achieve results, a manager is present.

School principals, meat market supervisors, service station operators, and factory supervisors are managers, just as the presidents of Air Canada, London Life Insurance, Imperial Bank of Commerce, and Falconbridge Nickel are managers. The prime minister is a manager, too, as are government agency heads, university deans, church pastors, and military commanders.

Managers are responsible for making decisions concerning the use of a firm's resources to achieve results. Managers are the catalysts who establish goals; plan operations; organize various resources — personnel, materials, equipment, capital; lead and motivate people to perform; evaluate actual results against the goals; and develop people for the organization.

The success of a particular business manager cannot be judged exclusively on short-run output. In other words, a manager may be said to be effective if his or her unit is earning a profit, or reducing costs, or increasing the market share for the company's products, or other such measurable results. Naturally, these accomplishments are important to any organization. However, a major challenge and, indeed, obligation of any manager is the development of people under his or her direction, and in doing this, long-term goals may be achieved more effectively. Developing competent and well-trained people who can be promoted to more responsible positions is a significant part of a manager's job. This is an excellent long-run measure of the effectiveness of a manager and contributes to the growth and success of the firm whether it is a manufacturing or service organization.

THE MANAGEMENT FUNCTIONS

In every organization, the work done by managers concerns the functions of planning, organizing, influencing, and controlling to achieve the organization objectives. A separate section of this text is devoted to each of these 4 management functions, which are introduced here.

Planning

The planning function of management is concerned with setting the objectives of the firm and deciding how these objectives are to be achieved. It is not enough to say that the overall objective of a company is to "make a profit" or "be the leader in the industry." Its plans must be specific and must indicate how the overall goal is going to be achieved. For example, Molson's might want to achieve a 30 percent share of the Canadian beer market and a 15 percent return on investment. In order to accomplish these goals, the company must develop step-by-step plans for producing and marketing its products. The overall organization objective is translated by managers into goals for each part of the firm; this is the planning process. The planning function — including decision making — is discussed in detail in chapters 3–5.

Organizing

After objectives and plans have been established, management must then organize the human and physical resources of the firm. The organizing function is concerned with developing a framework that relates all personnel, work assignments, and physical resources to one another. This framework is usually termed the **organization structure** and is designed to facilitate the accomplishment of the organization's objectives.

Since firms' goals and resources differ, the organization structure in each firm is unique. Firms within one industry may have similar organization structures (for example, Steel Company of Canada and Algoma Steel), but no two structures are exactly the same. Firms that provide different products or services may have very diverse organization structures (for example, Imperial Oil and Algonquin College). The organizing function of management is discussed in chapters 6–9.

Influencing

The third management function, influencing, is concerned with stimulating members of the organization to undertake action consistent with the plans. Using the influencing, or directing, function managers effectively motivate, lead, and communicate with employees in the organization. These three factors have a major impact on the type of corporate culture that exists within the firm. Topics relating to influencing are presented in chapters 10–13.

Controlling

Ensuring that the objectives and plans of the organization are achieved is known as the controlling function of management. The purpose of establishing controls is to ensure proper performance in accordance with the plans. Through the establishment of controls, managers are able to compare actual performance with the predetermined plan. In the event of unsatisfactory performance, managers take corrective action. For instance, if a firm's costs for producing a product are higher than planned, top management must have some means to recognize the problem and take the appropriate action to correct it. The controlling function is discussed in chapters 14 and 15.

Coordination

Some management writers consider coordination as a separate function of management. However, in our view **coordination** involves the integration of the functions of planning, organizing, influencing, and controlling. Being a manager should not be viewed as performing separate and distinct functions. For instance, the planning function is usually thought of as preceding controlling, but results of the controlling process may cause future plans to be altered. Coordination is necessary throughout the management process and in this text will not be considered as a separate and distinct function of management.

Managers must coordinate the functions, physical resources, and personnel of their firm so that the organization goals can be achieved efficiently and effectively. As such, coordination represents an overall concern of all managers and is achieved when people, resources, and functions blend together harmoniously to achieve quality results.

Management Functions at Various Managerial Levels

As illustrated in Exhibit 1-3, the basic functions of planning, organizing, influencing, and controlling are performed by managers at every

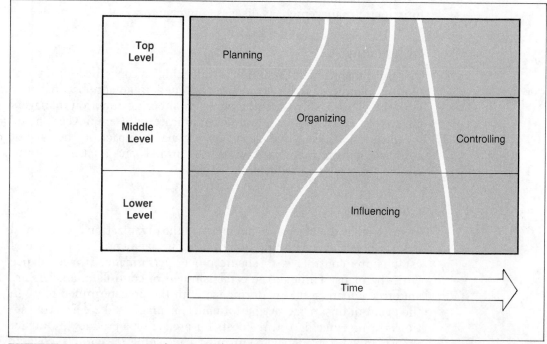

EXHIBIT 1-3   Management functions at various managerial levels

level within an organization. The amount of time and effort devoted to each function, however, will likely depend on the level of a manager. As shown in the exhibit the amount of time that lower-level managers spend on planning is much less than that spent by top management. The lower-level manager must devote considerable time and effort in influencing and controlling the work of others — accomplishing routine tasks and putting out daily fires. As managers move to higher levels in the organization, a greater percentage of their time is devoted to planning and less to influencing (although they may spend increased time influencing external groups like government, unions, or consumers). The amount of time spent on the controlling function is fairly consistent at all levels of management except for the uppermost level, such as for the president or chief executive officer. At this high level, the chief executive is concerned with overall control of resources essential to the survival of the firm. Finally, the amount of time devoted to the organizing function is fairly consistent at all levels.

MANAGERIAL ROLES

Management writers have long recognized that, when the complexities of managerial work are reduced to the 4 functions of planning, organizing, influencing, and controlling, much of the dynamics of what a manager does on a day-to-day basis is lost. In an attempt to overcome this problem, Henry Mintzberg of McGill University has developed a view of managerial work that captures some of the uncertainty, complexity, frustration, and excitement of the typical management job.[2]

Mintzberg did a detailed analysis of the work behavior of 5 chief executive officers. Overall, he found that managers worked long hours, were involved in intense activity, and often were interrupted before they could finish the task they were working on. Because of these factors, a manager's job can be frustrating and tiring, but also very rewarding.

More specifically, Mintzberg notes that managers are given formal organizational authority to run their own units, and they derive status from this authority. This status, in turn, causes them to get involved personally with subordinates, peers, and superiors. Each of these groups provide managers with the information they need to make decisions.

The formal authority and status aspects of management jobs result in managers playing 3 major roles as they carry out their work duties. The **interpersonal role** requires the manager to interact with other significant people both inside and outside the organization. When playing this role, a manager may be a figurehead — for example, performing ceremonial duties like breaking ground for a new building, a leader — for example, motivating subordinates, or a liaison — for example, dealing with people outside the firm.

The second major managerial role is the **informational role**. This role requires the manager to both gather and disseminate information. The manager may be a monitor — for example, analyzing travel costs of salespeople, a disseminator — for example, giving subordinates information they can use to perform their jobs better, or a spokesperson — for example, forwarding desired information to individuals outside the manager's unit or outside the organization.

The third major managerial role is the **decisional role**. This role requires the manager to use the information available to make decisions that will help the manager's unit function effectively. When carrying out this role, the manager may be an entrepreneur — for example, identifying a new product opportunity, a disturbance handler — for example, settling conflicts among subordinates, a resource allocator — for example, deciding how resources should be distributed within the manager's department, or a negotiator — for example, resolving a potential grievance with the union steward.

Mintzberg's "roles" approach to management gives considerable additional insight into what is required in the demanding job of managing. As you think about these roles, you'll have no difficulty concluding that the day-to-day work of a manager can be busy and challenging.

MANAGERIAL SKILLS

In order to be effective, a manager must possess and continually develop several essential skills. Exhibit 1-4 illustrates a number of skills that are important to a manager's overall effectiveness. As can be seen, the relative significance of each skill varies according to the level an individual manager occupies within an organization.

Technical Skill

The ability to use specific knowledge, methods, or techniques in performing work is referred to as **technical skill**. Technical skills are considered to be crucial to the effectiveness of lower-level managers because they have direct contact with employees performing work activities within the firm. The lower-level manager must provide technical assistance and support to personnel within the work unit. For example, a supervisor of keypunch machine operators must possess specific knowledge of the methods and techniques of operating the keypunch machines so that he or she may train newly hired operators and answer technical questions of the operators. The importance of technical skills to higher levels of management within the organization usually diminishes because the manager has less direct contact with day-to-day problems and activities.

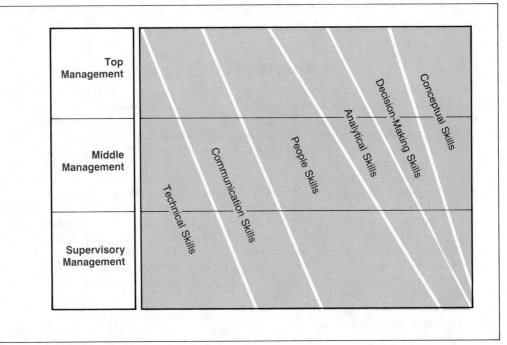

EXHIBIT 1-4   **Essential skills necessary at various levels of management in an organization**

Communication Skills

The ability to provide information in spoken and written forms to others in the organization for the purpose of achieving desired results is referred to as **communication skills**. They are skills that are vital to the success of everyone, but most especially managers who must achieve results through the efforts of others. Surveys of practicing managers consistently show that they value people with the ability to write in a clear, concise, and an organized fashion. Such surveys also indicate that aspiring managers must have the ability to make formal presentations and to communicate effectively one-on-one with subordinates, peers, and subordinates. Clear presentation of ideas shows people what they have to do, rather than causing misunderstandings or confusion. A person without these skills will experience considerable difficulty climbing the promotions ladder.

Communication skills are equally important at each level within the organization. Because of the importance of communication, Chapter 12 of this text is devoted to communication and related methods to improve managerial effectiveness.

MANAGEMENT IN PRACTICE

Managers of the Future

The turbulent 80s have brought the demand for managers with a unique set of skills. Perhaps the most important of these is an ability to articulate the corporations's purpose and set of values. A company's survival in the marketplace will be dependent on the manager's adeptness in communication. Tom Watson of IBM and Robert Noyce of Intel Corporation achieved this, and the potency of their messages gave their companies market dominance. Unfortunately, others, such as Ford and Xerox, were not as quick to see the importance of communication and their market shares declined.

Managers will have to become as nimble as entrepreneurs because changes are occurring at a rapid pace. Research and development in technology and new markets should be the focus of a manager's decisions, not short-term productivity.

According to Franz Tyaack [chief executive officer] of Westinghouse Canada, Inc., today's management system is outdated and worn out. It is a system perfected around 1900 which works on the premise that the blue-collar workforce is composed largely of poorly educated, recently arrived immigrants. This militaristic model is prevalent in both public and private North American enterprises. Under this system, human resources are wasted and there is much job dissatisfaction. The task for tomorrow's manager is to understand his or her business well, know when changes are necessary, and communicate effectively with employees.

SOURCE M. A. Wente, "Remaking the Management Mind," *Canadian Business* (January 1983): 23, 24, 82, 83.

People Skills

The ability of a manager to understand, work with, and get along with other people is referred to as **people skills**. These skills are essential at every level of management within the organization but are particularly significant at lower levels where supervisors have frequent and direct contact with operating personnel. Managers have people skills if they are able to create a climate for effective motivation and leadership. In chapters 10–13 the importance of people skills and the ways to develop them are discussed in detail.

Analytical Skills

Analytical skills are a manager's use of logical and scientific approaches or techniques in the analyses of problems and business opportunities. Although important at all levels of the organization, analytical skills tend to be relatively more significant at the level of top management. Lower-level managers tend to operate in a fairly stable or predictable atmosphere with specific guidelines for their performance. By contrast, top managers function in an atmosphere that is subject to considerable complexities and uncertainties. Analytical skills are crucial in this kind of corporate culture.

Decision-Making Skill

The ability of a manager to select a course of action from several alternatives is known as **decision making skill**. Decision-making skills are essential to managers as they perform the functions of planning, organizing, influencing, and controlling. Making effective decisions is an important skill for managers at all levels within a firm, but it is relatively more important to top managers than to lower-level managers. Many presidents have indicated that decision-making skills are essential to successful performance. Top management's primary responsibility is to make effective decisions, whereas lower levels of management are primarily concerned with executing or implementing decisions made by top management. In Chapter 5, we discuss the decision-making process. Every manager must be able to make decisions.

Conceptual Skills

Conceptual skills allow a manager to understand the complexities of the overall organization and how each department contributes to the accomplishment of the firm's objectives. These skills are crucial to the success of top-level executives for they must be concerned with the "big picture" — assessing opportunities in the environment external to the firm and determining overall objectives, plans, and strategies. Top managers must have the ability to see how each part of the organization interrelates and contributes to the primary goals of the firm. Moving down the managerial hierarchy, conceptual skills become less important because other skills are more important to the success of lower-level managers. For instance, first-level supervisors are able to refer to operating manuals to discover the capabilities of a particular piece of equipment whereas top-level managers must use their conceptual skills to determine what products will be produced with the equipment.

Professional managers recognize that they must develop and practice all of the managerial skills to be effective in accomplishing organization and personal goals. Managers cannot concentrate their efforts on one or only a few of these skills. The blending of the skills in the proper proportions based on the particular level occupied by the manager results in success.

The Relationship between Skills and Functions

The difference between management skills and management functions can be confusing. However, the relationship is really quite straightforward — management skills are necessary to perform management functions. For example, communication and people skills are necessary to perform the influencing function; technical skills are necessary to perform the controlling function; and analytical and conceptual skills are needed to perform the planning function. Since managers perform the functions of planning, organizing, influencing, and controlling, they ought to have some competence in each of the managerial skills. As shown in Exhibit 1-4, the emphasis on the various skills changes as a manager moves from the supervisory level to top management.

BASIC SCHOOLS OF MANAGEMENT THOUGHT

In order to improve our understanding of current management concepts, we think it is helpful to discuss the historical development of management thought. Most of current management practice is based on management theory developed in this century. Management theory has changed over time, mainly to meet changes in business and the rise of service firms in Canada. The influence of management concepts from other countries, especially from Japan, is discussed later.

Classical School of Management

The oldest and perhaps most widely accepted school among practitioners has been called the **classical school of management**. The classical school attempted to provide a rational and scientific basis to the management of organizations. The primary contributions of the classical school of management include the following:

- The application of the scientific method to management
- The classification of the basic management functions: planning, organizing, influencing, and controlling
- The development and application of specific principles of management.

In essence, classical management concepts have significantly improved the practice of management and have led to substantial improvements in performance within organizations.

As a result of the industrial revolution, people were brought together to work in factories. This was in marked contrast to the previously used handicraft system where people worked separately in small shops or in their own homes. Thus, industrialization created a need for the effective management of people and other resources in the emerging organizations. In other words, there was a need for efficient planning, organizing, influencing, and controlling of work activities performed by specialized labor.

In response to changing conditions in the late nineteenth century and during the early part of the twentieth century, there was an intensified and dedicated interest in management as a process and as a

MANAGEMENT IN PRACTICE
The Universality of Management

The universality of management is a concept discussed and accepted by most management writers. By this they mean that the functions of management (planning, organizing, influencing, and controlling) must be performed in all organizations. Because of this fact, some assert that a person who is a good manager can be successful in any organization, whether it is in the private or public sector, and whether or not it is profit oriented. Thus, a person who is successful in an industrial firm should also be successful in an insurance company. Or, a person who has been successful in a private sector firm should also be successful as the leader of a political party (for example, Prime Minister Brian Mulroney was formerly the president of Iron Ore Company of Canada, Ltd.).

Other management writers disagree with this idea and say that each industry or kind of business is different enough that success in one says nothing about success in the other. They point to the large differences across firms and the even larger differences across industries or sectors of the economy; they argue, further, that success is difficult to achieve in one organization, much less several.

Which of these two arguments is most reasonable?

---

science. It was apparent to many — especially Frederick Taylor, Harrington Emerson, H. L. Gantt, Frank and Lillian Gilbreth, Henri Fayol, and Chester Barnard — that management could be made more effective and efficient.

Scientific Management

Taylor, Emerson, Gantt, and the Gilbreths, were primarily interested in developing a scientific basis for the management of work. The interest and research efforts of these people gave rise to **scientific management**. Frederick Taylor, generally recognized as the father of scientific management, was convinced that management was a process in which the scientific method should be used. The scientific method provides a logical framework for the analysis of problems. It basically consists of: defining the problem, gathering data, analyzing the data, developing alternatives, and selecting the best alternative. He believed that following the scientific method would provide a means to determine the most efficient way to perform work. Instead of abdicating responsibility for establishing standards, for example, management would scientifically study all facets of an operation and carefully set a logical and rational standard. Instead of guessing or relying solely on trial and error, management would go through the time-consuming process of logical study and scientific research to develop answers to business problems. Taylor's philosophy can be summarized in these 4 principles:

- The development and use of the scientific method in the practice of management (finding the "one best way" to perform work)
- Using scientific approaches to select employees who are best suited to perform a given job

- Providing the employee with scientific education, training, and development
- Encouraging friendly interaction and cooperation between management and employees but with a separation of duties between managers and workers.

Taylor stated many times that scientific management would require a revolution in thinking on the part of both the manager and the subordinate. His motives were not confined solely to advancing the interests of the manager and the enterprise. He believed sincerely that scientific management practices were for the mutual benefit of the employee and the employer through the creation of a larger productive surplus. Thus, the organization would achieve higher output, and the worker would receive a greater income.

The greater part of Taylor's work was oriented toward improving management of production operations. The classic case of the pig-iron experiment at the Bethlehem Steel Company illustrates his approach.[3] The task was simple, so much so that most managers would tend to ignore it. Laborers would pick up 42 kg pigs of iron from a storage yard, walk up a plank onto a railway car, and drop them at the end of the car. In a group of 75 laborers, the average output was about 12.7 t per worker per day. In applying the scientific method of study to this problem of getting work done through others, Taylor developed:

- An improved method of work (motion study)
- A prescribed amount of rest on the job (fatigue study and rest periods)
- A specific standard of output (time study)
- Payment by the unit of output (incentive wages).

Using this approach, the average per worker per day output rose from 12.7 t to 48.8 t. Under the incentive system, the daily pay rose from $1.15 to $1.85, an amount substantially higher than the going rate in the community.

Taylor's dedication to the systematic planning and study of processes pervaded his entire life. With a technically designed tennis racket, he became part of the United States National Doubles Tennis Championship team. When he played golf, he used specially designed clubs for a predictable type of lie. When he used a particular putter, his friends refused to play because of its accuracy. A famed novelist reported that Taylor died of pneumonia in a hospital with his stopwatch in his hand.

Frank and Lillian Gilbreth concentrated on motion analysis to develop the one best way. H. L. Gantt developed a control chart that is used to this day in production operations. Harrington Emerson developed a set of twelve principles of efficiency. Emerson's principles state, for instance, that a manager should carefully define objectives, use the scientific method of analysis, develop and use standardized procedures and methods, and reward employees for good work.

General Management Theory

Henri Fayol and C. I. Barnard, in contrast to Taylor, Emerson, Gantt, and the Gilbreths, attempted to develop a broader theory concerned with general management. Fayol's thesis was that the fundamental functions of any manager consist of planning, organizing, commanding, coordinating, and controlling. He attempted to evolve empirically a number of general principles that, if followed, would improve the practice of general management.

Chester Barnard's ideas, expressed in his classic book, *The Functions of the Executive*, have significantly influenced the development of the theory and practice of management.[4] Barnard, a practicing manager, was president of New Jersey Bell Telephone. Although he made numerous contributions to the development of management thought, his concept that the most important function of a manager is to provide the basis for cooperative effort, directed toward goals of the organization, was highly significant. Barnard believed that the degree of cooperation depends upon effective communications and a balance between rewards an employee receives and contributions made by employees.

Behavioral School of Management

In the 1920s and 1930s, some observers of business management became concerned with what they felt was a shortsightedness and incompleteness in the scientific management approach. In particular,

---

MANAGEMENT IN PRACTICE

Scientific Management in Troubled Times

Until very recently, the scientific management ideas of Frederick Taylor were widely accepted. During the period 1920–1970, managers seemed to have the view that managing was like following a recipe. If the right ingredients were put into the business, an acceptable level of profit would automatically result.

Recently, the environment of business has become complex, and management writers are now saying that high performing companies are those that stress corporate culture rather than management techniques. Corporate excellence is more likely to result from motivated people than from the application of scientific management techniques. Viewing the manager as a tradesman is therefore "out"; viewing the manager as an entrepreneur is "in."

It is understandable that a techniques-oriented system developed after scientific management was proposed. Managers at all levels in organizations were rewarded for short-term performance, even if this performance was gained at the expense of the long-run viability of the company. The new view, strongly influenced by the Japanese system of management, is that managers must concern themselves with the long-run health and survival of the firm. If they don't, they will discover that they are unable to compete as the environment of business changes.

SOURCE   Adapted from Maurice Hecht, "Real Managers Don't Need Theories Anymore," *Executive* (January 1984): 32–35.

Elton Mayo and F. J. Roethlisberger began to point out that the approaches advanced by scientific management were not necessarily the most efficient, nor did they always work as intended.[5] The human factors of business organizations had been largely ignored. The field of human relations emerged from the work of Elton Mayo who has become recognized as the father of the human relations movement, and, thus, the **behavioral school of management** was developed.

Human Relations Movement

The project that had the most to do with the beginning of the concern for human relations in business was the Hawthorne experiments conducted at the Western Electric Company between 1927 and 1932. In these experiments, researchers attempted to prove the validity of generally accepted principles of management. Several experiments to determine the relationship between working conditions and productivity were conducted by varying working conditions within the plant.

In one experiment, the researchers established test groups where changes in lighting, frequency of rest periods, and working hours occurred, and control groups where no changes were made. When rest periods and other improvements in working conditions were introduced to the test group, productivity increased as expected. However, the researchers were surprised when output continued to increase when the various improvements in working conditions that had been introduced, such as rest periods, were removed. As a result of these changes, the scientists expected a decrease in productivity. Contrary to these expectations, production still continued to improve in most instances. Obviously, everything had not been controlled in the experiment; the human mind was still free and uncontrolled.

The results of these experiments prompted Mayo and his fellow researchers to conclude that when employees are given special attention by management, output is likely to increase regardless of the actual changes in the working conditions. This has become known as the **Hawthorne Effect**. To gain a deeper understanding, Mayo and Roethlisberger followed up the experiments at the Hawthorne plant with an intensive interviewing program and an investigation of informal cliques, groupings, and relationships initiated by the members of the organization. The basic conclusion from the intensive interviewing program was that the needs of the individual and the role of the informal group have a significant impact on the performance of the work group.

Some researchers conceive of a total overlapping of interests between the organization and its members and contend that the objectives of both classical and behavioral approaches are identical. Much behavioral research does support the thesis that reasonable satisfaction of the needs and desires of those people who work within and contribute to the enterprise will lead to greater output. A management approach that ignores or deemphasizes the human element will often result in only partly accomplished objectives, reduced creativity, and general dissatisfaction.

Modern Behavioral Management Science

Since the early experiments of Mayo and Roethlisberger at the Hawthorne plant, there has been an increased interest in and application of behavioral science in management. The human relations approach has evolved into **behavioral management science**. In recent years, considerable research has been conducted for the purpose of developing techniques to use people more effectively in organizations. The contributions — theories and research applications — of such well-known behavioral scientists as Abraham Maslow, Douglas McGregor, Chris Argyris, Frederick Herzberg, and Rensis Likert have provided considerable insight into approaches for increased managerial effectiveness.

While we discuss in considerable detail the specific contributions of each of these behavioral scientists in chapters 10 and 11 on motivation and leadership, we mention the basic concepts of behavioral management science briefly here.

Behavioral scientists have, in general, criticized classical management and organization theory as not being responsive enough to the needs of employees. Some of the behavioralists' specific criticisms include:

• Jobs have been overly specialized
• People are underemployed
• Management has exercised too much control and has prevented employees from making decisions of which they are capable
• Organizations and management have shown too little concern about a person's needs for recognition and self-fulfillment.

Behavioral scientists argue that the design of work has not changed enough to keep pace with changes in the needs of today's employees and the working environment they confront. In today's complex, affluent, and rapidly changing society, employees cannot be treated as interchangeable parts within the organization. Today's worker has a higher level of education and tends to possess higher expectations for improvements in the working environment along with a desire for more diverse and challenging work. This has placed increased pressure on management to be responsive to these changes and to provide an environment designed to meet these needs.

Other Schools of Management Thought

While our previous discussion focused on the classical and behavioral schools of management, it should not be concluded that these two basic schools represent the only possible approaches or theories of management. Harold Koontz, in attempting to clarify what he has described as a "management theory jungle," identified eleven schools or approaches to the study of management.[6] Each of the schools in Koontz's classification is identified and briefly described in the following table.

Koontz's Classification of the Theories of Management

Empirical or Case Approach

In this school, management is studied through case examples of the successes and failures of practicing managers. This approach can assist managers in developing basic generalizations to support theories or principles of management. However, this method of learning about management may create illusions for current managers because the future is quite likely to be considerably different from the past. An analysis of past experiences of managers may not prove to be very helpful in solving current managerial problems.

Interpersonal Behavior Approach

According to this school of thought, management is concerned with accomplishing results through others. Therefore, the study of management should concentrate on interpersonal behavior and the study of psychology. This school focuses on the study of motivation and leadership. While the study of human behavior in organizations is important, a manager's knowledge of management is incomplete if that's all a person understands.

Group Behavior Approach

By applying research findings of sociology, anthropology, and social psychology, this approach explains management in terms of group behavior. According to this view, effective management requires a thorough understanding of behavioral patterns of group members within the organization. However, rigid adherence to this approach may cause managers to place more emphasis on organization behavior and not on other equally fundamental concepts of management.

Cooperative Social Systems Approach

An outgrowth of the interpersonal and group behavior approaches, the cooperative social systems school of management has often been referred to as the "organization theory" approach. While all managers perform in a cooperative social system, this approach does not explain complexities of modern management. Social systems is a broader concept than management, and it overlooks a number of principles, techniques, and factors that are important to effective management.

(table cont'd.: Koontz's Classification of Management Theories)

Sociotechnical Systems Approach

The sociotechnical systems approach is based on the work at the Tavistock Institute in England. It was discovered that the technical system — the machines and methods used — has a strong influence on the social system within the working environment. Personal attitudes of group members were strongly influenced by the technical system of the work place. A major task of management is to make sure that the social and technical systems are harmonious. While closely related to industrial engineering, the approach has made a significant contribution to the practice of management. It does not, however, provide an overall theory of management.

Decision Theory Approach

The major responsibility of managers is to make decisions, according to the decision theory approach to management. While many who study and/or practice management agree that decision making is an essential skill, the approach overlooks other skills and requirements of management. In some cases, the actual making of the decision may be relatively straightforward.

Systems Approach

The systems approach to management concentrates on the effective and efficient use of resources in order to produce desirable products and/or services. The systems approach requires that the physical, human, and capital resources be interrelated and coordinated within the external and internal environment of an organization.

Mathematical or Management Science Approach

This school or approach to management uses mathematical models, concepts, and symbols in solving managerial problems, particularly those requiring decisions. Advocates of the school argue that management can be made more scientific through the use of mathematical and simulation models. Many advocates argue that the mathematical or management science approach offers a complete school of management. Other theorists and practitioners believe that mathematical models are tools of analysis, not a separate school of thought.

Contingency or Situational Management

Contingency or situational management refers to managers' abilities to adapt to meet particular circumstances and constraints a firm may encounter. In other words, managerial action depends upon circumstances within the situation. That is, "no one best approach" will work in all situations. Applying a situational approach requires that managers diagnose a given situation and adapt to meet the conditions present. The difficulty with this approach is that few management writers have prescribed precisely what a manager should do in a given situation.

(table cont'd.: Koontz's Classification of Management Theories)

Managerial Roles Approach

Henry Mintzberg of McGill University observed and studied what managers actually do in managing and identified the primary roles of managers.[a] He concluded that executives do not always perform the traditional managerial functions of planning, organizing, directing, controlling, but instead perform a variety of other activities. According to Mintzberg, managers have three dominant roles: interpersonal, informational, and decision making. In the interpersonal role, a manager acts as a figurehead, leader, and liaison person. In the informational role, a manager serves as a monitor, disseminator, and spokesperson. In the decision-making role, a manager acts as entrepreneur, disturbance handler, resource allocator, and negotiator. A difficulty that arises is that roles Mintzberg identifies inadequately describe managerial activities and functions. Such important roles as those of goal setting, strategy identification and implementation, developing the organization, and selecting and developing managers are not included.

Operational Approach

According to Koontz, these theories are certainly applicable to the study of management, but our interest in them must not necessarily be limited to managerial aspects and applications. The operational approach to management indicates that the foundations for management science and theory are drawn from a number of other schools and approaches. The operational approach recognizes that there are significant concepts, principles, theories, and techniques that comprise the effecive practice of management. This approach draws on pertinent knowledge from other fields of study including political science, sociology, social psychology, psychology, mathematics, economics, decision theory, general systems theory, and industrial engineering. We believe that the operational approach provides a logical framework for the study of management theory and practice.

SOURCE Harold Koontz, "The Management Theory Jungle Revisited," *Academy of Management Review* 5, no. 2 (April 1980). Reprinted with permission of the author and *Academy of Management Review*.

[a]Henry Mintzberg, "The Manager's Job: Folklore and Fact," *Harvard Business Review* 53, no. 4 (1975): 49–61.

One of the most important recent schools of management thought to emerge is the contingency, or situational, school. Gordon Allan, president of Gordon Allan Consultants of Toronto, noted as far back as 1971 that managers must be flexible and adapt to the characteristics of specific situations if they hope to be effective.[7] They must be able to change their managerial style to fit the demands of the situation. Failure to do so will result in inappropriate management behavior, in less satisfied employees, in lowered organization productivity, and in an overall reduction in organization effectiveness.

OPENING INCIDENT REVISITED

Lawton Manufacturing Ltd.

Marshall Cizek had a rather unpleasant introduction to the practice of management — perhaps because he did not understand what management is all about. In this chapter, we defined management as the accomplishment of organizational objectives through the efforts of other people. Cizek's experience suggests that he was ignoring this fundamental aspect of management. He was trying to do most of the work himself; he was acting as if he was still a maintenance mechanic whose job was to repair machinery. This situation had changed, but Cizek didn't seem to realize it.

In order to become effective managers, individuals must understand what the functions of management are. Planning, organizing, influencing, and controlling are introduced in Chapter 1 and are discussed in detail in the remaining chapters of this text.

In his new position, Cizek became a lower-level manager. As such, he should have been making certain decisions about how to spend his time. Exhibit 1-4 indicates that managers at the lower levels in an organization must allocate varying amounts of time to all the basic functions of management, but most should be spent on influencing others. Cizek allocated very little time to any of the functions and was particularly remiss with respect to influencing. As a result, he had little real influence with his subordinates. In fact, they had gone to the plant superintendent about his "meddling" in their work, rather than talk to him.

Overall, Cizek did not seem to understand the difference between managing the work of others and actually doing the work himself. Until he understands this distinction, he will have serious troubles in any management position.

SUMMARY

Effective management is essential to the success of every organization: whether the organization is a profit-oriented firm or a not-for-profit organization; whether it operates in the public or private sector; whether it produces a physical product or an intangible service; or whether it is a sole proprietorship, partnership, or a corporation. Management influences the lives of all members of an organized society. For individuals, knowledge of management is valuable as evidenced by the fact that organizations actively recruit students who have a concentration in management. All individuals can gain a better understanding of and appreciation for management in order to function more effectively in an organization. Our study of management provides:

- A knowledge of and insight into the responsibilities of managing people and other resources
- An understanding of the problems of operating a business firm
- An opportunity to learn the skills essential to making effective managerial decisions
- An understanding of basic principles of management
- The ability to identify and cope with internal and external environment forces that affect performance
- The skills and attitudes to continue your professional development.

Canadian society is dominated by large organizations in which people must work together effectively to accomplish goals. The degree of success of all organizations — business and nonbusiness — is determined to a great extent by the quality and overall effectiveness of management. What is management? Who is a manager? What do managers do? What roles do managers play in work performance? What skills are needed for good management? In answering these questions, it is important to realize that there is no one best approach to management that is effective in every situation.

Management is the process of planning, organizing, influencing, and controlling to accomplish organizational goals through the coordinated use of human and material resources. A manager is anyone, regardless of level within a firm, who directs the efforts of other people in accomplishing goals. A manager is the catalyst who makes things happen by *planning* what is to be achieved, *organizing* personnel and other resources to achieve the plan, *influencing* or *directing* people, and comparing results achieved to the planned performance. In order to be effective, managers need to possess and develop several essential skills, including: technical, communication, people, analytical, decision-making, and conceptual. These skills must be mixed in the proper proportion based on the particular level occupied by the manager.

While we can agree that every organization requires good management, there is considerable disagreement as to the most effective way to manage. Historically, two different approaches to management have developed. The classical school, including the work of Frederick Taylor, Henri Fayol, and C. I. Barnard, attempted to provide a rational and scientific basis for management. Major contributions of scientific management include the application of the scientific method to management and the classification of the basic management functions.

The behavioral school of management is concerned with the human element in the organization. The early "human relations" era, which resulted primarily from the Hawthorne experiments in the late 1920s and early 1930s, evolved into behavioral management science. Behavioral scientists have criticized classical management theory as being unresponsive to the needs of employees, overspecializing jobs, underemploying and overmanaging people, and showing too little concern about a person's need for recognition and self-fulfillment. In today's world, management has little choice but to be more responsive to the needs of employees if improved performance is to be achieved. Harold Koontz identified 11 schools of management. One of the eleven — the operational approach — indicates that the foundations of management science and theory are drawn from approaches found in other disciplines. Another of these schools — Allan's contingency approach — stresses the flexibility required when the basic functions of management are performed.

REVIEW QUESTIONS

1. Define management. Who is a manager and what does a manager do?
2. List some factors that may account for the success and effectiveness of a manager.
3. Why is the study of management important?
4. List and briefly describe 3 managerial roles and 6 managerial skills important to effectiveness. How are the skills relevant to managers operating at different levels in the organization?
5. What is the classical school of management? Identify the basic contributions of this school of management.
6. Frederick Taylor is known as the father of scientific management. Why? What is scientific management and Taylor's philosophy?
7. Identify briefly the contributions to management theory of:
   a. Henri Fayol
   b. C. I. Barnard
   c. H. L. Gantt
   d. Harrington Emerson.
8. Discuss the behavioral school of management. How and why did the movement originate?
9. What specific criticisms did behavioral scientists have of traditional or classical management theory?
10. Harold Koontz coined the phrase "management theory jungle" as he described the various approaches to the study of management. What do you believe he meant and what were the various schools of management he identified?

EXERCISES

1. Interview three managers from different types of organizations (for example, talk to managers in a bank, a retail store, a manufacturer, or a college/university). Have a list of prepared questions including, but not limited to, the following:
   a. How did you become a manager?
   b. What does your job as a manager entail? Describe your major functions.
   c. Why are you a manager?
   d. What skills are necessary for success as a manager?
   e. What advice would you give a person interested in a career in management?
   f. Is management a profession?
   g. Can a person learn to be a better manager? if so, how?

2. Review the employment classified ads in the *Globe and Mail* or a Saturday edition of a large city newspaper. Make a list of the types of managerial jobs, the companies offering employment, and the qualifications needed to obtain the positions. What is your basic conclusion after this review, in terms of the availability of managerial positions and the necessary qualifications for obtaining a position?

CASE STUDY

From Engineering to Management

Jack Esselmont recently had received a promotion to the position of manager of engineering at Keystone Home Products Ltd., a medium-sized firm producing a diverse line of consumer household products. Esselmont had an electrical engineering degree and had been with the company for 9 years since graduating from Queen's University.

Esselmont's record as a design engineer was excellent. He had developed three new products, one of which was now marketed in the United States and England. The department Esselmont worked in was widely respected as an industry leader in innovative product design and in research and development.

Not only was Esselmont a good engineer, he was also popular with almost everyone in the company. Throughout his 9 years with Keystone, Esselmont had kept up to date in his field by reading engineering journals and by attending meetings of electrical engineers where new technical developments were discussed. Because of his technical and engineering experience with the company and his ability to get along with people, top management felt confident in promoting Jack Esselmont to the position of manager of engineering.

For the first few months, Esselmont's department ran fairly smoothly. He continued to be heavily involved in actual research and new product design, but his subordinates didn't seem to mind too much — at least, they didn't say anything. As time went on, however, Esselmont began to feel frustrated because managing the department was starting to interfere with his ability to do the research and design work that he liked so well. He tried to compensate by working longer hours, but Esselmont found he didn't have the "creative spark" he used to.

The situation continued to deteriorate, as Esselmont found himself becoming less interested in either the management or the research functions in his department. He felt "burned out," lacking the motivation to do his job. To make matters worse, some of his engineers began to express the views that Esselmont was too heavily involved in research and design work, that he should concentrate on managing, so the engineers could do what they were paid for.

At about this time, Esselmont heard rumors that top management was having serious doubts about his ability to manage the engineering department. These rumors concerned him deeply, so he decided to make an appointment with his boss to see if he could straighten out the mess he had got into.

QUESTIONS

1. What is the basic problem confronting Jack Esselmont as a manager? What are the causes?
2. How does being a manager differ from being an engineer? Be specific.
3. Did top management make a mistake in promoting Esselmont to the position of engineering manager?
4. What skills are important for Esselmont as a manager? Why?
5. Does being a good engineer guarantee success as a manager? Why or why not?

CASE STUDY

From Assistant Foreman to President

Today, Phillip Garrick becomes president of Canadian Controls Ltd., a producer of high-quality control mechanisms. When the previous president had announced his retirement, Garrick had been identified as the likeliest choice to assume the post. He was respected for his competence in the field and for his ability to work with employees at all levels of operations. Garrick is early this morning, not so much to work, as to think. Sitting in his new office, his thoughts go back to his earlier days with the company.

Twenty years ago, Garrick had graduated from a community college. With a diploma in industrial management and no business experience, he had been hired as assistant foreman on the production line. "Those were the days," thinks Garrick. "Seemed as though there was a problem to solve every minute. Thank goodness for the standard procedures manual and a foreman who was patient enough to answer all my questions. Didn't have to make too many critical decisions back then."

Garrick's thoughts pass next to the time when he was taken off the production line and promoted to middle management. "Noticed a few changes," he remembers. As foreman, he had been primarily concerned with meeting daily production requirements; as production manager, he had had to plan weeks, often months, in advance. Just as at the lower level of management, the people and communication problems remained; Garrick seemed to think the reports he then had to write were much longer. Still, the major change was that he had had to do more creative thinking. Chuckling, he recalls the time he'd gone to the files for a standard procedure to respond to an unusual problem confronting him and found there wasn't one; he'd felt momentarily frustrated that he had to handle the problem without assistance. However, as his analytical, decision-making, and conceptual abilities increased, he found himself using his technical skills less.

Phillip Garrick's promotion 5 years ago to vice-president of planning was a major accomplishment in his career, as he had been in a tight competition with three well-qualified managers. He'd heard through the grapevine that he had been promoted over the others mostly because he was able to think for himself. But, even his past training had not fully prepared Garrick for the demands of this job; he had had to learn much of it on his own. Rather than think weeks or months into the future, as vice-president of planning, Garrick had to envision years ahead.

Garrick recalls that at first he had not realized how many people outside of production he had to coordinate. Marketing and finance had to be tied into production; although the process of planning for all three departments had been a difficult one, Garrick realized that his conceptual and decision-making skills had increased significantly through it. He had long left behind the "good old standard procedures manual."

Today, as Garrick looks at the gold plate bearing his current title as "President," he wonders what changes are in store for him at this top level of management. What new requirements will be placed on him? A twinge of excitement and challenge tells him he knows he can face and cope with them. What skills must he develop to continue to be successful?

QUESTIONS

1. As the president of Canadian Controls, what specific skills will Garrick need to be effective? Reference to Exhibit 1-4 provides insight into this question.
2. How do the demands of different levels of responsibility change as a manager progresses up the hierarchy of an organization?
3. What general recommendations would you offer Garrick?

CASE STUDY
A Business Opportunity

While working on their seminar case which was due in three days, Fred Dillinger, an accounting major, and Katherine Mandu, a marketing major, discussed what they were going to do when they graduated from Southern Alberta Institute of Technology (SAIT) in a few weeks. During their discussion they were joined by Rocky Allen, an administration major, who had a similar concern. As it turned out, Rocky had just received a $100,000 bequest from the estate of his uncle Woody and was thinking of starting a business. Fred indicated that he had just received a scholarship of $50,000 for maintaining a 3.75 point average in accounting over his six quarters at SAIT, and he was also considering starting his own business. Katherine revealed that she had just been awarded $75,000 from Economics instructor Keynes for being the only student to earn an A in Economics 201 in his fifty years at SAIT. She went on to tell them that not only was she interested in being in business but she had a great idea about which one to try.

Katherine had done a marketing survey of the students at SAIT and had found that they would welcome an establishment that would provide such activities as pool, bowling, and mini golf, while supplying beer, as long as it was not too far from SAIT. Through her research she discovered a company that would supply a pre-packaged pool hall, bowling alley, games arcade, miniature golf, and pizza center for $200,000 delivered. They also guarantee that their package would pass the Alberta Liquor Control Board requirements for the serving of beer.

Rocky and Fred became quite excited by Katherine's idea; the three decided to approach it the way they had learned to do case studies. They gathered the following facts:

- The package would cost $50,000 to erect.
- The business would require a C-1 lot of at least 30 m × 45 m.
- Equipment would cost $2,500 per month to lease.
- Preopening costs (advertising, promotions) would run about $10,000.

SOURCE Adapted from a case by Garry E. Veak, Southern Alberta Institute of Technology. Reprinted by permission.

- Two locations are available:
  - The former "Filler's Station" directly across from SAIT for $200,000.
  - A former Imperial service station and restaurant, "EAT HERE AND GET GAS," about 4 km away for $150,000.
- The first location can be purchased with a downpayment of $60,000 and monthly payments of $1,654.26 (15 years at 12 percent). Monthly utilities are $525. Monthly taxes are $500.
- The Imperial station can be purchased with a downpayment of $45,000 and monthly payments of $1,240.70 (15 years at 12 percent). Monthly utilities are $525. Monthly taxes are $414.
- The package can be purchased with a downpayment of $20,000 and monthly payments of $2,321.68 (15 years at 13.75 percent).
- Wages and salaries would be $3,000 per month.
- Rocky, Fred, and Katherine can only borrow an extra $5,000 each.
- Currently a "safe" investment would generate a 10 percent return.
- Rocky, Fred, and Katherine can each find a job with an annual income of about $24,000 if they choose not to go into this business.
- The former "Filler's Station" could produce a gross profit of $19,500 per month.
- The former Imperial station could produce a gross profit of $15,000 per month.

QUESTIONS

1. Advise Katherine, Fred, and Rocky about what form of business — sole proprietorship, partnership, or corporation — makes the most sense for their proposal. (None of them wants to be a minority owner.) Why is your choice more suitable than the other two? (*Hint:* Consult an introduction to business text's section on forms of business ownership.)
2. Indicate what will be involved in each of the basic management functions for this type of organization.
3. Suppose these SAIT graduates make their proposal a reality. Should they hire managers, or manage the business themselves?

NOTES

[1]*The Canadian Business Failure Record* (Dun and Bradstreet Canada Ltd., 1982): 4.

[2]Henry Mintzberg, "The Manager's Job: Folklore and Fact," *Harvard Business Review* 53, no. 4 (1975): 49–61.

[3]Frederick W. Taylor, *The Principles of Scientific Management* (New York: Harper, 1911): 41–47.

[4]Chester I. Barnard, *The Functions of the Executive* (Cambridge, Mass.: Harvard University Press, 1938).

[5]F. Roethlisberger and W. J. Dickson, *Management and the Worker* (Cambridge, Mass.: Harvard University Press, 1935).

[6]Harold Koontz, "The Management Theory Jungle Revisited," *Academy of Management Review* 5, no. 2 (April 1980).

[7]Gordon Allan, "Management Flexibility," *The Canadian Personnel and Industrial Relations Journal* 18 (May 1971): 13–21.

REFERENCES

Boone, Louis E., and Johnson, James C. "Profiles of the 801 Men and 1 Woman at the Top." *Business Horizons* 23, no. 1 (February 1980): 47–53.

Cook, Curtis W. "Guidelines for Managing Motivation." *Business Horizons* 23, no. 2 (April 1980): 61–70.

Cummings, L. L. "The Logics of Management." *Academy of Management Review* 8, no. 4 (October 1983): 532–538.

Drucker, Peter F. *Management: Tasks, Responsibilities and Practices.* New York: Harper, 1974.

Fayol, Henri. *General and Industrial Management.* New York: Pitman, 1949.

George, Claude, Jr. *The History of Management Thought.* Englewood Cliffs, N.J.: Prentice-Hall, 1972.

Hay, Christine D. "Women in Management: The Obstacles and Opportunities They Face," *Personnel Administrator* 25, no. 4 (April 1980): 25–31.

Hecht, Maurice. "Real Managers Don't Need Theories Anymore." *Executive* 26, no. 1 (January 1984): 32–35.

Kantrow, Alan M. "Why Read Peter Drucker?" *Harvard Business Review* 58, no. 1 (January-February 1980): 74–83.

Koontz, Harold. "The Management Theory Jungle Revisited." *Academy of Management Review* 5, no. 2 (April 1980): 175–189.

McGregor, Douglas. *The Professional Manager.* New York: McGraw-Hill, 1967.

Mintzberg, Henry. "The Manager's Job: Folklore and Fact." *Harvard Business Review* (July-August 1975): 49–61.

_____. *The Nature of Managerial Work*. New York: Harper, 1973.

Newman, William H., ed. *Managers for the Year 2000*. Englewood Cliffs, N.J.: Prentice-Hall, 1978.

Olivia, Terence A., and Capdevielle, Christel M. "Can Systems Really Be Taught? (A Socratic Dialogue)." *Academy of Management Review* 5, no. 2 (April 1980): 277–281.

Roethlisberger, F. J., and Dickson, W. J. *Management and the Worker: An Account of a Research Program Conducted by the Western Electric Company Hawthorne Works, Chicago*. Cambridge: Harvard University Press, 1939.

Stewart, Rosemary. *Choices for the Manager*. Englewood Cliffs, N.J.: Prentice-Hall, 1982.

Wells, Jennifer, ed. "Remaking the Management Mind: How Companies and Business Schools are Trying — Painfully — To Change Their Ways." *Canadian Business* 56, no. 10 (October 1983): 36.

Wente, M. A. "Remaking the Management Mind." *Canadian Business* 56, no. 1 (January 1983): 23.

The External Environment

Farlane Mining and Smelting Ltd.

James Farlane is the president of Farlane Mining and Smelting Ltd. which has operations at eight locations in Ontario and Quebec. As Farlane arrived at his office yesterday, several problems that had been building for weeks came to a head. The most pressing problem concerned the latest union contract. Negotiations had not been progressing well and the union was threatening to go on strike at midnight tomorrow. The main point of disagreement was a wage increase for union members that the company thought it could not afford.

Over the past two years, the company had been directed to meet federal pollution regula-

tions with its smelter. In the last three months, some emission-control devices had been installed; an inspector is due today. Farlane knew that, for the smelter to meet the legal requirements, the company would need substantially more equipment than had already been bought. In Farlane's assessment, the company simply cannot afford to spend more on pollution-control equipment because the increase in the company's cost structure would make it uncompetitive. Farlane was, however, sensitive to the adverse reactions of townspeople who lived near the smelter; he'd read articles in the local papers expressing increasing dissatisfaction with the company for polluting the air and water. The debates over acid rain had produced additional negative publicity for Farlane's company. Farlane feared the federal inspector would not be sympathetic to the pollution-control efforts made so far.

Farlane thought ahead to the company's upcoming annual meeting. He knew the company's shareholders would not be happy when he reported a 13 percent decline in earnings per share. The reasons for this decline were clear — wage increases granted to employees, expenditures for pollution-control equipment and generally depressed prices in the industry — but Farlane knew that the shareholders wanted earnings per share to grow, not decline.

Farlane had also noticed a recent trend among the company's customers; they were pressuring the company to lower prices on several products. Farlane had requested marketing reports to track the pricing of the company's competitors, fearing his customers might switch. Farlane was troubled about this problem because a drop in sales would make all the other problems facing him that much more difficult to resolve.

KEY TERMS

unions	systems approach	technology
shareholders	system	structure
social responsibility	standards	centralized
ethics	situational approach	decentralized
	objective	

LEARNING OBJECTIVES

After completing this chapter you should be able to
1. Describe the major external environment factors that can affect a firm.
2. Explain the systems approach to management and describe the basic components of a business system.
3. Describe the situational approach to management and identify the major situational factors successful managers must balance.

In Chapter 1, we introduced the concept of management; we also talked about what managers do in business and nonbusiness organizations. That discussion was directed largely toward the specific activity of managers within an organization. James Farlane's experience indicates that managers must also be concerned about activities outside the firm they work for. Changes in the environment external to an organization can have a major impact on it.

In this chapter we describe the eight major external environment factors that managers must deal with if they are to be successful. We then discuss two complementary problem-solving ideas — the systems approach and the situational approach — that help managers to cope effectively with the external environment. The systems approach views the business organization as part of a larger system of interrelated parts. This approach assumes that changes in the external environment also affect the internal workings of the firm. The situational approach builds on the systems approach and helps the manager to realize that different external situations require different managerial styles.

THE EXTERNAL ENVIRONMENT

Managing an organization is not accomplished in a vacuum. Many interacting external factors can affect the performance of managers and the firms they work for. Exhibit 2-1 shows the major external environment factors that can affect firms in Canada: (1) government, (2) competitors, (3) the work force, (4) unions, (5) shareholders, (6) suppliers, (7) customers, and (8) the general public. Each of these can constrain the behavior of a firm's managers. These external factors can work singly or in combination, and their impact may be difficult to predict.

Several general observations about all eight factors can be made. First, managers at different levels in the management hierarchy have differing degrees of involvement with the external environment of the firm. Generally speaking, the closer to the top of the firm's hierarchy managers are, the more their work will be affected by the external environment. First-line supervisors have relatively little management concern for activities outside the firm; vice-presidents, on the other hand, may spend a great deal of their work time dealing with consumer groups, labor unions, or government agencies.

Second, these external environment factors may be in conflict with one another as well as with the business firm. Customers want lower prices and workers want higher wages; but, since a firm has limited resources, it cannot satisfy fully the demands of both groups. When faced with conflicts like this, managers often try to compromise to satisfy some of the demands of each group. However, this tactic can be frustrating since each group may be persuasively vocal in its claim that all its needs should be met.

Third, the importance of a given external environment factor to a manager depends to some extent on that manager's specific responsibilities in the firm. The vice-president of personnel in a unionized manufacturing company may serve as the head of the firm's bargaining team when the labor contract is up for review. At that time, the most important external environment factor the vice-president of personnel will have to manage will be the union; at other times, that same vice-president may be more concerned with general labor market conditions. A superintendent in a pulp and paper mill may be concerned mainly with a steady flow of raw materials from suppliers. But, if townspeople living downstream from the mill report sudden increased amounts of effluent in the river, that same manager's responsibilities will expand. Probably, the plant superintendent will find that an aspect of government becomes the most significant environment factor to manage.

Fourth, the business firm may have some control over certain external environment factors but little control over others. Business managers cannot change the size and composition of the labor force, nor the number of competitors their firm faces. They can, however, have some impact on government, shareholders, suppliers, unions, and the general public.

Finally, each of the eight environment factors is complex. A brief discussion of them cannot capture all the possible ways they affect business managers. Given this fact, our purpose here is to describe the factors briefly and to suggest some of the more obvious ways they can influence managers as they carry out their planning, organizing, influencing, and controlling functions.

Government

One of the most obvious external factors Canadian managers must deal with is the law — federal, provincial, and municipal legislation. Government legislation covers a wide range of business activities, having a direct impact on the organization and its managers. A sample of such legislation is shown in the following table.

Canadian Legislation Affecting Business Activity

Federal Law	Major Provisions
Conciliation Act	Assists in the settlement of labor disputes through voluntary conciliation.
Industrial Disputes Investigation Act	Provides for compulsory arbitration of labor disputes by a government-appointed board.
Privy Council Order 1003	Recognizes the right of organized labor to bargain collectively with management.

(table continues on pp. 46–47)

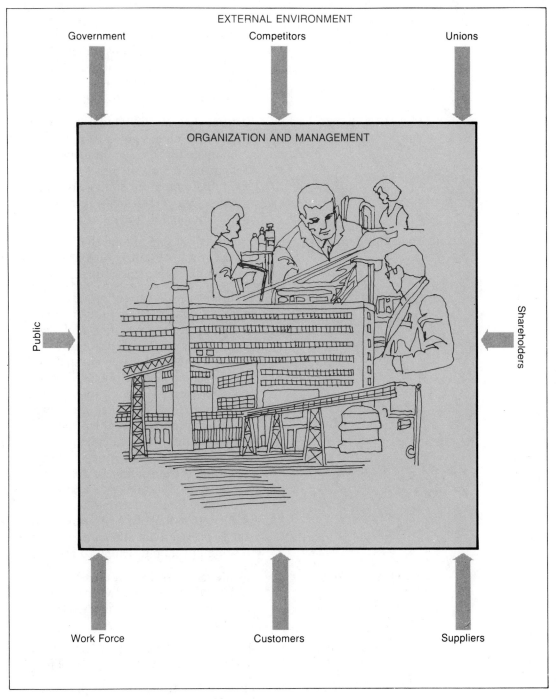

EXHIBIT 2-1   External environment factors

(table cont'd.: Legislation Affecting Business)

Canada Labour Code	Deals with the personnel practices of firms, with provisions on fair employment practices, standard hours of work, employee health and safety, and discrimination in employment practices.
Canadian Human Rights Act	Ensures that any individual who wishes to obtain a job has an equal opportunity to compete for it, by prohibiting discrimination (on the bases of age, race, sex, religion, marital status, and ethnic origin) in the recruitment, selection, promotion, and dismissal of personnel.
Food and Drug Act	Prohibits the sale of food that contains any harmful substance; also prohibits misleading advertising of food.
Combines Investigation Act	Prohibits a wide variety of business practices which lessen competition and/or harm the consumer. Includes prohibitions on (1) mergers and monopolies which lessen competition, (2) misleading advertising, (3) illegal trade practices — for example, setting abnormally low price in an attempt to bankrupt competitors, (4) bait and switch selling — baiting a consumer with an advertised low price and then switching the consumer to a higher-priced item, (5) resale price maintenance — manufacturers' attempts to force retailers to sell above a minimum price, and (6) promotional allowances — given to some buyers but denied to others.
Weights and Measures Act	Regulates weighing and measuring devices; also concerned with the implementation of the metric system in Canada.
Hazardous Products Act	Regulates the labelling, advertising, and sale of potentially dangerous products.
Consumer Packaging and Labelling Act	Ensures adherence to packaging and labelling guidelines. All prepackaged goods must, for example, state the quantity in English and French in metric units.

(table cont'd.: Legislation Affecting Business)

Textile Labelling Act	Regulates the labelling, importation, and sale of consumer textile articles.
Canada Water Act	Controls water quality in fresh and marine waters.
Environmental Contaminants Act	Establishes limits on the amount of airborne substances that may be discharged into the atmostphere.

Legislation affecting business activity is not something new. The Conciliation Act was passed in 1900; other laws regulating business have been on the books for many years. Whenever government perceives that business is acting in an undesirable way, it creates legislation to rectify the problem. For example, in the late 1800s, when many children worked in industry, legislation regulating the employment of children was passed. This legislation directly affected business firms by prohibiting children below a certain age from working.

The federal laws described in the table show also that all areas of the firm are affected by government activity. Personnel managers, for example, must be up to date on legislation regarding discrimination in employment practices. Production managers must be aware of pollution laws. Marketing managers must abide by advertising and pricing regulations. Government legislation therefore has a profound impact on all areas of the typical business firm.

On certain occasions, government legislation can be controversial. Foreign ownership and investment in Canada is one controversial area. In an attempt to reduce the perceived negative impact of foreign ownership of Canadian business, the Liberal government established the Foreign Investment Review Agency (FIRA) to screen new foreign investment in Canada. Its purpose was to ensure that significant benefits from foreign investment accrued to Canada. This federal legislation had a major impact on companies that wanted to be bought by foreign firms because they could be prevented from doing so by FIRA. Many complaints were levelled at FIRA during the 1970s and early 1980s; the argument was made by business managers that the agency had made Canada an unattractive place for foreigners to invest. When the Progressive Conservative government was elected in 1984, it quickly changed the name of the agency to "Investment Canada" and embarked on a strategy of encouraging appropriate foreign investment.

Controversy can also erupt between business and government at the provincial level. Consider Quebec's language law (Bill 101). This legislation, designed to protect and promote the French language, contained provisions prohibiting certain business practices conducted in English. All signs, menus, and employment advertisements, for instance, had to be printed in French only. Many business firms complained about the costs incurred to alter their firms to French only. They pointed out that much of their commerce was with businesses elsewhere, where the language of business is English. The language law and other legislation of the Quebec provincial government have caused many business firms in the 1980s to move out of the province. The long-run effect of this legislation on business activity in Quebec is not yet clear.

As a third example of controversial legislation, consider the dispute about metric conversion in Canada. Many Canadian consumers were opposed to converting to metric because it would require them to learn a new system of measurement. Many business firms, however, wanted to convert to metric because it is a more straightforward system than the imperial and because it would make trade with European countries easier. The federal Liberal government announced its commitment to metric conversion in 1972, and changes began to be noticeable by the late 1970s. Various pockets of resistance were evident — for example, in Ontario, some gasoline dealers and small grocery stores continued pricing by imperial measures — but the shift was clearly happening. As much of the general public — the voters — still expresses resistance to metric use, current legislators are considering the abandonment or delay of metric conversion. They point to the United States, where conversion is voluntary and very slow. However, many Canadian business firms have expressed opposition to any change of policy because they had already spent a great deal of money on metric conversion. In addition, the education system has converted wholly to metric measures. Likely, most business with direct contact with the general public will continue to use both systems simultaneously; that way, they meet the requirements of both external environment factors.

Competitors

Unless an organization is in the unusual position of having a monopoly in the market it serves, it will have to cope with competitive goods and services. A decision made by one firm may have a substantial impact on other firms in the market. Gasoline prices provide a common example. In recent years, service stations have watched their competitors very closely; in some cities prices vary little, within a tenth of a cent per litre. Weekend "gas wars" have erupted — to the delight of consumers — with service stations near one another lowering their prices several times a day in response to competitors' decreases.

The Work Force

The number and characteristics of individuals in the work force form a major external factor that business firms must take into account. In

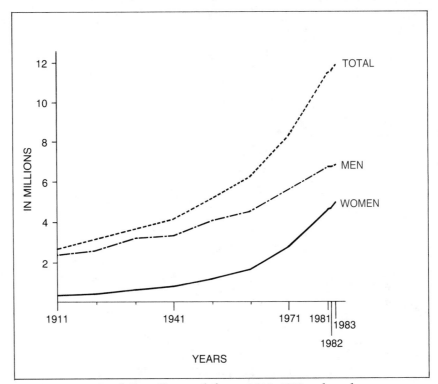

EXHIBIT 2-2   Total Canadian work force, 1911–1983, selected years

SOURCES *Historical Statistics of Canada,* ed. F. H. Leacy, series D123 (1911–1971) (Ministry of
Supply and Services Canada, 1983); Statistics Canada, *The Labour Force,* cat. no. 71-001
(1981–1983). Used with permission of the Minister of Supply and Services.

1983, the Canadian work force was comprised of approximately 12
million people, nearly double the figure for 1961. (See Exhibit 2-2.)
During the 1980s, the work force will continue to increase in size but
at a much slower rate than that experienced over the last 20 years. It
is also likely that the high unemployment levels evident in the early
1980s will continue throughout the decade. (See Exhibit 2-3.)

The industries that will absorb these additional workers will likely
be different from those that dominate current employment in Canada.
The goods-producing industries, such as construction, mining, and
manufacturing, are expected to remain relatively stable in terms of
employment. But job opportunities in service industries, such as health
care, trade, repair and maintenance, government, transportation, banking, and insurance are expected to increase. (See Exhibit 2-4.) Employment in service industries will likely constitute an increasing proportion
of total employment in Canada.

The composition of the labor force is also changing. While the participation rate for men continues to decline, it is rising sharply for
women. (See Exhibit 2-5.) Women currently have improved opportunities to move into occupations that traditionally have been closed to

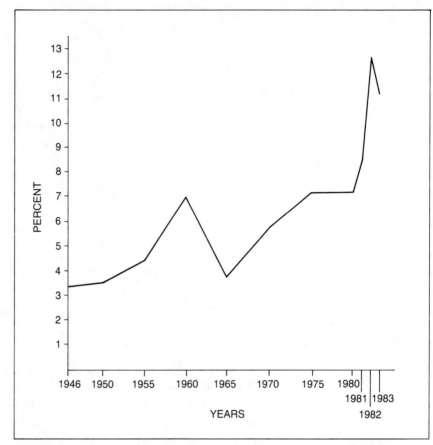

EXHIBIT 2-3 **Unemployment rates in Canada, 1946–1983, selected years**

SOURCES *Historical Statistics of Canada*, series D491–497 (1946–1975) (Ministry of Supply and Services Canada, 1983); Statistics Canada, *The Labour Force*, cat. no. 71-001 (1980–1983). Used with permission of the Minister of Supply and Services.

them, for example, computer sales, public accounting, and top management. This trend is expected to continue.

The number of white-collar workers is also expected to increase more rapidly than the number of blue-collar workers through 1990. The increased use of computers and the shift from goods-producing to service-producing firms are largely responsible for this growth in white-collar jobs. This trend started many years ago and is evidence that our economy has reached a high level of industrial maturity. This can also be seen in the steadily declining employment in agriculture. (See Exhibit 2-6.)

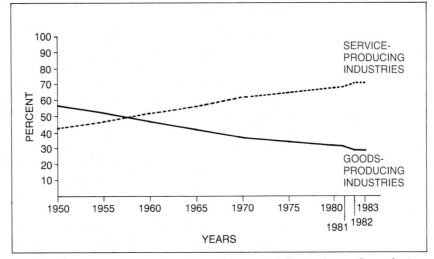

EXHIBIT 2-4 Proportion of total Canadian employment in goods-producing and service-producing industries, 1950–1983, selected years

SOURCE Statistics Canada, *The Labour Force*, cat. no. 71-001 (1980–1983). Used with permission of the Minister of Supply and Services Canada.

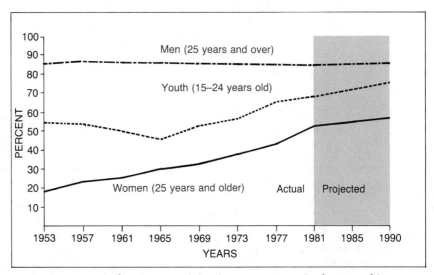

EXHIBIT 2-5 Employment participation among certain demographic groups, 1953–1990, selected years

SOURCES Historical data based on: Statistics Canada, *Labour Force Survey*, a projection developed by the Labour Market Development Task Force; Department of Finance projection from Participation Rate and Labour Force Growth in Canada (July 1981): 57. Used with permission of the Minister of Supply and Services Canada.

NOTE: The historical series break in 1975, the year in which major revisions were made to the labor force survey. The most abrupt break occurs in the case of the less-than-25 group. Prior to the revisions, this group consisted of 14–24-year-olds. It was revised to consist of 15–25-year-olds.

Unions

Unions consist of employees who have joined together for the purpose of presenting a united front in dealing with top management. Unions are an external environment factor because they are third parties dealing with company management. The union, rather than the individual employee, negotiates an agreement with the firm; so, while individual employees are part of the internal environment of the firm, their union is a part of the external environment.

Through collective bargaining, organized labor has influenced the pattern of employee-management relations in business firms. In Canada, approximately 32 percent of the total labor force is unionized. (See Exhibit 2-7.) Even among nonunion firms that try to maintain their nonunion status, unions have an impact. Current wage levels, fringe benefits, and working conditions for millions of employees reflect decisions made by unions and management through collective bargaining.

Shareholders

People who are owners and who share in a corporation's profit (or loss) are referred to as **shareholders**. They are vitally interested in the firm's operating effectiveness. The price of the shares and the dividends paid are also of major concern to shareholders. Managers actually operate the firm but, since the shareholders own the company, managers must be sensitive to the needs of shareholders as an external environment factor.

Because shareholders have a monetary investment in the firm, they may at times challenge programs considered by management to be beneficial to the organization. Managers may be forced to justify the merits of a particular program in terms of how it will affect future

MANAGEMENT IN PRACTICE

Unionization at Eaton's

For many years, Eaton's employees have been nonunion. However, in 1984, the Retail, Wholesale, and Department Store Employees Union was certified as the bargaining agent for employees at two Eaton's stores. A retail analyst from a Montreal brokerage firm had predicted a union drive because department stores had frozen wages and reduced staff levels dramatically during 1980–1982. A research and education director for the Ontario Retail Council believes there were also other contributing factors. Part-time jobs used to be taken by people who were between jobs, but that era has passed. People have begun relying on these jobs, and the lower wages associated with them have become unacceptable.

To discourage further inroads by labor unions, retail outlets will need to improve working conditions and employee wages and benefits. However, this may reduce profits and put downward pressure on share prices.

SOURCE Frances Phillips, "Union Claims Second Eaton's Store," *The Financial Post* (April 21, 1984): 4.

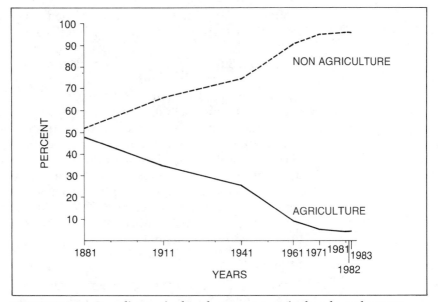

EXHIBIT 2-6   Canadian agricultural versus nonagricultural employment, 1881–1983, selected years

SOURCES *Historical Statistics of Canada*, series D1-7 (1881–1971) (Ministry of Supply and Services Canada, 1983); Statistics Canada, *The Labour Force*, cat. no. 71-007 (1981–1983). Used with permission of the Minister of Supply and Services.

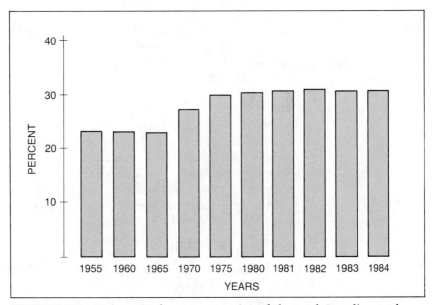

EXHIBIT 2-7   Union members as proportion of the total Canadian work force, 1955–1983, selected years

SOURCE Department of Labour, *Directory of Labour Organizations in Canada* (Ministry of Supply and Services Canada, 1984): xxvi. Used by permission.

profits. For instance, if managers recommend that equipment be bought that will lower pollutants, they will likely have to justify the purchase to shareholders with regard to how it affects the long-term profitability of the firm. Shareholders are concerned with how expenditure decisions relate to increasing revenues or decreasing costs.

Another means by which some shareholders have influenced some firms is through shareholder activism. A small group of shareholders may try to force a corporation to take a certain action in order to avoid negative public relations. For example, during the 1960s, a group of Dow Chemical shareholders asked the firm to stop manufacturing items used in the war in Vietnam. The last thing most corporations want is criticism of the firm in the headlines of major newspapers. Such action was virtually unheard of before 1960 and, although shareholder activism's goals are rarely fulfilled, it usually succeeds in increasing the firm's sensitivity to its public image.

Suppliers

A manufacturing firm cannot operate effectively unless it is continuously supplied with needed raw materials. Lack of adequate supplies can cause the manufacturing process to be inefficient or to cease altogether — even if the firm has sufficient capital and employees. Managers must try to minimize the negative impact of supplier failure. For instance, a steel strike can affect a manufacturing firm's ability to produce its regular product. Similarly, a computer company which produces data-processing services would likely have to delay its operations if it was unable to secure the needed forms to process the customer's output. Suppliers of both service and goods-producing industries can be a crucial external factor. When supplies fail, managers should have contingency plans ready.

Customers

The people who actually use a firm's products and services also must be considered part of the external environment. Because sales are critical to a firm's survival, managers have the task of ensuring that its business practices do not antagonize the members of the market it serves. If customers or consumers think a firm's employment, pricing, or pollution policies are unreasonable, for instance, they may refuse to buy the firm's products or services.

The General Public

Canadian society as a whole also exerts considerable pressure on managers. The general public is not always willing to accept the actions of business without question. Pressure has been brought to bear on business with respect to such issues as product safety, minority and women's rights, and advertising.

As an external environment factor, the general public can affect managers through government. Public pressure can be effective if a

MANAGEMENT IN PRACTICE

Business Is Listening

In the 1980s, managers will be required to expand their thinking about how business firms fit into the overall Canadian society. Franz Tyaack, [chief executive officer] at Westinghouse Canada, Inc. and Robert Blair, CEO of Nova, an Alberta corporation, feel that business organizations must strike a balance between the numerous constituencies in their external environment. One of the most important constituents is government, and there will almost surely be more interaction with government during the next few years. Although some firms view this as a nuisance and an intrusion into their operations, Tyaack and Blair say that business managers must be realistic and recognize the interactive relationship business will have with government. No longer can a firm close a plant or lay a pipeline across the tundra and then claim that society has no stake in that decision.

SOURCE M. A. Wente, "Remaking the Management Mind," *Canadian Business* (January 1983): 82.

sufficiently large segment of society elects representatives who will support legislation to control the business activities at issue. In the 1970s and 1980s, for example, public concerns about pollutants have been expressed so widely that business firms are now much more conscious of how their activities will affect air and water quality. The general public can also act directly to affect an organization; consider the impact "right-to-life" advocates have as members of hospital boards.

Two concepts — corporate social responsibility and business ethics — must be considered when discussing the public as part of the external environment. **Social responsibility** is defined as the firm's "obligation to constituent groups in society other than shareholders and beyond that prescribed by law or union contract."[1] **Ethics** are contemporary standards or principles of conduct that govern the actions and behavior of individuals within the organization.

If a firm is to remain acceptable to the general public, its managers must be able to explain its purpose satisfactorily. This can be a most difficult challenge. Recent surveys have indicated that the general public does not have a favorable perception of business; as many as 50 percent of those surveyed have expressed displeasure with the actions of business. The public also has an exaggerated view of overall business profitability. When asked what a typical business firm earns on each dollar of sales, many people think profits are almost thirty cents (30 percent) per dollar of sales when in reality profits are usually about five cents (5 percent) on each sales dollar.

Managers must remember that the employees of the firm are also members of the general public. If an organization has 10 000 employees, these individuals will have an influence over a larger number of people who are not directly connected with the firm — for instance, their families, friends, and neighbors. Therefore, a firm should maintain clear communications with its employees so that the management's perspective of an issue is told.

TALKING TO MANAGERS

Dr. John R. Evans
Allelix Inc.

Looking for ways to take part in what's expected to be a $100 billion, worldwide market arising from the application of biological processes and mechanisms to industrial and commercial uses? Consider a visit to Allelix Inc.'s brand new $20-million biotechnology center in the city of Mississauga, adjacent to Toronto.

Allelix is probably Canada's major entry in the race to endow organisms with abilities that will create products in fields as diverse as forestry, medicine, and food. Basically, Allelix's work force of 90 scientists (a research scientist in biotechnology can expect to make up to $60,000 a year, five years after his or her Ph.D.) is trying to gain genetic control of certain enzymes that can produce desirable products. Running an operation dedicated to the industrialization of this microscopic world calls for a special blend of intel-

lectual, entrepreneurial, and administrative skills. It took more than a year to find and attract the men who filled the jobs in June 1982 of president, scientific director, and commercial director. In February 1983, Allelix rounded out top management by appointing 54-year-old John Evans as chairman and chief executive officer.

Q: We laymen are mildly terrified of work being done in biotechnology. Are we justified in our fears?

Evans: Those involved in this field face major ethical considerations. No one can rule out that some variant in a process might not be harmful. But, consider these two important aspects. First, experience suggests that mutants — the ones we change in these organisms — tend not to survive very well. We have to nourish them and support them, and sometimes they die out when we try to scale up. This lack of adaptive processes, which characterize natural organisms, is a protection.

Second, wherever one is producing new organisms, one must impose control systems. In a facility like ours, even though we don't believe there is a danger and even when we're using standard organisms that already exist, we use careful control systems so that they are separately vented and looked after. If we came up with an organism that seemed to have toxic effects, we should have to be extraordinarily careful with it. Most of the organisms we deal with are already present in nature, and all we're doing is changing one characteristic. It's pretty hard to imagine that's going to be a threat to society down the road.

Q: It's been more than 30 years since the proposal for the structure of DNA. Where are we now in terms of developing commercially useful products using biotechnology?

Evans: First-generation biotechnology firms dealt primarily with products for humans: insulin, growth hormones, interferons, blood products. That began in the early 1970s and those companies are just now bringing to market a few of the products that are a little simpler in their characteristics. In the next five years, we'll see quite a lot of such products.

Q: Your challenge must be in selecting areas of research.

Evans: That's the greatest dilemma because we don't have an established marketing system to send back directing signals about which niche to cultivate. You see some general market opportunities which you can assess but you don't know whether the science will be far enough advanced to take you to those.

A company such as ours at this stage has a heavy orientation to "science-push" rather than "market-pull" in determining its activities. We have very few marketing people on staff and we have a great diversity of product possibilities. We supplement our own market analysis by working with people who are major commercial actors in different fields.

I expect that there will be three different approaches to commercialization. Where we have a major flow of product possibilities and where the market is not already dominated by difficult-to-budge entities, we will develop products at Allelix itself or spin off Allelix subsidiaries to handle the production side and, maybe, even the marketing aspect up to distributor level. The second option is for us to licence out the products to a group that already has a position in the market. Some of our earliest products may go in that direction because we don't want to develop the necessary management until we know more about where our best lines are likely to emerge. A third possibility is joint ventures, in which we join with somebody who can bring something to the table in a commercial position, both in terms of market analysis and in marketing and distribution skills.

Q: So research and development is the main thrust?

Evans: I would hate to see that disappear from Allelix. The aim is certainly not to run a little research and then market. I hope that at the end of a decade Allelix will be a very strong research and development enterprise with a knowledgeable group that attracts others to work with it in scientific areas. I hope it would also have proven most effective in identifying commercial niches.

Q: Your scientists are coming together here for the first time. How does the lack of shared previous experience affect Allelix?

Evans: In any organization, there's a tendency to seek a compartmental comfort. We hope that won't happen because interactions among scientists in major areas of scientific activity are of great importance. The key breakthroughs will come in the overlapping areas of scientific development. A management challenge is to create an atmosphere that encourages crossing the classical scientific disciplinary boundaries to allow linkage of the intelligence that exists in different areas. If people are rewarded for moving their own projects forward exclusively, they're going to be reluctant to give their time to helping others move their projects forward. We have to give value to the support an individual gives to a project outside his or her area.

Q: You offered scientific staff equity in Allelix. Is this a strong motivator?

Evans: I thought it would be. But so far, it is not. The critical issue is whether this is going to be a reasonably stable enterprise or a fly-by-night. Some biotechnology groups have depended on hype to float an equity issue. A great strength of Allelix is that its shareholders have made a commitment which will sustain the core scientific staff for 8 to 10 years. That means a chance to get some worthwhile intermediate and long-term product development under way. In other companies, there's a tendency to press on short-term issues that could go to market quickly; these aren't as rewarding financially or scientifically to the individuals concerned.

Q: Where does Canada stand against other countries in this technology?

Evans: The overwhelming leader is the United States. Over the last 20 years, Americans have made major investments in the basic biological sciences and in molecular biology, stimulated by cancer research programs. The amount of private-sector investment through the large chemical, pharmaceutical, and agribusiness companies is enormous. It's primarily a private-sector and university development there. If you think of the United States in the first rank, and Japan and Europe in the second rank, then Canada is in the third. Whether we can move up into the second rank depends on whether we can bring some kind of coordinated approach to industry, universities, and government laboratories.

SOURCE   Adapted from Dean Walker, "Allelix Offers a New Hybrid That Could Take Root," *Executive* (April 1984): 52–57. Reprinted by permission.

THE SYSTEMS APPROACH: THE BUSINESS SYSTEM

In order to be successful, managers must understand and be capable of coping with the many environment factors that confront them each day. Managers must also be able to see how the functions of planning, organizing, influencing, and controlling interrelate. A concept that helps managers to perform the management functions and to respond effectively to environment factors is the **systems approach**. A **system** is an arrangement of interrelated parts designed to achieve objectives. Through the systems approach, managers are better able to understand and work with the various units within the organizaton to interrelate and coordinate the accomplishment of the goals of the firm.

Successful managers have found that the systems approach aids significantly in managing organizations. In any organization, management's job is to use resources (inputs) in an efficient manner to produce or achieve desirable products and/or services (outputs). Although the systems approach is useful in managing any type of organization, our illustration of its usage is applied specifically to a business firm. (See Exhibit 2-8.)

Resources/Inputs

A business enterprise uses certain inputs that are processed into outputs (products and/or services). This interaction with the external environment suggests that organizations are operating in an open system; for instance, the organization depends on other systems for its inputs. Just as people cannot live long without food and water, a dynamic business system cannot survive without resources that keep it alive. These resources or inputs may be human (employees to run the plant) or nonhuman (fuel for the factory, supplies or information). The resources needed by the system vary according to the objectives or goals of the firm. If, for example, a watch manufacturer has the objective of making high-quality watches, the inputs needed are likely to be highly trained craftspeople and quality equipment and materials. A manufacturer of lower-quality watches may need different inputs, such as mass-production equipment and less-skilled employees.

Processing Resources/Inputs

Resources or inputs are processed within the organization to create desired outputs in the form of products or services. This processing includes every aspect of the firm except managerial talent. It contains the necessary equipment, employees, and structure needed to convert resources into outputs. The processor for a university includes the faculty, the nonmanagerial staff, and the buildings required to maintain the university. The president, vice-presidents, deans, department heads, and other managerial personnel are not considered part of the processor.

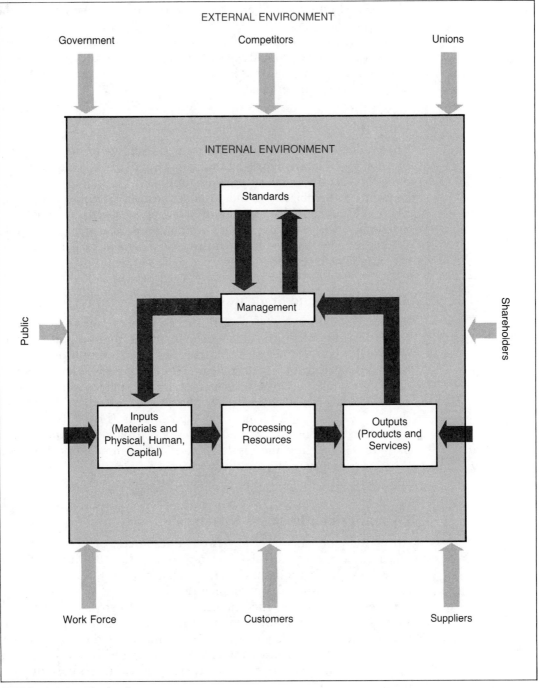

EXHIBIT 2-8 The business system

The desired outputs of the processor vary with the objectives of the firm. The Ford Motor Company takes steel, aluminum, and glass and converts them into automobiles and trucks. A hospital changes patients into healthy people; a school changes uninformed students into knowledgeable ones; and a retail store changes products on the shelves into desired consumer goods.

Outputs

The products and services are the result of outputs of the conversion process. Once inputs (physical, human, capital) are converted to outputs, they return to the external environment. These outputs should conform to the objectives and goals of the firm (discussed in greater detail in Chapter 3). The output of IBM is largely information-processing machinery, while the output of Ontario Hydro is energy. A different system may be required for each firm to reflect the goals of each and the output required.

Management and Standards

Viewing the business system still further, note the information feedback to management (the arrow in Exhibit 2-8 from outputs to management). Managers use this information to ensure that outputs are being produced according to standard. **Standards** provide management with basic guidelines for desired performance. If standards are not being achieved, management must make changes to correct any deviations; these may be a result of incorrect inputs, such as defective parts or unqualified employees. As inputs are processed and transformed into outputs, a problem could result because of low morale of employees. Whatever the cause, management's task is to identify any deviations and make corrections in line with company objectives.

Dynamics of a Business System

All of the components of any firm — resources, processor, output, management, and standards — operate as a system. But it cannot be a closed system that fails to take into consideration the external environment. The external environment affects how the business system operates. For instance, the union may decide to strike and, thereby, shut down the processor. Suppliers may not be able to provide the material necessary to keep the processor going. Government legislation may be passed that places certain restrictions on the firm. Competitors may develop an innovative product that makes the firm's current products obsolete.

The business system is dynamic, constantly changing. The systems approach provides managers with a means of viewing the interrelationships of internal and external factors. Many factors must be considered if the goals of the organization are to be achieved.

THE SITUATIONAL APPROACH

Managers use the systems approach to management to analyze inter-relationships that exist within all organizations. Another concept — the situational approach — builds upon the systems approach and provides managers with a broader appreciation of the management process. The **situational approach** stresses management flexibility to adapt to meet particular circumstances and constraints that a firm may encounter. It is not a new concept; in *The Prince* (1512), Nicoló Machiavelli wrote:

> Therefore, you ought to know that there are two ways to fight: by using laws, and by using force. The former is characteristic of man; the latter, of animals. . . . Therefore, since a prince must perfect his knowledge of how to use animal attributes, those he must select are the fox and the lion. Since the lion is powerless against snares and the fox is powerless against wolves, one must be a fox to recognize snares and a lion to frighten away wolves.

Machiavelli was telling his prince that he must be capable of making decisions based on the demands of a particular situation; nothing is consistently either yes or no. In using this approach, managers recognize that many different types of situations can exist and they should use a variety of strategies to respond to them.

Although there is an unlimited number of specific circumstances or constraints managers may encounter, it can be classified in six major categories:

- External environment
- Objectives
- Technology
- Structure
- Personnel
- Managerial style.

Not only must managers recognize that these factors exist, they must be capable of aligning or synchronizing them through the help of the systems approach to achieve the best results. Situationally oriented managers must be constantly aware of these factors and the manner in which they interact. Managers should recognize that no one best approach to management meets the needs of all organizations.

External Environment

Earlier in this chapter, we discussed the main factors that comprise the external environment. These factors constantly affect the way managers perform their assigned tasks. The situational approach counsels managers to be aware of possible pressures or changes in the external environment and to solve problems with the objectives of the organization in mind.

Objectives of the Organization

An **objective** describes the result a firm wants to accomplish. For example, a beverage company may want to achieve a 20 percent market share for a new soft drink. Or, a nightclub might want to reduce employee turnover to 5 percent during its next fiscal year.

Objectives are influenced by the external environment of the firm. If environment changes are dramatic enough, objectives may have to be completely abandoned. For example, when saccharine was banned by legislation in 1977, companies making products using saccharine had to remove them from grocers' shelves. Knowing the government was preparing this legislation, the saccharine producers had to rethink their product strategies. This, in turn, forced them to set different profit objectives with products that did not contain saccharine.

In highly uncertain environments, such as ones for professional sports teams, objectives may be subject to rapid change. In more stable and predictable environments, such as those for Bell Canada or B.C. Hydro, managers are able to establish more specific and steady objectives. As external environment requirements change, the objectives of a firm that desires to survive and prosper must also change.

Technology

Knowledge about how to use skills, methods, and equipment to convert resources into desired products and/or services is called **technology**. In the situational approach to management, technology can be characterized on the basis of how well it is understood. If the technology is well understood and a firm knows exactly what it is doing, a routine can be developed and applied uniformly. If the technology is complex and rather uncertain, the organization is more dependent on people for effective operations. The technology for manufacturing hand calculators is more straightforward than that for teaching students. In turn, the technology for teaching students is better developed than the technology for curing mental illness.

Structure

As used here, **structure** means the manner in which the internal environment of the firm is organized or arranged. If most major decisions are made primarily by top-level executives, the organization is **centralized**. If lower-level supervisors and managers are permitted to make significant decisions, the structure is more **decentralized**. Organization structures are discussed in Chapter 7.

Personnel

Hire good people and let them use their strengths is the general philosophy toward personnel held by many effective managers. But be-

MANAGEMENT IN PRACTICE

Adjusting to Technological Change

As technological changes are introduced into the printing industry, some companies' older workers are experiencing difficulties, according to Gary Brickell, president of Brickell and Associates, a Toronto-based consulting firm. The experienced workers in most printing firms are very knowledgeable about mechanical printing presses, but they have difficulty coping with the new computer-controlled presses. Retraining is possible but is expensive and time-consuming. As a result, many firms are hiring younger workers who are more ambitious and who are eager to learn the new technology. Their interest and enthusiasm should cause increased productivity in the printing industry. This is an important goal for these firms, since competition has become intense and increasing productivity is one of the obvious ways to cope with competitors.

SOURCE Wayne Gooding, "High-Tech Adjustments Can Be Tough," *The Financial Post* (January 14, 1984): S3.

cause each employee differs in terms of goals, aspirations, background, experiences, and personality, some employees are a better match with one organization than another. It has been found that employees tend to move toward the firm that possesses an environment most compatible with their goals and needs. If a firm has a need for individuals with skills that are different from those currently available in the organization, changes may have to be made. This is a predicament facing Canadian workers of the future. Technological changes will affect thousands of jobs over the next 20 years. For instance, robots are taking the place of some automobile assembly-line workers, and other applications are sure to follow. Managers need a work force that can keep pace with the technological advances of the firm, either through retraining or hiring personnel with different skills.

Managerial Styles

There are basically two managerial styles: autocractic and participative. With the autocractic style a manager's attitude is, "I will make all the decisions." With the participative style a manager encourages worker involvement in decision making. The situational approach says that both styles are workable under certain conditions because different situations call for different managerial styles. This issue is examined in more depth in Chapter 11.

Balancing the Situational Factors

Thus far we have discussed the systems and situational approaches as if they were separate and distinct. This is not really the case, since the systems approach provides a manager with the ability to balance the situational factors. It is how these factors interact, rather than any one factor taken separately, that is significant.

Both the systems and situational approaches must be interrelated if a manager is to be effective. The organizational system must take into consideration the situational factors. (See Exhibit 2-9.) These factors must be balanced if good results are to be achieved. As the situational factors change, the system may need to be modified. For instance, if the objectives of the firm alter (the firm switches to diversification as opposed to concentration on only one product), the situational factors will likely be out of balance. New technologies may be required in order to achieve the new objectives. New workers will likely be needed; if the structure is not one that can accommodate these new employees or if the firm finds that it is having difficulty recruiting the type of people necessary to bring about these changes, the situational factors will need further realignment. As the factors are altered, the system must change to adapt to the restructuring of the situational factors.

A manager must be capable of recognizing when the situational factors are out of balance and bringing them back into line by changes to the system. Any of the situational factors may require other factors to be modified. Thus, maintaining proper alignment of the factors ensures that the firm is operating at all times with the best system to meet the objectives of the organization.

Underwood, the leading producer of typewriters many years ago, failed to recognize the changing trends toward mechanization of the office. These changes were the impetus for the development and sale of electric typewriters, which later became standard equipment in virtually every office. Underwood, however, continued to produce manual typewriters. A competitor, IBM, recognized the trends and brought its basic conditions into alignment with the environment. IBM adapted its organization objectives, technology, structure, personnel, and management approach to meet the needs of a changing environment. IBM has since become the leading manufacturer of electric typewriters and many other electronic office products. Underwood (which merged with Olivetti in 1966 to become Underwood-Olivetti) belatedly noted the changing market conditions and entered the electric typewriter business, but it has been unable to reestablish its former dominant position in the typewriter industry.

Management must attempt to balance the various factors in the most effective manner with the assistance of the systems approach. We can also demonstrate the necessity for a situational approach to management by contrasting different types of organizations. It would be inappropriate to try to manage a college or university in the same way as a large manufacturing corporation. Though the management functions are the same in all types of organizations, their performance depends on the situation. Both the systems and situational approaches are important to managers in the performance of their jobs.

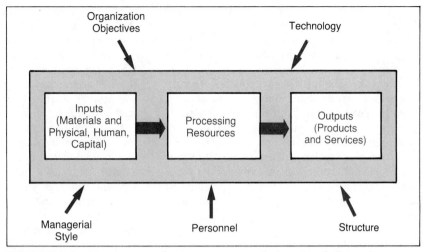

EXHIBIT 2-9   Management from a systems and situational viewpoint

OPENING INCIDENT REVISITED

Farlane Mining and Smelting Ltd.

Manager James Farlane was experiencing pressure from a variety of factors in the environment external to his company, and he was wondering if he could satisfy all of them. The material in this chapter indicates that eight significant environment factors can affect any business firm. For Farlane Mining and Smelting, at this particular time, four have assumed prominence: (1) the union, (2) government, (3) shareholders, and (4) customers. Each of these groups is asking for something that will cost the company money. Since monetary resources are limited, Farlane cannot agree to exactly what each group wants. Rather, he will have to compromise — try to give each group enough of what it wants and still keep the firm in business.

Farlane must contend with the further complication that one group or environment factor may be in conflict with another as well as with the company. For example, the union wants higher wages, but shareholders want higher

earnings per share. The goals of these two groups are in conflict since money is limited. As another example, the federal government requires the company to install more pollution-control equipment, which will cost money; at the same time, some customers want lower prices. Decreasing prices would reduce both profits and the company's ability to buy more pollution-control equipment. It will also reduce their ability to pay higher wages.

There are no easy solutions to the problems facing Farlane Mining and Smelting. But, since firms that cannot satisfy the demands of important external environment groups run the risk of being forced out of business, Farlane must do something. He might present the company's financial problems to the union and see if it will consider wage concessions in return for job security. A number of companies across Canada in the last several years have used this strategy successfully. He might also try to get an extension on complying with federal pollution regulations, giving the company time to sort out some of its other problems and generate the capital necessary to purchase the additional pollution-control equipment. The government is likely to be reasonable about such an extension; after all, it does not want to bankrupt the firm.

Farlane's presentation to the shareholders at the annual meeting must point out these conflicting pressures and must demonstrate the need for shareholder patience. The crises will pass. If the proper actions are taken, earnings per share should increase and shareholders will benefit in the future. About the customers, Farlane may not be able to do much. In a free economy, customers can purchase wherever they are getting the best deal. Farlane Mining and Smelting must remain competitive if it is to stay in business. The requested marketing survey will indicate which competitors are likely to pose the major threat; Farlane may try an advertising campaign stressing product quality as a counter strategy, rather than lowering the prices.

This series of crises demonstrates the complex interaction of the various external environment factors facing business managers. To be successful, managers must be able to cope with considerable uncertainty and anxiety. They must also be able to find creative ways to satisfy the conflicting demands of groups in the firm's external environment.

SUMMARY

The job of managing is not accomplished in a vacuum. Many interacting external factors can affect a manager's performance. Major external environment factors include: government, competitors, the work force, unions, shareholders, suppliers, customers, and the general public.

One of the most important external factors managers must cope with is the law, the maze of regulations from federal, provincial, and municipal governments. Such regulations range from protection of the air, water, and land to prohibition of discrimination in hiring based on age, race, color, sex, religion, or national origin. Regarding competition, managers must remember that a decision made by another firm may affect their own company. The nature of the Canadian labor force as a whole will be quite different as more women and white-collar workers enter the work force; increased use of technology will also bring changes to employment practices. Unions, too, must be considered an external environment factor because they become essentially third parties when dealing with the firms in which unionized employees work. Shareholders are vitally interested in the firm's operation and, since they own the company, their needs must be considered by managers. Managers must be aware of suppliers in the external environment, because lack of supplies could cause the manufacturing process to be reduced or to stop, even though the firm has sufficient capital and employees. The customers — the people who buy and use a firm's products or services — are a crucial factor in the firm's external environment. Finally, the general public can affect managerial decisions, usually working through its elected representatives to legislate changes to business practices.

The systems approach is a concept that helps managers to perform the management functions and to respond to external environment considerations effectively. A system is an arrangement of interrelated parts designed to achieve objectives. Successful managers have found that the systems approach is a significant aid because it leads them to consider the factors inside and outside the firm that have an impact on one another and on the firm itself. In any organization, managers use resources (inputs) in an efficient way to produce or achieve desirable products and/or services (output). Standards provide managers with basic guidelines for desired performance. All the components of any firm — input, processor, management, and standards — operate as a system.

The situational approach to managing builds on the systems approach, giving managers a greater appreciation of the management process. The situational approach requires that managers adapt to meet particular circumstances and constraints that a firm may encounter. Although the number of such circumstances and constraints is unlimited, it can be classified into six major categories: the external environment, objectives, technology, structure, personnel, and managerial styles. Not only must managers realize that these factors exist, they must be capable of aligning or synchronizing them through the situational and systems approaches to achieve the best results.

REVIEW QUESTIONS

1. Identify and describe the eight major external environment factors that can affect a manager.
2. How is the Canadian work force expected to change by the year 1990?
3. Define a system. Why does a manager need to understand the systems approach?
4. What are the components of a business system? How do they interrelate?
5. Define the situational approach to management. Identify and define the six categories of situational factors that a manager must align or balance to achieve the best results.

EXERCISES

1. Consider the following objectives from two different firms:
   Firm A: Our goal is to be an innovator in the creation of new products and services.
   Firm B: Our goal is to mass produce products that have a proven record of success.

Given these different objectives, how might the situational factors of technology, structure, personnel, and managerial style be different? Are there factors from the external environment that would be different for each firm?

2. Listed below are three different managerial positions. Describe and discuss the major environment factors that would likely affect these positions.
   a. President of Falconbridge Nickel Ltd.
   b. President of a community college or a university
   c. Owner and operator of a 7-11 convenience store in a major Canadian city.

CASE STUDY

The Toy Environment

Carson Toys Ltd. produces a line of children's toys. The company had always been successful, but recent reports showed that sales of two of Carson's most successful nonseasonal toys were down substantially. If allowed to continue, this would have a negative effect on profits, so Jonathan Carson, president of Carson Toys, called in Martha Bucyk, the vice-president of marketing, for an explanation. She gave several possible reasons for the decline.

First, Bucyk said that she had been told by several of Carson salespersons that some customers were placing trial orders with a toy manufacturer in Taiwan. This manufacturer produced two high-quality toys which were very similar to two of Carson's toys. The major difference was the price. In Canada the imported toys sold at retail for 75 percent of the retail price of Carson's two toys. Bucyk, suggested that retail toy buyers were growing more price conscious, because the uncertain economy in Canada was causing customers to demand more for their money.

Bucyk also suggested that the recent increase in the cost of plastic had led to a reduction in the thickness of the plastic used to make several Carson products, including the two problem products. She thought that this had hurt the company's reputation for making quality toys. In fact, Carson had received 150 letters from retail customers complaining about "shoddy"

toys, and three customers said they were reporting the problem to Consumer and Corporate Affairs Canada. They claimed that their children had received cuts on their hands from jagged pieces of plastic, which became exposed when the toys broke during normal play. Bucyk and Carson worried about this. They knew that three competitors had removed several unsafe toys from the market. Bucyk suggested, however, that this was a production problem and not directly her concern.

Bucyk's third suggestion for decreased sales was the declining birth rate in Canada. The two problem toys appeal to children between the ages of two and four, she pointed out, and so, with the number of potential users declining, Carson Toys cannot be surprised if sales also decline.

She suggested, too, that many parents were complaining about the tremendous volume of advertising aimed at children and that the constant bombardment of television commercials was "bad" for them. Carson had concentrated its advertising on Saturday-morning children's television shows and several parents had written to Carson and accused the company of "taking advantage" of children. Bucyk also knew that the government was investigating these complaints from parents and that restrictive legislation was possible. As a result, the company had decided several months ago to reduce its advertising. However, they may have been too late and these complaints may have caused the decline in sales.

Finally, Martha Bucyk reminded Carson that more and more toys were now being sold through "price-cutting" discount stores. Carson had always refused to sell through discount stores because many toy store owners said they would stop buying their products if they did. The discount stores had become a major problem, Bucyk noted, and something had to be done in order for Carson to remain competitive in non-discount stores.

QUESTIONS

1. List and describe briefly the external environment factors affecting Carson Toys Ltd.
2. How are these environment factors causing problems for Carson Toys Ltd.?
3. Develop a plan of action for dealing with each one of these environment factors.

CASE STUDY

The Roberts Cultivator

Jim Roberts, the president of Roberts Implements Ltd., contemplated his situation in mid-December 1984. His firm manufactured a specialized line of farm implements — the Roberts cultivator — in a rural Saskatchewan community of approximately 2000 people. He employed 47 people on a two-shift basis. The cultivator was sold primarily in Manitoba, Saskatchewan, and Alberta.

After increasing dramatically from $320,000 and $15,000 in 1976 to $810,000 and $90,000 in 1983, sales and profits levelled off in 1984 as farm incomes, with which farm implement sales were directly correlated, stabilized. Because of these good years the firm was in solid financial shape. The outlook for 1985, however, was uncertain. Agricultural experts were divided, although most considered that grain prices would remain low for 1985. Furthermore, other experts predicted a dry growing season in 1985 which, if it occurred, would adversely affect yields. Roberts had evidence that inventories of competitive firms were increasing. In addition, there was pending legislation on farm implement warranties that would increase manufacturing costs.

Roberts was considering whether he should reduce his planned output for the coming year. It would mean cutting back to a work force of 30. He anticipated that, if he did so, the workers laid off would have difficulty finding other jobs, and this would affect adversely the image of his firm in the community. On the other hand, if he did not decrease production, his firm could increase market share if the anticipated market decline did not occur.

QUESTIONS

1. List and describe briefly the external environment factors affecting Roberts Implements Ltd.
2. How are these environment factors causing problems for Roberts Implements Ltd.?
3. Develop a plan of action for dealing with each one of these environment factors.

NOTE

[1] Thomas M. Jones, "Corporate Social Responsibility, Revisited, Redefined," *California Management Review* 22 (Spring, 1980): 59–60.

REFERENCES

Allen, Robert E., and Keaveny, Timothy J. "Does the Work Status of Married Women Affect Their Attitudes toward Family Life?" *Personnel Administrator* 26 (June 1979): 63–66.

Appley, Lawrence A. "New Directions for Management." *Supervisory Management* 26 (February 1981): 9–12.

Dam, André van. "The Future of Management." *Management World* (January 1978): 3–6.

Davis, Tim R. V. "The Influence of the Physical Environment in Offices." *Academy of Management Review* 9, no. 2 (April 1984): 271–283.

Fram, Eugene H., and Deubrin, Andrew. "Time Span Orientation: A Key Factor of Contingency Management." *Personnel Journal* 60 (January 1981): 46–48.

Gooding, Wayne. "High-tech Adjustment Can Be Tough." *Financial Post* (January 14, 1984): S3.

Graeff, Claude L. "The Situational Theory: A Critical View." *Academy of Management Review* 8, no. 2 (April 1983): 285–291.

Grayson, C. Jackson. "Productivity's Impact on Our Economic Future." *Personnel Administrator* 24 (December 1979): 21, 23.

Jacobs, Bruce. "Keeping Fast-Track Managers on the Rise." *Industry Week* (November 10, 1980): 34.

Leslie, C. E. "Critical Issues Confronting Managers in the '80s." *Training and Development Journal* 34 (January 1980): 14–17.

Luthans, Fred, and Stewart, Todd I. "A General Contingency Theory of Management." *Academy of Management Review* 2 (April 1977): 181–195.

Marsh, Robert M., and Minnari, Hiroshi. "Technology and Size as Determinants of Organizational Structure of Japanese Factories." *Administrative Science Quarterly* 26 (March 1981): 33–57.

Mintzberg, Henry. "The Manager's Job: Folklore and Fact." *Harvard Business Review* (July-August 1975): 49–51.

Nicholson, Joan; Cooper, Toby; Peterson, Russell; Henderson, Hazel; and Densen, James. "How Business Treats Its Environment." *Business and Society Review* 33 (Spring 1980): 56–65.

Rieder, George A. "The Role of Tomorrow's Manager." *Personnel Administrator* 24 (December 1979): 27–31.

Rosen, Gerald R. "Can the Corporation Survive?" *Dun's Review* 114 (August 1979): 40–42.

Schwartz, Gail G., and Niekirk, William. "New Shakedowns in the Workplace." *Canadian Business* 57 no. 5 (May 1984): 85.

Stout, Russell. "Formal Theory and the Flexible Organization." *Advance Management* 446 (Winter 1981): 44–52.

Wooton, Leland M. "The Mixed Blessings of Contingency Management." *Academy of Management Review* (July 1977): 431–441.

II

Planning and Decision Making

3

The Planning Process

Allyn and Bacon, Publishers

Allyn and Bacon is a publisher of educational textbooks. In 1983, they decided to expand their Canadian publishing activities. To achieve this goal, they hired Dennis Bockus from a rival company; his job was to build up the list of Canadian textbooks published by Allyn and Bacon.

Before 1983, the Canadian books that Allyn and Bacon had published were the result of almost random opportunities identified by its sales representatives in their discussions with university professors and community college teachers. The company's efforts to find new projects increased with its decision to expand its Canadian publishing. Bockus and the salespeople

uncovered publishing possibilities in business, chemistry, education, engineering, English, environmental studies, French, history, political science, psychology, social work, and sociology. Bockus was faced with more opportunities than he could evaluate in a year. He realized that he must devise a strategy to determine which projects would get top priority.

In order to develop this strategy, a two-day meeting was arranged at a rural inn with Bockus, Gerry FitzGerald (the general manager), and Jerry Smith (the marketing manager). At this isolated place, the managers were free from the normal interruptions that would occur at their regular office. Their goal at this two-day meeting was to determine what objectives they should set for the company's publishing program during the next 2 to 3 years. FitzGerald was left to decide how a strategy could be developed that would satisfy the needs of the 3 managers and win their support.

KEY TERMS

planning process
objectives
plans
strategic planning
standards
policies
procedure
rules
reactive planning

forecasting
demand forecasting
trend line
cyclical variation
seasonal demand
random demand
moving average
exponential
 smoothing

regression analysis
time series analysis
integration
diversification
retrenchment
performance results
 standards
process standards

LEARNING OBJECTIVES

After completing this chapter you should be able to
1. Describe the planning process.
2. Explain the types of organization objectives a firm must consider.
3. Explain the strategic planning sequence.
4. Define standards and recognize the various types of standards that may be established.
5. Distinguish among a policy, a procedure, and a rule.
6. Describe the concept of reactive planning and its importance to managers.

All managers need to be effective planners. Whether the organization they work for sells products or services, operates in the private or public sector, or is a profit-oriented or not-for-profit organization is immaterial. Each of these types of organization needs planning. Managers are responsible for planning — it is one of the four basic management functions.

In Chapter 2, we discussed the impact on organizations facing uncertainty in their external environment. Some people might argue that such uncertainty makes planning fruitless. However, a systematic consideration of the constraints and opportunities in the external environment may lead to strategies that allow an organization to cope more effectively. Managers who undertake such studies understand the value of planning. Without it, the organization is simply hoping that things will work out all right.

Reportedly, many managers do not like to spend time planning. They prefer to be active, energetic individuals, accustomed to making rapid decisions and achieving goals daily. Because much of their work has this day-to-day perspective, they have difficulty thinking about the future. But, in order to continue meeting realistic daily goals, managers must be prepared for the future.

Planning is important at all levels of management, although its focus differs from the bottom of the firm to the top. There are four major differences. First, lower-level managers must develop plans that will fit the overall objectives established by top management. Second, the amount of time spent on planning by lower-level managers is not as great as by top management. Third, the timeframe for planning is shorter for lower-level managers. Finally, lower-level managers focus more on internal factors, while top management deals with both internal and external factors.

We begin this chapter with a brief overview of the planning process. We then discuss organization objectives. We note several different types and discuss the benefits and problems of setting objectives. Next, we describe the strategic planning process — that part of the total planning process concerned with reaching organization objectives. The chapter concludes with a discussion of standards, rules, policies, and procedures — specific types of plans that help organizations achieve their goals.

THE PLANNING PROCESS: AN OVERVIEW

Determining objectives and the courses of action needed to obtain these objectives is referred to as the **planning process**. The planning process presented in Exhibit 3-1 serves as a guide for the entire chapter. This process is appropriate whether planning is done by top or lower-level management.

The process begins with a mission statement — the reason the firm is in business. The mission of Canadian National Railways is to provide transportation, while the mission of Great West Life Assurance is to achieve excellence in the development and distribution of financial services. Each managerial level in every organization has a mission — its reason for existence.

Objectives or goals that serve as the desired end results can be established once the mission statement is determined. Objectives are set at each managerial level in the organization. However, lower-level

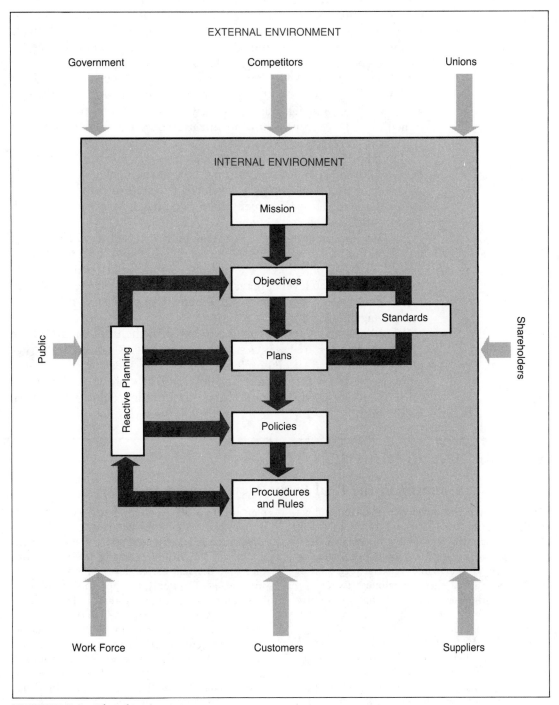

EXHIBIT 3-1   The planning process

objectives must be consistent with objectives of top management. For example, a top management objective for General Motors of Canada might be to "provide automobiles that satisfy consumer desires for safety, comfort and style"; a lower-level objective in the same company might be to "produce 42 Chevettes each hour at the Brantford plant."

Plans are then developed to specify the manner in which objectives are to be accomplished. Plans tell how the desired end results are to be achieved. Determining how organization objectives will be achieved is referred to as strategic planning.

Standards determine whether the objectives in the form of plans have been achieved. Standards are norms, or criteria, to which something can be compared. A plan may be developed to enable sales to be increased by 10 percent. This 10 percent then becomes a standard by which performance can be compared.

Policies are predetermined, general guides established to provide direction in making decisions. Policies are based upon a thorough analysis of corporate objectives. They help in the formulation and achievement of plans. Each level of management can establish policies; however, lower-level policies must be in agreement with policies of middle and top management.

Procedures and rules are created to assist in the implementation of plans. **Procedures** are a series of steps created to assist in the accomplishment of some special project or endeavor. **Rules** are very specific and detailed guides to action, set up to direct or restrict the action fairly narrowly. A rule may prohibit smoking in certain work areas, for example.

MANAGEMENT IN PRACTICE

Planning in the Real Estate Development Industry

Canadian real estate developers had tremendous success during the 1960s and 1970s in developing both commercial and residential real estate. The downtown areas of many Canadian cities attest to that. However, the recession of 1981–1983 caused these developers to revamp their planning processes (which had been fairly rudimentary) to cope with the changed economic environment.

A study of 6 major Canadian real estate developers by Peter Barnard Associates of Toronto revealed similar planning processes across the 6 companies. Most plan five years in advance and rely heavily on information from the sales staff in the field. The information filters up to the chief financial officer who puts a business plan together and ensures that it is consistent with overall corporate objectives.

Executives in this industry are enthusiastic about the benefits of planning. In spite of the fact that the real estate development industry must respond quickly to opportunity, systematic planning is not seen as something that "gets in the way of quick action." Rather, it gives management a framework in which to decide on the investment opportunities that best suit the company. In the companies surveyed, planning also encouraged dialogue between corporate planners and divisional managers, something that is often missing in large organizations.

SOURCE   Rod Lawrence, "Developers Adjust to Change," *Executive* (February/March 1983): 51–53.

The successful planner does not operate in a vacuum and must be flexible enough to respond to changing external and internal conditions. When managers at any level prepare to adjust to unanticipated occurrences, they are using reactive planning. Reactive planning can occur at any phase of the planning process.

The planning process is dynamic and should be constantly evaluated and modified to conform to both current and anticipated situations.

ORGANIZATION OBJECTIVES

Objectives affect the size, shape, and design of an organization, and they are important in motivating and directing personnel. In order to appreciate the importance of objectives in an organization, the types of objectives that a firm may consider are discussed next. This is followed by a presentation of the process of establishing objectives and the range of objectives that a firm must consider.

Types of Objectives

The creation of specific organization objectives is no simple task. As we discussed in Chapter 2, numerous external factors exert their influence on a firm. These external environment factors are competition, shareholders, customers, unions, suppliers, the labor force, the general public, and government. Because of these external factors, an organization usually has more than one objective, and the emphasis may change depending on the impact of a particular environment factor or group of factors. At least three main types of objectives can be identified for Canadian business firms.

- **Economic objectives** — survival, profit, and growth
- **Service objectives** — creation of economic value for society
- **Personal objectives** — goals of individuals and groups within the organization.

Economic Objectives

Survival is a basic objective of all organizations: the one goal common to all. Whether an organization is producing products or services that are useful takes second place to the concern of just staying in business. A firm cannot easily account to higher societal objectives when it does not know whether it can meet the next payroll. An anonymous fellow once noted: "It's difficult to remember that your initial objective was to drain the swamp when you're up to your neck in alligators."

In order to survive, a business firm must at least break even — that is, it must generate enough revenues to cover costs. But business firms want more than mere survival — they are in business to make a profit. Profit provides a vital incentive for continued, successful operation.

Not-for-profit organizations obviously do not pursue profit, but they do have economic objectives that focus on organization survival. Their goal is to continue to provide their services to those who need them. The United Way, for example, sets an objective each year regarding the amount of money it needs to carry out its programs.

Growth may be a major objective of both profit and not-for-profit organizations. In an effort to avoid failure, an organization may seek unrestricted growth; sometimes this growth can become an end in itself, blinding the organization to economic objectives. There are, of course, certain advantages that come with expansion. In profit-oriented companies, growth may help them to compete more effectively in the marketplace. In not-for-profit organizations, growth may help them to generate revenues more effectively and to have more impact on society.

Service Objectives

Profit alone is often viewed as the primary motive for being in business. While it is true a business firm cannot survive for long without making a profit, the old question, "Which comes first, the chicken or the egg?" may have meaning when discussing the profit versus the service objective. If a firm cannot consistently create a product or service that consumers want or can use, it will not stay in business long enough to make a profit. To accomplish the economic objective, a firm must produce goods consumers want. The creation of economic value constitutes the major goal of business organizations within Canada's economic system.

Service objectives are often even more important in not-for-profit organizations. In fact, they may be the major reason the organization exists. For example, agencies running provincial drug- and alcohol-abuse programs do not provide a profit to the government, but their service is beneficial to society in general.

Personal Objectives

Organizations are made up of people who have different personalities, backgrounds, experiences, and goals. Most likely, their personal goals are not identical to the objectives of the organization. If the difference in one individual's goals is significant, that employee may choose to withdraw from the firm. However, "withdrawal" does not necessarily mean departure from the organization. For instance, an employee may not feel that he or she can afford to quit. Major differences between the employee's goals and the organization's goals can result in "withdrawal" through minimum work effort, absenteeism, and even sabotage. Employees are not the only ones whose goals, when they differ from those of the organization, can affect that organization. For instance, a shareholder can cease to provide support for the organization by selling his or her shares.

If the organization is to survive, grow, and earn a profit, it must attempt to provide a match between its goals and the goals of groups who have contact with the firm. Some possible goal differences between the organization and these various groups may be seen in the table below. It is not unusual for particular groups or members to feel their personal goals are in conflict with the goals of other individuals related to the organization. For instance, some customers may believe that higher wages will make the prices of products higher, while the union may believe that shareholder dividends are too high. Managers have the difficult task of reconciling these conflicts.

Possible Goal Differences between the Organization and Groups who Have Contact with the Firm

Group	Possible Goal
Organization	Maximize profits
Management	Earn promotions, higher salaries, or bonuses
Employees	Increase wages and bonuses
Government	Obtain adherence to all government legislation, laws, and regulations
Competition	Attain a greater share of the market
Customers	Buy quality product at lowest price
Shareholders/owners	Increase dividends
Public	Protect the ecological environment
Unions	Gain greater influence for union members

Establishing Objectives

Objectives are established by an organization's managers. When these objectives are developed, the mission of the firm and the desires of the shareholders must be considered. Because diversity of personality, background, experience, and personal goals exists among individuals, objectives of two firms may differ, even though they both produce similar products.

MANAGEMENT IN PRACTICE

Planning at CWNG

Until a few years ago, Canada Western Natural Gas (CWNG) was able to develop business plans for up to five years in advance. The onslaught of the recession in the early 1980s changed all that. Once planning had been just a matter of basing future performance on past performance; the new planning process had to be much more complicated.

The focus of the new process is on an understanding of the corporate mission, the company's objectives, and the basic rules for achieving them. The road to success is created through the awareness of the external environment and the impact it has on the company. CWNG has created a planning and control group to support the main planning group at the company. Strengths and weaknesses in the planning system are constantly being evaluated. An assessment of management's responsibility to customers, governments, shareholders, employees, and suppliers is important for a successful business.

The real key to successful planning for CWNG is realizing that future prospects for growth and development will be much less dramatic than in the past because of increased government regulation, an economy that is more difficult to predict, and several other factors.

SOURCE   Adapted from "Forecasting and Planning," *Oilweek* (January 30, 1984): 14, 15, 17.

The person or persons charged with the responsibility of establishing overall corporate objectives vary from business to business. At times, the president or chairperson of the board provides the major thrust in goal creation. At other times, a group of top-level executives develops corporate goals. Whatever the source, these objectives provide the course toward which future energies of the firm will be directed.

Objectives should be well thought out and concisely stated. They should not constrain lower management to the degree that no further decision making is possible. An objective permits the greatest possible freedom for lower-level management while still providing direction to achieve a specific result.

Overall organization objectives should be accompanied by priorities that should not be altered too frequently. Obviously, major decisions have far-reaching and drastic effects on areas such as personnel requirements, managerial styles, and organizational structure. For instance, a firm dedicated to maintaining a high-quality product needs a priority to recruit individuals capable of achieving the goal of quality. Also, a more participative structure may be required to keep skilled employees. Thus, once a particular corporate objective has been stated, the effects of the decision will be felt throughout the organization for a long time.

Problems Encountered in Establishing Objectives

Numerous difficulties can arise when creating objectives. Here are three types of problems that may be encountered.

Real versus Stated Objectives

The real goals of any organization may be at odds with its stated goals. Objectives are often the result of power plays and pressures that come from circumstances in the marketplace or from internal tensions. The personal goals of the board of directors, outside creditors, lower-level managers, employees, shareholders, and labor unions are bound to be different. Because of these differences, the stated goals are at times different from the real goals of the organization. Goals are often significantly altered by individuals and groups who seek to adapt the organization to their narrower purposes. For example, a manager may claim that his objective is to make decisions that will benefit the company, but he actually makes decisions only after considering how his own career will be affected.

To determine the real goals of an organization, one must look at the decisions and actions that occur from day to day. Managers' actions speak louder than words. What functions or groups actually receive the major share of the resources? What type of behavior is accorded the greatest rewards by managers? A prison may specify its major objective as rehabilitation of prisoners; but, if it has only 2 counselors on its payroll while it employs 500 guards, the facts go against the stated goal. A manufacturing firm may say its chief objective is to produce high-quality products; but, if it employs only a few quality-control inspectors and does not stress the importance of quality to its workers, the firm's real objective is inconsistent with its stated objective.

Multiple Objectives

At times, an organization may have multiple and sometimes conflicting goals that must be recognized by management. For instance, what is the major service goal of a university? Is the primary objective of the university to provide education for students, or to conduct research to advance the state of knowledge, or to provide community service? In some universities, research is given the first priority in money, personnel, and privilege. In others, the teaching goal is dominant. In still others, an attempt is made to be all things to all people. However, given limited funds, priorities must be established in most cases. One can debate the priority of goals for such institutions as a mental hospital (therapy? or confinement?), a church (religion? or social relationships?), a prison (rehabilitation? or confinement?) a vocational high school (skill development? general education? or keeping young people off the streets?), a medical school (training students for medical practice? or for basic research?), or an aerospace firm (research information? or usable hardware?). At some point, choices and priorities must be made.

Goal Distortion

Once overall objectives and a pattern of priorities are established for an organization, managers must set and pursue goals that conform to them. Unfortunately, managers occasionally get sidetracked and emphasize the achievement of goals that are not significant to the overall organization. This problem can arise when an unimportant goal is easy to quantify, while an important goal is difficult to quantify. For example, in universities, the primary goal of excellence in education is difficult to quantify. Administrators may, therefore, be tempted to overstress what can be quantified — for instance, the number of books and articles published by faculty members. A particular book or article may indeed contribute to excellence in education, but the contribution is difficult to measure.

In another example, a government agency may measure how many dollars it distributes to its constituency because this is easy to quantify. It may then argue that it is effective because it has distributed increasingly large amounts of money over time. It may not be obvious that the agency is really achieving its goals by spending more money.

Goal distortion also occurs when one department in an organization overemphasizes its particular functions and loses sight of the overall objectives of the organization. In a business firm, for example, marketing managers may pursue sales with great vigor. This is not surprising, since that is marketing's function. However, if they pursue sales to the exclusion of other important organization objectives (for example, researching new areas of their marketplace), the total organization may suffer. If the organization permits its aggressive marketing department to be more important than its after-sales service department, then this imbalance also creates goal distortion. Organizations that stress functional activities always risk goal distortion because personnel and managers in each functional area may become so involved in that specific area that they lose sight of the organization's overall objectives.

STRATEGIC PLANNING

Determining how the organization objectives will be achieved is referred to as **strategic planning**. The two basic stages in strategic planning are determining the strategy, and developing the specific plans to implement the strategy. Long-range strategic planning usually covers a timeframe extending 5 years or more into the future. Of course, this timeframe can vary depending on the purpose of the organization and its technology. For instance, it may be unrealistic for the Toronto Argonauts to plan 10 years into the future; too many factors can change — a star player may be sidelined by an injury or a rookie may develop much faster than expected. A long-range plan for 2 or 3 years may be more realistic. On the other hand, long-range strategic planning for Canadian General Electric may be more than 10 years, and for B.C. Forest Products it may be 30 years or more.

Long-range planning depends, to a large extent, on how far the organizaton can look into the future with a reasonable expectation of being accurate. What should be the strategic plan of Pepsi-Cola Canada Ltd. since it has a goal of being number one in the soft-drink industry? Should the company diversify into other soft drinks, add new product lines other than soft drinks, add new plants, and/or expand into other markets? How long should such changes take to be implemented?

Logically, firms that establish an overall long-range strategic plan ought to be more effective than those that do not develop such a plan. In recent years, long-range planning has received increased emphasis in Canadian business firms. Firms that recruit executives for other companies report that their clients increasingly want managers with some background in strategic planning and forecasting. As further evidence of the importance of strategic planning, consider the fact that many companies have established planning departments with responsibility for developing three-, five-, and ten-year plans for their organizations. Most of the top Canadian firms have a position called "vice-president of planning" or some variation of that title. Even firms that do not have a vice-presidential planning position usually have permanent committees that are actively involved in long-range strategic planning.

The specific tasks to be accomplished in strategic planning are determined by corporate objectives and the type of business in which the

MANAGEMENT IN PRACTICE

Planning in High-Tech Industries

Denzil Doyle opened Digital Equipment of Canada Ltd.'s first sales office in the 1960s. When he resigned as president of Digital in the early 1980s, the company was selling $250 million worth of computers each year and employed over 1700 people. At present, he is the head of Doyletech Corporation, a Kanata, Ontario company that helps high-tech companies get organized and running.

Doyle stresses the critical importance of a business plan. In his view, nothing significant happens to a high-tech idea until the people with the idea develop a business plan and then give

that plan to venture capitalists for consideration. Doyle says that the business plan for a high-tech venture should include a clear statement of why investors should put their money into the venture. The product should also be described and its benefits stated. Market share objectives, channels of distribution, costs of marketing, pricing, and product strategies should also be included. Detailed revenue projections using different assumptions (for example, optimistic and pessimistic) should also be presented.

SOURCE   Alan Morantz, "Denzil Doyle: A Man for the High-Tech Season," *Executive* (August 1983): 22–24.

firm is engaged. Gary R. Miller is director of corporate planning for Morrison-Knudsen Company, Incorporated, a construction, engineering, and real estate development corporation. Miller says that one of the biggest tasks an organization has is to develop an understanding of what long-range planning is and what it can do — not only for the corporation but for the individual. Specific projects in a variety of businesses for which strategic planning can be used may be seen in the following table. As one might expect, the type of project varies according to the company involved. The particular planning projects also tend to be directed toward accomplishment of overall company objectives.

Long-Range Planning Projects

Primary Products of Firm	Type of Planning Projects
Automotive tires	Assess effects of energy crisis New product diversification Help ailing product lines
Computers	Research new business markets Acquisitions Venture analysis
Aircraft	New product development
Natural gas	Acquisitions Raw materials supply research Diversification
Catalog order and retail department store	Expansion of facility Corporate financing Marketing directions
Railway transportation	Major construction projects Capital expenditure Market growth
Steel	Overall industry or business capital Spending policies and trends Timing of major investments
Pharmaceuticals	Plant location planning New product development Overall business strategy
Cosmetics and toiletries	Expansion New business Resource allocation
Petroleum	Finding new energy sources New/expanded petrochemical plants Technology and personnel needs

Strategic planning is an important part of the total planning process. Developing a strategic plan for an organization is costly, complicated, and time consuming. Yet, substantial benefits can accrue if the strategic plan is done properly. The steps in the strategic planning sequence are shown in Exhibit 3-2.

State the Mission

As is the case with the total planning process, the starting point for strategic planning is the determination of the mission of the firm. The mission must be clearly understood by all members of the organization. For example, the mission of Canadian General Electric is to provide quality electrical products to a wide range of users including government, industry, and ultimate consumers. The mission of Ontario Hydro is to provide reliable electrical power to the people of that province. If a firm is to survive, its mission must be one that provides some clear benefit to society.

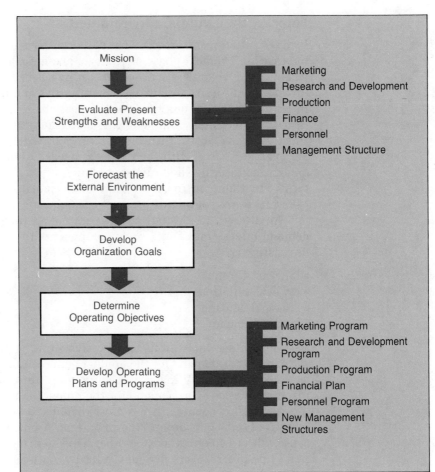

EXHIBIT 3-2
Strategic planning sequence

Evaluate Present
Strengths and Weaknesses

The next step in the strategic planning sequence is to analyze the present strengths and weaknesses of the firm. This involves an analysis of resources necessary for the accomplishment of these objectives — personnel, materials, money, physical plant, and machines. The strength/weakness evaluation should encourage the firm to be more reasonable in its expectations. If, for example, one of its strengths is strong management talent, this quality should be incorporated into strategic planning.

Some companies have success obtaining government contracts because they have a reputation for possessing strong management talent and effective planning systems. Other firms are successful in the consumer market because they have a reputation for after-sales service. An analysis of a firm's strengths and weaknesses permits planners to formulate realistic long-term goals. This competence profile may well lead to an alteration of the kind of business the firm will pursue.

Forecast the External Environment

Planners' attempts to predict what will occur in a firm's future is called **forecasting**. The next phase of strategic planning, goal setting, cannot be done properly unless serious forecasting has been done. Forecasting involves identifying anticipated opportunities and threats to the firm in its external environment. For the best chances of survival of the firm, its forecast environment will match its strengths. However, if this is not the case, the firm's long-term goals will have to be modified. For example, a firm with the strengths needed to manufacture a high-quality engineering slide rule should modify its goals to meet the external environment's need for hand-held calculators.

Several terms commonly used in forecasting are illustrated in Exhibit 3-3. An attempt to estimate the demand for a firm's product is called **demand forecasting**. The 4 basic components to consider in demand forecasting are:

- long-term trend
- cyclical variation
- seasonal demand
- random demand.

As you can see in Exhibit 3-3, the **trend line** projects the long-run estimate of the demand for the product being evaluated. Long-run projections are typically made 5 years or more into the future. In this instance, the long-run demand for the product is increasing.

But a business planner needs more than just a long-run trend. **Cyclical variation** occurs around the trend line. A business recession may cause sales to go down; on the other hand, demand may be above the trend line in a recovery period. Cyclical variations occur over periods

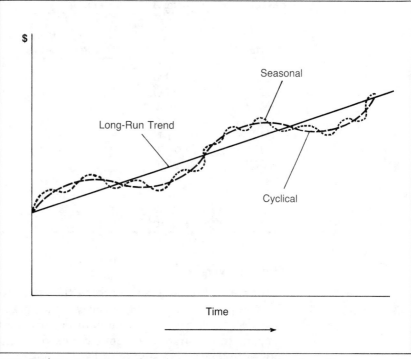

EXHIBIT 3-3
Forecasting

NOTE: Random patterns are not shown because we do not know when they will occur.

greater than one year but less than five, with the typical cyclical span being three years. Cyclical variation is important because of the severe peaks and valleys associated with the demand for some products. Even though there is an overall trend for increased demand for the product, sales may currently be in a valley because of cyclical variations; this situation may affect production, inventory, and labor requirements.

Managers often need to evaluate demand patterns in a shorter timeframe than cyclical, known as **seasonal demand**. This forecast period is typically twelve months or less. During a twelve-month period the demand for many products fluctuates drastically. Electric shaver sales are concentrated heavily in the holiday seasons; swim suits are sold in the spring. Knowledge of these seasonal demand patterns is important to business planners to anticipate production, inventory, and labor requirements.

Finally, **random demand** may cause exasperation for business planners. Random demand follows no pattern. Whether it is unexpectedly high or low, random demand causes disruptions in the orderly conversion of inputs to outputs. By definition, it occurs for reasons that business managers cannot anticipate, even with the most sophisticated forecasting techniques.

Four widely used forecasting techniques are: (1) moving averages, (2) exponential smoothing, (3) regression analysis, and (4) time series analysis.

EXHIBIT 3-4   Moving Average Example

Quarter	Actual Demand	Three-Quarter Moving Average	Five-Quarter Moving Average
Q1	3000	–	–
Q2	2350	2767	–
Q3	2950	2758	3075
Q4	2975	3342	3025
Q1	4100	3275	3065
Q2	2750	3133	3548
Q3	2550	2533	2980
Q4	2300	2683	2915
Q1	3200	3092	3035
Q2	3775	3442	–
Q3	3350	–	–

Moving Averages

A simple technique for smoothing the effects of random variation is through the use of moving averages. Since planners do not want business decisions based on a random occurrence that may never again happen, they attempt to remove this one-time occurrence through moving averages. As shown in Exhibit 3-4, the different time periods are averaged to get both a three-quarter and a five-quarter **moving average**. The greater the number of months that are averaged, the less effect the random variations will have on the demand estimate. To compute a three-quarter moving average, periods 1, 2, and 3 are averaged. This provides the first figure for the three-quarter moving average. To get the next quarter's estimate, the first quarter is dropped and the fourth quarter is added and again averaged. Through the use of moving averages, the effects of random variation are reduced and the demand estimate is smoothed.

Exponential Smoothing

One of the major difficulties associated with moving averages is that their calculation requires a large amount of historical data. When the exponential smoothing technique is applied, planners need only three types of data:

- the forecast from the previous period
- the actual demand that occurred in this forecast period
- a smoothing constant.

While the first two pieces of data are relatively easy to obtain, determining the smoothing constant requires that managers personally identify what they consider to be a good response rate. This smoothing constant depends to a large extent on the past demand for the product.

If it has been relatively stable, the smoothing constant will likely be small. However, if the product is experiencing rapid growth, managers may wish to have a large smoothing constant to ensure that the firm is keeping up with the actual demand.

Consider how **exponential smoothing** helps to forecast goals for two entirely different products; one has a stable demand and the other has rapidly increasing demand. A low smoothing constant (perhaps 0.05) might be chosen for the stable product and a high smoothing constant (0.50) for the rapid-growth product. Assume that in both instances the previous forecast was 1000 units and actual demand was 2000 units. Two entirely different projections for future demand result:

New forecast   = Past forecast + Smoothing constant
                                         (Actual demand − Past forecast)

New forecast
(Stable product)   = 1000 + 0.05 (2000 − 1000)
                      = 1050 units of forecast demand

New forecast
(Rapid-growth product)   = 1000 + 0.50 (2000 − 1000)
                      = 1500 units of forecast demand.

If the product has stable demand, there is no reason to believe that a rapid surge in sales will occur through other than perhaps random fluctuation. However, when a high smoothing constant is chosen, managers realize that demand shifts rapidly and requires swift action in order for the business to be competitive. The identification of the proper smoothing constant is crucial to forecasting with exponential smoothing.

Regression Analysis

With the increased use of high-speed computers and sophisticated statistical packages, managers have at their disposal a useful tool for forecasting — regression analysis. It has gained respectability for forecasts ranging from estimating product demand to development of profiles of successful versus less successful employees within a particular firm.

Regression analysis is used to predict one item (known as the dependent variable) through knowledge of one or more other items (the independent variables). Managers must first determine what they need to predict, then identify the independent variables to determine if they actually are capable of predicting a particular outcome. Suppose, for instance, a manager wants to determine the relationship that advertising and size of the sales force has on company sales. The basic equation follows:

$$Y \text{ (company sales)} = \text{Advertising } (X_1) + \text{ sales force size } (X_2)$$
dependent variable   independent variable(s)

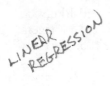

If there does exist a relationship the equation that might result is:

$$Y = 2(X_1) + 4(X_2).$$

This result means that, for each added dollar spent on expanding the sales force, total sales would increase by four dollars. However, for every dollar spent on advertising, total sales would increase by only two dollars. Once this manager has determined how reliable this model is, she might use it toward developing a marketing plan to achieve the greatest company sales.

Time Series Analysis

Another approach to the use of regression is **time series analysis**, in which the same mathematical approach is used except that the independent variable is expressed in units of time. For instance, planners might want to project the number of car sales in a particular region for the coming year (for example, 1985). In order to make this projection, planners would need the car sales for previous years, as shown in Exhibit 3-5. Given these data, the manager turns the work over to a financial analyst who provides the following equation:

$$Y \text{ (quto sales)} = 21\,230 + 310 \text{ (year)}.$$

Substitute the year (85) into the equation:

$$Y = 21\,230 + 310 \text{ (85)} = 5120.$$

Thus, the estimated number of cars that will be sold in this district for the year 1985 is 5120. The $-21\,230$ represents a constant that results from the calculation of the regression equation. As with the regression analysis example, the manager must study these statistics to determine the reliability of the model. But the analysis provides the manager with a valuable tool for planning and making decisions.

Managers have a wide variety of forecasting techniques available to them. However, those discussed above — moving averages, exponential smoothing, regression analysis, and time series analysis — are particularly valuable for making the kinds of assessments of the external environment that are required in strategic planning. Regardless of the specific forecasting technique that is used, managers must try to estimate what the external environment might look like at some point in the future. Once forecasting is accomplished, the next step in the planning process — developing organization goals — can be pursued.

EXHIBIT 3-5
Auto sales

Cars Sold	Year
400	1972
600	1973
1550	1974
1500	1975
1500	1976
2400	1977
3100	1978
2600	1979
2900	1980
3800	1981
4500	1982
4000	1983
4900	1984

Develop Organization Goals

Once the firm is aware of its strengths and weaknesses and the nature of its forecast environment, the firm's managers can proceed with strategic planning to develop its long-term goals. These goals are developed

in view of both the strengths of the firm and the forecasted environment. If the strengths are not consistent with the changes predicted
in the environment, certain capabilities of the firm may need to be
developed in order for the objectives to be achieved.

Determine Operating Objectives

With the long-term goals of the organization identified, the objectives
of each of the functional departments such as marketing, production,
finance, personnel, and research and development can be identified. If
the organization objective of a firm is for it to become the market share
leader, the various functional areas in the firm will have to work together toward ensuring it. Marketing's operating goal may be to increase sales by 20 percent; production's goal may be to guarantee product
availability; personnel's goal may be to provide an appropriately trained
work force to manufacture the product; and finance's operating goal
may be to make money available so that all of the foregoing can be
achieved.

Develop Operating Plans and Programs

The last step in the strategic planning sequence is to detail operating
plans and programs for each functional area of the firm. In marketing,
for example, key decisions should be made concerning such factors as
product mix, sales promotion, advertising, and pricing. With respect
to production, plans may relate to changes in technology, flexibility
of current facilities, and inventory levels. Plans could include a research
and development program that will play a key role in determining the
types of products offered by the firm in future years. Plans concerning
personnel must cover future skills needed and the level of skills among
current employees.

Programs developed for all of a firm's resources obviously require
financing. Perhaps the greatest restraint is the availability of money
to implement the total long-range program. Profit planning, retention
of earnings, and development of short- and long-range capital resources
are all important elements of this plan.

An administrative plan must be developed so that all these functional
programs can be implemented. Proposed organizational structures should
be designed with the emphasis on the types of decisions necessary to
accomplish the tasks required by the program. In locating the appropriate decision maker, key concern is with the importance of the decision as indicated by the amount of money involved, the number of
organizational units affected, the duration of the effect of the decision,
and the possibility of reversing it once it is made. In addition, a control
system must be designed to provide operating information so that corrections may be made when actions and environment are significantly
different from the planned program.

**Robert F. Black
Eddie Black's Limited**

Great-grandfather made and sold boots in Beaverton, Ontario. Grandfather owned a store at Spadina and Lonsdale in the old village of Forest Hill, when those streets weren't much more than wagon trails. Father started Eddie Black's radio and appliance store in 1930. "We are," acknowledges Robert F. Black, president of Eddie Black's Limited, the Ontario chain of specialty photography stores, "a merchant family."

The descendants of these storekeepers now have 100 crisply designed outlets in Ontario and a space-age photofinishing laboratory in a $5-million headquarters on the outskirts of Toronto. Careful market analysis and astute investment have kept up a pace of growth that did not pause for the recent recession. Sales grew to almost $59 million last year from $28.4 million in 1978. Profits have almost kept that pace too — earnings last year were about $5.6 million, up from just under $2 million in 1978.

Bob Black's been a part of the company since working during the Christmas school break in 1945 at his father's store. He just never went back to school. This put an end to his plans to become a veterinarian, but gave him his first spin as an entrepreneur.

Q: You are adding about a dozen stores a year. Why are they all in Ontario?
Black: Look at the marketplace. Outside of Ontario, going east, we'd have to go to Montreal. We weren't anxious to go into the Quebec environment of the last few years. Going west, the marketplace is Winnipeg, which is not as big as North York [a part of metropolitan Toronto], and then Calgary and Edmonton. It's not too enticing to go 1500 km to find 500 000 people.

Q: Yet, you must be close to saturation in Ontario.
Black: That's becoming true. Ontario growth is not as buoyant as it was five years ago. Every community now has a shopping center and we're in most of them.

Q: What's the strategy? go to the United States?
Black: It's a possibility. We could locate an office 500 km south of Toronto and pick up 20 million people in a 250 km radius.

Q: Who is your main competition?
Black: The department stores are fairly strong competitors in cameras and allied products. The specialty stores compete more for the carriage trade with sophisticated products for the serious amateur or some professionals. We don't chase that business. We gave up the semiprofessional business years ago because we felt that the well-informed customer would not be particularly loyal. We thought it might be more sensible to go to where the people are and offer convenient facilities for the middle-of-the-road picture taker who likes good quality but is not deeply involved. That's why we wanted to try shopping centers in the 1950s when they were new.

Q: How do you win out in competition in that middle area?

Black: We try to be innovative. When the photography business began to grow after World War II, most of the people in it were either studio operators or people who liked taking pictures. There weren't many people in the business with merchandising know-how. On the other hand, we were raised in merchandising by a high-profile entrepreneur. My father was not a good executive in managing finances, inventory and warehousing, but he was a great entrepreneur. We saw the weakness of running a company without proper systems. When we finally took over, we had to dismiss a lot of my father's employees because the systems had been poor and the temptations too great.

Q: What gives you an edge?
Black: Our mix of merchandise and how we blend the finishing work and equipment sales.

Q: Is the money in selling film and processing rather than cameras?
Black: It is and it isn't. Certainly, the margin in popular cameras, from 5 percent to 30 percent, would make a shoe merchant sick. But the equipment is not only technical, it is also fashionable. So we're vulnerable there. When we have a 5 percent markup and an item stops selling, it's difficult to clear out. We have to stay on top of everything with sophisticated inventory control. From the perspective of margins, cameras provide our lowest profits. The average person shoots about 6 or 7 rolls of film a year. At $10 a roll, that's $60 to $70 a year spent by the average camera user who will have spent anything from $15 to $500 for the camera.

Q: The technology has changed and middle-priced cameras can be quite sophisticated. What has that meant to the average shooter?
Black: We were lucky when we decided to go out into the shopping centers. Then, cameras had become much simpler, and more people could take more pictures more easily.

Q: For a while there was a surge in popularity of instant photography. Did that scare you?
Black: It did. At Christmas 1976, 40 percent of all cameras sold processed the film in the camera. That rattled us because there is virtually no profit in selling instant cameras or instant film. Shortly after Christmas we had a session to decide what to do. We'd already started offering a larger print for Kodak's Instamatic Camera. To make us noticeable against instant pictures, we decided to print 4" x 6" (10 cm × 15 cm) pictures on all film sizes. That wasn't exactly new; other finishers had offered it as an option. However, we sold nothing but those prints. We spent $500,000 to convert equipment and had to train staff. In the spring of 1977, we produced the larger prints across the board. To convey bigness, we created our elephant symbol and had a commercial made right in a shopping center with an elephant delivering a roll of film to our counter. We had albums created to fit the pictures. We promoted it very strongly. It was highly successful. That was a gamble that really paid off. Instant pictures never did come back to the acceptance of 1976. They eventually settled into a niche as a party novelty, a fun thing.

Q: Is there a new threat now from electronic photography?
Black: It's coming. It's been set back for a while by innovations in film. Electronic photography isn't just over the horizon; it's down the road somewhere.

Q: What are you doing about the exploding market for videotape records?
Black: We're not in the VTR business yet. But we want that business when it comes. When a VTR becomes one-piece and truly portable, we'll be in there.

Q: How do you personally exercise control over what's going on?
Black: We have a concept of central distribution. Everything funnels out from one central source: finishing supplies, toilet paper, paper clips, whatever. Things work better when managers can walk around and be part of everything. I can walk into the lab or a store and, from 35 years' experience, know from what's happening whether it's right or wrong. We also look at the computer printouts, read reports, check inventory — do all that. But managers still need that personal contact to know that they're satisfied with what's happening.

SOURCE   Adapted from Dean Walker, "Black's *Is* Photography: And Don't They Know it," *Executive* (January 1984): 36–39. Reprinted by permission.

GRAND STRATEGIES

We have described in general terms much of the nature of strategic planning. Next we consider three grand strategies which often grow out of that process.

Integration

Organization strategists sometimes choose to unify control of a number of successive or similar operations: this is an **integration** strategy. When companies combine, they become integrated. Integration also includes a company taking over a portion of an industrial or commercial process previously done by other firms. Integration need not involve ownership, only control; supply and marketing contracts are forms of integration. Integration toward the final users of a company's product or service, as when Tandy Corporation opened its Radio Shack stores, is forward integration. A company taking control of any of the sources of its inputs, such as raw materials or labor, is practicing backward integration. Buying or taking control of competitors at the same level in the production and marketing process is horizontal integration.

Backward and forward integration are usually designed to accomplish one or both of two purposes: capturing additional profits or obtaining better control. Backward integration gains better control of suppliers. Forward integration gains better access to customers. Obviously, if a supplier or an intermediate customer is making exorbitant profits, vertical integration may be justified on this basis alone. Vertical integration may also be justified when a firm can perform the functions of suppliers or intermediate customers effectively and efficiently. If better control of sources of supply or access to customers is the only objective, it may be better not to buy the business. Taking over customers or suppliers often involves a firm's management in businesses with which it is unfamiliar. To avoid this, while obtaining control, some companies make franchise agreements with intermediate customers and long-term supply agreements with suppliers.

Diversification

Diversification is increasing the variety of products or services made or sold by a business firm. Diversification may be conglomerate or concentric. Conglomerate diversification means going into businesses unrelated to the firm's current businesses; concentric diversification means going into businesses related to the firm's current businesses. As a grand strategy, diversification usually has reduction of risk as its purpose. A company involved in a number of different businesses avoids having "all its eggs in one basket." Ideally, when some of a conglomerate firm's businesses decline, others will be on the increase. Of course, diversification into related businesses may not appear to serve the risk reduction objective as well as conglomerate diversification. However, concentric diversification may be more successful in improving profitability because the managers of the concentrically diversifying firm know something about the business they are buying.

Diversification often occurs as a byproduct of bargain hunting by corporate strategists. Even if the preference is for a related merger candidate, corporate level strategists may opt for a firm in an entirely different business because it is deemed to be greatly underpriced. Diversification can also be a product of a desire for growth.

Retrenchment

Another grand strategy is **retrenchment**, the reduction in the size or scope of a firm's activities. Few top managements are willing to do this except in emergencies. Although growth is often intrinsically an organization objective, retrenchment seldom is. When a retrenchment strategy is proposed, the firm's goal may be plain survival. Actually, retrenchment should be considered as workable an option as growth. Prompt elimination of losing businesses has been the hallmark of many successful companies.

STANDARDS

Managers need to express objectives and plans to employees and they need ways to find out if objectives are being met. Both needs are met by standards, policies, and procedures and rules.

A norm, or criterion, to which something can be compared is referred to as a **standard**. Standards specify what constitutes proper behavior or conditions; they help determine whether objectives in the form of plans have been achieved. As such, they provide the link between planning and controlling. Referring once again to Exhibit 3-1, we can see that standards provide a way for determining if a plan is being properly implemented. It would be foolish to establish objectives and not be able to determine if they have been achieved. But, as is described in Chapter 14, standards provide the starting point for the controlling process.

In business, standards can be created to cover nearly every aspect of a situation. Standards can be divided into two main categories. Standards for which desired results are relatively simple to specify are classified as **performance results standards**. On the other hand, standards that evaluate functions that are difficult or impossible to formulate are referred to as **process standards**. Examples of both types of standard are seen in the table on the next page.

Examples of Standards

Type of Standard	Example
Performance Results	
Quantity	Forty units should be produced each day.
Quality	Each part should have a mass of 1.5 kg ± 0.01 kg.
Time	Project is scheduled for completion by January 1.
Cost	Labor costs should not exceed $2 per unit.
Process	
Function	The procedure in handbook A-1 should be followed when writing up a sales order.
Personnel	The probationary period for new employees is three months.
Physical factors	Only two workers at a time are permitted in the security area.

Performance Results Standards

The major areas to be evaluated with performance results standards relate to:

- The quality of work
- The quantity of work
- The time needed to complete work
- The cost of work.

Quality standards are usually derived from the design of the firm's products or services. For a physical product, standards would exist for consistent quality of form, dimensions, strength, color, and durability. Often quality-control inspectors collect information from production and compare it with established requirements. For a service, quality standards would exist for consistent, fair treatment of all customers.

Quantity standards relate to the number of items produced during a specific time period. For instance, a factory time study may result in a requirement that 50 units per hour be produced by a certain machine operator. An employment interviewer for a personnel agency may be required to place a minimum of 15 applicants a week. In an automobile assembly plant, the standard might be 60 vehicles produced each hour on the assembly line.

Standards governing time are often related to the quantity standards as shown in those examples. The most common example of a time standard relates to completion of a report on a particular date. Most firms' annual report must be completed in time for presentation at the annual meeting of their shareholders.

Cost standards are established to ensure that a project is completed within set cost limits. These standards are extremely important, for it is embarrassing and financially unwise to complete a project on time only to find that the costs are significantly higher than expected and they wipe out whatever profits mights have been realized. Annual and monthly budgets constitute a well-known example of cost standards. Standard cost systems are also designed to enable managers to make more effective decisions governing ongoing action.

Process Standards

Managers attempt to specify and control performance through process standards. For example, a hotel may hire a highly qualified chef for its finest restaurant; this would be a standard of personnel. Or the hotel may develop standards for the best service through job descriptions and standard operating procedures for all hotel staff. These are standards of function. Finally, standards that attempt to provide superior physical factors in terms of equipment, furnishings, lighting, ventilation, or privacy may be drawn up. These are physical factors standards. The operating assumption here is that the best people, using the latest in methodology and equipment, might reach maximum efficiency without having to establish specific standards of quality, quantity, time, and cost. Process standards can be applied for manufacturing firms, but are often crucial to service organizations.

POLICIES

A **policy** is a predetermined, general course or guide established to provide direction in making decisions. As such, policies should be based on a thorough analysis of organization objectives. Policies cover the important areas of a firm such as personnel, marketing, research and development, production, and finance. A company that collects debts may have a policy that says: "No collection agent shall accept from any client or debtor gifts that are substantial enough to cause undue influence on the decision-making behavior of the collection agent." This policy does not tell the agents exactly what gifts they can accept, but it does state that the agents must not let these gifts interfere with their collection responsibilities.

To formulate policies, managers must have knowledge of, and skill in, the area for which the policy is being created. However, there are certain generalizations that apply to the establishment of policies. The most important has already been stated: policies must be based on a thorough analysis of organization objectives. There are several other general principles that can help managers create appropriate policies.

- *Policies should be based on known principles and, as much as possible, on facts and truth.* It is a fact that each province has passed legislation for safety in the work place. It is not a fact that a satisfied employee is automatically a productive employee.
- *Subordinate policies should be supplementary, not contradictory, to superior policies.* A policy for a company division should not conflict with an overall corporate policy.
- *Policies of different divisions or departments should be coordinated.* They should be directed toward the entire organization rather than favoring a particular department, such as sales, engineering, purchasing, or production, to the detriment of the whole.
- *Policies should be definite, understandable, and in writing.* If a policy is to guide actions, persons concerned must be aware of its existence; this requires the creation of understandable directives in a definitive written form. These sets of guides record the memory of the organization, which it uses to help cope with future events.
- *Policies should be flexible and stable.* The requirements of policy stability and flexibility are not contradictory; one is a prerequisite to the other. Stable policy alters only in response to fundamental and basic changes in conditions. New government regulation can represent such a basic change in conditions that it can have a major impact on a firm's employment policies. The higher the organizational level, the more stable the policy must be. Changing the direction of the enterprise is a much more complex and time-consuming task than changing the direction of a department or section. The higher the organizational level, the more policy resembles principle; conversely, the lower the level, the more it resembles a rule.
- *Policies should be reasonably comprehensive in scope.* Policies conserve an executive's time by making available a previously determined decision. Managers should organize their work in such a way that subordinate personnel can handle the routine and predictable work, while they devote time to the exceptional events and problems. If the body of policies is reasonably comprehensive, the cases that arise that are not covered by policy constitute exceptions.

PROCEDURES AND RULES

When a firm's broad policies have been established, more specific plans may need to be created to ensure compliance with them. Procedures and rules might be thought of as restrictions on the actions of lower-level personnel. They are usually established to ensure adherence to a particular policy. Although the terms *procedure* and *rule* are similar, they refer to discrete ideas.

Procedures

For most policies, there is an accompanying procedure to indicate how that policy should be carried out. A procedure is a series of steps established for the accomplishment of some specific project or endeavor. Procedures are developed to assist in the implementation of plans or to indicate steps to be taken for repeated activities. For example, most companies have a clear procedure for reimbursing salespeople for their monthly traveling expenses. Salespeople fill out a form indicating where they traveled during the last month; they also attach any appropriate receipts. If they do not follow this procedure, their travel expense cheque may be held up or not approved.

Rules

A rule is a specific and detailed guide to action, set up to direct or restrict action in a fairly narrow manner. For example, a company with a printing shop may have a "no smoking" rule there because many flammable chemicals are used in printing.

An illustration of the difference among policies, procedures, and rules is shown in the table below (and on pp. 100–101). Clearly, procedures and rules may overlap as to definition. Taken out of a sequence of steps, a procedure may actually become a rule.

Policies, procedures, and rules are designed to direct action toward the accomplishment of objectives. If managers could be assured that all persons doing work were thoroughly in agreement with and completely understood basic objectives, then policies, procedures, and rules would not be needed. Apparently, objectives at times are unclear and even controversial. Thus, all organizations have a need for policies, procedures, and rules that are more definitive and understandable than the overall objectives on which they are based.

Examples of Policies, Procedures, and Rules

Policy	It is the policy of the company that every employee is entitled to a safe and healthful place in which to work. The company desires to prevent accidents from occurring in any phase of its operation. Toward this end the full cooperation of all employees will be required.
	Management will view neglect of safety policy as just cause for disciplinary action.
Procedure	The purpose of this procedure is to prevent injury to personnel or damage to equipment by inadvertent starting, energizing, or pressurizing equipment that has been shut down for maintenance, overhaul, lubrication, or setup.

(table cont'd.: Examples of Policies, Procedures, and Rules)

1. Each maintenance mechanic assigned to work on a job will lock out the machine at the proper disconnect with his or her safety lock and keep the key in his or her possession.
2. If the maintenance mechanic does not finish the job before the shift change, he or she will remove this safety lock and put a seal on the disconnect. The mechanic will hang a danger tag on the control station, stating why the equipment is shut down.
3. The maintenance mechanic coming on with the next shift will place his or her lock on the disconnect along with seal.
4. On completion of the repairs the area supervisor will be notified by maintenance that work is completed.
5. The supervisor and the maintenance mechanic will check the equipment to see that all guards and safety devices are securely in place and operable. Then the supervisor will break the seal and remove the danger tag from the machine.

Rules

The following rules are intended to promote employee safety:

1. The company and each employee are required to comply with provisions of the provincial health and safety regulations. You will be informed by your supervisor about specific rules not covered here that apply to your job.
2. Report promptly all accidents that occur on the job or on company premises. This should be done whether or not any injury or damage resulted from the incident.
3. Horseplay, practical jokes, wrestling, throwing things, running in the plant, and similar actions will not be tolerated — they can cause serious accidents.
4. Observe all warning signs, such as No Smoking or Stop. They are there for your protection.
5. Keep your mind on the work being performed.
6. Familiarize yourself with the specific safety rules and precautions that relate to your work area. Learn the procedure for orderly exit in case of fire.

(table cont'd.: Examples of Policies, Procedures, and Rules)

7. Approved eye protection must be worn in all factory and research lab areas during scheduled working hours or at any other time work is being performed.
8. Approved hearing protection is required when the noise level in an area reaches limits established by provincial legislation.
9. Adequate hand protection should be worn while working with solvents or other materials that might be harmful to skin.
10. Wearing rings or other jewelry that could cause injury is not allowed for persons working in the plant and lab.
11. Good housekeeping is important to accident prevention. Keep your immediate work area, machinery, and equipment clean. Keep tools and materials neatly and securely stored so that they will not cause injury to you or others.
12. Aisles, fire equipment access, and other designated "clear" areas must not be blocked.
13. Learn the correct way to lift. Get help if the material to be lifted is too heavy to be lifted by one person. Avoid an effort that is likely to injure you.
14. Only authorized employees are allowed to operate forklifts and company vehicles. Passengers are not allowed on lift equipment or other material handling equipment except as required in the performance of a job.
15. Learn the right way to do your job. If you are not sure you thoroughly understand a job, ask for assistance. This will often contribute to your job performance as well as your job safety.
16. Observe safe and courteous driving habits in the parking lot.

REACTIVE PLANNING

Robert Burns wrote: "The best laid schemes of mice and men / Go oft awry" — a sentiment still applicable in today's business world. Events can occur so rapidly that plans may be useless before they can be fully implemented. Even though a plan is properly developed, external and internal disturbances often occur that result in modification or even elimination. Prudent managers recognize that unforeseen events can happen and that they must anticipate such disruptions and deal effectively with the new conditions. When managers at any level prepare to adjust to unanticipated occurrences, they are using reactive planning. **Reactive planning** is a systematic way of modifying objectives; long-range planning; policies, procedures and rules; and standards to adapt to the external environment. Managers who use reactive planning are employing a true situational approach to planning.

Referring again to Exhibit 3-1, reactive planning encompasses all phases of the planning process. Suppose, for instance, that a paint firm's competition alters its product in a way that affects the product plans of the firm. Reactive planning must quickly take effect, or the firm's own plans could be a failure. Changes in the firm's plans could affect not only long-range planning but also policies, procedures, rules, and even standards. Examples that reinforce the need for reactive planning are numerous. For instance, a new government policy may have a drastic effect on a long-range business plan; it can even change organization objectives. A new regulation calling for the total removal of lead from paint would affect the plans of both firms in the earlier example. Also, an unanticipated stoppage in the supply of a raw material, as with the oil embargos of the 1970s and 1980s, certainly brings reactive planning into play.

Reactive planning does not mean that a firm has to wait for an unanticipated situation to occur before it responds. Management should attempt to anticipate these contingencies as far as possible. Naturally, not all situations can be anticipated, but managers who try to anticipate possible deviations stand a much better chance of coping with new situations.

UNINTENDED SIDE EFFECTS OF PLANS

Every plan is likely to have certain undesired effects, and managers must not be blinded by all of the possible good results of a plan. Managers must anticipate the negative as well as the positive results of a plan. In many instances, a possible counterproductive effect of a plan can be headed off by appropriate action. For example, if a top manager suddenly asks for weekly output figures in kilograms, he may cause frantic juggling of orders to ensure high kilogram runs on Thursday and Friday. This misguided objective in turn, is likely to lead to missing some delivery promises for smaller orders. Rather than abolish the new output reports, thereby harming the control function, the top manager can ask for such reports on a semimonthly basis. The additional time should provide the flexibility for lower managers to meet both delivery dates and kilogram output standards. Looking at an important index too frequently can produce some undesirable side effects.

One unintended side effect of planning is that the individuals who have to carry out the plan may resist it. This opposition is particularly likely if employees feel that the plan has negative implications for their long-term employment prospects, or if the plan upsets normal working patterns. For example, if management develops a plan for installing a new computer complex, employees may resist it for fear of losing their job to the computer. Or, employees may resist attempts by management to change the objectives that the organization is pursuing. People who have worked in an organization for a long time become comfortable with the objectives they are used to pursuing, and any significant change in these can cause serious employee opposition. In situations where executives want to institute plans that are a major departure from past practice, it is important that they get as many employees as possible committed to the plans. The issue of implementing change in an organization is discussed in detail in Chapter 13.

The fact that a plan may have some negative effects is not usually adequate justification for its abandonment. Management needs to anticipate negative consequences and make provisions for handling them. Additional subordinate participation can reduce some of the adverse effects; education, patience, participation, and more effective reward systems can remove many more. Specialization cannot be abandoned, but efforts can be made to ensure that various functional units communicate, coordinate, and work together.

OPENING INCIDENT REVISITED

Allyn and Bacon, Publishers

In the opening incident, FitzGerald, Bockus, and Smith were trying to set objectives for Allyn and Bacon's publishing program for the next 2 to 3 years. How did they do it?

First, the 3 managers tried to define the corporation's identity: why does Allyn and Bacon exist, and what does the Canadian company hope to accomplish? The mission statement that they finally created defined their concern with producing educational materials — rather than just books — for Canadian post-secondary use (not just subjects that had specific Canadian content).

The second step in the managers' planning process was to analyze the external environment facing them. They examined the patterns of enrollments in various subject areas and agreed that they would not publish in areas of small or declining enrollments. They also evaluated the textbooks available from Allyn and Bacon's competition; the managers found that, in some high enrollment areas, so many good textbooks had already been published that it did not make sense to publish more.

The third step was for the 3 managers to identify honestly the strengths and weaknesses of their company and to capitalize on its strengths. They decided that, in the short-run, the company would take on a limited number of projects so that the marketing department could put full emphasis on each project.

The 3 managers now had the basis for a corporate strategy. The company would not pursue certain subject areas because the market was too small or because the competition was too well entrenched. The subject areas not excluded for these reasons would form the basis for Allyn and Bacon's Canadian publishing strategy. Bockus could now request specific market research from Smith's personnel. Further, Bockus could establish information networks in these subject areas and could ignore the others. This strategy would make him far more efficient in his work.

As a result of this two-day meeting, implementation plans for 30 specific projects were developed. One of those plans was for the textbook you are now reading.

SUMMARY

Setting objectives and deciding on the courses of action needed to obtain these objectives is referred to as the planning process. Overall organization objectives toward the desired result are established first. Then plans are developed to specify how objectives are to be accomplished. Standards are developed to determine if the objectives in the form of plans have been attained. Appropriate policies, procedures, and rules are then created to specify in greater detail the manner in which the plan will be achieved. Yet successful planners do not operate in a vacuum and must be flexible enough to respond to changing external and internal conditions. This is referred to as reactive planning and must be designed with the planning system. Plans should be constantly evaluated and modified to conform to both current and anticipated situations.

The three main types of business objectives are economic, service, and personal. If the organization is to survive, grow, and earn a profit, it tries to match its goals and the goals of groups who have contact with the firm. Some of the problems encountered in establishing objectives include conflicts between real and stated objectives, multiple objectives, and goal distortion.

The determination of how organization objectives will be achieved is referred to as strategic planning. The two basic stages of strategic planning are determining the strategy and developing the specific plans to implement the strategy. The primary difference between planning by lower-level management and planning by top management is the external environment in which the two levels of management operate.

Policies, procedures, and rules are formulated to implement plans. A policy is a predetermined, general guide established to provide direction in making decisions. A procedure is a series of steps established for the accomplishment of some specific project or endeavor. A rule is a specific and detailed guide to action that is set up to direct or restrict action in a fairly narrow manner.

REVIEW QUESTIONS

1. What are the steps involved in the planning process?
2. What are the main types of objectives that can be identified for business firms in our society?
3. Describe and briefly discuss the strategic planning sequence.
4. Define standards. Why is it important for managers to develop clearly defined standards?

5. Distinguish by definition among policies, procedures, and rules.
6. What is meant by the term *reactive planning* as it relates to the planning process?
7. What are some unintended side effects of plans?

EXERCISES

1. It has been stated in the text that a firm can have multiple objectives. What do you consider would be the objectives of the following firms and organizations with regard to their interrelationship with society?
   a. Ford Motor Company
   b. Canadian Pacific Airlines
   c. Peat, Marwick, and Mitchell
   d. The Toronto Blue Jays
   e. The Girl Guides
   f. Revenue Canada.
2. Assume that your objective is to obtain, straight A's in your courses next term. Develop a plan; policies, procedures, and rules; and standards that could help you achieve this goal.

CASE STUDY

Undue Influence?

Heather Odom is the head of the purchasing department of a large federal government agency. Her department is responsible for purchasing items ranging from paper clips to computer software; annual purchases of the department exceed $10,000,000. Odom has two people reporting to her who contact and buy from visiting salespeople. One Monday morning, Odom is called into her boss's office. Her supervisor informs her that Paul Hayles, one of Odom's purchasing agents, has been accepting substantial gifts from potential suppliers.

The agency has a policy forbidding acceptance of gifts from suppliers if these gifts are substantial enough to cause undue influence on the purchasing agent. The agency believes purchasing agents might be influenced to buy from suppliers willing to sweeten a deal with such gifts. In the extreme, such influence could cause purchasing agents to buy inferior products for the agency. Odom's supervisor requests a quick resolution to this problem.

Odom meets with Hayles later that day and asks him about the gifts. Hayles readily admits he accepted gifts from three different suppliers and that he purchased some items from them. However, Hayles denies that he had purchased the items because he had been given a gift by the salesperson. Odom reminds Hayles of the agency's policy forbidding acceptance of suppliers' gifts which might influence purchasing behavior. Hayles says he is aware of the policy and reassures Odom that his purchasing decisions are not influenced by the gifts. Odom is under the impression that Hayles will continue to accept gifts.

After Hayles leaves, Odom sits in her office wondering what she should do and what she'll tell her supervisor.

QUESTIONS

1. What is the problem here and why has it arisen?
2. What should Odom do now:
    a. regarding Paul Hayles?
    b. in her report to her supervisor?

CASE STUDY

Objectives and Plans at West-Can

West-Can Stores Ltd. operates a chain of convenience stores in western Canada. (See Exhibit 3-6 for a partial organizational chart of the company.) Duties for store managers are specific; top management of the company believes that profitability is possible only if a tight rein is kept on operations at the retail level.

Top management strives for uniformity of operation in all areas, including ordering, stocking, customer check-out procedures, and managers' attitudes generally prevailing within a store. Because of the routine nature of work and because of a concerted effort by top management to foster conformity in store managers' duties, there tends to be little discretion on the part of managers regarding day-to-day store operations.

This general lack of freedom to make decisions extends to the supervisory level. Virtually all supervisors are promoted from the ranks of "successful managers" within West-Can. As a result, those individuals who conform best to the convenience store orientation are promoted. Typically a supervisor has responsibility for 3 to 5 stores. Normal duties include picking up the previous day's receipts, verifying daily accounting records, monitoring physical conditions of the stores, and making employment recommendations. Most matters not recognized as standard operating procedures are resolved at a higher managerial level.

The authority of district managers is also limited, though to a lesser extent than that of supervisors. Typically district managers have responsibility for approximately 15 stores, with 3 supervisors reporting directly to them. Although their district is considered a profit center, their ability to control profits is restricted to routine matters. From a practical standpoint, success or failure of a district manager depends on the degree of conformity he or she is able to obtain from managers within his or her area of responsibility.

Any decisions that are not covered by standard operating procedures must be made at the division manager level. The division manager is also responsible for establishing objectives and formulating plans. All division managers are promoted from the ranks after successful accomplishment of the duties of a store manager, supervisor, and district manager.

Bob Harrison was recently promoted to division manager, moving up through West-Can's ranks in only 10 years. The area manager called Harrison in last Wednesday and questioned him about his objectives and plans for the coming year. When Harrison said he did not have them

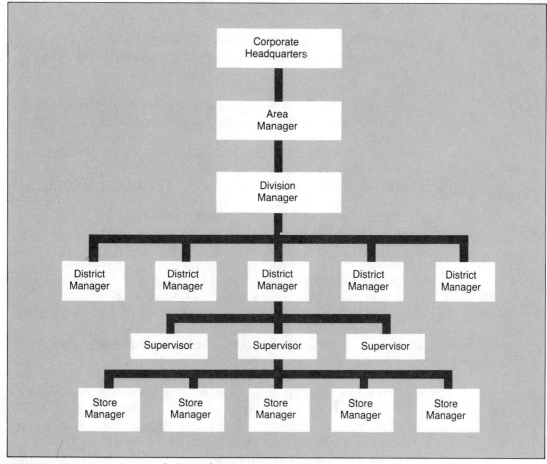

EXHIBIT 3-6   Organizational chart of West-Can Stores

and was not really sure what was expected, the area manager became rather puzzled.

"Bob," the area manager said, "you are expected to do much more creative thinking now than in the past. You can let your subordinates take care of daily routines. Your job is much more encompassing. The very survival of West-Can depends on how well your objectives and plans are formulated."

Harrison returned to his office in a state of controlled panic. He really had no idea how to go about setting objectives because higher managers had always told him clearly what to do. He thought back to his positions as store manager, supervisor, and district manager. In each of those jobs he had felt quite secure because

operating procedures had been spelled out for him. Now he felt as if his area manager had set him adrift with no guidelines. What was he going to do?

QUESTIONS

1. Why does the area manager believe the "very survival" of West-Can depends on how well district managers' objectives and plans are formulated?
2. Harrison's situation is not uncommon. How could a firm ensure that people such as Bob are equipped to handle the planning function?
3. Assess the managerial style at West-Can.

REFERENCES

Allen, David. "Establishing a Financial Objective — A Practical Approach." *Long Range Planning* 12 (December 1979): 11–16.

Allen, L. A. "Managerial Planning: Back to the Basics." *Management Review* 70 (April 1981):15–20.

Anderson, Carl R., and Paine, Frank T. "Managerial Perceptions and Strategic Behavior." *Academy of Management Journal* 18 (December 1975): 811–823.

Bowman, Edward H. "Risk/Return Paradox for Strategic Management." *Sloan Management Review* 21 (Spring 1980): 17–31.

Camillus, John C., and Grant, John H. "Operational Planning: The Integration of Programming and Budgeting." *Academy of Management Review* 5 (July 1980): 369–379.

"Forecasting and Planning." *Oilweek* (January 30, 1984): 14.

Fox, H. W. "Frontiers of Strategic Planning: Intuition or Formal Models." *Management Review* 70 (April 1981): 44–50.

Goldstein, S. G. Mike. "Involving Managers in System-Improvement Planning." *Long Range Planning* 14 (February 1981): 93–99.

Gup, Benton E. "Begin Strategic Planning by Asking Three Questions." *Managerial Planning* 28 (November 1979): 28–31.

Hailden, B. T. "Date and Effective Corporate Planning." *Long Range Planning* 13 (October 1980): 106–111.

Herbert, Theodore T. "Strategy and Multinational Organization Structure: An Interorganizational Relationships Perspective." *Academy of Management Review* 9, no. 2 (April 1984): 259–270.

Kahalas, Harvey. "Planning Types and Approaches: A Necessary Function." *Managerial Planning* 28 (May-June 1980): 22–27.

Kudla, R. J. "Elements of Effective Corporate Planning." *Long Range Planning* 9 (August 1976): 82–93.

Lebell, D., and Krasner, O. J. "Selecting Environmental Forecasting Techniques from Business Planning Requirements." *Academy of Management Journal* 20 (July 1977): 373–383.

Lindsay, W. M., and Rue, L. W. "Impact of the Organization Environment on the Long Range Planning Process: A Contingency View." *Academy of Management Journal* 23 (September 1980): 385–404.

Lorange, Peter. *Implementation of Strategic Planning.* Englewood Cliffs, N.J.: Prentice-Hall, 1982.

McCaskey, Michael B. "A Contingency Approach to Planning: Planning with Goals and Planning without Goals." *Academy of Management Journal* 17 (June 1974): 281–291.

Martin, John. "Business Planning: The Gap between Theory and Practice." *Long Range Planning* 12 (December 1979): 2–10.

Michael, Steven R. "Feedforward versus Feedback Controls in Planning." *Managerial Planning* 29 (November-December 1980): 34–38.

_____ . "Tailor Made Planning: Making Planning Fit the Firm." *Long Range Planning* 13 (December 1980): 74–79.

Naylon, T. H. "Organizing for Strategic Planning." *Managerial Planning* 28 (July 1979): 3–9.

Pearson, G. J. "Setting Corporate Objectives as a Basis for Action." *Long Range Planning* 12 (August 1979): 13–19.

Pekar, Peter P. "Planning: A Guide to Implementation." *Managerial Planning* 29 (July-August 1980): 3–6.

Ratcliffe, Thomas A., and Logsdon, D. J. "Business Planning Process — A Behavioral Perspective." *Managerial Planning* 28 (March 1980): 32–38.

Robinson, Richard B. Jr., and Pearce, John A. II. "Research Thrusts in Small Firm Strategic Planning." *Academy of Management Review* 9, no. 1 (January 1984): 128–137.

Simmons, William W. "Future of Planning." *Managerial Planning* 29 (January-February 1981): 2–3.

Snyder, N., and Glueck, W. F. "How Managers Plan the Analysis of Manager's Activities." *Long Range Planning* 18 (February 1980): 70–76.

Stephenson, E. "Assessing Operational Policies." *Omega* 6 (1976): 437–446.

Taylor, Bernard. "Strategies for Planning." *Long Range Planning* (August 1975): 437–446.

Thomapoulis, Nick T. *Applied Forecasting Methods*. Englewood Cliffs, N.J.: Prentice Hall, 1980.

Thune, Stanley S., and House, Robert J. "Where Long-Range Planning Pays Off." *Business Horizons* 13 (August 1970): 81–87.

Townsend, Robert. *Up the Organization*. Greenwich, Conn.: Fawcett, 1971.

Vancil, Richard F., and Lorange, Peter. "Strategic Planning in Diversified Companies." *Harvard Business Review* 53 (January-February 1975): 81–90.

Vesper, Volker D. "Strategic Mapping — A Tool for Corporate Planners." *Long Range Planning* 12 (December 1979): 75–92.

Wente, M. A. "Remaking the Management Mind." *Canadian Business* 56 no. 1 (January 1983): 23.

Word, E. Peter. "Focussing Innovative Effort through a Convergent Dialogue." *Long Range Planning* 13 (December 1980): 32–41.

Management by Objectives: An Approach to Planning

OPENING INCIDENT

Algonquin Food Products Ltd.

William Klassen, marketing department manager at Algonquin Food Products Ltd. was reviewing a memo from the president. Marie Beliveau, accounting department head, stopped by his office and asked him if he wanted to go for coffee.

"Yes, I need a break from this goals memo from the president," replied Klassen. "You know,

I'll never understand him or this so-called participation planning system. Here's another memo that dictates the latest objectives my department is supposed to achieve. No one in my department had a chance for input or discussion of these objectives. Most of them are unrealistic and many are unattainable."

"Frustrating, isn't it?" agreed Beliveau. "My

department couldn't meet the last set of objectives, and nothing I say seems to make a difference."

"Why doesn't the president ask us about the goals before he decides to impose them?" Klassen continued. "Isn't that how our Management-by-Objectives system is supposed to operate? And another complaint I have is about all these forms we have to fill out! I'm not sure the president even reads them. But, if he does, he'll probably use them against me this time next year. I really can't see how any of this is going to increase the performance in marketing."

Beliveau chuckled, "Come on, Bill; give up on trying to change the president for now. Let's get a cup of coffee and talk about more pleasant things."

KEY TERMS

management by
  objectives
activity trap
action plans

routine objectives
problem-solving
  objectives
innovative objectives

personal
  development
  objectives
team objectives

LEARNING OBJECTIVES

After completing this chapter you should be able to
1. Explain what management by objectives (MBO) is about and describe the historical development of MBO.
2. Explain the essential elements of the MBO process.
3. State the types of objectives used in MBO programs.
4. Identify the characteristics of MBO objectives for both individuals and teams.
5. Describe the application of MBO at Investors Syndicate.
6. List and describe briefly the primary benefits and potential problems with MBO programs.

William Klassen's experience illustrates that, in goal-oriented organizations, people are influenced — in this case negatively — by the goals set by top management. Most people want to know what's expected of them; most people, whether managers or subordinates, would also like to have some involvement in determining what is expected. Most employees of organizations feel they have ideas that will benefit the company. Logically, involving such employees in setting objectives for their work makes more sense than simply imposing objectives on them. If people are allowed to participate in setting their work objectives, they will probably work more enthusiastically to achieve them.

In this chapter, we examine what is probably the most widely used management technique designed to achieve this enthusiasm: management by objectives (MBO). We begin by describing the background and development of MBO. We then discuss the MBO process as it should be practiced. We note several types of objectives that can be set using MBO. Then, as an illustration, the application of MBO at one large Canadian company is described in some detail. The chapter concludes with an examination of the benefits and problems associated with MBO; we also make some suggestions about how to increase the chances that MBO will be effective.

MANAGEMENT BY OBJECTIVES (MBO)

During the past two decades few developments in the theory and practice of management have received as much attention and application as MBO. It directs managers' attention toward specific targets or results that the organization must attain to be successful. In an MBO system, the efforts of management are goal directed as opposed to being activity centered.

Whether profit or not-for-profit, private or government, all organizations are concerned with achieving objectives; the attainment of objectives should be the primary concern of management. We defined management as the process of planning, organizing, influencing, and controlling to accomplish organization goals through the coordinated use of human and material resources. An MBO system causes management to focus its attention on the objectives — the results. In essence, MBO is "simply common sense, in that it is a reflection of the purpose of managing itself."[1]

Effective management practice concentrates on establishing and attaining measurable goals. **Management by objectives** (MBO) is a management technique that provides a systematic and organized approach that allows management to attain maximum results from available resources by focusing on achievable goals. Above all else, MBO represents an overall philosophy of management that concentrates on achieving results. As such, it forces management to predict and plan for the future as opposed to simply responding or reacting on the basis of guesses or hunches. It provides a more systematic and rational approach to management and helps prevent "management-by-crisis," "firefighting," or "seat-of-the pants" methods. MBO emphasizes measurable achievements and results and is designed to lead to improvements in both organizational and individual effectiveness.[2] The approach depends heavily on active participation at all levels of management.

Background and Evaluation of MBO

Peter Drucker was first to describe "management by objectives" in 1954 in *The Practice of Management*.[3] According to Drucker, managers' primary responsibilities are to balance a number of demands and objectives in all areas where performance and results directly affect the survival, profits, and growth of the business. Drucker stated that specific objectives must be established in the following areas:

- market standing
- innovation
- productivity
- worker performance and attitude
- physical and financial resources
- profitability
- managerial performance and development
- public responsibility.

Drucker argued that the first requirement of managing any enterprise is "management by objectives and self-control." As originally described, an MBO system was designed to satisfy three managerial needs.

First, MBO would provide a basis for more effective planning. Drucker had in mind what might be called the systems approach to planning — that of integrating objectives and plans for every level within the organization. The basic concept of planning consists of making things happen as opposed to just letting things happen. According to Drucker, MBO is a planning system requiring each manager to be involved in the total planning process by participating in establishing the objectives for his or her own department and for higher levels in the organization.

MBO is designed to improve communications within the organization since managers and employees frequently discuss and reach agreement on performance objectives. In the process, there is frequent review and discussion of the goals and plans of action at all levels within the firm.

Third, Drucker thought that the implementation of an MBO system would encourage the acceptance of an increasingly participative approach to management. By participating in the process of setting objectives, managers and employees develop a better understanding of the broader objectives of the organization and how their goals relate to the total organization.[4]

One of the foremost advocates of MBO, George Odiorne, contends that special efforts must be undertaken to avoid the **activity trap**.[5] This trap exists when managers and employees become so enmeshed in performing assigned functions that they lose sight of the goal or reasons for their performance. As a result, they justify their existence by the energy and sweat expended and avoid questioning whether they have accomplished any result deemed necessary to overall effectiveness. While some managers are always busy, their efforts are not focused on the most important goals of the organization.

Another advocate of MBO, Douglas McGregor, had stressed a slightly different aspect. McGregor, who favored MBO because of its usefulness as a performance appraisal method, thought that the essence of MBO is management by integration and self-control. McGregor's philosophy of MBO was based on what he termed Theory Y. (Theory X and Theory Y are explained in detail in Chapter 10 — Motivation.) The basic assumption in Theory Y is that individuals are responsible human beings capable of exercising self-direction and self-control in achieving organization goals if they are committed to the goals.

In McGregor's approach, individual managers establish their own short-term performance objectives and develop plans to achieve these goals. Although the manager's boss provides assistance in goal setting by creating a climate for effective participation and commitment, the goals are set by the subordinate, not the superior.

The Historical Development of MBO

In its early years, MBO was primarily concerned with evaluating the performance of managers. With this emphasis, MBO did not always stress overall corporate objectives. Nevertheless, MBO did provide a means for reducing the subjectivity in performance appraisal by developing specific objectives and performance standards for each position. An MBO performance appraisal system provided an alternative to traditional performance evaluation, which was often based on perceived personality traits of the individual being appraised. It encouraged individuals being rated to participate actively in the process of establishing specific performance goals and in appraising progress toward their accomplishment.

When MBO is used only as an appraisal system, the program will likely receive only mild support from top management. As an appraisal system, responsibility for implementation of the program essentially comes from the personnel department; management's involvement is usually limited to the completion of the paperwork associated with the program. Substantial paperwork can be generated when MBO is used because managers and their subordinates must fill out various forms indicating what they hope to accomplish in the coming year. Performance reviews conducted annually or semiannually normally involves only subordinates and their bosses.

When MBO is used only as an appraisal system it is also possible that management views less productive employees as making greater contributions to the overall success of the firm than persons who are much more productive. Management may fail to recognize the difference in the levels of difficulty of goal achievement and overall contributions of different employees. For example, with rigid implementation of an MBO appraisal system, Milly Chang, a highly productive employee, may have attained 90 percent of her targeted goals. However, Wayne Miller, in the same department, may have achieved 100 percent of his goals, but his goals may have been much less demanding and ambitious than Chang's. Management should recognize the differences in the degree of difficulty in the goals of Chang and Miller and reward them accordingly.

MBO continues to be used in some companies simply as a performance appraisal system. However, if the MBO program does not proceed beyond the performance evaluation stage, its effectiveness will be limited. Performance appraisal is only one part of the MBO system; it has the most impact if it is preceded by the setting of objectives.

During the late 1960s, MBO began to be incorporated into the planning and control processes of organizations. Specific objectives for each department had to fit into the overall plans of the company. All of this activity was controlled through the use of budgets. Results-oriented performance appraisals continued to be an integral part of the MBO program, but there was considerably more top management support than during the earlier phase. In addition, since the MBO program was part of the budget process, management had the primary responsibility for its success. With this approach, the emphasis on training and development of personnel was increased throughout the organization.

Since the early 1970s, MBO has evolved into a system of management designed to integrate key management processes and functions in a logical and consistent manner. Anthony Raia, a leading advocate of MBO as a system of management, believes that MBO consists of "overall organizational goals and strategic plans; problem-solving and decision-making; performance appraisal, executive compensation, manpower planning, and management training and development."[6] MBO programs that have experienced success have included these characteristics:

- Direction and thrust come from top management, but managers at all levels are actively involved in the process.
- Increased need for teamwork involves more groups in establishing goals, action planning, and reviewing performance.
- Goal setting is more flexible and covers longer time spans.
- Performance reviews occur more frequently.
- There is more emphasis on individual growth and development.[7]

THE MBO PROCESS

Earlier we defined MBO as a systematic and organized approach that allows managers to attain maximum results from available resources by focusing on achievable goals. However, this definition of MBO does not provide significant insight into the total process. MBO should be constantly reviewed, modified, and updated. The dynamics of an MBO system are illustrated in Exhibit 4-1.

Top Management's Philosophy, Support, and Commitment

Any MBO program is doomed from the start without the absolute and enthusiastic support of top management. It is because of the lack of top-level commitment that so many MBO programs fail. To be effective, MBO must be consistent with the philosophy of top management. Implementing an effective MBO program is difficult if the chief executive lacks trust in the subordinates or is not personally committed to a participative style of management. A chief executive cannot introduce MBO by simply giving an order or a directive. Lower-level managers must be convinced of the merits of the system and meaningful participation in the process. MBO relies on the participative approach to management; this requires the active involvement of managers at all levels in the organization.

Establish Long-Range Goals and Strategies

Every successful MBO program must have long-range goals and the strategies to accomplish these goals. Long-term plans are developed by thoughtful determination of the basic purpose or mission of the organization. In Chapter 3, we noted that to develop long-range goals, the top management of a firm must answer such questions as these:

• What is the basic purpose of the organization?
• What business are we in and why?
• What business should we be in?

Long-range planning is essential if top management is to identify areas needing improvement.

Long-term goals and strategic planning can be illustrated by considering a company whose mission is to produce and market agricultural implements. Several long-term goals and strategies consistent with this mission may be developed. The company may have a goal both to increase its rate of return on shareholder investment to 15 percent after taxes and to achieve a share of 25 percent of the total Canadian market for agricultural implements within 7 years. This is a long-range goal because it extends beyond one year. The firm's strategic plan — the means to attain the stated goal — might include substantial quality improvements in the agricultural implements they produce. These changes might create a greater demand for the firm's products. If the firm is able to control costs and generate greater sales volume, its long-term goals should be attained.

Establish Specific Organization Objectives

After long-range goals and plans are established, top management must set specific objectives to be attained within a given time period. These

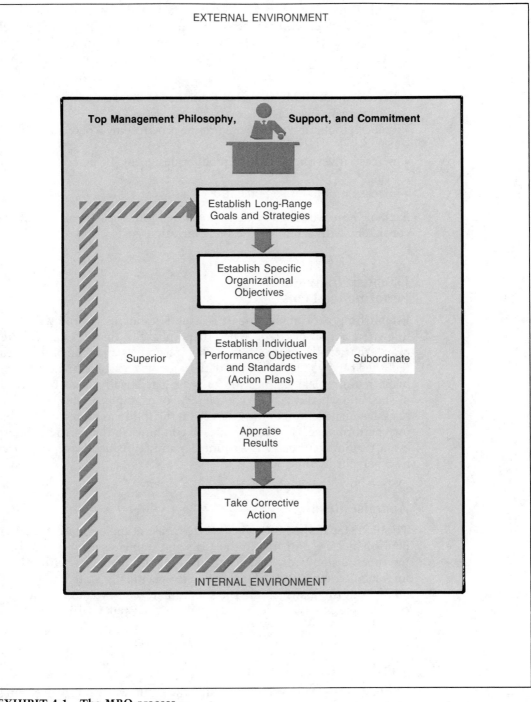

EXHIBIT 4-1   The MBO process

objectives must support the overall purpose and key result areas. Usually they are expressed as precise and quantifiable targets covering such areas as productivity, market, and profitability. Returning to the agricultural implements manufacturer, specific organization objectives might be:

- Increase sales of self-propelled combines to 8000 units — an increase of 10 percent over last year.
- Reduce production costs per combine produced by 5 percent over last year.
- Increase investment in new product design by 10 percent over last year.
- Increase profits by 10 percent over last year.

Each of these would be further subdivided into department objectives consistent with attaining these organization goals.

Establish Individual
Performance Plans

Establishing performance objectives and standards for individuals is known as action planning. The crucial phase of the MBO process requires that challenging but attainable objectives and standards be established through an interaction with superiors and subordinates. **Action plans** require clear delineation of what specifically is to be accomplished and when it is to be completed. For example, a salesperson and his sales manager might have agreed on the following standards for his own performance: (1) increase sales of combines in the north Saskatchewan region by 10 percent by June 30, and (2) reduce travel expenses by 5 percent by June 30.

Appraise Results

The next step in the MBO process is to measure and evaluate the actual performance as compared to the goals and standards established. Having specific standards of performance provides managers with a basis for such a comparison. When goals are specifically stated and agreed on by both the manager and the subordinate, self-evaluation and control become possible. We discuss performance appraisal in detail in a later chapter.

Take Corrective Action

Although an MBO system provides the framework for goal setting, managers in the organization must take action to correct areas where results are not being accomplished according to the plans. Such action may take the form of changes in personnel, the structure, or even the goals themselves. Other forms of corrective action may include providing additional training and development of individual managers or employees to enable them to achieve the desired results better. Corrective action should not automatically have negative connotations. Original objectives can be renegotiated without any penalty or fear of loss of job.

TYPES OF OBJECTIVES

Many kinds of objectives can be developed using MBO. These depend on the job and the organization in which they are being performed. Regardless of the job or organization, however, there are four basic types of objectives: routine, problem solving, innovative, and personal development. The following table shows how some of these objectives might be classified in a manufacturing firm.

Examples of Objectives in an MBO Program in a Manufacturing Company

Position	Objective	Type of Objective
Production manager	Achieve a 10 percent reduction in late production reports by December 31.	Routine
	Reduce product rejects caused by inferior quality from 8 percent to 5 percent by December 31.	Routine
Finance and accounting manager	Correct problem of low rate of return on the firm's assets by achieving 12 percent annual rate of return by December 31.	Problem solving
	Attend 2-week executive development program on improving leadership effectiveness by June 1.	Personal development

(table cont'd.: Examples of MBO Objectives in a Manufacturing Company)

Manager of engineering, research, and development	Develop and test 3 new products for entry into the market by June 1.	Innovative
	Employ 10 recent university engineering graduates — 4 mechanical engineers, 4 electrical engineers, and 2 industrial engineers — by September 1.	Routine
Marketing manager	Peform market tests on 2 products developed by Engineering, Research, and Development by June 30.	Routine
	Design and implement a new and more effective advertising program within a budget of $250,000 by August 31.	Innovative
Personnel director	Develop and implement program to reduce turnover of engineers and computer programmers from 30 percent to 20 percent by December 31.	Innovative
	Complete 3 courses toward MBA degree by August 31.	Personal development

Routine

Routine objectives are recurring day-to-day activities that must be performed. They represent standards of performance. As indicated in the table, a routine objective for a production manager might be to reduce product rejects caused by inferior quality from 8 percent to 5 percent by December 31. For a marketing manager, a routine objective could be to perform market tests on 2 new products by June 30.

Problem Solving

Problem-solving objectives are concerned with correcting a situation that is creating difficulties for the individual or the firm. The basic management task is that of solving problems. For example, a problem for the manager of finance and accounting may be a low rate of return on the firm's assets. To correct this problem, a problem-solving objective for the manager of finance and acounting is to achieve a 12 percent annual rate of return by December 31.

Innovative

Innovative objectives are concerned with unusual or special accomplishments, such as the development of new methods or procedures. MBO goal-setting sessions provide an opportunity for innovative goals to be developed and stated. Designing and implementing a new and more effective advertising program by the marketing manager within a budget of $250,000 by August 31 could well be an innovative objective designed to increase sales of the company's products and overall market share.

Personal Development

Personal-development objectives provide the opportunity for each individual to state his or her personal goals and action plans for self-improvement and personal growth and development. Almost all MBO systems include a section on personal growth and development goals. Examples of personal development goals might include a statement such as "completing a 2-week executive development program on improving leadership effectiveness by June 1" by the finance and accounting manager. Personal development goals are important because of their potential for helping individuals improve their current skills, preparing them for increased responsibility and career advancement, and improving their current performance.

SETTING OBJECTIVES

The actual setting of objectives is the heart of the MBO process and is considered one of the most difficult activities. Managers must decide how much involvement subordinates should have in setting objectives. As well, managers must settle the question of whether objectives should be targeted for individuals or for groups.

Who Should Set Objectives?

MBO objectives may be set (1) by the superior, (2) by the subordinate, (3) jointly, or (4) jointly with the aid of a staff specialist. (See Chapter 7 for a discussion of the staff specialist concept.) When superiors are completely in charge of goal setting, problems often occur. Rather than involving subordinates in the process, they impose a specific, quantitative, and time-bounded goal on employees. This is not MBO but probably should be referred to as RBO (rule by objective). The following conversation between the president of a holding company and the president of one of his subsidiaries illustrates RBO. The subsidiary president had expressed doubt as to whether he could meet the budget goal. The holding company president's reply was: "Do I pay you a lot of money? Do I argue with you over what you want to spend? Do I bother you? Then don't tell me what the goals should be. . . . My board and my shareholders want me to make my numbers. The way I make my numbers is for you guys to make your numbers. So, make your numbers!"[8]

Most MBO programs require some type of joint determination of objectives between superiors and subordinates. The advantage of having an MBO specialist is that it assures that meetings will actually take place and that help and advice will be available. The joint process can comprise any number of variations. The closest to RBO would be an initial determination of goals by the superior; these would be given to the subordinate, whose reaction would be requested. At the other extreme, the subordinate could set his or her goals and give them to the superior for a reaction. A middle ground is to have both superior and subordinate come to the meeting with a set of tentative objectives; final objectives will be agreed on after some negotiation.

Objectives for Individuals

In order for MBO to achieve maximum results, objectives for each individual should be carefully developed. They should be limited in number, highly specific, challenging, and attainable. The number of objectives for each individual should range from 4 to 8. Having more than 8 leads to spreading oneself too thin, thereby diminishing overall effectiveness. Each objective should be assigned a priority, perhaps ranging from 1 to 3. In this way, should time and resources prove to be more limited than anticipated, the individual has a basis for deciding which objective to pursue.

Perhaps the most emphasized characteristic of good objectives is that they should be stated in specific terms. In most instances, this means quantification and measurability. For example, goals have far less impact when stated in such terms as "improve the effectiveness of the unit," "keep costs to a minimum," or "be alert to market changes." At the performance review, the employee should be able to look back and definitely answer the question, "Did I do it or not?" For instance, a goal stating that production will be increased by 1000 units is much clearer than one that merely encourages increased production. Therefore, in writing objectives, a special attempt should be made to phrase them in terms of volume, costs, frequency, ratios, percentages, indexes, degrees, or phases. It is particularly important to place time limits on each objective. In 10 of 11 studies that examined the impact of such specific goals on performance, evidence was found supporting the contention that specifically stated goals increased the level of accomplishment.[9]

Developing challenging and attainable objectives requires a delicate balance of opposing forces. Yet both are essential in motivating the subordinate. Obviously, managers desire that objectives be set at such a level that employees must make special efforts. Some researchers have pointed out that, if promotion and salary are related to success in attaining objectives, as they should be, the participatory approach may well be asking the subordinate to construct a "do-it-yourself hangman's kit."[10] Jean Bishop, a hospital supply sales representative, might indicate to her sales manager that she plans to sell $200,000 in surgical instruments and supplies during the next 3 months. Since no one in the company has ever accomplished this level of sales in a 3-month period and since Jean sold only $200,000 during the entire last year, it is highly unlikely that she will attain her goal. Jean has just hung herself because her goal is unrealistic and unattainable.

In the initial phases of new MBO programs, one of the more common errors is the establishment of objectives that are unattainable. This is particuarly the case if the time period for review is 6 to 12 months. Anything seems possible with that much time. The superior must not allow excessively high goals to be set because this may cause a decline in future expectations and performance of the individual. Attention must be given to obstacles that affect accomplishment, for example the availability of resources necessary for performance. The impact of other personnel on the subordinate's performance must be recognized and discussed.

Research indicates that challenging objectives lead to greater accomplishment only if the subordinate truly accepts the goal as reasonable and only if goal accomplishment actually leads to organization rewards. Challenging goals with a history of past success will lead to continued success. A series of failures creates a mental set that makes attainment increasingly more difficult. Subordinates with self-assurance do well in relation to challenging goals. The subordinates' assessment of the probability of success should be that they at least have a 50-50 chance of achieving the objectives.

Group Objectives

The accomplishment of goals often requires that individuals cooperate as a team. There are many factors that can affect the attainment of **group** or **team objectives**. For instance, if a sales manager sets a specific objective of selling 50 000 units by March 1, it cannot be done if production does not manufacture that number of units. One of the most recommended approaches to overall goal setting involves team meetings to establish group goals. Team goal setting requires an open and supportive corporate culture. In general, MBO is more effective and achieves more positive results when applied in an organization with an open and supportive culture. Consider this instance: "a medium-size service company experimented with the team approach and decided to ignore individual objectives altogether, reasoning that too much interlinking support and cooperation are required to blame or reward any individual for the production of any single end result."[11]

If team goal-setting sessions are to be used as a prelude to the more typical individually oriented meeting, some training in group processes most likely is necessary. It is difficult enough for a manager to establish an open and participatory climate with an employee. It is far more complex and challenging to try to do so in a group. Programs of training directed toward this end go under the title of organizational development, a subject discussed in Chapter 13. The following is a suggested sequence in an MBO team approach: (1) team meetings of top executives to set overall organizational objectives; (2) team meetings at unit level; (3) individual person-to-person goal-setting sessions; (4) individual reviews of accomplishments; (5) team meetings at unit level to review progress and accomplishment; and (6) review at the top level to determine the degree of overall organization success.[12] The team goal-setting process improves the chances of success of the MBO program because it improves coordination and communication within the organization.

MANAGEMENT IN PRACTICE

Application of MBO at Investors Syndicate Limited

Investors Syndicate has used MBO since 1974 to motivate its sales force in selling a wide range of financial services. Investors is a private corporation and a wholly owned subsidiary of Power Corporation. It has over 1000 salespeople across Canada, making it the largest direct sales force of any company in the financial sector. Investors also owns Great West Life Assurance Company and Montreal Trust. Its major competitors are banks, trust companies, and insurance companies. Investors Syndicate has offices in every major metropolitan area of Canada. It also has offices in smaller cities such as Kelowna, British Columbia; Red Deer, Alberta; Dauphin, Manitoba; St. Catharines, Ontario; and Ste-Hyacinthe, Quebec. Its salespeole are paid on a straight commission basis.

During the early 1970s, top management of Investors observed that MBO was a useful management technique being used by a variety of business organizations. Representatives from Investors attended MBO seminars; they reported that the concept might be successful for Investors in the sales function. (A partial organization chart of the sales function at Investors is shown in Exhibit 4-2.) After reading a great deal of literature on the subject of MBO, top management concluded that, if MBO is to succeed, five key concepts must be stressed:

Concept 1: *Company purpose* The basic reason the company is in existence (its mission) must be understood by all employees. The mission of Investors is to satisfy clients in need of general and comprehensive financial planning. Through product development and an efficient sales distribution system, Investors assists in implementing financial plans and providing effective on-going service.

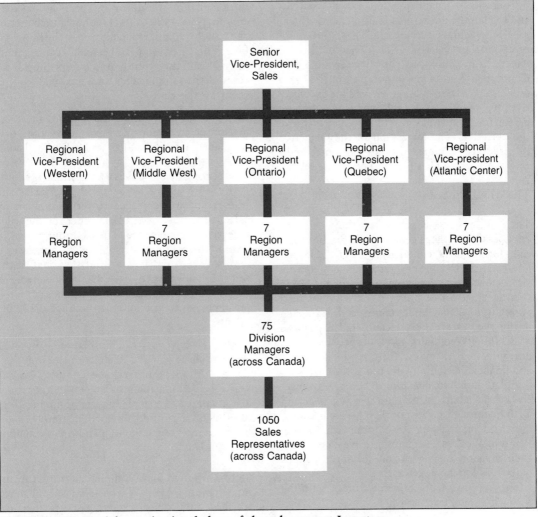

EXHIBIT 4-2 Partial organizational chart of the sales area at Investors

Concept 2: *Activities* The tasks that employees must perform so that the company can fulfill its mission must be clearly stated. In the sales area, this means calling on commercial and household clients and informing them of the wide range of financial services that are available from Investors. It also includes salespeople studying to improve their product knowledge, communication skills, prospecting abilities, and administration of their franchise.

Concept 3: *Responsibilities* The "key result areas" in which each employee must perform well need to be outlined. The Concept 3 activ-

ities are grouped into related areas, usually of four to five key responsibilities.

Concept 4: *Measurement* Effectiveness standards and performance indicators must be developed.

Concept 5: *Objectives* The specific results (objectives) that each salesperson will attempt to achieve must be stated.

These five concepts are constantly referred to at Investors. When the vice-president of sales asks for a "Concept 5", his people know what it is and the criteria that are valid for it.

Concepts 3, 4, and 5 are used to set objectives and to plan the activity the salesperson will engage in to achieve these goals. These three concepts form the basis for the "Objective Record Sheet." (An example is shown in Exhibit 4-3.) Concepts 3–5 form the action part of the MBO program. When a salesperson has set an objective (for example, 2 sales calls per day), that same person must establish an activity plan to achieve the objective. The lower half of the Objective Record Sheet requires the salesperson to indicate the activity plan in detail.

The MBO Process

The MBO process begins when the vice-president of sales develops general goals for the entire sales force. These general goals may be based on, for instance, last year's performance or on desired growth over last year's performance. This sets the stage for Planning Week which is held annually in 35 regional centers across Canada during the first week of December. The purpose of Planning Week is to give salespeople the opportunity to: (1) review their personal, career, and financial accomplishments of the past year, (2) relate individual results to the goals, objectives, and plans of the total company, and (3) think through and restate their personal, career, and financial goals for the coming year. During Planning Week, sales representatives meet with their division managers and set specific sales objectives for the next year.

The setting of objectives involves working through five distinct steps:

Step 1: *Determining Franchise Operating Costs* Since each sales representative in essence owns a franchise, the first step is to determine the costs of operating each franchise. Once expenses are projected, the salesperson can compute the level of income required to make the franchise profitable.

Step 2: *Determining Personal Requirements* Each salesperson then decides on personal financial needs; for instance, each asks: "How much money do I need to live on for the next year?"

Step 3: *Determining Total Financial Requirements* Steps one and two are combined to establish the salesperson's total financial re-

quirement for the upcoming year. Included in this analysis is the goal set for how much money the franchise wants to make. Thus, the franchise operating costs (Step 1), personal requirements (Step 2), and the profit requirements (Step 3) determine the salesperson's total financial requirement for the year.

Step 4: *Activity Plan* This requires the preparation of an action plan to achieve the goals developed in the Steps 1, 2, and 3. Detailed guidance is provided here, so that the salesperson can set realistic objectives. (An example is shown in Exhibit 4-4.) The activity plan tells the salesperson in very specific terms how many sales calls must be made in order for the sales objective to be reached. The example shown in Exhibit 4-4 is a realistic one taken from actual company records. This exhibit says that, if the salesperson wants to make $30,000 per year, he or she will have to make 46 approaches per week (an approach is an attempt to contact a possible client).

Step 5: *Productivity* The final step involves the completion of the "Sales Information System — MBO Summary Sheet." (See Exhibit 4-5.) Detailed instructions for completing it are also given to salespeople to assist them in filling out this important document. This information becomes the basic data for planning throughout the company.

Steps 1 through 5 are completed during the annual Planning Week. When the salespeople have finished, their objectives are given to their division managers. They discuss the objectives with each of their salespeople and come to a consensus on what individual sales goals will be. Each division manager then forwards the proposed objectives for his or her division to the appropriate region manager. This process continues all the way up to the vice-president of sales (refer to Exhibit 4-2) who gives final approval to the total company sales objectives for the coming year.

Negotiation is an important element of the MBO process at Investors. On occasion, a salesperson will set a goal that the manager considers to be either too low or too high. When this occurs, negotiation between the salesperson and the manager is needed until a goal is developed that is satisfactory to both. Investors has found

EXHIBIT 4-3
Objective
record sheet

	OBJECTIVE RECORD SHEET/ RELEVE D'OBJECTIFS
Time-frame	*REGION-DIVISION*

	CONCEPT 3. (Major Responsibilities/Responsibilités Majeurs)
FULL YEAR	PERSONNEL (REGION MANAGER)

CONCEPT 4. (Measurements/Mesures)	Priority/ Priorité
PER DIVISION: No. of Interviews; No. of Tests; No. of Terminations; Net Increase; No. sent to Career Development Seminars; $ spent on personnel prospecting	1

CONCEPT 5. (Objectives/Objectifs)

To hire 24 reps — approximately 12 for each division — 8 of these hirings to be experienced — female market to be explored.

Dates	PROGRAM OF ACTIVITIES/ PROGRAMME D'ACTIVITÉS	Objectives Objectifs	Results Resultats
Jan. & Sept.	1) Hold Management meeting to set up Co-op Personnel recruiting budget.	2	2
Jan., Mar., Apr., Jun., Oct. & Dec.	2) Hold Career Information nights in conjunction with Division Managers.	6	5
	3) Handle all screening personally up to the In-Depth Interview.	—	—
	4) Make 6 contacts personally each month.	6	6
Jan., Apr., Jul., Oct.	5) Ask all representatives for names of possible recruits at least quarterly.	4 ea.	

M Dionne

MANAGER/DIRECTEUR

ACTUAL PERFORMANCE/RESULTATS OBTENUS:

Financial Requirements	$ 30,000	**Approaches Objective**		2,025
divided by: income per sale ratio ÷	200	divided by: number of weeks to be worked in the coming year ÷		44
Sales Objective	150	**Weekly Approaches Objective**		46
multiplied by: presentations per sale ×	3	Convert sales objective to a production objective:		
Presentations Objective	450			
multiplied by: contacts per presentation ×	3	Average production per sale		15,000
Contacts Objective	1,350			
multiplied by: approaches per contact ×	1.5	multiplied by: sales objective ×		150
		Production Objective		$2,250,000

EXHIBIT 4-4 Activity plan

SALES INFORMATION SYSTEM — MBO Summary Sheet
PLANNING WEEK MBO SUMMARY SHEETS

REPRESENTATIVE NAME	REP. NO.	REGION OFFICE	R.O. NO.	DIVISION OFFICE	DIV. NO.

ACTIVITY	ACTUAL 1983			MBO 1984			
MONTHLY	PRODUCTION 1983	APPS	PLANS	PRODUCTION 1984	% INC. (Dec.)	APPS	PLANS
January							
February							
March							
April							
May							
June							
July							
August							
September							
October							
November							
December							
TOTAL							

ACTIVITY BY	ACTUAL 1983			MBO 1984		
PRODUCT	YTD S.I.S.	EST. DEC.	TOTAL 1983	MBO 1984	DIFF. 83–84	% INC. (Dec.)
Income Deferral Certificates						
MAP — Guaranteed						
Equity Funds						
Debt Funds						
RRSP — GIC						
MAP — Equity						
Annuities						
Group Products						
GIC — Montreal Trust						
Insurance						
Dollar Averaging						
Money Builder						
RHOSP						
GIC — Investors						
Installment GIC						
Term Certain Annuity						
Investors Real Property Fund						
Canamerica Money Fund						
TOTAL						

PRODUCTION INCREASE _____ %   Rep. _____   Reg. Mgr. _____

Div. _____   R.V.P. _____

EXHIBIT 4-5   Sales information system — MBO summary sheet

that resolving problems through negotiation early in the planning process helps prevent major disagreements later.

Recognition is also an important part of the MBO system at Investors. Various awards are given for different levels of sales performance, and these awards are publicized. (See Exhibit 4-6.) Each salesperson works at his or her own level of ability; most salespeople earn awards and are recognized for their achievements. Each salesperson therefore feels that he or she is making a positive contribution to the company, as well as his or her career.

Summary of MBO at Investors

Investors has found that the MBO system is well suited to its sales function. The goals of salespeople can be stated in quantitative terms and the salesperson can tell clearly whether or not he or she has achieved the goals originally established. Senior Vice-President of Sales, Sterling McLeod believes that the MBO system is valuable; he notes that Investors' salespeople often set much more challenging goals for themselves because of this system. The company has reached or exceeded its objectives each year since the MBO system was introduced. Between 1980 and 1983, Investors' sales nearly doubled, despite the fact that the Canadian economy was not strong during that period.

McLeod notes that about 75 percent of Investors' salespeople conscientiously fill out the MBO forms, and that MBO has made a noticeable difference in their sales performance. A few salespeople do, however, view MBO as something of a game of paper shuffling and, for them, MBO may not be so helpful. Given this, McLeod says Investors' managers must sell MBO to the staff instead of trying to enforce it. In McLeod's view, many companies that have tried to enforce MBO discovered that its employees resisted the system instead of enthusiastically using it to improve their own financial well being.

McLeod also points out that, by itself, MBO would not have had a dramatic impact; Investors simultaneously emphasized career planning along with MBO. Together, they have had very positive effects. People can use MBO to do long-range planning for their careers; this encourages them to achieve yearly goals.

Overall, MBO appears to have had a positive effect on the performance of salespeople at Investors Syndicate. Once the salespeople have set specific goals, they are motivated to perform the activities necessary to achieve them. The feedback they get in terms of satisfaction and recognition completes this process.

PRODUCTION QUALIFICATIONS AND BENEFITS	
$15,000 per week average	Qualifies a new representative to attend the Career Development Center — Initial Seminar — to be presented with Qualified Financial Planner Certificate.
$20,000 per week average	Qualifies a new representative to attend the Career Development Center — Advanced Seminar — to be presented with Advanced Financial Planner Certificate.
$500,000	Qualifies you for free personalized letterhead.
$1,000,000	Qualifies you for overwriting on all personal production.
$1,500,000	Qualifies you for the No Limit Performance Bonus.
$2,000,000	Qualifies for you the Millionaire plaque, for free personalized Millionaire stationery and calling cards plus an announcement in your local newspaper.
$8,000,000	Qualifies you to receive Investors' beautifully designed diamond ring in recognition of an outstanding sales achievement.

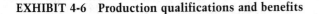

EXHIBIT 4-6   Production qualifications and benefits

SUMMARY EVALUATION OF MBO

Like other management techniques designed to improve an organization's effectiveness, MBO has both benefits and costs associated with it. We next examine these benefits and costs and draw some conclusions about the value of MBO for organizations.

Benefits of MBO Programs

Organizations using MBO have experienced several benefits. A good MBO system:

- Results in better overall management and the achievement of higher performance levels. MBO provides an overall results-oriented philosophy of management that requires managers to do detailed planning. Managers also must develop action plans and consider the resources and control standards needed.

- Provides an effective overall planning system. MBO helps managers avoid management by crisis.

- Forces managers to establish priorities and measurable targets or standards of performance. MBO programs sharpen the planning process. Rather than just saying "do your best" or "give it your best shot," managers who request specific goals force specific planning. Such planning is typically more realistic because MBO calls for a scheduled review at a designated future date. Subordinates make sure that they can obtain the resources necessary for goal accomplishment and that obstacles to performance are discussed and removed. MBO encourages planning of a logical sequence of activities before the start of action.

- Clarifies the specific role, responsibilities, and authority of personnel. Objectives must be set in key result areas and individuals responsible must be given adequate authority to accomplish them. A production plant superintendent who has a goal of producing 10 000 units a day must be given the authority to organize and direct resources to achieve this level of production.

- Encourages the participation of individual employees and managers in establishing objectives. If the process of MBO has been undertaken on a joint and participatory basis, increased commitment will likely be evident.

- Facilitates the process of control. Periodic reviews of performance results are scheduled, and information collected is classified by specific objectives. Subordinates must relate what was accomplished rather than concentrate on descriptions of what they did or how hard they worked. MBO also stimulates improvement in the performance of superiors, who are forced to clarify their own thinking and to communicate it to subordinates.

- Provides opportunity for career development for managers and employees. Personal development goals are often part of the set of objectives developed in joint sessions. MBO often demonstrates areas where employees need additional training. Priorities establish realistic guides for effort, as well as enabling concrete demonstration of goals accomplishment. This, in turn, allows for a more realistic and specific annual performance review, which, of course, is crucial in deciding on promotions, pay increases, and other organization rewards.

- Other specific strengths of an MBO system might include:
  - Lets individuals know what is expected of them.
  - Provides a more objective and tangible basis for performance appraisals and salary decisions.
  - Improves communications within the organization.
  - Helps identify promotable managers and employees.
  - Facilitates the enterprise's ability to change.
  - Increases motivation and commitment of employees.[13]

Potential Problems with MBO Programs

Although there are numerous benefits attributed to MBO, there may also be problems that may be encountered, such as:

- MBO programs often lack the support and commitment of top management. Without it, employees may conclude that MBO is not very important, and they will not seriously work at making it a success. Even with top management support, care must be taken to ensure that participation of all employees is part of the process.

- Certain people may believe that quantitative goals cannot be set for their jobs. A social worker may argue that social work does not lend itself to the setting of quantified objectives because the occupation deals with people and their personal problems. In fact, goals for virtually all jobs can be quantified but, if people do not believe it can be done, they may be hostile to the idea of MBO.

- The implementation of an MBO system can create a paper mill if it is not monitored closely. If people in the system spend an excesssive amount of time filling out MBO forms, they will have less time to pursue the important goals of the organization.

- There may be a tendency to develop short-run goals at the expense of long-run goals. If this happens, organization members will spend their time stressing goals that reduce the chance of long-run survival for the firm. For example, if marketing managers focus solely on selling the company's existing products and do not conduct market research for new products, the company may eventually find itself with an obsolete product line.

- The goals set may not be the most important ones for the organization. Goals may be set simply because they can be quantified or because everyone agrees on them. However, if they are not the important goals toward which the organization should be striving, little will be accomplished by using MBO to achieve them.

Toronto management consultant Gordon Allan has pointed out that Management by Objectives may cause rigidity in the organization if objectives are simply developed by top management and imposed on lower-level managers.[14] In order for an organization to cope with rapid change, develop new products or services, and keep in tune with its external environment, it must develop objectives that take into account the skills, needs, abilities, and aspirations of the people who must achieve them.

Assessing the Effectiveness of MBO Programs

In a review of 185 MBO studies, Kondrasuk found that there are numerous arguments pro and con as to the effectiveness of MBO.[15] Many organizations have adopted MBO on faith, often as a result of questionable case studies or unsubstantiated testimonies. According to another study, there is "relatively little empirical evidence to demonstrate the impact of MBO on any aspect of organizational or individual behavior, including job performance."[16]

As illustrated in Exhibit 4-7, MBO achieved positive results in 153 organizations, a ratio of 9 to 1, positive to not positive. Case studies and surveys show a much higher level of effectiveness for MBO than do experiments. According to Kondrasuk's analysis, there are: "tendencies for MBO to be more effective in the short term (less than two years), in the private sector, and in organizations removed from direct contacts with the customer. We may conclude that MBO can be effective, but questions remain about the circumstances under which it is effective."

However, approximately 50 percent of large organizations use some form of MBO, indicating its acceptance as a management concept. Despite complaints by managers and researchers, most surveys and case studies of the application of MBO indicate considerable satisfaction with the concept. A number of conclusions regarding MBO can be drawn from the responses of 279 personnel administrators representing a cross-section of private and public sector organizations.[17] The conclusions are:

- MBO has been successful in the majority of organizations.

- Effectiveness of an MBO program is not dependent on the type or size of the organization.
- Extensive ongoing training is a fundamental ingredient for a successful MBO program.
- Increased frequency of managerial reviews leads to a more effective MBO program.
- The overall results of MBO programs have not met the expectations of participating managers. Performance did not improve as much as expected.
- Most studies on MBO have tended to emphasize the positive and underrate the negative consequences.
- The major problems associated with an MBO program include insufficent review and evaluation of goals, lack of support of the philosophy of MBO throughout the organization, inadequate participation of employees in goal setting, difficulty in quantifying goals, and too much paperwork required.

Improving the Effectiveness of MBO Programs

MBO programs can be made more effective if management adheres to the following guidelines:

- Secure top management support and commitment.
- Specify the overall objectives of the program and communicate them throughout the organization.
- Emphasize MBO as an overall philosophy or system of management rather than just a performance appraisal technique.
- Allocate adequate time and resources to instruct each person in the organization in the nature and philosophy of the system.
- Recognize that goals must be realistic and attainable and that they must contribute to the overall purpose of the organization.
- Be willing to modify the goals as changes in the external environment dictate. Continuous review is a must.

EXHIBIT 4-7   MBO effectiveness as applied in 185 organizations

Research Approach	Positive	Mixed	Not Positive	Ratio of Positive : Not Positive
Case Studies	123	8	10	12:1
Surveys	9	2	1	9:1
Quasi-experiments	20	3	4	5:1
True experiments	1	2	2	1:2
Totals/Average	153	15	17	9:1

SOURCE   From Jack N. Kondrasuk, "Studies in MBO Effectiveness," *Academy of Management Review* 6, no. 3 (1981): 425. Used with permission.

- Be sure to clarify responsibility and authority relationships so that everyone understands what's expected in the MBO system.
- Insist that goals be written and stated in measurable terms to be attained within a specified period of time.
- Make the goal-setting process a joint activity between superiors and subordinates.
- Recognize that MBO will not solve all managerial problems.

OPENING INCIDENT REVISITED

Algonquin Food Products Ltd.

The way MBO has been implemented at Algonquin Food Products certainly leaves something to be desired, at least according to William Klassen. Several of the potential problems mentioned in this chapter have become problems at Algonquin. Klassen is particularly upset that he is never consulted about what goals are realistic and attainable for his department. As noted in the chapter, when unrealistic goals are imposed by a supervisor, subordinates are generally not enthusiastic about pursuing them.

Klassen is also concerned that the MBO system is merely a "paper mill." If employees feel that MBO only means filling out forms each year, they aren't likely to think it can be useful; in such a company, it probably won't be. Klassen also believes that no one will look at his results.

This implies that top management is not genuinely committed to the MBO process at Algonquin. Klassen fears that, even if top management does look at his performance goals, the MBO system will be used against him rather than to help his department perform better in the future.

In general, Algonquin has violated most of the basic rules about MBO. Therefore, the system will likely not be beneficial to the firm. A close reading of this chapter should help you think of ways top management at Algonquin could have avoided the situation that has developed. The material on the MBO process is particularly important; an understanding of what MBO is supposed to do reduces the chance of faulty implementation.

SUMMARY

The attainment of organization objectives is the primary concern of management. An approach that aids in goal achievement is management by objectives (MBO). MBO represents an overall philosophy of management — a way of thinking about planning — that concentrates on measurable goals, targets or results. It provides a systematic and rational approach to management and helps prevent management by crisis. To be effective, MBO depends on active participation at all levels of management.

The application of MBO in organizations has progressed through three stages — from an emphasis on performance appraisal, to one on planning and control, and most recently to an integrated system of management. The MBO process consists of several important steps: attaining top management commitment and involvement; establishing long-range goals and strategic plans; defining specific organization objectives; establishing performance objectives and standards for individuals (action planning); measuring results achieved (appraisal); and taking corrective action to ensure the attainment of the desired results (control). The types of objectives established in MBO programs include routine, problem solving, innovative, and personal development. Objectives should be limited in number, stated in specific and measurable terms, and should be challenging and attainable.

MBO offers both benefits and potential problems for managers. Some of the primary advantages of MBO are that it provides an effective planning system; forces managers to establish priorities and specific standards of performance; clarifies specific roles, responsibilities, and authority of personnel; encourages participation in goal setting; aids in control; assists in career development for managers and employees; provides a more objective basis for performance appraisal as well as promotion and salary decisions; and tends to increase the motivation and commitment of personnel. The major problems that may be encountered in using MBO include lack of support and commitment of top management; difficulty in establishing goals; creation of a "paper mill"; tendency for goals to concentrate too much on the short run; and the time-consuming nature of the process.

Numerous Canadian companies use MBO. Investors Syndicate Limited instituted MBO in 1974 and now uses MBO for its 1000 person sales force across Canada. The MBO process has worked well at Investors and has been associated with a dramatic increase in sales.

Research evidence indicates that MBO has been effective in most organizations; however, one study concluded that MBO tends to be more effective in the short term, in private-sector firms, and in organizations removed from direct contact with customers. While we may not yet be able to deliver the final judgment on the effectiveness of MBO, it is estimated that about 50 percent of large organizations use some form of MBO. This widespread use suggests that organizations find MBO useful.

REVIEW QUESTIONS

1. What is management by objectives (MBO)? Explain its value to management.
2. Compare and contrast Drucker's view of MBO with that of Douglas McGregor.
3. Briefly describe the three distinct phases MBO programs have passed through.
4. What are the basic steps in the MBO process? Explain each briefly.
5. What are the four types of objectives that can be established in MBO programs? Explain and provide examples of each type of objective.
6. What are the basic characteristics of objectives and how are objectives determined?
7. Briefly discuss the benefits and costs of an MBO system. Which are the most significant and why?

8. Has MBO been effective as a management system?
9. What suggestions for improving the effectiveness of MBO could you offer an organization?

EXERCISES

1. Apply the managment by objectives concepts discussed in this chapter by developing clear-cut personal goals for yourself to cover the next year. Be sure to include specific goal statements and completion times for routine, problem solving, innovative, and personal development. Also include specific action plans to ensure goal accomplishment.
2. Visit a firm in your area that uses MBO and ask several managers within the company about their reaction to the program. This is an excellent class project that could be part of a tour of a local business.

CASE STUDY

MBO at York Investments Ltd.

York Investments Ltd. provides a wide range of financial services to consumers and business firms. The company introduced a management by objectives (MBO) program two years ago. Top management of the firm was convinced that MBO would significantly improve the company's overall effectiveness in planning and would provide a system for more accurate evaluation of personnel. Prior to the implementation of MBO, the company had no formal planning system and had used a performance appraisal system that primarily evaluated such factors as quantity of work, quality of work, judgment, and adaptability. The performance factors were rated from 1 (very poor, unacceptable performance) to 5 (exceptional performance). All personnel including managerial employees were evaluated using this system. The considerable dissatisfaction with this rating system was the primary reason for York Investments to implement an MBO system. At the beginning of each year, overall company objectives as well as department goals are formulated and communicated to managers throughout the firm. The following is a description of the company's MBO program as it is applied in the Accounting Services Department.

Jean Stelmach, the accounting services manager, has four supervisors reporting to her. These supervisors are responsible for accounts payable, accounts receivable, payroll, and customer services. At the beginning of each year, Stelmach discusses the company and department objectives with each of her four supervisors.

The payroll supervisor is George Patrick, an RIA who has been with York for 9 months. He had 4 years of experience in payroll operations at another company. He is considered to be a competent supervisor with 8 clerks reporting to him. The department processes the payroll for almost 1000 employees. Patrick and Stelmach had agreed on the following goals for the payroll department during Patrick's first year as supervisor:

1. Establishment of a consistent account reconciliation program for the 160 payroll-related accounts in the general ledger by June 1.
2. Establishment of a cross-training program for the payroll clerks by June 1.
3. Creation of written documentation for all of the payroll department procedures by September 1 (in accordance with the company's broader statements on policy and procedure).

4. Reduction of employee turnover to 15 percent during the year.

During the year, the company experienced rapid growth, adding an average of 10 employees per month. Turnover of clerical personnel in the payroll department began in February. Within the first 4 months, payroll lost 3 experienced employees. These personnel changes required considerable on-the-job training for the new employees. Near the end of the year, Stelmach reviewed the progress of the payroll section with Patrick. The results were as follows:

Objective 1 Not accomplished. A consistent reconciliation program has not been implemented.

Objective 2 Not accomplished. A cross-training program has not been devised. Several duties have been reassigned as new employees were hired, and some jobs have been slightly redesigned.

Objective 3 Not accomplished. Written documentation has increased, but no substantial progress was made during the year toward developing an overall detailed payroll procedures manual.

Objective 4 Not accomplished.

Stelmach expressed disappointment with the overall performance of payroll. She asked Patrick why payroll had experienced these problems. Patrick agreed the results were not attained as planned but believes employee turnover greatly affected payroll. "Of the three people I hired," he said, "only one was as effective as those who quit."

QUESTIONS

1. If you were Jean Stelmach, how would you rate the performance of George Patrick, the payroll supervisor?
2. Evaluate the MBO program as it is used by the company. Does it meet the criteria for a successful program as discussed in the chapter?
3. Should Patrick be retained? Why or why not?

CASE STUDY

MBO Program at Federation Stores

Top management at Federation Stores Limited, a chain of 21 retail stores, recently decided to implement an MBO program throughout its organization. Sam Maryk, manager of the Calgary store, has just completed reviewing his objectives for the new program with his district manager, Ray Gibb. As a result of this meeting, Maryk is both confused and irritated.

Three weeks before, Maryk had received a letter from Gibb outlining top management's MBO program, pointing out how it would improve efficiency and increase each store's profit contribution to Federation Stores. The letter noted that objectives would be used to measure performance and that salary increases and promotions would in future be directly related to that performance. Gibb had included instructions for store managers to list the objectives each considered appropriate for his or her store, then to wait for his visit to discuss them.

Maryk had realized that he and the two assistant managers of the Calgary store had a lot at stake in establishing realistic objectives for their store. After discussing the situation, Maryk and the assistant managers selected objectives that they thought would be appropriate for their store. They selected performance levels that were improvements from the past year but could be exceeded. Among others, they selected the following objectives:

• Increase selling efficiency as measured by the ratio of sales salaries to sales by 10 percent.
• Reduce inventory shortage to 2 percent of sales.
• Reduce register shortage to 0.05 percent of sales.
• Improve customer service to the extent that there are 20 percent fewer complaint letters mailed to the home office.

The district manager had arrived late for the MBO review visit, so that there had not been much time for discussion. After scanning the objectives Maryk submitted, Gibb explained that profit improvement was really what the home office was interested in. Rather than trying to monitor separate objectives from the Calgary (or any other) store, the home office had decided that a 12 percent profit improvement would be a reasonable objective for Maryk's store. This single objective would facilitate the monitoring of performance by the home office and would also reduce the amount of information the store would have to submit. The visit was cut short because Gibb had to attend a home office meeting on the advertising budget to be allocated to individual stores.

QUESTIONS

1. What problems does Federation Stores have with its MBO program?

2. What mistakes, if any, did the home office make in trying to establish its MBO program? Did the MBO system at Federation meet the criteria for an effective program as discussed in the chapter?

3. Will using profit as the sole measure of performance have the results the home office desires? Why or why not?

4. Did Maryk have the right approach to setting goals?

5. What indicators of poor communications were apparent?

6. How could MBO have been implemented at Federation Stores so that the problems were avoided? Be specific.

NOTES

[1]Harold Koontz, "Making MBO Effective," *California Management Review* 20 (Fall 1977): 5.

[2]Anthony P. Raia, *Managing by Objectives* (Glenview, Ill.: Scott, Foresman, 1974): 10–12.

[3]Peter F. Drucker, *The Practice of Management* (New York: Harper, 1954).

[4]Peter F. Drucker, *Management Tasks, Responsibilities, Practices* (New York: Harper, 1974).

[5]See George S. Odiorne, *Management by Objectives* (Belmont, Cal.: Pitman, 1965), and *Management Decisions* (Englewood Cliffs, N.J.: Prentice-Hall, 1969).

[6]Raia, 14–15.

[7]Raia, 14–18.

[8]Wendell L. French and Robert W. Hollman, "Management by Objectives: The Team Approach," *California Management Review* 17, no. 3 (Spring 1975): 19.

[9]Raia, 14–18.

[10]Gary P. Latham and Gary A. Yukl, "A Review of Research on the Application of Goal Setting in Organizations," *Academy of Management Journal* 18, no. 4 (December 1975): 829.

[11]W. J. Reddin, *Effective Management by Objectives* (New York: McGraw-Hill, 1971): 16.

[12]Richard E. Byrd and John Gowan, "MBO: A Behavioral Science Approach," *Personnel* 51, no. 2 (March-April 1974): 48.

[13]See Koontz, 5–7.

[14]Gordon G. Allan, "Management Flexibility," *The Canadian Personnel and Industrial Relations Journal* 18 (May 1971): 13–21.

[15]Jack N. Kondrasuk, "Studies in MBO Effectiveness," *Academy of Management Review* 6, no. 3 (1981): 419–430.

[16]Kondrasuk, 419–430.

[17]Robert C. Ford, Frank S. McLaughlin, and James Nixdorf, "Ten Questions About MBO," *California Management Review* 23, no. 2 (Winter 1980): 90.

REFERENCES

Babock, R., and Sorensen, P. F. Jr. "MBO Checklist: Are Conditions Right for Implementation?" *Management Review* 68 (June 1979): 59–62.

Bologna, J. "Why MBO Programs Don't Meet Their Goals." *Management Review* 69 (December 1980): 32.

Denny, W. A. "Ten Rules for Managing by Objectives." *Business Horizons* 22 (October 1979): 66–68.

Dowst, S. "Classify Your Objectives." *Purchasing* (April 25, 1979): 38.

Ford, C. H. "MBO: An Idea Whose Time Has Gone?" *Business Horizons* 22 (December 1979): 48–55.

Ford R. C. "MBO: Seven Strategies for Success." *SAM Advanced Management Journal* 42 (Winter 1977): 4–13.

Ford, R. C., et al. "Ten Questions about MBO." *California Management Review* 23 (Winter 1980): 48–55.

Haines, W. R. "Corporate Planning and Management by Objectives." *Long Range Planning* 10 (August 1977): 13–20.

Jackson, J. H. "Using Management by Objectives: Case Studies of Four Attempts." *Personnel Administrator* 26 (February 1981): 78–81.

Koontz, H. "Making MBO Effective." *California Management Review* 20 (Fall 1977): 13–15.

Lopata, R. "Key Indicators: Simpler Way to Manage." *Iron Age* (January 26, 1981): 41–44.

Migliore, R. Henry. *MBO: Blue Collar to Top Executive.* Washington, D. C.: Bureau of National Affairs, 1977.

Muczyk, J. P. "Dynamics and Hazards of MBO Application." *Personnel Administrator* 24 (May 1979): 51–61.

Pack, R. J., and Vicars, W. M. "MBO — Today and Tomorrow." *Personnel* 56 (May 1979): 68–77.

Schneier, C. E., and Beatty, R. W. "Combining BARS and MBO: Using an Appraisal System to Diagnose Performance Problems." *Personnel Administrator* 24 (September 1979): 51–60.

Tosi, H., et al. "How Real Are Changes Induced by Management by Objectives?" *Administrative Science Quarterly* (June 1976): 276–306.

Weitzul, J. B. "Pros and Cons of an MBO Program." *Best's Review* 81 (January 1981): 72–73.

Wiehrich, H. "TAMBOL Team Approach to MBO." *University of Michigan Business Review* 31 (May 1979): 12–17.

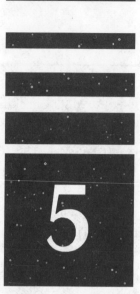

5

Managerial Decision Making

Mackie Real Estate

Mackie Real Estate is a small but rapidly growing firm in a western Canadian city. The company's two main activities are traditional residential real estate sales and speculative buying and selling of commercial property. For the latter activity, the four managers of the firm meet once a month to determine if any good opportunities exist.

At the last meeting a dispute arose over the speculative purchases. One manager had heard that the provincial government was likely to purchase one of three blocks of land in the next 6 months in order to build a power plant. If the

company could buy the land first and then sell it to the government, Mackie could realize a tidy profit. The managers' dispute centered on which of three available blocks of land the company should buy.

Block 1 costs $40,000. The managers estimate that there is a 0.2 probability that the government will purchase Block 1 for its power plant. If it does, the company could make a $40,000 profit; if the government doesn't buy it, Mackie will still make a $5,000 profit because the land is inflating in value.

Block 2 costs $60,000, and the managers estimate that there is a 0.5 probability that the government will build the power plant on it. If it does, the company will make a $50,000 profit; if it doesn't, Mackie will lose $25,000 because the land will decline in value.

Block 3 costs $100,000 and the probability of the government buying it is 0.3. If it does, the company could make $110,000; if it doesn't, Mackie will lose $35,000.

Which purchase should Mackie's managers make?

KEY TERMS

decision making	problem content	physical models
personal decisions	payoff relationships	schematic models
professional decisions	state of nature	mathematical models
professional decision maker	intuition	management information system
routine decisions	scientific approach	microcomputer
nonroutine decisions	hypothesis	minicomputer
decision maker	risk	telecommuting
	model	

LEARNING OBJECTIVES

After completing this chapter you should be able to

1. Define decision making and distinguish between making personal and professional decisions and making routine and nonroutine decisions.
2. Describe the basic approaches to decision making.
3. Explain the decision-making process.
4. Identify the primary factors affecting the decision-making process and describe the requirements for decision making.
5. Relate the importance of model building to a manager.
6. Describe the role of management information systems in the decision-making process and understand the impact of computers on management.

Managers make decisions. The manner in which they resolve organization problems determines their success as managers. In fact, decision making can be viewed as synonymous with managing, since it accounts for a large portion of managers' jobs. Merely because individuals have managerial titles does not mean that they can manage. Many individuals with elaborate titles are not managers because they are not decision makers. The key to whether a person should be classified as a manager is whether he or she is in a position to choose from among alternatives to make the needed decision and has the authority to implement it.

Managers who have the authority but refuse to make decisions are not carrying out their jobs. One of the most important qualities for success as a manager is to not procrastinate on decisions, hoping problems will go away if ignored. True, a decision to do nothing may, in its broadest sense, imply that a choice has been made. However, a pattern of failure-to-decide does not give a person the right to be called a manager.

Increasingly, managers are being measured by the results of their decisions. Companies do not want dynamic failures; they want individuals who are equipped properly to make correct decisions. This does not mean that managers must be right 100 percent of the time; no one is perfect. But, successful managers have a higher ratio of success to failure than less successful managers.

In this chapter, we first define decision making. The requirements for decision making are discussed. We then examine two basic approaches to decision-making as well as some factors that affect the decision-making process. Next, we describe the key steps in the decision-making process. We also note the usefulness of models to managers when analyzing possible alternatives. One crucial element to decision making is the information available to managers. We end the chapter with a discussion of management information systems and some of the business roles of computers in decision making.

MAKING DECISIONS

Decision making is the process of evaluating alternatives and making a choice among them. The concept of a definite process in making decisions is important, since some people overstress the time at which one alternative is chosen. This unbalanced emphasis ignores the analysis that led to the point at which the alternative could be chosen.

Everyone makes decisions every day. However, before anyone even thinks about actually making the decision, he or she either is confronted with a problem or sees an opportunity. Thus, people make problem decisions or opportunity decisions. Once an individual identifies the choice as a problem or an opportunity, that person must identify and analyze the alternatives that are available. The alternative that promises to resolve the problem most effectively or takes best advantage of the opportunity is chosen after careful analysis. The choosing of this alternative is defined as the decision point.

To place decision making in perspective, we need to distinguish between such classifications of decisions as personal versus professional decisions and routine versus nonroutine decisions.

Making Personal versus Professional Decisions

Although a similar thought process exists in making either personal or professional decisions, managers should be aware of the differences between the two. Here is a brief overview of personal and professional decision making.

Personal Decisions

A wide variety of decisions are considered personal. Decisions to study, to go on a date, to watch television, or to go to bed early are examples of personal decisions made routinely by university and college students. **Personal decisions** can, of course, affect business firms. If you purchase a Ford instead of a Chevrolet, you will have a positive effect on the Ford Motor Company and a negative effect on General Motors.

A portion of any manager's time is spent discussing employees' personal problems and what can be done about them. Managers should recognize that employees experiencing difficulties in their personal lives may bring these problems to the job. Thus, a manager may be involved to some degree in the personal decisions of employees, whether the manager wants to be or not.

Professional Decisions

Virtually every gainfully employed person is required to make **professional decisions** — decisions that are part of the work he or she performs. Professors make decisions concerning the nature of the information they present to their students. Physicians diagnose problems and prescribe treatments. Scientists formulate hypotheses and design experiments for testing them. Managers of baseball teams, football coaches, politicians, plumbers, and clergy — in fact, most employed people — are required to make decisions as part of their professional lives. Yet the administrator in a business organization is labeled a manager, whereas many of the other decision makers are not. Managers are expected to be **professional decision makers**; their reason for being a manager is to make decisions.

Why are organization managers labeled professional decision makers whereas people in many other occupations are not? The answer is visibility. The manager of an organization operates in an open environment. A managerial decision affects many people (customers, shareholders, employees, the general public). The business manager sees the results of decisions reflected in the firm's earnings report, the welfare of employees, and the economic health of the community and the country. Decisions made by business managers may be no more or no less crucial that those of the physicians or scientists, but their decisions affect a greater number of people. Managers' careers cannot be made by only one good decision. Their careers must be marked by a series of decisions that are acceptable. Hence, Levitt contends, unlike the lawyer, scientist, or physician: "The manager is judged not for what he knows about the work that is done in his field, but by how well he actually does the work."[1] To survive, the manager must be able to make professional decisions.

Making Routine versus Nonroutine Decisions

Managers are continually confronted with the need to make a variety of decisions. Professional decisions may range from such major ones as whether to build a new plant or to enter a new business to rather routine decisions, such as deciding from which supplier to purchase the washroom paper towels. The two basic categories of professional decision making are routine and nonroutine.

Routine Decisions

Most managers make numerous routine decisions daily in the performance of their jobs. **Routine decisions** made by managers are governed by the policies, procedures, and rules of the organization, as well as the personal habits of the managers. Decisions related to appropriate disciplinary action if an employee has violated company safety rules or settling disputes among employees over vacations may be governed by company policies, procedures, and rules. Deciding when to go to lunch or how to organize daily activities are examples of routine personal decisions that may be determined largely by habit.

Since routine decisions are relatively straightforward for managers to make, they free managers for more challenging and difficult problem solving. Many organizations set policies, procedures, and rules that provide a framework for decision making. Some firms have routine decisions made by a computer system; these are often called programmed decisions. However, managers are little more than robots if they simply adhere to the rule book and do not exercise personal judgment.

Nonroutine Decisions

While routine decisions may take up a considerable portion of a manager's time, individuals make or break it as managers on the basis of the success of their nonroutine decision-making ability. **Nonroutine decisions** are those made when managers deal with unusual problems or situations. Decisions to expand to foreign markets, build a new production plant, or buy a more advanced computer system are examples of nonroutine or out of the ordinary decision situations. While these are examples of nonroutine decisions made by top management, managers at all levels in the organization make nonroutine decisions. For instance, nonroutine decisions made by a lower-level manager might include firing an employee or changing the layout or work flow procedures in his or her department.

Exhibit 5-1 illustrates the relationship between the level of management and the proportion of routine and nonroutine decisions made at each level. As managers progress to higher levels, their proportion of nonroutine decisions increases. Nonroutine decisions require managers to exercise creativeness, intuition, and good judgment in solving nonroutine problems.

REQUIREMENTS FOR DECISION MAKING

As previously stated, the most important quality that a business manager needs is the ability to make correct decisions. This one quality often separates the successful from the less successful managers. Certain conditions that must be present before a decision can be made are: a decision maker, a problem, various alternatives, payoffs, and states of nature.

The Presence of a Decision Maker

While Harry Truman was president of the United States, he kept a plaque on his desk that stated: "The buck stops here." He was the

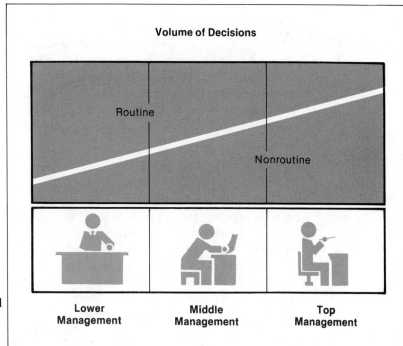

EXHIBIT 5-1
Managerial levels and the amount of routine versus nonroutine decisions

person responsible and he made the final decision. The **decision maker** has the responsibility for choosing the course of action that will take up an opportunity or solve a problem within the area for which he or she is accountable.

The role of decision maker may be assumed by an individual manager or by a group. If a group is making a decision, an outsider may have difficulty identifying who has the most influence during deliberations. The important thing is that a decision maker exists. If no one in the group is willing or able to make the decision, actions that should be taken will not be taken.

Problem Content

The **problem content** includes the internal or external environment within which the problem exists, the decision maker's knowledge of that environment's factors, and the changed environment that will exist after a choice is made. Because of the significance of the particular problem content of one decision, what may be optimum in one organization may result in complete failure in another. For instance, if a nonunion firm decided that, because of reduced sales, 10 percent of its work force must be laid off, the least productive workers would likely be the first to be laid off. On the other hand, a unionized firm facing the same circumstances would have to adhere to the labor-management agreement; it would likely lay off employees with the least seniority, even if these workers were highly productive.

Courses of Action

With a decision problem, a manager should develop more than one alternative from which to choose. Alternatives may be many or few in number. They may merely represent the option of doing something or doing nothing. A good decision maker, however, attempts to identify and analyze as many alternatives as possible within given time and resource restrictions.

Payoff Relationships

The various courses of action must be analyzed with the decision's objective in view. **Payoff relationships** are established to measure the costs or profits of alternative courses of action. When the profits and costs associated with a particular alternative cannot be expressed mathematically, managers may have difficulty making the decision. For example, decision making is made easier if a manager can state that a particular decision will save $50,000 as opposed to expressing an opinion that costs will be lowered.

MANAGEMENT IN PRACTICE

A Decision-Making Problem

Suppose you are considering two possible part-time positions at a pizza restaurant that has recently opened. One of the positions is for an assistant manager and the salary is based on commission. The alternative is as a pizza cook for which you will be paid $6.00 an hour.

Because the pizza house is relatively new, a trend has not been established as to the sales potential of the business. However, based on the experience within the community, you estimate that there is a 20 percent chance of high sales, 50 percent chance of average sales, and 30 percent probability of low sales. You recognize that these states of nature will have an impact on the amount of money you could receive from the assistant manager's position. As an assistant manager, you estimate the payoff for high sales will be $10.00 an hour, for average sales it will be $7.00 an hour, and for low sales it will be $2.00 an hour. However, you will receive $6.00 an hour no matter what the sales are if you choose the job as a pizza cook. The payoff relationship between each alternative and the states of nature is provided in Exhibit 5-2. You are now in a position to analyze the two alternatives.

Which job should you take? One way to make the choice is to compute the expected value of each job. The expected value is computed by multiplying the probability of each state of nature by the payoff associated with each. For this problem, you will have two expected values because you have two job alternatives. They are as follows:

$$\text{pizza cook} =$$
$$0.2(6.00) + 0.5(6.00) + 0.3(6.00) = \$6.00$$

$$\text{manager} =$$
$$0.2(10.00) + 0.5(7.00) + 0.3(2.00) = \$6.10$$

For the expected earnings for the pizza cook position, multiply the probability of the high sales state of nature (0.2) by the payoff associated with high sales ($6.00). Add to that total the sum of the probability of the average sales state of nature (0.5) times its payoff ($6.00) plus the probability of the low sales state of nature (0.3) times its payoff ($6.00). The job value of the pizza cook position is $6.00. Do the same analysis for the assistant manager job; the expected value for it is $6.10. If you want the job that has the highest expected value, you will take the assistant manager position.

However, you should consider other facts before you make the decision. Your financial situation may prevent you from accepting the risk of receiving only $2.00 an hour if sales are poor. Other alternatives also might have been analyzed. For instance, you may have other jobs available to consider. You may think the experience gained from the assistant manager job outweighs any money you might earn. Full evaluation of the solution, of course, cannot be done until the job is actually taken.

EXHIBIT 5-2   The pizza house job matrix

Alternatives	High Sales	Average Sales	Low Sales
Probabilities	0.20	0.50	0.30
Hourly wage	$ 6.00	$6.00	$6.00
Commission	$10.00	$7.00	$2.00

State of Nature

The **state of nature** refers to the probability that various situations could occur for a course of action. For example, when a weather reporter says: "There's a 20 percent chance of rain," rain would be one state of nature and no rain would be another. If the state of nature never offered a choice, everyone would be an excellent decision maker. Choice is required when the precise relationships among alternatives are known and the problem is to identify the probability of success or failure in terms of the decision's objective. Choice may come about because of uncertainty about the future environment or because precise relationships among alternatives are not known. Anyone who has played five-card draw poker understands uncertainty about the future and the imprecise relationships that can exist. The good decision maker, like a good poker player, studies the situation thoroughly in the hope that his or her decisions will be correct more often than not. Because of the state of doubt, most decision makers will never be 100 percent correct.

APPROACHES TO DECISION MAKING

Two basic approaches to decision making are intuition and research. Each is briefly discussed and broadened to include the professional decision maker.

Intuition

Individuals who rely on intuition make their decisions based on accumulated experience. **Intuition** is insight acquired through experience and accomplishments rather than through a formal reasoning process. Experience has a reputation for being a good teacher. You will discover that many business recruiters place major emphasis on the business experience students have gained while in university or college and on extracurricular activities they have participated in. The recruiters believe the learning process for a particular job may be shortened if a student has been active in other endeavors while in school. But business managers who make decisions relying only on intuition base judgment on their "feel" for the situation. Alternatives are chosen on the basis of a hunch. If decision makers confront situations to which they have not been exposed previously, wrong decisions may result. The intuitive approach to decision making has several obvious shortcomings:

- Learning from experience is usually random.
- Although experience is valuable, no one can assess its value. No one can guarantee that experience equals learning.
- What is learned through experience is necessarily limited by any individual's experiences.

- Conditions change and experiences of the past may not be good indicators of current or future conditions.[2]
- The question may be asked, "Do you have 20 years of experience or do you have one year of experience 20 times?"

Research and the Scientific Method

The **research** approach to decision making is systematic, stressing that the scientific method be used in problem solving. The **scientific approach** can be conveniently divided into four distinct but interrelated phases: observation of events, formulation of hypotheses, experimentation, and verification.

Observation of Events

The first step in the scientific method requires that a person explore fully the relationships among the elements of a system and want to know how and why they produce a particular outcome. The process begins by observing an occurrence and then asking why it happened.

Hypothesis Formulation

The second step in the scientific method requires the creation of an explanation as to the hows and whys of the observed event. A **hypothesis** is a tentative statement of the nature of relationships

---

MANAGEMENT IN PRACTICE

Intelligence and Decision Making

Intelligence, as measured by IQ tests, seems to be related to a person's success in school, but it apparently doesn't have much to do with how successful a person is in his or her business career. Successful executives generally score fairly well on IQ tests, but that is not what distinguishes them from unsuccessful executives. Accordingly, psychologists are increasingly searching for something called "practical intelligence."

This involves discovering the mental processes that are critical in work situations. Recent research suggests that the most successful executives are those who are cognitively complex; they have the ability to plan strategically without being locked in to one course of events and they have the capacity to acquire much information on which to base decisions, but they are not overwhelmed by that information. They are also able to grasp relationships among rapidly changing events.

Professor Siegfried Streufert assessed managerial thinking styles in a simulation in which executives spent several hours making decisions based on data such as investments abroad, raw materials, and the stability of foreign governments. He found that executives who displayed greater cognitive complexity did a better job of making decisions which took into account the complicated relationships among these factors.

SOURCE Daniel Goleman, "Super IQ Not the Key to the Executive Suite," *Globe and Mail* (August 21, 1984): L9.

that exist. A hypothesis provides an explanation of the cause that brought about the observed effect. For instance, you might formulate the hypothesis that a relationship exists between turnover and job satisfaction.

Experimentation

The third step in the scientific approach to decision making is experimentation. A manager subjects the hypothesis to one or a series of tests to determine whether the tentatively stated relationship does in fact exist. Tests either support the hypothesis or prove it to be unsound.

Verification

The final step in the scientific method is verification of the findings obtained from the experiment. Sometimes this may take the form of another experiment or a series of experiments. Such is the case when a marketing researcher finds that a sample market is highly receptive to a new product and then verifies these results in additional test cities when the product is actually sold to consumers.

Which Approach Is Better?

The professional decision maker must adopt an approach that uses the best features of both the intuitive and the scientific approaches. All information that managers are able to obtain should be used to assist in making decisions. Intuition is an essential part of good research because experience can provide valuable insight into what may occur if a certain decision is made. The research approach, on the other hand, forces the decision maker to evaluate critically what is known and to recognize what is unknown before jumping to a decision based solely on a hunch. Professor Ralph C. Davis's classic statement summarizes the need for a bond between these two approaches in this discussion of the professionally trained executive:

> A man who has nothing but background is a theorist. A man who has nothing but practical experience is a business mechanic. A professionally trained executive is one in whom there is an effective integration of these two general types of experiences, combined with adequate intelligence regarding the types of problems with which he must deal.[3]

THE DECISION-MAKING PROCESS

Managers make decisions by choosing among various courses of action. It is often as simple as deciding whether or not to work overtime or as complicated as deciding on the future objectives of the firm. If an organization is to be successful, it must have managers who are willing and able to make decisions that will be best for the firm. As such, decision makers are the architects of an organization. They have the ability to develop solutions to problems that occur in their area of responsibility.

The process managers follow to make decisions is shown in Exhibit 5-3. As illustrated, all decisions must be made within the constraints of both the internal and external environment. The internal and external factors surrounding the decision maker may change, based on whether the decision is made by top, middle, or lower-level management, but the general process does not. For instance, a president will likely have to consider the views of shareholders when making a decision to build a new plant. A production supervisor, on the other hand, will have to consider internal company policy when thinking about terminating an employee.

We should note that the implementation of a decision does not complete the decision-making process. The arrows in Exhibit 5-3 indicate

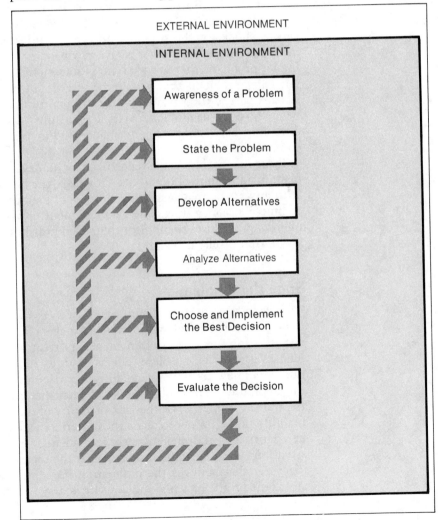

EXHIBIT 5-3
The decision-making process

that there is constant reevaluation and feedback to every phase of decision making. The outcome — whether good or bad — provides information that influences future decisions. Decision making is thus an on-going, dynamic process. For example, if a manager makes the decision to implement a new work procedure and it proves unsatisfactory, a different alternative would likely be chosen. If the new procedure works, a learning process has resulted. Successful managers learn from their mistakes. Less successful managers make the same mistake repeatedly and wonder why their decisions are consistently wrong.

Awareness of a Problem

The first step in making a decision is to be aware that a problem exists. If a manager doesn't realize a problem exists, nothing can be done to solve it. We have all heard the answer to the question: "Why are you doing it this way?" The stock answer: "We've always done it that way" causes shock for the person who is truly interested in problem recognition. The stock answer is given by people who have stopped looking for problems that need solving. Professional managers will always recognize problems that need to be solved, but they should also spend at least part of their time looking for opportunities to make decisions where no obvious problem exists. Opportunity decisions can mean the difference between good performance and marginal performance for a company.

Typically, problems are recognized by managers when they perform planning and control functions. However, the problem itself may deal with any of the management functions of planning, organizing, influencing, and controlling. The establishment of plans and the development of procedures to monitor their accomplishment makes managers aware that problems exist.

State the Problem

The second step in the decision-making process is to define the problem as clearly and concisely as possible. Managers must solve the problem, not its symptoms. Too often managers treat symptoms and do not identify the actual problem. Let us assume, for instance, that a large number of new employees are failing a particular portion of their training (symptom). The problem may be identified as: (1) the difficulty of the training material, (2) the lack of ability of the employees, or (3) the inability of the trainer to teach the material in an understandable manner. Until the training manager can identify the real problem, the situation cannot be remedied. Consider the top management of a manufacturer that believes the problem of its company is: not making a sufficient profit. Not making a profit is a symptom, but it is not the actual problem. The problem might be ineffective cost controls, excessive inventory, high turnover of personnel, or a multitude of other factors. Whatever the instance, identification of symptoms rather than causes can hurt the decision-making process and result in inappropriate decisions being made.

Develop Alternatives

Once the problem has been identified, the alternative courses of action that might solve it must be stated. The number of alternatives that can be generated is limited by: (1) the information available to the decision maker, (2) the time available to make the decision, and (3) the importance of the decision. Obviously, however, the best decision cannot be made if it is not considered as an alternative course of action. For instance, the company that was not making a profit might consider a number of alternatives, such as cost control or incentives to workers, to correct the cause of the problem. However, if the correct alternative is not considered, the problem cannot be solved.

Managers can use several ways to generate alternatives. An organization that wants to introduce a new product can, for example, conduct marketing research in order to develop information about several product alternatives. Stated more generally, managers can rely on information to develop alternatives. We discuss information systems in more detail later in this chapter.

Another way to develop alternatives is to ask subordinates for their input on various problems. Since subordinates often are very knowledgeable about specific aspects of the organization, consulting them will often uncover useful alternatives.

MANAGEMENT IN PRACTICE

Japanese Decision Styles

Although it is unusual, there are some North Americans working for major Japanese companies. In their positions, they can observe Japanese decision-making styles. Thomas Cappiello, a public relations man for the trading company Nissho Iwai, notes that a good leader in Japan is one who doesn't make decisions; instead, he or she finds out what the decision is. In a similar vein, Geoffrey Tudor of Japan Air Lines points out that, if Japanese managers try to make an important decision unilaterally, they are removed from their jobs — in a face-saving way. John Macklin, an executive for Fujitsu, observes that, if a company president wants a certain decision made, he may first plant the idea with a few subordinates; then he'll let them do the analysis on the problem and make the decision. He will then compliment them on a good idea and decision.

Apparently these practices are widespread. In terms of individual participation in decisions, this type of environment can be very motivating. Ronald McFarland, a supervisor at Isuzu Motors, says that one satisfying aspect about Japanese companies is that the ideas of even new employees are listened to.

SOURCE   Adapted from "Outsiders in Japanese Companies," *Fortune* (July 12, 1982): 114–128.

TALKING TO MANAGERS

Dr. Heleen McLeod
Alberta Education

Heleen McLeod is the Director of Special Educational Services for Alberta Education. The mandate of this branch is to develop policies which will result in the initiation, maintenance, and improvement of educational programs to meet the special educational needs of gifted, talented, or disabled students in all Alberta schools. McLeod studied at the University of Alberta, receiving a Ph.D. in Counselling Psychology and an M.Ed. in Educational Psychology. She was Assistant Superintendent with the Edmonton Public School Board and held positions of Supervisor Teacher Staffing, Director of Counselling Services, teacher, and counsellor with that board. In addition, McLeod has been employed as a consulting psychologist to the Edmonton General Hospital and to the Westfield Diagnostic and Treatment Centre and has operated a private psychology practice.

Q: Is there some particular aspect of your job that requires unusually careful attention during decision making?

McLeod: Yes — determining how money to be spent on special educational needs for students will be allocated to, and spent in, the various school jurisdictions in the province. As one might expect, this can be a very emotional issue, so Special Educational Services has had to take great care when making allocation decisions.

Q: Could you briefly indicate how you make these allocation decisions?

McLeod: We are in the midst of changing the system. Previously, each school system applied for money to provide programs for special-needs students (those with mental or learning disabilities, physical or multiple disabilities, and deaf or blind children). Our branch then reviewed the applications and decided on the basis of established criteria how much money each school jurisdiction would receive. School jurisdictions that knew how to play the application game and had good programs already in place got a larger proportion of the funds, while jurisdictions that weren't as adept at the application process or hadn't developed programs received less.

About a year ago, Alberta Education decided to change this procedure. We changed some of the criteria for allocating funds. For example, we used to require that a given school have 3 to 5 special students within a certain category before we would allocate funds to set up a special class. Now we allocate money on the basis of a commitment to provide services to students with special educational needs. To demonstrate such commitment, we require that the school board have policies relating to serving those special educational needs. So, our emphasis has gone from being funding-based to being policy-based. Now, we provide a block rate of $135 per resident student to each school jurisdiction, to be spent on such special programs and services. We have decentralized decision making, since the school jurisdiction is expected to use block funding in the most appropriate way. An obvious result of this system is that school jurisdictions have increased responsibility to provide good services with the money they are allocated. With increased discretion on how to spend the money, they can be more responsive to local needs and conditions and can no longer simply blame "the government" if things don't go well.

Q: How did you decide on this new system for allocating funds?

McLeod: This is only part of a new Management and Finance Plan, which is a current thrust of Alberta Education. This plan is meant to provide — within policy directions established by the province — increased local responsibility, flexibility, and discretion to school jurisdictions regarding the use of provincial funds. Initially, committees were set up to develop the new system and to prepare people for the change. Interestingly, some departmental staff thought that school jurisdictions wouldn't use wisely the money they were given. But we finally agreed that we had to decentralize decision making in order to get better decisions. Decision making regarding the use of special educational funds now rests with the local school jurisdictions instead of the province, with Alberta Education regional offices monitoring the use of funds. Our committees also identified some potential snags in the new system. For example, if a very small school division were to have an unusually large number of disabled students, the $135 per student might be insufficient. We therefore decided to set up a contingency fund for such situations.

Q: What is your philosophy of decision making in the day-to-day aspects of management?

McLeod: Well, as a general statement, I try to push decision-making as far down the hierarchy as possible. I feel that the people who work for me will be more motivated to do their jobs well if they have the right to make many of the decisions that affect them.

Q: Can you give a specific example?

McLeod: We are in the process of developing a manual that will explain all the details and implications of the Management and Finance Plan. I met with my staff and discussed what the objectives of the manual were, but indicated that they would decide what should actually go into the manual. This is a major job, and they will have to make many decisions before it is eventually completed. Once it is completed, I hope they will feel a sense of ownership for it. Likely, they would not feel that way if all details of the finished manual were simply imposed on them from above. Expecting them to make many of the decisions about what to include will also increase their understanding of the new system.

Q: What do you do if a subordinate suggests something that you don't agree with?

McLeod: I try to think objectively about it and try to ensure that I don't disagree simply because I didn't think of it first. Even if I don't agree with the idea, I may allow the subordinate to proceed on the project because, after all, that person has worked more closely on it than I have and may have more insights about the problem. I have very competent staff members and they understand the organization in which we work. However, if I can't agree with a project or the way it is being done, the project may need to be adjusted or discontinued. I don't think we've ever come to the point of not going ahead with a project, since generally we can work differences through by discussing them and coming to an understanding of each other's point of view. On occasion, I will discuss issues with my supervisor or directors of other branches to get a fresh point of view on the matter.

My supervisor takes the same approach with me on many occasions. I send status reports on various projects to him and make suggestions for how I think things should be done. He retains the right to reject my suggestions, but he doesn't generally exercise that right. That motivates me to work harder on a given project.

One of the things I have to do is make sure that suggestions my subordinates make are politically acceptable. People lower in the hierarchy may not be aware of the agendas of certain people further up the line. So, I try not to reject new ideas, but they must be presented in a way that is acceptable.

Q: What do you feel is necessary for good management decision making?

McLeod: Three things. First, you must have good information on which to base your decision. While you can get overwhelmed by data if you're not careful, you need sound and sufficient information to make good decisions. Second, you need to involve people in the decision-making process. If you simply try to impose a decision on them, they will usually resist it. Third, you must recognize that the rational decision may not be the one that will be implemented. Emotional considerations play a big role in many decisions.

A third way for managers to generate alternatives is to use their experience and knowledge about their job. This approach works best for routine problems, but it does not often yield innovative alternatives. To develop more innovative alternatives, management might use group brainstorming. In brainstorming, individuals are encouraged to come up with as many ideas as possible, no matter how outrageous or unworkable they might seem at first. Criticism of these alternatives is not allowed until a later phase in the decision-making process. This lack of criticism is designed to encourage people to come up with lots of alternatives. (Brainstorming in quality circles as a motivation tool is discussed in Chapter 10.)

Analyze Alternatives

Each alternative or potential solution to the problem must next be analyzed with respect to how it will interact with external and internal environment conditions. In this step, managers must provide answers for the question: "What will happen if this course of action is taken?" Consider that an optimum decision at times cannot be implemented. An external environment factor may force a manager to make a less than optimum decision. For instance, an airline may want to expand service from a particular airport. However, the public may object to the increased noise, or the Canadian Transport Commission may not approve of additional flights. The airline may have to decide on another, less than optimum alternative.

Choose and Implement the Best Alternative

The ability to select the best course of action from several possible alternatives separates the successful managers from the less successful ones. The alternative offering the highest promise of attaining the objective, taking into consideration the overall situation, should be selected. This final step may sound easy, but it is the toughest part of a manager's job. Fear of making the wrong decision sometimes causes managers to make no decision at all. In this final stage, weak managers sometimes fail.

Firms generally pay high salaries to managers who have a reputation for making the correct decision the majority of the time. Anyone can have the hindsight to criticize the manager who made a wrong decision, but it is much more difficult to be the manager with responsibility to make a decision under tremendous time pressures.

Directly or indirectly, the manager who makes a decision must implement it. When the decision means that other people must take action, the actual decision maker must make certain that the appropriate steps have been taken. It is here that the decision-making process often falls short. Some managers, because they are action oriented, believe that once the decision has been made, it will automatically be implemented. Good managers monitor the situation to ensure that their decisions are put into practice.

Evaluate the Decision

No decision-making process is complete until the decision has been exposed to the realities of the business environment. Evaluation requires an objective assessment of how the decision has solved the problem. This process is the one by which managers learn and develop useful experience. Without this step, the decision-making process has no value beyond providing an immediate solution to a problem. Perhaps for this reason, some firms stress decentralized management in which lower-level managers are provided the opportunity to become more involved in the decision-making process.

The evaluation step provides younger managers with decision-making experience. Intuition and judgment increase with more exposure to decision making. Through decentralization, individual managers do not have to wait until they are finally promoted to a higher-level position before being given the opportunity to make decisions. It is better to make a poor decision at a lower level and learn from this experience than to make a more crucial decision at a higher level and be wrong.

MANAGEMENT IN PRACTICE

The Ethics of Personnel Decisions

Most writing about decision making stresses the procedural aspects of the process. Aspiring managers are told that good decision making results when the problem is first identified, facts are gathered that are relevant for the problem, and then these facts are used to analyze promising alternatives to determine which one should be chosen.

These activities are important, but managers should consider at least one other factor when making decisions. There are ethical dimensions to most business decisions. For example, when economic times are good, a company may experiment with hiring from minority groups. Likely, the company will be praised for using ethics in its hiring decisions. However, when economic times are bad, the company may lay off workers;

the recently hired minority workers may be among the first to go. Concern will then be expressed that the company is behaving unethically. What is a reasonable decision in such a situation? The answer depends on the criterion used to make the decision.

Top management may believe that its decision to vary the size of the work force based on promising economic conditions is reasonable. If some other criterion, such as maximizing the well-being of workers, is used, the decision to lay off workers because of adverse economic conditions is less justifiable. Which criterion should top management use? In a pluralistic society like Canada's, this question will never be answered conclusively. Instead, government, business, and labor can each debate with particular views.

FACTORS AFFECTING THE DECISION-MAKING PROCESS

Three factors — risk, time, and organization politics — can have a major impact on the decision-making process.

Risk

Risk is a probability that an incorrect decision may have an adverse effect on an organization. Risk is a factor that all managers consider, consciously or unconsciously, when making decisions. The president of a small book publishing firm, for example, is thinking of paying a $50,000 advance to a well-known author to write a book. If the book sells well, the firm could make $250,000; if it doesn't sell well, the publisher will lose the $50,000 advance, plus about $30,000 in developmental and promotional costs. The president decides that the risk of losing $80,000 could put the company out of business. The $50,000 advance is too high a risk; if the author will not accept less, the publisher must try another alternative.

The purchasing manager at General Motors frequently signs contracts that exceed $1 million each for automobile parts. The risk involved in each decision to sign, however, is typically low. The parts will be used and, as part of vehicles, will be sold. But, even the loss of $1 million would not have as disastrous an effect on General Motors as the loss to the publisher. The relative risk must be weighed in each decision. Generally, as risk related to a decision increases, more time and effort will be devoted to the process of making that decision.

Time

The amount of time a manager can devote to making a decision is often a critical factor to be considered. A manager would prefer to have sufficient time to develop and analyze thoroughly all alternatives prior to making a decision. Most business people are not afforded this luxury; they must make decisions under pressure, when they often do not have sufficient time to analyze all alternatives. Suppose, for instance, that a customer of yours offers to purchase your product in bulk, but at a slight discount. Although the firm will make a profit on this order, the profit is not as large as normally obtained. Today you have no other orders to choose from; tomorrow you may have. However, the decision must be made today or your buyer will go to another manufacturer. You are truly under time pressure. It is much easier to make decisions when you have enough time to analyze all the alternatives; managers often do not have the extra time to decide.

Organization Politics

Managers in all kinds of organizations know that rational factors are not the only ones to consider when making decisions. Organization politics can also influence managerial decision making. Status, power, prestige, convenience, and ease of implementation are political influences on decision makers. This means that managers may debate at length about which alternative is the politically correct one. For example, if a company is trying to decide whether to break into a new market, some people in the organization will favor it and some will oppose it. Each side will try to influence its point by bringing to bear both rational and political arguments. The final decision may be based partly on rational grounds — the company will make more money — and partly on political grounds — the president wants to do it. The issue of organization politics is discussed in detail in Chapter 8.

MODEL BUILDING

A procedure managers often find useful in all phases of the decision-making process is model building. A **model** is defined as an abstraction of a real situation. It is an attempt to portray reality without having to work directly with the real situation. For instance, suppose a manager must make a decision involving many millions of dollars about where to build a new factory. Once funds have been spent on the plant, the decision is irreversible. But, if a three-dimensional model of the proposed building is used, the manager can develop alternatives and analyze them prior to making the real decision and spending real money. Physical models, however, are not the only types used by managers in all organizations.

MANAGEMENT IN PRACTICE
But You Can't Quantify That!

Quantifying significant variables when making decisions is useful because many decision-making techniques require numerical values. However, difficulties arise when decision makers attempt to quantify, for instance, the value of a park to community residents, the value of preserving a vanishing species of animal, or the value of a human life. Can such variables be quantified? Why quantify them?

Suppose an automobile manufacturer is alerted to a design flaw in a current model that may be dangerous to human life. Should the manufacturer correct the flaw? Suppose that, after doing some research, the company concludes that: (1) the flaw will cost $20 million to fix, (2) 23 people will die if it is not fixed, and (3) class-action suits against the company by relatives of those killed will amount to $10 million.

In purely quantitative terms, the company should not fix the flaw because at most it will cost them $10 million and 23 deaths. However, this alternative implies that the manufacturer has a quantitative value for a human life: $434,782 ($10 million ÷ 23 people). This sounds rather mercenary; if the manufacturer did not fix the flaw, it would likely not be willing to admit that it made the decision on this basis.

However, the fact remains that the value of a human life can be quantified in a given situation — as long as the decision maker doesn't mind being thought heartless. To avoid such an accusation, most people prefer to talk in generalities about issues like this and managers prefer to say: "You can't quantify that!"

In business, models can be expressed in many ways and can have many meanings, because managers deal with highly complex business systems that can be simplified to be understood. Model building provides the means for simplifying a complex situation. The model builder must first determine the purpose of the model as it is to depict the real situation. The purpose of the model should be consistent with the overall objectives of the firm. Next, the model builder decides which parts should be included: a major advantage of model building. If certain components would be included in the real situation but have no effect on the problem under consideration, they can be omitted. Finally, the model builder must define the interrelationships that exist among the parts. The understanding of these interrelationships is vital in model building. The model is a tool for extending the manager's understanding of the organization.

Models are more widely employed than commonly realized. Many times a manager may not even realize a model is being used. If a manager envisions what would occur if a particular decision is made, model building is actually taking place, because the manager has a picture (model) of the relationships that will result if a particular decision is made.

One means by which to examine models is through the language the model-builder employs. By language, we mean the technique chosen to communicate understanding. Models may use physical, schematic, or mathematical "languages."

Physical Models

Physical models were among the first to be used for management and are the most familiar. Systems represented by physical models can include people, ships, airplanes, automobiles, houses, dams, shopping centers, factories and retail stores. **Physical models** generally look like the system they represent. Physical models can, however, be more abstract representations. A photograph captures the physical appearance of a person as does a portrait, but, in painting the portrait, the artist can deemphasize or exaggerate features.

Schematic Models

Line drawings, flowcharts, graphs, maps, organization charts, and similar items that represent the major features of a particular system are **schematic models**. Schematic models may or may not be related in scale to the object being abstracted. Elements of a highway system are represented by road maps, which are two-dimensional scale models. Schematics depicting electrical circuitry for stereos, tape decks, or televisions usually are not drawn to scale.

Schematic models have been widely used for management to define components of the organization and to analyze problems. Schematics are used to describe processes and procedures as well as physical components. Computer programmers use schematic models — flowcharts — to illustrate the steps that must be accomplished in writing a program. Although schematic models are useful to managers in each major business function, production and operations management personnel have used them more than others.

Mathematical Models

A mathematical equation that defines and represents the relationships among elements of a system is a **mathematical model**. These models portray in quantitative terms the essential elements and interrelationships among elements of the systems they describe. For a mathematical model to represent reality, a manager must know a good deal about that reality. In many instances this can be a problem. The primary limitation to the application of mathematical models in assisting managers is the constraint imposed by the inability to measure the relationships among elements of the environment.

MANAGEMENT INFORMATION SYSTEMS

In this chapter, we focus on managerial decision making. In several places, we stress the importance for managers to have good information on which to base decisions. In the concluding section of this chapter we look at management information systems (MIS) and how they aid decision makers.

A Definition of an MIS

All organizations have some sort of system — either simple or sophisticated — for getting the information they need to make decisions. A **management information system** (MIS) can collect, analyze, organize, and disseminate information from both internal and external sources so that managers can use it to make decisions beneficial to the organization. A good MIS gives managers information on past and present organization activities and makes some projections about future activities. An effective MIS provides managers with information that is timely, accurate, and useful. In short, the MIS helps managers perform the four basic functions of management — planning, organizing, influencing, and controlling.

Because computers have had such an impact on information, many people assume that a computer must be a part of any business MIS. A computer is not an automatic element of an MIS, although increasing numbers of organizations are using computers in their MIS because they can analyze large amounts of data quickly. We discuss the role of computers in MIS later; for now, keep in mind that: (1) a computer need not be used in an MIS and (2) even when one is used, a computer is only one part of the total MIS.

A crucial distinction in discussions of MIS is the one between "data" and "information." "Data" refers to unanalyzed facts about an organization's operations. Data become information only when used for some sort of analysis. "Information" is anything relevant and useful to practicing managers, including analyzed data. A good MIS takes data and converts them to information managers can use to help make decisions.

The Need for an MIS

Managers in all organizations rely on information to make decisions. Consider the need for information for making decisions by managers in the functional areas of production, marketing, and personnel.

Production managers need information on plant capacity utilization in order to determine whether plant expansion will be necessary if demand increases. They also need regular information on such items as production costs, labor costs, order backlogs, and machine breakdowns.

Marketing managers need information on sales trends so that they can coordinate their activities with those of the production people. They also need information on new product development, new product sales trends, selling costs, marketing research, and sales territories.

Personnel managers need information on workforce turnover and absenteeism, employee skill levels, labor markets, and wage levels in order to decide how to mobilize the firm's human resources in the most effective way. Managers in each functional area constantly need information in order to make good decisions. This information can be supplied by the MIS.

Information Needs at Different Levels of Management

Managers at different levels in the organization (top, middle, and lower) need different kinds of information, and they usually need it at different time intervals.

Top management uses the MIS to set overall corporate policies and strategy to ensure organization growth and survival. Because these kinds of decisions have a long-term impact on the organization, this information is generally needed at most quarterly and, perhaps, only yearly. The most useful information for top management deals with whether the general direction of the organization is profitable and whether changes would increase the chance that goals will be reached.

Middle managers put into operation the overall plans and strategies that top management has developed. They use the MIS to set up control procedures and to allocate resources toward organization objectives.

Because this information is more specific, middle managers need information on a weekly or monthly basis. The information most useful to middle managers indicates whether the operational systems put into place can reach top management's overall objectives.

Lower-level managers ensure that the goods or services offered by the organization are actually produced. They use the MIS to determine what raw materials they need, to develop work schedules, and to make sure that materials and people are in the right place at the right time so that production activities are not held up. Because these activities are very detailed, lower-level managers need information on an hourly or daily basis. The information most useful at this level centers on whether goods and services have been produced on schedule and whether customers are getting the products they want when they want them.

The following table summarizes these and other ideas regarding the different information needs at different management levels.

Information Requirement by Division Category

Characteristics of Information	Management Level	
	Operational	Strategic
Source	Largely internal ———————►	External
Scope	Well defined, narrow ———————►	Very wide
Level of aggregation	Detailed ———————►	Aggregate
Time horizon	Historical ———————►	Future
Currency	Highly current ———————►	Quite old
Required accuracy	High ———————►	Low
Frequency of use	Very frequent ———————►	Infrequent

SOURCE: G. Anthony Gorry and Michael Scott Morton, "A Framework for Management Information Systems," *Sloan Management Review* (Fall 1971): 59. Reprinted by permission.

Developing an MIS

An MIS may be developed for a particular department in an organization, or one may be developed for the total organization. When an organization decides to develop a company-wide MIS, it must realize that it will probably take many months before the new system is fully operational. Determining the information needs of an organization is not a simple matter, so considerable time must be allocated to the process. As well, top management must give its wholehearted support to the development process; without it, the MIS will probably not generate the information that the organization really needs, nor will it be used by those who are supposed to benefit from it.

Robert G. Murdick has proposed that the development of an organization-wide MIS proceeds essentially through four stages.[4] In the first stage, an MIS task force is selected to determine the information needs of the company. This study includes the internal and external environment of the firm and the influence these areas have on the information that is needed. The information needs of all the major areas of the firm are identified, and any possible constraints on the development of the system are noted.

In the second stage, the task force proposes various MIS designs that might be used. The performance requirements the organization will need of its MIS are identified. Managers and workers in the organization are asked for their input into the system.

In the third stage, the proposed MIS design is tested to see whether it will generate the information that is needed. Based on feedback from managers in the firm, necessary revisions to the system are made.

In the final stage, many specific operational activities are performed. For example, forms for data collection are designed, training programs are written, computer software is developed (if a computer is part of the system), and files are developed. This stage concludes with a final test of the new system. The same four stages are used for a department-wide MIS.

Implementing an MIS

The implementation of an MIS constitutes a major change to an organization. Great care must be taken to ensure that the change will be accepted by the people who must work with the new system. Whenever an organization decides to install an MIS, it runs the risk of making all sorts of mistakes. We next look at some mistaken assumptions often made during the implementation process and then present some suggestions for avoiding problems during the installation of an MIS.

Russell Ackhoff has described the five most common misapprehensions people have about an MIS:[5]

- More information is better. Often, an MIS is introduced on the assumption that managers suffer from a shortage of relevant information. While managers may lack some of the information they should have, it is more likely that they have an overabundance of irrelevant information. They may therefore be spending excessive amounts of time analyzing information that is not very helpful to them. If an MIS simply generates additional irrelevant information, the MIS is not serving its purpose.

- Managers actually need all the information they request. Managers often ask for a great deal of information, particularly on issues about which they may not know very much. They do this because they think that more information may help them break through to a solution. If the designer of the MIS gives managers all the information they request, this MIS may simply worsen the information overload referred to in the first point.

- If managers are given all the information they need, they will make better decisions. Just having information on which to base a decision does not guarantee managers will make a good decision. If managers cannot use information effectively, those managers will not make good decisions no matter how much information is provided.

- More information communication means better performance. In most cases, an MIS can provide more current information about what the various parts of a firm are doing. Some people assume that this alone will allow managers in all parts of the firm to coordinate their activities and that this coordination will increase the performance of the total organization. These results are certainly possible, but information dissemination alone does not constitute either communication or coordination.

- Managers do not have to understand how the MIS works in order to use it. MIS designers try to make the system as easy as possible to use, but usually do not stress that managers understand it. As a result, managers may be unable to evaluate the system properly and may end up being controlled by the MIS instead of the other way around.

This formidable list constitutes mistakes that can reduce the effectiveness of the MIS. Fortunately, many lessons have been learned during the last 20 years about MIS. An MIS can be implemented effectively with the following general guidelines in mind.

Users should be involved in the design and implementation of the system. Perhaps the most fundamental lesson that has been learned is that the manager/user must be involved in the MIS development process. Management information systems are normally developed by systems analysts who have technical expertise but, possibly, little knowledge of the manager's job. Therefore, they must get input from the managers who are actually going to use the system. Managers who are consulted by the systems analysts in the MIS design and implementation are more likely to accept and use the system and are more able to revise the system as management needs change. If the manager/user is bypassed initially, he or she may never accept or use the system.

Time and cost factors associated with the system must be accurately assessed. During the early stages of MIS design, all concerned parties must have a reasonable estimate of what the MIS will cost and when it will be operational. It is frustrating for users to be told repeatedly that the system "isn't quite ready yet." Top management become displeased when their new system is not only behind schedule, but also costlier than originally planned.

"Human problems" need attention. The introduction of an MIS can lead to significant changes in the way people relate to one another and to the amount of information they have about each other. In both these cases, people may become unhappy. Suppose a company institutes a computerized MIS and finds that its most effective approach is to combine the purchasing and inventory functions. The people in these two areas may be unhappy that the distinctive nature of their work has disappeared. They may also be required to work with new people. These kinds of problems should not be underestimated; productivity may be affected negatively as people try to retaliate against the system that imposed an uncomfortable working environment on them. An MIS that is technically sound but is opposed by the firm's employees likely will not work as well as an MIS that has some technical flaws but is enthusiastically supported by workers and managers.

The MIS performance goals must be stated at the outset. Both designers and users must understand just exactly what the MIS is supposed to achieve once it is operational. In many instances, managers are surprised to learn that the MIS will not do something they assumed it would do. Careful specification of just what management can expect from the system before it is implemented is important for avoiding problems further down the line.

Understandable training and directions for users must be provided, especially when a computer is part of the MIS. Many managers are fearful of computers, so systems analysts must provide easy-to-understand directions and training manuals on how to use the MIS. If these are not provided, the chances are that system use will decline. Training and documentation must be geared to managers, not computer experts.

Computers and MIS

Because an MIS is likely to include a computer, its manager/users need to be somewhat computer literate. This does not mean that managers must become data-processing experts any more than it means that they must become professional accountants. But, just as managers need some accounting knowledge to understand and interpret financial reports, they need to know something about what computers can and cannot do. At the minimum, managers need to know enough about computers to make good decisions regarding their use.

Computers were first used in business firms in the early 1950s shortly after they were developed. Early use was restricted to extremely mechanical, high-volume work like processing employee paycheques and keeping track of inventory. As computer technology improved, computer usage expanded in business. During the 1960s and 1970s, computer programs were developed to deal with frequently recurring routine decisions. We referred to these as programmed decisions earlier. Computers make fine tools for an MIS. Further changes in computer technology now occur with such tremendous speed that we cannot foresee uses that may eventually develop. Managers must be aware of such innovations and how they can benefit their organization in order to remain competitive in this rapidly changing world.

Choosing a Computer for the MIS

Too many firms purchase or lease a computer and then attempt to design their MIS around the computer. If a computer is needed to provide accurate, timely, and useful information, the computer should be chosen on the basis of how well it converts raw data into useful information. Choosing a computer may not be an easy task since a wide variety of computers is available. The selection should be made with the firm's specific needs to fit the design of its MIS.

The smallest version is the **microcomputer**. The availability of microcomputers has permitted many smaller firms to buy their own computer system.[6] In large organizations, recent trends suggest increasingly that individual managers are using microcomputers.

Minicomputers are larger and more powerful than microcomputers. They are able to handle more sophisticated programs and to store greater amounts of information than micros.

The largest mainframe computers are capable of handling vast amounts of data and of processing several programs at virtually the same time.

The Impact of the Computer on Management

The rapid developments in computer technology are having an enormous impact on managerial decision making. Some computer equipment can be carried in a briefcase, permitting a manager to work almost anywhere. Computer hookups from office to home have added a new dimension to the work-at-home routine, called **telecommuting**. Moving the computer terminal into the home has permitted businesses to reach labor markets that might not otherwise be reached. However, managers must be trained to cope with this new working relationship. Some managers find it quite difficult to supervise workers they do not see regularly. Also, some workers find working at home an isolating experience because they are left out of office politics, gossip, and coffee breaks with friends.[7]

The office of the future is expected to change dramatically because of the computer. Specialized work stations are being created for professionals and managers in an attempt to increase worker productivity.[8] These work stations should provide executives with access to information by the touch of a button.

In spite of the positive aspects of information synthesis offered by a computer, some middle and lower-level managers are worried. While it is true that they will be able to monitor their subordinates more effectively, they know that they in turn will be monitored more closely by their superiors. This monitoring could create anxiety and unhappiness, especially for managers who may be insecure about their positions. Some managers may dislike the fact that they must supply information to the MIS specialists rather than directly to their superiors. Such managers may feel a loss of control. Another potential problem for middle and lower-level managers is that the MIS allows top management to centralize decision making; some middle and lower-level managers may consider they have lost some discretion. Some managers fear that a computerized MIS will actually do away with some managerial positions.

Top management does not share these concerns because generally it is benefiting from the MIS. The managers at the top of the firm with an effective MIS will be getting timely, accurate information about what is going on throughout the organization; they feel in control. As a result, they are usually favorably impressed by an MIS. However, top management should be aware of other managers' concerns and try to allay them.

MANAGEMENT IN PRACTICE

An Example of an MIS

Now that we have described the basic idea of MIS, we present a brief example of how it works in practice. We consider an MIS at work in the personnel area of an organization.

The goal of the personnel function is to ensure that appropriate human resources are available when the organization needs them. (The personnel function is described in detail in Chapter 9.) In order to do a good job, personnel managers need information about several aspects of human resource management. (See Exhibit 5-4.) They need (1) information about potential employees and their characteristics, (2) financial data about payroll and budgets, and (3) job data regarding the number and type of jobs that need

to be filled. These three factors constitute the inputs to the MIS. The information developed through these three input areas is combined into data bases. These data bases can be manipulated to provide outputs, such as wage and salary programs, promotion plans, and fringe benefit reports. The entire system of inputs, transformation, and output makes up the MIS. It allows personnel managers to make sound decisions regarding the use of the firm's human resources.

An MIS can be developed for any area of the firm — production, marketing, or engineering — or for the entire firm.

OPENING INCIDENT REVISITED

Mackie Real Estate

The managers at Mackie Real Estate can use mathematical analysis to help decide which speculative investment to make. Since they are able to attach numbers to the important variables in the problem, they can use the kind of analysis that was used in the part-time job problem in this chapter.

The expected value of each of the three alternatives must be computed. For each alternative there is a chance of gaining — if the government later buys the block of land the company buys

now — and a chance of losing — if the government does not choose the block of land the company buys. The general formula for expected value is: the probability of gaining multiplied by the amount won plus the probability of losing multiplied by the amount lost. The expected values for the three alternatives are:

$$\text{Block 1} = 0.2(40) + 0.8(5) = 12.0$$
$$\text{Block 2} = 0.5(50) + 0.5(-25) = 12.5$$
$$\text{Block 3} = 0.3(110) + 0.7(-35) = 11.5$$

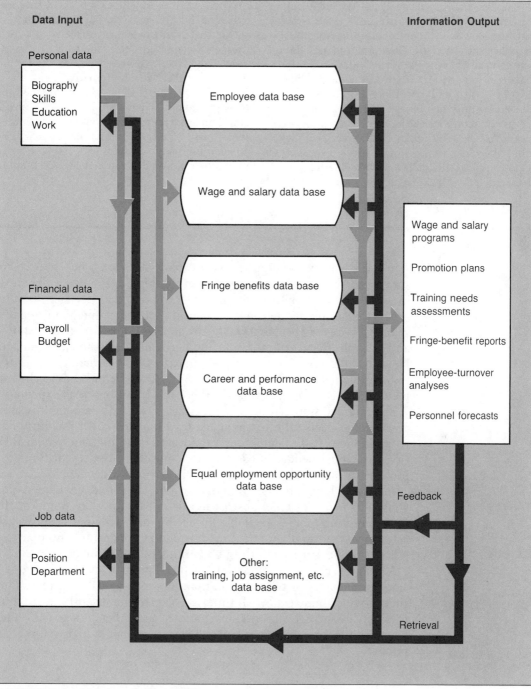

EXHIBIT 5-4 An example of an MIS

SOURCE Lawrence J. Gitman and Carl McDaniel Jr., *Business World* (New York: Wiley, 1983): 182. Reprinted by permission.

Based on this simple analysis, Mackie should buy Block 2 because its expected value is the highest. However, other important factors must be taken into account. How much money does the company have to use for speculation? In this case they have $100,000; so, they could buy both blocks 1 and 2 and have more of a chance than by buying only one block. Another factor concerns the relative risk preferences of the managers. Are they risk-takers or risk-averse? If they are risk-averse, they will buy Block 1, because they can't lose any money on it no matter what happens. If the Mackie managers are risk-takers, they will want to buy Block 3 because they can make the most money if the government chooses it. Another factor is lost investment opportunities elsewhere. Can this company invest its money and do even better elsewhere than it can with any of these three alternatives?

This brief analysis shows that even when the facts to make a decision are quantified, considerable uncertainty may still exist about what the best course of action is. Each decision will be affected by many variables and, likely, no two individuals would develop and analyze them in precisely the same way.

SUMMARY

A person who has the authority to make decisions, but refuses to, should not be classified as a manager. Making decisions is the most important responsibility of a manager. The actual decision-making process is simple to state but is often difficult to implement. Once a manager is aware a problem exists, the problem should be clearly stated, and then alternatives to the solution of the problem can be developed. Next, each alternative is analyzed and the best alternative is chosen to be implemented. The decision-making process continues as the implemented decision is evaluated to be sure it will work as expected.

Before a decision can be made, certain basic requirements must be achieved. A decision must be made by a manager with the authority to implement it. Problem content, courses of action, and payoff relationships must be identified. A major consideration is identifying the probabilities in the state of nature for a particular decision.

Model building allows alternatives to be identified, developed, and analyzed. A model is an abstraction of a real situation. Some of the most common models available for use by managers include physical, schematic, and mathematical models. These models let the manager portray the real situation through various means indirectly.

Management information systems (MIS) provide another way to assist the manager in the decision-making process. MIS is a technique that provides managers with timely, accurate, and useful information to assist in the decision-making process. Some benefits of MIS have been significantly enhanced since the development of high-speed computers.

REVIEW QUESTIONS

1. Define and discuss the process of making decisions. How important is it to a manager?

2. Distinguish between personal decisions and professional decisions. Why are managers expected to be professional decision makers?
3. What effect do risk, time, and organization politics have on managers when making decisions?
4. Discuss the strengths and weaknesses of decisions based on intuition and decisions based on the research or scientific method.
5. What are the basic requirements for decision making?
6. Distinguish among physical models, schematic models, and mathematical models. Give an example of each as it might help to make a business decision.
7. What is an MIS? Discuss some benefits and some potential disadvantages of using a computer in an MIS.
8. What is telecommuting? How might it affect organizations if its use increases?

EXERCISES

1. Everyone makes decisions. Take a one-hour period during the day and list the top 5 decisions you made. Were they based primarily on intuition? the scientific or research approach? or the professional decision-making process? Why?
2. Make a list of the different types of models you observe during a 24-hour period.
3. Develop a decision-making problem in which there are 2 courses of action and 3 states of nature. Remember that the probabilities must total one.

CASE STUDY

A Request for Special Favors

Bill Paquette is the manager of the payroll department at Plains Insurance Company. Bill reports to the company comptroller. A major function of the department is processing the company biweekly payroll for the more than 1000 employees of the company. The work load in payroll is oriented toward tasks and deadlines. The work load is even more demanding during holiday periods, such as Thanksgiving, Christmas, and New Year's.

At the beginning of December, Betty Friesen, a 20-year-old clerk, informs Paquette that she needs to take a week of vacation between Christmas and New Year's in order to "visit her family during the holidays." Since the payroll is processed every other week, it has been customary for the payroll department manager and clerical personnel to schedule vacations during the weeks that the payroll is not processed. Betty, an efficient worker, has been employed since March and became eligible for one week of vacation in October. (An employee is eligible for one week of vacation after 6 months, or for two weeks on the completion of one year.) At the time Friesen was hired, specific vacation arrangements were not discussed, only the minimum time for eligibility.

Friesen's request for a one-week vacation during the holiday period would make it difficult for the payroll department to meet its deadlines. The department will lose 2 days during the period because Christmas Eve and Christmas Day are holidays. Paquette is concerned about getting the payroll processed that week; with Friesen away, the deadlines would be more difficult to meet.

Paquette and Friesen discussed work load requirements during the week in question. He told her the department needs her effort that week, particularly since it is a short week. Friesen responded by saying: "My husband has made plans for us to go and he says we're going." Paquette considers Friesen a satisfactory worker, but wonders about her commitment to the job and company. He is also concerned about the effect on other members of the department if he approves Friesen's vacation request.

QUESTIONS

1. What decision should Bill Paquette make regarding Betty Friesen's request for vacation? Demonstrate how Paquette could make the decision using the decision-making process developed in this chapter.
2. In making the decision, what additional situational factors should be considered, other than the fact that Friesen intends to take the time off against the wishes of her supervisor?

CASE STUDY

A Decision To Move a Bank Teller

Wayland is a small town in Saskatchewan. Two new farm-related industries recently opened factories in the area and created an increase in Wayland's general business activity. Because of the increased business, the largest of the three banks in town began to notice long waiting lines at tellers' windows. On the basis of a questionnaire sent to its customers, the bank's executives decided to open a new drive-through facility. The bank purchased a vacant lot across the street and built one drive-through window facility. Room for expansion was possible if the new service proved to be as popular as expected.

Eight tellers were employed by the bank. All were considered good workers and had good relations with the customers. Ada Penner, aged 48, was chosen by a bank vice-president to be the teller in the new drive-through facility. She had been with the bank for 9 years. The reasons given for her selection were that: (1) she can serve customers rapidly; (2) she has a responsible attitude toward the work to be accomplished (she helps others when her work is finished and the other tellers seek her advice when they have a problem); and (3) she works well without supervision. An additional teller was employed inside the bank to take Penner's place.

The opening day for the new window was hectic, but, thanks to Ada Penner's organization and work habits, the opening was considered to be a success by the customers and by bank officials. Penner complained of a headache, but she attributed it to opening day jitters. Through the next week, Ada Penner's headaches increased, and she was becoming despondent. The next week, she was late twice and made some errors on her accounts. The bank president then told the vice-president to reevaluate his choice of Ada Penner as the teller for the new drive-through facility.

QUESTIONS

1. What other factors should the vice-president have considered prior to moving Ada Penner to the new drive-through facility?
2. What do you believe are the causes of the difficulties that Penner experienced?
3. At what point did the decision-making process break down?
4. Would you remove Penner? Why or why not?

NOTES

[1]Theodore Levitt, "The Managerial Merry-Go-Round," *Harvard Business Review* 52 (July-August 1974): 120.

[2]First four items adapted from Alvar O. Elbing, *Behavioral Decision in Organizations* (Glenview, Ill.: Scott, Foresman, 1970): 14.

[3]Ralph C. Davis,*The Fundamentals of Top Management* (New York: Harper, 1951): 55.

[4]Robert G. Murdick, "MIS Development Procedures," *Journal of Systems Management* 21, no. 12 (December 1970): 22–26.

[5]Russell L. Ackhoff, "Management Misinformation Systems," *Management Science* (December 1967): 147–156.

[6]Jay Daniel, Conger, and Fred R. McFadden, *First Course in Data Processing With BASIC, COBOL, FORTRAN, RPG* (New York: Wiley, 1981): 167.

[7]"The Potential For Telecommuting," *Business Week* (January 26, 1981): 94.

[8]"Will The Boss Go Electronics, Too?" *Business Week* (May 11, 1981): 106.

REFERENCES

Archer, Earnest R. "How to Make a Business Decision: An Analysis of Theory and Practice." *Management Review* 69 (February 1980): 54–61.

Bass, Bernard M. *Organizational Decision Making.* Homewood Ill.: Richard D. Irwin, 1983.

Brown, Rex V. "Do Managers Find Decision Theory Useful?" *Harvard Business Review* 51 (May-June 1970): 78–89.

Daniel, D. W. "What Influences a Decision? Some Results from a Highly Controlled Defense Game." *Omega* 8 (November 1980): 409–419.

Fischhoff, Baruch, and Goitein, Bernard, "The Informal Use of Formal Models." *Academy of Management Review* 9, no. 3 (July 1984): 505–512.

Grayson, C. Jackson, Jr. "Management Science and Business Practice." *Harvard Business Review* 51 (July-August 1973): 41–48.

Grindlay, Andrew. "MIS Organization: Perhaps It's Time to Change." *Business Quarterly* 48, no. 4 (Winter 1983): 9–17.

Grove, Andrew, S. "Decisions, Decisions." *Canadian Business* 57, no. 2 (February 1984): 62.

Harrison, J. Richard, and March, James G. "Decision Making and Post-decision Surprises." *Administrative Science Quarterly* 29, no. 1 (March 1984): 26–41.

Henderson, John C. "Influence of Decision Style on Decision Making Behavior." *Management Science* 26 (April 1980): 371–386.

Hogarth, Robin M., and Mankridakis, Spyors. "Value of Decision Making in a Complex Environment — An Experimental Approach." *Management Science* 27 (January 1981): 93–107.

Hughes, Robard Y. "A Realistic Look at Decision Making." *Supervisory Management* 25, no. 1 (January 1980): 2–8.

Kirby, Peter G. "Quality Decisions Start with Good Questions." *Supervisory Management* 25, no. 8 (August 1980): 2–7.

Mangrum, Claude T. "Determining the Right Regimen of Managerial Exercises." *Supervisory Management* 26, no. 2 (February 1981): 26–30.

McKenny, J. L., and Keen, P.G.W. "How Managers' Minds Work." *Harvard Business Review* 52, no. 3 (May-June 1974): 79–90.

Mayer, Alan D. "Mingling Decision Making Metaphors." *Academy of Management Review* 9, no. 1 (January 1984): 6–17.

Pitz, Gordon F.; Sachs, Natalie J.; and Heerboth, Joel. "Procedures for Eliciting Choices in the Analysis of Individual Decisions." *Organizational Behavior and Human Performance* 26, no. 3 (December 1980): 396–408.

Roy, Delwin A., and Simpson, Claude A. "Export Attitudes of Business Executives in a Smaller Manufacturing Firm." *Journal of Small Business Management* 19 (April 1981): 16–22.

Simon, Herbert A. *The New Science of Management Decision*. rev. ed. Englewood Cliffs, N.J.: Prentice-Hall, 1977.

——— . "Rational Decision Making in Business Organization." *American Economic Review* 69, no. 4 (September 1979): 493–513.

Tjosvald, Dean. "Effects of Crisis Orientation on Manager's Approach to Controversy in Decision Making." *Academy of Management Journal* 27, no. 1 (March 1984): 130–138.

Vroom, Victor H. "A New Look at Managerial Decision Making." *Organizational Dynamics* 1, no. 4 (Spring 1973): 66–80.

Wright, Peter. "The Harassed Decision Maker: Time Pressures, Distractions and the Use of Evidence." *Journal of Applied Psychology* 59, no. 5 (October 1974): 555–561.

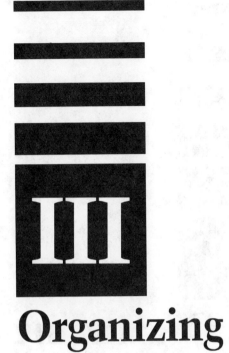

Organizing

The Organizing Process

Richter's Hardware Stores

Karl Richter grew up in Winnipeg's North End. He exhibited an entrepreneurial attitude early in life and, by the time he graduated from university with a degree in marketing, he had already been involved in several small-scale operations. He returned home after graduation in 1964 to take over his father's hardware store to refine his entrepreneurial skills. He thought this would give him an opportunity to put into practice some ideas he had learned at university.

Richter threw himself into work with great vigor. After carefully analyzing the Winnipeg market, he added some completely new product lines, expanded others, and discontinued some altogether. He streamlined record-keeping by instituting a mechanized data processing system. Within 3 years, profits and sales had increased dramatically. Encouraged by this success, Richter opened 2 new stores in Winnipeg in 1967. These were also successful and, by 1970, the company employed 51 people. (See Exhibit 6-1.)

Richter decided to expand farther west in the next few years, since he thought that the Winnipeg market was getting saturated. He branched out regionally to include such cities as Brandon, Portage La Prairie, Dauphin, and Regina. By 1980,

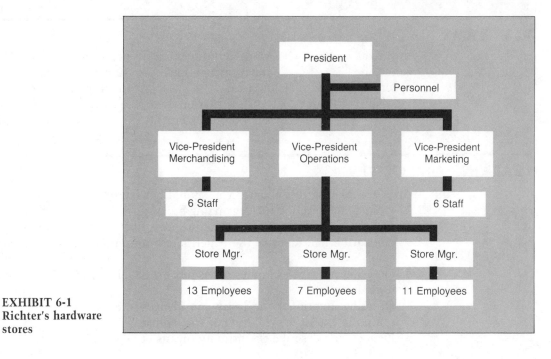

**EXHIBIT 6-1
Richter's hardware
stores**

the company employed 103 people at 16 different locations. Richter observed that these regionally dispersed stores were reasonably successful, but not as profitable as the new Winnipeg stores.

Over the next several years the company expanded to include Saskatoon, Calgary, and Edmonton. By 1984, the company had 29 stores and 203 employees. At this point, difficulties began. The financial statements for 1984 showed that the company overall was still making a profit, but far below expectations. Richter therefore called a meeting of the 3 vice-presidents to get their views on what was wrong.

The meeting was not pleasant. All three complained that in the last several years their jobs had become almost impossible. The marketing vice-president complained that she was forced to spend promotion money in new markets that she really didn't know much about. She noted that her travel expenses were up considerably. The merchandising vice-president complained that he was unsure about what product lines to carry in the different regions. He implied that the marketing vice-president didn't seem interested in cooperating with merchandising. He

noted several sales ads that had recently appeared in local papers for products the company didn't even have in stock. The marketing vice-president retorted that it wasn't her job to coordinate the two functions.

The operations vice-president wasn't happy either. He claimed that regional store managers paid little attention to his suggestions for store operations. The regional store managers pointed out that the operations vice-president didn't have any knowledge about their local markets and that he shouldn't try to impose unreasonable ideas on them from the head office.

Richter listened to these and other complaints for 3 hours. He heard of discord among members of the top management team and apathy among employees at the retail outlet. Head office employees in the marketing, operations, and merchandising functions seemed reasonably content, but some couldn't see how their particular job fit into the total scheme.

Richter knew the company could not survive financially if it had another couple of years like the last one. After the meeting with his vice-presidents, he was concerned about the satisfaction and motivation levels of his employees.

KEY TERMS

organization
function
specialization or
    division of labor

work simplification
functionalization
vertical
    differentiation
span of management

horizontal
    differentiation
functional similarity
departmentation

LEARNING OBJECTIVES

After completing this chapter you should be able to
1. Define and describe the organizing process.
2. In terms of organizational structure, describe a function and specialization and identify the benefits and limitations of specialization.
3. Describe and give examples of the process of vertical and horizontal differentiation.
4. Describe functional similarity and identify the factors that determine the extent to which it can be applied.
5. Identify and describe the primary means of departmentation.

The managerial function of organizing is important for all types of organizations — a university, military unit, church, hospital, government agency, or manufacturer. Once the objectives and plans have been developed and stated, managers must organize; they must design a structure that will bring together human resources and inputs to function in an orderly manner. In this part of the text, we discuss the concepts, principles, and practices of the basic management function of organizing.

Organizations, large or small, have at least three common characteristics:

• They are composed of people.
• They exist to achieve goals.
• Each has some degree of structure that results in a definition and limitation of the behavior of its members.

Earlier, we defined an organization as two or more people working together in a coordinated manner to achieve certain goals. To be effective, managers must be capable of organizing human resources, physical factors, and functions (production, marketing, finance, and personnel) in such a way that the goals of the organization are achieved. In chapters 8 and 9, we discuss the organizing of human resources.

In chapters 6 and 7, we discuss the process of organizing through functions.

THE PROCESS OF ORGANIZING

The basic management function of organizing is illustrated in Exhibit 6-2. Both the internal and external environments of an organization affect the organizing process. Internally, the process is affected by the availability of human and physical resources, as well as departmentation requirements and the specific delegation of authority. Externally, the managers' organizing process is affected by such factors as government legislation, the general public's desire for clean air and water, the marketing strategies of competitors, and the desires of shareholders. Managers perform the steps of the organizing process by:

- Establishing what is to be accomplished (objectives)
- Determining the type of work that needs to be accomplished (functions)
- Assessing human resources
- Assessing physical resources requirements
- Grouping the functions, physical resources, and human resources into an organizational structure (functionalization and departmentation)
- Assigning the obligation to perform a certain job (responsibility) and the right to make decisions or take action to accomplish the job (authority)
- Assigning specific work activities
- Determining if the job was accomplished (accountability of personnel).

The primary purpose of the organizing function is to achieve an effective and efficient blending of the essential ingredients for the success of the organization: people, physical resources, and structure. This coordination is imperative if the firm is to achieve its goals. Without good organizing, chaos may result. When the organizing function is performed effectively, personnel understand the goals of the firm, as well as the role and functions they are expected to fulfill. In addition, all persons have a clearer understanding of their responsibility and to whom they report and are accountable, as well as how their work relates to the work of others in the organization. In this chapter we discuss the organizing process (the upper half of Exhibit 6-2). In Chapter 7, we discuss the delegation of responsibility and authority (the lower half of Exhibit 6-2).

The organizing function must be closely integrated with the planning function. In fact, the first step in organizing is the establishment of objectives, as shown in Exhibit 6-2. Before managers can determine what functions or resources are needed, they must clearly define objectives. Managers must know what is to be accomplished. Once goals and plans have been established, the organizing process begins.

MANAGEMENT IN PRACTICE

The Organizing Process at CSL

Bruce Lougheed was a systems engineering manager for 10 years with a major computer company; recently, he resigned his position to form a computer services company, which he has named Computer Systems, Limited (CSL). Lougheed and two partners, Gerry Zakus and Marion Spence, are making plans to develop a computer services firm specializing in the development, installation, and maintenance of computer software systems for life insurance companies.

The goal for CSL is to provide high-quality, specialized computer services to life insurance companies at a profit. After establishing the objectives for the new company, the three partners determine that the functions CSL must accomplish include: systems engineering and design, programming development, and the installation and maintenance of computer systems. Based on these functions, the human resources required for CSL are: highly trained systems analysts, computer programmers, and marketing personnel, as well as a clerical support staff. In addition to the personnel required, physical resources, such as capital, computer equipment, office space, and office furnishings, are essential. The partners must determine not only the type of personnel needed but also the number of specialists

needed for each major function. Recruiting will be Zakus's major task. In addition, they must secure sufficient capital from banks, other shareholders or other sources to begin and continue operations. Spence will be responsible for finding the funds to lease office space, purchase or lease equipment, employ and compensate personnel, and pay for supplies.

Lougheed realizes that he must coordinate the functions and the physical and human resources into a workable organizational structure. He decides that 3 departments are needed: (1) systems design and programming, (2) installation and maintenance, and (3) marketing. In this newly formed company, personnel will perform a wide variety of tasks; but, as CSL grows, they will perform more limited, specialized functions. Once the functions have been grouped into a coordinated organizational structure, Lougheed will assign appropriate levels of responsibility, authority, and accountability to all employees. The final phase of the organizing function is the assignment of specific work activities. For instance, the marketing manager must perform such work activities as calling on potential customers, designing promotion and advertising, and recruiting and training sales personnel.

FUNCTIONS

Once objectives have been planned, the organizing process begins. Managers determine the types of functions or work that must be performed within the organization. A **function** is a type of work activity that can be identified and distinguished from other work activities. On a hockey team, several distinct functions must be performed effectively if the team is to win games. Players on the team perform the functions of checking, shooting, penalty-killing, defending, and goal-keeping. A good team has specialists for each of these activities. A baseball team needs a pitching staff consisting of starters, short-relievers, long-relievers, and a stopper. Infielders and outfielders specialize in defense at a particular position, like first base or shortstop, but must also produce offensively. Most teams also hire specialists for both batting and running bases.

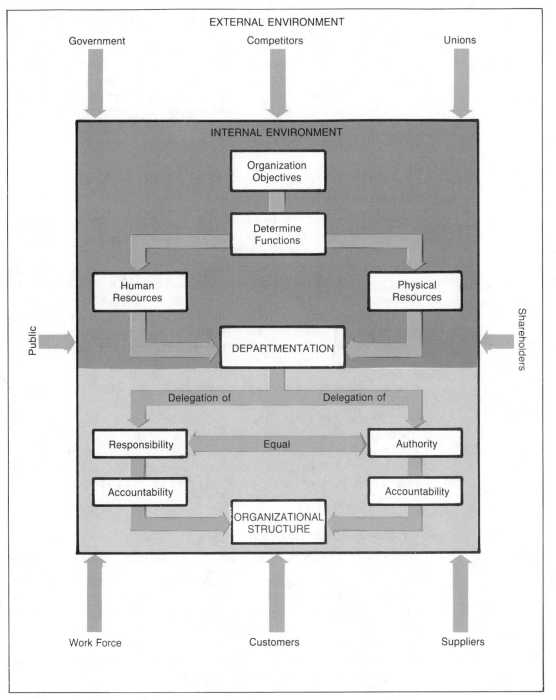

EXHIBIT 6-2   The organizing process

Basic work functions can be defined in any organization. The major functions of a manufacturer are production, marketing, and finance. For a retailing company, the basic functions are buying and selling of merchandise and extending credit. The major functions in a bank include depositing or receiving customers' money and making loans to borrowers. At a university or college, teaching, research, and service are the primary functions that must be performed. Functions performed by an individual within the organization must be identified, defined, and separated from the work performed by other people.

Specialization

Specialization or division of labor is a major element of the organizing process. It is essential for the achievement of efficiency in mass-production industries. In fact, most work activities performed in nearly all organizations are of a specialized nature. In many of today's organizations, specialization of labor is often referred to as **work simplification**, which organizes jobs into small, highly specialized components. Organizations have several options as to the degree of specialization associated with each job. For instance, if a company produces small transistor radios, several different approaches might be available, such as:

- Each employee assembles the entire radio (low degree of specialization).
- Each employee assembles several major components of the radio, perhaps the plastic casing and primary transistor circuit board.
- Each employee assembles one component of the radio, the casing.
- Each employee performs a few routine operations, such as putting the knobs on for tuner and volume control (high degree of specialization).

Advantages of Specialization

Specialization or work simplification offers the following advantages:

- Allows workers to concentrate skills on a narrow range of work, thus increasing work output.
- Permits managers to supervise a larger number of employees.
- Facilitates the selection and training of workers to perform identical activities, so that jobs can be learned in less time.
- Leads to more efficient utilization of workers because they can develop and practice specialized skills.
- Contributes to better consistency of quality in products or services.
- Facilitates the achievement of complex goals.

A worker who is able to concentrate skill and effort on a small number of tasks can usually achieve a higher level of output than a worker who must perform a large number of tasks. In manufacturing electronic components, output per worker tends to be much higher when employees perform highly specialized work activities. Similarly, high performance results are apparent in many fast food restaurants where employees perform specialized functions, such as cooking hamburgers or french fries, contrasting the more traditional restaurants where employees perform a wide variety of jobs.

In addition to higher output, specialization may permit a manager to supervise a larger number of employees. A manager may be able to supervise effectively 30 to 50 workers who perform the same specialized tasks. If workers perform diverse tasks, the number of employees a manager can supervise effectively is fewer.

Generally, a more specialized job can be learned more quickly than a job involving numerous work activities. When training time is reduced, workers become productive at a faster rate. For instance, the time required to train a worker to cook french fries or prepare milkshakes is minimal compared to the time required to learn all the jobs performed in a fast food restaurant.

Work simplification leads to a more efficient utilization of employees because they can develop and practice their specialized skills. A worker can be more efficient and produce more by concentrating on one or a few activities. A professional football player is usually a highly trained specialist; rarely does one player perform more than a few specialized activities. Most place kickers in professional football specialize only in kicking extra points and field goals. Quarterbacks, linemen, and running backs all specialize in what they do best. By specializing, the players continually refine and improve their individual skills.

Specialization contributes to consistently higher-quality products and services. In an age of specialization, most people are employed as specialists. Many students who choose to pursue a degree or diploma in business administration specialize in accounting, computer science, finance, management, or marketing. Few professions demonstrate the move to specialization more than medicine. As more is learned about each phase of medicine, entire careers emerge concentrating on a specific part of the body or a specific symptom. Forty years ago most medical doctors treated all ailments of all members of the family. Now, most physicians specialize in, say, pediatrics, cardiology, gynecology, or gerontology. By specializing in a narrow range of the medical profession, such physicians can offer their diagnosis and treatment based on the current research and technology of that specific field.

Finally, specialization facilitates the achievement of complex goals. The successful completion of any complex project usually requires many different specialists. For example, the development of Canada's oil resources in the oceans or the prairie tar sands would not be possible without the work of thousands of specialists. A large amount of knowledge about ecology, climate, production processes, and extraction techniques is critical to the success of Canada's energy plans.

Disadvantages of Specialization

Despite the advantages of the specialization of labor, its application may not always be desirable. In some organizations, certain jobs have become oversimplified. Too much specialization in the design of jobs may create boredom and fatigue among the employees; for example, some people would find it difficult work on an assembly line tightening a bolt 1000 times a day. Typically the highest degree of specialization is found in assembly line work, which sometimes results in employee turnover, absenteeism, and a deteriorating quality of output. These negative consequences of specialization may cause an increase in operational costs.

Another disadvantage of specialization is that it can cause employees and managers to become too involved in their own area of specialization. When people in organizations work at highly specialized jobs, they may fail to see the overall objectives the organization is trying to achieve. Specialization can also lead people to think that their specific function is the most important, when, in fact, all the different functions must be integrated and coordinated for effective organization operation.

Specialization has been a well-entrenched concept in Canada for many years because Frederick Taylor's scientific management ideas have had a major impact on managers. Some companies, however, are finding that specialization doesn't always lead to higher productivity. Many companies are beginning to experiment with ways to achieve high productivity without breaking each job into tiny parts. Currently, the most popular approach is job enrichment, a concept in which jobs are designed so that workers do a larger, not smaller, part of a function. We discuss job enrichment further in Chapter 10.

Functionalization

The process of differentiating functions as the organization grows is known as **functionalization**. In a newly formed small organization, an owner/manager performs all the major functions of the business, such as providing the necessary financing, procuring materials, designing the product, and making and selling the product. (See "Two-Person Firm" in Exhibit 6-3.) As the volume of business grows, the work required will increase beyond the capacities of one person. At this point, functionalization begins as additional personnel are employed.

Vertical Differentiation

As a business grows, additional workers are added to perform certain functions. Functionalization requires that two levels of organization be created: managerial and operative. (See "Two-Level Organization" in Exhibit 6-3.) Managerial employees may still perform operative work in addition to directing the operative employees. For example, the manager may retain the sales and finance functions and allocate the production work to new employees. This is **vertical differentiation**.

As the volume of business continues to grow, additional personnel will be added and more operative functions differentiated and allocated. (See "Three-Level Organization" in Exhibit 6-3.) The original person may now serve in the capacity of full-time manager. As such, he or she manages the work of the supervisors, who now constitute the second management level. They, in turn, supervise the work of the operative workers who constitute the third level in the organization.

The process of adding personnel has its limits because one manager cannot supervise an unlimited number of personnel. This limitation is usually referred to as the **span of management** or span of control. According to the span of management, there is a limit to the number of employees a manager can effectively supervise or control. This principle is an organizational generalization based on the theory that managers cannot effectively supervise a large number of people (for example 100), but they can supervise more than one. When a manager's span

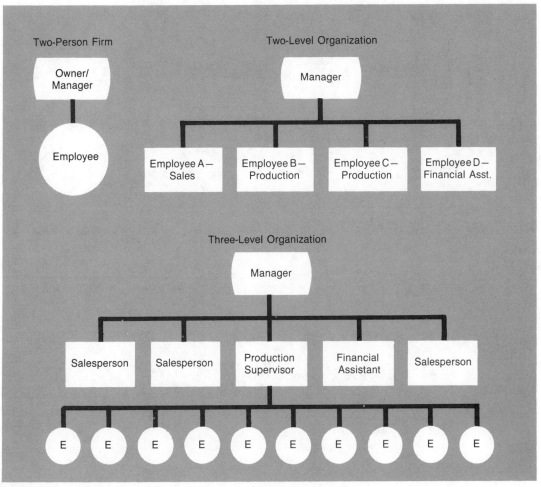

EXHIBIT 6-3   Functional differentiation: vertical and horizontal

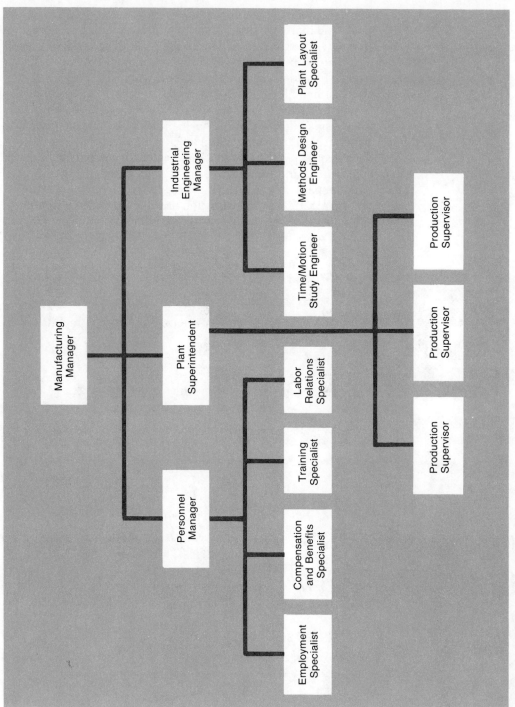

EXHIBIT 6-4 Development of staff departments

of management is excessive, one of the employees may be designated a supervisor, and subordinates are placed under this person's direction. The newly appointed supervisor is still responsible to the original manager. This creates three levels in the organization and does not overwork the capacities of one manager. The span of management is discussed in greater detail in Chapter 7.

Horizontal Differentiation

The first direction of organizational growth from the one-person enterprise is usually downward. However, at some point, growth of the firm will cause a splitting out of functions, forming outward levels in the organization called **horizontal differentiation**. Personnel performing these functions will be newly appointed. Ordinarily, horizontal differentiation occurs because the original manager finds that certain functions can be more effectively and economically performed by a specialist. For example, a manager may find sales a weak area because of ineffective or inadequate training programs. Therefore, a sales trainer would be employed to take over that phase of the business so the manager can devote more time to other areas. Horizontal growth usually occurs at the supervisory levels first in the organization and at lower levels as additional workers are required. As the organization grows, horizontal differentiation usually results in functions being split off that are the most complex and are least similar to any other functions of the firm.

If the organization continues to grow, the sales specialist may find that the volume of work exceeds the time available to do it. The second stage of horizontal differentiation is likely to be the creation of a formal department. An additional employee will probably be hired to assist the original specialist and a chain of command in this specialized area has now been formed. Growth at this point becomes vertical differentiation again.

As shown in Exhibit 6-3, horizontal differentiation usually occurs in several areas of an organization. Recall the example of the sales trainer. Other areas that usually grow are marketing research, labor relations, design, and engineering. Sometimes several functions need to be grouped together under a single manager to reduce the span of management. This grouping ensures coordination and compatibility among the functions. For example, training, employment, and labor relations might be combined to create a personnel department. (See Exhibit 6-4.)

The ideal result of the process of vertical or horizontal differentiation is to facilitate the accomplishments of the organization's goals through the use of specialists. The benefits of creating additional specialists in any organization — profit or non-profit — must exceed their costs. If a firm has doubled the size of its sales force without splitting out the training function from the work of the sales manager, employing a sales training specialist may add greater benefit than it will cost the company.

Grouping Functions: Functional Similarity

Objectives determine the work to be performed. The total work load must be divided among the available personnel. Individual jobs, or units of responsibility, are created by selecting and grouping functions into individual assignments. The basic guide that governs this process is **functional similarity**. Work that is similar in content and activities is grouped together following the principle of functional similarity. In Exhibit 6-5, functions J, L, and Q are shown to be sufficiently similar in objectives and content to comprise the work assignments for Job 1, a press operator. Therefore, a person with the skills and abilities necessary to execute this job must be found. Job 2, the quality control inspector, consists of functions AA, G, B, and X. The same principles also guide managers in the creation of sections, departments, and divisions. Jobs with similar objectives and requirements are grouped to form a section. A person with the background necessary to supervise these functions effectively should be assigned as the manager.

Although functional similarity is desirable, the extent to which it can be applied depends on several factors we note in this section.

Sufficient Volume of Work

Grouping similar functions occurs when a sufficient volume of work demands some specialization. In the small firm, personnel perform a wide assortment of jobs. But, as volume of work increases, the concept can be applied more rigorously. For example, compare the operations of a small grocery store versus those of a large supermarket. In the small store, one person might perform such functions as stocking shelves, working in the produce section, cashiering, and packing groceries. In the large supermarket, personnel will tend to specialize in one or only a few of the basic functions. It's common to have individual managers for each function in the larger supermarkets. A low volume of work would limit functionalization.

Tradition, Preferences, and Work Rules

Even though the tasks may be similar, traditions, personal preferences and work rules may prevent their assignment to a certain individual. For example, installing electrical conduit is quite similar to running water piping. However, few plumbers would be willing to install conduit and few electricians would willingly run water pipes. People associate a set of behavioral expectations, duties, and responsibilities with a given position.[1] In this way, grouping by functional similarity would be limited. In unionized organizations, formal work rules often prohibit, for instance, the assignment of plumbers to electrical work or electricians to plumbing.

EXHIBIT 6-5
Illustration of
functional similarity

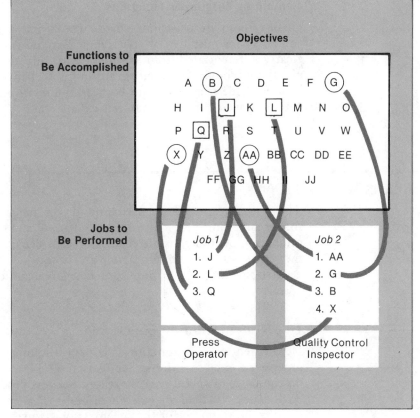

Functions Similar in Different Areas of the Organization

A third limitation to grouping by functional similarity is that two areas of the organization may perform similar functions that must stay within each area. For example, the function of inventory control would appear to fit logically with the purchasing area. Purchasing buys the material and keeps records of inventory levels. However, production uses these materials and, in scheduling, must work with these same inventory records. Inventory control could be placed in either area, but is unlikely to be wholly within either.

Separation of Functions for Control or Motivation

A fourth limitation is the occasional separation of similar functions for purposes of control or motivation. For instance, inspection is a function of production; inspectors frequently work side by side with production employees. However, the inspector should not be unduly influenced by the production manager's interest in quantity and cost. Therefore, inspection, although similar to production, might be separate from production to protect its independence.

Combining Dissimilar Functions

Finally, there are occasions when two dissimilar functions must be combined for purposes of effective action and control. Purchasing is clearly differentiated from selling in a manufacturer but, in a department store, buying and selling are so interdependent that one person is often made responsible for both. In the retail business the attitude is that "a well-bought coat or hat is half sold."

DEPARTMENTATION

The process of grouping related functions or major work activities into manageable units to achieve more effective and efficient overall co-ordination of an organization's resources is **departmentation**. The primary bases of departmentation are function, product, customer, geographic territory, and project. In large organizations, several of these bases may be used.

Departmentation by Function

Departmentation by function is perhaps the most common means of grouping related functions. (See Exhibit 6-6.) Departments are formed on the basis of specialized functions, such as production, marketing, engineering, finance, or personnel, and assists managers to use efficiently the resources of the organization. However, departmentation by function may create problems for managers in the sense that employees in these specialized functions may become more concerned with their own department than with the overall company. Departmentation by function is especially useful for firms whose external environment is stable and where technical efficiency and quality are important.[2]

EXHIBIT 6-6
Departmentation by function

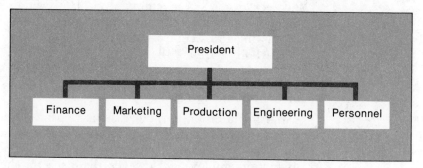

Departmentation by Product

The product basis of departmentation is used when top management wants to emphasize product lines. This type of departmentation enhances the use of specialized knowledge of particular products or services and is often used by rather large companies that have diverse products. For example, a large electronics firm might be organized into three product divisions. (See Exhibit 6-7.)

Firms manufacturing and selling technologically complex products are often structured this way.[3] Since 1916, General Motors had been divided into five product divisions: Chevrolet, Pontiac, Oldsmobile, Buick, and Cadillac. Because of what GM executives call "creeping complexity," the company recently reorganized into only two divisions — one comprised of Chevrolet, Pontiac, and GM Canada and a second comprised of Buick, Cadillac, and Oldsmobile. Small cars will be designed and manufactured by the first division and intermediate and large cars by the second division.[4]

EXHIBIT 6-7
Departmentation by product

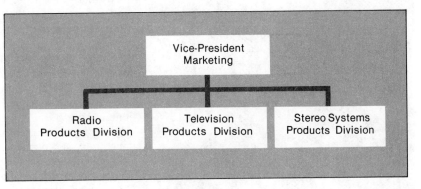

Departmentation by Customer

Departmentation by customer is used by organizations that have a special need to provide high quality service to different kinds of customers. As illustrated in Exhibit 6-8, a manufacturing company might have industrial, government, and consumer products divisions. Large retailers and banks use customer departmentation to provide a wide variety of services. Businesses and members of the general public have different needs for such organizations.

EXHIBIT 6-8
Departmentation by customer

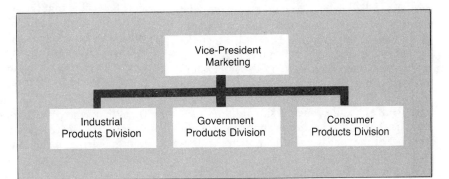

TALKING TO MANAGERS

Tom Ward
Genstar Shipyards Ltd.

Tom Ward is Operations Manager for Genstar Shipyards Ltd., a Vancouver firm that specializes in the custom building and repair of icebreakers, research vessels, ferries, tugs, and barges. The company has sales in excess of $30 million and employs 200 to 400 workers. It is the second largest shipyard on Canada's west coast; in peak periods, it has delivered a new ship every 2 months. Ward is responsible for the overall operations of the shipyard. His duties include: (1) reviewing and approving project cost estimates that have been developed by the shipyard's estimators and engineers, (2) writing proposals for custom-built vessels, and (3) setting work schedules once a shipbuilding contract has been awarded to the company. He is a member of the management committee and reports to the president.

Ward works closely with 2 full-time new construction Project Managers (PMs), who have degrees in marine engineering in addition to considerable shop floor experience. Each ship the company builds is treated as a project, and the PMs have the responsibility of seeing that each project is finished on schedule, to specification, and within budget. Some projects employ up to 400 people, making the PM's job a major administrative function. Each PM has a small clerical staff to assist in this work.

Q: What is the dollar value of a typical project, and how long does it take to complete?
Ward: The value of each project varies widely and can range from a low of about $2 million for a small tugboat, to a high of nearly $60 million for a state-of-the-art icebreaker. Projects run from a minimum of 4 months to a maximum of 2 years.

Q: What does a PMs job involve?
Ward: The Project Manager is responsible for the initial development of a master schedule for the vessel's design and construction. In conjunction with the estimating, technical, and purchasing departments, he identifies items of machinery and outfit which are critical to this schedule; if necessary, he will negotiate with the ship owners and designers to modify the specifications to allow equipment to be used whose availability and quality satisfies both the shipyard's schedule and cost budgets and the owners' performance requirements. During this period, the PM interacts with all departments having input into both the technical and the commercial aspects of the construction contract; he also familiarizes himself with the overall intent, requirements, preferences, and priorities of the customer. Once there is an agreement that the master schedule satisfies both the ship owners' and builder's requirements, the PM is responsible for seeing that the schedule and budget are adhered to. After launching and completion of outfitting, the PM oversees the trials of the ship and her delivery to the owner. He will then act as the main contact between the shipyard and owners during the guarantee period — usually 1 year after delivery.

Q: What kind of authority does a PM have?
Ward: The PM derives most of his authority from reporting to the same level that the shipyard superintendents report to. He has specific authority to decide the construction sequence and how many workers will be assigned to each

phase of the project. He makes these decisions after consulting the project plans and the time-frame in which the project must be completed. He does not have authority to hire, lay off, or fire workers employed on the project — this remains with the worker's functional supervisor, the department foreman; but the PM works with all the foremen to determine when the work force should be increased or decreased. Shipyards employ many different trade skills — steelworkers, welders, carpenters, painters, pipefitters, electricians, and machinists — and the PM must be knowledgeable about the collective agreement the company has with various trade unions.

The PM also approves purchase orders being placed with outside suppliers and subcontractors. Throughout the project, he is required to keep a close eye on costs committed to purchase orders, and he has to work closely with the accounting department in approving accounts payable. In the event of any dispute arising with these outside sources, the PM's approval is required for payment of their invoices. In many companies, the PM does not have this type of authority, but we have found that it is beneficial.

Q: Do the workers on a project report to — the PM or the foreman?
Ward: The workers report to the foreman, and the foreman takes direction from the PM. The PM can often decide which worker he wants assigned to a project. If the PM and the foreman disagree about which particular tradesmen or how many of them in a specific trade will be on which project, the PM can appeal to the foreman's superintendent. He usually gets his way on staffing issues, because those levels on our projects are so important and both understaffing or overstaffing can have a serious effect on the project schedule and cost.

Q: Are there other disagreements that arise between a PM and the foremen?
Ward: Yes. For example, a foreman might think work on some aspect of the ship's construction ought to be done in a particular way, and the PM might think it should be done in some other way. If the disagreement is a question of sequencing the work, the PM will usually prevail; but, if the disagreement is about specific trade practices, the foreman will generally get his way. As another example, a foreman may try to assign more tradesmen to a project than the PM thinks necessary. The foreman may do this to give himself a cushion in meeting his schedule. In these cases, the PM usually wins out because he has the total project schedule and budget in mind, whereas the foreman may be thinking only of the work that his particular crew is doing.

Q: Do the two PMs ever have disagreements with each other?
Ward: Sometimes. However, it is important that a high level of communication and trust exist between the two PMs because they must think about how all the shipyard's contracts can be most effectively dealt with. Each PM is drawing from the same common pool of tradesmen and helpers, so they must be flexible in their demands and keep the good of the total company in mind when making their respective staffing decisions. The better the quality of each worker loading schedule developed from the master construction schedule, the less will be the potential for conflict in this area.

Q: What kind of skills does a PM have to possess to be effective?
Ward: Three basic skills, really. First, the PM must be very strong in his interpersonal skills. He has to be able to instill enthusiasm and push the project forward at as fast a pace as possible. However, should a disagreement arise between a PM and a foreman, the PM must be sensitive enough to know when to push hard for his point of view and when to ease off. Second, the PM must have good administrative skills so that he can keep track of the total project, its physical progress, and the extent of committed costs at all times. Finally, he must possess good technical skills so that he can communicate effectively with the technical people on the project. This allows the PM to assess accurately how well the work is progressing and to deal with any technical problems that might arise.

Q: On balance, how has the project management structure worked for Genstar Shipyards?
Ward: It is really the only structure that makes sense for us. Since time is of the essence in every construction contract we enter into and costs have to be closely monitored, the project structure is necessary. It focuses our efforts on the activities that are needed to get the job done, and that helps us meet our time deadlines. It is very gratifying to see a finished ship leaving.

Departmentation by Geographic Territory

Departmentation according to geographic territory is used by organizations that have physically dispersed and/or independent operations or markets to serve. The marketing function of the company shown in Exhibit 6-9 is organized into the Western, Central, and Atlantic regional divisions. Geographic departmentation offers the advantages of better service with local or regional personnel, often at less cost.

EXHIBIT 6-9
Departmentation by geographic territory

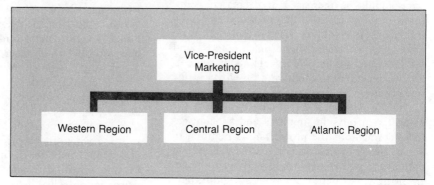

Departmentation by Project

Departmentation by project is a method of bringing together personnel with various work backgrounds to form a team. Exhibit 6-10 provides an illustration of departmentation for the special project of developing an aircraft plan. Engineer B and Financial Planner C are to accomplish this special project. The team has been assigned a specific task or objective to be accomplished within a given time period. On completion of the project, Engineer B and Financial Planner C will return to their regular work assignments. Departmentation by project has received considerable usage in recent years by the construction and aerospace industries. We discuss project departmentation in more detail in Chapter 7.

Departmentation: A Combination Approach

Unless the organization is quite small, it is likely that several different bases for departmentation will be used. No one form of departmentation can meet the needs of most firms, particularly in such firms as Bell Canada, Massey Ferguson, Canadian Pacific, or Alcan Aluminum. An organization chart illustrating various forms of departmentation is shown in Exhibit 6-11. In this case, the manufacturing company is departmentalized by type of functions performed (engineering, production, marketing, and so on), type of products (industrial and consumer), and geographic territory. The precise form of departmentation a firm chooses must be based on its particular needs.

EXHIBIT 6-10
Departmentation
by project

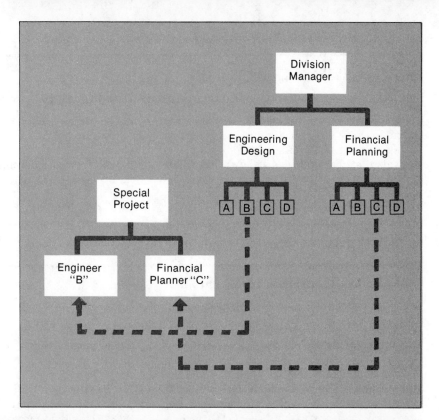

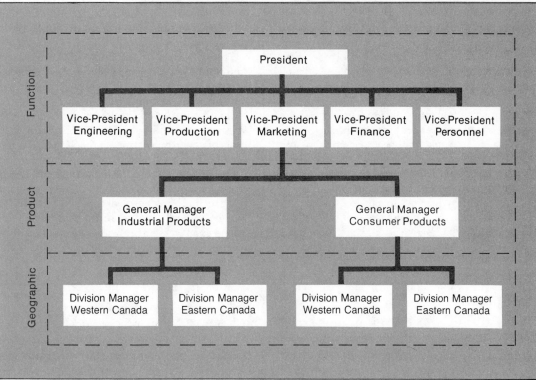

EXHIBIT 6-11   Organizational chart illustrating departmentation

MANAGEMENT IN PRACTICE
Departmentation in Practice

In practice, it may or may not be easy to decide what basis of departmentation a company is using. Consumers Distributing, for example, is organized at the top level as shown in Exhibit 6-12. This firm is clearly organized using departmentation by function; the key functions that the company must perform (store operations, finance, or development) are the basis for the various departments.

The basis for departmentation is not as clear at Continental Group of Canada Ltd. There are elements of both functional departmentation (finance, operations) and product departmentation (metal products and automotive). (See Exhibit 6-13.) This combination of bases of departmentation is more common in Canadian firms than pure departmentation.

OPENING INCIDENT REVISITED
Richter's Hardware Stores

Karl Richter had made numerous improvements to his hardware chain but their success has been limited. The basic problem here is that Richter has concentrated on expansion without giving much thought to the structural implications of doing so. Richter has added product lines and expanded regionally without adequately preparing existing managers and without altering his head office's perspectives of the organization.

Some of the specific manifestations of this problem are indicated in the dispute between the marketing and merchandise vice-presidents. The lack of coordination between them is probably caused by the company's unstructured growth. This problem would not have arisen back in the days of the smaller company because these two managers would have been operating in only the Winnipeg market; coordinating their product lines and inventory would have been easier. The expanded structure contributed to this current problem by forcing managers into specialized jobs but not allowing them to see the organization-wide perspective; they have difficulty making suggestions about how to head off these problems.

An additional problem is that Richter has added new outlets at various locations and is running into the problem of distance from his head office. The vice-president of marketing in Winnipeg really didn't know about some of these distant markets, yet her job was to advertise in them. This kind of problem could be resolved by changing the structure to set up a regional office in certain areas instead of doing everything from head office.

The structure of the company is based on function. During expansion, this basis contributes to the company's problems because the top management is having increasing difficulty coordinating the diverse regions where Richter has stores. One obvious alternative is to use another basis of departmentation. Perhaps the most reasonable is departmentation by geographic territory. Richter might appoint two vice-presidents, one for the Winnipeg area, and one for the outlying region. Under each of these vice-presidents would be marketing, merchandising, and operations managers. If growth continues, a third vice-president could be added, dividing the outlying region.

SUMMARY

An organization can be defined as two or more people working together in a coordinated manner to achieve group results. To be effective, managers must be capable of organizing human resources and functions to ensure the achievement of the firm's goals. The primary purpose of

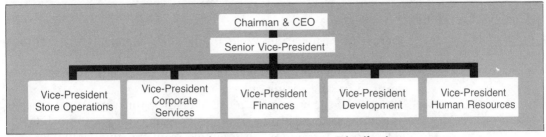

EXHIBIT 6-12   Departmentation by function at Consumers Distributing
SOURCE   Annual Report, Consumers Distributing (1980).

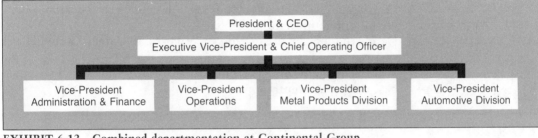

EXHIBIT 6-13   Combined departmentation at Continental Group
SOURCE   Annual Report, Continental Group of Canada Ltd. (1980).

the organizing function is to achieve an effective and efficient blend of the essential elements of the organization that lead to success.

A function is a type of work activity that can be identified and distinguished from other work. Functions performed by individuals within the organization must be identified, defined, and separated from the work performed by others.

Work simplification or specialization of function is the traditional approach to work design; jobs are organized into small, highly specialized components. Despite the numerous advantages of specialization, certain jobs have been oversimplified in some organizations and at times have led to work that is boring and fatiguing for employees.

The process of differentiating functions as an organization grows is known as functionalization. In vertical differentiation more levels of authority are added. Horizontal differentiation involves the splitting out of functions and dividing the work responsibilities, forming horizontal (or equal authority) levels in the organization. The ideal result of the process of vertical or horizontal differentiation is to accomplish organization goals through the use of specialists. Specialization of function is usually accomplished by the process of departmentation. Departmentation involves grouping related functions or major work activities into manageable units to achieve more effective and efficient overall coordination of the resources of the firm. The primary bases of departmentation are function, product, customer, geographic territory, and project. In most organizations, a combination of these bases of departmentation is used.

REVIEW QUESTIONS

1. Define an organization. What are the three characteristics common to all organizations?
2. Describe the process of organizing. What tasks must managers perform in the organizing process?
3. In terms of the organizing process, define a function. What types of functions are needed for a community drama group? a football team? a fast foods restaurant? an assembly plant for small appliances?
4. Define specialization. What are the advantages and disadvantages of specialization?
5. Distinguish by example and definition between vertical and horizontal differentiation.
6. Define the concept of functional similarity. What factors could limit the use of this concept?
7. What does the term *departmentation* mean? What are the primary bases of departmentation?

EXERCISES

1. Specialization has both advantages and disadvantages. List the specialized education and training required for the following professions. Which profession(s) are possible with your present level of education and training? Which could you achieve?
   a. an electrical engineer
   b. a neurosurgeon
   c. a machine operator
   d. a college president
   e. a personnel manager.
2. Assume that you are production manager for a firm offering photocopying and some printing services. The firm currently is experiencing much growth and success with its services; two new stores have opened in the past year. As a result, you have hired 15 new employees over the last 6 months to keep up with demand. Describe the horizontal and vertical differentiation you would implement in the company for maximum efficiency as the organization continues to grow.

CASE STUDY

The Organization of Quality Control

Richard Boas is production manager for Memorand Ltd., a small component parts manufacturer in the Maritimes. He has been with the firm for 15 years and has progressed from foreman to his current position. Boas is completely dedicated to the company and its future. He has passed up numerous opportunities for a higher paying, more prestigious position with competing firms to remain with Memorand because he likes his job and the employees.

Kathy Wells is currently in charge of the quality control section with Memorand and reports directly to Boas. She has been with the company for 10 years, having started as department secretary to Boas. He has supported Wells getting a degree and has allowed her to take time off to attend classes at the local university. After several years of attending courses, she recently obtained a degree in operations management with a specialty in quality control. Because of the patience and support Boas gave her, Wells has a strong loyalty to Boas and to Memorand.

Memorand has been awarded a very lucrative contract by CBU Ltd., with the provision that Memorand would produce the parts within 3 weeks. If Memorand completes the order on time, it may obtain additional contracts from CBU that would increase overall company sales by at least 10 percent a year. The order comes at a time when business has been relatively bad for Memorand — the firm had been considering a reduction of its work force.

On the second day of production, Wells discovered a problem and requested a meeting with Boas. This conversation took place:

Wells: Dick, the quality of the parts we're making for CBU is not as good as those we normally make. I believe we should slow down and inspect all the parts to ensure that we don't send out an inferior product.

Boas: Are the parts below standard?

Wells: No, but about 45 percent of the parts are marginal. I believe that, if we want to improve our chances of obtaining additional orders, we must slow down the production line.

Boas: If we slow down the production line, Kathy, we won't make the deadline we promised CBU. If we don't make the deadline, most likely Memorand will not even have a chance to receive follow-up contracts. I expect you to meet the production schedule like everyone else.

After receiving such a firm demand, Wells left the office. She thought her position was right but didn't know what more to do.

QUESTIONS

1. Would you reorganize the reporting relationships of the production department and the quality control section to ensure that the conflict experienced by Wells and Boas would not occur in the future? Why or why not? If you would reorganize, how?
2. If you agree with Wells, what do you think she should do? Discuss.
3. Do you believe Boas was correct in his assessment of the situation? Discuss.

CASE STUDY

Materials Organization at Newco

Newco Manufacturing Company, based in Hamilton, employed 210 workers in the production and assembly of small electrical motors. Tom Baryluk, the new materials manager, knew one of his first tasks was to improve the organization in his department. Baryluk reported to the vice-president of manufacturing, Charles McDowell. Baryluk had 12 people in his department; they performed functions like stocking, receiving, inventory control, purchasing, and outside sales.

Because the workflow was not easily predictable, the previous materials manager told the department's personnel to do whatever they thought necessary. Jobs included working the parts issue windows while mechanics were ordering parts, stocking the parts bins when time permitted, receiving parts when deliveries were made, and shipping orders to customers. These same employees answered the phone and handled outside sales as required. Frequent employee complaints had been made about inadequate pay, unclear work assignments, and lack of competent leadership.

Baryluk had received a rather detailed account about the materials operation from McDowell. McDowell described the materials department as performing poorly, because of a lack of overall direction, ineffective organization, and incompetent personnel. McDowell described several of the department's personnel as "dope heads" or "long hairs" who did as little work as possible. The turnover rate had been over 200 percent per year for the past 3 years. McDowell suggested that Baryluk "clean house" by firing most of the employees in the department and start with a fresh crew.

Baryluk was surprised by McDowell's comments and concerned about the complaints of the personnel in the department. He considered finding a new position, but chose not to leave the company until he had given the assignment his best efforts for at least a few months.

QUESTIONS

1. Using concepts and principles discussed in this chapter, what actions would you recommend Baryluk take to improve the materials department?
2. What type of organization chart would you recommend Baryluk develop?
3. Should Baryluk "clean house" as suggested by McDowell? Why or why not?

NOTES

[1] W. G. Astley and A. H. Van de Ven, "Central Perspectives and Debates in Organization Theory," *Administrative Science Quarterly* (June 1983): 248.

[2] R. L. Daft, *Organization Theory and Design* (St. Paul, Minnesota: West Publishing, 1983): 227.

[3] T. T. Herbert, "Strategy and Multinational Organization Structure: An International Relationships Perspective," *Academy of Management Review* (April 1984): 263.

[4] "Can GM Solve Its Identity Crisis?" *Business Week* (January 23, 1984): 32–33.

REFERENCES

Alexander, E. R. "Design of Alternatives in Organizational Contexts: A Pilot Study." *Administrative Science Quarterly* 24 (September 1979): 382–404.

Bobbitt, H. R. Jr., and Ford, J. D. "Decision-Maker Choice as a Determinant of Organizational Structure." *Academy of Management Review* 5 (January 1980): 13–23.

Cherman, C. "Organizing for Strength." *Personnel Journal* 58 (July 1979): 437–438.

Dalton, D. R.; Todor, W. D.; Spendelini, J.; Fielding, J.; and Porter, L. W. "Organization Structure and Performance: A Critical Review." *Academy of Management Review* 5 (January 1980): 61–64.

Gerwin, D. "Relationships between Structure and Technology at the Organizational and Job Levels." *Journal of Management Studies* 16 (February 1979): 70–79.

Handy, C. "Shape of Organizations to Come." *Personnel Management* 11 (June 1979): 24–27.

_____ . "Through the Organizational Looking Glass." *Harvard Business Review* 58, no. 1 (January-February 1980): 24–27.

Herbert, Theodore T. "Strategy and Multinational Organization Structure: An Interorganizational Relationships Perspective." *Academy of Management Review* 9, no. 2 (April 1984): 259–270.

Huber, G. P., et al. "Optimum Organization Design: An Analytic Adoptive Approach." *Academy of Management Review* 4 (October 1979): 567–578.

Naylor, T. H. "Organizing for Strategic Planning." *Managerial Planning* 28 (July 1979): 3–9.

Pavett, Cynthia M., and Lau, Alan W. "Managerial Work: The Influence of Hierarchical Level and Functional Specialty." *Academy of Management Journal* 26, no. 1 (March 1983): 170–177.

Scanlon, K. "Maintaining Organizational Effectiveness — A Prescription for Good Health." *Personnel Journal* 58, no. 5 (May 1980): 381–386.

Slocum, J. W. Jr., and Hellriegel, D. "Using Organizational Designs to Cope with Change." *Business Horizons* 22 (December 1979): 65–76.

Authority, Responsibility, and Organizational Structure

The Faculty of Administration

Frank Singh was the head of the management department in the Faculty of Administration at a large university. John Gebhart was an Associate Dean in the same Faculty. Singh and Gebhart had attended college together and both had come to the university about 15 years ago. They remained good friends, often lunching together and talking over Faculty business. Two years ago Gebhart had given up the position of head of the management department to become the Asso-

ciate Dean for Graduate Studies and Research. Singh had been chosen as Gebhart's replacement. (See Exhibit 7-1 for the current organizational structure of the Faculty of Administration.)

One function Singh performed as department head was assigning classes to the members of his department. Recently he completed this activity and sent each member in his department his or her schedule for next year, including

Gebhart's classes. Soon after the schedules were distributed through the faculty mailboxes, Gebhart approached Singh about his schedule, noting that he had been assigned two sections of the Organization Behavior course in the MBA program. Gebhart asked Singh if the two sections could be combined so that both full- and part-time students could be handled in one class. Singh said that he was reluctant to do so. He had heard various faculty members complaining that administrators (associate deans and department heads) only taught two classes per year, while regular faculty members were required to teach five classes. He was afraid that, if he let Gebhart teach only one class, the criticism would be even greater and he would be accused of "playing favorites." (It was well known that Singh and Gebhart were friends.)

When Singh expressed this concern tactfully, Gebhart said that he wasn't interested in faculty members' views about the teaching loads of administrators. Gebhart said that he was working hard at his job and that members of Singh's department shouldn't question how many classes administrators teach. Singh raised his own concern that members of his department might accuse him of favoritism if he assigned only one course to Gebhart. Singh said he would like to leave Gebhart's schedule as it was, with Gebhart teaching two sections of the Organization Behavior course.

At this point, the two were interrupted in their discussion and the matter was left unresolved. Since it was Friday afternoon, Singh had the weekend to mull over his problem. He didn't want this incident to affect his friendship with Gebhart, but he also didn't want to be accused of favoritism by members of his department. Either result might reduce his ability to lead the management department effectively.

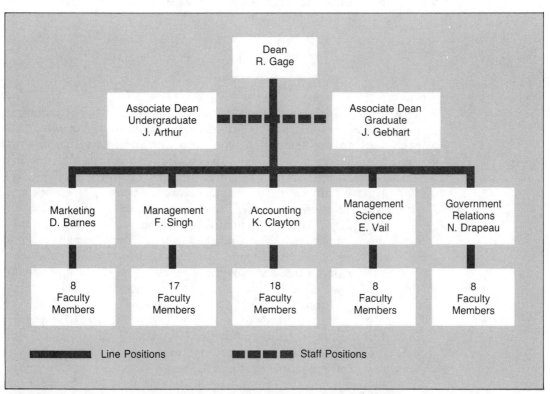

EXHIBIT 7-1 Organizational structure of the Faculty of Administration

KEY TERMS

delegation	single accountability	line organization
responsibility	chain of command	line and staff
authority	span of management	organization
centralization	organizational structure	functional authority
decentralization	functional structure	project organization
accountability	divisional structure	matrix organization

LEARNING OBJECTIVES

After completing this chapter you should be able to
1. Distinguish between authority, responsibility, and accountability.
2. Identify the advantages and disadvantages of centralization and decentralization.
3. Define delegation and describe the reasons for delegation.
4. Explain the basic principles related to authority, responsibility, and accountability.
5. Define span of management and identify the factors affecting it.
6. Identify the basic types of organizational structures and the advantages and disadvantages of each.

The incident with Singh and Gebhart illustrates just how frustrating it can be when functional relationships are unclear and/or when expectations are ambiguous. In order to perform effectively in any organization, managers must have a clear understanding of what's expected of them and what levels of responsibility and authority they possess. The primary purpose of an organizational structure is to clarify and communicate roles of managers and other personnel within the firm. As described in Chapter 6, organizing is the process of bringing together functions, human resources, and inputs for the purpose of achieving the objectives of the firm. There, we discussed the various functions that must be performed and how these functions might be grouped. In this chapter, we discuss patterns for organizing the functions, people, and formal relationships that exist in organizations.

What concepts and principles should managers understand and apply in performing the organizing function? We first discuss the ideas of delegation of responsibility, authority, and accountability. Next, we present several guidelines that can be used by managers to determine how well they are performing the organizing function. In the final section of the chapter, we discuss the concept of organizational design and the main types of organizational structures.

The first portion of the organizing process was described in Chapter 6. The remainder of the organizing process (see lower half of Exhibit 6-2) is presented in this chapter. As can be seen in the exhibit, an interrelationship exists among the concepts of delegation, responsibility, authority, and accountability.

DELEGATION

The process of making specific work assignments to individuals within the organization and providing them with the right or power to perform those functions is **delegation**. Delegation is one of the most significant concepts or practices affecting a manager's ability to perform the organizing function. However, delegation creates a risk for managers in that they are ultimately responsible for either the success or the failure of an operation. As a result, some managers attempt to reduce the risk by avoiding delegation and doing tasks themselves. Yet delegation of responsibility and authority is essential if managers are to provide opportunities for the development of people. One of the greatest failures of managers is the unwillingness or inability to delegate responsibility and authority.

**EXHIBIT 7-2
Reasons for
Delegation**

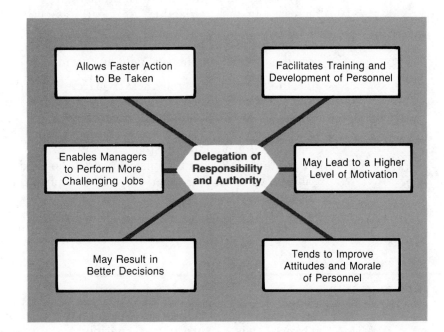

Delegation is essential if the work of the organization is to be accomplished effectively and efficiently. Some of the more significant reasons why delegation is important to the organizing process are illustrated in Exhibit 7-2.

Delegation of responsibility and authority generally leads to quicker action and faster, better decisions. Action can be taken much faster by subordinates if they do not have to go to their superiors for each decision. If an employee has a question about routine work procedures and the supervisor is required to go to the next level of management for a decision, the action is delayed and both employee and supervisor may become frustrated waiting for a decision. In general, when routine matters are handled at a higher level than necessary, time is wasted and work output is reduced. Delegation reduces these negative factors.

Delegation is an important facet of training and developing personnel in the organization. Employees or managers cannot learn to perform certain functions or make decisions unless they are given the opportunity. Delegation of responsibility and authority is essential if the firm wants to develop its personnel to assume more challenging and demanding jobs in the future. In addition, delegation may lead to higher levels of motivation among personnel since they believe they are being trusted and their managers have confidence in their abilities. Delegation not only builds the confidence of personnel but also improves attitudes and morale generally.

Through delegation of routine matters, managers are freer to perform especially challenging jobs. Delegation is a way to extend managers' capabilities; evidence suggests that managers recognize this. A recent study about graduating MBAs and practicing managers revealed that increases in task variability are clearly associated with increasing delegation.[1]

Despite these reasons for delegating responsibility and authority, certain potential problems should be considered:

- If employees do not tell their managers what they are doing, the managers may lose control and may not have time to correct any situation in which a problem occurs.
- Delegation can fail if the degree of responsibility and authority is not clearly defined and understood.
- If an employee given responsibility or authority does not possess the ability, skills, and/or experience to accomplish the jobs or make decisions, delegation can prove disastrous.
- Problems can result if an employee is given responsibility for a job but is not given sufficient authority to perform the task.

RESPONSIBILITY

Responsibility is an obligation to perform work activities. For example, if James Lewis, a manager, is responsible for the data processing center, he has an obligation to plan, organize, influence, control, and coordinate the work of computer operators and analysts. That's not all. He also has the obligation for the maintenance of the computer equipment and programs, plus numerous other activities that are essential to the success of the data processing department.

Responsibilities or obligations to perform certain functions must be clearly defined. Nothing is more frustrating to managers or workers than being unclear about the nature, scope, and details of their specific job responsibilities. For instance, consider the following conversation between Suzanne Belle, a lower-level manager for a large insurance company and her superior, Phil Reeve:

Belle: Is my unit responsible for processing the new commercial fire insurance policies or should Joe Davis's unit handle them?

Reeve: I don't think it really matters too much which unit handles these new policies as long as it's done correctly and thoroughly.

Belle: But what am I expected to do?

Reeve: I'll get back to you later on this — I'm busy at the moment.

Obviously Reeve's responses create ambiguous expectations for Belle. She doesn't know what her specific responsibilities are with regard to the new commercial fire insurance policies and gets no clarification from Reeve. Accomplishing the objective of processing the commercial fire insurance policies may be quite difficult. In order to perform any job adequately, an individual must understand the objectives, functions, and specific responsibilities. As was illustrated in Exhibit 6-2, objectives, functions, responsibilities, and authority must be closely integrated for the most effective organization.

Personnel in the organization are delegated responsibilities or work assignments by their superiors. When a manager delegates a responsibility to a subordinate, a relationship based on an obligation exists between the two. However, managers should remember an important point: managers cannot relieve themselves of any portion of the original responsibility; delegation allows only for someone else to do the work. Responsibility is a series of obligations established between two management levels in an organization.

AUTHORITY

Once managers have assigned responsibilities, they must delegate the authority necessary to accomplish the job. Viewed in terms of management, **authority** is the right to decide, to direct others to take action, or to perform certain duties in achieving organization goals. The concept of authority comprises at least 3 key characteristics:

- Authority is a right.
- Exercising authority involves the making of decisions and taking actions or performing of duties.

• Authority is used to achieve organization goals.

Authority is absolutely essential for managers to organize and direct the use of resources to attain the goals of the organization.

Division of Authority

Delegation of authority and responsibility cannot and should not be separated. In fact, a widely accepted basic principle of management states that authority should equal responsibility. In other words, a manager who is given a job to do (responsibility) should have adequate authority (or rights) to get the job done.

The concept as stated sounds good in theory. Yet one of the most common complaints of lower-level managers is that they have more responsibility than authority. Authority deals with rights, and these must be made specific in terms of the responsibility delegated. For example, if a supervisor is made responsible for staffing a department, he or she can be delegated any one of these degrees of authority:

• Rights to recruit, screen, and hire all personnel
• Rights to recruit, screen, and hire subject to prior approval from a higher-level manager
• No rights to recruit and screen (This function has been delegated to the personnel department, but the supervisor can accept or reject candidates.)
• No rights to hire. (The supervisor must take whomever the personnel department sends.)

In the last instance, the supervisor is responsible for getting a job done but lacks the authority to perform the job adequately by hiring personnel he or she considers best qualified.

Amount of Authority: Centralization versus Decentralization

Management must determine the appropriate degrees of responsibility and authority to be delegated. If, generally, a limited amount of authority is delegated, the organization is usually characterized as centralized. If, generally, a significant amount of authority is delegated to lower levels, the organization is described as decentralized.

Centralization and decentralization are theoretical extremes, with many gradations between. The real issue is not whether a company should decentralize but rather how much. In determining how decentralized an organization is, the nature and location of decision making must be assessed. In a structure using **centralization**, individual managers and workers at lower levels in the organization have a rather narrow range of decisions or actions they can initiate. By contrast, in a decentralized organization, the scope of authority to make decisions and take actions is rather broad for lower-level managers and workers. For example, in a highly centralized organizational structure, top management makes all decisions regarding, for instance, the hiring or firing of personnel, or the approval of purchasing of equipment and supplies. In a decentralized structure, lower-level managers may make these decisions.

Although recent trends in Canadian businesses seem to favor decentralization, a decentralized organization cannot be assumed to be better or more effective than a centralized organization. **Decentralization** is advocated by those who believe that lower-level managers should be given responsibility to make decisions. Such advocates believe that, when all decisions and orders come from one central source, organization members tend to act like robots — unthinking executors of someone else's commands. Decentralization usually creates a climate for more rapid growth and development of personnel, a primary responsibility of managers.

In addition to the different impacts on human behavior evident between decentralization and centralization, other factors can affect managers' decisions. Centralization generally:

- Produces uniformity of policy and action
- Results in few risks or errors by subordinates who lack either information or skill
- Utilizes the skills of central and specialized experts
- Enables closer control of operations.

Decentralization generally:

- Produces speedier decision making by reducing consultation
- Results in decisions that are more likely to be adapted to local conditions
- Results in greater interest and enthusiasm on the part of subordinates to whom authority has been entrusted (These expanded jobs provide excellent training experiences for possible promotion to higher levels.)
- Allows top management to use its time for more study and consideration of the basic goals, plans, and policies of the organization.

To what extent should authority be decentralized? Top management of an organization, in making this decision, must consider the organization's size and complexity, its geographic dispersion, the competence of its personnel, the adequacy of its communications system, the degree of organizational uniformity, the risk of costly poor decisions, and the history of the organization.

Size and Complexity of the Organization

The larger the organization, the more authority managers are forced to delegate. If the firm is engaged in many separate businesses, the limitations of expertise will usually lead to decentralization of authority to the heads of these units. Each major product group is likely to have different production problems, varying kinds of customers, and varied marketing channels. If speed and adaptability to changing conditions are necessary to success, decentralization is a must.

MANAGEMENT IN PRACTICE

Decentralization: A Key to Good Decisions

A rigid hierarchy in an organization may be the cause of poor decisions by top management and poor implementation by workers. The larger the hierarchy, the more information is filtered on its way up and down. Stephen Ferris, a management consultant for Berkley Developmental Resources, Inc. in Toronto, says that many top executives are isolated from the realities of the world around them because they have surrounded themselves with yes-men who screen out bad news and allow only good news to pass through. Too often a manager is so far removed from the lower levels in the organization that he or she has never even been into the factory or met a customer.

The remedy for this kind of problem is a more decentralized structure that stresses smaller work units, multidirectional communication (lateral, diagonal, and vertical), and shared decision making. Gordon Fehr, CEO of Pfizer Canada, Inc. of Montreal, says that his firm tries to have its decisions made as far down the hierarchy as possible. The best decisions are made by the people who know the work and the consequences of different actions. He thinks that decentralized decision making improves the effectiveness of decisions and the productivity and commitment of employees.

SOURCE   Adapted from M. A. Wente, "Remaking the Management Mind," *Canadian Business* (January 1983): 24.

Geographic Dispersion of the Organization

When the difficulties of size are compounded by geographic dispersion, the organization has a greater need for decentralization. General Motors Company is a prime example of decentralization because of size and geographic dispersion. However, not every decision or every function should be decentralized. Control of operations may have to be pushed down to lower levels in the organization, while control of financing may remain centralized. Because of the increasing complexity of government legislation affecting employment practices, centralization of labor relations is often established for purposes of uniformity throughout the company.

Competence of Personnel Available

A major limiting factor in many organizations is the adequacy or inadequacy of present personnel. If the organization has grown under centralized decision making and control, subordinates may be ill-equipped to start making major decisions. They were hired and trained to be followers, not leaders or decision makers. In some convenience store chains this deficiency has developed into a major problem. Store managers are promoted to supervisors because they are able to perform basic store functions, not because they make sound decisions. Supervisors are promoted to general managers not because they have made good decisions, but because they can ensure that lower managers follow standard operating procedures. A person who eventually makes it to the top is not equipped to cope with the large number of decisions to be made that are not based on established practices and procedures.

The chain will have few managers who are proven capable of independent thought and action; many may already have left the centralized firm.

Adequacy of Communications System

Size, complexity, and geographic dispersion lead to the delegation of larger amounts of authority to lower levels in the organization. Managers can seek to avoid decentralization through the development of a communication system that provides for speed, accuracy, and great amounts of information needed for top management to exercise centralized control. In effect, although size and geography may preclude being on the spot, a firm can try to control subordinates by detailing standards of performance and process and by ensuring that information flows quickly and accurately to the central authoritative position.

Uniformity of Policy Desired

If top management wants all its employees to behave consistently with respect to certain policies, the organization will be highly centralized. For example, if top management wants all customers to pay the same price for a certain product, it will not give its salespeople the authority to set or change prices. If, however, top management wants to "charge what the traffic will bear," it might allow salespeople to charge different prices to different customers. Top management must realize that, in a decentralized organization, not all lower-level managers will make the same decision when confronted with a certain problem. Therefore, if it is important that all employees follow a uniform policy — for example, obeying antitrust laws — then the organization will have to be centralized. If uniformity of policy is not critical, the organization may be increasingly decentralized.

Cost of Decisions

If the cost to an organization of a bad decision is going to be high, the right to make that decision will likely be centralized. The right to make decisions with low monetary risk may be given to lower-level managers. For example, a foreman would probably be allowed to spend a small amount of money on machine maintenance, but that same foreman would not have the authority to buy new machinery.

History of the Organization

The way in which the organization has grown over the years also influences the amount of decentralization. If the organization has grown by acquiring other organizations, it will tend to be more decentralized. This is because the addition of new products or services may involve top management in areas where it has no particular expertise. The managers of the acquired companies will likely have considerable freedom in running them.

If a company grows simply by selling more of what it is already involved in, it may remain fairly centralized. This is because top management of the company knows a great deal about its products and services and hence is able, if it wishes, to centralize decision-making authority at the top of the organization.

ACCOUNTABILITY

Once a person has been delegated sufficient authority to complete the task for which he or she is responsible, the person can be held accountable for results. **Accountability** is the final responsibility for results that a manager cannot delegate to someone else. Managers are accountable not only for their own actions and decisions but also for the actions of their subordinates, even though the responsibility and authority may have been delegated to their subordinates.

Before managers can be held accountable for results, they should be sure that certain conditions exist. First, responsibilities must be thoroughly and clearly understood. An individual who is unaware of what is expected should not be held accountable. Second, the person must be qualified and capable of fulfilling the obligation. It would be unwise to assign the responsibility and authority for performing engineering or accounting functions to individuals having no previous educational background and/or experience in these areas. Finally, sufficient authority to accomplish the task must be delegated. Assigning a manager the total profit responsibility for a department but no authority to hire or fire employees would mean that insufficient authority has been delegated. This manager should not be held accountable for results.

PRINCIPLES RELATED TO AUTHORITY, RESPONSIBILITY, AND ACCOUNTABILITY

Several important principles relate to the concepts of authority, responsibility, and accountability. These principles are summarized in the table on the opposite page and are then discussed briefly.

Single Accountability

Perhaps the most widely known principle of management governing the relationship of accountability is **single accountability,** also referred

Principles of Authority, Responsibility, and Accountability

Principle	Definition of	Reason for	Possible Causes of Violation	Possible Results of Violation
Single Accountability	A person should report to only one superior	Clarity and understanding, to ensure unity of effort and direction, and to avoid conflicts	Unclear definition of lines of authority	Dissatisfaction or frustration of employees and perhaps lower efficiency
Authority Should Equal Responsibility	The amount of authority and responsibility should be equal (responsibility = authority)	Allows work to be accomplished more efficiently, develops people, and reduces frustration	Fear on the part of some managers that subordinates might "take over"	Waste of energies and dissatisfaction of employees thereby reducing effectiveness
Chain of Command	There should be a clear definition of authority in the organization ("to go through channels")	Clarity of relationship avoids confusion and improves decision making and performance	Uncertainty on the part of the employee or a direct effort by the employee to avoid chain of command — often over disagreement with superior	Poor performance, confusion and/or dissatisfaction
Span of Management	There is a limit to the number of employees a manager can effectively supervise	Increased effectiveness in direction and control of a manager	Overloading a manager due to growth in number of personnel	Lack of efficiency and control resulting in poor performance

to as unity of command. Ideally, each employee should answer to only one immediate superior. Single accountability enables better coordination and understanding of what is required and improves discipline. An employee with two or more superiors can receive contradictory orders. Although single accountability is a sound concept, it does have certain limitations. Single accountability does not exist in many organizations, as we note later in this chapter. As the size of an organization increases, a person may be accountable to more than one superior.

Equal Authority and Responsibility

We have already noted that authority should equal responsibility. When this happens, the likelihood is much higher that work will be performed more efficiently and with a minimum amount of frustration on the part of personnel. By not delegating an adequate amount of authority with responsibility, managers are wasting employee energy and resources; dissatisfaction often results.

Suppose, for example, that a sales manager is given the responsibility of achieving certain sales goals but is not given the authority to discipline or reward salespeople. This situation is undesirable because the sales manager cannot do what is necessary to motivate the salespeople to achieve the organization's sales goals. Not an extreme case, many organizations inadvertently create situations where authority and responsibility are not equal. In universities, for example, department heads often face this problem. They are given the responsibility for developing high performance in teaching and research among faculty members, yet often do not have the authority necessary to attain it.

The Chain of Command

The principle of a **chain of command** suggests that there should be a clear definition of authority in the organization. This concept is often referred to as the scalar chain. Following this principle is crucial to management because its application clarifies relationships, avoids confusion, and improves decision making — leading to more effective performance. When the chain of command is in effect, a person communicates in the organization by going through channels established up and down the chain.

Span of Management

The number of employees a manager can effectively supervise is referred to as the **span of management**. The span of management, or span of control as it is sometimes called, is a fundamental principle related to the organizing function. Adherence to it enables the manager to achieve maximum effectiveness in organizing, motivating, and controlling personnel. According to the span of management principle, the number of employees a manager can effectively supervise or control is limited. The precise number or "span" varies according to the situation.

Determining the number of potential relationships that a manager might have with a certain number of subordinates was the subject of research by A. V. Graicunas, a management consultant during the 1930s. Graicunas derived a formula to determine the potential interactions or relationships that were possible when a manager had a given number of employees.[2] Graicunas's formula is: $R = n + n(n - 1) + n(2^{n-1} - 1)$, where R represents the number of relationships or interactions and n is the number of subordinates reporting to the manager.

According to Graicunas's formula, a manager with 2 employees would have 6 potential relationships. For example, if Ed has 2 subordinates, Joan and Sasha, the following interactions are possible.

EXHIBIT 7-3
Possible relationships with different number of employees

Employees	Potential Relationships
1	1
2	6
3	18
4	44
5	100
6	222
7	490
8	1080
9	2376
10	5210
11	10 342
12	24 708

Number of Relationships

2	Ed may meet and talk with Joan *or* Ed may meet and talk with Sasha	= *direct relationships*
2	Ed may meet and talk with Joan with Sasha present *or* vice versa	= *group relationships*
2	Joan may interact with Sasha without Ed *or* Sasha may meet with Joan without Ed	= *cross-relationships*

6

As Exhibit 7-3 shows, each additional employee a manager supervises creates a substantial number of additional relationships.

Factors Affecting the Span of Management

In most private and public-sector organizations, spans of management have historically been relatively narrow, usually ranging from 6 to 15 employees per manager. More restricted spans of management permit closer supervision of personnel but tend to create tall organizational structures with a large number of levels; this result may cause difficulties in communications. Larger or wider spans result in relatively fewer levels or flat organizations and greater freedom for the individual employee. (See Exhibit 7-4, in which both organizations have a total of 29 employees.) While managers agree that the span of management is a fundamentally valid concept, the exact number of subordinates that one manager can effectively supervise cannot be determined precisely. However, a number of factors affect the span of management:

- Complexity of the work
- Degree of similarity to other work
- Degree of interdependence with other work
- Stability of the organization and situation
- Degree of standardization of the work
- Qualifications, skills, expertise, and experience of the manager
- Qualifications, skills, experience, and motivation of the employees
- Type of technology.

In general, the more complex the work, the narrower the span of management. The span can be wider if a manager is supervising employees performing similar jobs. If jobs are closely interlocked and interdependent, a manager may have greater problems with coordination, creating the need for a rather limited span of management. Similarly, if the organization is operating in a rapidly changing environment, a narrow span may prove to be more effective. On the other hand, the establishment of numerous standards increases predictability and provides the basis for effective control, thereby resulting in a wider effective span. Another key factor affecting the span of management is the qualifications of managers and nonmanagerial personnel. Man-

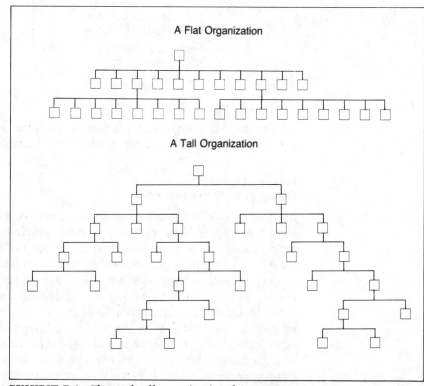

EXHIBIT 7-4   Flat and tall organizational structures

agers and employees who are highly skilled, experienced, and motivated generally can operate with wider spans of management and with less supervision. But narrow spans may result in a higher commitment to the organization.[3]

Finally, technology can have a significant impact on the span of management. Joan Woodward, a British researcher who conducted studies in 100 English manufacturing firms, discovered that the type of technology had a significant impact on the spans of management actually used in businesses. Woodward classified production technology on the basis of:

- Unit or small batch processing (made-to-order goods such as custom-tailored clothing)
- Mass production (assembly-line operations)
- Process production with continuous long runs of a standardized product (such as oil, chemicals, or pharmaceuticals).

She discovered that spans of management were widest in those firms using mass production technology. The jobs in mass production tend to be more routine and similar to one another, thereby leading to wider effective spans of management.[4] Unit and process production had narrower spans.

ORGANIZATIONAL STRUCTURES

In Chapter 6, we discussed functional areas within an organization as part of the basic management function of organizing. We also discussed the ideas of specialization and departmentation that help organizations to perform those important functions more effectively. In this chapter, we discuss additional concepts that managers use in organizing: delegation of responsibility and authority, accountability, and the span of management. Throughout our discussions, the possible **organizational structure** has been noted as crucial to effective organizing. The choice of type of departmentation and of overall organizational structure can be as significant to new companies as to companies that have been in existence for many years. If top management of an existing company assesses that its organizing function is ineffective, it may decide that reorganization — changing the structure — will improve performance.

Although the complex hierarchies of large businesses spring to mind at the mention of organizational structures, every firm has a structure. A smaller firm may not have a diagram or chart of its organizational structure, but a structure exists nevertheless. Small businesses usually have straightforward structures that may be informal and highly changeable. By contrast, larger, more diverse, and more complex organizations usually have a strictly formalized structure. But that doesn't mean the structure of larger firms is so rigid that it cannot change.

Determining the most appropriate organizational structure is not a simple matter. Considerable experimentation and analysis is necessary before a firm is in a position to adopt a suitable structure for its particular kind of work. Even so, changes in the firm's external environment or in its overall objectives may result in further structural experimentation or analysis. The frequency with which some companies reorganize is an indication of how actively they are searching for the most workable structure. Newly formed high-technology companies are likely to reorganize frequently; but, as noted earlier, some long-established Canadian industrial firms may introduce structural changes to improve their effectiveness.

The structure of an organization provides guidelines essential for effective employee performance and overall success. The structure defines and clarifies the lines of responsibility and authority within the firm and assists management in coordinating overall operation. The structure of an organization is shown in its organizational chart, which depicts diagrammatically a firm's formal structure at a point in time. An organizational chart does not indicate the extent to which authority is delegated, what the organization's objectives are, the comparative importance of the various jobs in the organization, or the informal relationships that spontaneously arise in the organization over time. (The informal organization is discussed in Chapter 8.)

A cursory glance at the organizational charts of several different organizations presents what appears to be an almost infinite variety of structures. However, a close examination of these structures shows that most of them fit into one of two basic categories: functional or divisional.

The Functional Structure

The oldest and most commonly used is the **functional structure**, similar in concept to departmentation by function. Both are established on the basis of the key functions the organization must perform in order to reach its objectives. In Chapter 6, we showed how departmentation by function would look in a traditional manufacturing firm. (Refer to Exhibit 6-6.) Examples of how a functional structure looks in other kinds of organizations are shown in Exhibit 7-5.

An analysis of the examples in exhibits 6-6 and 7-5 clearly shows that the work of the various functional areas must be coordinated by some higher authority. In the manufacturing firm in Exhibit 6-6, the functions of personnel, engineering, production, marketing, and finance must be coordinated by the president because not one of these functional areas can by itself achieve organization goals.

Advantages of the Functional Structure

Functional structure is common because it has several advantages. First, it encourages specialization of labor. Specialization normally leads

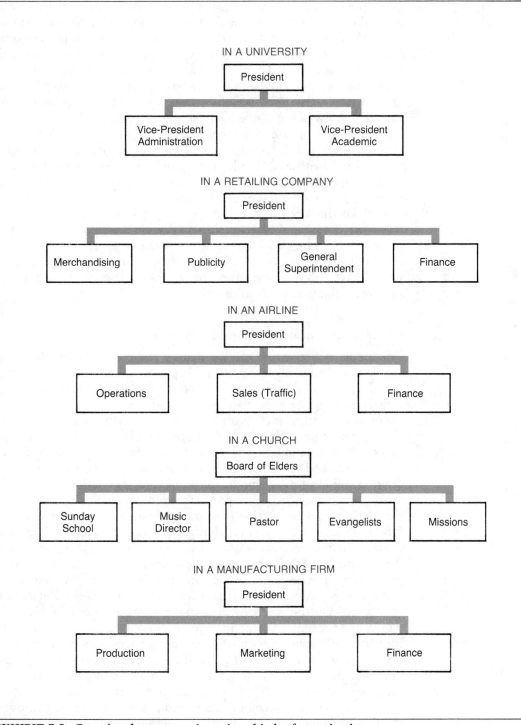

EXHIBIT 7-5 **Functional structures in various kinds of organizations**

to efficiency in the performance of tasks. A person who is a specialist in marketing, for example, will likely do a better marketing job than a person who must know a little about marketing in addition to other jobs. The functional structure therefore promotes a career path for people with specialized skills. Second, employees understand the structure. It is easy for employees to understand that specialized functional areas exist in the firm and that these specialized areas must work together. As well, employees in each of the areas work with people who have training similar to theirs; task accomplishment is enhanced because these employees see that they have something in common with their coworkers. Finally, functional structure eliminates duplication. In the functional structure, there is only one marketing department, or one production department. With only one department in each of the key functions, it has tight control over the activities being performed and little duplication of activities occurs. It is very unlikely that two departments would each be working on, say, the effects of advertising on sales without being aware that another group was working on the same question. Rather, all work is centrally coordinated; duplication is minimal.

Disadvantages of the Functional Structure

The functional structure can have some disadvantages. Employees do not have a systems perspective. Perhaps the major failing of the functional structure is that employees become overly concerned with activities in their own specialized area and are not concerned enough about coordinating their work with other areas of specialization. A classic example of this problem is the conflict that arises between marketing and production in many firms. Marketing wants a diverse product line and short delivery times in order to maximize sales; production wants a limited product line and long production runs in order to minimize costs. Another potential problem with functional structure is that no one function is accountable for results. Since no single function can achieve organization goals by itself, each one can argue that it is blameless if the organization as a whole doesn't perform well. If a company suffers a financial loss, who is to blame? marketing? production? personnel? finance? The answer is usually not clear.

A serious disadvantage of a functional structure is the lack of training for top management. Since each manager in a functional structure works in a specialized area, he or she may not be getting good training for truly top management positions. The top person in an organization must be able to see how all parts of the organization work together, but a person who has come up through the ranks in a specialized area may have difficulty seeing the significance of functional areas outside his or her own specialization. As a result, certain functions (those of the person's previous experience) may get preferred treatment and the total organization suffers.

The Divisional Structure

The functional structure's disadvantages can make it inappropriate for some companies. In fact, many companies have adopted instead the **divisional structure**. The organization is broken down into divisions; each division operates as a semiautonomous unit and as a profit center. The divisions may be formed on the same basis as departmentation by product, customer, or geography. (Refer to exhibits 6-7, 6-8 and 6-9.) Whatever basis is used, each division operates almost as a separate business. Divisional performance can be assessed each year by the parent company because each division behaves as a separate company. Firms with this structure are often called conglomerates.

Advantages of the Divisional Structure

The divisional structure is suitable for some companies because of its advantages. First, expansion is facilitated. If the parent company wishes to expand into additional lines of work, it can simply add another division to focus on this new line of work. Since many companies seem very interested in growth, this advantage is important. Second, accountability is increased. Each of the divisions is responsible for reaching its own profit targets; thus, there is much more discipline than in the functional structure. Managers within each division must think constantly in terms of actions that will generate profits for the division.

A further advantage of the divisional structure is that expertise is built within each division. If a division is organized around products, the managers within that division will have detailed knowledge about those products. If a division is organized around geography, managers in that division will have detailed knowledge about local markets. Knowledge of this type benefits the division and increases the chance of good performance. Finally, divisional structure allows for training for top management. Since the head of a division is really acting in the role of a chief executive overseeing all functional areas, the divisional structure is a good training ground for top managers. A person who successfully headed a division could likely take over an independent company because of his or her previous experience as a top manager. Also, since one firm will have several divisions — each with its own "top management" — it will have a pool of experienced managers as candidates for promotion.

Disadvantages of the Divisional Structure

In spite of these substantial advantages, the divisional structure has some potential problems. Certain activities, for example, may be duplicated. It is quite likely that two (or more) divisions in a conglomerate could be working on the same problem. If these different divisions do not communicate with each other about what they are doing (and often they do not), costly duplication can result. If two divisions are working on a new rust-inhibiting paint but are unaware of each other's work, much less may be accomplished and higher costs incurred than if their work were coordinated. This duplication of effort is probably the greatest disadvantage of the divisional structure. A further disadvantage may be that specialists' communication is limited. Each division in a conglomerate will have specialists (chemists, engineers, or geologists) with skills that are relevant for that division. The communication between, say, engineers working in different divisions may be infrequent. Various studies have shown that ideas often emerge when specialists have in-person discussions about problems they are working on.

Another serious disadvantage is that the conglomerate may have no strategy for adding divisions. One of the criticisms of the divisional structure is that the parent company can become involved in such a diverse set of activities that no one has an overview of the entire organization. In the 1970s, for example, many conglomerates were forced to get rid of certain divisions because they were performing poorly, but no one in the parent company knew enough about the divisions' activities to take appropriate remedial action.

Whether an organization uses a functional or divisional structure, it must make a decision about whether or not to use staff experts. If it decides not to use them, the firm maintains a simple line organization; if it does use them, the firm has a line and staff organizational structure. The distinction between these two organizational structures is discussed below.

Line Organization

A structure using **line organization** shows the direct, vertical relationships among different levels within the firm. A pure line organization would consist of personnel managing only those functions essential to the successful existence of the firm. In a line organizational structure, authority follows the chain of command. Exhibit 7-6 is an illustration of a simple three-level line organizational structure for a manufacturing company. Several advantages are associated with the pure line organizational structure.

- A line structure can simplify and clarify responsibility, authority, and accountability relationships within the organization. The levels of responsibility and authority of personnel operating within a line organization are precise and understandable.
- A line structure promotes fast decision making and allows the organization to change directions more rapidly, since few people must be consulted when problems arise.
- Since pure line organizations are small, a feeling of closeness of management to the employees is easily promoted and all personnal usually have an opportunity to know what's going on within the firm.

Despite these advantages, line organization also has certain disadvantages. The major disadvantage is its increasing lack of effectiveness as the firm grows larger. At some point, speed and flexibility do not offset the lack of specialized knowledge and skills. In other words, a line structure may force individual managers to wear too many hats, thereby reducing their effectiveness. In a line organizational structure, the firm may become overly dependent on one person or a few key people who can perform numerous jobs. If the organization is to remain purely line, one solution is for management to seek help by creating additional levels of organization to share the managerial load. This, however, will result in a lengthening of the chain of command and a consequent loss of some of the values of speed, flexibility, and central control.

Line and Staff Organization

Suppose Bill Smith starts a company and over a period of several years the firm grows and becomes quite successful. Smith (now president) heads an organization that looks like the one shown in Exhibit 7-7. This is a line organization: all the positions in the organization are in the direct line of authority from the top of the firm down to the bottom.

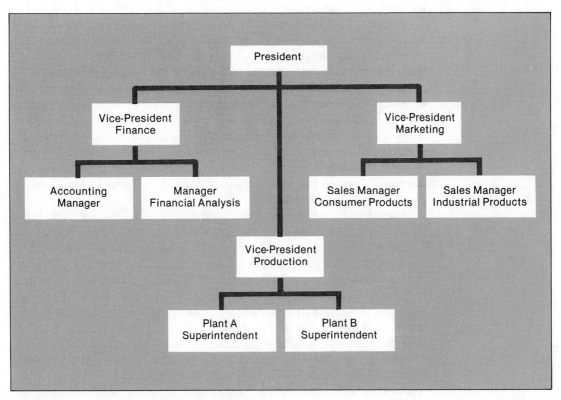

EXHIBIT 7-6 A line organizational structure

Each level in the organization is subordinate to the ones above it, and there are no advisory specialists. This structure might work very well as long as the company does not get too large. However, with increased growth the need for specialized experts almost surely will emerge. If these experts are added to the organization, the structure is called a **line and staff organization**. Depending on the organization, these experts might be personnel experts, legal advisors, market researchers, accountants, industrial engineers, or computer programmers. (See Exhibit 7-8.)

The line and staff structure preserves the authority relationships in organizations in the face of primary and secondary goals. In the line and staff organization, certain functions are considered central to goal attainment (line functions), and others are considered secondary (staff functions). The principle of line and staff relationships states that line personnel have command authority in their functional areas; staff personnel, on the other hand, are said to have the right to provide advice to line personnel in their (staff) field of expertise. Strictly speaking, it is incorrect to say that line functions are more important and staff functions are less important, since in some instances staff functions, while secondary in relation to goals, are nevertheless quite significant. In these situations, staff people usually possess **functional authority**, which can make them equivalent to the line, although such situations are generally temporary.

An example of the temporary prominence of a staff expert in a coal mine operation would be a safety engineer. While safety is not a primary function of the organization — it is not the organization's main objective to produce safe mines — safety is nevertheless so crucial to productivity that the safety engineer is given the equivalent of line authority. This permits the production manager of the mine to retain full (line) authority and accountability over the complete operation of the mine but, should the situation require, allows the safety engineer to exert influence in matters of mine safety. In this instance, the production manager would likely have a general safety orientation and training, whereas the safety engineer would be highly specialized in the field of safety engineering.

Four separate types of specialized staff units can be identified: (1) personal, (2) advisory, (3) service, and (4) control. Personal staff (for example, the executive assistant to the president) assist specific line managers but generally do not act for them in their absence. Advisory staff (for example, personnel, marketing research) advise line managers in areas where the staff has particular expertise. Service staff provide a specific service to line managers (for example, testing and interviewing of prospective applicants by the personnel department). Control staff (for example, accounting, quality control) are those with the responsibility of controlling some aspect of organizational performance, although they theoretically still only provide advice.

It is possible for one unit to perform more than one of these functions. For example, the personnel department may advise line managers on

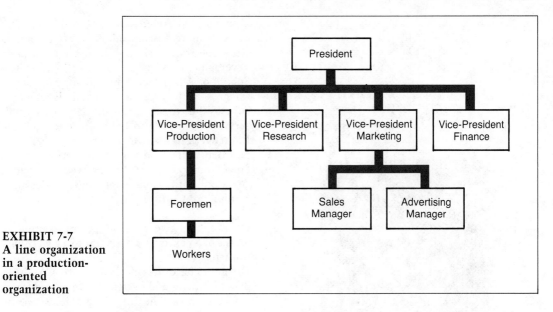

EXHIBIT 7-7
A line organization in a production-oriented organization

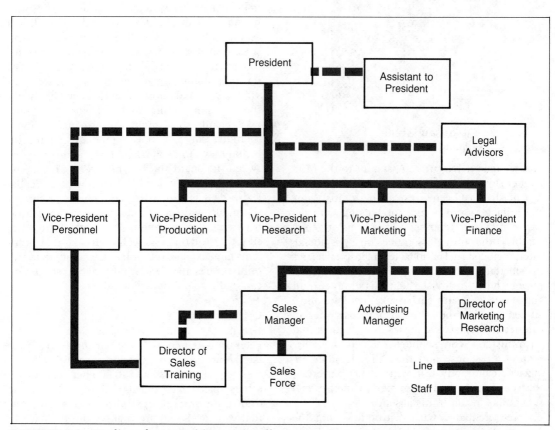

EXHIBIT 7-8   Outline of a typical line and staff structure in a production- oriented organization

TALKING TO MANAGERS

Susan Green
Executive Assistant

Susan Green is Executive Assistant to the Minister of Hospitals and Medical Care for the province of Alberta. Green is responsible for managing the minister's office, and for liaising with departmental staff; Members of the Legislative Assembly; other ministers' offices on a provincial, interprovincial, and national level; hospital boards in Alberta; the media; and the public. It is her responsibility to advise the minister on current and sensitive health care issues, review policy, and ensure that the minister is prepared for all cabinet and legislative duties. She ensures that all ministerial correspondence receives the appropriate response and that all telephone inquiries are promptly dealt with. She also oversees the scheduling of the minister's itinerary and acts on his behalf in his absence.

Green graduated with distinction from the University of Alberta in 1974 with a Bachelor of Arts in recreation administration and has worked toward a Masters degree in community development. A recent graduate of the Banff School of Advanced Management, she has also taken a variety of professional development courses during her career in the Alberta public service. From 1974 to 1979, Green was a Senior Intergovernmental Officer in the Alberta Department of Federal and Intergovernmental Affairs. From 1979 to 1983, she served as Executive Assistant to the Honourable Mary LeMessurier, Minister of Culture.

Q: Can you give us some specific examples of duties of an executive assistant to a government minister?
Green: The duties of an Executive Assistant (EA) are many and varied. An MLA may want advice on how a health care problem of a constituent might be addressed, or when new hospital or nursing home beds will be added to his or her constituency, or how to deal with hospital boundary disputes. Departmental staff will call seeking advice and clarification on policy directives from the minister. I might call my counterpart in the federal government asking for information on any number of issues. I will provide background information to the media should the minister be unavailable. I work with hospital boards throughout the province, helping them to resolve a variety of problems. That resolution may only come about after a meeting between the board and the minister, or it may be something easily handled by a few phone calls. I also deal with constituents and members of the public who may, in some way, have been frustrated by the system. In general, I must ensure that the office is well managed, that problems are expeditiously handled, and that the minister has all relevant information so that he can make sound policy decisions.

Q: Are most EA positions similar?
Green: At some very fundamental level, yes. Each of us is here to serve our respective ministers; but EAs vary in terms of specifics. Some EAs receive as little as $20,000 per year, while others make over $50,000. Some have a great deal of informal power, while others have virtually none. Some are highly educated, while

others have little formal education. Some have considerable technical training, while others are strong in administration.

I have had two EA positions and each was quite different. For instance, many health care issues, including the development of the Canada Health Act, have been foremost in the minds of Canadians over the past 2 years. Naturally, this entailed considerable policy review, very involved federal/provincial interchanges, and responses on the minister's behalf to sometimes very stiff public criticism.

Q: Exactly what kind of authority do you have?
Green: My authority comes directly from the minister. I am expected to be acting on his behalf at all times. This means I have to be very sensitive to those issues that require actual ministerial approval and those that do not. I suppose I could state it most succinctly this way: on many matters which are purely administrative, I have considerable latitude in terms of authority. For example, if there is a departmental regulation that may be punitive in an exceptional case, I could ask the department to suspend the rule in the interest of compassion for an individual. I would have little formal authority if a major policy issue was at stake, such as a change in legislation. It is the minister who is ultimately answerable to the public and the minister must provide this input. Even there, though, I could give the minister both editorial and substantive advice on draft legislation. Whether or not he would incorporate my views would naturally be his decision.

Q: When you are seen as not speaking directly for the minister, do people still see you as having authority?
Green: It depends. People may have difficulty deciding how much authority I have on a given issue because they don't know how extensively (or if) the minister and I have already discussed it. I suppose they are always wondering whether I have the minister's ear on some issue or not. If they perceive that I do, they will probably be influenced by my views. If they think I'm giving an opinion on my own, they probably won't be unduly influenced. You must recognize that, in a job like mine, formal authority is only part of the total equation. The ability to influence

people is crucial precisely because my formal authority is often ill-defined.

In this general vein, I would also like to say that it is not enough for an EA to just do the job well; you must be able to work effectively with people and go beyond the minimum expected from you. If you do that, people are more likely to respect you and cooperate with you, even though you may not have any formal authority over them. To be effective in this job, you must understand how the system works, and that includes both the formal and informal system. It is particularly important to understand the informal system; if you don't your career will suffer.

Q: Are you saying that organization politics plays a big role in your job?
Green: I think organization politics plays a big role in almost any managerial job.

Q: Do you have any difficulties coping with organization politics?
Green: I don't think so, but I recently read a management consulting report that said that one of the reasons many women experience some difficulty in management is that they have not learned the skills necessary to engage in effective political behavior. Regardless of what people may think of political behavior, it is an important element in management jobs.

Q: Do you experience any frustration because you do not have formal authority to order people to do something you want done?
Green: No. First, I request information or recommend that a particular action be taken because I am representing the minister and believe that the response is essential for the minister to carry out his duties effectively. Second, I believe I have a management style which motivates people to get information for me, or to give me help when I need it. If you accept the idea that people want to do a good job and that they are interested in the development of their careers, and you keep those things in mind when you deal with people, you can usually structure your requests in such a way that other people will help you out when you need it. With that kind of support, you should be quite successful in management. However, you can't demand that kind of support; you have to earn it.

the appropriateness of recognizing a particular labor union. That same department may also provide a service by procuring and training needed production and sales personnel. The personnel department also exercises control by, for instance, auditing salaries actually paid to ensure conformity to line-approved pay ranges.

Some staff units are predominantly one or another in character. For example, a staff economist may advise the establishment of long-range plans, a maintenance staff unit repairs plant and equipment, and a quality control staff enforces authorized product standards. The potential for conflicts in coordination between line and staff tends to increase from advice to service to control. Advice can be ignored, but service is needed, and control is often unavoidable.

There are both advantages and disadvantages of a line and staff organizational structure. The primary advantage is that it uses the expertise of specialists. The actions of a manager can be more systematic by concentrated and skillful analysis of business problems. In addition, the manager's effective span of management can be widened — he or she can supervise more people. Some staff personnel may operate as an extension of a manager to assist in coordination and control.

Despite the fact that a line and staff structure allows for increased flexibility and specialization, it may create conflicts. When a firm introduces various specialists into its organization, its line managers may believe they have lost authority over certain specialized functions. These managers do not want staff specialists telling them what to do or how to do it, even though they recognize the specialists' knowledge and expertise. To maintain good working relations, a firm should introduce staff personnel without destroying single accountability. The right of the line manager still remains, although the ability to exercise this right may have been considerably weakened. The problem is not so much the type of structure but the individual personnel within it. Some staff personnel have difficulty adjusting to the role of adviser, especially if line managers are reluctant to accept their advice. Staff personnel may resent not having authority, causing further conflict.

Another potential problem of a line and staff structure is that staff specialists often seek to enlarge their personal influence by assuming line authority in their specialty. Since the fundamental purpose of all staff is to produce greater economy and effectiveness of operation, staff should attempt to introduce changes that result in more efficiency. These changes will not always be welcomed by line personnel. Thus, the introduction of specialized, noncommand personnel into what was a fairly simple organizational structure can create ambiguity about authority and responsibility.

Functional Authority

A pure line organizational structure has very limited use of specialists by management. The line and staff organizational structure frequently uses specialists. If a staff specialist is given authority over a line man-

MANAGEMENT IN PRACTICE

The Executive Assistant

The executive assistant position exists in many organizations. People who are executive assistants are usually one of three types. First, they can be staff people up from the ranks. For example, Lyn Johnson is the executive assistant to the president of Shell Oil. In her position she organizes most of the president's official encounters with people outside Shell Oil. This involves assisting the president in choosing speaking engagements, helping with speech writing, and keeping him up to date on a variety of issues.

Another kind of executive assistant is the one with a few years of line experience, who is a "comer" in the company but needs some high-level experience. Ben Heineman of Northwest Industries takes bright young executives, makes them his special assistant for a couple of years, and then puts them into top line positions. One former assistant, for example, became president of one of Northwest's chemical subsidiaries and then moved up to vice-president of Northwest.

The third type of executive assistant is one who may be as old or older than the boss. This may be a person who realizes that he or she won't make it to a top line position, but who likes having the power that goes along with reporting to a top executive.

Other people in the organization are often suspicious of executive assistants because they don't know how much power the assistant has or how favorably the boss views the assistant. Another potential problem is that the executive assistant can lose his or her own identity in the shadow of the boss. One executive assistant quit soon after his boss did because he found he had no reputation or identity as an executive in his own right.

SOURCE Walter Kiechel, "The Executive Assistant," *Fortune* (November 15, 1982): 177–180.

ager with regard to the staff person's specialty, a **functional authority** relationship has been created. Functional authority is typically limited to the areas in which the staff person is an expert. The chain of command of line authority and the notion of single accountability is broken, creating multiple accountability.

Although few firms are established completely on a functional authority basis, increasing numbers of companies have some staff specialists with functional authority over some line executives. If a firm considers a function to be crucial, it may need the specialist to exercise direct rather than advisory authority. The violation of single accountability is undertaken deliberately. The possible losses resulting from confusion or from conflicting orders from multiple sources may be more than offset by increased effectiveness in the performance of the specialty.

Good examples of specialties that have been given functional authority in many organizations include quality control, safety, and labor relations. (See Exhibit 7-9.) Quality control is a prominent function in most manufacturing organizations, and its level of authority and stature within organizations has increased over the years. A staff quality control department would merely advise; if, however, that unit is given the authority, or right, to issue orders (for example, to correct defects) in its own name, it has functional authority.

Likewise, safety and labor relations specialists may exercise functional authority over personnel in other areas of the organization, but only in relation to their specialties. A safety manager may issue compliance guidelines and give direct interpretations of provincial health and safety regulations; a labor relations specialist often will have complete authority in contract negotiations with the union. In each of these examples, the traditional chain of command has been split. As long as this splitting process is restricted, coordination and unity of action are not in real danger. Many organizations that use functional authority attempt to confine its impact to managerial rather than operative levels. Thus, a department supervisor may have to account to more than one superior, but the employees are protected from this possible confusion.

Despite the advantages of functional authority, two potential problems can result: (1) the conflicts from the violation of the principle of single accountability, and (2) the tendency to keep authority centralized at higher levels in the organization. If functional authority is used extensively, the line department supervisor may become little more than a figurehead. The overall structure can become complicated when corresponding functional specialists work at various levels in one organization.

Project and Matrix Organizations

The line and line and staff structures have been the traditional approaches. The primary concern of these forms of managerial organizing has been the establishment and distribution of authority to coordinate and control the firm by emphasizing vertical, rather than horizontal, relationships. However, work processes may flow horizontally, diagonally, up, or down, depending on the problem and distribution of talents. Work requirements often result in the need for organizing, based on the specific nature of work projects. Two forms of organizing that have emerged to cope with this challenge are referred to as project or matrix organizations. The key element in both project and matrix organizations is the creation of a structure in which managers and professionals have more than one superior.

A **project organization** provides a highly effective means by which all of the necessary human talent and physical resources can be focused for a time on a specific project or goal. It is a temporary organizational structure designed to achieve specific results by using a team of specialists from different functional areas within the organization. The team focuses all of its energies and skills on the assigned project. Once the specific project has been completed, the project team is broken up and personnel are reassigned to their regular positions in the organization. Many business firms and government agencies make use of project teams or task forces to concentrate their efforts on a specific project assignment like the development of a new product or new technology or the construction of a new plant.

The project organization is used extensively by Canadian firms. The construction of hydroelectric generating stations is a case in point. These large-scale projects are headed by a project manager who oversees all aspects of the construction. When the station is completed, it is turned over to the operating people and then becomes part of the traditional structure of the provincial hydroelectric utility. The project organization is also used in the technological development in the prairie tar sands. The extraction of energy resources from this area is a unique and complex activity; the project organization has proven useful for coordinating the many elements needed to extract oil from the tar sands.

Project organization is most appropriate when work is:

• Definable, in terms of both a specific goal and target date for completion that have been established
• Unique and unfamiliar to the existing structure
• Complex, with respect to interdependence of activities and specialized skills necessary to accomplishment
• Critical, in terms of possible gain or loss
• Temporary, with respect to duration of need.

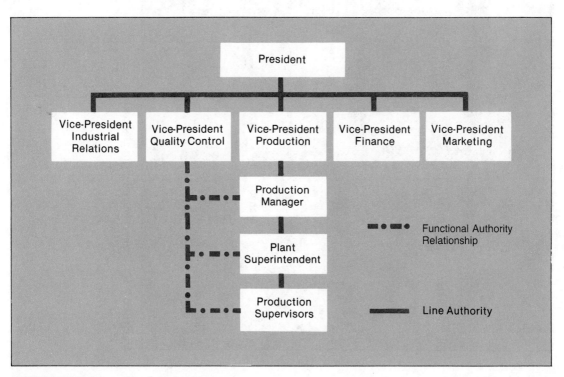

EXHIBIT 7-9 Functional authority

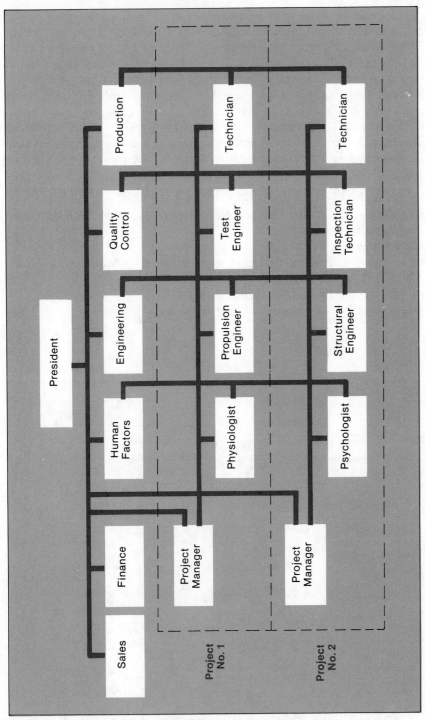

EXHIBIT 7-10 Project organizational structure

Exhibit 7-10 illustrates a simplified project organization that is attached to an existing structure. Personnel are assigned to the project from the existing structure and work under the direction and control of the project manager. The project manager specifies what effort is needed and when work will be performed, while the individual department managers may decide who in their unit is to do the work and how it is to be accomplished. Home base for most personnel is the existing department — engineering, production, purchasing, personnel, or research and development.

The authority over the four project members is shared by both the project manager and the functional managers in the existing structure. The specialists are temporarily on loan to spend a portion of their time on the project assignment. However, authority of personnel seems to be one of the crucial issues of the project organization. A deliberate conflict has been established between the project manager and managers within the existing structure. The authority relationships are overlapping, presumably in the interest of ensuring that all problems will be covered.

Project managers and department heads are often forced into using means other than formal authority to accomplish results. Informal relationships become more important than formal prescriptions of authority. In the event of conflict and dispute, discussion and consensus are required rather than forceful compliance by threat or punishment. Full and free communication, regardless of formal rank, is required among those working on the project. More attention is allocated to roles and competence in relation to the project than to formal levels of authority.

Project organizations are temporary attachments to existing structures. When this concept is introduced in a more lasting form, it is usually referred to as a **matrix organization**; it is often used when the firm must be highly responsive to a rapidly changing external environment. For example, an electronics firm operating in a highly competitive market with rapidly changing technology might find that the matrix organization facilitates quick response to this environment. The matrix organization, however, requires the use of an effective coordinating mechanism to offset the negative effects of dual authority.[5] Matrix organizational structures have been used successfully in such industries as banking, chemicals, computers, and electronics.

Matrix organizations have functional managers and product managers. Functional managers are in charge of such specialized resources as production, quality control, inventories, scheduling, and selling. Product managers are in charge of one or more products; they are authorized to prepare product strategies and call on the various functional managers for the necessary resources. When a firm moves to a matrix organizational structure, its functional managers must realize that they will lose some of their authority and will have to take some direction from the product managers, who have budgets to purchase internal resources.

Despite limitations, the effectiveness of the project and matrix organizations demonstrates that people can work for two or more managers and that managers can effectively influence those over whom they have no clear authority. The possibility of conflict and frustration is a risk, but the opportunity for prompt, efficient goal accomplishment is great.

OPENING INCIDENT REVISITED

The Faculty of Administration

Frank Singh, head of the department of management, was wondering how to resolve the scheduling problem that had arisen between himself and John Gebhart, the associate dean of the faculty. Singh was concerned that he would get complaints no matter what decision he made. If he agreed with Gebhart, he would be accused of favoritism; if he agreed with members of his department, Gebhart would be dissatisfied.

This incident demonstrates how problems can arise in organizations when authority and responsibility are not equal and when job responsibilities are not clearly stated. Singh believes he has the responsibility to assign Gebhart's class load, but doesn't feel he has the authority to do so. The inequality of authority and responsibility is causing Singh some difficulty, but the solution to his problem is quite straightforward.

Singh shouldn't be deciding how many classes Gebhart should teach because Gebhart doesn't report to Singh. Exhibit 7-1 clearly shows that Gebhart reports to the dean, not to Singh. Therefore, the only person who has the authority to determine Gebhart's teaching load is the dean. The dean should decide what proportion of Gebhart's time should be spent teaching and what proportion should be spent on administrative work; once this information is conveyed to Singh, he can assign the number of classes that the dean thinks is appropriate. Singh should not get caught up in trying to make a decision he has no authority to make.

Situations like this can and do arise frequently in organizations. Why? Perhaps people get so involved in trying to get their work done that they forget to analyze fundamental issues like equating authority and responsibility.

SUMMARY

Determining the appropriate levels of responsibility and authority is essential to sound organizing. Derived from functions, responsibility is an obligation to perform certain work activities. It is crucial to the success of a firm that responsibilities be clearly defined. Once responsibilities have been assigned to personnel, superiors must then delegate enough authority to get the job done. Authority is the right to decide, to direct others to take action, or to perform certain duties in achieving an organization's goals. A basic principle of management is that authority should equal responsibility. The process of making specific work assignments to individuals within the organization and giving them the authority to perform these functions is known as delegation. Delegation is an important concept if work is to be accomplished and people in the organization are to develop expertise. Once authority has been delegated, an individual can then be held accountable for results. Accountability is the final responsibility for results that a manager cannot delegate to someone else.

Depending on the extent of the delegation of authority, an organization is said to be either centralized or decentralized. In a centralized organization, decisions are made primarily by top management, whereas in a decentralized structure, lower-level managers in the organization play a more active role in making decisions. The four important principles of authority, responsibility, and accountability that must be considered in the delegation process are:

- *Single accountability.* A person should have only one superior.
- *Authority should equal responsibility.*
- *A chain of command.* Clear definition of authority (through channels).
- *Span of management.* A limit to the number of people a manager can supervise effectively.

The means for organizing the functions, resources, and the formal relationships is the organizational structure, of which there are two basic types: functional and divisional. Within both these general categories we can find three other structural variations: line, line and staff, and project or matrix. A line structure is the simplest and most basic. The line and staff structure allows for increased flexibility and specialization with the introduction of staff specialists who serve as advisers. However, it creates conflicts over authority. In the line and staff structure, staff specialists are given authority to issue orders in designated areas of work. Finally, project and matrix organizational structures provide a means by which all of the necessary human talent and physical resources are allocated for a time to a specific project.

REVIEW QUESTIONS

1. Define and illustrate the following:
   a. responsibility
   b. authority
   c. accountability.
2. What is meant by centralization and decentralization?
3. What are the advantages and disadvantages of centralization and decentralization?
4. Briefly describe the primary factors to be considered in determining the degree of centralization that is appropriate for an organization.
5. What is meant by delegation? Identify 4 reasons for delegating and 4 limitations of delegation that managers should consider.

6. Identify and briefly define 4 significant principles of management governing authority, responsibility, and accountability relationships. What are some possible causes for and results of the violation of these principles?
7. What are the advantages and disadvantages of wide and narrow spans of management? What factors affect the span of management?
8. Identify the two basic types of organizational structures. Draw a chart to illustrate each.
9. Briefly discuss the strengths and weaknesses of each type of organizational structure identified in number 8.
10. What is the difference between a "line" and a "line and staff" organizational structure?
11. What is functional authority? Why is it used?
12. Under what circumstances are project and matrix organizational structures most appropriate?

EXERCISES

1. Analyze the organizational charts of a local retail store, a bank, a manufacturing company, and your college or university. How is each organized and what are the bases of departmentation used? What changes, if any, would you suggest in the structure of these organizations? Draw new charts if necessary.
2. Go to the library and review 2 current journal articles describing corporate reorganizations. At the next class meeting report to the class one example of a company that has been reorganized. In your three-minute presentation briefly describe the company as well as the reasons for and advantages of the reorganization.

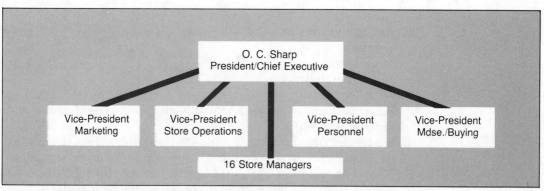

EXHIBIT 7-11 Organizational structure of Sharp's

CASE STUDY

Managing Growth at Sharp's

At 07:00, O. C. Sharp unlocks his office door. He has been arriving at this same office at this precise hour, 6 days a week for the past 19 years; that was when he took over as president of Sharp's Department Stores from his father, who had turned a family-operated dry goods business into a 3-store firm. Under O. C. Sharp, the business has grown to a 16-store firm in 10 Ontario cities. O. C. Sharp is considered by business colleagues to be a shrewd businessman and a far-sighted planner, even though some question his paternalistic attitudes toward his employees.

During his 19 years as chief executive at Sharp's, Sharp pioneered the development and implementation of modern management systems, including MBO, as well as extensive planning, policy, and procedure systems. The organization and its president have a reputation as an effective and efficient machine. (Exhibit 7-11 shows the current organizational chart at Sharp's.)

Sharp obviously knows how to operate a department store successfully; few others have the success he enjoys in this highly competitive field. Each store in the firm handles operations in the same way because Sharp has constantly overseen the writing and revision of "operating procedures." These "OPs", as Sharp calls them, give step-by-step methods for all phases of operation; they are discussed and updated at monthly managers meetings. Sharp, the 4 vice-presidents, and all store managers attend these meetings. A typical meeting would involve 4 to 5 hours reviewing, discussing, and updating the OPs and the remaining time on discussions of merchandise, buying, scheduling of company-wide sales, store expansion plans, and selection and training of personnel.

On this particular morning, though, Sharp's mind keeps turning over a conversation he'd had the day before with one of the vice-presidents. They had both been expressing disappointment over recent stunted sales volume and the slowdown in the growth rate of the business. Sharp recognized some time before that he had been finding it increasingly difficult to add new stores. He'd always believed he could manage a chain of 25 or 30 stores with equal success using his OP system. What's troubling him this morning is the realization that he can't seem to stay on top of all activities in the 16 stores he has now. He wonders if he needs to change some facet of the business, or if he's just getting too old to manage as president.

QUESTIONS

1. What do you think is the source of Sharp's Department Stores' recent slump? If O. C. Sharp consulted you, what advice would you give him?
2. Refer to Exhibit 7-11. Evaluate the strengths and weaknesses in the current organizational structure of Sharp's Department Store chain.
3. What changes to the organizational structure or the reporting relationships would you suggest, in order to respond to any weaknesses you've found?

CASE STUDY

Who Has the Authority?

Doughboy Snack Foods is a large bakery with approximately 300 employees. Located in Toronto, the company is 18 years old, is unionized, and features a wide line of products, including cakes, snack foods, and an extensive array of breads. Doughboy ships its products all over eastern Canada. The bread distribution department — the largest — consists of one department head, one supervisor, one assistant supervisor, three leadmen (very experienced employees), and eight regular employees.

James Martens is the first-shift supervisor; he

has been with Doughboy since it opened. Before coming to the company, he owned and operated a cabinet shop with one employee, Sam Morris. Martens is a no-nonsense, autocratic manager. He makes all the decisions and passes them along to the second-shift supervisor who is Martens's assistant and his former employee, Morris. Before Martens leaves each day, he writes down what needs to be done and leaves Morris in charge. Morris has been with Doughboy for 5 years, having got the job through Martens. Martens was also responsible for recommending Morris for his promotions to leadman and to assistant supervisor.

The employees in the bread distribution section are the highest paid in the company. Most of them are happy with the company and look forward to a long employment. However, one employee of this section is currently experiencing some problems. Terry Murphy is the second-shift leadman but, until 2 months ago he was the third-shift leadman, a position he held for over 3 years. Murphy accepted the job on the new shift because Martens assured him he could have Saturdays and Sundays off. However, from the first day on the new job, Murphy has been assigned weekend duty because he is the most experienced employee on the shift. Murphy spoke with Morris, his shift supervisor, and asked for weekends off. Morris explained the need for the present schedule and gave Murphy the impression that, if he wanted to continue with the company, the present schedule was his only choice. Company policy dictated that after an employee accepts a job it's up to the managers to establish working hours. Also, nothing in the union contract stated that employees' schedules couldn't be changed after they accepted a specific job. But Murphy can't help feeling betrayed by the undesirable schedule and annoyed with Morris for not giving him the hours he had expected when he joined this shift.

To complicate Murphy's position in this situation further, as he was returning home with some furniture in the back of his truck one afternoon, Murphy spotted Martens. Murphy stopped the truck and explained that he was moving the furniture to his home and asked Martens if it would be all right for him not to work that evening. Martens consented to let him off, and Murphy figured that, since company policy stated that he had to give at least 2 hours' notice of personal business, he would have an excused absence. Murphy came into the office the next day, and noticed that Morris was not in the office. Murphy knew that Morris was responsible for the attendance records for his shift, so he checked the records while waiting for Morris to return. He was surprised by the notation "unexcused" beside his name for the previous evening and then he felt angry because, as far as he was concerned, he had followed policy for an "excused" absence.

Murphy had always been a hard-working employee, but he'd begun to feel Doughboy was not treating him fairly. He became sullen and began to be lax in his work. As a matter of fact, the next shift suffered from a lack of productivity of Murphy's group.

QUESTIONS

1. What problems relating to authority and responsibility relationships exist in the bread distribution department?
2. What do you believe should be done to prevent a recurrence of the types of problems Terry Murphy is having?

NOTES

[1]J. D. Ford and W. H. Hegarty, "Decision Makers' Beliefs About the Causes and Effects of Structure: An Exploratory Study," *Academy of Management Journal* (June 1984): 281.

[2]A. V. Graicunas, "Relationships of Organizations," *Papers on the Science of Administration*, eds. L. Gulick and L. Urwick (New York: Columbia University Press, 1947).

[3]L. W. Fry and J. W. Slocum, Jr., "Technology, Structure, and Workgroup Effectiveness: A Test of a Contingency Model," *Academy of Management Journal* (June 1984): 236.
[4]Joan Woodward, *Industrial Organization: Theory and Practice* (London: Oxford University Press, 1965): 52–62.
[5]J.L.C. Cheng, "Interdependence and Coordination in Organizations: A Role-Systems Analysis," *Academy of Management Journal* (March 1983): 160–161.

REFERENCES

Arnold, John D. "The Why, When, and How of Changing Organizational Structures." *Management Review* (March 1981): 17–20.

Benson, Robert. "Delegation: A Tough Skill to Learn but Worth the Cost." *Canadian Business* (December 1982): 138.

Gibson, James L.; Ivancevich, John M.; and Donnelley, James H. Jr., *Organizations: Behavior Structure and Processes*. Dallas: Business Publications, 1981.

Graeff, Claude L. "The Situational Theory: A Critical View." *Academy of Management Review* 8, no. 2 (April 1983): 285–291.

Haynes, M. E. "Delegation: There's More to It Than Letting Someone Else Do It." *Supervisory Management* 25 (January 1980): 9–15.

Herbert, Theodore T. "Strategy and Multinational Organizational Relationships Perspective." *Academy of Management Review* 9, no. 2 (April 1984): 259–270.

Karasek, R. A. Jr. "Job Demands, Job Decision Latitude for Job Redesign." *Administrative Science Quarterly* 24 (June 1979): 285–308.

Logges, J. G. "Role of Delegation in Improving Productivity." *Personnel Journal* 58 (November 1979): 776–779.

Ouchi, W. G. "Relationship between Organizational Structure and Organizational Control." *Administrative Science Quarterly* 22 (March 1977): 206–216.

Peters, T. J. "Beyond the Matrix Organization." *Business Horizons* 22 (October 1979): 15–27.

Potter, B. A. "Speaking with Authority: How to Give Directions." *Supervisory Management* 25 (March 1980): 2–11.

Rousseau, D. M. "Assessment of Technology in Organizations: Closed versus Open Systems Approaches." *Academy of Management Review* 4 (October 1979): 531–542.

Waterman, H. Jr.; Peters, J.; and Phillips, R. "Structure Is Not Organization." *Business Horizons* 23, no. 2 (June 1980): 14–26.

Wente, M. A. "Remaking the Management Mind." *Canadian Business* (January 1983): 24.

The Informal Organization

The Publishing Department

Ginny DeVor is one of 46 employees in the publishing department of a large government agency. She has been on the job for 3 years. While having coffee with several colleagues one afternoon, she learns that the head of her department is being promoted to a new job in another agency. Not surprisingly, there is much discussion and rumor about who the new head will be.

The department is presently composed of two distinct groups of people — the younger climbers and the older, more established workers. There is animosity between the two groups on several issues, including the criteria for promotion. The young workers feel that performance should be

the criterion, while the older workers argue that seniority should be used. DeVor is a member of the younger group and would like to become the new head. She also knows that Carl Ryan, the informal leader of the older group, assumes he will get the job because he has been in the department for 11 years.

Several years ago, the department adopted the practice of using a 4-person selection committee to recommend to the agency director who the new department head should be. Members are elected to the selection committee at a meeting of the entire department. The director is not required to accept the committee's choice, but he is reluctant to ignore it because he really believes in participative management.

In the month before the election of the selection committee members, DeVor makes a point of cultivating friendships. In one-on-one meetings with various members of the department, she determines their likes, dislikes, fears, and hopes. She makes a point of going to lunch with various groups in the department and participates discreetly in ongoing discussions about the qualities the new head should possess. Before long, she finds that all the members in the young group — and even some of the older workers — are quietly urging her to apply for the head's job.

Given this support, DeVor becomes more open in her strategy. In the week before the meeting when the selection committee will be elected, she consults many members of the younger group; they agree to nominate 4 members from their group and then concentrate all their votes on those 4 candidates. They also agree to nominate 7 or 8 members from the older group in order to split that group's votes over a larger number of nominees.

At the meeting, 4 candidates favorable to DeVor are elected. Various supporters come by her office after the meeting to congratulate her and to say the important activity in choosing a new head has already been done. All that remains is the formality of the selection committee going through the motions of selecting the new head.

One month later, it is announced that Ginny DeVor is the new department head.

KEY TERMS

group	cohesiveness	status symbol
norms	synergism	power
role	grapevine	organization
contact chart	status	politics

LEARNING OBJECTIVES

After completing this chapter you should be able to

1. Explain how group goals, norms, roles, leadership style, and structure differ in both the formal and informal organizations.
2. Describe the importance of cohesiveness, size, and synergism in the informal organization.
3. Identify the benefits and costs of the informal organization.
4. Explain the concepts of status, status sources, and status symbols.
5. Relate the importance of understanding power and organization politics.

To this point, we have talked about managers occupying positions in the formal structure of organizations without much reference to them as people. Chapters 6 and 7 outlined the types of formal structures and functions managers must consider when organizing. Chapters 8 and 9 consider how the human element affects and is affected by the organizational structure. In a general sense, inserting the human element into an organization blunts the clear, logically designed official structure that so appeals to some managers. These managers are proud of the formal structure they have created precisely because it is logical and orderly. (See Exhibit 8-1.) Everyone knows exactly who he or she reports to and the task each is expected to do. Some managers believe their organizing function is fulfilled and their work will run itself because of the orderly formal structures they have developed.

This is a false hope. When the orderly structure designed by managers is peopled, it is often drastically altered to conform to people's wants and needs. The way a company is formally organized and the ways employees actually interact may be enormously different. An illustration of the way the informal group operates within the formal organization is shown in Exhibit 8-2. Mary, the president by title, actually has little influence; Alice is recognized as the most influential decision maker (even by Mary herself). Ira, Tan, and Sam defer to and confer with Alice rather than Mary; all three compete with one another for Alice's attention, hoping for promotion if Mary steps aside. Alice is so busy she hasn't noticed that Kelly and Harry, who report to her, dislike each other and try constantly to undermine one another's efforts. Denis, taking advantage of the hostility between Kelly and Harry, deals more often with Alice than with his own supervisor, Ira. Edie, who also reports to Ira, wonders who's really in control and who should be doing Denis's neglected work. Marilyn and Ceta, although they report to Tan as his employees, are both more interested in him as a member of the opposite sex. Bibi, Ceta's friend, is more interested in the romance in the adjacent area than in working for her supervisor, Sam. Jerry, who also reports to Sam, spends much of his time trying to influence Mary because he is sure she will one day take back her rightful authority.

Overall, Exhibit 8-2 makes one key point: employees often do not conform to the formal structure that has been prescribed. Rather, they develop spontaneous friendships and relationships based on criteria that are not derived from the formal structure. They sometimes choose their own informal leaders and allegiances; these leaders may or may not be those selected by the formal organization. Managers must be aware of the informal organization if they want their formal structures to work toward effective organizing.

In this chapter, we examine the nature of the informal organization and attempt to gain an appreciation of the influence — both positive and negative — it can have on the formal organization. To further your understanding of the dynamics of day-to-day operations in organizations, we also discuss the concepts of status, power, and organizational politics. The objective of this chapter is to give you an appreciation of the factors a manager must consider when dealing with the informal organization. Failure to deal with such issues effectively will almost certainly guarantee managerial failure.

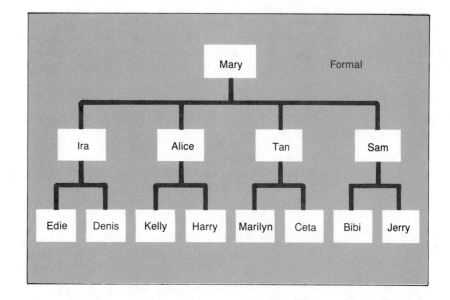

EXHIBIT 8-1
The formal
organization

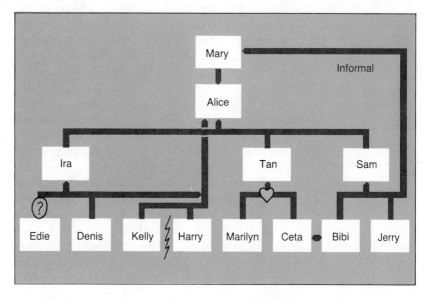

EXHIBIT 8-2
The informal
organization

COMPARING FORMAL AND INFORMAL ORGANIZATIONS

In Chapter 7 we examined some types of formal organizational structures and discussed their potential impact on employee behavior. In
addition to the formal structure as set out in the organizational chart,
another structure exists that is also important in determining employee
behavior. This structure is called the **informal organization** and refers
to the patterns of behavior and influence that arise out of the human

interaction occurring within the formal structure. While formal and informal organizations are similar, they have some important differences. Because the informal organization can exert a strong influence on employee behavior, managers must understand its nature, how it works, in what ways it affects behavior, and how it can be used in the management of organizations. Examples of behavior in the informal organization are many and varied; here are a few:

- A production worker restricts output to conform to the norm of the rest of the work group.
- Management plans a major announcement for employees; the message is leaked earlier through the grapevine.
- The manager of a department may find that during the baseball season the leader of the company baseball team appears to exert more influence than the line managers.
- A potentially conflict-laden meeting proceeds rationally — most of the disagreements on issues were worked out the night before over a few drinks.

In other words, any employee behavior that occurs beyond that prescribed by the formal organization is a result of the informal organization.

In general, the informal organization emerges because the formal structure does not satisfy all employee and organization needs. The exact form the informal organization will take depends on the specific deficiencies in the formal structure and in employee need satisfaction. Managers do not have a choice as to whether or not the informal organization will develop; informal relationships *will* be formed within any formal structure. Managers should try to understand, rather than to suppress, the informal organization and to channel its energies toward organization goals.

Another reason for the existence of the informal organization is the employees' need for predictability and stability in interpersonal relationships and social processes. The formal organization is unable to provide them, since formal structures are generally designed from a mechanical, rational perspective, not a behavioral one. The personal relationships that develop from on-the-job interaction provide the necessary security and predictability that individuals need, resulting in the informal structure parallel to the formal one.

The formal and informal organizations have common attributes, but the manifestations of these attributes differ significantly. Informal organizations represent the human side of organizations and are dependent on the nature of individuals in the organization; formal organizations, since they are not spontaneous, are usually highly structured and give less emphasis to human considerations. In one sense, the formal organization is "how it should be" and the informal organization is "how it actually is." The table opposite summarizes many of the differences between formal and informal structures. In the discussion that follows, several key differences between formal and informal organizations, noted in the table, are analyzed in more detail.

A Comparison of Formal and Informal Organization Characteristics

Characteristic	Informal Organization	Formal Organization
Structure		
Origin	Spontaneous	Planned
Rationale	Emotional	Rational
Characteristics	Dynamic	Stable
Position terminology	Role	Job
Goals	Member satisfaction	Profitability or service to society
Influence		
Base	Personality	Position
Type	Power	Authority
Flow	Bottom up	Top down
Control mechanisms	Physical or social sanctions (norms)	Threat of firing, demotion
Communication		
Channels	Grapevine	Formal channels
Networks	Poorly defined, cut across regular channels	Well defined, follow formal lines
Speed	Fast	Slow
Accuracy	Moderate	High
Charting the organization	Contact chart	Organization chart
Miscellaneous		
Individuals included	Only those "acceptable"	All individuals in work group
Interpersonal relations	Arise spontaneously	Prescribed by job description
Leadership role	Result of membership agreement	Assigned by organization
Basis for interaction	Personal characteristics, ethnic background, status	Functional duties or position
Basis for attachment	Cohesiveness	Loyalty

Group Goals

A **group** exists when 2 or more people join together to accomplish a desired goal. Workers in sections, departments, and divisions have formal goals directed toward accomplishment of the mission of the organization. The informal organization also has goals, although managers often do not recognize them. For example, a group of employees may be more interested in socializing on their coffee breaks than in thinking about better ways to do their work. This does not mean that the informal organization group cannot contribute to the achievement of organization goals; rather, it means that the social needs of the group must be satisfied as they pursue organization goals. If the goals of the informal organization group are consistent with those of the formal organization, productivity will normally be high; if they are contrary to those of the formal organization, the firm will probably suffer in some way.

Norms

The formal organization has its performance standards, and the informal organization has its **norms**, or standards of behavior expected from group members. Those who violate group norms are encouraged to conform. Informal pressures to conform to group norms are often more powerful than the official sanctions used by managers to enforce conformance to organization standards. A worker who is a good producer — highly acceptable to the formal organization — may be ostracized by the informal organization until his or her production falls back in line with the informal group's norms. Group norms are unwritten rules that new members, if they are to remain members, gradually learn. Norms that are frequently understood include: how hard one should work, whether one should be friendly, the degree to which one should cooperate with managers, and whether one should be innovative.

Roles

The concept of role is broader than that of its counterpart in the formal organization — the job. A **role** consists of the total pattern of behavior expected of a person. In the formal organization it includes, but goes beyond, the official content of the job description. If a person is officially designated a supervisor, pressure may be exerted to dress, talk, and act similar to other supervisors in the organization. If managers in a firm dress formally, the manager who fails to wear the proper "uniform" is not fulfilling the expected role.

Individuals in an informal group also are expected to act out a role. Whether an informal group of employees is supportive of its managers has a major impact on the roles of the group members. If the group decides it should not support a decision made by top management, the pattern of its behavior (role) may reflect indifference or slowing down on the job. Failure to conform to the expected role may result in a member's psychological ejection from the informal group.

A person may have many roles that he or she must constantly play. For instance, when working toward a doctorate, one of the authors was at times a student, a teacher, a consultant, and a military officer. For each of these activities, the author needed a different role; failure to change roles immediately at the proper time often resulted in difficulties. Being a military officer on the weekend with considerable authority, followed on Monday morning by the learning role of a doctoral student was sometimes not easy. Supervisors working in firms who return to school part-time often encounter similar difficulties.

Leadership

In the formal organization, leaders (managers) are placed in their position of authority by top management. By filling a particular supervisory position, the individual is designated the leader. An entirely different procedure is at work in selecting a leader for the informal organization. The informal group leader emerges from the group. No formal election is held; rather, the process of identifying a leader occurs gradually. Typically, the person who adheres closest to the norms of the group is the leader. No formal title is attached to this individual, but this person is looked to for guidance in achieving the group's goal. Should the informal leader begin to deviate from group norms, another leader who is closer to the group norm will emerge to take his or her place.

Structure

Although it is sometimes difficult to chart, the informal organization has its own structure. As with the formal structure, informal groups may also have different levels in a chain of command. Sometimes managers may chart the informal organizational structure, but the members themselves rarely diagram their structure. Successful executives know that an organizational chart cannot capture who has the real influence and authority in an informal organization.

The informal structure constantly changes as different members enter into and exit from the group. The structure is heavily based on the communication patterns that develop among group members. If many people attempt to get advice from one individual, this individual is often the informal leader and the structure develops around this person. Just as formal organizations have vice-presidents, the informal group may have an equivalent counterpart. The informal structure evolves and changes, rather than being formally laid out, but it is often more effective than the structure of the formal organization.

One means by which the structure of an informal organization may be studied is through the use of a **contact chart**. This chart can be developed to identify the connection that an individual has with other members of the organization. Many contacts do not follow the formal organization chart. (See Exhibit 8-3.) In various instances, certain levels of management are bypassed; others show cross-contact from one chain of command to another. Based on the number of workers contacting an employee, individual 19 appears to be very popular and is likely an informal leader.

One difficulty with a contact chart is that it does not show the reasons for relationships that do develop. Also, these contacts could work either for or against the organization. Individual 19 in Exhibit 8-3 could be assisting other employees in doing their work or could be stirring up trouble for the organization and promoting disharmony among company employees. Once managers have identified the major contact points, they are in a position either to encourage or discourage the individual within the work group.

Cohesiveness

The degree of attraction that the group has for each of its members is referred to as **cohesiveness**. It has importance to both the formal and informal organizations. It is identified by such attitudes as loyalty to the group, a feeling of responsibility for group effort, defending against outside attack, friendliness, and congeniality. Cohesive informal work groups are powerful instruments that can work for or against the formal organization. For instance, a highly cohesive group whose goals are in agreement with organization objectives can use this strength to assist the firm in increasing productivity. On the other hand, a highly cohesive group that is not in agreement with organization objectives can have an extremely negative effect on the accomplishment of the firm's goals. Because of this potential power, some managers attempt to reduce group cohesion in order to maintain control.

Size

The size of the formal work group is determined by the needs of the organization; the size of the informal organization is determined by the kinds of satisfactions that the informal group members want. Because interpersonal relationships are the essence of informal organizations, the informal group tends to be small so that its members may interact frequently.

Since many organizations consist of thousands of members, the initial approach to managerial organizing must be formal in nature: the design of official units, definition of jobs, and establishment of relationships for authority, responsibility, and accountability. Within this formal organization, many small, informal work groups will be spontaneously established and — so managers hope — will be aligned with overall organization objectives.

Synergism

Synergism means the whole is greater than the sum of its parts. In the context of an organization, **synergism** can mean that, when 2 or more people work together, they can do more in total than what would have been possible by each person working separately. Synergism also comprises the possibility of accomplishing tasks that could not have been

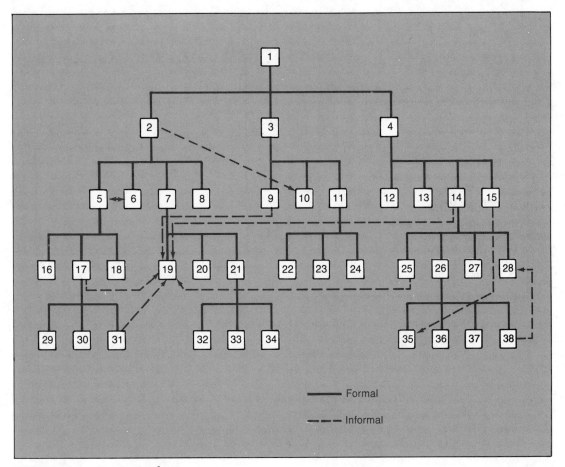

EXHIBIT 8-3   A contact chart

done at all by 2 people working alone.[1] The concept of synergism has implications for both the formal and informal organizations. Managers need to recognize that greater effort may be achieved when 2 workers cooperate. However, through the synergistic effect, the informal organization achieves more power because people in groups have much more influence than each individual has alone.

BENEFITS AND COSTS OF THE INFORMAL ORGANIZATION

Managers often have mixed emotions about informal work groups. On the one hand, the work group is capable of contributing to greater organizational effectiveness. On the other, the informal organization is not without its drawbacks. If managers are properly trained to understand and work with informal groups, the benefits should exceed

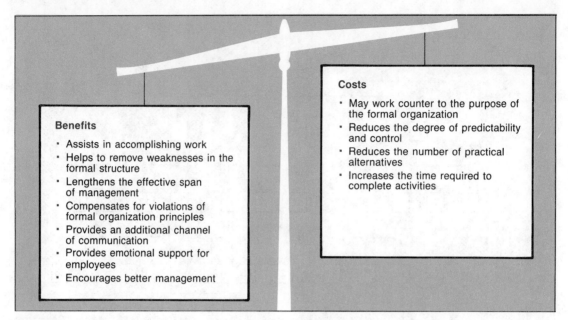

Benefits

- Assists in accomplishing work
- Helps to remove weaknesses in the formal structure
- Lengthens the effective span of management
- Compensates for violations of formal organization principles
- Provides an additional channel of communication
- Provides emotional support for employees
- Encourages better management

Costs

- May work counter to the purpose of the formal organization
- Reduces the degree of predictability and control
- Reduces the number of practical alternatives
- Increases the time required to complete activities

EXHIBIT 8-4 Benefits and costs of the informal work group

the costs. (See Exhibit 8-4.) However, if management is not careful, the scale may tip the other way so that the costs exceed the benefits.

Benefits of the Informal Organization

Managers cannot destroy the informal organization, fortunately—because it is capable of providing significant benefits to an organization. These potential values are discussed below.

Assists in Accomplishing Work

For a manager to be effective, his or her subordinates must be permitted a certain degree of flexibility in performing their assigned tasks. Advance approval of every move is detrimental to achieving success. If people in a business acted only when they were told to act, followed standard instructions to the letter at all times, and contacted others only when duly authorized, the business would have to cease operations.

Occasionally a formal command will be unsuitable or inadequate for the situation. If the atmosphere in an organization is prominently traditional, subordinates may exhibit malicious obedience by executing a command faithfully despite personal knowledge that their action will ultimately result in failure. Unions working to rule provide an example of this activity. Many managers have discovered that subordinates can follow every directive to the letter and yet fail miserably. If more faith is placed in informal relationships, subordinates may voluntarily adapt the formal order to the requirements of the actual situation. When a work group is loosely structured, it is often able to achieve organization objectives more effectively.

Helps To Counter
Weaknesses in the Formal Structure

The formal organization often has a number of gaps that the informal group can fill. Consider a person who is promoted to a position that exceeds his or her capabilities. This condition is not unusual for a newly promoted manager. He or she must be given time to get used to the position and, possibly, to make some mistakes because of inexperience. While the new manager is learning how to do the job properly, the informal organization can fill in the gaps in his or her knowledge and experience. For example, experienced employees can show the new manager how certain tasks are done and why they are done that way. The formal organizational chart says the new manager is the boss but, by admitting temporary weaknesses caused by inexperience, help may be obtained from subordinates. In effect, deficiencies in the formal structure have been countered when the new manager acquires operational information that could lead to decision making through the informal organization. As the new manager gains more experience, this kind of reliance on the informal organization will decline.

Broadens the Effective
Span of Management

As we indicated in Chapter 7, the number of people a manager can supervise effectively is limited. As individuals and small groups learn to interact more cohesively and are permitted to do so, their manager need not devote so much time to each individual worker. This informal cooperation could contribute to a broadening of a manager's formal span of management.

Compensates for
Violations of Formal Principles

The development of informal relationships can compensate for the violation of certain traditional principles of formal organizations. For instance, even though authority should equal responsibility, the principle is often violated. As a result, employees try to develop informal contacts with personnel over whom they have no formal authority. Favors are traded and friendships form. Employees quickly learn that the formal prescription of authority often is not a sufficient base for operation. Yet this informal compensation still does not negate the desirability of having responsibility equal authority.

Provides an Additional
Channel of Communication

The informal means by which information is transmitted in an organization is called the **grapevine**. To some traditional managers, the grapevine constitutes an obstacle to be destroyed. They seek to channel and control most, if not all, communications through the official chain

of command. However, the grapevine can add to organizational effectiveness if managers use it for their own purposes. Clues to the changing informal structure can be gained through the grapevine; managers
can even circulate unofficial information through the grapevine.

Use of the grapevine does not decrease the importance of the official
channels of communication and command. Although the grapevine
can spread much information in a short time, it cannot provide the
authority necessary for much of the action that will take place.

Provides Emotional and Social Support for Employees

Many managers find out the hard way that employees need emotional
support while they are working. Over half of all voluntary resignations
in many Canadian businesses are estimated to occur within the first
6 months of a person's employment. These are often a result of poor
hiring and orientation procedures, when little help is provided the new
employee in joining and being accepted within work groups. Friendships, or at least speaking acquaintances, are essential to a satisfactory
working environment for most people. In one hospital the termination
rate among janitorial personnel was high; research disclosed that the
janitorial staff felt isolated and uncomfortable when working alone
among physicians, nurses, and patients. Hospital management formed
cleanup teams of janitors; the new work teams reduced the negative
feelings, and the turnover rate declined considerably.

Encourages Better Management

Awareness of the nature and impact of the informal organization often
leads to better management decisions. The acceptance of the fact that
formal relationships will not enable full accomplishment of organization goals stimulates managers to seek other means of motivation.
If most of the work is done informally, managers will seek to improve
their knowledge of the nature of the people in general and of their
subordinates in particular. Managers should realize that organizational
performance can be affected by the workers who grant or withhold
cooperation and enthusiasm. Means other than formal authority must
be sought to develop attitudes that support effective performance.

Costs of the Informal Organization

The informal organization is not without its drawbacks. If a manager
is hostile toward informal work groups or tries to suppress their activities, these drawbacks are more likely to emerge. We discuss some
of the possible costs of the informal organization below.

May Work against the Formal Organization

Most managers realize that individuals and groups can and sometimes
do work contrary to the formal goals of an enterprise. If the goals of

the informal group were always the same as those of the formal organization, few managers would oppose its existence. However, on occasion, informal organizations engage in tactics like work restriction, pressuring workers to exhibit disinterest in company requirements, disloyalty, insubordination, and unauthorized actions that hurt the organization. When these tactics are used, they usually frustrate and anger managers who then try to suppress the informal organization. Unfortunately, suppression attempts will take time and will probably make the informal organization dig in its heels even more.

Reduces Degree of Managerial Control

Some managers feel uncomfortable with the informal organization because they believe it reduces their ability to predict how well subordinates will work. Some subordinates may have much more informal influence than their position in the formal organizational chart suggests they should have. A basic purpose of an organization is to ensure predictability and control of individual behavior so that individuals will work effectively toward organization goals. Accomplishing this purpose depends, however, on people interpreting and executing formal guidelines. If managers recognize and accept the possibility of a good outcome from permitted flexibility, they also must accept the risks that accompany this lower degree of control. The informal element can and does add much to an organization's effectiveness; it also can and does add more uncertainty.

Reduces the Number of Practical Alternatives

A study of military combat units during World War II concluded that the natural unit of personal commitment was the informal group, not the total formal organization.[2] The soldiers reported that one of their major reasons for moving forward in combat was to avoid letting the other fellow down. The solidarity developed in the informal group greatly strengthened the motivation of individual members.

The significance of this finding creates problems in businesses when transferring personnel. If natural groups are broken up by moving individual members in and out of them, a degree of motivation and cooperation is reduced. This potential loss may mean that managers should think in terms of moving groups around, rather than individuals. If managers wish to capitalize on the considerable values issuing from the development of primary work groups, they must lose some flexibility in the making of decisions.

Increases the Time Required To Complete Activities

If the cooperative efforts of the informal work groups can be aligned with the objectives of the firm, managers have the best of both worlds.

254

TALKING TO MANAGERS

Charles W. McDougall
Royal Victoria Hospital

Charles W. McDougall is an administrator at the
Royal Victoria Hospital in Montreal. An 863-
bed facility, the hospital is associated with McGill
University and provides major research and
teaching components along with patient care.
McDougall reports to the vice-president of corporate affairs who reports to the president. About
60 percent of his time is devoted to project
administration, the planning of new building and
renovation being undertaken by the hospital. The
remainder of his time is spent managing such
line functions as maintenance of buildings, care
of equipment, and security. In total, he is responsible for coordinating the efforts of about
75 people, most of whom are consultants, and

administering a budget of about $16 million
per year.

Q: What are the main formal groups that must
interact within the hospital?
McDougall: We have over 200 physicians located full-time in the hospital. There are senior
administrators, finance people, nurses, hospital
service workers, laboratory workers, professional service workers, and members of the
auxilliary services. Many of the groups are represented within their professions or by unions,
of which we have 17 locals.

Q: How are the interests and concerns of all
these various groups represented and served in
the operation of the hospital?
McDougall: A lot of the actual policy of the
hospital is determined by committees. About a
third of my time is related to committee activities. I serve on 7 major committees, including
the Property Committee, the Management Advisory Committee, the Management Information Systems Master Group, the Equipment
Committee, the Space Committee, the Building
Coordinating Committee, the Interdepartment
Coordinating Committee, and about 8 planning
task forces. A basic function of the committees
is to rationalize the competition for limited resources.

Q: Is there a lot of competition among members of the committees? One would expect the
politics to become intense in the effort to sway
a committee to one or another point of view.

The collective power generated can be quite phenomenal. Managers
will find, however, that informal work group activities, such as gos-
siping, betting pools, long coffee breaks, and general horseplay, are time

McDougall: First of all, let me explain that the committees do not vote; they work by consensus, although the chairperson may exert considerable influence to establish a consensus in some situations. Members do tend to argue from the background base that they represent and to favor the needs of their own constituents, but no one wants to close the door completely on anyone. After all, they all need to work together in the future. Resources do tend to be spread around. Of course, the way that happens may sometimes be an extension of self-interest. Security has a very low profile and low priority in the allocation of resources for equipment, but, if a few microcomputers have been stolen from various departments and offices, funds for security cameras to watch the unguarded exits may be approved hastily. Without that kind of incident, the security director lacks the power base to have his requests supported.

The workings of most of the committees are quite smooth, but in the Space Committee, groups get very territorial. Department directors "own" space within the hospital. When they need additional space for some reason, they can usually only get it by expropriating space from someone else. Committee work becomes more difficult on such occasions.

Q: Are there situations in which the existence of informal relationships or groups undercuts or, perhaps, enhances the accomplishment of management policy?
McDougall: The situation at the Royal Victoria Hospital seems to work against the formation of informal groups. Perhaps there are so many formal structures created by the depart-

ments and the interdepartmental committees that most possible informal groups have been made formal.

Informal relationships still exert considerable influence, of course. There was a situation a while ago when the president authorized the creation of some new office space for one department. This was a small department, and the new space would represent a significant increase in its size. The decision was made without the approval of the Space Committee. In my mind, the decision occurred primarily due to the informal relationships that exist around the president. The chief of that particular unit is a physician with an international reputation. Keeping key people from becoming world travellers is a legitimate concern, but now I have the problem of where to place the dominoes. So far I have managed to relocate the occupants of 3 offices that adjoin the department. Finding the additional required space is proving more difficult.

Unlike other places I have worked I have little social interaction here outside the formal structures. There is almost an ethic among managers that discourages social intercourse.

In some ways this situation makes a manager's work more difficult. Socialization produces some commonality of goals. I once worked for a hospital where several managers met every 2 weeks to play penny-ante poker. Many of the hospital's problems were sorted out at those games. Here I don't have access to such chances to talk things over in a relaxed social setting. This situation here may result in more rational decision-making processes, but it is certainly more demanding. I feel that I am more effective as a manager when I can work through informal channels as well as formal ones.

consuming and may be detrimental to efficient operations. These acts will tax the patience of managers who have specific goals to reach within strict deadlines. Yet, if an effective work group is to be established, some of these activities will have to be permitted and some even encouraged. Managers must realize that, despite concern for goal accomplishment, they must allow the group time and opportunity to maintain itself in good working order. People can usually sustain action for a longer period of time under an informal atmosphere than they can when in a rigid, controlled, and formal situation.

STATUS, POWER, AND ORGANIZATION POLITICS

So far, we have noted that the formal organization organizes jobs rationally so that overall organization goals will be achieved. We also noted that the informal organization may facilitate or inhibit the achievement of these goals. Other significant concepts are related to, but go far beyond, the simple distinction between formal and informal organizations. These concepts — status, power, and organization politics — are material to an understanding of how organizations really work.

Status

A person's rank or position in a group is called **status**. The concept of status has considerable effect on the morale and productivity within an organization. Status is an inevitable component of human relationships in all aspects of life, as well as in business. In this section, we examine the sources of status in business organizations, the symbols that denote status levels, and the functions of a status system.

MANAGEMENT IN PRACTICE

Status Symbols at Ontario Hydro

Most large companies spell out status symbols quite clearly, and Ontario Hydro is no exception. It has very detailed specifications regulating office size and furnishings for its managers. For example, the office sizes are as follows:

Chairman	56 m²
Executive Vice-President	46 m²
Vice-President	37 m²
Directors	32 m²

Office furnishings are also specified in detail.

For example, directors get no extras except 2 plants and a couch; vice-presidents are allowed 3 plants and several pieces of furniture; the executive vice-president gets even more plants and furniture; and the chairman gets two glass walls, a television and videotape machine, even more furniture, and custom white carpet.

SOURCE Jerry Amernic, "The Perks of Power," *The Financial Post Magazine* (November 1, 1982): 78.

Status Sources

The sources of status, or social rank, can be of both an informal and a formal nature. Examples of these sources are:

Formal Organizational Sources	Personal Sources
Occupation or job	Education
Organizational level	Age
Job title	Seniority
Salary	Ethnic origin
Authority	Religion
	Parentage
	Gender
	Competence
	Associates

Certain jobs are accorded more prestige than others. In the most general sense, white-collar jobs have higher status than blue-collar jobs. But within this broad classification additional distinctions are made. For example, electricians have more status than cleaners, even though both are blue-collar jobs. Computer programmers have more status than office clerks, even though both are white-collar jobs. Even finer distinctions can be made. Long-distance telephone operators have more status than local operators; cafeteria personnel who serve beef have higher status than those who serve fish; and graduate students have higher status than undergraduates.

The status of occupation depends on: (1) the rank accorded the occupation by one's peers or by society, and (2) the job's level within the enterprise structure. The former is defined by the informal organization, while the latter is indicated by the formal organization. The status given a job by the informal organization may or may not be consistent with the status given to it by the formal organization. For example, a maintenance crew may occupy a relatively low position on the formal organization chart, but, because they do critical repair work that keeps the entire factory running, they may have very high status. Their status may also be high because they can move around the factory, whereas other workers must stay at one machine.

Status Symbols

A visible, external sign of one's social position is known as a **status symbol**. A stranger can enter an office and, if aware of status hierarchies, is able to recognize who has status quickly by reading the various symbols. Status symbols do vary from firm to firm; most firms provide managers in the higher-status positions with increasingly elaborate office furnishings. In one organization, however, the high-status positions are given antique roll-top desks, whereas lower jobs come equipped with new, shiny, modern furniture. Symbols sometimes change with the times. Some typical items that can be status symbols (or perquisites) in business are:

- Job titles
- Pay
- Bonus or stock plans
- Size and location of desk or office
- Location of parking space or reserved parking
- Type of company car assigned
- Secretaries or researchers
- Privacy
- Use of executive clubs or sports facilities
- Cocktail party invitations
- Office furnishings, including rugs, pictures, tables, and bookcases
- Privileges, including freedom to move about, not punching a time clock, and freedom to set working hours and to regulate coffee breaks
- Ceremonies of induction
- Number of windows in office.

Many status symbols are within the control of managers and constitute the basis for conflicts. Executives have been caught down on their hands and knees measuring to compare the sizes of offices. Windows are counted, steps from the president's office are paced off, secretaries who can take fast dictation are sought (even though the supervisor may never give dictation), parking space is fought for, and company cars are wangled.

Some companies have tried to abolish all status symbols by equalizing privileges, offices, and furnishings. Other companies have eliminated executive dining rooms; some use open-landscaped offices. In most universities, the position of department head is rotated among

---

MANAGEMENT IN PRACTICE

Status Symbols at Crows Nest Resources

Large companies are not alone in specifying status symbols. Even small firms seem concerned about spelling out what managers at various levels are allowed to possess in the way of status symbols. Crows Nest Resources is a Calgary-based coal mining company with only 600 employees. Its office area specifications are as follows:

President	30 m²
Vice-Presidents	28 m²
Managers	21 m²
Others	14 m²

As far as furnishings are concerned, the president gets 2 plants and expensive Chippendale furniture; the vice-presidents get one plant and walnut furniture; managers get no plants and even cheaper furniture; and others get nothing beyond a desk.

SOURCE Jerry Amernic, "The Perks of Power," *The Financial Post Magazine* (November 1, 1982): 78.

department members, thereby reducing the status attached to the position. In some businesses, windowless buildings have been constructed, office sizes are standardized, and only one type of company car is available.

Generally speaking, these official attempts to do away with status symbols fail. People want to distinguish their position in the company from the position occupied by other people, and status symbols fulfill this desire. If certain status symbols are not formally allowed, others will emerge. If no one's office has a window, some other criterion (desk size, thickness of carpet, size of plants) will be used to rank people. An individual wants other people to know where he or she stands in the status hierarchy, and status symbols indicate that position with more impact than a job title alone.

Status Functions

Status produces certain positive conditions within the organization. First, status assists in meeting people's social needs. Most employees want the respect of others. Recognition of their abilities and accomplishments becomes tangible through status symbols. Also, status facilitates informal channels of communication in the organization. Even a person's job title conveys subtle messages that help other people process information; an opinion about a computer coming from an electronics expert with programming experience (whose job title states these credentials) is likely to be more valuable than the opinion of a computer salesperson — even if the information is identical. Status can carry influence that helps people weigh alternatives. Clearly, status can act as motivation for managers or for employees who wish to become managers. The perquisites and influence of status provide incentive for managers to perform well and be considered promotable. Nonfinancial incentives can be as satisfying as additional money; if many managers are paid the same salary, the managers may feel motivated to compete for the nonfinancial status symbols. Higher-level managers can develop more comprehensive and coordinated incentives to provide further motivation and, by their awarding of status symbols, indicate approval or disapproval toward managers.

Power

We noted in Chapter 7 that authority is the right to command others. **Power** is the ability to influence the behavior of another person. Managers in organizations have little trouble understanding the role and importance of power. In a study, each of 10 department managers was asked to rank himself or herself and 20 other department managers based on how much influence each had.[3] Only one manager asked what was meant by "influence." The overall results showed that there were virtually no disagreements in the ranking of the top 5 and bottom 5 managers on the list, even though ranking 21 people is not an easy task.

Power is an emotionally laden term, particularly in cultures that emphasize individuality and equality. To label a manager pejoratively as a power seeker is to cast doubt on that manager's motives and actions. Some of these negative views are the result of earlier writings which suggested that power is evil, that it corrupts people, that it is largely comprised of brute force, and that the amount of power is in limited supply.

Not a great deal of systematic analysis of power in organizations has been conducted. Possibly this research may have been neglected because 3 groups affected by power — students, managers, and the general public — want to believe that all behavior in organizations is rational.[4] The management students prefer to believe that they are entering a career in which they rationally allocate resources for the good of society than to believe that they will be involved in power struggles with other people. Practicing managers may be reassured to believe that their careers are based on rational considerations of merit, not on power. Similarly, the general public takes comfort in the belief that businesses allocate the resources of society in an efficient and rational way.

Sources of Power

The sources of power are many and varied. Power may come from the formal organization, the informal organization, or the individual. Power derives nominally from formal authority as a result of position. Significant power results from a person's place in a formal position of authority within the organizational structure. Authority carries with it the ability to reward or punish employees for comparative work performance. Managers who have this ability have power over other people. They have direct influence over other persons by promising to give a reward if they work as required, or by threatening them with punishment if they do not. Many people use this source of power to get other people to do what they want for both work and personal goals they may have.

Another source of power is expertise or specialized knowledge. Even an individual with limited formal authority can have considerable power or influence by his or her particular expertise. Expert power often creates problems for managers. A computer programmer may become so familiar with a system that his or her supervisor cannot adequately supervise the computer expert; the supervisor may feel that he or she cannot even reprimand the programmer for fear of losing the expertise the worker possesses.

Another major problem can develop in line and staff relationships — the line has the power that issues from authority, whereas the staff has the power that issues from knowledge. The formal right to manage a firm remains, but the capacity to manage it has been diluted and spread among experts. The person possessing knowledge and expertise has power regardless of the formal authority relationships within the organization.

Individuals who have earned respect in an organization have power. The particular personality and characteristics of an individual will also affect the degree to which other persons wish to identify and be associated with that person. If a person is liked and respected, that person is likely to influence others. If he or she is associated with persons occupying high and visible power positions, that individual probably holds even more influence. If a person has access to many sources of power, he or she may get exaggerated responses to requests. The president of a large enterprise inquired about hiring procedures currently in effect. After a 3-week delay, he received a comprehensive and detailed report covering all facets of hiring, with an emphasis on the current status of minority group members. At this point, it was discovered that a friend of the president's had a son who wanted a summer job but, because the young man had already found a position elsewhere, the president was no longer interested.

Power versus Formal Authority

The discussion of various sources of power illustrates how the concept of power extends far beyond that provided by formal authority. We might view the concept of power in terms of this simple formula:

$$\text{Power} = \text{Formal Authority} \pm \text{Informal Influence.}$$

A manager's power is heavily dependent on the informal influence he or she can exert. The knowledge (informal influence) that a computer programmer can use greatly increases his or her power. Also, notice the plus or minus sign regarding the impact of informal influence: a person can actually lower his or her power level below the formal authority level because of the poor use of informal influence. Even though placed in a formal position, a manager may be limited in accomplishing a job because of a limited amount of power.[5]

Significance of Power to Managers

Research has shown that a good manager must have a concern for acquiring and using power. A number of studies found that over 70 percent of managers have a higher need for power than does the general population.[6] The better managers have a stronger need for power than a need to be liked by others. This need for power is not a desire to be dictatorial, nor is it necessarily a drive for personal enhancement. Rather, it is a concern for influencing others on behalf of the organization. It is a need for socialized power rather than for personal power. When managers feel a greater need to be liked than a need to influence others, they tend to be less effective in many organizations.

The control of situational factors, both in and out of the organization, is of significant concern to the modern manager. It has been noted that, when organizations grow so large and complex that no one individual has the capacity to manage all of the interdependencies, a dominant managing group will develop. This coalition is sometimes formalized into a presidential or executive office. It will exist, however, whether or not it is actually recorded on a chart. If the president of the firm depends on the vice-president of finance to develop the crucial programs, that vice-president is likely to be a member of the dominant coalition and have actual power in excess of that suggested by the official chart. Within the organization, smaller and sometimes more temporary coalitions are formed so that a task involving significant interdependencies can be executed. The formation, use, and dissolution of such coalitions are sometimes collectively called **organization politics**.

Organization Politics

Organization politics is one of the most pervasive yet elusive concepts in organizational behavior. An understanding of this subject is crucial for anyone with serious career aspirations in top management. In today's complex organizations, individuals do not move rapidly up the hierarchy unless they have a good grasp of the political aspects of their work environment.

Consider the results of a study which analyzed 149 managers in a manufacturing firm over a 5-year interval.[7] During the period, 47 percent were promoted, 14 percent were given a lateral transfer, 22 percent

---

MANAGEMENT IN PRACTICE

A Power Struggle at Birks

Henry Birks & Sons Ltd. is the largest jewelry chain in Canada (1983 sales were $265 million). The firm has 4000 employees and 111 stores across Canada; it also has 68 stores in the United States. The firm was started in 1879 in Montreal by Henry Birks. Down through the years, succession had passed from eldest son to eldest son without any hint of disagreement. At least that was true until 1976 when a family member was fired and an internal power struggle began.

The fired family member, Robbie Birks, sued for $3 million for wrongful dismissal. In addition, his father Victor, vice-chairman of Birks, was fired with 3 days' notice after 53 years of service. He also sued the company, claiming that a voting trust agreement he had signed in 1968

should be annulled because he did not understand the impact it would have on his control of the company. Victor Birks won his suit in a court decision handed down in 1980, but that decision was overturned in 1983; the opposition (headed by Drummond Birks) essentially gained complete control of the company.

Industry observers predict that Drummond Birks will continue to head the company for many years and, when he retires, one of his 3 sons will take over the business. Whether there will be further disagreements at that time remains to be seen.

SOURCE Rod McQueen, "Brawl in the Family," *Canadian Business* (March 1984): 62–68.

stayed in their jobs, and 17 percent were demoted. The individuals who were promoted exhibited the following characteristics: (1) they understood the complex nature of the organization and the overlapping responsibility that resulted; (2) they recognized that it was more important to get along with their peers than with their subordinates, if they wanted to get ahead in the company; (3) they felt they had great freedom on the job; (4) they recognized that good performance was not automatically rewarded; and (5) they recognized that it was more important to seize the opportunity to become known than simply to do a good job and hope for the best.

These comments by successful practicing managers are probably not unusual. To demonstrate the diversity of situations in which political activity is important, consider the following examples from actual organizations:

Bill reports to the vice-president of marketing for a provincial utility. He is aggressive and considers himself top-management material. By ingratiating himself with the vice-president's secretary, Bill is able to gather considerable evidence that the vice-president is frequently out of the office on nonbusiness activities. Bill informally presents this evidence to certain key members of the board of directors who belong to the same country club that Bill's father does. Two months later the vice-president is fired and Bill is chosen as his replacement.

Marsha is a sales representative with a major computer manufacturer. One Thursday afternoon her boss informs her that an important customer is arriving at the airport and that she is to pick him up. Marsha feels complimented that her boss has chosen her for the job. Moments later, however, Marsha's boss says: "By the way, don't take your car. It isn't good enough for the customer. I think it's time you bought a new one." Marsha feels threatened by this comment, since she can't afford a new car.

Bob is majoring in business. Last Friday, he cut his Principles of Management class to play in an intramural basketball playoff game. After class on Monday he went to the professor's office and said: "I missed class last Friday — did we do anything important?" Bob wondered why the professor looked so disgusted.

Joanna and Kirk are management trainees for a major food marketing company. They do not particularly like each other. Both are in line for a promotion and both are members of the new-product committee. At a meeting of the committee, Kirk makes what appears to be an impressive presentation. However, Joanna observes aloud that his argument contains a major logical flaw. Although no decision is made at that time, Joanna notices that Kirk's proposal is quietly dropped from the agenda for the committee's next meeting. When the next promotion is announced, Joanna gets it.

Louis is a finance professor in a large business school in central Canada. He has very strong views about nearly everything and he expresses them vigorously at faculty meetings. When Louis first came to the university, his comments had some impact, but as time passed people paid less and less attention to him. A recent faculty meeting was typical. The Strategic Planning Committee chairman presented a report proposing a new administrative position for the faculty. With the best of intentions, Louis asked what experience other universities had had with this type of position. Several committee members gave vague responses, and it was clear that the Strategic Planning Committee had not analyzed the issue in much depth. Louis therefore suggested that this analysis be done before a person was hired for the proposed position. He was amazed and infuriated when his suggestion was rejected and the committee's recommendation was approved instead.

Ron is the top regional sales manager of a major food products company. He is also an excellent golfer. Last week he was asked to join a foursome composed of his boss (the national sales manager), the vice-president of marketing (his boss's boss), and the president of the firm. Ron knew that these people were critical to his career, and he wanted to make a good impression. So he played his best and shot a 71, the lowest score by far in the group. He left the golf course in great spirits. When Ron entered his boss's office the next morning he was greeted by: "Ron, what in the world were you trying to prove yesterday? *Nobody* beats the president at golf!" His boss then curtly dismissed him. Ron felt depressed about the incident for several days.

Incidents like these happen every day in organizations. They demonstrate that some individuals (Bill and Joanna) are able to assess the realities of organization life and then act in a way that is beneficial to their careers. Other individuals (Marsha, Bob, Kirk, Louis, and Ron) seem to have difficulty doing so. As a result, their careers are impeded and they don't get what they want.

Organization politics has been described as a "network of interaction by which power is acquired, transferred, and exercised upon others."[8] The individuals participating actively in organization politics are working with and through many people. As such, politics transcend the traditional structural boundaries. In the process of these interactions the medium of exchange is power. The shrewd office politician acquires power and transfers it to another person when it can purchase something of value. Organization politicians use this medium of exchange in the network that they establish to exert pressure on others in order to gain their desired result. Just like the accountant, the office politician has a balance sheet. When power is transferred, something is received in return. To the politician, a favor given now is power to be extracted in the future. Thus, everyone is a politician to a certain extent; some are better at it than others.

The Universality of Political Behavior

Political behavior in organizations is both universal and inevitable. It can be observed in all kinds of organizations — manufacturing firms, government agencies, service organizations, churches, the military, or universities. In this sense, political behavior is like the informal organization; any attempt to suppress it is certain to fail because the forces that encourage it are so potent.

What are these forces? Perhaps the most fundamental is self-interest, what people do to improve their own financial situation, status, or ego. While most people understand such behavior, they also recognize that, since organizations are made up of many different people, their self-interests are likely to clash. When people observe that what they are pursuing may be thwarted by someone else — as happens frequently — political behaviors are likely to be used.

Another reason political behavior is so widespread is that an organization has limited resources. An organization must therefore decide which of many possible goals it will pursue. Various groups or individuals in the organization will normally be in conflict with one another over which goals are going to be pursued and, in the process of trying to win, these groups are likely to indulge in political behavior. Such tactics are particularly likely if little objective evidence exists about the goals the organization should pursue.

Self-interest and limited resources guarantee that political behavior will be evident in all organizations. Some individuals believe that, in certain kinds of organizations, political behavior doesn't exist. For instance, might not charitable organizations pursuing goals that society values have no political behavior because employees use their energies to pursue those goals? Unfortunately, this view ignores the two realities we've noted: individuals pursue their own self-interests, and organization resources are limited. Individuals in such organizations who ignore these realities may be surprised, shocked, and dismayed at the behavior of others. Conversely, those who take these realities into account will find that they can often predict the behavior of others.

The Dynamics of Political Behavior

If all actions could be foreseen, perhaps organization members would have little need for politics. They could also assume that all conflicts could be resolved in some rational manner acceptable to everyone. Inasmuch as neither of these two circumstances is likely, individual members will be asked to adjust and accommodate to varying conditions and pressures. Though going exclusively by the official rules could, under certain circumstances, be construed as one form of political behavior, adjustment or accommodation usually requires additional future interactions. It sometimes involves a bending of the rules, an exchange of favors, or offers of a reward for cooperation. Some management students are shocked to discover that merely doing their job will not earn them rewards they might expect.

To make the implications of politics clearer, consider this situation. An engineer heading up an industrial engineering department has developed a new procedure for processing work in the production department. According to the formal rules, she would elect to follow the first suggestion listed below. The others listed are *not* formally required and can be construed as various forms of adjustment and accommodation.

1. The engineer submits the recommendation for approval by the line executive. She provides supporting data and presents persuasive arguments. This failing, the engineer appeals to a common line superior who will decide the case and issue an order accordingly.
2. The engineer attempts to get to know the line executive on a personal basis through casual conversation, enquiries about respective backgrounds, and the like.
3. The engineer attempts to simulate a friendship that is not genuine.
4. The engineer arranges to go to lunch with the line executive in the company dining room to promote her views on a casual basis.
5. The engineer invites the line executive to lunch away from the company premises at her own expense.
6. The engineer offers to exchange favors that are possible within the regular operating rules and policies; for example, she agrees to do an immediate restudy of a particular job rate that has caused serious difficulties between the line executive and the union.
7. The engineer agrees to a favor involving a slight bending of the procedures and policies; for example, she agrees to delay introduction of a new method and rate, even though fully developed and ready to go, at the request of the line executive.
8. The engineer agrees to a favor involving a more serious bending of the procedures and policies; for example, she "discovers" that the particular job rate (in item 6) is too tight, when it is not, and loosens it up for the benefit of the line executive.
9. The engineer agrees to cover for the line executive if, for example, the line executive wishes to use the industrial engineering department as an excuse for failing to meet schedules because of presumed work interferences.
10. The engineer, with the assistance of understanding accountants, agrees to a transfer of industrial engineering budget funds to the line executive's department.

Many other possible actions might have been tried to persuade the line executive to cooperate. The available alternatives depend on the extent of power possessed by the two parties. In instances where one has control over items or services that can be adapted to personal as well as organizational use, the power is even greater. Cases are on record in which personal furniture has been constructed on company time with company materials, or personal cars have been repaired in company motor pools.

The degree of political behavior is limited not only by formal organization restrictions but also by personal codes of ethics and conscience. The fact that at times office politics may be unethical should not preclude a discussion of the subject. That such actions as in the

MANAGEMENT IN PRACTICE

Politics at Manitoba Hydro

Manitoba Hydro is a provincially owned and operated utility whose mandate is to promote efficiency and economy in the supply and use of electric power. In 1979, the Tritschler Commission conducted hearings about alleged mismanagement of the organization. Among other conclusions, the commission reported that Manitoba Hydro had predicted power shortages that never materialized, had underestimated construction costs of new generating plants, and had expanded when its financial position was weak.

Several political principles and how they operated at Manitoba Hydro are noted below:

Principle 1. Groups within organizations vie with one another for status and power. In a province where 90 percent of the electricity is generated by water, it is not surprising that hydraulic construction engineers were a powerful group.

Principle 2. Changes in the external environment of the organization will favor one group over another. The rapid growth in demand for electricity in the 1960s increased the organizational power of the hydraulic engineers.

Principle 3. Organizational power considerations are as important, if not more so, than economic or rational considerations in making organization decisions. At Manitoba Hydro, hydraulic engineers produced the demand forecasts and did the planning for future generating stations. Impartial decisions were therefore not likely to be made.

Principle 4. Powerful groups will use political means to stay in power. When the predicted demand for electricity did not materialize, the engineers attempted to manipulate the environment to increase demand. For example, rates were kept artificially low and deals were made to sell power to the United States.

SOURCE Adapted from Roger Hall, "Some Emerging Principles of the Politics of Organizational Decisions" (Paper presented at the Administrative Sciences Association of Canada Conference, 1980).

example do exist in various business firms is undeniable. Few businesses are run completely and rigidly by the book, and political behavior cannot be condemned outright. Some accommodations are constructive, whereas others may be destructive of both organized activity and individual morals.

Is Political Behavior Positive or Negative?

Until recently, the majority of people who analyzed organizations or worked in them assumed that political behavior was negative. However, many researchers and managers are now accepting the idea that political behavior has positive aspects. At least political behavior is now accepted as a fact of organization life; an improved understanding of it can lead to better results for both organizations and individuals. However, many people still see it as undesirable, so we examine the major arguments made by the opponents of political behavior. For each of these arguments, the counter arguments made by the supporters of political behavior are presented.

People may be treated unfairly when political decisions are made. Ethnic minority groups argue, for example, that employment decisions are made not on the basis of competence, but on the basis of ethnic origin. (This practice is, of course, illegal, but that doesn't stop it from happening.) Opponents of political behavior also argue that it causes decisions to be made on mysterious criteria by an in-group that does not really have to answer to anyone. The existence of this in-group (frequently called the "old-boy network") is often considered unreasonable in a democratic society. The implication of the argument is that the old-boy network will make decisions based on something other than "rational" or "merit" grounds and that competent people may not be given a chance to show their merit; thus, overall organization performance will suffer.

The supporters of political behavior reject this line of reasoning. They argue that the old-boy network benefits organizations because it is efficient: (1) decisions can be made quickly and accurately on the basis of personal contacts, and (2) the organization benefits because the decision maker feels confident about the results when a decision is made on this basis. Information is crucial in making good decisions, and supporters argue that political decision making gives better results than decision making on a traditional basis.

Opponents of political behavior also believe it distorts the decision-making process so that decisions made may be bad for the organization or for society as a whole. Opponents of political behavior feel that the political maneuvering going on in organizations is caused by individuals' desires to improve their career prospects. While this motivation is not negative by itself, it is often carried to extremes. The motivation of self-interest for survival runs strong in most people, often strong enough to induce them to act in order to further their own careers without regard to the harm they may cause to other individuals, the organization, or society as a whole. The most widely cited example is that of the executive who comes to shape up a weak division. Typically, some drastic actions are taken in the short run, and performance often does improve noticeably. After a couple of years, the executive is promoted to another position on the basis of his or her successful past performance. But what happens after the executive leaves the division? Sometimes productivity declines and it appears that the executive is really missed. However, performance might have declined even if he or she had stayed, because the executive generated increased profits in the short run only by reducing training, maintenance, or other such expenditures. Thus, the executive's pursuit of personal goals (promotion) induced him or her to make decisions that were bad for the organization.

Supporters of political behavior agree that some executives behave this way; they respond by pointing out that, in a free society, individuals should be allowed to pursue their self-interest as long as they are not breaking the law. The supporters of political behavior also point out that individuals will always debate about what goals an organization should pursue and the behavior that is acceptable in the pursuit of these goals. When disagreements arise, they must be resolved in some way. Supporters of political behavior argue that the most effective and efficient mechanism for resolving these conflicts is the use of power. Hence, political behavior is functional for individuals and organizations because it provides a mechanism for resolving conflicts that might otherwise be unresolvable.

Opponents of political behavior also claim that use of it and use of power allow an organization to ignore internal and external groups that may be unhappy with what the organization is doing. The essence of the criticism is that certain individuals and groups inside and outside organizations are prevented from being heard because the people in power ignore them. What's worse, the people in power stay there by using all sorts of unfair tactics. The most obvious example is the refusal of corporations to do voluntarily what consumer groups believe they should do, such as controlling pollution or not publishing pornography. Consumer advocates respond by attempting to get laws passed requiring that these actions be taken by corporations.

Supporters of political behavior reject this line of reasoning and argue that the reverse is true — political behavior forces an organization to behave realistically both internally and in its relations with its external environment. Supporters agree that, in every organization, people at the top try to retain their positions. At the same time, however, many pressures for change are at work, both internally and externally. If the organization does not deal with these changes, it will find itself in deep trouble. For example, many of the traditional manufacturing industries in Canada find themselves unable to compete with foreign firms because they are unwilling or unable to adapt to fundamental changes in their industry. Often, political behavior on the part of certain managers in the firm is the only way to move the organization in a direction that will ensure survival.

Opponents argue that organization politics is inefficient and time-consuming. The negotiation, bargaining, conflict, and strategy development that is so evident in political behavior takes up people's time unduly. Opponents express concern that people in organizations will expend so much effort on political behavior that they will have little time or energy left for pursuing organization goals. As a result, organization performance will suffer.

Supporters of politics argue that political decisions are made as quickly as rational decisions. They argue that rational processes take a great deal of time, too, because information must be formally gathered and analyzed, and its meaning debated by many people. Political processes, they claim, are more informal and tend toward private rather than public discussions of various issues. Therefore, political decisions may be made quicker than those made on a rational basis.

Opponents of political behavior note that political processes allow certain individuals to have too much power while other individuals have too little. This is perhaps the most fundamental criticism of political behavior. Central to this argument is the idea that power corrupts people and that power differences between people should therefore be minimized. The best way is to eliminate political behavior.

In response to this criticism, supporters of political behavior make 3 points. First, it is not possible to minimize power differences between people because of the pyramidal structure of organizations, and because people differ in their abilities and inclinations to behave politically. Second, the most powerful individuals and departments in organizations are usually those who cope with important uncertainties the organization is facing. Power is therefore a way of inducing people to act (for example, to cope with uncertainty) in ways that increase organizational effectiveness. Third, individuals who are able to solve key problems rise to positions of power, further increasing organizational effectiveness. At a society-wide level, an interesting trend is evident regarding the kinds of individuals who become chief executives. In the early twentieth century, the major problem facing organizations was how to satisfy rapidly increasing demand. In this environment, production-oriented people often became presidents of corporations. By the 1930s and 1940s, production problems had been largely resolved and the main problem was how to sell what was being produced. Then, sales-oriented people rose to positions of power. More recently, the unsettled financial environment has given finance- and accounting-oriented people more power to attain positions as chief executives.

We believe that, managed properly, political behavior and the use of power can be helpful to an organization. Unfortunately, the current understanding of organization politics does not allow us to state simple rules for effectively managing politics and the use of power. Keep in mind that any attempt to regulate political behavior closely may be doomed to failure. Somehow, people always find ways to get around the rules that other people make. Perhaps the following quote helps to compromise all the conflicting perspectives:

> Power — because of the way it develops and the way it is used — will always result in the organization suboptimizing its performance. However, to this grim absolute, we add a comforting caveat: If any criteria other than power were the basis for determining an organization's decisions, the result would be even worse.[9]

OPENING INCIDENT REVISITED
The Publishing Department

Ginny DeVor in the publishing department wanted to become promoted ahead of an older, more experienced person who was an informal leader of an important group. DeVor's success was, in part, a result of her sensitivity about organization politics.

DeVor's tactics consisted of cultivating friendships before the time when these friendships could be used to secure votes. In order to get the job, DeVor knew that the selection committee's decision must favor her; the most direct approach was to influence the nomination and election of committee members. With 4 sympathetic members on the selection committee, DeVor realized they likely would choose her as the new department head.

DeVor's behavior in the opening incident is quite consistent with the definition of politics presented in this chapter. Carl Ryan was probably unhappy with the outcome because he wanted the job. If Ryan was insensitive to or aloof from office politics, he may have disapproved of the tactics used by DeVor's supporters; he would probably say they were unfair.

Whether the political activities behind DeVor's appointment as department head are in themselves positive or negative is difficult to say. At the individual level, some people are hurt and some people are helped by political behavior. At the organizational level, if political behavior results in a more capable individual being promoted, the organization benefits and the net

effect is positive. Of course, the definition of *capable* is crucial. In this case, some would argue that DeVor was more capable than Ryan because she saw what was necessary to get the job. Individuals who aspire to positions of authority must be sensitive to influential organization characteristics, and DeVor certainly was sensitive. On the negative side, this perspective of "capable" might allow DeVor to rationalize doing whatever is necessary to get her preferred decisions in her daily job performance, which could be undesirable to the publishing department or the agency itself.

All individuals must make their own decisions about how involved they will be in organization politics. Clearly, all sorts of people are prepared to become heavily involved in an attempt to further their careers. Their activities will have an impact on other members of the organization as well as people in the society at large.

SUMMARY

The manager of the formal organization establishes what employees should do through organizational charts and job descriptions. However, the official structure is only part of organizing. Another structure emerges consisting of informal relationships created, not by officially designated managers but, by any and all organization members.

A group exists when 2 or more people join together to accomplish a desired goal. Both the formal and informal organization have goals, although managers often do not like to recognize the existence of those of the informal organization. The formal organization has performance standards, and the informal organization has norms that are standards of behavior expected from group members. The concept of informal role is broader than that of its counterpart in the formal organization (the job). A role consists of an individual's total pattern of expected behavior. Norms and roles shape the dynamics of informal organization relationships. Informal group leaders emerge from the group. The informal organization also has its structure, which is constantly changing and is rarely diagrammed.

The degree of attraction that the group has for each of its members is referred to as cohesiveness. The size of the informal organization is a major factor determining its effectiveness. Because interpersonal relationships are the essence of the informal organization, the informal group tends to be small so that its members may interact frequently. Synergism creates the possibility that when 2 or more people work together, they can do more than would have been possible by working separately. Although some managers attempt to reduce the influence of the informal organization, they are rarely successful; it continues to exist and brings with it both benefits and costs to the organization.

Status, power, and organization politics are concepts that all managers constantly observe. A person's rank or position in a group is referred to as status. Status symbols are visible signs of a person's social position and official influence in the organization. Status assists in meeting the needs of an individual, aids in the communication process, and serves as a motivational device for managers.

Power refers to the ability of one person to influence the behavior of another person. As with status, it is neither completely formal nor informal. The primary sources of power are: formal authority; rewards; punishment; expertise; and identification with individuals who are respected. Power is important to managers because it permits them to benefit others on behalf of the organization.

Organization politics is the means by which power can be acquired, transferred, and exerted on others. Through office politics, adjustments and accommodations are made to varying conditions and pressures. Some degree of political action will occur in any organization regardless of the caliber of people involved or the degree of formalization of organization rules and regulations. Opponents and supporters of organization politics continually debate its impact on organizations.

REVIEW QUESTIONS

1. Describe how group goals, norms, roles, leadership styles, and structure differ in both the formal and informal organizations.
2. What effect do cohesiveness, size, and synergism have on the informal organization?
3. In your own words, describe the costs and benefits that may be attributed to the informal work group.
4. What is the purpose of a contact chart?
5. Define: *status; power; politics.*
6. What are the 3 functions of status?
7. In your own words describe the various sources of power. What is the significance of the understanding of power to a manager?
8. What is the role of politics in today's business organization?

EXERCISES

1. Develop a contact chart for an organization of which you are a member. Interpret the results.

2. Identify 3 groups of which you are a member. What are the various status symbols in the group?
3. Collect 5 articles from your local newspaper that relate to the use of power. Describe how power was used to obtain results or why it failed to achieve results.

CASE STUDY

The Young Accountant

Dave Maddala was recruited to work as an accountant for Bradford Ltd., a manufacturer specializing in producing oil field parts. Dave brought with him an impressive record from his university years, both as an excellent student and his involvement in all forms of campus activities. Also, Dave worked intensely for the chartered accountancy firm that employed him while he studied for his CA exams. Generally, people felt comfortable around Dave, and his opinions were well respected by the students, faculty, and fellow workers.

Donald Dean, the department head, took great pride in having hired Maddala once he was fully qualified. Dean bragged to his superiors about how he was able to attract Maddala to Bradford Ltd. As expected, when Maddala began with Bradford, he started with the same intensity that earned him the respect earlier. Maddala learned the job quickly and within a short time was identifying and initiating changes that could improve operations. He followed the chain of command and cleared each modification with Dean. This pleased Dean, for he was able to take the credit for the changes with his superiors.

In the department, 10 other accountants reported to Dean. They soon came to recognize Maddala's expertise; they began to go to him with their particular problems, since Maddala's easy-going personality made it easy for others to talk to him. Even though Maddala was junior in age, he was regarded as a true professional. As time went on, employees would even go to him with their personal problems.

A strange situation ultimately developed. If an employee had a problem, he or she would first go to Maddala. If he could not solve it, he would go to Dean. Upward communication was going entirely through Maddala.

Although Dean did not have a reputation for political sensitivity, he recognized what had evolved. Although the department had gained in efficiency since Maddala had joined the firm, Dean did not like his loss of power. He even felt that his career was in jeopardy. Dean reasoned that the only way to eliminate this threat was to ensure that Dave was either transferred or pressured to resign.

Dean immediately began a harassment campaign. He reprimanded Maddala in front of his peers. Anything Maddala recommended Dean immediately disapproved. It did not take long for the other employees to recognize that, if they associated with Maddala, they were in trouble. Various instances of subtle discipline were in store for those who even spoke to Maddala. Ultimately, Dean's strategy worked; Maddala quit. But, 6 of Dean's best accountants also resigned and his department was thrown into complete confusion.

QUESTIONS

1. Why did Dave Maddala become an informal leader?
2. To what extent was Maddala a threat to his supervisor, Donald Dean? How noticeable and influential are status, power, and politics in this situation? Discuss.
3. How can a strong informal group affect the operations of a department such as accounting?
4. Evaluate Dean's position at Bradford Ltd. once Maddala resigned.

CASE STUDY

Power Play

Robert Henri grew up on a farm near Bedford, Quebec. His parents were disciplinarians, conservative in their views, and over the years helped him to develop a strong sense of right and wrong. He had been happy through childhood because his parents stressed the value of hard work and harmony in the family.

After Henri graduated with an engineering degree from Laval University, he went to work for Latimer Hydraulics, a firm which specialized in the custom manufacture of liquid pumping systems for agriculture and industry. Customers approached the company with a specific problem and its hydraulic engineers would design a system to meet the customer's need. Since the systems were custom-made, testing them was an important function.

Henri was a first-rate engineer, and his boss, Charles Toland, soon recognized Henri as a valuable addition to the company. Henri was given increased responsibility in a variety of areas and he always performed well. Four years after Henri joined the firm, a major contract was landed by Latimer Hydraulics. The contract involved building a state-of-the-art system for Creighton Manufacturing, and Henri was named chief engineer on the project. In that role he had the responsibility of overseeing all aspects of the contract, including final testing of the system.

Design and production went well for the first four months. The work was proceeding on time, and preliminary test results were positive. However, 3 weeks before the new system was to be ready, Henri received the results of a test on a major component of the system, indicating that it did not work. The tests were repeated, but the results were the same. Henri therefore began to redesign in order to remedy the defect. He also informed Toland that additional time would be needed to complete the project. At that point the following conversation took place:

Toland: I'm sorry, but I can't give you any additional time to complete the project. The customer needs it in 3 weeks. Just sign the test report saying that the system works and we'll get it working later. We've done that before when we had problems.

Henri: I can't do that. The system doesn't work! It wouldn't be right.

Toland: As the chief engineer, you've got to sign the test report.

Henri: I won't sign it until the system is working.

Toland: Now, Robert, listen to reason. This contract is going to put Latimer on the map! You want to be part of that, don't you? Now sign the report.

Henri: You can sign it if you want. I won't be part of a deception like that. It's unethical.

Toland: Well, I'm going to have to sign it. I'm sorry to say this, but I'm going to remove you as chief engineer, effective immediately.

Disappointed and somewhat shocked, Henri continued to argue his point. Toland seemed unable to understand. The next day, Henri resigned.

Several months later, Henri read in the paper of a problem that had developed between Latimer Hydraulics and Creighton Manufacturing involving a pumping system that didn't work. The paper noted that, after some negotiations between Latimer and Creighton, a satisfactory arrangement had been worked out. It also noted that Charles Toland had been promoted to executive vice-president of Latimer Hydraulics.

QUESTIONS

1. What factors contributed to Robert Henri's resignation? What could he have done to avoid the situation that led up to it?
2. Evaluate Toland's decision as a manager.
3. What would you have done in this situation?

NOTES

[1]Arthur D. Sharplin, Northeast Louisiana University, unpublished working paper (December 1981).

[2]Samuel A. Stouffer, et al., *The American Soldier* (Princeton: Princeton University Press, 1949): vol. 2, 1974.

[3]G. R. Salancik and J. Pfeffer, "Who Gets Power — And How They Hold On To It: A Strategic Contingency Model of Power," *Organizational Dynamics* 5 (1977): 3.

[4]J. Pfeffer, *Power in Organizations* (Boston: Pitman, 1980): 7.

[5]Derived from working papers developed by Robert M. Noe III, East Texas State University (April 1981).

[6]David C. McClelland and David H. Burnham, "Power is the Great Motivator," *Harvard Business Review* 54 (March-April 1976): 102.

[7]F. H. Goldner, "Success vs Failure: Prior Managerial Perspective," *Industrial Relations* (October 1970): 457–474.

[8]John M. Pfiffner and Frank P. Sherwood, *Administrative Organization* (Englewood Cliffs, New Jersey: Prentice-Hall, 1960): 311.

[9]Salancik and Pfeffer, 20.

REFERENCES

Allen, R. W., et al. "Organizational Politics: Tactics and Characteristics of Its Actors." *California Management Review* 22 (Fall 1979): 77–83.

Amernic, Jerry, "The Perks of Power." *The Financial Post Magazine* (November 1, 1982): 76.

Astley, W. Graham, and Sachdewa, Paramjit, S. "Structural Sources of Intraorganizational Power: A Theoretical Synthesis." *Academy of Management Review* 9, no. 1 (January 1984): 104–113.

Briscoe, Dennis R. "Organizational Design: Dealing with the Human Constraint." *California Management Review* 23 (Fall 1980): 71–80.

Cobb, Anthony T. "An Episodic Model of Power: Toward an Integration of Theory and Research." *Academy of Management Review* 9, no. 3 (July 1984): 482–493.

Franklin, J. E. "Down the Organization: Influence Processes across Levels of Hierarchy." *Administrative Science Quarterly* 20 (June 1975): 153–164.

Hall, R. H., et al. "Patterns of Interorganizational Relationships." *Administrative Science Quarterly* 22 (September 1977): 457–474.

Harragan, Betty Lehan. *Games Mother Never Taught You*. New York: Warner Books, 1977.

Herker, C., and Aldrich, H. "Boundary Spanning Roles and Organization Structure," *Academy of Management Review* 2 (April 1977): 217–230.

Hodge, John. "Getting Along with the Informal Leader." *Supervisory Management* 25 (October 1980): 41–43.

Lincoln, J. R., and Miller, J. "Work and Friendship Ties in Organizations: A Comparative Analysis of Relational Networks." *Administrative Science Quarterly* 24 (June 1979): 181–199.

Lucas, H. C. Jr. "MIS Affects Balance of Power." *Management Accounting* 61 (October 1979): 61–68.

March, James G., and Feldman, Martha S. "Information in Organizations as Signal and Symbol." *Administrative Science Quarterly* 26 (June 1981): 171–186.

Mayes, B. T., and Allen, R. W. "Toward a Definition of Organizational Politics." *Academy of Management Review* 2 (October 1977): 672–678.

McKenna, R. F. "Blending the Formal with the Informal System." *Journal of Systems Management* 26 (June 1975): 38–41.

McQueen, Rod, "Brawl in the Family." *Canadian Business* (March 1984): 62.

Miles, R. H., and Perreault, W. D. Jr. "Organizational Role Conflict: Its Antecedents and Consequences." *Organizational Behavior and Human Performance* 17 (October 1976): 19–44.

Miller, J. "Isolation in Organizations: Alienation from Authority, Control, and Expressive Relations." *Administrative Science Quarterly* 20 (June 1975): 260–271.

Mintzberg, Henry. "Power and Organization Life Cycles." *Academy of Management Review* 9, no. 2 (April 1984): 207–224.

Moschis, G. P. "Social Comparison and Informal Group Influence." *Journal of Marketing Research* 13 (August 1976): 237–244.

Pfeffer, Jeffrey. *Power in Organizations.* Marshfield Ma.: Pitman, 1982.

Quick, J. C. "Dyadic Goal Setting and Role Stress: A Field Study." *Academy of Management Journal* 22 (June 1979): 241–252.

Quinn, R. E. "Coping with Cupid: The Formation, Impact, and Management of Romantic Relationships in Organizations." *Administrative Science Quarterly* 22 (March 1980): 57–71.

Roos, L. L. Jr., and Hall, R. I. "Influence Diagrams and Organizational Power." *Administrative Science Quarterly* 25 (March 1980): 57–71.

Schmidt, S. M., and Kochan, T. A. "Interorganizational Relationships: Patterns and Motivations." *Administrative Science Quarterly* 22 (June 1977): 230–234.

Schriensheim, C. A. "Similarity of Individually Directed and Group Directed Leader Behavior Description." *Academy of Management Journal* 22 (June 1979): 345–355.

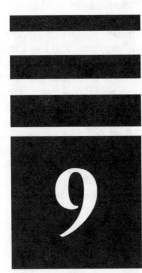

9

Staffing the Organization

OPENING INCIDENT

Condor Steel

Douglas Gardner is the plant superintendent of Condor Steel's rolling mill in Hamilton. He has been with the company for 27 years, is highly regarded, and runs the mill with a very firm hand. His mill has the highest efficiency rating of the 8 mills operated by Condor.

As is typical of large Canadian manufacturers, the personnel department at Condor plays a substantial role in recruiting both blue- and white-collar workers. It cannot, however, dictate to line management who they should hire. Recently, Karen Mercato, the personnel administrator, developed a list of candidates for a newly established quality control managerial position

in the plant. When Mercato and Gardner met to discuss the candidates, the following exchange took place:

Gardner: I've looked over these candidates and, in my mind, the only person who could handle the job is Bill Prosser. He's been in the plant for 7 years and has some on-the-job training that will be valuable. I've talked to him on several occasions and I know I could work well with him because we see eye-to-eye on production.

Mercato: Of course, you have the final say on hirings, but I think I should warn you that you'll have problems if you choose Prosser. I know Monica Stewart really wants that job and she has been here longer than Prosser. Remember that she has some formal academic training in quality control. Gilles Ferrier is also a strong candidate — he held a quality control position at Inland Steel before he came to work for Condor. Do you think you should ignore these two candidates?

Gardner: Stewart and Ferrier may look good on paper, but they just won't work out. I have a sixth sense about people on the job. Besides, neither of those two are compatible with what I want to do. Take Stewart, for example. She won't be able to cope with all the hassling she'll get from the guys in the plant. Ferrier is tough enough, but he hasn't earned respect out there because he hasn't worked in the plant long enough. The person who takes this job will have to work under pressure, and he's got to be strong to take the deadline demands. Prosser is the only one who will fit in, so I'm going to choose him.

Mercato: Doug, you can't refuse a job to candidates on the grounds that they won't fit in or because they're the wrong sex. You'll have to form some more valid reasons for not considering them. Either Ferrier or Stewart may file a complaint with the human rights commission saying they weren't fairly considered for the job.

Gardner: That's ridiculous! I've considered them fairly and I've concluded that they won't be able to handle the job. You know, Karen, I'm getting sick and tired of government rules about who we can hire, promote, and fire. In our business, we've got to make hard, quick decisions so that the mill works at peak efficiency. The company's got to remain competitive so that we can beat out foreign competition. Why don't you let me run this mill the way I see fit? So far I've done that very well without advice from outsiders and I'm going to continue my way until somebody forces me to do otherwise.

Mercato: Well, Doug, I hope we don't have any legal hassles about this. A commission enquiry could cost Condor a lot of money and goodwill.

Gardner: Don't worry about it. I'll handle it.

KEY TERMS

personnel planning
recruitment
selection
training and
  development
organizational
  development
performance
  appraisal
compensation
health
safety

staffing process
job analysis
job description
job specification
work load analysis
work force analysis
employment
  requisition
recruitment
screening interview
employment
  application

testing
validity
reliability
interview
patterned
  interview
unstructured
  interview
stress interview
orientation
assessment center

LEARNING OBJECTIVES

After completing this chapter you should be able to
1. Identify and briefly describe the basic functions related to human resources that must be accomplished if the firm's employment needs are to be met.

2. State the predominant laws that affect the staffing process.
3. Describe what is involved in human resources planning and recruitment.
4. Explain each phase of the selection process.
5. State some special considerations involved in selecting managerial personnel and identify some techniques for identifying managerial talent.

The success of a firm depends, to a great extent, on its effectiveness in selecting quality personnel. A firm will not profit if it has high market potential for a product or service but no capable personnel to direct the effort to achieve the market potential. The need for sound selection and development practices is crucial for all types of organizations — banks, retail stores, manufacturing plants, hospitals, schools, and professional sports teams.

In this chapter we examine human resource management. We first describe the basic human resource management activities to be performed if an organization is to make effective use of its personnel. Second, we note the legal framework within which an organization's personnel function operates. Government regulation has become increasingly important in recent years and will have a substantial future impact on the personnel function. Third, we describe in detail the key elements in the staffing process. Finally, we discuss briefly the special problems that are encountered in executive recruitment.

MANAGEMENT OF HUMAN RESOURCES

Managers must work with the firm's human resources if organization goals are to be achieved. The firm must attract, select, train, motivate, develop, and retain qualified people. Employees must also be permitted to satisfy at least some of their own personal needs. Six basic activities must be performed in a firm to utilize its human resources effectively: (1) staffing, (2) training and development, (3) compensation, (4) health and safety, (5) employee and labor relations, and (6) personnel research.[1]

Staffing: Personnel Planning, Recruitment, and Selection

An organization should determine in advance how many workers and what kinds of skills are needed to accomplish the firm's objectives. This analysis of future personnel requirements is **personnel planning**. **Recruitment** involves encouraging individuals with the needed skills to make application for employment with the firm. **Selection** is the process of identifying those individuals who will best be able to assist the firm in achieving its goals. These 3 tasks must be carefully coordinated if the firm is to manage its human resources to its best advantage.

Training and Development

Training and development (T&D) programs help individuals, groups, and the entire organization to become more effective. Training is needed because people, jobs, and organizations are always changing. T&D should begin at the time individuals join the firm and continue throughout their careers. Large-scale T&D programs are called **organizational development** (OD). The purpose of OD is to alter the firm's internal environment so that employees can become more productive.[2]

A management technique that is closely associated with T&D is performance appraisal. Through **performance appraisal**, employees are evaluated to determine how well they perform their assigned tasks. Managers identify both strong points and areas for improvement; any obvious deficiencies can often be amended through T&D programs.

Compensation

The issue of what constitutes a fair day's pay has been a major concern of managers for decades. Employees must be provided with adequate and equitable rewards for their contributions to organization goals. **Compensation** includes all rewards individuals receive as a result of their employment. As such, it is more than monetary income. The reward may be one or a combination of:

- Pay: The money that a person receives for performing jobs.
- Benefits: Additional financial rewards other than base pay, such as paid holidays, medical insurance, and retirement programs.
- Nonfinancial: Nonmonetary rewards that an employee may receive, such as enjoyment of the work performed and a pleasant working atmosphere.

Health and Safety

Health refers to the employees' physical and mental well-being. **Safety** involves the protection of employees from injuries caused by work-related accidents. These topics are important to managers because employees who enjoy good health and work in a safe place are more likely to be productive; forward-thinking managers support safety and health programs. Today, because of government legislation, all organizations have to become concerned about their employees' safety and health.

Employee and Labor Relations

As we noted in Chapter 2, millions of Canadian workers belong to labor unions. Business firms are required by law to recognize unions and bargain with them in good faith; this relationship has become an accepted way of life for many employers. However, the majority of workers in Canada (68 percent) still do not belong to unions. Nevertheless, people in nonunion organizations are often knowledgeable about union goals and activities. Often, nonunion firms try to satisfy the needs of their employees to persuade them that a union is not necessary for individuals to achieve their personal goals. Thus, unions influence even organizations that are not unionized.

Personnel Research

The personnel manager's research laboratory is the work atmosphere. Research needs permeate all human resources management. For instance, research may be conducted to determine the type of workers who will be most helpful to the firm. Or, it may be directed toward determining the causes of certain work-related accidents. Or, it may involve study and analysis of compensation packages that might increase worker motivation or satisfaction. Personnel research will be increasingly important to all kinds of organizations in the future.

MANAGEMENT IN PRACTICE

Employee Assistance Programs

In the mid-1970s, employee assistance programs (EAPs) were introduced in an attempt to reduce turnover, absenteeism, industrial accidents, and poor employee performance caused, for instance, by depression, money problems, or alcohol abuse. When EAPs are used, companies contract with psychologists and social workers to provide free counseling to employees.

The popularity of EAPs has grown considerably among governments, unions, and large private-sector employers. However, smaller firms still have some reservations about them. Smaller firms usually do not have personnel departments that could implement the programs, and many are simply not aware of the success other companies have had with them.

An alternative to each company having its own EAP is to form a consortium whereby a group of companies supports one EAP. Since 1976, the London Employment Assistance Consortium in Ontario has looked after 10 companies, including firms like 3M Canada, Kellogg, Salada, GM Diesel Division, and Canada International Paper.

Companies using EAPs claim savings of $4 to $15 for every dollar invested. When they were first introduced, there was strong opposition. Management questioned their effectiveness, unions saw them as a disciplinary tool, and employees doubted whether problems they revealed would be kept confidential. Yet, through the years, guidelines for running successful EAPs have led to positive ratings from government, labor, and industry.

SOURCE Michael Salter, "Helping Employees With Personal Problems Pays Off," *Financial Post* (February 11, 1984): 18.

LEGAL ASPECTS OF STAFFING

The main external environment factor that affects managers performing the staffing function is legislation concerning human resources management. When managing human resources, managers must deal with 4 basic categories of laws: (1) antidiscrimination laws, (2) health and safety laws, (3) labor relations laws, and (4) compensation laws.

Antidiscrimination Laws

The key federal antidiscrimination legislation is the Canadian Human Rights Act of 1977. The goal of this Act is to ensure that any individual who wishes to obtain a job has an equal opportunity to compete for it. The Act applies to all federal agencies, Crown corporations, and business firms that do business interprovincially. Thus, it applies to firms like the Bank of Montreal, Air Canada, Telecom Canada, Canadian National Railways, and many other public and private sector organizations that operate across Canada. However, even with such wide application, the Act effects only about 10 percent of Canadian workers; the rest are covered under provincial human rights acts.

The Canadian Human Rights Act prohibits a wide variety of practices in the recruitment, selection, promotion, and dismissal of personnel. The Act specifically prohibits discrimination on the basis of: age, race and color, national and ethnic origin, physical handicap, religion, gender, marital status, or prison record (if pardoned). Some exceptions are permitted with respect to these blanket prohibitions. Discrimination could not be suggested against a blind person who was refused a position as a train engineer, bus driver, or crane operator. Likewise, a firm could not be charged for discrimination if it did not hire a deaf person as a telephone operator or as an audio engineer.

These situations are fairly clear-cut, but many others are not. For example, is it discriminatory to deny women employment in a job which requires routine carrying of objects with a mass of more than 50 kg? Ambiguities in determining whether discrimination has occurred are sometimes circumvented by referring to the concept of "bona fide occupational requirement." This concept means that an employer may choose one person over another based on overriding characteristics of the job in question. If a fitness center wanted to hire only women to supervise its women's locker room and sauna, it could do so without being discriminatory because it established a bona fide occupational requirement.

Even with reference to the bona fide occupational requirement concept, other uncertainties remain. Consider 3 cases: Would an advertising agency be discriminating if it advertised for a male model of about 60 years in age for an ad that is to appeal to older men? Would a business firm be discriminating if it refused to hire a person as receptionist because the applicant was overweight? Would a bank be dis-

MANAGEMENT IN PRACTICE

The Impact of Human Rights Legislation

Years ago, a company could hire anyone it liked. Times have changed. With the advent of the Canadian Human Rights Act and its provincial counterparts, management has found that it must be careful not to violate anyone's human rights.

Take the case of the man who applied for a job as a coach cleaner for Canadian National Railways. The company originally refused to hire him because he had curvature of the spine. But 3 medical specialists testified at a Canadian Human Rights Commission hearing that the man's condition would not affect his ability to do the job. The man was awarded $15,400 in lost wages and was promised that he would be given the next coach cleaner position that came open.

While awards like this are the exception rather than the rule, the case demonstrates the kinds of issues that are now being scrutinized in Canada. In 1982, the Canadian Human Rights Commission handled 444 complaints. Almost half of these were dismissed; 96 others were settled by conciliation, and 61 were either withdrawn or settled during the investigation. Regardless of the outcome of the case, companies have found that dealing with alleged human rights violations is time-consuming and frustrating. Recruitment practices must therefore be closely monitored to ensure that human rights violations do not occur.

SOURCE   Keith McLean, "Legal Liability: Why Your Hiring Practices May Be Discriminatory," *Canadian Business* (February 1984): 114–115.

criminating because it refused to hire an applicant whom the personnel manager felt wouldn't fit in because of his appearance?

We might speculate that the advertising agency is not discriminating, the business firm might or might not be discriminating, and the bank would probably be accused of discrimination, but we can't be sure. The human rights legislation cannot specify all possible situations; so, many uncertainties remain regarding what the law considers to be discriminatory and what it considers to be acceptable. Nevertheless, the spirit of the legislation is clear, and managers must try to abide by it.

Enforcement of the federal Act is carried out by the Canadian Human Rights Commission. The commission can either respond to complaints from individuals who believe they have been discriminated against, or launch an investigation on its own, if it has reason to believe that discrimination has occurred. During an investigation, data are gathered about the alleged discriminatory behavior and, if the claim of discrimination is substantiated, the offending organization or individual may be ordered to compensate the victim.

Each province has also enacted human rights legislation to regulate organizations operating in that one province. These provincial regulations are similar in spirit to the federal legislation, with many minor variations from province to province. All provinces prohibit discrimination on the basis of race, national or ethnic origin, color, religion, sex, and marital status, but some do not address issues like physical handicaps, criminal record, or age. Enforcement of provincial legislation is handled by provincial human rights commissions.

Health and Safety Laws

The purpose of health and safety laws is to ensure that employees do not have to work in situations that are dangerous to their physical or mental well-being. These laws are an outgrowth of the undesirable conditions that existed in many Canadian firms at the close of the nineteenth century and the beginning of the twentieth century. While much improvement is evident, Canada still has some problems in the area of workplace health and safety. In a recent study of 6 western industrialized nations, Canada had the worst safety record in mining and construction, and was next to worst in manufacturing and railways.

In Canada, each province has developed its own workplace health and safety regulations. Provincial health and safety laws are very similar from province to province. The Ontario Occupational Health and Safety Act of 1978 is illustrative; parts of it are described briefly below.

The Ontario Act requires that all employers make sure that equipment and safety devices are used properly. Employers must also indicate to workers the proper way to operate machinery. At the job site, supervisors are charged with the responsibility of seeing that workers use equipment properly. Workers are also required by the Act to behave appropriately on the job. Employees also have the right to refuse to work on a job if they believe it is unsafe; a legal procedure exists for resolving the dispute.

Provincial health and safety regulations provide for the establishment of joint health and safety committees. These committees must be composed of people from both managerial and worker levels. Their purpose is to identify possible hazards in the work place and to make suggestions as to how these hazards can be reduced. The Ministry of Labor in each province also appoints inspectors to enforce workplace health and safety regulations. If the inspector finds a sufficient hazard, he or she has the authority to clear the work place. In most provinces, inspectors can come to a firm unannounced to conduct an inspection.

Labor Relations Laws

One of the crucial areas many Canadian managers must handle is labor relations laws. These laws affect both union and nonunion firms, although union firms will have more daily experience with them. During the past 80 years, several major pieces of federal legislation have been passed dealing with labor relations. The key acts are noted in the table on the opposite page.

In addition to the various federal acts, each province has enacted a labor relations Act. Each is similar to the federal Act in its provisions, but each contains many minor variations. The provincial acts prohibit a wide variety of practices by both labor and management. For example, a manager cannot interfere with the formation of a union, nor can a manager discriminate against a person who is involved in the formation of a union. A union cannot ask management to dismiss an employee simply because the employee has been expelled from the union, nor can the union interfere with the formation of an employers' association.

Compensation Laws

The federal and provincial governments have all enacted legislation dealing with many issues regarding compensation for employment. These laws stipulate such matters as minimum wages, hours of work per day or week before overtime must be paid, statutory holidays, overtime rates, maternity leave, and termination of employment. As with other human resource legislation, compensation laws differ slightly in each jurisdiction. Managers must be aware of the federal laws and the provincial or territorial laws where their organization operates.

THE STAFFING PROCESS

The **staffing process** involves planning for future personnel requirements, recruiting individuals, and selecting from those recruits employees who are most likely to fulfill the needs of the firm. Exhibit 9-1 illustrates the basic steps in the staffing process. In the sections below, we discuss each of these steps.

Four Federal Labor Relations Acts

Industrial Disputes Investigation Act	The first major legislation dealing with labor-management relations, it prohibited work stoppages while a 3-person board (one person each from labor and management, and a neutral chairperson) investigated the dispute.
Privy Council Order 1003	This order guaranteed labor's right to organize and bargain collectively with management.
Industrial Relations and Disputes Investigation Act	Similar to PCO 1003, but applied only to employees of the federal government.
Public Service Staff Relations Act	Gave government workers the right to strike or to have compulsory arbitration.

Human Resources Planning

Plans provide the means whereby the objectives of the organization may be achieved. Therefore, human resources planning is necessary to assure that the organization will have the right numbers and kinds of people available when and where they are needed to perform useful work. Human resources planning, when performed properly, can:

- Enable managers to anticipate shortages and surpluses of labor, allowing the development of plans for avoiding or correcting problems before they become serious
- Permit forecasts of recruitment needs for both numbers and types of skills sought
- Help analyze sources of supply of labor in order to focus recruitment efforts on the most likely sources
- Provide for identification of replacements or backup for present key managers from either inside or outside the organization
- Integrate personnel plans with financial plans and forecasts.[3]

Job Analysis

The process of determining the human qualifications required to perform each job is a **job analysis**. It requires identifying the responsibilities and operations of a job, leading to the development of a job description and job specification. Several methods may be used in conducting job analyses including:

- Observations of and interviews with present employees performing the jobs
- Questionnaires completed by present employees or supervisors of the work
- Analysis by experts
- A diary of activities performed by present employees.

Job Description

The job description is a product of job analysis. As shown in the adjacent insert, a **job description** summarizes the purpose, principal duties, and responsibilities of a job. A job description includes statements on:

- Duties to be performed
- Supervision given and received
- Relationships with other jobs
- Equipment and materials needed
- Physical working conditions.

Job descriptions facilitate the recruitment process by clarifying the specific nature of objectives and responsibilities of jobs. They are also

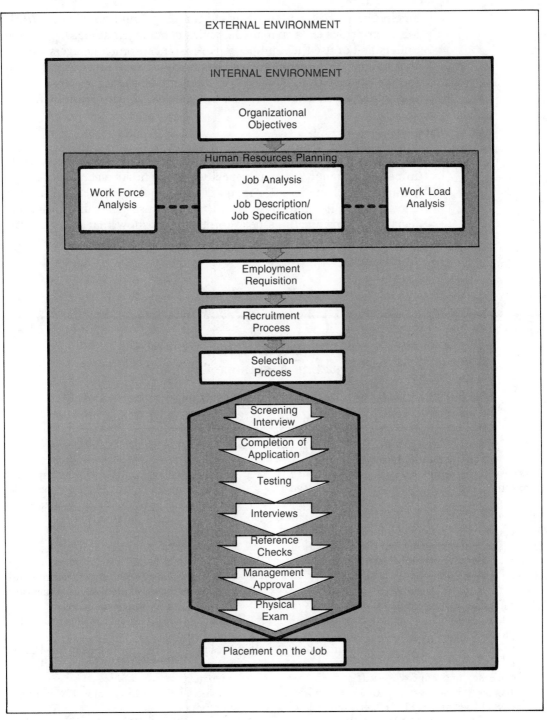

EXHIBIT 9-1   The staffing process

a helpful tool in the orientation and training of new employees. While job descriptions exist in many large firms, managers sometimes do not understand or use them properly. For instance, some managers believe that having job descriptions restricts flexibility and creativity in staffing the organization. However, to be useful to managers, job descriptions must be translated into a statement of human requirements.

Job Specifications

The statement of the minimum acceptable human qualities necessary to perform the job is the **job specification**. The job specification pinpoints such characteristics required for the job as: education, experience, personality, and physical abilities. Because of antidiscrimination legislation, organizations need to be able to show that other characteristics are job related. The job specification is the standard to which the applicant is compared in each step of recruitment.

Job Description
Great West Life Assurance Company

JOB TITLE Senior Benefits Clerk	CLASSIFICATION	C5
DEPARTMENT Personnel Benefits	DEPT. 158 WA 85·04·23	
DIVISION Corporate Resources	COMMITTEE SECRETARY	

General Purpose

To assist in the initial set up and maintenance of benefit records (manual and computer) for the on-going administration of all Company Benefit Programs for Staff and Agents. To provide Staff and Agents with up-to-date information regarding their benefits, ensuring that this information is correct and promptly received.

Duties

1. Maintains computer and manual records of benefit programs for Staff and Agents.
2. Checks the calculation and coding of benefits for new staff and agents, terminations, and changes.
3. Processes and approves staff and agents changes to benefits, for instance, group life, AD&D, Dependent Life, Health and Dental (excluding Evidence of Insurability Forms).
4. Assists in year-end procedures and preparation of benefit summaries.
5. Provides assistance and advice and answers questions on all Benefit Plans (for example, questions on health and dental claims) for Staff and Agents on a daily basis, both by phone and in written form.
6. Prepares pension quotations for checking by the Personnel Benefits Administrator.
7. Checks the calculation of pension refunds.
8. Is responsible for calculation of deferred annuities and issuing certificates.
9. Assists in annual indexing of pension and disability pensions.
10. Is responsible for conversions of life, health, and disability conversions and health extensions.
11. Assists in preparation of monthly premium statements.
12. Is responsible for ensuring long-term disability payments and benefit deductions are handled accurately.

Work Load Analysis

Not only must we know the type of person required for a job but also the number of people necessary to meet organization needs. Determining the number of personnel needed by an organization requires a prediction of future work loads.

Work load analysis involves estimating future types and volume of work to be performed. It requires that forecasts of work volume be prepared. These forecasts are then translated into person-hour requirements. Work programs are often stated in terms of units produced, products assembled, boxes packed, customer calls, or vouchers processed. These are then converted into the number of person-hours by a time study of the units or by averaging past work experience. For example, to produce a specified number of products will require 1000 person-hours of work during a 40-hour work week. By dividing 1000 person-hours by 40 hours, the work load personnel needed would be 25 workers.

---

13. Is responsible for the administration of all applications, changes, and balancing of the Individual Retirement Annuity Plan.
14. Assists in the administration of the Profit-Sharing/Savings Plan in respect of the annual enrollment, terminations, re-entries, and withdrawals.
15. Is responsible for annual enrollment and processing of applications for Accidental Death and Dismemberment Insurance.
16. Handles special projects: for instance, ad hoc increases, statistical studies, and benefit surveys.

Job Specifications

I. Education and Experience   High school education with an aptitude for analytical and mathematical work. Some Company experience in an area using mathematical skills and well-developed communication skills: 2–3 years' experience preferred.

II. Responsibility Level   Works with confidential information (salaries, increases, personal family information).
   Reports to Personnel Benefits Administrator under general supervision.

III. Contacts   Extensive phone and written contact with Staff and Agents (at all levels) regarding their benefits.
   Extensive phone and written contact with other departments, Commission Administration, Payroll, Staff and Agents Claims, Marketing Actuarial Programming, and Group Pensions.
   Some outside Company contacts — Trustees of Profit-Sharing/Savings Plan, other insurance and trust companies.

IV. Job Knowledge   Detailed knowledge about all the Company Benefit Plans and how to calculate benefits under these plans.
   Detailed knowledge of coding procedures and how to read computer output to ensure that there are no errors.
   Good knowledge of department routines and procedures, especially those occurring at year-end.

V. Supervisory Responsibility   Nil.

JOB ANALYST _wA_ CHECKED BY _KH_ APPROVED BY _EH_ DATE _85.04.23_

Work Force Analysis

After determining the number of workers required, personnel research needs a work force analysis. A **work force analysis** consists of identifying the skills of current personnel to determine if work loads can be handled by these employees. If the work cannot be performed by the present work force, individuals will have to be recruited from outside the firm. In some organizations a computerized personnel data bank (human resources information system) assists in providing this information. The following is typical of the information included:

- Personal history: age, sex, marital status, and similar data
- Skills: education, job experience, and training
- Special qualifications: membership in professional organizations and special achievements
- Salary and job history: present salary, past salary, dates of raises, and various positions held
- Company data: benefit plan, retirement information, and seniority
- Capacity of individual: test scores and health records
- Special preferences of the individual: geographic location and work assignments.

Employment Requisition

In most large organizations, an **employment requisition** is issued whenever a job becomes available. The requisition is the product of an analysis of a company's personnel requirements and must be closely coordinated with the job specification. In firms where job specifications are detailed, employment requisitions are usually brief, typically including such information as the job title, starting date, pay scale, and a brief summary of principal duties.

MANAGEMENT IN PRACTICE

Promotions in the Banking Industry

Canada's 5 major banks rank in size among the top 100 banks in the world. Thus, the position of chairman and CEO carries a lot of power: power to squeeze a developing country, to veto major corporate loans, and even to dictate how a business in trouble should operate.

There used to be a standard way of becoming a bank chairman and CEO in Canada. The age-old rags-to-riches notion was very true: start working at a bank at age 16 and gradually work up to a top management position.

The Bank of Montreal was the first bank to bring in outsiders rather than promoting someone from within the ranks of the bank itself. These outsiders gave the bank a fresh outlook and an open mind on modernization.

Merely promoting from outside is not a guarantee of long-term success, however. William Mulholland was brought into the Bank of Montreal in the mid-1970s to "shake up the organization." Profits went up sharply after his arrival and, by 1981, earnings per share were $6.16. Recently, earnings per share have slid to $3.87; critics say that Mulholland's style was right for turning the bank around, but not right for running it on a long-term basis.

SOURCES   Roderick McQueen, "Heirs Apparent," *Canadian Business* (February 1983): 26, 28 and "Bank of Montreal Loses Ground to Rivals," the *Globe and Mail* (November 24, 1984): B1.

Recruitment

The process of searching for prospective employees and encouraging them to apply for available jobs is referred to as **recruitment**. Personnel recruitment can range from locating individuals within the firm who are qualified to conducting a sophisticated and extensive search for a new president.

Personnel can be recruited using internal and/or external sources of qualified applicants. There are advantages and disadvantages of both internal and external sources of applicants. Internal recruitment, or promotion from within, is an important source of personnel for positions above the entry level. Promotion from within has several advantages; it

- Increases morale of employees
- Improves the quality of selection since an organization usually has a more complete evaluation of the strengths and weaknesses of internal applicants than those from outside the firm
- Motivates present employees to prepare for more responsible positions
- Attracts a better quality of external applicants for entry-level jobs if chances for promotion from within are good
- Assists the organization to use personnel more fully.

Despite the advantages of internal recruiting, several disadvantages should be considered; two of these are: (1) the supply of qualified applicants may be inadequate; and (2) internal sources may lead to inbreeding of ideas — current employees may lack new ideas on how to do a job more effectively.

External sources of applicants permit an organization to overcome the disadvantages of recruiting internally. The major advantage of external recruitment is the new ideas that come into the firm with new people. If a firm promotes strictly from within, its personnel may develop a narrow view of the business and may fail to adopt innovative or creative ideas that will help the firm prosper. External recruitment is also needed to maintain a constant labor force since workers do retire, leave the firm, or die.

Keep in mind the distinction between sources and methods of recruitment. Sources of recruitment refers to the location of potential employees. Possible sources of recruitment include high schools and vocational schools, technical schools, community colleges, universities, competitors, and unsolicited applicants. Methods of recruitment are the means by which job applicants may be encouraged to seek employment with the firm. Some methods are advertising, employment agencies, recruiters, and employee referrals. Essentially, the firm must first determine where potential employees may be found and then use the appropriate methods to encourage them to apply. Only when a firm has applicants for a job can the selection process begin.

⊙━ㅍ

THE **Great-West Life** ASSURANCE COMPANY • HEAD OFFICE - WINNIPEG, CANADA

APPLICATION FOR EMPLOYMENT   CAN.

SURNAME		GIVEN NAMES (CIRCLE NAME USED)		

PRESENT ADDRESS			POSTAL CODE	HOW LONG?

TELEPHONE	ALTERNATE TELEPHONE	SOCIAL INSURANCE NUMBER	

HAVE YOU EVER APPLIED FOR EMPLOYMENT WITH THIS COMPANY? NO ☐ YES ☐ WHEN?	HAVE YOU EVER BEEN EMPLOYED BY THIS COMPANY? NO ☐ YES ☐ WHEN?

DATE AVAILABLE TO COMMENCE EMPLOYMENT	TYPE OF WORK FOR WHICH YOU ARE NOW APPLYING	PERMANENT ☐ SUMMER ☐ TEMPORARY ☐ PART-TIME ☐

ARE YOU LEGALLY ENTITLED TO WORK IN CANADA? ☐ YES ☐ NO	SALARY EXPECTED

LANGUAGES:
ENGLISH – ☐ WRITTEN ☐ SPOKEN   FRENCH – ☐ WRITTEN ☐ SPOKEN   OTHER – ☐ WRITTEN ☐ SPOKEN

EDUCATION	NAME OF SCHOOL	ENTERED MONTH YEAR	LEFT MONTH YEAR	GRADE/LEVEL COMPLETED	DEGREE/DIPL. OR CERT. OBTAINED	OVERALL AVERAGE	COURSE TAKEN AND/OR MAJOR SUBJECT
HIGH SCHOOL		NOT REQUIRED	NOT REQUIRED				
UNIVERSITY OR COMMUNITY COLLEGE							
OTHER							

IF COMPLETED HIGH SCHOOL WITHIN LAST 2 YRS. LIST COURSES, THEIR NUMBERS AND MARKS FOR FINAL YEAR. UNDERLINE SUBJECT LIKED MOST, CIRCLE SUBJECT LIKED LEAST.

HAVE KNOWLEDGE OF			OTHER SKILLS
TYPING ☐ (WORDS PER MIN.)	COMPUTER LANGUAGES ☐	SPECIFY _____	
DICTAPHONE ☐	WORD PROCESSING ☐	TYPE OF EQUIP. _____	
CALCULATORS ☐	KEY PUNCH ☐	TYPE OF EQUIP. _____	

PLANS FOR FUTURE EDUCATION

LIST PREVIOUS EMPLOYMENT IN ORDER BEGINNING WITH THE PRESENT OR LAST EMPLOYER

COMPANY	POSITION	DATE STARTED	REASON FOR LEAVING
ADDRESS TELEPHONE NO.	SUPERVISOR OR MANAGER	MONTH YEAR DATE LEFT	
DEPARTMENT	SALARY START FINISH $ $ PER _____	MONTH YEAR	

BRIEFLY OUTLINE DUTIES PERFORMED

COMPANY	POSITION	DATE STARTED	REASON FOR LEAVING
ADDRESS TELEPHONE NO.	SUPERVISOR OR MANAGER	MONTH YEAR DATE LEFT	
DEPARTMENT	SALARY START FINISH $ $ PER _____	MONTH YEAR	

BRIEFLY OUTLINE DUTIES PERFORMED

FOR COMPANY USE   (EMPLOYMENT HISTORY CONTINUED ON REVERSE)

DEPARTMENT NUMBER	TYPING W.P.M.	SOURCE	TEST SCORE	START DATE	SALARY	PREV. EXPER. GWL ☐	TRAINING UNIV. ☐
DIVISION NUMBER	DATE TESTED			REPLACING		YRS.___	BC ☐
JOB NAME		CLASS				OTHER ☐	HS ☐
REPORTING TO LOCAL	PROB. ☐ REGULAR ☐			INTERVIEWER(S)		YRS.___	OTHER

E15CAN-7-82M

EXHIBIT 9-2   An employment application form

EMPLOYMENT HISTORY CONTINUED

COMPANY		POSITION	DATE STARTED		REASON FOR LEAVING
ADDRESS	TELEPHONE NO.	SUPERVISOR OR MANAGER	MONTH	YEAR	
			DATE LEFT		
DEPARTMENT		SALARY / START / FINISH / $ / $ PER _____	MONTH	YEAR	
BRIEFLY OUTLINE DUTIES PERFORMED					

COMPANY		POSITION	DATE STARTED		REASON FOR LEAVING
ADDRESS	TELEPHONE NO.	SUPERVISOR OR MANAGER	MONTH	YEAR	
			DATE LEFT		
DEPARTMENT		SALARY / START / FINISH / $ / $ PER _____	MONTH	YEAR	
BRIEFLY OUTLINE DUTIES PERFORMED					

REFERRED FOR EMPLOYMENT BY	NAMES OF ACQUAINTANCES EMPLOYED BY THIS COMPANY

LIST HOBBIES, CLUBS TO WHICH YOU BELONG OR HAVE BELONGED*, SPORTS, POSITIONS OF LEADERSHIP HELD, AND OTHER SPARE-TIME ACTIVITES

*NOT REQUIRED TO LIST THOSE WHICH WOULD DISCLOSE RACE, RELIGION, COLOUR, SEX, AGE, MARITAL STATUS, POLITICAL BELIEF, NATIONALITY, PHYSICAL OR MENTAL HANDICAP, ETHNIC OR NATIONAL ORIGIN OR FAMILY STATUS.

GIVE BELOW TWO REFERENCES WHO ARE NEITHER RELATIVES NOR FORMER EMPLOYERS

NAME	ADDRESS	TELEPHONE NO.	OCCUPATION
NAME	ADDRESS	TELEPHONE NO.	OCCUPATION

Are you aware of any current health condition or disability that could affect performance on the job and/or attendance record?
☐ No ☐ Yes   If Yes, please elaborate.

_____

_____

_____

Do you require reasonable accommodation or special work conditions to perform the type of work for which you are applying? ☐ No ☐ Yes
If Yes, please elaborate.

_____

_____

_____

In connection with my application for employment I hereby consent that The Great-West Life Assurance Company conduct and/or cause to be conducted a personal investigation. I understand that any misleading or incorrect statements render this application void, and, if employed, may be cause for my termination.

_____   _____   _____
DATE   CITY   SIGNATURE

The Selection Process

The ultimate objective of recruitment is to select individuals who meet the requirements of the job. This is primarily a matter of comparing applicants' skills, knowledge, and education to the requirements of the job description/job specification. There are several steps in the selection process. (Refer to Exhibit 9-1.)

Screening Interview

Screening interviews are typically used to eliminate the obviously unqualified applicants for such reasons as excessive salary requirements, inadequate education, inability to speak coherently, or lack of job-related experience. An applicant who appears to qualify for a position is asked to complete an employment application.

Employment Application

Almost all organizations use a form for **employment application** in selecting new employees. The application collects objective biographical information about an applicant, such as education, work experience, special skills, general background, marital status, and references. (See Exhibit 9-2 for an example of an employment application.) Information obtained from the employment application significantly assists managers in selecting quality personnel. Some organizations design and use a weighted application blank by determining relationships between biographical facts and job success. For example, one bank discovered that newly hired secretaries are least likely to quit the job if they are over 35 years of age, married, not college graduates, and have more than 3 years of experience.[4] Biographical analyses can also be used to predict the quality of job performance. Remember that information requested on an employment application should not lead to discrimination against applicants. Questions referring to an applicant's age, sex, race, religion, national origin, or family status may violate government regulations.

Testing

Traditionally, **testing** has been an integral component in the selection process. Tests have been used to screen applicants in terms of skills, abilities, aptitudes, interest, personality, and attitudes that cannot be objectively judged in other ways. Tests to determine specific skills such as typing or shorthand are in wide use. However, in recent years many organizations have reduced or eliminated their psychological and intelligence pre-employment testing programs because some tests have been found to be instruments of discrimination.

In order to meet legal requirements, tests must possess both validity and reliability. **Validity** of tests is concerned with the relationship between the score on the test and actual job performance. A test is valid if the score on the test can predict job success. Validity is highly

MANAGEMENT IN PRACTICE

Personnel Tests and Hiring Decisions

Because the cost of hiring a manager is getting extremely high, many Canadian companies do extensive testing of applicants before a hiring decision is made. Imperial Oil, Maclean Hunter Ltd., Ontario Hydro, the federal government, and many others use personnel tests when they are recruiting people.

Companies which do personnel testing incur rather substantial expenses (one Toronto testing firm charges $750 for each person tested), but most companies think that the benefits exceed the costs. Warren Shepell, an industrial psychologist, argues that companies which simply interview prospective managers will hire the right person only about half the time, but if they conduct job-related tests, their batting average increases to about 75 to 80 percent.

Some of the tests which are administered are very controversial. For example, the Rorschach inkblot test is designed to get candidates to reveal their inner thoughts based on what they say about a pattern of inkblots. Interpreting a test like this is very difficult. As another example, some firms administer handwriting tests, claiming that certain conclusions can be drawn from the way a person writes. Some of these tests may be discriminatory, but so far Canadian courts have not ruled on the issue.

SOURCE Andrew Tausz, "Probing Before Hiring Can Ease Personnel Grief," *Executive* (April 1984): 40–45.

specific in nature. A test may be valid for one objective and invalid for another. For instance, an IQ test may be valid for measuring abstract intelligence, but it will probably be far less valid in predicting the on-the-job success of a supervisor.

Reliability is concerned with the degree of consistency of test results. If a test possesses high reliability, a person tested a second or third time with the same test, under the same conditions, will obtain close to the first score.

An organization choosing to use testing in the employment process should be careful to avoid potential discriminatory aspects of tests and use tests only as an aid in the process, not as the determining factor.

Interviewing

The **interview** is the most widely used and probably the most important method of assessing the qualifications of job applicants. In general these are several objectives in interviewing job applicants:

- Assessing potential for advancement
- Determining the ability to get along with others
- Assessing personality
- Determining if the person will fit into the organization.

The selection process can choose between two basic types of interviews: direct (patterned) and unstructured (nondirect). In recent years, increased interest has been shown in the use of a directed or patterned interview. In **patterned interviews**, the interviewer follows a predetermined series of questions in interviewing applicants. The interviewer

TALKING TO MANAGERS

Brian Peto
Credit Union Central

Brian Peto is the Personnel Supervisor at Credit Union Central, an organization which is a co-operative financial intermediary within the province of Manitoba. Credit Union Central provides financial opportunities, services, representation, and leadership for member organizations, the majority of which are credit unions. Credit Union Central is often called "the credit unions' credit union." While it does perform some of the traditional functions of a credit union (for example, making loans), its major focus is on the provision of services to credit unions on a basis similar to that of a trade association.

Past President of the Human Resource Management Association of Manitoba, Peto received his diploma in Business Administration from Red River Community College in 1975; he is currently working on a B.A. in administrative

studies. He started his career working full-time for Eaton's as a Personnel Representative. He joined Macleod's in 1977 and helped develop its personnel support function. From 1980 to 1984, Peto was the personnel manager at Burroughs Canada, a major computer manufacturer. In 1984, he joined Credit Union Central of Manitoba. As personnel supervisor, Peto is responsible for developing and administering many of the personnel services that are sold to Manitoba credit unions, such as analyzing compensation packages, recruiting individuals for managerial positions, or evaluating organizational effectiveness.

Q: How is the personnel services activity at Credit Union Central different from that in most personnel departments?

Peto: The difference is that we provide personnel services to independent credit unions around the province of Manitoba. Each credit union is completely autonomous and doesn't have to use our services if it doesn't want to. This contrasts with the situation normally found in companies that have their own personnel departments; staff feel duty-bound to use them whether they do good work or not. For example, if a manager in a credit union doesn't like the quality of service we're providing, he or she can go to some other organization and contract with it to do the work. Or, if a credit union is trying to recruit a general manager, it could use a management consulting firm to find one. This doesn't often happen, however, because we have a proven track record in providing good personnel services. The important point is that we don't have any authority over the line managers in the credit unions.

Q: Do the various credit unions in Manitoba have their own personnel departments?

Peto: Some credit unions are large enough to have full-time personnel staff, but even then they rely on Central's Human Resource Department for support. The majority of credit unions do not have their own departments and therefore rely on the "trade association" principle in using our resources.

Q: What specific kinds of services does your department provide to the credit unions in Manitoba?

Peto: Basically, our service can be divided into the two main areas of personnel services and training. Personnel services include recruitment, personnel policy development, employee benefits, compensation, relocation, and counselling. As far as training goes, we concentrate on the training of management and staff of credit unions, as well as the training of volunteers who serve on the boards of the credit unions.

Q: Can you give us a couple of specific examples?

Peto: Well, suppose the board of directors of a credit union wanted to hire a general manager. Normally the directors would come to us and indicate what kind of a person they are looking for; that's often somewhat dependent on the size of the credit union — they range in size from 2 employees to over 100. Based on the directors' preferences, we then draw up a job specification and begin advertising the opening for potential candidates. For some of these jobs, we get many applicants, so we may have to do considerable screening. After the screening and in conjunction with the board directors, we develop a short list of candidates that they will want to interview. We are normally asked to attend these interviews in order to answer candidates' technical questions about working conditions, conditions of employment, or moving policies, and to help the board with the interview process. The board directors then make the final decision about who will get the job.

As another example, we provide training for tellers at credit unions in two main areas: how to sell services that credit unions offer, and how to do the technical work required in a teller's job. Our department sets up this training and designs it with the credit unions in mind. I would like to point out again that, if a credit union doesn't like what we're doing, it can stop using our training services. So we've got to be responsive to their needs.

Q: In your experience, what role does the personnel department play in most organizations?

Peto: In all four of the companies I've worked for, the personnel function has definitely been a staff function. I have always been in the role of consultant to line managers and have rarely had any authority over their activities. So, I have had to prove that the work of the personnel department is valuable to them. I think I have been able to do that successfully, and I've noticed that, once line managers accept that the personnel department is doing a good job, they come to rely on it for a wide range of services. In order to get to the point where personnel is seen as a desirable service, people who work in it must be able to empathize with line managers and see the organization from their perspective.

Q: How do you ensure that work gets done in the proper way and at the right time?

Peto: I think it is important to make sure people understand exactly what they are supposed to do. It is not enough to give brief directions and then assume that workers are clear on what is to happen. Taking a little more time on the front end to ensure that the worker knows exactly what to do is an important part of the controlling function of a manager's job. It is also important for a manager to check work in progress and to give workers enough authority to do the work properly. For example, if I ask one of my employees to develop data on salary ranges for the credit union system, they must have the authority to gather these data. Of course, they also have to exercise discretion when factoring in market peculiarities and other variables that might distort the data. Once they have salary ranges for one class of jobs — for example, tellers — I usually have them check with me on what they had done so far. If the research looks good, they can then proceed to the next phase, which might be salary ranges for branch managers or secretaries.

Q: How much discretion can you give workers and still carry out your control responsibilities?

Peto: Quite a bit. I've found that, if you make it clear that you expect people to make their own decisions and not come running to the boss all the time, that they will usually exercise good judgment. If you have high expectations, you'll get high performance from people. Feedback is also very important in the control process. You've got to let people know how they're doing, whether it's good or bad. It's easier to give people good news than bad news, but feedback in both areas is necessary.

asks questions and records the applicant's responses. The patterned interview usually yields complete, consistent, and reliable information about an applicant. Also, its use permits easy comparison of several applicants and minimizes interviewer bias and prejudices.

Unstructured interviews have no predetermined interviewing strategy or list of questions. Broad, open-ended approaches, such as "Tell me about yourself," are part of the unstructured interview. The unstructured interview may be useful in assessing such characteristics of an individual as ability to communicate, personal values and personality.

Other types of interviewing techniques have also been used for special purposes. One of these techniques, the group interview, has been frequently used in the selection of managerial trainees. Group interviews are used where a small group of 5 or 6 applicants is observed and evaluated in discussions by 2 or more company managers or interviewers. Another technique, the panel interview, is a situation in which an applicant is interviewed by several people at the same time.

The **stress interview** is another approach that is sometimes used in the selection of managers and potential managers. The stress interview deliberately puts the applicant on the defensive — perhaps by having the interviewer say something like "I don't think you're qualified for this job" — and then observes how the applicant reacts. The logic here is that managerial jobs contain much stress and, if an applicant can handle stress during an interview, he or she may make a good manager.

Regardless of the type of method used, the interview is the most important element in the selection of new personnel. Since most managers must rely on interviewing when selecting new employees or evaluating candidates for promotion, following sound practices is essential. The following guidelines are helpful in conducting effective interviews:

- Plan for the interview: review job specification and description as well as the applications of candidates.
- Create a good climate for the interview: try to establish a friendly, open rapport with the applicant.
- Allow sufficient time for an uninterrupted interview.
- Conduct a goal-oriented interview: seek the information needed to assist in the employment decision.
- Avoid certain types of questions: try not to ask leading questions or questions that may imply discrimination.
- Seek answers to all questions and check for inconsistencies.
- Record the results of the interview immediately on completion.[5]

Over the years, the interview, much like testing, has received considerable criticism concerning its ability to predict success on the job. In interviewing an applicant for employment, many factors influence the decision of the interviewer. For example, the interviewer may allow a first impression of an applicant to influence unduly the outcome of the interview. In a large insurance company, the personnel manager was a great believer in the importance of initial impressions in evaluating applicants for jobs. He placed considerable emphasis on his initial reactions to an applicant's handshake, speed of walking, and eye contact. For male applicants, the personnel manager strongly believed that, if the applicant had a firm handshake, maintained good eye contact when meeting others, and could keep up with the personnel manager's fast walking pace, the applicant was both confident and aggressive. Many managers rely on similar, but sometimes questionable practices in selecting personnel.

Interviews can be instruments of discrimination and, for this reason, they have received close scrutiny in recent years. Charges of possible discrimination have led to an increase in the use of the patterned interview, since it has significantly higher reliability and validity than other methods of interviewing.

An effective means of assessing the success of an organization's interviewing process is to compare performance of employees with the evaluation of these same employees when they were first interviewed for the job. This objective evidence is an indication of the effectiveness or validity of the interview in predicting job success for that organization.

Background and Reference Checks

Once an applicant successfully clears the interviewing hurdle, the practice of many organizations is to conduct background and reference checks. The purpose of checking a person's background and references is to verify the information provided by the applicant in the interview and on the employment application.

Reference checks may or may not yield useful information. Suppose an employee left a previous job because he was not performing up to par. Would a reference check detect this? If the applicant's former manager didn't want to hurt the person's chances of getting another job, or was relieved to get rid of a problem employee, she might not indicate that the employee was a problem. In this case, the person doing the reference check would not really find out anything useful. Another problem with reference checks is the increasing concern about employee privacy. Possibly, as privacy laws become more refined, employers will be reluctant to say much about former employees for fear of being prosecuted for releasing confidential information. Some organizations now have official policies that bar managers from disclosing any information about former employees beyond the years worked and the positions held. Even recommendations are not permitted.

Management Approval

In most large organizations, many of the selection steps are performed by a personnel department. However, the personnel department does not usually make the final decision as to which person is selected for a particular position. Under most circumstances, the manager or supervisor who will be the immediate superior of the new employee will make the final hiring decision. The selection decision is usually made after interviewing all the applicants and reviewing the recommendations of the personnel department. The immediate supervisor knows the needs of his or her department and is in the best position to evaluate the qualifications and characteristics of prospective employees. The supervisor or manager should be able to identify factors in the applicant's background or work experience that would help the new employee fit into the department.

Physical Exams

After a prospective employee has successfully completed the other phases in the selection process, he or she must usually pass a physical exam. The physical exam has at least these 3 basic goals:

- To determine if the applicant can meet the physical demands of the job
- To provide a record to protect the organization against claims for previously incurred injuries
- To prevent communicable diseases from entering the firm.

Placement on the Job: Orientation

Once individuals have been selected for a particular position, they need an orientation to the organization. **Orientation** is the process of introducing the new employee to the organization. Every new employee goes through an orientation period regardless of whether the firm has a formal orientation program. New recruits must learn the ropes or rules of the game if they are to succeed. Much new employee orientation takes place on an informal basis — during coffee breaks, at lunch, or during work — through interactions with longer-term employees. However, most organizations have formal orientation programs designed to acquaint new personnel with the formal items they should know. The table opposite lists these important items.

SPECIAL CONSIDERATIONS IN SELECTING MANAGERIAL PERSONNEL

In recruiting and selecting nonmanagerial personnel, it is usually possible to use more objective factors in identifying potentially successful employees. However, more subjective judgment is often involved in selecting managerial personnel. In selecting managers, many intangible factors like people skills, leadership ability, planning and decision-making skills, attitudes, and personal characteristics are the focus of

An Orientation Outline

1. History and nature of the business
2. Goals of the company
3. Basic products/services provided by the firm
4. Organizational structure
5. Policies, procedures, and rules covering such areas as:
    a. Work schedules
    b. Salaries and payment periods
    c. Physical facilities
    d. Attendance and absenteeism
    e. Working conditions and safety standards
    f. Lunch and coffee breaks
    g. Discipline and grievance
    h. Parking
6. Company benefits:
    a. Insurance programs
    b. Pension and/or profit-sharing plans
    c. Recreation programs — bowling, tennis, or golf
    d. Vacations and holidays
7. Opportunities:
    a. Advancement, promotion
    b. Suggestion systems
8. Specific department responsibilities:
    a. Department functions
    b. Job duties/responsibilities/authority
    c. Introduction to other employees in work group

MANAGEMENT IN PRACTICE

Executive Succession

Planning who the future top executives of a company will be is an important job for Canadian companies. With the increasingly difficult economic atmosphere facing Canadian firms, companies must have capable top executives leading them.

At Hewlett-Packard Canada Ltd., the key to good planning is performance appraisal, according to Brian Wright, the personnel manager. The firm has a large number of training programs which are designed to improve managerial capability. In addition, the company identifies 2 or 3 people who are possible presidential successors. One of the key factors in determining who should be the chief executive is the company's corporate strategy. The strategy will determine the kind of people that are needed to make it work. Overall, succession planning requires that companies clearly identify their needs and then pursue people who can satisfy those needs.

SOURCE Adapted from "Training: A Good Way To Spot Future Executives," *The Financial Post* (May 5, 1984): 24.

evaluation. These intangibles may be much more difficult to assess than such factors as typing ability, filing ability, and manual dexterity, which are measures for lower-level workers.

The recruitment and development of quality managerial personnel is essential to the continuing success of every organization. Because of this need, organizations must be concerned with identifying persons with managerial potential.

Determining Executive Needs

Decisions concerning the number of executives required by an organization involve a comparison of: (1) predicted future needs, and (2) present inventory of talent. Determining needs for managerial personnel requires an inventory of personnel currently available within the organization. The inventory is not simply a counting of heads; it includes a catalog of present and potential abilities and attitudes. It is an assessment not only of skills, experience, and abilities but also of personal motivation. Sometimes, a person who appears to be properly prepared for a promotion indicates a desire to transfer, to change occupational area, or to remain on the present job.

In making up the inventory, a decision must be made about which personnel to include. Certainly, present lower- and middle-managers will be included. In some companies all salaried personnel compensated on a monthly or semimonthly basis are included. Each lower-level manager may be asked to submit recommendations of employees with the potential for advancement. For each individual included, detailed information must be gathered to supplement and update existing data, such as education, experience, performance ratings, health, psychological test results, recreational interests, hobbies, and civic involvement. Such data can be computerized in order that: (1) assessment as to current adequacy of talent reservoirs can be made, and (2) searches can be made to fill particular vacancies arising.

Many companies maintain backup organizational charts to show listings of available talent for each key managerial position in the organization. These charts usually include the names of at least two individuals as replacements for each key position. They also include an assessment of eligibility for promotion for each of the key positions.

Techniques for Identifying Managerial Talent

Identifying individuals with potential executive talent has become an increasingly significant activity in large organizations. In general, the activity has taken two directions: (1) determining the material personal characteristics or behaviors that seem to predict managerial success, and (2) establishing managerial talent assessment centers.

Personal Characteristics

Over the years, considerable interest has been shown in determining the personal characteristics related to managerial success. Major companies, such as AT&T, Sears, General Electric, and Standard Oil, have engaged in research within their firms to identify a series of traits or characteristics necessary for success. The studies related such measures of job performance as productivity, salary level, and quality of work of successful managers with personal characteristics and attitudes of these managers. Some of the characteristics of managers included in these studies were grades in college, level of self-confidence, organized and orderly thought, personal values of a practical and economic nature, intelligence, nonverbal reasoning, and general attitudes.

While a few studies showed a relationship between these kinds of factors and managerial success, for the most part, studies of personal characteristics of managers have not yielded very accurate predictions of managerial success.

Assessment Center

In an effort to improve managerial selection, researchers have developed a second technique for identifying talent in recent years. This approach is the **assessment center** designed to provide the systematic evaluation of the potential of individuals for future management positions. In the typical assessment center, a series of activities is designed to test the potential manager's skills, abilities, attitudes, and judgment. The table on page 304 illustrates a 3-day assessment center that uses a number of different bases on which to evaluate executive candidates. The basic assessment center idea was developed in the 1950s by AT&T and has grown in popularity in both Canada and the United States.

The assessment center procedure usually has 5 steps. The first step involves participants in several activities designed to test the effectiveness of their behavior in simulated, but realistic management situations. For example, a participant might be asked to chair a committee meeting or do a performance appraisal. While the participant is going through these exercises, several assessors observe.

The second step requires individual assessors to draw some conclusions about the participant's planning ability, leadership skills, and communication skills.

In the third step, the assessors pool their individual evaluations and develop a group consensus about how well each of the participants performed during the simulations.

Step four is the preparation of the assessment center report. This report summarizes the participant's behavior during the simulations and notes the participant's strong and weak points.

The final step involves giving the assessment center report to the participants and having one-on-one discussions with them about its

A Typical Schedule for an Assessment Center

Day 1
Orientation of dozen candidates
Break-up into groups of four to play a management game (observe and assess organizing ability, financial acumen, quickness of thinking efficiency under stress, adaptability, leadership)
Psychological testing (measure and assess verbal and numerical abilities, reasoning, interests, and attitudes) and/or depth interviews (assess motivation)
Leaderless group discussion (observe and assess aggressiveness, persuasiveness, expository skill, energy, flexibility, self-confidence)

Day 2
In-Basket exercise (observe and assess decision making under stress, organizing ability, memory and ability to interrelate events, preparation for decision making, ability to delegate, concern for others)
Role-playing of employment or performance appraisal interview (observe and assess sensitivity to others, ability to probe for information, insight, empathy)
Group roles in preparation of a budget (observe and assess collaboration abilities, financial knowledge, expository skill, leadership, drive)

Day 3
Individual case analyses (observe expository skill, awareness of problems, background information possessed for problems, typically involving marketing, personnel, accounting, operations, and financial elements)
Obtainment of peer ratings from all candidates.
Staff assessors meet to discuss and rate all candidates

Weeks later
Manager with assessor experience meets with each candidate to discuss assessment with counseling concerning career guides and areas to develop

contents. The report can also be given to the personnel people to help them decide what additional training and development individuals might need or want.

OPENING INCIDENT REVISITED

Condor Steel

The material in this chapter is relevant to the hiring situation apparent at the Condor Steel Mill run by Doug Gardner. The legal aspects of recruiting, hiring, and promoting people have changed substantially in the past 20 years, and managers must consider them. Formerly, managers had considerable discretion in these areas, but many laws now exist that prohibit activities which used to be widely accepted.

Two problem areas are raised in the Condor incident. The first is the issue of overt discrimination against women in promotions. Gardner is convinced that Stewart cannot handle the quality control job because she couldn't cope with the "hassling she'll get from the guys in the plant." Mercato and Gardner do not mention any bona fide occupational qualification for the job in question; Gardner may put Condor into difficulty if Stewart goes to the human rights commission.

Second, Gardner is ignoring Ferrier, another qualified individual who also has a good claim on the job, because his experience is from another firm. Gardner has apparently decided that Prosser is the man who can best handle the job, but how he came to this conclusion is not clear. Gardner obviously likes Prosser — and may feel he can control him — but beyond that he provides very little evidence that Prosser is better suited for the job than the other 2 candidates.

Gardner says he has a "sixth sense about people on the job," but this evidence will not be acceptable if one of the candidates goes to the human rights commission. Gardner is apparently relying on subjective factors in this decision, which may cause him legal problems.

From Gardner's point of view, he is being unduly dictated to by government and his decision making is being interfered with by Mercato. Gardner looks back on his successful career and wonders why he has to defend his choice to a personnel officer who isn't even a line executive. This incident shows the kind of conflict that can arise between line managers and staff specialists. Each party is competent in his or her area and, when faced with a person who disagrees, each may defend his or her position vigorously.

SUMMARY

People are the most important asset of any organization. Most firms today realize that acquiring and developing quality human resources is essential if the organization is to survive and grow. In most large firms, a human resources or personnel department is responsible for administering the organization's staffing function. However, every manager, regardless of function, must understand and participate in the staffing process.

The 6 basic functions related to human resources are staffing, training and development, compensation, health and safety, employee and labor relations, and personnel research. Staffing primarily involves personnel planning, recruitment, and selection. Training and development programs are designed to assist individuals, groups, and the entire organization to become more effective. Compensation includes all rewards individuals receive as a result of their employment. Health and safety programs are designed to enable workers to have a safe and healthy work place. Employee and labor relations involve dealing with a union or developing an atmosphere where employees believe a union is unnecessary. Personnel research is directed toward gaining a better understanding of human relations problems.

Every manager involved with human resources management is affected by government legislation. Both the federal and provincial levels of government in Canada have passed laws that affect the way managers deal with the recruitment, hiring, promotion, and dismissal of employees. The key federal legislation is the Canada Human Rights Act, which prohibits discrimination on the basis of race and color, national origin and culture, gender, physical handicap, marital status, age, religious beliefs, and pardoned prison record.

The staffing process involves planning for future personnel requirements, recruiting individuals, and selecting from those recruits employees who fulfill the needs of the firm. The process of determining the human qualifications required to perform the job is called job analysis. A job description summarizes the purpose, principal duties, and responsibilities of the job. The statement of the minimum acceptable human qualities necessary to perform the job is the job specification. Work load analysis involves estimating the types and volume of work that needs to be performed if the organization is to achieve its objectives. Work force analysis consists of identifying the skills of current personnel to determine if work loads can be handled by these employees.

In most large organizations, an employee requisition is issued whenever a job becomes available. Recruitment may then begin. The ultimate objective of recruitment is to select individuals who are most capable of meeting the requirements of the job. Selection from among those recruited applicants is the next step. The steps in the selection process are: (1) screening interview, (2) completion of application, (3) testing, (4) interviews, (5) reference checks, (6) management approval, (7) physical exam. Once individuals have been selected, they need an orientation to the organization.

REVIEW QUESTIONS

1. Describe and discuss the different phases in the staffing process.
2. Distinguish between a job description and job specification.
3. What are the major federal and provincial laws that affect the staffing process?
4. Describe the advantages and disadvantages of promotion from within.
5. What are the general objectives that need to be achieved in interviewing job applicants?
6. What steps are involved in the personnel selection process?
7. What is the purpose of an assessment center? Discuss.

EXERCISES

1. Assume you are a personnel director for firms with a vacancy that requires the skills identified below. What phase(s) of the personnel

selection process do you believe would require special attention?
   a. Faculty member for a major university that stresses research
   b. A general laborer for a construction firm
   c. A skilled welder for work on an assembly line
   d. A senior secretary who is required to take dictation and type 70 words per minute
   e. A first-level production supervisor.
2. Consult the personnel wanted section of a major weekend newspaper. Evaluate the positions that are available for the following career fields. Can you detect a general pattern of job requirements that are needed for an applicant?
   a. Personnel manager
   b. Computer specialist
   c. Car salesperson
   d. Production supervisor.

CASE STUDY

Absenteeism of a Long-Service Employee

Quality Business Forms Ltd. has a policy stating that employee absenteeism should not exceed four days during a 90-day work period without medical verification. If an employee does not have medical reasons for excessive absences, he or she may be subject to disciplinary action.

Ed Thompson has been employed by Quality for 21 years. In the past 3 years he has had an abnormal number of absences, which his supervisor chose to ignore because of Thompson's long tenure with the company. Thompson's supervisor was transferred and another individual in the department, Alice Randall, assumed the supervisory position. She immediately advised Thompson that his absenteeism was excessive and that it would have to cease or disciplinary action would be taken. Thompson claimed that he was injured 5 years previously on his job and that his absences were a result of that injury. A review of his health records was undertaken; no injury had ever been reported.

Thompson's attendance improved during the first 6 months under Randall's supervision but began to deteriorate during the latter part of the year. Warned again about the absenteeism, Thompson repeated his previous excuse. At this point, Randall contacted the personnel manager for assistance. Randall was advised that further disciplinary steps should be taken along with a complete physical evaluation by the corporate medical doctor. The physical exam was given immediately and no physical abnormalities were found.

This information was given to Thompson verbally by the doctor, but he did not accept the findings. He was then counseled by the personnel manager, his supervisor, and his department manager. Thompson listened intently to what was said and took notes. He was told that the next step in the disciplinary procedure would be dismissal if his absenteeism continued. He said he understood and that he would work when he felt able and would not work when he did not feel able.

Thirty days later Thompson and Randall were called in to the personnel office at 09:00 and Thompson was terminated. It was a shock to him that he had actually been fired, since the president of the company had to approve the termination of employees with a long service record. A discrimination charge was filed, but was dropped after no grounds could be established. A Workers' Compensation Board claim came in but could not be substantiated.

QUESTIONS

1. Do you agree with the standards developed by the firm with regard to absenteeism?
2. Can you think of reasons for Ed Thompson's absenteeism that could have called for a different reaction from his employer?
3. What responsibilities does an employer have about when a long-term employee should be terminated?
4. How much documentation is really needed to be fair to the employee? to the employer?

CASE STUDY

The Harried Department Head

Ron Colindale was the head of the department of management at a large university. Total university enrollment for the past year was approximately 20 000 and had been increasing slowly each year, despite earlier predictions that it would decline in the 1980s. Demand for spaces in the business school was even higher than that for the university as a whole. For example, last year, 1345 students applied for admission to the business school; only 485 were admitted because of limited teaching staff.

Unlike many other faculties on campus, the business school was actively recruiting teachers in an attempt to satisfy the demand for management education. As a department head, Colindale was responsible for recruiting, but he was rapidly becoming frustrated by the rigid rules and regulations he had to follow. Two factors were at the root of his frustration: (1) very few people who had a PhD in business could be attracted to teaching, and (2) recruiting rules were very strict. Colindale had discovered, for example, that, if he wanted to hire an American, he had to prove that no equally qualified Canadian applicants were available. Colindale didn't have any particular preference for American faculty but, since many more candidates with PhDs were produced in the United States than in Canada, he would have more candidates to choose from.

Explicit directions had been provided for the wording and publication timing of advertisements Colindale wanted to place in various university journals. The wording directions concerned both the Canadian-American issue and the gender bias issue. Although no laws demanded that a certain number of women be hired, the university required that equal opportunity be heavily emphasized in the ads. Colindale considered himself personally supportive of equal opportunity, but he found himself starting to worry about satisfying the restrictions confronting him. For the timing deadlines, Colindale's ad had to appear in at least 2 consecutive issues, at least 60 days before the closing date for applications.

The rules and regulations did not stop there. Once Colindale had received curriculum vitae from various candidates, he had to meet with a committee of faculty members from his department. This committee — one member of which had to be a woman — would choose the 3 most promising applicants and invite them for an interview. Several lengthy meetings occurred, during which Colindale and one committee member disagreed persistently about the qualifications of several applicants.

Colindale finally had the following discussion with the Dean of the Faculty of Business, Gene Moeller:

Colindale: You know, Gene, this recruiting is starting to get me down.

Moeller: What's the problem?

Colindale: Well, all these rules and regulations make it difficult to do an efficient job of staffing my department. Every time I turn around there's another restriction. Making sure I'm adhering to all these rules sure takes a lot of time.

Moeller: But these rules are designed to ensure equal treatment for all applicants.

Colindale: I know, but I have to get special permission to make decisions that managers in other organizations could do in the normal course of their work.

Moeller: Like what?

Colindale: Well, take the initial screening of applicants: surely I should be able to do that on my own? I could then present my short list of candidates to the recruiting committee and we could decide which candidates to have in for an interview. I have spent hours involved in detailed discussions of every applicant with all the committee members. I don't have the time to do that and keep up my teaching, administrative work, and research.

Moeller: I'd like to help, but I'm afraid you don't have any alternative in this area. The recruiting rules are quite specific. But you've done a good job so far; keep up the good work and don't let it get you down. Well, it's time for the dean's council meeting, Ron. Nice talking to you.

QUESTIONS

1. What circumstances have motivated the university to state recruiting regulations so specifically?
2. What federal laws are relevant for this case?
3. What should Ron Colindale do? Why?

NOTES

[1] This section is based on the discussion in R. Wayne Mondy and Robert M. Noe III, *Personnel: the Management of Human Resources* (Boston: Allyn and Bacon, 1981): 8–11.

[2] Lester A. Digman, "Let's Keep the OD People Honest," *Personnel* 56 (January-February 1979): 23.

[3] Lewis E. Albright, "Staffing Policies and Strategies," *ASPA Handbook of Personnel and Industrial Relations*, edd. Dale Yoder and Herbert Heneman (Washington, D.C.: Bureau of National Affairs, 1974): vol. 1, 4–21.

[4] Stanley R. Jovack, "Developing an Effective Application Blank," *Personnel Journal* 49 (May 1970): 421.

[5] C. Harold Stone and Floyd L. Ruch, "Selection, Interviewing, and Testing," in *ASPA Handbook of Personnel and Industrial Relations*, edd. Dale Yoder and Herbert G. Heneman (Washington, D.C.: Bureau of National Affairs, 1979): 152–154.

REFERENCES

Breaugh, J. A. "Relationship between Recruiting Sources and Employee Performance, Absenteeism, and Work Attitudes." *Academy of Management Journal* 24 (March 1981): 142–147.

Bucalo, J. "Personnel Directors: What You Should Know Before Recommending MBO." *Personnel Journal* 56 (April 1977): 176–178.

Byham, William C. "Assessment Centers for Spotting Future Managers." *Harvard Business Review* 40 (July-August 1970): 158.

Campbell, Andrew. "Hiring for Results — Interviews that Select Winners." *Business Quarterly* 48, no. 4 (Winter 1983): 57–61.

Collins, E.G.C., and Blodgett, F. B. "Sexual Harassment: Some See It — Some Won't." *Harvard Business Review* 59 (March-April 1980): 77–94.

Davies, G. S. "Consistent Recruitment in a Graded Manpower System." *Management Science* 22 (July 1976): 1215–1220.

Dhanens, T. P. "Implications of the New EEOC Guidelines." *Personnel* 56 (September 1979): 32–39.

Gandz, Jeffrey, and Rush, James C. "Human Rights and the Right Way to Hire." *Business Quarterly* 48, no. 1 (Spring 1983): 70–77.

Greer, Charles R. "Countercyclical Hiring as a Staffing Strategy for Managerial and Professional Personnel: Some Considerations and Issues." *Academy of Management Review* 9, no. 2 (April 1984): 324–330.

Heflich, D. L. "Matching People and Jobs: Value Systems and Employee Selection." *Personnel Administration* 26 (January 1981): 77–85.

Henderson, J. A. "What the Chief Executive Expects of the Personnel Function." *Personnel Administration* 22 (May 1977): 40–45.

Higgins, James M. "A Manager's Guide to the Equal Employment Opportunity Laws." *Personnel Journal* 55 (August 1976): 406–412.

Hoffman, W. H., and Wyatt, L. L. "Human Resources Planning." *Personnel Administration* 22 (January 1977): 19–23.

Hollingsworth, A. T., and Preston, P. "Corporate Planning: A Challenge for Personnel Executives." *Personnel Journal* 55 (August 1976): 386–389.

Malinowski, F. A. "Job Selection Using Task Analysis." *Personnel Journal* 60 (April 1981): 288–291.

Marr, R., and Schneider, J. "Self-Assessment Test for the 1978 Uniform Guidelines on Employee Selection Procedures." *Personnel Administration* 26 (May 1981): 103–108.

McLean, Keith, "Legal Liability — Why Your Hiring Practises may be Discriminatory." *Canadian Business* 57, no. 2 (February 1984): 114–115.

McQueen, Roderick. "Heirs Apparent." *Canadian Business* 56, no. 2 (February 1983): 26.

"Probing Before Hiring Can Ease Personnel Grief." *Executive* 26, no. 2 (February 1983): 40–45.

Salter, Michael. "Helping Employees with Personal Problems Pays Off." *Financial Post* (February 11, 1984): 18.

"Training: A Good Way to Spot Future Executives." *The Financial Post* (May 5, 1984): 24.

IV
Influencing

10
Motivation

OPENING INCIDENT

Baylor's Department Store

George Homenchuk was the vice-president of operations for Baylor's Department Store in Edmonton. For the past 20 years the store had surveyed its customers annually about their feelings toward the store. The last 3 surveys had shown a disturbing trend — customers felt that the salesclerks in the store were unfriendly and not very helpful. These feelings had been reflected in sales; the data Homenchuk had before him revealed that both absolute sales volume and profit margins had declined for the last 3 years.

Homenchuk believed the problem was very serious, so he called a meeting of Baylor's executive committee to deal with it. In attendance were the vice-presidents of marketing, finance, personnel, and merchandising. After a lengthy meeting with considerable input from the personnel vice-president, the executive committee decided that the real problem was low motivation levels among salesclerks. These low motivation levels apparently had resulted in indifferent attitudes toward customers. Several executives at the meeting commented that rumors had filtered up to them that clerks on the floor were not happy because they felt they were being ignored by management.

The vice-president of personnel, Lise Daniels, pointed out that Baylor's conducted attitude surveys of employees from time to time, and these revealed: (1) salesclerks did not find their jobs interesting; (2) they received little feedback on how well they were doing; and (3) they felt that there were inequities across departments in terms of workload. A discussion then ensued about how these attitudes could be improved. Daniels pointed out that, since the salesclerks were on straight salary, they were all paid the same amount of money regardless of their sales. She suggested that the clerks be put on commission; if so, Daniels argued, salesclerks would show much more interest in customers and therefore would sell more. She cited evidence from a number of organizations showing that the introduction of an incentive system had resulted in increased output by employees and increased profit for the organization.

Some of the members of the executive committee thought that this step was rather drastic and that employee turnover would surely increase if the system were implemented. They cited evidence from companies where this had happened. Other members thought that an incentive scheme really wouldn't solve the problem of poorly motivated employees because money wasn't a good motivator of people. In view of these disagreements, Homenchuk scheduled a second executive committee meeting for one week later, to allow the members time to mull over the problem and to come up with a workable solution.

KEY TERMS

motivation	need for achievement	reinforcers
motive	need for power	equity theory
Theory X	need for affiliation	job design
Theory Y	expectancy theory	job rotation
self-fulfilling	expectancy	job enlargement
prophecy	valence	job enrichment
hierarchy of needs	reinforcement theory	quality circles
E-R-G theory	organizational	Theory Z
hygiene factors	behavior	Seven S Model
motivators	modification (OBM)	

LEARNING OBJECTIVES

After completing this chapter you should be able to
1. Define motivation and explain some basic philosophies of human nature.
2. Distinguish between the motivation theories of Abraham Maslow and Clayton Alderfer.
3. Explain the motivation theory of Frederick Herzberg.
4. Describe the work of David McClelland as it relates to motivation.
5. Explain how expectancy theory, organizational behavior modification, and the self-fulfilling prophecy might be applied in business.
6. Explain job design and its relationship to job enrichment and job enlargement.

The problem facing Baylor's Department Store is, unfortunately, a common one in all kinds of organizations. Increasingly, researchers and employers report that today's employees do not respond to managers in the more compliant way their earlier counterparts did. Apparently the prosperity of the post–World War II era has caused fundamental changes in the way workers view their jobs — although recessions can produce further changes. Still, managers cannot ignore employees' views of their jobs without ignoring the basic management function of influencing.

Influencing is the management function of directing or stimulating the members of an organization to follow its plans and objectives, to work efficiently, and to help the firm to prosper. Managers can influence employees — as well as other managers — through motivation, through their leadership, through effective communication and handling of conflict, and through the development of the organization's culture. This part, chapters 10 to 13, deals with each of these topics. This chapter discusses motivation.

Throughout history, managers in diverse kinds of organizations have made a variety of assumptions about what motivates workers. Threats and abuse were common in slave labor organizations; even paid workers were thought to work only out of economic necessity. In the 1930s and 1940s the view that money was the only effective motivator was widespread. In the 1970s and 1980s, however, workers have increasingly been saying that they want something more from their jobs. They talk of wanting to be "fulfilled" by their job and by doing work that has "meaning." Comments like these imply that money by itself is not sufficient to motivate workers. Unfortunately, they don't suggest any specific motivators that managers can use to influence workers to produce enthusiastically.

Managers need to keep informed about worker needs, attitudes, and desires. Many workers appear to be generally suspicious of management, unimpressed by money, unconcerned about productivity. Motivating workers with these views presents a genuine challenge to managers in the 1980s. This challenge exists when managing either blue- or white-collar workers. Until recently, more attention was directed at blue-collar workers; now, white-collar workers are also becoming more difficult to motivate. Some are refusing transfers and promotions in the interest of pursuing leisure-time or family-oriented activities. Absenteeism is becoming common and a general apathy seems to pervade the white-collar ranks in some firms.

In view of these developments, a manager must ask: "How can I create a climate that will motivate my employees to perform most effectively and efficiently?" To answer this crucial question, in this chapter we analyze what is known about human motivation and how these findings can be applied in the work place. We begin by defining the term "motivation." We then describe several philosophies of human nature and show how these philosophies influence managerial behavior and subordinate motivation in the work place. In the third section of the chapter, we present the most popular motivation theories. They provide considerable insight into human behavior and are useful for improving an understanding of what motivates various employees. The fourth section is a discussion of the role of money as an employee motivator. The fifth section analyzes the important issue of job design and how it influences employee motivation. The chapter concludes with a discussion of what are usually called "Japanese management techniques" and indicates how these techniques can have a positive impact on employee motivation.

THE PROCESS OF MOTIVATION

Motivating the modern Canadian worker is considerably more complex than the simple application of the carrot-and-the-stick approach used by many managers in the past. **Motivation** is the process of influencing or stimulating a person to take action by creating a work environment whereby the goals of the organization and the needs of people are satisfied. In an organization, personnel are motivated if they perform their jobs efficiently, effectively, and eagerly.

In Exhibit 10-1, a model of motivation is illustrated. Everyone has certain needs. A person cannot be motivated until a need is activated; this need activation is referred to as a **motive**. Motives explain why people engage in certain behavior; they are the drives or impulses within an individual that cause the behavior.

An aroused need (motive) will cause a person to search for a way to satisfy the need. Once a way is found, it will be followed with some type of behavior directed toward a particular goal that the person has learned will satisfy the need. For example, a person may feel a need to associate with other people. He or she will search out other individuals and associate and interact with them in the hope of obtaining the goal of friendship.

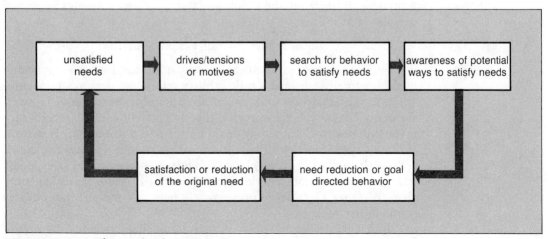

EXHIBIT 10-1 The motivation process

This simple explanation of motivation does not represent the complexity of the process. Any single act by a particular person may be reflecting a number of different needs. Striving for a promotion may be caused by a need for material possessions or by a need for recognition. The same act by another person may be caused by a different set of needs. One person may seek friendships to satisfy his or her need for association with other people, whereas another individual may wish to use friendships for advancing a career. One person seeks recognition through hard work; another seeks it by being the office clown or practical joker. The same need can be expressed in different ways.

To motivate employees to perform well, managers have traditionally relied on the use of rewards (increased pay, job security, good working conditions) or punishments (dismissal, demotions, reprimands). However, current managers cannot rely on the manipulation of pay, benefits, or working conditions to motivate workers to perform effectively. Rather, managers must create a work atmosphere that will bring out the potentials within every person. Specifically, managers should create a work atmosphere in which employees will want to be productive, contributing members of the organization.

To achieve this goal, managers must be aware of basic human needs and how these needs influence work behavior. Managers cannot assume that all people are alike, but they can assume that there is a reason for each subordinate's behavior. Managers should not condemn any act as stupid or senseless because, in the eyes of the person who committed it, the behavior makes sense. Instead, managers should try to understand why the behavior occurred. Stated more formally, managers must understand the forces that instigate behavior.

Researchers and practicing managers generally accept the idea that employee performance is the result of many factors, some of which are not known to the manager, and some of which may not even be consciously understood by the worker. They also agree that the two most important variables in explaining employee performance are employee motivation and employee ability. These variables appear to be related as follows:

$$\text{performance} = \text{motivation} \times \text{ability}.$$

As we have noted, motivation is evident if employees eagerly and enthusiastically perform a task. Ability refers to a person's task competence. The distinction between ability and motivation is relevant for many situations. For example, if 2 offensive linesmen are vying for a starting position, they may do so with equal enthusiasm. However, if one of them weighs 80 kg and the other weighs 115 kg, the coach will likely pick the heavier player. In a business situation, 2 salespeople may pursue customers with equal vigor, but if one sells much more than the other, the sales manager would have to conclude that one has more ability at sales.

Admittedly, these two examples are somewhat extreme. Most managers face situations where: (1) the difference between ability and

MANAGEMENT IN PRACTICE

Productivity Improvement at Cardinal

Cardinal Meat Specialists of Mississauga, Ontario sells meat to retail outlets such as The Keg and Swiss Chalet restaurants. In 1982, it introduced a productivity gain-sharing program in an attempt to increase employee productivity. The program measures productivity gains on a division basis (not an individual one) and the value of any productivity gains is evenly split between management and workers. For example, a 30 percent gain produces a 15 percent bonus to each worker's paycheque.

The program has worked very well at Cardinal. Productivity increased 17 percent within 10 weeks of the program's introduction. It continued to increase, and in 1983 productivity was 34 percent higher than before the program was introduced. As well, absenteeism and turnover have declined to nearly zero, according to Jack Boulet, the controller at Cardinal.

SOURCE   Sandra Bernstein, "Morale Booster: Productivity Gain Sharing Helps You Get More From Your Workers," *Canadian Business* (April 1984): 122.

motivation is not quite so clear, and (2) performance may not be clearly defined. Nevertheless, an understanding of the formula noted above gives considerable insight into an important part of a manager's job: getting employees to perform at a satisfactory level. The formula allows managers to assess various situations much more effectively because they can emphasize the variable that seems to be causing unsatisfactory performance. In some situations employee motivation levels are the problem, but in others ability is the issue. The solutions to the problems of lack of ability and lack of motivation are quite different; managers will obviously be more effective if they define the problem correctly.

In the above formula, a very low score on either motivation or ability will result in low performance overall. For example, people who are extremely nervous about speaking in front of a large audience (low ability) will not perform well at this task, no matter how motivated they are. The formula also implies that a high score on one variable can overcome a moderate score on the other variable. Thus, a person with relatively low ability, but high motivation, might outperform another person with high ability, but low motivation. This situation occurs frequently in professional sports when a supposedly superior team — one with players with more ability — gets beaten by a team with less talented players.

PHILOSOPHIES OF HUMAN NATURE

In order to create an atmosphere conducive to a high level of employee motivation, managers must gain some understanding about basic philosophies of human nature. The assumptions that managers make regarding other people's behavior are a major factor in determining the climate for motivation. Some supervisors, for instance, still believe that employees are basically uninterested in what the organization is doing and are there simply because of economic necessity. These supervisors reason that such employees certainly won't have much of value to say about how to improve the organization's performance. Other supervisors might assume just the opposite. Managers' positive or negative views of human nature have a major impact on the motivational levels of the people working for them.

McGregor's Theory X and Theory Y

In 1960, Douglas McGregor stressed the importance of understanding the relationship between motivation and philosophies of human nature.[1] In observing the practices and approaches of traditional managers, McGregor concluded that managers usually attempt to motivate employees by one of two basic approaches. He referred to these approaches as Theory X and Theory Y. **Theory X**, or the traditional view of management, suggests that managers must coerce, control, or threaten employees in order to motivate them. In contrast, McGregor proposed an alternative philosophy of human nature; **Theory Y** suggests that managers basically believe people are capable of being responsible and mature. Thus, employees do not require coercion or excessive control by the manager in order to perform effectively. McGregor's basic belief was that Theory Y is a more realistic assessment of people.

The table opposite illustrates the different assumptions of these two philosophies of human nature. The Theory Y assumptions represent managers' high degree of faith in the capacity and potential of people. If managers accept the Theory Y philosophy of human nature, they will seriously consider managerial practices like these: (1) abandonment of time clocks, (2) flexible working hours on an individual basis, (3) job enrichment, (4) management by objectives, and (5) participative decision making. All these practices are based on the belief that abilities are widespread in the population and each person can be trusted to behave in a responsible manner. Thus, management would create an atmosphere that would permit workers to realize their potential. McGregor did not advocate Theory Y as the panacea for all managerial problems. The Theory Y philosophy is not utopian, but McGregor argued that it does provide a basis for improved management and organization performance.

Argyris's Maturity Theory

The research of Chris Argyris has also aided managers in developing a more complete understanding of human behavior. Argyris emphasized the importance of the process of maturity. He suggested that there is a basic difference between the demands of the mature personality and the demands of the typical organization. Argyris concluded

MANAGEMENT IN PRACTICE

Increasing Motivation through Profit Sharing

Palliser Furniture of Winnipeg instituted a profit-sharing plan in 1978. Of the firm's 800 employees, all 600 who are eligible belong to the plan. David DeFehr, head of management information systems at Palliser, says the plan works as follows: 20 percent of the company's profits go into a pool; payout from the pool has ranged from 0 percent to 17 percent of an individual worker's salary, depending on the year's profits. The employee can take the cash, or put it into a deferred profit sharing plan which works like an RRSP.

The plan has resulted in better employee morale and significant productivity gains for the company. Employees also are more interested in their work, produce higher quality output, and maintain equipment better than before the system was implemented.

SOURCE Jack Francis, "Profit Sharing Gaining Ground," *Winnipeg Free Press* (June 8, 1984).

A Comparison of McGregor's Theory X and Theory Y Assumptions about Human Nature

Theory X	*Theory Y*
The average person inherently dislikes work and will avoid it if possible.	The expenditure of physical and mental effort in work is as natural as play or rest.
Because of the dislike of work, most people must be coerced, controlled, directed, and threatened with punishment to get them to perform effectively.	People will exercise self-direction and self-control in the service of objectives to which they are committed.
The average person lacks ambition, avoids responsibility, and seeks security and economic rewards above all else.	Commitment to objectives is a function of the rewards associated with achievement.
Most people lack creative ability and are resistant to change.	The average person learns, under proper conditions, not only to accept but to seek responsibility.
Since most people are self-centered, they are not concerned with the goals of the organization.	The capacity to exercise a relatively high degree of imagination, ingenuity, and creativity in the solution of organization problems is widely, not narrowly, distributed in the population.

SOURCE Based on Douglas McGregor, *The Human Side of Enterprise* (New York: McGraw-Hill, 1960).

that, if plans, policies, and methods/procedures are prescribed in detail, an employee will need to be submissive and passive, which suggests a Theory X type of organization. In this type of organization, subordinates are expected to concentrate on the orders as given and not question or attempt to understand these orders in a broader perspective. In brief, such a detailed prescription may ask individuals to work in an atmosphere where:

- They are provided minimal control over their workaday world.
- They are expected to be passive, dependent, and subordinate.
- They are expected to have a short time perspective.
- They are induced to perfect and value the frequent use of a few shallow abilities.
- They are expected to produce under conditions leading to psychological failure.[2]

When the mature employee encounters these conditions, 3 reactions are possible:

- An employee may escape by quitting the job, being absent from work, or attempting to climb to higher levels in the firm where the structure is less rigid.
- A person can fight the system, exerting pressure on the organization by means of informal groups or through formally organized labor unions or ombudsmen.
- The most typical reaction by employees is one of adaptation by developing an attitude of apathy or indifference. The employee plays the game, and pay becomes the compensation for the penalty of working.

According to Argyris, adaptation is the least representative of good mental health.

Managers cannot assume that all employees are mature, as defined by Argyris, or are Theory Y types, as defined by McGregor. These assumptions may be valid when managers are dealing with highly educated professional, technical, and managerial employees, but security may mean more to the industrial worker than to the highly educated professional. The industrial worker may value the freedom of private thought permitted by the highly structured and repetitive tasks that others may find boring.

It could be argued that a highly structured atmosphere requires employees to act in an immature manner. In fact, managers have conditioned employees to prefer that type of behavior. Many people can and have adjusted to tightly regimented work situations that Argyris contended demand immature behavior. One need only observe workers on an assembly line to recognize this interpretation. The resulting condition is one of indifference and apathy, which may be a successful, acceptable adaptation. However, only a fraction of the jobs in Canadian business are of the highly structured, totally controlled type. To the degree that an open job market operates effectively, some matching of varying human needs and organization demands will be possible.

The philosophies of human nature discussed here provide the basis for a manager's approach to motivation and leadership. As such, the theories of both McGregor and Argyris should be kept in mind as we discuss human motivation in this chapter and leadership in Chapter 11.

Motivation: The Self-Fulfilling Prophecy

One of the major problems that managers can counter with their influence is the **self-fulfilling prophecy**: what a manager expects from a subordinate is what the subordinate will give the manager. J. Sterling Livingston argues that:

- A manager's expectations of employees and the way he or she treats them largely determine their performance and career progress.
- A unique characteristic of superior managers is their ability to create high performance expectations that subordinates fulfill.
- Less effective managers fail to develop similar expectations and, as a consequence, the productivity of their subordinates suffers.
- Subordinates, more often than not, appear to do what they believe they are expected to do.[3]

The work of McGregor and Argyris suggests a solution to the problem of the self-fulfilling prophecy: a manager should develop high expectations of subordinates rather than low expectations, since both tend to be self-fulfilling prophecies. A manager communicates expectations through both verbal and nonverbal means. The manager's facial expressions, eye contact, body posture, or tone of voice can indicate approval and high expectations or just the reverse.

Numerous studies support the notion of the self-fulfilling prophecy. In one such study, 18 elementary school teachers were informed that about 20 percent of their students were intellectual "bloomers." The teachers were told that these youngsters would achieve remarkable progress during the school year. In actuality, the 20 percent sample of students was chosen at random and did not differ in intelligence or abilities from the remainder of the students in the classes. The only variable was the teacher's expectations of the group. The students actually did achieve significantly greater progress during the school year. Thus, the teachers' expectations of the students became a self-fulfilling prophecy.

Similar results have been achieved by managers. More often than not, if managers have high expectations of their employees, the employees' performance will meet those expectations. For example, the high expectations of the manager of a large computer center at a major university substantially changed the life and work of a janitor. The manager believed that the janitor, with limited formal education, had the potential to become a computer operator. The computer center manager had high expectations and believed that the cleaner could learn the new job. After several months of training, the former janitor did become a successful computer operator, eventually training others. This example illustrates how the high expectations of one person can have a significant positive impact on the actions of another.

Many businesses have not developed effective managers rapidly enough to meet the needs of their organization. As a consequence, organizations are not developing their most valuable resource — talented young men and women. In fact, the self-fulfilling prophecy seems to have the greatest potential impact on younger employees and managers. By failing to create high expectations or provide training and development of their personnel, firms are experiencing high costs from excessive employee turnover. Also, managers who fail to communicate high expectations may significantly damage the attitudes and career aspirations of younger personnel.

Managers in every organization, who are interested in high productivity, must meet the challenge of encouraging the development of managers who will treat their employees in ways that contribute to high performance, career development, and personal satisfaction. Effective managers who have high expectations of subordinates tend to build the employees' self-confidence and develop their performance capabilities. By contrast, ineffective managers tend to create a climate of negative or low expectations of subordinates. As a result, employees' level of motivation and performance is lower, and their self-esteem and careers may be damaged.[4]

MOTIVATION THEORIES

There are nearly as many theories of motivation as there are psychologists who develop them. Because of the large differences from one theory to another, the acceptance of one may mean that another theory will be rejected. None of the theories provides a universally accepted approach that explains all human behavior. However, a basic understanding of these theories is useful to managers as they attempt to motivate people in their organizations. Our purpose in presenting different theories of human motivation is not to identify one as superior. Rather, it is to develop a thought process that will ultimately lead managers to understand human motivation and how it affects their specific work situation.

Maslow's Hierarchy of Needs

Many psychologists believe that there are certain patterns or configurations of human needs, although there obviously are individual differences. A common approach to establishing this need pattern is to develop a universal need hierarchy. Abraham Maslow has proposed one widely accepted pattern, which is illustrated in Exhibit 10-2. Examples of how an organization might help to satisfy these basic needs are also

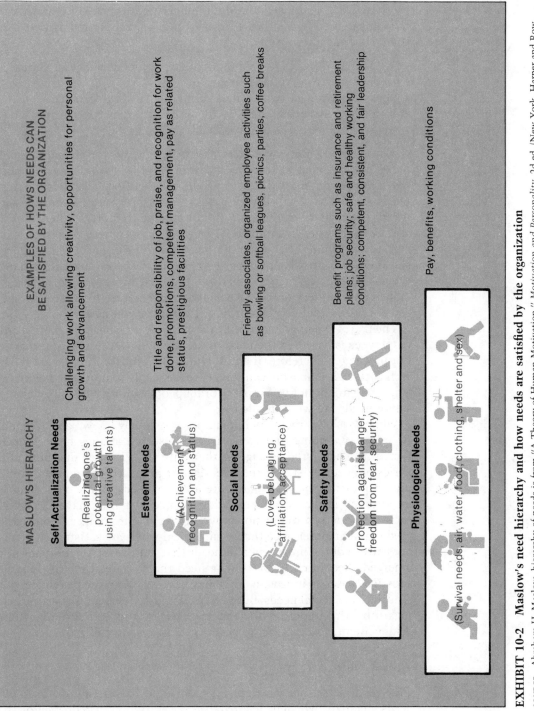

MASLOW'S HIERARCHY

EXAMPLES OF HOWS NEEDS CAN
BE SATISFIED BY THE ORGANIZATION

Self-Actualization Needs

(Realizing one's potential growth using creative talents)

Challenging work allowing creativity, opportunities for personal growth and advancement

Esteem Needs

(Achievement recognition and status)

Title and responsibility of job, praise, and recognition for work done, promotions, competent management, pay as related status, prestigious facilities

Social Needs

(Love, belonging, affiliation, acceptance)

Friendly associates, organized employee activities such as bowling or softball leagues, picnics, parties, coffee breaks

Safety Needs

(Protection against danger, freedom from fear, security)

Benefit programs such as insurance and retirement plans; job security; safe and healthy working conditions; competent, consistent, and fair leadership

Physiological Needs

(Survival needs; air, water, food, clothing, shelter and sex)

Pay, benefits, working conditions

EXHIBIT 10-2   Maslow's need hierarchy and how needs are satisfied by the organization

SOURCE   Abraham H. Maslow, hierarchy of needs is from ''A Theory of Human Motivation,'' *Motivation and Personality*, 2d ed. [New York, Harper and Row, 1970]. Reprinted by permission of author and publisher.

presented. Maslow states that individuals are motivated to satisfy certain unsatisfied needs. His theory of human motivation is based on the following assumptions:

- Needs that are not satisfied motivate or influence behavior. Satisfied needs do not motivate behavior.
- Needs are arranged according to a hierarchy of importance.
- An individual's needs at any level on the hierarchy emerge only when the lower-level needs are reasonably well satisfied.[5]

According to Maslow's **hierarchy of needs** theory, an individual's needs are arranged in a hierarchy from the lower-level physiological needs to the higher-level needs for self-actualization. The physiological needs are the highest priority because, until they are reasonably satisfied, the higher-level needs will not emerge to motivate behavior.

A person is never completely satisfied on any need level but, if a sufficient amount of gratification of lower-priority needs exists, he or she then seeks to satisfy upper-level needs. Maslow suggested that a typical person might be 85 percent satisfied in physiological needs, 70 percent in safety needs, 50 percent in love needs, 40 percent in self-esteem needs, and 10 percent in self-actualization needs.

The use of the universal needs hierarchy by a manager in motivating employees is based on the idea that reasonably well-satisfied needs do not motivate. Therefore, if an individual's lower-level needs are fairly well satisfied, managers cannot use these needs to motivate behavior. Thus, pay might not be a motivator for people whose physiological and safety needs are well satisfied.

While Maslow's theory of human needs is widely known and accepted by many practicing managers, several research studies have contradicted it. These studies suggest that only two or three distinct categories of needs exist, not the five Maslow proposed. In addition, some critics question the order of the hierarchy of needs. While considerable importance is placed on physiological needs if they have not been satisfied, a person might not move up the hierarchy in an orderly or predictable manner once the physiological needs are satisfied. A clear-cut pattern of the progression of needs that require satisfaction has not emerged. According to Maslow, a need that has been relatively well satisfied ceases to motivate. This may be the case for the physiological, security, and social needs. But such a conclusion may not be warranted regarding the upper-level needs of esteem and self-actualization, achievement, recognition, or acceptance of responsibility.

Alderfer's E-R-G Theory

Clayton Alderfer has developed a more modern version of Maslow's needs hierarchy, which he referred to as the existence-relatedness-growth, or **E-R-G theory**.[6] Alderfer's theory is an attempt to make Maslow's theory more consistent with knowledge of human needs. The table below illustrates the relationship between Alderfer's and Maslow's theories of human needs. Alderfer's classification condensed Maslow's ideas into three categories of needs:

- **Existence Needs**: types of physical or material needs
- **Relatedness Needs**: relationships with other people
- **Growth Needs**: All forms of creative efforts to achieve or gain recognition to satisfy needs for esteem and attain high degree of personal fulfillment.

Alderfer's and Maslow's Theories: A Comparison

Needs theories	Level 1	Level 2	Level 3
Maslow's hierarchy of needs theory	Physiological needs	Social needs, security needs	Self-fulfillment needs, esteem needs
Alderfer's E-R-G theory	Existence needs	Relatedness needs	Growth needs

In contrast to the satisfaction of existence and relatedness needs, the importance of growth needs may increase as an individual achieves satisfaction of these needs. According to the E-R-G theory, each level becomes increasingly abstract and more difficult to satisfy. While some individuals follow a logical progression in satisfying needs from level 1 through 3, some people experience frustration. A person who is unable to satisfy growth needs reverts back one level and concentrates on the more concrete relatedness or existence needs. For example, an assembly-line worker who has a job that fails to satisfy his need for recognition or personal satisfaction might concentrate on improving his personal relationships and friendships with other employees and on gaining additional pay and job security.

Herzberg's Motivation-Hygiene Theory

One of the most widely known and controversial theories of motivation is the motivation-hygiene theory of Frederick Herzberg.[7] His theory grew out of research on factors that led to job satisfaction. Herzberg proposes that job satisfaction and job dissatisfaction are not opposite ends of the same continuum. Instead, there exist two significantly different classes of job factors, one of which influences job satisfaction, and the other job dissatisfaction. Thus, there are two different continuums.

One class, referred to as **hygiene factors**, makes up a continuum ranging from "dissatisfaction" to "no dissatisfaction." As illustrated in Exhibit 10-3, hygiene factors relate to the environment and are external to the job. Herzberg indicates that these factors do not cause job satisfaction; rather their absence causes dissatisfaction. Hygiene factors "maintain" an employee; they do not make a person healthy but rather prevent unhealthiness. An organization that meets the hygiene needs of its employees will eliminate dissatisfaction but will not motivate employees to work harder.

The second class of factors, referred to as **motivators**, makes up a continuum leading from "not satisfied" to "highly satisfied." As illustrated in Exhibit 10-3, the work itself, recognition, achievement, possibility of growth, and advancement are motivators. These are concerned with the work itself rather than its physical, administrative, or social atmosphere. If the worker is to be truly motivated, the job must contain motivators.

Herzberg's theory suggests that a clear delineation exists between motivators and hygienes. Pay, for example, is categorized as a hygiene factor for each individual, but pay may be a dissatisfier to some individuals and a satisfier to others. Thus, it can be argued that hygiene and motivation factors should not be considered as absolute categories.

Specific criticisms of Herzberg's theory include:

- The research methodology using the critical incident technique of asking people to reflect on experiences may cause people to recall only the most recent experiences. Also, analysis of the responses derived from this approach is highly subjective.
- The theory is most applicable to knowledge workers — managers, engineers, accountants, and other professional-level personnel. Thus, it is not possible to say that the findings apply equally to other occupational groups. Most studies have shown that, when the employees are professional- or managerial-level employees, the theory is applicable. However, studies of lower-level or manual workers are less supportive of the theory.
- The theory focuses too much attention on "satisfaction" or "dissatisfaction" rather than on the performance level of the individual. Satisfaction may or may not be directly related to job performance.

Despite these criticisms, Herzberg's two-factor theory has made a significant contribution toward improving a manager's basic understanding of motivation. As a result, managers should be aware of the potentially successful application of the theory as the work force becomes increasingly better educated and develops higher expectations of management.

There is a fairly close relationship between Maslow's hierarchy of needs theory and Herzberg's motivation-hygiene theory. (See Exhibit 10-4.) Herzberg's motivators are similar to the esteem and self-actualization needs in Maslow's hierarchy. The hygiene factors closely correspond to the physiological, safety, and social needs. Herzberg's basic

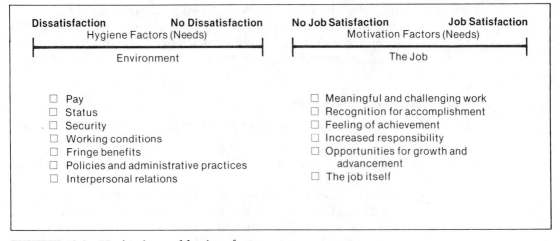

Dissatisfaction	No Dissatisfaction	No Job Satisfaction	Job Satisfaction

Hygiene Factors (Needs)   Motivation Factors (Needs)

Environment   The Job

☐ Pay
☐ Status
☐ Security
☐ Working conditions
☐ Fringe benefits
☐ Policies and administrative practices
☐ Interpersonal relations

☐ Meaningful and challenging work
☐ Recognition for accomplishment
☐ Feeling of achievement
☐ Increased responsibility
☐ Opportunities for growth and advancement
☐ The job itself

EXHIBIT 10-3   **Motivation and hygiene factors**

contention is that most organizations give inadequate attention to the motivation factors in the work place. Most of the efforts of managers are concentrated on meeting the low-level needs, which are satisfied by the hygiene factors. But, just because the hygiene or maintenance needs are satisfied — by good pay, benefits, or working conditions — does not mean that the individual's performance will be positively influenced. To achieve effectiveness, the organization must satisfy both the hygiene and the motivation needs of its employees. Most organizations have given considerable attention to the hygiene needs but inadequate attention to the motivation needs of their personnel. This imbalance is understandable since hygiene needs can be met in a more tangible or specific manner than can the motivational needs. It may be easier to provide employees with improved pay, fringe benefits, or working conditions than with a job that is more responsible or challenging.

Advocates of Herzberg's two-factor theory of motivation suggest that managers can assist employees in meeting their motivational needs by providing employees with more challenging and responsible jobs. According to Herzberg, increasing the level of autonomy, skill variety, task significance, and feedback will lead to better job performance and more satisfied employees. (This is known as job enrichment, which will be discussed later in this chapter.)

McClelland's Manifest Needs Theory

Whereas Maslow's theory stresses a universal hierarchy of naturally existing needs, the research of David McClelland emphasizes that certain needs are learned and socially acquired as the individual interacts with the environment. McClelland's manifest needs theory is concerned with how individual needs and environmental factors combine to form 3 basic human motives: the need for achievement (*n Ach*), the need for power (*n Pow*), and the need for affiliation (*n Aff*). As previously noted, motives explain behavior. McClelland conducted numerous studies in an attempt to define and measure basic human motives.

Need for Achievement

A person with a high **need for achievement** (*n Ach*) is an individual who:

- Wants to take personal responsibility for finding solutions to problems
- Is goal oriented
- Seeks a challenge — and establishes moderate, realistic, and attainable goals that involve risk but are not impossible to attain
- Desires concrete feedback on performance
- Has a high level of energy and is willing to work hard.

People exhibiting a high *n Ach* have found the above pattern of behavior personally rewarding. McClelland's research has shown that a high *n Ach* is probably a strong or dominant need in only a small proportion of the population. Persons high in the need for achievement gravitate toward entrepreneurial and sales positions. In these occupations, individuals are better able to manage themselves and satisfy the basic drive for achievement.

Need for Power

A high **need for power** means that an individual seeks to influence or control others. Such an individual tends to be characterized by the following types of behavior:

- Is concerned with acquiring, exercising, or retaining power or influence over others
- Likes to compete with others in situations that allow him or her to be dominant
- Enjoys confrontations with others.

McClelland suggests that 2 basic aspects of power exist: positive and negative. Positive power is essential if a manager is to accomplish results through the efforts of others. Negative power is evident when an individual seeks power for his or her own personal benefit; negative power may be detrimental to the organization.[8]

Need for Affiliation

The **need for affiliation** is related to the desire for affection and establishing friendly relationships. A person with a high need for affiliation is an individual who:

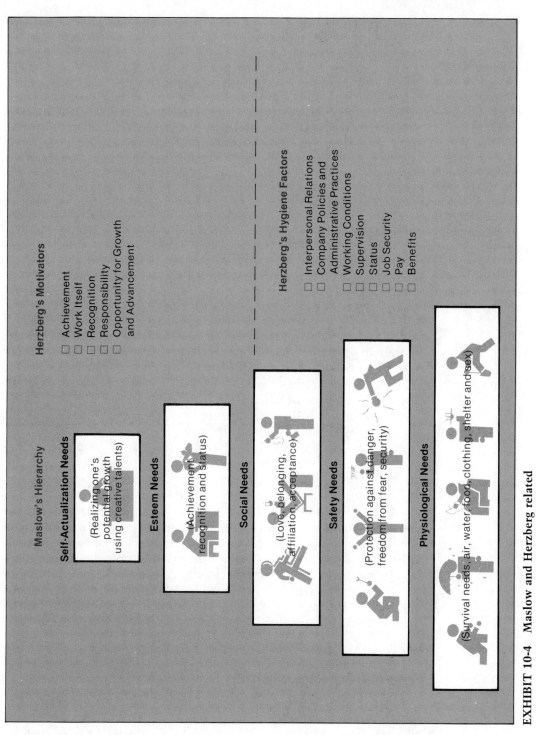

EXHIBIT 10-4 Maslow and Herzberg related

- Seeks to establish and maintain friendships and close emotional relationships with others.
- Wants to be liked by others
- Enjoys parties, social activities, and bull sessions
- Seeks a sense of belonging by joining groups or organizations.

To varying degrees, everyone possesses these 3 motives. However, one of the needs will tend to be more characteristic of an individual than the other two.[9] People in a given culture may have the same needs, but the relative strength of those needs differs. Each of the 3 motives evokes a different type of satisfaction. For example, the achievement motive tends to evoke in managers a sense of accomplishment, whereas a manager may have a feeling of being in control or influencing others when the power motive is prevalent. According to this theory, the probability that an individual will perform a job effectively and efficiently depends on a combination of:

- The strength of the motive or need relative to other needs
- The possibility of success in performing the task
- The strength value of the incentive or reward for performance.

The most effective mixture of these 3 motives depends on the situation. In studies of over 500 managers, it was concluded that the most effective managers have a high need for power, a moderate need for achievement, and a low need for affiliation. These managers tended to use their power in a participative manner for the good of the organization. Managers had a moderate need for achievement, but it was not strong enough to interfere with the management process. Persons with high needs for both power and achievement have high managerial motivation, but they may not make the best managers.[10] After all, management is the achievement of goals through the efforts of others, not shoving others aside to do the work alone.

Outstanding sales personnel tend to be high in the need for achievement and moderately high in the need for power. Entrepreneurs who develop ideas and promote specific enterprises tend to be high in achievement motivation. They delight in solving problems personally and in getting immediate feedback on the degree of success. Entrepreneurs sometimes are unable to make the transition to top management positions. Their need for personal achievement gets in the way of the requirements for effectively influencing the organization's employees.

Vroom's Expectancy Theory

Managers must develop an understanding of human needs and the variety of organizational means available to satisfy the needs of employees. However, the needs approach to motivation as developed by Maslow, Alderfer, and Herzberg does not adequately account for differences in individual employees or explain why people behave in certain ways to pursue goals. Victor Vroom developed an approach to motivation known as **expectancy theory** that attempts to explain behavior in terms of an individual's goals, choices, and the expectations of achieving these goals.[11] This theory assumes that people can determine which outcomes they prefer and make realistic estimates of the chances of obtaining them. The key concept of expectancy theory is that motivation depends on: (1) an individual's **expectancy** (his or her perception of the probability) that a particular outcome will occur as a result of certain behavior, and (2) the value (**valence**) an individual places on a specific outcome.

These factors — expectancy and value — determine motivation. Both must be present before a high level of motivation can occur. In other words, a high expectancy or a high value alone will not ensure motivation. For example, if an employee had a low expectancy (perceived little chance) of receiving a pay increase but placed a high value on money, the employee would not be highly motivated to work hard to obtain the increase.

All employees in an organization do not share the same goals or values regarding pay, job security, promotions, benefits, or working conditions. For example, a supervisor in the systems and programming division places a high value on receiving a promotion to a more challenging and responsible position. She perceives that excellent performance in her current supervisory position is essential to achieving her desired promotion. Her manager recognizes the value that she places on a promotion. Therefore, the manager attempts to let her know that there is a high probability she can be promoted if she performs effectively in her current position. Thus, she will seek to perform well in order to achieve the promotion. Another employee, an office supervisor, values stability and job security and is not interested in a promotion because he does not want more responsibility. Thus, he will not be motivated by an opportunity for a promotion.

A key factor in the expectancy model is what the employee perceives as desirable, not what the manager believes the employee should consider to be desirable. A manager's ability to motivate employees therefore depends on a thorough knowledge of each individual employee's background, goals, or experiences. The manager needs to identify what sparks motivation in each employee.[12]

A major contribution of expectancy theory is that it explains how the goals of employees influence their behavior on the job. The employees' behavior depends on their assessment of the probability that the behavior will actually lead to the attainment of the goal.

A manager who wishes to use the expectancy model of motivation should:

• Ensure that employees have sufficient training to do the task assigned
• Remove organizational obstacles to good performance
• Instill in employees the confidence to perform well
• Select organization rewards that will meet specific employee needs

- Communicate clearly the relationship between rewards and performance
- Administer the reward system consistently and equitably so that employees will perceive a relationship between performance and the rewards they receive.

Skinner's Reinforcement Theory

B. F. Skinner's **reinforcement theory** is concerned with the ways in which behavior is learned as the result of either positive or negative consequences. People tend to repeat behaviors that produce pleasant outcomes and tend not to repeat behaviors that have negative outcomes. Behavior that is reinforced will be repeated; behavior that is not reinforced will not be repeated. If a worker wants additional pay, and he learns that, by working harder his pay increases, he is likely to continue this action. On the other hand, if he discovers that pay increases may be obtained by playing office politics, he may engage in this practice.

Skinner contends that people's behavior can be controlled and shaped by rewarding (reinforcing) desired behavior while ignoring undesirable actions. Over time, the reinforced behavior will be repeated, whereas the unrewarded behavior will be extinguished and will disappear. Punishment of undesired behavior is to be avoided since it may contribute to feelings of restraint and actions of rebellion. Thus, over a period of years, a conditioner can control human behavior without the person becoming aware of being controlled. In his book, *Beyond Freedom and Dignity*, Skinner said that people can be controlled and shaped while at the same time feeling free.[13]

Skinner's theory of shaping behavior is useful to managers, but you should not assume that human behavior is simple to understand and/or modify. The primary shaping technique suggested by Skinner is organizational behavior modification.

Organizational behavior modification (OBM) rests on two fundamental concepts: (1) people act in ways they find most personally rewarding, and (2) people's behavior can be shaped and determined by controlling the rewards they receive. In OBM, rewards are termed **reinforcers** because the goal is to stimulate continuation of the rewarded behavior. Which reinforcers actually work in motivating people is determined by a manager's trial and error and experience. What is successful with one employee may not work with another because the needs and wants of the two differ. Praise is used most frequently because it is most readily available. However, it becomes less effective whenever it becomes predictable or is continuously applied. Money is also used, as are public or private letters of commendation, time off, and increased status.

In OBM, punishment is rejected as a reinforcer because it suppresses the undesired behavior while at the same time stimulating anger, hostility, aggression, and rebellion. And at times, it is difficult to identify the punishment. In one prison, placing prisoners in solitary confinement on bread and water turned out to be a status symbol and led to repetition of offenses. When the bread and water was changed to baby food, the status symbol disappeared, leading to a significant reduction in the number of undesirable acts. When undesired behavior is not rewarded, it tends to disappear over time.

In reinforcing desired behavior in a positive fashion managers must allocate the rewards soon after the behavior occurs so that the person perceives a clear and immediate link. Fast and accurate feedback of information to the performer in itself constitutes a reinforcer.

Organizational behavior modification has been used successfully in a number of organizations to improve performance. In one firm, positive reinforcement was used to reduce absenteeism.[14] Each day an employee came to work on time, he or she received a playing card. At the end of the week, the highest poker hand received $20. Over a 3-month period, the absenteeism rate of the experimental group decreased 18 percent, whereas that of a control group actually increased. Michigan

MANAGEMENT IN PRACTICE

Behavior Modification at Burroughs Memorex

Burroughs Memorex is one of Canada's major producers of computer products. In the early 1980s, its Winnipeg plant was experiencing several problems, including poor quality, failure to meet schedules, high scrap costs, and less-than-ideal labor relations. In an attempt to resolve these problems, the company introduced a behavior modification program called Performance Management.

The first step was to train 75 managers and supervisors how to use behavior modification properly. Once the training had been completed, supervisors identified their "key result areas." They then began applying behavior modification principles in order to improve performance in these key result areas. Both verbal and written positive reinforcement was given to employees who had achieved the standards which had been set. Output graphs were also posted in the factory so that all workers could see the extent to which they were achieving quality and output goals. An incentive system for rewarding good suggestions was also implemented.

The behavior modification program has had dramatic effects. Consider the following: In 1981, the "arrival quality" of the plant's shipments was only 59 percent — only 59 percent of the customers were happy with the product and how it worked when it arrived at their plant. The workers set a goal of 80 percent arrival quality in 1982; they actually achieved 83 percent. They then set a goal of 90 percent for 1983 and achieved 91 percent. Arrival quality during 1984 was 93 percent.

Another example: Scrap costs on a certain part in 1981 were running at $6,500 per week. One employee discovered that these costs were incurred by improper handling of the product; he therefore wrote up a 20-minute training program that indicated the proper way to handle the part. His program is now used to train all people who handle the part in question. After being made aware of the cause of the problem, the employees set a goal to reduce scrap costs to $2,500 per week. Feedback graphs were also posted in all departments who handled the part and appropriate reinforcement applied for improved performance. Scrap costs are now down to $400 per week.

SOURCE   Interview with Carole Postnieks, Manager of Training and Development, Burroughs Memorex, Inc.

Bell Telephone identified these desirable behaviors among its operators: (1) service promptness in answering calls, (2) shortness of time taken to give information, (3) use of proper references in handling the call, and (4) attendance.[15] Praise and recognition were adopted as the dominant reinforcers. The results were an improvement in attendance by 50 percent and above standard productivity and efficiency levels.

The Emery Air Freight OBM program was a major success story.[16] It used the simple reinforcers of information feedback and praise to condition employee behavior. In responding to customer questions about service and schedules within a standard 90-minute period, performance moved from 30 percent of the standard to 90 percent within a few days. Employees were provided with feedback charts through which they could monitor their own performance. Employees who did not achieve the desired results were reminded of the goal, then praised for their honesty. This 90 percent achievement remained stable for over 3 years. As a result of the application of OBM, estimated savings to Emery Air Freight were placed at $650,000 per year.

If a manager wants to use OBM, the following actions are necessary:

- Identify the desired performance in specific terms, for example, improving attendance rates or answering a certain number of questions in a certain period of time.
- Identify the rewards that will reinforce the desired behavior, for example, praise, money, time off.
- Make the reward a direct consequence of the behavior.
- Select the optimum reinforcement schedule.

Despite the successes achieved by behavior modification, it has been criticized as being a manipulative and autocratic approach to management because employees are conditioned to change their behavior in the direction required by management and the organization. Some critics argue that OBM is not consistent with the theories of such behavioral scientists as Maslow, Argyris, or McGregor. The assumption underlying their theories is that people are motivated by their own internal needs and are capable of a degree of self-control; OBM assumes that the causes of human behavior are in the environment and therefore external to the individual.

Adams's Equity Theory

Equity theory assumes that individuals consider the ratio of their inputs on the job to the outcomes they receive and then compare this ratio with the input/outcome ratio of others doing similar work.[17] If the worker perceives an inequity, he or she will be motivated to resolve the inequity. Managers must deal with employees who continually compare the pay and rewards they are receiving with the rewards other employees receive. The degree of perceived equity is important to each employee. When an employee receives compensation from the organization, his or her perceptions of equity are affected by: (1) comparison of the compensation received to such factors as input of effort, education, or training, and (2) the comparison of the perceived equity of pay and rewards received compared to other people. For example, even though an employee values money and expects that it will be paid if he or she performs, comparisons will be made to the rewards received by others. Thus, if the employee likes money and believes that an $800 raise will be forthcoming when performing well, motivational force decreases if he or she perceives that other employees are receiving $1,000 for the same performance level.

THE ROLE OF MONEY IN MOTIVATION

The role of money in motivation has been debated vigorously for many years. In the early part of the twentieth century, Frederick Taylor's views about money were widely accepted. (See Chapter 1.) In Taylor's view, workers would do a job in a certain way only if they were given the monetary incentive to do so. By the 1930s, this "economic man" view of workers was challenged by research like the Hawthorne studies which suggested that workers were also motivated by intangible factors like friendship, respect, and belonging to a group.

The function of pay in our society today is quite complex. Each of the motivation theories discussed makes some direct or indirect statement about the role of money in motivation; in the following paragraphs, we present some summary comments about the role of money in motivation by referring to these motivation theories.

One of the difficult aspects of compensation is that financial rewards have multiple meanings. In addition to being the obvious means by which workers can satisfy basic needs, pay can be an indication of social status, social value, and competence. Therefore, workers can also satisfy higher-order needs with their paycheques. To complicate the situation even more, their perceptions of the degree to which their lower-order needs are satisfied may change as their income rises; so, while workers may have their basic needs relatively satisfied, a pay increase may serve only to increase their level of expectations regarding the lower-order needs. For example, if eating hamburgers 4 times a week satisfies people's need for food, increasing their wages may simply cause them to change their eating habits from hamburger to steak as a result of higher expectations of satisfaction. Possibly, eating steak may also satisfy other needs, like status.

Perceptions of need satisfaction are determined by expectations, which are in turn determined by comparisons with what other individuals are receiving relative to the responsibility of their jobs. Individuals generally feel an inequity if comparisons show that they are receiving less than others with similar inputs. Equity theory is very useful here, since it states that the relative levels of perceived pay are as important as absolute levels of actual pay.

**William Dimma
A. E. LePage Ltd.**

William Dimma, 54, has followed a winding trail to the presidency of Canada's largest real estate company. With an engineering degree and an MBA, he spent 20 years climbing close to the top at Union Carbide Canada Ltd. He then left the work force in 1970 to take his doctorate in business administration at Harvard. After graduation, Dimma spent a couple of years as dean of administrative studies at York University. It was a challenging job but in working for a university he discovered something about himself that he thinks applies to many other executives: the struggle to make a company profitable is a drug-fix he cannot easily do without. Thus, when Beland Honderich invited him into Torstar, the expansion-minded communications group, he couldn't resist. He was Torstar's president until

moving over to A. E. LePage Ltd. in 1979, where his responsibilities are virtually equal to those of the chairman and chief executive, Gordon Gray.

Q: Three-quarters of your people are on straight commission. Is it getting harder to find people with that sort of entrepreneurial approach these days?

Dimma: Society is less entrepreneurial than it was 25 years ago but there's still a very strong demand for and good supply of entrepreneurial people who are prepared to take chances on the down side as long as there's an up side. In real estate the up-side potential is very significant. There are people who make a great deal of money year in, year out, selling real estate — an amount of money it would be very difficult to make on a salary. We have agents who make as much as most corporation presidents. There is a rather limited number of jobs around for corporation presidents, whereas there's lots of opportunity for good people in real estate.

Q: Your younger people had only experienced boom markets when the recession came along. Did a lot of them find they weren't as entrepreneurial as they thought? Did you lose people?
Dimma: All the real estate firms had turnover between July 1981 and August 1982, when the residential market was so weak. Yet our good people continued to do well. It's surprising the number of people who continued to earn really good money. There's no question that the people who came into the market during the boom of 1979 through to the first half of 1981 had difficulty adjusting to a buyer's market. While I can't say I'm delighted that we ran into that kind of economy, it did re-establish the traditional values of hard work and intelligence.

Q: Your best people make a lot of money. But you do other things as well to motivate people, such as letting employees buy shares. With 1100 employee shareholders, how do you establish policy?
Dimma: About 87 percent of the company is owned by the employees. We have one outside shareholder, The Toronto Dominion Bank which, for historical reasons, has 13 percent ownership of the company, a passive investment. We have two classes of plan under which you can acquire

shares. The employee stock purchase plan is wide open. You can acquire shares in that plan when you've been around for a year. We're not interested in encouraging people who have demonstrated that they trade shares. We're looking for people who will hold their shares. But, subject to that, those people can acquire shares and we encourage them to. We usually have a share issue every year. In addition, there's a voting trust of the most senior 55 to 60 people who own about 50 percent of the stock. Control of the company is vested in the voting trust.

Q: A. E. LePage is almost a two-president company; you and Gordon Gray share responsibilities. What does he offer? What do you offer? How do you avoid stalemates?

Dimma: By happenstance or good fortune or design, I'm not sure which, we complement each other. Gordon is about 70 percent entrepreneur and 30 percent manager; I'm about 70 percent manager and 30 percent entrepreneur. So there's a nice balance. He spends a higher percentage of his time on the entrepreneurial side of the business. I spend a higher percentage on the managerial and administrative side. Having said that, however, we work so closely together that we check almost everything with the other. Each month we go away for a day, out of the building, away from the phone, and talk about the problems of the business. We keep a list of ongoing items so that we don't get distracted and don't keep moving like a bee from flower to flower. We want to *solve* some problems. Our list generally runs to about 300 items and we'll review maybe 15 or 20, try to push some forward, try to come to an agreement and put them into execution.

We also talk about the strategy of the firm a great deal, long-term direction, where we want to be, new businesses we want to be in, acquisitions. And we talk about policies, areas where we need more control, areas where we can decentralize. The philosophy of the firm is to decentralize as much as possible, subject to good financial control. We want as many profit centers as we can manage. We have about 200 of them.

Q: Let's look at the life and times of Bill Dimma. After about 20 years in the work force, why did you go back to school? After finishing your studies, why did you choose academia over the business world?

Dimma: From time to time throughout my career at Union Carbide, I wondered whether the more contemplative life geared to teaching or research would suit me. I didn't want to spend my entire career in one institution. I have a reasonably high need for change and for a fair level of excitement and I didn't really want to retire at age 65 saying I'd had 43 years with one institution. I would always have wondered whether I should have done something else. The question was whether I would go right into another business institution or have a fling at something a little offbeat. I could afford to go back to Harvard even though I had two small kids at the time. We all went down to Boston and lived there for three years.

It was a marvelous experience. Everybody ought to take some time in their life to go off and think about things on a more basic level. A businessman's life is hectic; there's not much time for thinking. I don't think my personality changed. But, by the time I'd finished the doctoral program, I was able to sort out pretty well what I wanted to do with my life. I had concluded that I wasn't going to make my life in academia, yet I felt I owed it to myself and, perhaps, to Harvard, to try the life for a while. So I went to York. I had no intention of getting into academic administration. I went as a professor expecting to stay two or three years and then move back into the private sector. But they were searching for a dean at about that time and the late George Edwards prevailed on me to throw my hat in the ring. So I became dean and tried academic administration. I accepted a five-year term but only stayed in the job about two years.

A combination of things led me not to stay my term. The financial constraints and underfunding of universities were getting to be crucial. It was clear there wasn't going to be enough money to do the things that needed to be done. Also I needed the excitement of the bottom-line motivation.

Most businessmen find that after a while. It's like a fix, a shot of narcotics. That bottom-line motivation is in your blood. I recognized that I needed it. As a university dean you have a cost center not a profit center. So I came back into the business world.

SOURCE   Excerpted from Dean Walker, "Conversation with William Dimma of A. E. LePage", *Executive* (May 1983): 44–48. Reprinted by permission.

Consider the concept of piece-rate or commission payment (incentive) systems and their potential impact on motivation. Perhaps a useful way to determine their impact is to examine the assumptions that underlie the incentive system concept:

- Employees desire to make more money and will change their behavior to meet this objective ("economic man" assumption).
- Employees can see a relation between their efforts and the rewards they receive (expectancy theory).
- Employees attach a net positive value to increasing their efforts to produce more (expectancy theory).
- Earning extra money will allow employees either to increase their perception of needs satisfaction or to satisfy needs not currently satisfied (Maslow).
- Employees have the ability to increase output (physiological assumption).
- Other conditions in the work atmosphere do not override the desire to increase output for financial rewards (Herzberg, expectancy theory).
- The worker perceives that other individuals in his or her comparison group receive similar rewards for similar efforts (equity theory).

Unsurprisingly, many piece-rate and commission payment systems are less than successful in view of all the criteria that should be met.

Gellerman has noted that, in order for money to motivate, pay increases must be extremely large to create the feeling of "wealth."[18] If a worker sees that increased effort will lead to a significant change in his or her standard of living, then pay can be considered a motivator. For this reason, incentive systems at higher echelons of organizations tend to meet with more success than do those on production-line systems. If top executives improve their performance, they stand to gain considerably from their efforts since some company bonus systems increase executive pay by as much as 50 percent. Production workers, on the other hand, are limited to much smaller absolute increases.

Herzberg maintains that pay is not a motivator but a hygiene: if it is satisfactory, workers will not be dissatisfied. If pay meets their expectations, they will do nothing differently because of it. Only when pay does not meet expectations do employees change their behavior. Consistent with both equity theory and Gellerman's position, payment above expectations will probably change behavior as the individual attempts to reduce the dissonance associated with the increased pay. Payment below expectations causes dissatisfaction and prevents a positive work climate from being established. The key point in this philosophy is that providing workers with what they expect will have no appreciable effect on their behavior.

The varied role that pay can assume is further demonstrated through McClelland's $n\,Ach$ theory. In the most literal sense, the high achiever is not motivated by pay. However, in actual job situations, it is easy to see how a supervisor can misinterpret the individual's motives and assume that the need for money — instead of the need for achievement — is operating.

In summary, if money is to motivate behavior, employees must both desire it and believe that it will be forthcoming if they behave in the manner prescribed. Determining the degree of importance of money to employees requires knowledge of each individual's current need level. If employees have a need for higher pay and expect to receive it if they perform more effectively, then pay can motivate performance.

JOB DESIGN AND MOTIVATION

Can managers enhance employee motivation, improve job satisfaction, and maximize production all at the same time? J. Richard Hackman and Greg R. Oldham contend that it is possible to improve the quality of work life while increasing worker productivity.[19] They challenge several traditional assumptions, such as:

- The basic nature of work is fixed and cannot be changed.
- Technology and work processes determine job design.
- All management can do is properly select and train personnel.

Work or job design has been identified as an approach that can assist in increasing productivity. **Job design** is the process of altering the nature and structure of jobs for the purpose of increasing productivity. Job design is concerned with the specific tasks to be performed, the methods used in performing them and how the job relates to other work in the organization. In their book, *Work Redesign*, Hackman and Oldham assert that, if managers wish to create a climate for a high level of motivation, reliable feedback on performance must be provided; there must be a sense that the worker is accountable for specific results and a feeling that the job has meaning beyond pay.[20] Workers get more satisfaction from completing a "whole and identifiable piece of work" than from producing indistinguishable pieces. Because of this, job design becomes an important concept in creating a motivational climate for today's work force.

Technology constraints on job design include the type of equipment and tools as well as the particular work layout and methods used in producing the product or service. Technology may make job redesign difficult and perhaps expensive though not impossible. For example, adapting or redesigning an assembly line may not be technically or economically feasible.[21]

Economic factors affect job design. Top management must decide if sufficient resources are available to the organization should it wish to redesign some or all of its jobs. Suggestions to redesign jobs may improve output and the level of worker satisfaction, but the cost may be prohibitive. Managers must continually balance the benefits of job design with the costs.

Job design is also affected by government requirements or regulations. Management may wish to design a job in a way that might increase worker performance but would violate labor laws or environmental or safety standards. Some proponents of work redesign have even urged the federal government to legislate guidelines for changes in work design.

If a company has a union, job design can be affected by the philosophy, policies, and strategies of the union. Typically, the contract between the company and the union specifies and defines the types of jobs and the duties and responsibilities of workers. Unions have traditionally opposed many work redesign experiments. They have perceived them to be attempts by management to squeeze more work out of the worker without any increase in wages. In order to maintain harmony and work efficiency, managers must foster cooperation with the union over job redesign.

Important considerations for job design are the abilities, attitudes, and motivation of personnel within the organization. Obviously, the design of particular jobs depends on the ability or training of present or potential employees. It would be ridiculous to design a job that would be considerably more complex than the ability level of employees available for the position. The ability and willingness of employees to be trained can limit job redesign.

Finally, management philosophy, objectives, and strategies may determine the degree of job redesign possible. Top management must be committed to the concept. Job redesign may allow employees to gain greater authority to determine how their jobs are performed and how they are managed. Thus, managers who identify with McGregor's Theory X assumptions would likely have difficulty with job redesign because it might give workers more discretion than the manager thinks is desirable.

Some approaches to job redesign require only minor changes in attitudes and behavior (for both managers and workers), while others require substantial change. Several approaches are discussed below.

Job Rotation

The simplest approach to job redesign is **job rotation**. When it is used, employees are rotated through several very similar jobs. For example, a production-line worker might be rotated every 2 weeks through several assembling jobs that require about the same level of skill. While job rotation does increase the variety in a worker's job, its impact on the worker to increase efficiency or productivity is doubtful. As a result, job rotation probably does not have a significant positive effect on employee motivation.

Job Enlargement

Job enlargement involves a horizontal expansion of worker duties, so that the worker learns several different jobs with somewhat different skill levels. For example, a production-line worker may work at several different jobs during the course of a day. These jobs would require the worker to use various skills. Compared to job rotation, job enlargement is more likely to increase worker motivation, but it also falls short of truly changing the worker's view of work. As a result, job enlargement is not likely to cause a substantial increase in worker motivation.

Job Enrichment

The most dramatic type of job redesign is called job enrichment. Strongly advocated by Frederick Herzberg, **job enrichment** refers to basic changes in the content and level of responsibility of a job so as to provide for the satisfaction of the motivation needs of personnel.[22] The individual is provided with an opportunity to derive a feeling of greater achievement, recognition, responsibility, and personal growth in performing the job. Although job enrichment programs have not always achieved positive results, such programs have demonstrated improvements in job performance and in the level of satisfaction of personnel in many organizations.

According to Herzberg, a number of principles are applicable for implementing job enrichment:

- Increasing job demands: Changing the job in order to increase the level of difficulty and responsibility of the job.
- Increasing a worker's accountability: Allowing more individual control and authority over the work, while retaining accountability of the manager.
- Providing work scheduling freedom: Within limits, allowing individual workers to schedule their own work.
- Providing feedback: Making timely periodic reports on performance to employees — directly to the worker rather than to the supervisor.
- Providing new learning experiences: Work situations should encourage opportunities for new experiences and personal growth of the individual.

If these 5 principles are adhered to, the result will be a substantially redesigned job for many workers, particularly those in mass production industries and in firms with repetitive clerical operations.

Consider the changes in job design that occurred in one company that manufactured pumps for washing machines. Prior to the implementation of job enrichment, the work was done in the traditional assembly-line fashion with the pump (containing 27 parts) assembled by 6 workers, each to assemble a small part of the pump. Each pump required approximately 1.75 min to complete. In a 2-step process, the job was enriched so that eventually one worker assembled the entire pump, inspected it, and placed his or her identifying mark on it. After the change, the company reported that: (1) assembly time had dropped to 1.5 min per pump, (2) product quality increased, and (3) cost savings were evident.[23]

This example demonstrates several of the principles of an enriched job noted above. First, by assembling the entire pump, the worker experienced increased job demands. Second, because the inspection function remained with the worker, the worker received feedback on how well the job had been performed. Third, the worker was allowed to determine individual work pace and procedures for completing the job, thereby increasing job freedom.

Quality Circles

Another technique that has been shown to be effective in enhancing motivation and achieving improved quality and productivity in several hundred American and Canadian companies is a concept known as quality circles.[24] In most firms, **quality circles** (QCs) consist of periodic meetings of small groups of employees who brainstorm ways to improve the quality and quantity of work.[25]

Consider how quality circles operate at Great-West Life Assurance Company, a large insurance company with Canadian head offices in Winnipeg. The company has an active productivity improvement program, which is based on the idea of employee participation in decision making and the use of quality circles. At present, 10 to 15 percent of Great-West's staff are members of quality circles; the goal is to increase eventually to 30 percent participation. Most of the quality circles operate in Winnipeg, but recently they have also been set up in Toronto and Vancouver, and in Denver, its American head office.

MANAGEMENT IN PRACTICE

Quality Circles at TRW

The Thompson Products Division of TRW in St. Catharines, Ontario implemented quality circles because it felt they would allow workers more involvement in their work and would promote improvements in cost reductions, product quality, productivity, and manager/worker teamwork.

To implement the concept, a steering committee made up of a cross section of workers and managers was formed. Each quality circle is made up of volunteers; maximum group size is 15 members. The groups meet once a week for one hour prior to the end of their shifts. A quality circle facilitator has been appointed from company staff to train quality circle group leaders.

The first quality circle was started in the die build area, which is concerned with the die sinking operation for dies used in the forge shop.

After some initial experimentation with team size, a quality circle composed of 10 people was formed. After only 2 months, the circle members made a presentation to management indicating how they wished to solve several important problems facing them. Management was impressed with the quality of both the presentation and the recommended solutions.

The benefit derived from use of quality circles goes beyond the specific problems that are solved. It also has allowed the firm to implement the behavioral theories of Maslow, Herzberg, McGregor and others. Using these motivation theories on the job also allows employees to satisfy more of their own personal needs.

SOURCE L. J. Knight, "Quality Circles in Action: A Canadian Experience," *CTM: The Human Element* (February 1983): 20–21.

Quality circles at Great-West Life are called "Innovative Change Teams" (ICTs). The objectives of the ICTs are to:

- Build an attitude of continuous improvement and problem prevention through creative thinking, open communications, and teamwork.
- Provide all employees with the opportunity to contribute ideas for change and to participate in decisions affecting their work.
- Achieve an enhanced quality of working life for employees, a higher level of productivity, and a superior quality of service to customers.

Each ICT is made up of volunteer members who meet once a week on company time to consider ways to do higher quality, more effective work. There are no monetary rewards for participation in an ICT. Each group has a leader who has received formal training in leading an ICT. The leader of a newly formed ICT is usually the group's supervisor, but the leader position often rotates after the group has been meeting for a while. Group leaders also train their group members. An agenda is prepared for each meeting; it may include discussion of several minor items, or the entire meeting may be devoted to a major issue. When a group has completed a given project — large projects may take 6 months

MANAGEMENT IN PRACTICE

Quality Teams at Burroughs Memorex's Winnipeg Plant

As part of a program to improve product quality and plant operations, Burroughs Memorex, Inc. implemented quality teams at its Winnipeg plant in 1981. Each quality team is made up of 8 to 10 people who meet once a week for one hour to brainstorm ways to improve operations. Problems may be raised by team members, or management may request that the team consider how to solve a particular problem. Although team membership is voluntary, 90 percent of eligible employees are participating. Quality team meetings take place on company time, but several teams have worked on projects on their own time.

Burroughs's use of the team concept differs from that of other companies in several significant ways. First, managers are involved on quality teams; in fact, they were the first to be trained. In many other companies, quality circles are composed solely of workers.

Second, all quality team members receive formal training in quality control and behavior modification — 32 hours in total. This training gives them valuable insights into what quality teams are supposed to accomplish and how they work.

Third, each team identifies levels for the ideas it comes up with. Level 1 solutions can be implemented without managerial approval; level 2 solutions must be submitted for managerial consideration because they affect other departments; level 3 solutions are taken to managers at the idea stage so that more information can be gathered regarding their feasibility.

Fourth, the formal presentations the quality teams make to higher levels of management are not so much designed to get approval, as they are for positive reinforcement for the people on the quality team.

Finally, because quality teams were implemented after a successful behavior modification program had been started (see page 333), a high level of trust had developed between workers and management. This earlier program made the quality team concept easier to implement and it was received with enthusiasm.

SOURCE Interview with Carole Postnieks, Manager of Training and Development, Burroughs Memorex, Inc.

or more — a presentation is made to management. All team members are encouraged to take part in these presentations.

ICTs at Great-West Life have become involved in both quality- and productivity-improvement projects. Projects have been completed in 4 general areas: (1) procedures/processes, (2) communications, (3) education and training, and (4) internal environment. A sample of the kinds of projects that have been completed in each of these areas is shown in the table below.

At Great West Life, ICTs have been set up to improve productivity and quality over the long run. As a result, the company has not yet begun to stress quantitative measurement of their impact. This will be possible once the idea of quality circles is firmly entrenched and employees feel comfortable with it. At present, the program looks promising; both employees and managers feel that quality circles have resulted in a higher quality of service, improved productivity, and improved employee satisfaction.

Sample of Quality Circle Projects at Great-West Life

Procedures/Processes
Improved system for receiving information from policyholders
Improvements to central file systems in several departments
Improved productivity in the Group Insurance Renewal Calculation
Improved use of central photocopy service to reduce cost and improve
  staff productivity

Communication
Developed newsletter to communicate information on new procedures,
  projects, and people
Improvements to circulation file system
Identified opportunities for improving productivity in the underwriting
  departments

Education and Training
Preparation of manual which provides medical and occupation infor-
  mation in uncomplicated language
Development of orientation program for new staff in Real Estate
  Accounting Department
Development of a "Helpful Hints Guide" to improve the use of com-
  puter terminals in the Actuarial Systems Department

Internal Environment
Recommendations on upgrading typewriter equipment to improve
  productivity
Redesigned office layout to improve efficiency
Improved telephone system

MANAGEMENT IN PRACTICE

Quality Circles at the Jim Pattison Group

Jim Pattison is one of Canada's best known entrepreneurs. In the late 1970s, he visited Japan and became interested in quality circles. Quality circles at his company involve regular meetings and workshops among nonmanagerial personnel. These sessions are designed to improve communications among workers, which in turn, should improve worker efficiency and product quality.

There are now more than 100 quality circles in the Pattison Group, and they are starting to show results. One company in the group, EDP, specializes in financial packages for business. A quality circle was introduced there in 1980 and, as a result, the number of jobs having to be redone has dropped from 15 percent to less than 3 percent.

The Pattison Group can quote many examples of how quality circles have improved company operations. One circle discovered that a better type of paint existed for a certain job; they also discovered that the company already had some of that paint in its storeroom.

SOURCE *Executive* (April 1984): 30.

MOTIVATION LESSONS FROM THE JAPANESE

William Ouchi's book *Theory Z* and Richard Pascale and Anthony Athos's *The Art of Japanese Management* describe management practices in a number of progressive North American companies that are similar to those successful Japanese firms have been using for years.[26] Ouchi identified Hewlett-Packard, IBM, Procter and Gamble, and Eastman Kodak as Theory Z organizations. **Theory Z** refers to an organization that shows a strong relationship between the company and its employees and demonstrates unusual responsibility toward its employees; the employees in turn show great loyalty toward the company. Theory Z companies tend to keep employees for their entire working life and avoid layoffs. The companies usually enjoy low employee turnover, low absenteeism, and high employee morale. The workers are more involved in their jobs with the company, a factor that leads to increased productivity and performance. Theory Z companies often develop their own traditions, ideals, and culture that fosters close to a family atmosphere. This atmosphere within the organization tends to bond its members — employees and managers — thereby facilitating decision making and communications within the company. All these practices have much in common with Japanese patterns and practices. Companies in North America have not necessarily imitated Japanese practices but have developed their own management style through the recognition of the types of employees who make up today's work force.

Pascale and Athos identify many of the same companies mentioned in the Ouchi study, Eastman Kodak, IBM, Hewlett-Packard, as practitioners of the Theory Z style of management. However, they also include: Delta Airlines, Boeing, and 3M as companies with management styles similar to Japanese firms. Pascale and Athos present what they refer to as a **Seven S Model**. This model attempts to identify what makes enterprises succeed or fail. The 7 S's are:

Strategy	Plan or course of action leading to the use of resources to achieve goals
Structure	Manner in which the firm is organized — type of departmentation, and responsibility and authority of managers
Systems	Policies, procedures, and methods that managers use in making decisions, implementing change, or communicating with others in the organization
Staff	"Demographic" characteristics of personnel within the firm
Skills	Distinctive capabilities of key personnel
Style	Patterns of behavior of key managers in achieving the organization's goals; cultural style of the organization
Superordinate goals	The overall purpose of the organization — guiding values and principles that integrate individual and organizational purposes.[27]

The first 3 elements, strategy, structure, and systems, are known as the "hard S's" or the more traditional elements that a company relies on for effective management. The other 4 factors, or "soft S's," are often not adequately addressed by firms. Pascale and Athos argue that the more successful and progressive companies address all 7 S's and give particular attention to the 4 soft S's. They place significant emphasis on what they refer to as "superordinate goals" — the glue that holds the other 6 S's together.

Well-managed companies, such as those described in Ouchi's *Theory Z* and Pascale and Athos's *The Art of Japanese Management*, usually have superordinate goals expressed in terms of the firm's responsibility to its employees, to its customers, and to the surrounding community.Thus, superordinate goals assist the firm in becoming more internally unified and self-sustaining over a period of time. For instance, at IBM, the goal of never sacrificing customer service is an example of a superordinate goal. Outstanding companies are usually quite advanced in their grasp of strategy, structure, and systems, but, unlike less successful firms, which rely primarily on these 3 S's, the best managed companies usually show great sophistication in the 4 soft S's as well. The most effective firms link their purposes and ways of realizing them to human values as well as to economic measures such as profit and efficiency.[28]

MOTIVATION: IMPLICATIONS FOR MANAGEMENT PRACTICE

From our discussion of the theories of motivation, several implications for managers can be derived. Management should recognize that many factors affect job performance, including: (1) skills and abilities of personnel, (2) levels of education and training of employees, (3) existing technology, and (4) available equipment and tools to perform the job. A manager may not be able to motivate an employee to better job performance if the employee does not possess the education, skills, training, and equipment to perform the job effectively. If any of these factors is inadequate, performance may be adversely affected. Employees may possess the necessary skills and be highly motivated to perform a certain job effectively, but their overall performance level may be quite low because they may not know how to do the job. This problem is sometimes overlooked by managers who believe that an employee is simply not motivated when in fact the employee does not understand what he or she is required to do, or lacks the proper training or equipment to perform efficiently and effectively. It does little good, and may cause considerable harm, if managers persist in driving employees in an effort to motivate them when motivation is not the problem.

- Managers must keep in mind that effective motivation is not so much something that a manager "does" to an employee as it is the creation of the climate where personnel will want to be productive and creative in their work.
- Managers must try to develop a better understanding of human behavior if they hope to create a climate that encourages greater employee performance and satisfaction.
- Human needs that are reasonably well satisfied do not motivate behavior. The lower-level needs on Maslow's hierarchy (physiological, safety, and social) are fairly well satisfied for most employees and therefore have little significant influence in motivating behavior. Thus, management should devote more of its attention toward providing a climate for the satisfaction of upper-level needs, such as esteem and self-actualization.
- Personnel have generally been underutilized and overmanaged. Organizations should try to provide more responsible and challenging jobs that allow a greater degree of individual self-control.
- Many managers hold Theory X assumptions regarding the behavior of their subordinates. These managers have created a climate of distrust and one that encourages immature actions on the part of employees. These conditions do not lead to more effective performance or a higher level of employee satisfaction.

OPENING INCIDENT REVISITED

Baylor's Department Store

If you were a member of the executive committee and attended the second meeting called by the vice-president of operations, what useful comments could you make about the role of money in motivation after reading this chapter? If you accept Herzberg's view of motivation, you would probably disagree with Lise Daniel's incentive scheme as a solution to the motivation problem; Herzberg does not see money as a motivator. He would instead propose a restructuring of the job so that it would be psychically rewarding to employees and would motivate them to sell enthusiastically.

If you accept Maslow's arguments, the role of money as a motivator is less clear. Money could be a motivator for any need, but is particularly likely for physiological and safety needs. For some needs, however, money is only one of the ways to achieve satisfaction. The need for status, for example, may be satisfied by having a certain job title even though the job does not pay very well. Thus, the role of money in motivation in

Maslow's theory is dependent on the level of the hierarchy at which the individuals find themselves as well as the general view of money the individuals have.

Equity theory says that money may be a motivator if people are underpaid or overpaid. If the person perceives an inequity involving pay, he or she will be motivated to resolve it. This motivation may, of course, be positive or negative, as the person may produce more *or* less. Baylor's, in this case, would have to determine if salary schedules for salesclerks are perceived to be equitable before implementing the incentive scheme.

Expectancy theory argues that money is a motivator if it is positively valent and no organization factors inhibit task performance. In the case of Baylor's, management would have to ensure that these two criteria are satisfied before an incentive scheme could be successfully implemented.

SUMMARY

Motivation is one of the most important and frequently discussed subjects in management. Today's employees are better educated, more highly skilled, and often do not respond to traditional values that may have motivated employees 20 or 30 years ago. Motivation is the process of influencing or stimulating a person to take action by creating a work atmosphere in which the goals of the organization and the needs of the people are satisfied. In an organization, personnel are said to be motivated if they perform their jobs effectively and efficiently. Management has traditionally relied on the use of rewards, such as increased pay, job security, good working conditions, or punishment — such as dismissal, demotions, or withholding rewards — to motivate employees. But today, management cannot rely on the manipulation of pay, benefits, or working conditions to motivate personnel to perform effectively. Motivation is a much more complicated process.

Managers must attempt to understand human nature and employees' basic needs if they are to create a climate for motivation. McGregor's Theory X and Theory Y and Argyris's maturity theory can help managers to develop a better understanding of human behavior. The theories of Maslow, Herzberg, McClelland, Vroom, Skinner, and Alderfer are also helpful to managers as they attempt to gain a more complete appreciation of basic employee needs and the reasons for their behavior.

Maslow's hierarchy of needs is a widely accepted theory, which suggests that people are motivated by unsatisfied needs. According to Maslow, a person's needs are arranged in priority from the basic physiological to the complex self-actualization needs. The key point for managers to accept is that needs that are fairly well satisfied do not motivate behavior. Alderfer's E-R-G theory classifies needs into 3 levels in order of progression — existence, relatedness, and growth. Each level of need becomes increasingly difficult to satisfy. Herzberg's motivation-hygiene theory classifies human needs into 2 categories — hygiene factors and motivators. The hygiene factors correspond to the lower-level needs on Maslow's hierarchy, while the motivators represent upper-level needs. Herzberg contends that, despite the fact that most managers and organizations concentrate on satisfying the hygiene needs, this action does not motivate employees. He believes firms should direct more attention to the motivators and to enriched jobs; but, at the same time, firms should not forget to be concerned about the hygiene needs. McClelland's theory stresses that certain needs are learned. He argues that each person's need for achievement, power, and affiliation affects his or her behavior in the work place.

The needs approach to motivation as developed by Maslow, Alderfer, and Herzberg does not adequately explain individual differences in the way people behave in accomplishing goals. Vroom's expectancy theory of motivation attempts to explain behavior in terms of an individual's goals, choices, and the expectations of achieving the goals. Employees are motivated by what they expect in terms of rewards as a result of their behavior. Skinner contends that behavior can be controlled and shaped by reinforcing desired behavior. The primary approach suggested by Skinner is organizational behavior modification (OBM), which has been successfully applied in a number of organizations. Under this approach, people act in the way they find most rewarding and, by controlling rewards, management can direct or modify employee behavior.

In addition to the major theories of motivation, managers should also develop an understanding of the role of money as a motivator. There is no simple relationship between pay and employee motivation, but an assessment of the popular motivation theories will give some insight into when money is likely to be a motivator and when it is not. If money is desired by an employee and the employee can see a clear connection between effort expenditure and money, it will likely be a motivator of behavior for that person.

Job design is the process of altering the nature and structure of jobs for the purpose of increasing productivity. Job design is concerned with the specific tasks to be performed, the methods used in performing the tasks, and how the job relates to the others in the organization. Some of the factors affecting work design include: technology, economy, government, unions, and management philosophy. Job rotation and job enlargement involve a horizontal expansion of duties, but add no responsibilities to the job. Job enrichment, on the other hand, creates basic changes in the content and level of responsibility of a job in an attempt to provide for the satisfaction of the needs of personnel.

Another technique that has been shown to be effective in enhancing motivation and achieving improved quality and productivity in several hundred North American companies is a concept known as quality circles. In most firms, quality circles consist of periodic meetings of small groups who get together to brainstorm ways to improve the quality and quantity of work.

North American firms are becoming increasingly interested in the motivation practices of Japanese companies, since Japanese workers are strongly committed to the firms they work for and are, as a result, extremely productive. Some policies of Japanese firms include lifetime employment, a high degree of responsibility toward employees, and an avoidance of employee layoffs.

REVIEW QUESTIONS

1. How would you define motivation?
2. Compare and contrast McGregor's Theory X and Theory Y. What are some examples of managerial practices that are consistent with a Theory Y philosophy of human nature?
3. What is Argyris's maturation theory? How does it apply to motivation?
4. What is the notion of the "self-fulfilling prophecy?" How is it related to management and motivation?
5. Relate Herzberg's theory of motivation to the theory developed by Maslow and Alderfer.
6. Describe McClelland's theory of human motives. How does it relate to motivation, and what are the basic characteristics of individuals described by the theory?
7. What is expectancy theory, and how can managers use it in the motivation process? Provide examples.
8. Briefly describe organizational behavior modification. How can it be used in motivating people? Give illustrations.
9. What is the role of money as a motivator? How important is the issue of equity of pay in terms of motivation? Explain.
10. What is meant by job enrichment, and how does it differ from job enlargement? How would you apply job enrichment? Give an example.
11. What are quality circles and how successful have they been in improving the quality and quantity of work?
12. What characterizes "Theory Z" type companies? How do the 7 S's relate to motivation in organizations?

EXERCISES

1. Interview 3 managers — for example, a bank president, a college dean, and a local retailer. Ask these managers to describe their

approach to creating a climate for motivating personnel within their organization. Compare their comments with the concepts on motivation presented in this chapter.

2. Using Maslow's hierarchy of needs as a guide, describe how your various needs have been satisfied on any job(s) you have held. Were any of your needs not met? Why or why not? How could they have been satisfied?

CASE STUDY

The Problem Chemist

Martin Stahl was the head of the research and development lab of Beltronics Ltd., a large manufacturing firm involved in the manufacture of plastic products for both consumer and industrial markets. In his role as laboratory head, Stahl supervised 11 chemists, all of whom had PhDs in chemistry. The R & D laboratory had a dual responsibility: (1) to do pure research on various chemical compounds and how they behaved, and (2) to take any promising results from the pure research output and see how they could be applied in the manufacture of plastic products.

The R & D lab had an excellent reputation inside and outside the company. A steady stream of new ideas and compounds had emerged from the lab over the last 10 years, and several major patents had been obtained during that period. Most of the members of Stahl's department had also published articles about their work in chemical trade journals. Stahl encouraged this because it gave the company a good reputation and it provided feedback and status to the chemists.

Stahl was on good terms with all but one of the staff chemists. Gary Blaski had been hired 7 years ago to give some additional expertise in the pure research area. Blaski had gone to school with one of Stahl's group and, on that person's recommendation, Stahl had hired Blaski. However, within about one year of Blaski's hiring, Stahl began to have problems with him. In Stahl's view, although Blaski was a fine chemist, he didn't seem to be motivated to do the kind of work the R & D lab was doing. Blaski showed little enthusiasm for the job, was often absent, and had very low productivity as measured by new patents granted, trade journal publications, and research projects completed.

Stahl had several discussions with Blaski about his performance, but Blaski rejected Stahl's position and argued that research can't be rushed. These discussions were often frustrating for Stahl, but he had gradually learned some things about Blaski. For example, he realized that Blaski craved recognition of any sort, no matter how insignificant. Stahl had attempted to use this knowledge to motivate Blaski by suggesting that Blaski get some of his work patented; this would mean considerable recognition. Blaski seemed interested in the idea, but somehow nothing ever came of it.

As time went on, Stahl became more and more unhappy with Blaski's nonchalant attitude and his subpar performance. He began increasing pressure on Blaski to improve his performance, but the interpersonal relations between the two worsened. Stahl noticed that Blaski seemed to be more and more unhappy; on one occasion Blaski offered the opinion that the other chemists didn't seem to like him. He even commented that his former school buddy seemed to be avoiding him. When asked why, Blaski said he didn't know, but that it was unfair that his peers didn't recognize his abilities.

One afternoon Blaski came to Stahl's office and requested permission to take time off from work (with pay) to attend a meeting of industrial chemists being held in another city. The following conversation took place:

Blaski: I'd like to go to the Industrial Chemists Association meetings. I think it's appropriate that the company pay for my travel and accommodations since I will be improving my work-related expertise by attending this meeting. I know you have reimbursed other people in the lab, and I think I should be treated the same way.

Stahl: I'm sorry, but I can't grant the request. Before laying out money for things like this, I need to see a considerable improvement in your work here.

Blaski: What do you mean?

Stahl: You know exactly what I mean. Your nonchalant attitude has got to change and your productivity must improve.

Blaski: I've told you this before, but you just don't listen. You can't rush research.

Stahl: The other chemists don't seem to be having any trouble meeting my productivity standards. I must not be "rushing" them. Why are you the only person who can't seem to do the job?

Blaski: You just don't realize that each person is unique. You're trying to make me fit into a certain mold and that's been weighing on my mind and reducing my productivity. If I were given more freedom to do my own thing, I would be more productive.

Stahl: When you demonstrate some productivity you'll get some freedom!

After Blaski left, Stahl wondered if he had been too harsh with him. However, he was at the end of his rope and had exhausted all the avenues he knew of to motivate Blaski.

QUESTIONS

1. Use each of the motivation theories in this chapter to analyze this problem. What solutions would each theory suggest?
2. Comment on Blaski's performance problems using the formula performance = ability × motivation.
3. What should Stahl do to motivate Blaski?

CASE STUDY

Motivating a Dissatisfied Manager

Alice Rose had been a district sales manager with Finn Productions for 10 years. She was recognized by her peers and supervisors as a person who ran a good department. However, everyone also realized that Rose was extremely ambitious and was seeking a higher-level management position. When one of her sales representatives did a good job in a particular quarter, Rose would attempt to take the credit. However, if a problem arose, it was never Rose's fault.

When the marketing manager retired, Rose applied for the position. The company decided to do a thorough search because of the responsibility and importance associated with the position. When the search was concluded, the decision was made to go outside for a person to fill the position. The consensus of top management was that Rose, although a good district sales manager, might have difficulties in working with her new peer group. They felt that she might alienate the other managers if she tried to take credit for their work.

Rose was furious. She had wanted that particular job for a long time and had dedicated all of her energies toward obtaining it. She became very despondent and her work deteriorated. The department functioned in spite of her, not because of her. Decisions were made slowly if at all, and she began to be late with her sales reports. Although her sales staff continued to be productive, Rose could not take the credit.

When the new marketing manager took over, one of the first major problems that he confronted was how to motivate Rose to her former level of performance. He recognized that Rose had been with the company for a long time, but something constructive had to be done. Rose was receiving an excellent salary for doing virtually nothing.

QUESTIONS

1. As the new marketing manager, what approach would you use to motivate Alice Rose?
2. Do you believe that Rose can be motivated to become a productive member of the organization once again? Why or why not? Discuss.

NOTES

[1] Douglas McGregor, *The Human Side of Enterprise* (New York: McGraw-Hill, 1960).

[2] Chris Argyris, *Personality and Organization* (New York: Harper, 1957).

[3] J. Sterling Livingston, "Pygmalion in Management," *Harvard Business Review* (July-August 1969).

[4] John L. Single, "The Power of Expectations: Productivity and the Self-Fulfilling Prophecy," *Management World* (November 1980): 19, 37–38.

[5] Abraham Maslow, *Motivation and Personality* (New York: Harper, 1954).

[6] Clayton P. Alderfer, "A Critique of Salancik and Pfeffer's Examination of Need Satisfaction Theories," *Administrative Science Quarterly* 22 (December 1977): 658–672.

[7] Frederick Herzberg, *Work and the Nature of Man* (Cleveland: World, 1966).

[8] David C. McClelland and David H. Burnham, "Power is the Great Motivator," *Harvard Business Review* 54 (March-April 1976): 103.

[9] David R. Hampton, Charles E. Summer, and Ross A. Webber, *Organizational Behavior and the Practice of Management* (Glenview, Ill: Scott, Foresman, 1978): 11–15.

[10] M. J. Stahl, "Achievement Power and Managerial Motivation: Selecting Managerial Talent with the Job Choice Exercise," *Personnel Psychology* (Winter 1983): 786.

[11] Victor Vroom, *Work and Motivation* (New York: Wiley, 1964).

[12] C. W. Kennedy, J. A. Fossum and B. J. White, "An Empirical Comparison of Within-Subjects and Between-Subjects Expectancy Theory Models," *Organizational Behavior and Human Performance* (August 1983): 124.

[13] B. F. Skinner, *Beyond Freedom and Dignity* (New York: Knopf, 1971).

[14] Ed Pedalino and Victor U. Gamboa, "Behavior Modification and Absenteeism," *Journal of Applied Psychology* 59 (December 1974): 694–698.

[15] W. Clay Hamner and Ellen P. Hamner, "Behavior Modification and the Bottom Line," *Organizational Dynamics* 4 (Spring 1976): 12.

[16] "At Emery Air Freight: Positive Reinforcement Boosts Performance," *Organizational Dynamics* 1 (Autumn 1973): 41–50.

[17] J. S. Adams, "Toward An Understanding of Inequity," *Journal of Abnormal and Social Psychology* 67 (1963): 425.

[18] S. W. Gellerman, *Management by Motivation* (New York: American Management Association, 1968).

[19] J. Richard Hackman and Greg R. Oldham, *Work Redesign* (Reading, Mass.: Addison-Wesley, 1980).

[20] Hackman and Oldham.

[21] John F. Runcie, " 'By Days I Make the Cars,' " *Harvard Business Review* (May-June 1980): 106–115.

[22] Frederick Herzberg, "One More Time: How Do You Motivate Employees?" *Harvard Business Review* 46 (January-February 1968): 53–62. See also Frederick Herzberg, "Motivation and Innovation: Who are Workers Serving?" *California Management Review* 22, no. 2 (Winter 1979).

[23] M. D. Kilbridge, "Reduced Costs Through Job Enlargement: A Case," *Journal of Business* 33 (1960): 74–80.

[24] "Will the Slide Kill Quality Circles?" *Business Week* (January 11, 1982): 108–109.

[25] "The New Industrial Revolution," *Business Week* (May 11, 1981): 85–98.

[26] William Ouchi, *Theory Z: How American Business Can Meet the Japanese Challenge* (Reading, Mass.: Addison-Wesley, 1981); Richard Pascale and Anthony Athos, *The Art of Japanese Management: Applications for American Executives* (New York: Simon and Schuster, 1981).

[27] Pascale and Athos, 81.

[28] Pascale and Athos, 178.

REFERENCES

Armstrong, J. "How to Motivate." *Management Today* 12 (February 1977): 60–63.

Berry, L. E. "Motivation Management." *Journal of Systems Management* 30 (April 1979): 30–32.

Collison, Robert. "The Japanese Fix." *Canadian Business* (November 1981): 37.

Cook, C. W. "Guidelines for Managing Motivation." *Business Horizons* 23 (April 1980): 61–69.

Davis, Tim R. V. "The Influence of the Physical Environment in Offices." *Academy of Management Review* 9, no. 2 (April 1984): 271–283.

Eastmond, Archie, "Motivation in the Broker's Office." *Canadian Insurance* (September 1982): 14.

Francis, Jack. "Profit Sharing Gaining Ground." *Winnipeg Free Press* (June 8, 1984): 46.

Gallagher, W. E. Jr., and Einhorn, H. J. "Motivation Theory and Job Design." *Journal of Business* 49 (July 1976): 358–373.

Gayle, J. B., and Searle, F. R. "Maslow, Motivation, and the Manager." *Management World* 9 (September 1980): 18–20.

Giblin, E. J. "Motivating Employees: A Closer Look." *Personnel Journal* 55 (April 1976): 68–71.

Hackman, J. R. "Is Job Enrichment Just a Fad?" *Harvard Business Review* 53 (September 1975): 129–138.

Hatuany, N., and Puick, V. "Japanese Management Practices and Productivity." *Organizational Dynamics* 9 (Spring 1981): 4–21.

Keys, J. Bernard, and Miller, Thomas R. "The Japanese Management Theory Jungle." *Academy Management Review* 9, no. 2 (April 1984): 342–353.

Kim, Jay S. "Effect of Behavior Plus Outcome Goal Setting and Feedback Satisfaction and Performance." *Academy of Management Journal* 27, no. 1 (March 1984): 139–149.

Klimoski, R. J., and Hayes, N. J. "Leader Behavior and Subordinate Motivation." *Personnel Psychology* 33 (Autumn 1980): 543–555.

Knight, Lou. "Quality Circles in Action: A Canadian Experience." *CTM: The Human Element* (February 1983): 20.

Latham, Gary P., and Steel, Timothy P. "The Motivational Effects of Participation versus Goal Setting on Performance." *Academy of Management Journal* 26, no. 3 (September 1983): 406–417.

McClelland, D. C., and Burnham, D. H. "Power Is the Great Motivator." *Harvard Business Review* 54 (March 1976): 100–110.

Miller, William B. "Motivation Techniques: Does One Work Best?" *Management Review* (February 1981): 47–52.

Neider, L. L. "Experimental Field Investigation Utilizing an Expectancy Theory View of Participation." *Organizational Behavior and Human Performance* 26 (December 1980): 425–442.

Norris, Dwight R., and Beibuhr, Robert E. "Attributional Influences on the Job Performance — Job Satisfaction Relationships." *Academy of Management Journal* 27, no. 2 (June 1983): 424–430.

Odiorne, G. S. "Uneasy Look at Motivation Theory." *Training and Development Journal* 34 (June 1980): 106–112.

Ouchi, William G. "Organizational Paragrams: A Commentary on Japanese Management and Theory Z Organizations." *Organizational Dynamics* 9 (Spring 1981): 36–42.

————."Theory Z Corporations." *Industry Week* (May 4, 1981): 49–51.

Peters, Thomas J. "Putting Excellence into Management." *Business Week* (July 21, 1980): 196–205.

Pinder, C. C. "Concerning the Application of Human Motivation Theories in Organizational Settings." *Academy of Management Review* 2 (July 1977): 384–397.

Quick, J. C. "Dyadic Goal Setting within Organizations: Rolemaking and Motivational Considerations." *Academy of Management Review* 4 (July 1979): 377–380.

Rosenthal, Robert. "The Pygmalion Effect Lives." *Psychology Today* (September 1973): 56–60.

Runcie, John F. " 'By Days I Make the Cars.' " *Harvard Business Review* (May-June 1980): 106–115.

Schmitt, N., and Son, L. "Evaluation of Valence Models of Motivation to Pursue Various Post High School Alternatives." *Organizational Behavior and Human Performance* 27 (February 1981): 135–150.

Speigel, D. "How Not to Motivate." *Supervisory Management* 22 (November 1977): 41–45.

Trautman, L. J., et al. "Managing People: Choosing the Right Motivator." *Mortgage Banker* 40 (August 1980): 34–37.

Ungson, Gerardo Rivera, and Steers, Richard M. "Motivation and Politics in Executive Compensation." *Academy of Management Review* 9, no. 2 (April 1984): 313–323.

11

Leadership

OPENING INCIDENT

Mission Chapel

The Mission Chapel is a nondenominational church located in the downtown section of a large Canadian city. The chapel's choir has 45 volunteers and performs each Sunday from September through June.

There are two distinct types of people in the choir. Ten people are experienced singers, with many years of formal music and voice training. The remaining 35 people have little or no musical training but are in the choir because they like to sing. The experienced singers are expected to help the inexperienced ones; in addition, the experienced singers do solo performances on a regular basis.

The choir director, Carolyn Barnes, is known throughout the city as an excellent musician. In addition to directing the chapel choir, she judges

various musical competitions held throughout the year and is the producer of a popular local television musical show. Barnes is paid a token salary of $5,000 per year for conducting the chapel choir. Practice is held for 2 hours on Wednesday evenings, at which time the choir works on a variety of numbers toward the goal of a good performance at the regular church service.

Barnes ran the choir with a firm hand. She decided which music was to be performed, the date on which it would be performed, who the soloists would be, the nature and timing of special concerts, and the structure of the Wednesday night practices.

In her opinion, she was very effective, since the current choir had placed first in all 3 competitions it had entered in the past 18 months.

Morale of the choir seemed very high and turn-over was fairly low (10 percent).

In spite of this success, Barnes had noticed two things that disturbed her. First, absenteeism was running at 20 percent at both the practice sessions and the regular Sunday services. She had tried to solve this problem by pointing out to choir members the importance of regular attendance, but this lecture had been ineffective. Second, certain of the choir members were con-tinually talking and cutting up during the practice sessions. This joking was annoying to Barnes and on several occasions she had made it clear that she was not going to tolerate it. These comments had not had any effect and the problems continued. Barnes wondered if her leadership style was appropriate for the situation and if she should change it in an attempt to solve these two problems.

KEY TERMS

leadership
formal power
reward power
coercive power
expert power
referent power
trait approach
Likert's systems of
  management
managerial grid
Ohio State leadership
  studies

initiating structure
consideration
path-goal theory
leadership
  continuum
Fiedler's contingency
  leadership model
leader-member
  relations
task structure

position power of the
  leader
Hersey and
  Blanchard's
  situational
  leadership theory
task behavior
relationship behavior
task-relevant
  maturity
leadership decision-
  making model

LEARNING OBJECTIVES

After completing this chapter you should be able to
1. Describe leadership and define the types of power a leader may possess.
2. Identify and describe the major leadership theories which advocate a universal leadership style.
3. Identify and explain the major situational leadership theories.
4. Describe the integrated approach to leadership.

Influencing through motivation can be most effective when a manager shows clearly that he or she is a leader. "What does it take to be an effective manager?" "What is the most effective leadership style?"

These questions have perplexed and challenged managers for generations. Literally thousands of research studies have been conducted to provide greater insight into these questions. However, such studies of leaders and the leadership process have not yielded any set of traits or behaviors that are consistently related to effective leadership. The basic conclusion that can be drawn from these studies is that there is no one most effective leadership style. What we do know is that effective leadership is absolutely essential to the survival and overall growth of every organization.

As we noted at the beginning of Chapter 1, nearly 60 percent of all new businesses fail within the first 6 years. Despite high salaries and excellent opportunities in large corporations, there continues to be a shortage of competent managers who are effective leaders. The lack of capable leadership is not just confined to business organizations but has also been felt in government, churches, education, and all other types of organizations. The problem is not a lack of people who want to be leaders or managers, but rather a scarcity of skilled people who are capable of performing effectively in leadership positions. The primary challenge of leadership or management is to guide an organization toward the accomplishment of its objectives. The leader achieves this by directing and encouraging employees of the organization to attain the highest level of performance possible within the limitation of available resources, skills, and technology.

Many large businesses, and even countries, have made successful turnarounds as a result of a change in leadership. Even though we don't have all the answers, a more complete knowledge of the skills, attitudes, and values that are related to effective leadership would greatly improve our ability to select, train, and develop more effective managers. This is precisely the purpose of this chapter. We first define "leadership" and compare it to "management." We next look at three universalist leadership theories; these theories assume that there is "one best way" to lead others, regardless of the situation. The next section examines several contingency leadership theories; these theories reject the universalist idea and argue that the most effective leadership style depends on a variety of situational factors. Finally, we present an integrative approach to leadership that should prove beneficial to individuals as they develop their leadership styles.

LEADERSHIP DEFINED

Leadership is the ability of one individual to influence other individuals positively in order to accomplish group goals. These group goals may or may not be consistent with the goals of the organization the group belongs to. (Recall our discussion of the informal organization in Chapter 8.) So, a leader may or may not have a positive effect on the achievement of an organization's goals. In this chapter, we are primarily concerned with managers as leaders.

We need to make a distinction between the terms "leader" and "manager." A manager is one who performs the functions of planning, organizing, influencing, and controlling and who occupies a formal position in an organization. For example, the sales manager is the individual who manages the sales staff of the company. A leader is anyone who is able to influence others to pursue certain goals. Is this sales manager both a manager and a leader? Not necessarily. The sales manager is certainly a manager because of the formal position he or she occupies. Whether the sales manager is also a leader depends on his or her ability to influence the sales staff to pursue certain goals.

The president of an organization may have a great deal of formal power but, if he or she is so disliked that employees will not allow themselves to be influenced positively, this president demonstrates very little leadership. He or she can coerce other individuals into doing some work — but that is not leadership.

Generally speaking, a good manager is a good leader, but a good leader may not be a good manager. Consider the following actual situation. A team of consultants had prepared a feasibility study for the president of a newly formed mobile home manufacturer. The study recommended that the new plant produce a relatively low-priced mobile home because the firm was in a low-income geographic area. However, the company hired a production manager with an excellent reputation who had several years of experience with a manufacturer of higher-priced, higher-quality mobile homes. Against the advice of the consultants and without the knowledge of the board of directors, the production manager decided to direct his production supervisors and workers to produce a higher-priced mobile home. The results proved to be disastrous for the newly established company. The sales staff was not able to sell these high-priced units; the firm had invested over $350,000 of its working capital in an inventory of mobile homes that it could not sell. This was a major factor contributing to the firm's bankruptcy within 9 months of its start-up. In this illustration, the production manager exercised effective leadership because he significantly influenced the behavior of his workers. However, he was an ineffective manager because he had the employees pursuing goals that were not in the best interest of the company.

Thus a company can fail, even though it has leaders who have been effectively influencing the behavior of others to accomplish goals, if these goals are inappropriate for the company. Also, it should be noted that a person can have the title of manager but have very little influence over the behavior and actions of others. Or, an individual might not carry the title of manager but be an important informal leader exercising considerable influence over the behavior of others in the work group.

Leaders are able to influence others because they possess power. We discussed the various types of power in Chapter 8. However, we will briefly review these below. Power can be in one or any combination of the following forms:

- **Formal power**:   Derived from authority or formal position in the firm
- **Reward power**:   Based on the leader's ability to administer and control rewards (such as pay, promotions, and praise) to others for complying with the leader's directives
- **Coercive power**:   Based on the leader's ability to administer and control punishments (such as the power to fire, demote, or reprimand) to others for not following the leader's requests
- **Expert power**:   Based on the special knowledge, expertise, technical skill, or experience possessed by the leader. For example, employees may view Frank Wilson, an engineer, as a "real pro" in the engineering department. While Wilson is not the manager of the department, other engineers and managers may go to him for technical assistance with structural design problems.
- **Referent power**:   Based on the leader's possession of personal characteristics that make him or her attractive to other people. Some individuals possess charisma, one form of referent power. Another form of referent power can be derived from one's association with another powerful leader.

ONE-BEST-WAY (UNIVERSALIST) LEADERSHIP THEORIES

Leadership research began in earnest in the early twentieth century and has been increasing in volume steadily. Leadership theories which were developed before 1970 often had a universalist flavor: they assumed that there was one best way to lead subordinates regardless of the situation the leader found himself or herself in. Three of the most popular universalist leadership theories are: (1) the trait approach, (2) Likert's System IV Management, and (3) Blake and Mouton's Managerial Grid.

The Trait Approach

The leader has always occupied a strong and central role in traditional management theory. Most of the early research on leadership attempted to: (1) compare the traits of people who became leaders with those who remain as followers, and (2) identify characteristics and traits possessed by effective leaders. Research studies comparing the traits of leaders and nonleaders basically failed to find any specific set of traits that differentiated leaders from nonleaders. While there was some tendency for leaders to be somewhat taller, more outgoing, more self-confident, and more intelligent than nonleaders, a specific combination of traits has not been found that would differentiate the leader or potential leader from the followers.

There has been considerable research to compare the traits of effective and ineffective leaders. Traits such as aggressiveness, ambition, decisiveness, dominance, initiative, intelligence, physical characteristics (looks, height, and weight), self-assurance, and other personality factors were studied to determine if they were related to effective leadership. The major question of this research was: "Could such traits differentiate effective from ineffective leaders?" Perhaps the underlying assumption to personal trait research has been that leaders are born, not made. Although research has demonstrated that this is not the case, some people still believe that certain inborn traits make a person a good leader. Research has not shown that any overall traits can distinguish effective from ineffective leaders.

However, the **trait approach** to the study of leadership is not dead. Edwin Ghiselli has continued to conduct research in an effort to identify personality and motivational traits related to effective leadership.[1] Ghiselli identified 13 personal trait factors. Subsequent research studies of these trait factors have ranked these in order of significance as illustrated in Exhibit 11-1. The 6 most significant traits are:

- Supervisory ability: The performance of the basic functions of management, including planning, organizing, influencing, and controlling the work of others.
- Need for occupational achievement: The seeking of responsibility and the desire for success.
- Intelligence: Creative and verbal ability, including judgment, reasoning, and thinking capacity.
- Decisiveness: Ability to make decisions and solve problems capably and competently.

EXHIBIT 11-1   Ghiselli's managerial traits

Traits[a]	Importance Value[b]
Supervisory ability (A)	100
Occupational achievement (M)	76
Intelligence (A)	64
Self-actualization (M)	63
Self-assurance (P)	62
Decisiveness (P)	61
Lack of need for security (M)	54
Working-class affinity (P)	47
Initiative (A)	34
Lack of need for high financial reward (M)	20
Need for power (M)	10
Maturity (P)	5
Masculinity-femininity (P)	0

SOURCE   James F. Gavin, "A Test of Ghiselli's Theory of Managerial Traits," *Journal of Business Research* (February 1976): 46. Reprinted by permission.
[a] A = ability trait; P = personality trait; M = motivational trait
[b] 100 = very important; 0 = plays no part in managerial talent

- Self-assurance: The extent to which the individual views himself or herself as capable of coping with problems.
- Initiative: Ability to act independently and develop courses of action not readily apparent to other people. Self-starter — able to find new or innovative ways of accomplishing goals.

In spite of the contributions of Ghiselli, the trait approach to the study of leadership has left many unanswered questions concerning what is required for effective leadership. Perhaps one of the major problems with the trait approach is defining who is effective. Does the mere fact that a person has a powerful position make that individual a leader?

Likert's Systems of Management

Rensis Likert, former director of the Institute for Social Research at the University of Michigan, developed a universal theory of leadership. Likert's theory consists of a continuum of styles ranging from autocratic to participative. **Likert's** 4 basic **systems of management** are: System I, Exploitative Autocratic; System II, Benevolent Autocratic; System III, Consultative; and System IV, Participative Team. Only the last style — System IV — was in the long run deemed best for all situations.[2]

System I — Exploitative Autocratic

In this kind of organization, managers make all the decisions. They decide what is to be done, who will do it, and how and when it is to be accomplished. Failure to complete work as assigned results in threats or punishment. Under this system, management exhibits little confidence or trust in employees. A typical managerial response with this system is: "You do it my way or you're fired." In System I, a low level of trust and confidence exists between management and employees.

System II — Benevolent Autocratic

In System II organizations, managers still make the decisions, but employees have some degree of freedom and flexibility in performing their jobs so long as they conform to specific procedures. Under this system, managers take a very paternalistic attitude: "I'll take care of you if you perform well." With System II, a fairly low level of trust is present between management and the employees; employees use caution when dealing with management.

System III — Consultative

In System III organizations, managers consult with employees prior to establishing the goals and making decisions about work. Employees have a considerable degree of freedom in making their own decisions as to how to accomplish the work. A manager using System III might say to an employee: "I'd like your opinion on this before I make the decision." Management tends to rely on rewards, as opposed to punishments, to motivate employees. Also, the level of trust between the employees and management is fairly high. This system creates a climate in which employees feel relatively free to discuss work-related matters openly with management.

System IV — Participative Team

System IV is Likert's recommended system or style of management. The emphasis in a System IV organization is on a group participative role with full involvement of the employees in the process of estab-

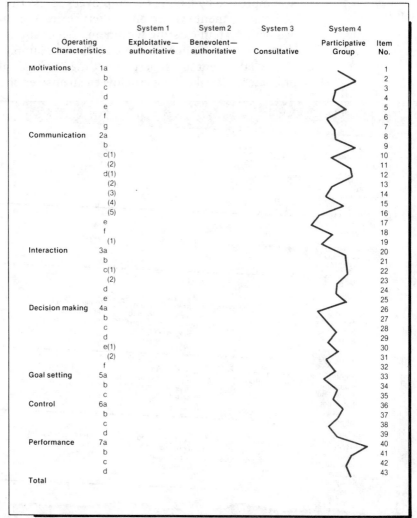

		System 1 Exploitative—authoritative	System 2 Benevolent—authoritative	System 3 Consultative	System 4 Participative Group	Item No.
Operating Characteristics						
Motivations	1a					1
	b					2
	c					3
	d					4
	e					5
	f					6
	g					7
Communication	2a					8
	b					9
	c(1)					10
	(2)					11
	d(1)					12
	(2)					13
	(3)					14
	(4)					15
	(5)					16
	e					17
	f					18
	(1)					19
Interaction	3a					20
	b					21
	c(1)					22
	(2)					23
	d					24
	e					25
Decision making	4a					26
	b					27
	c					28
	d					29
	e(1)					30
	(2)					31
	f					32
Goal setting	5a					33
	b					34
	c					35
Control	6a					36
	b					37
	c					38
	d					39
Performance	7a					40
	b					41
	c					42
	d					43
Total						

EXHIBIT 11-2 Likert chart—management systems

SOURCE Rensis Likert, *The Human Organization* (New York: McGraw-Hill, 1967). Reprinted by permission of author and publisher.

NOTE: Management system used by the most productive plant (Plant L) of a well-managed company, as seen by middle and top managers.

lishing goals and making job-related decisions. Employees feel free to discuss matters with their managers, who display supportive rather than condescending or threatening behavior. Likert argues that the entire organization should be designed along System IV lines, with work being performed by a series of overlapping groups. The leader provides a link between the group and other units at higher levels in the organization. This concept is often referred to as the linking-pin theory. Decision making is widespread throughout the enterprise, with the power of knowledge usually taking precedence over the power of authority.

Measurement of the type of style in the Likert framework is usually accomplished by having the employees assess the organization culture and management system on a Likert scale. A profile showing the management system existing within an organization is developed through this survey of opinion (Exhibit 11-2). For example, when the question, "To what extent are superiors willing to share information with subordinates?" is asked, the employee can answer on the continuum from

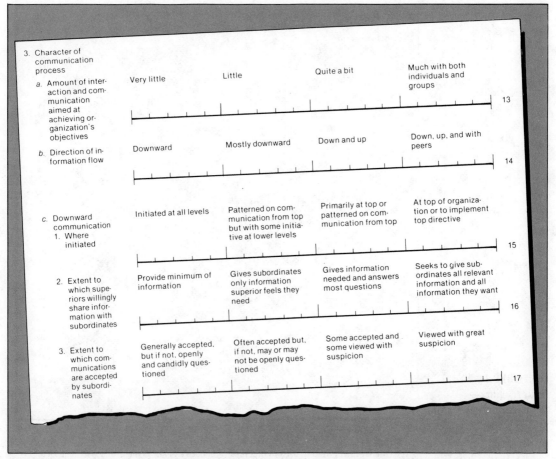

EXHIBIT 11-3   Sample of questions on Likert Scale relating to organization communications

SOURCE   Rensis Likert, *The Human Organization* (New York: McGraw-Hill, 1967). Reprinted by permission.

"provide minimum information" all the way to "seeks to give subordinates all relevant information and all information they want." (See question 3c2 in Exhibit 11-3.) It has been found that the positions on these scales can be significantly altered through organizational and management development programs. (See Chapter 13.)

Blake and Mouton's Managerial Grid

Perhaps the most widely known of all leadership theories is the **managerial grid** developed by Robert R. Blake and Jane S. Mouton.[3] The managerial grid is illustrated in Exhibit 11-4. The two dimensions of

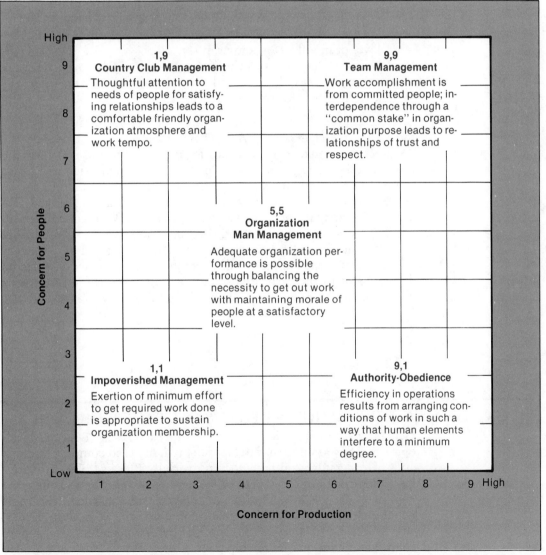

EXHIBIT 11-4 Blake and Mouton's managerial grid

SOURCE Robert R. Blake and Jane Nrygley Mouton, *The New Managerial Grid* (Houston: Gulf Publishing Company, 1978): 11. Reprinted by permission of the authors and publisher.

the 9 × 9 grid are labeled "concern for people" and "concern for production." A score of 1 indicates low concern and a score of 9 shows a high concern. The grid depicts 5 major leadership styles representing the degree of concern the leader has for "people" and "production."

- 1,1 **Impoverished Management:** The manager has little concern for either people or production.
- 9,1 **Authority-Obedience:** The manager stresses operating efficiently through controls in situations where human elements cannot interfere.
- 1,9 **Country Club Management:** The manager is thoughtful, comfortable, and friendly, and has little concern for output.
- 5,5 **Organization Man Management:** The manager attempts to balance and trade off concern for work in exchange for a satisfactory level of morale — a compromiser.
- 9,9 **Team Management:** The manager seeks high output through committed people, achieved through mutual trust, respect, and a realization of interdependence.[4]

According to Blake and Mouton, the first 4 styles listed are not the most effective leadership styles. They strongly suggest that only the 9,9 position of maximum concern for both output and people is the most effective. They argue that using the 9,9 team approach will result in improved performance, lower employee turnover and absenteeism, and greater employee satisfaction. The use of job enrichment and subordinate participation in managerial decision making contributes to this 9,9 situation, where both the organization and its members are accorded maximum and equal concern. The managerial grid concept has been introduced to many managers throughout the world since its development in the early 1960s and has influenced the management philosophies and practices of many of them.

SITUATIONAL (CONTINGENCY) THEORIES OF LEADERSHIP

Generally speaking, situational leadership theories are a recent development. They assume that the leadership issue is so complex that one style of leadership is unlikely to be universally effective. These theories have identified a wide variety of factors that determine the effectiveness of a given leadership style at a given point in time. The most popular situational leadership theories are: (1) The Ohio State leadership studies, (2) House's Path-Goal theory of leadership, (3) Tannenbaum and Schmidt's leadership continuum, (4) Fiedler's contingency leadership model, (5) Hersey and Blanchard's situational leadership theory, and (6) Vroom and Yetton's decision-making model.

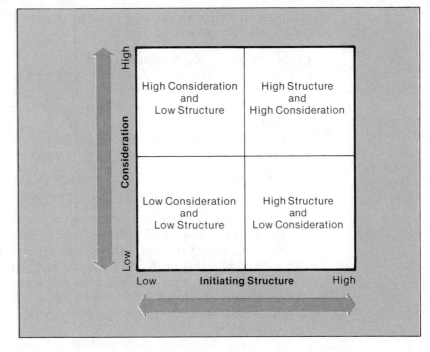

**EXHIBIT 11-5
Ohio State
leadership model**

Ohio State Leadership Studies

Beginning in 1945, researchers in the Bureau of Business Research at Ohio State University made a series of detailed studies of the behavior of leaders in a wide variety of organizations. The key concern of the **Ohio State leadership studies** was the leader's behavior in directing the efforts of others toward group goals. After many studies, researchers identified 2 important dimensions of leader behavior:

1. **Initiating Structure**: the extent to which leaders establish goals and structure their roles and the roles of subordinates toward the attainment of the goals.
2. **Consideration**: the extent to which leaders have relationships with subordinates characterized by mutual trust, respect, and consideration of employees' ideas and feelings.

Initiating structure and consideration were identified as separate and distinct dimensions of leadership behavior. As illustrated in Exhibit 11-5, there are 4 basic leadership styles representing different combinations of leadership behavior. A manager can be high in both consideration and initiating structure, low in both, or high in one and low in the other. Although the Ohio State studies are often cited as a Universalist theory of leadership, the one most effective combination that meets the needs of all situations was not suggested by their model. Rather, the combination or appropriate level of initiating structure and consideration was determined by the demands of a particular situation.

Among the many situational variables that must be related to leadership behavior are:

- Expectations of the people being led
- Degree of task structuring imposed by technology
- Pressures of schedules and time
- Degrees of interpersonal contact possible between the leader and subordinates
- Degree of influence of the leader outside of the group
- Congruency of style with that of one's superior.

The following observations can be made with regard to the type of leadership styles proposed in the Ohio State model:

- If a group expects and wants authoritarian leadership behavior, it is more likely to be satisfied with that type of leadership.
- If group members have less authoritarian expectations, a leader who strongly emphasizes initiating structure will be resented.
- If the work situation is highly structured by technology and the pressures of time, the supervisor who is high in consideration is more likely to meet with success measured by absenteeism, turnover, and grievances.
- If task structuring precludes individual and group self-actualization, it will be useless to look for motivation from this source.
- When subordinates have little contact with their supervisor, they tend to prefer a more autocratic style.
- If employees must work and interact continuously, they usually want the superior to be high in consideration.

Path-Goal Theory of Leadership

Robert House, extending the Ohio State studies, developed what he termed the **path-goal theory** of leadership.[5] This approach to leadership is closely related to the expectancy theory of motivation discussed in Chapter 10. House concluded that managers can facilitate job performance by showing employees how their performance directly affects their receiving desired rewards. In other words, a manager's behavior contributes to employee satisfaction and acceptance of the manager if it increases goal attainment by employees. According to the path-goal approach, effective job performance results if the manager clearly defines the job, provides training for the employee, assists the employee in performing the job effectively, and rewards the employee for effective performance.

Four distinct leadership behaviors are associated with the path-goal approach:

- **Directive:** The manager tells the subordinate what to do and when to do it (no employee participation in decision making).
- **Supportive:** The manager is friendly with and shows interest in employees.

- **Participative:** The manager seeks suggestions and involves employees in decision making.
- **Achievement oriented:** The manager establishes challenging goals and demonstrates confidence that employees can achieve these goals.

Following the path-goal theory, a manager may use all 4 of the leadership behaviors in different situations. For instance, a manager may use directive behavior when supervising an inexperienced employee and supportive behavior when supervising a well-trained, experienced worker who is aware of the goals to be attained. The primary focus of the path-goal approach is on how managers can increase employee motivation and job satisfaction by clarifying performance goals and the path to achieve those goals.[6]

Tannenbaum and Schmidt's Leadership Continuum

Robert Tannenbaum and Warren H. Schmidt described a series of factors that they thought influenced a manager's selection of the most appropriate leadership style. Their approach advocated a continuum of leadership behavior supporting the notion that choosing an effective leadership style depends on the demands of the situation. As illustrated in Exhibit 11-6, leadership behavior ranges from "Boss-Centered" to "Subordinate-Centered," which is similar in concept to the other dimensions of leadership behavior discussed. Tannenbaum and Schmidt

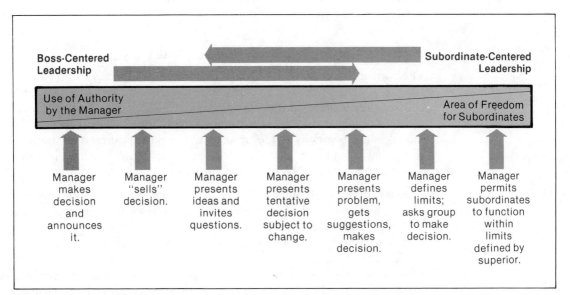

EXHIBIT 11-6 Continuum of leadership behavior

SOURCE Exhibit from Robert Tannenbaum and Warren H. Schmidt, "How to Choose a Leadership Pattern," *Harvard Business Review* (May/June 1973). Reprinted by permission of the President and Fellows of Harvard College and of the *Harvard Business Review*.

emphasized that a manager should give careful consideration to the following factors before selecting a leadership style:

- **Characteristics of the manager:** background, education, experience, values, knowledge, goals, and expectations
- **Characteristics of the employees:** background, education, experience, knowledge, goals, values, and expectations
- **Requirements of the situation:** size, complexity, goals, structure, and culture of the organization, as well as the impact of technology, time pressure, and nature of the work.

According to the **Tannenbaum and Schmidt leadership continuum**, a manager may engage in a more participative leadership style when subordinates:

- Seek independence and freedom of action
- Understand and are committed to the goals of the organization
- Are well educated and experienced in performing the jobs
- Seek responsibility for decision making
- Expect a participative style of leadership.

If the above conditions do not exist, managers may need to adopt a more autocratic or "boss-centered" leadership style. In essence, managers must be able to diagnose the situations confronting them and then choose a leadership style that will improve their chances for effectiveness. The most effective leaders are neither "task centered" nor "people centered" but, rather, are flexible enough to select a leadership style that fits their needs as well as the needs of their subordinates and the situation.

Fiedler's Contingency Leadership Model

The contingency theory developed by Fred E. Fiedler has received considerable recognition as a situational approach to leadership.[7] **Fiedler's contingency leadership model** suggests that there are a number of leadership styles that may be appropriate, depending on the situation. His model's framework is made up of 8 significantly different situations and 2 basic types of leadership orientations. Three major elements determine whether a given situation is favorable to a leader:

- **Leader-member relations:** the degree to which the leader feels accepted by subordinates. The culture may be friendly or unfriendly, relaxed or tense, and threatening or supportive.
- **Task structure:** the extent to which goals are clearly defined and solutions to problems are known.
- **Position power of the leader:** the degree of influence over rewards and punishments, as well as official authority possessed by the leader.

The concept of leader-member relations is similar to the consideration or relationship behavior concepts, while task structure and position power are closely related to initiating structure or task behavior

Framework of Fiedler's Contingency Leadership Model

Situation	Degree of Favorableness of Situation to Leader	Leader-Member Relations	Task Structure	Position Power of Leader
1	Favorable	Good	Structured	High
2	Favorable	Good	Structured	Low
3	Favorable	Good	Unstructured	High
4	Moderately Favorable	Good	Unstructured	Low
5	Moderately Favorable	Poor	Structured	High
6	Moderately Favorable	Poor	Structured	Low
7	Moderately Favorable	Poor	Unstructured	High
8	Unfavorable	Poor	Unstructured	Low

SOURCE Edwin B. Flippo and Gary M. Munsinger, *Management*, 4th ed. (Boston: Allyn and Bacon, 1978): 381. Reprinted by permission.

as discussed previously. By mixing these 3 elements, the 8 situations can be identified. (See the table.)

These 8 situations show varying degrees of favorableness of a situation to a leader — the leader's influence and control over the group. A leader has maximum influence in situation 1 and very little in situation 8. Research evidence indicates that a task-oriented, controlling leader will be most effective when the situations are either very favorable (1, 2, and 3) or very unfavorable (8). The more permissive, considerate leader performs more effectively in the intermediate situations, which are moderately favorable to the leader (4, 5, 6, and 7). Another way to illustrate Fiedler's framework is seen in Exhibit 11-7. The task-oriented style of leader is more effective in situations 1, 2, 3, and 8 while the relationship-oriented style is more effective in situations 4, 5, 6, and 7. As demonstrated by Fiedler's theory, the most effective leadership style is contingent on several situational factors.

Hersey and Blanchard's Situational Leadership Theory

Paul Hersey and Kenneth Blanchard have developed a situational leadership theory that has attracted considerable attention on the part of managers.[8] **Hersey and Blanchard's situational leadership theory** is based on the notion that the most effective leadership style varies according to the level of maturity of the followers and demands of the situation. Their model uses 2 dimensions of leadership behavior — task and relationship. These are similar to the classifications used in the Ohio

State leadership model and Blake and Mouton's managerial grid. Hersey and Blanchard argue that an effective leader is one who can diagnose the demands of the situation and the level of maturity of the followers and use an appropriate leadership style. Their theory is based on a relationship among these factors:

- The amount of **task behavior** the leader exhibits — providing direction and emphasis on getting the job done
- The amount of **relationship behavior** the leader provides — consideration of people, level of emotional support for people
- The level of **task-relevant maturity** followers exhibit toward the specific goal, task or function that the leader wants accomplished.

The key concept of their leadership theory is the level of task-relevant maturity of the followers. Maturity is not defined as age or psychological stability. The maturity level of the followers is defined as:

- A desire for achievement — level of achievement motivation based on the need to set high but attainable goals
- The willingness and ability to accept responsibility
- Education and/or experience and skills relevant to the particular task.

A leader should consider the level of maturity of his or her followers only in relation to the work or job to be performed. Certainly employees are mature on some tasks when they have the experience and skills as well as the desire to achieve and are capable of assuming responsibility. For example, an accountant may be very mature when preparing quarterly tax reports for Revenue Canada, but may not exhibit the same level of maturity when preparing written audits of the company's operations. The accountant does not need much direction (task-related behavior) from the manager when preparing tax reports, but may require considerably more supervision and direction when preparing and writing audits. The accountant may not have the skills and/or motivation to prepare audits but, with proper training, direction, and encouragement, can assume greater responsibility in this area.

As illustrated in Exhibit 11-8 the appropriate leadership style used by a manager varies according to the maturity level (represented by M1 through M4) of the followers. There are 4 distinct leadership styles that are appropriate given different levels of subordinate maturity. As the task-relevant maturity level of followers increases, the manager should reduce task behavior and increase relationship behavior. These are illustrated by the classifications of the styles as:

S1 — Telling	High task
	Low relationship
S2 — Selling	High task
	High relationship
S3 — Participating	High relationship
	Low task
S4 — Delegating	Low relationship
	Low task

**EXHIBIT 11-7
Appropriateness of
leadership styles
to situation**

SOURCE Adapted from
Edwin B. Flippo and Gary
M. Munsinger,
Management, 4th ed.
(Boston, Allyn and Bacon,
1978): 381. Reprinted by
permission.

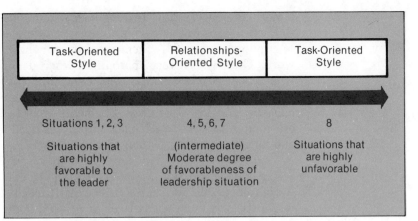

**EXHIBIT 11-8
Situational
leadership**

SOURCE Paul Hersey and
Kenneth Blanchard,
Center for Leadership
Studies, California
American University,
1977. Reprinted by
permission.

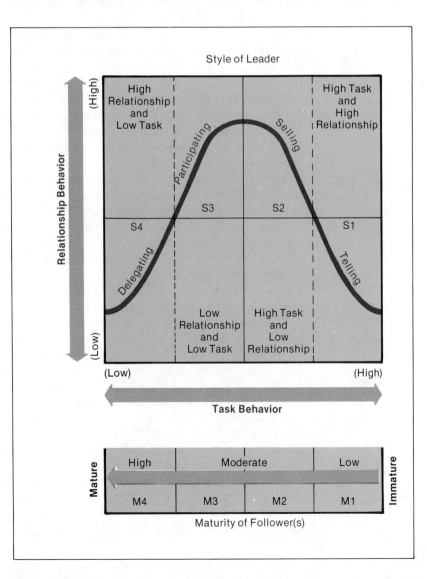

With the S1 (Telling) high-task, low-relationship leadership style, the leader uses one-way communication, defines the goals and roles of employees, and tells them what, how, when, and where to do the work. This style is very appropriate when dealing with subordinates who lack task-relevant maturity. For example, in supervising a group of relatively new, inexperienced employees, a high level of task-directed behavior and low-relationship behavior may be an appropriate leadership approach. Inexperienced employees need to be told what to do and how to accomplish their jobs.

As employees learn their jobs, the manager begins to use an S2 leadership style. There is still a need for a high level of task behavior, since the employees do not yet have the experience or skills to assume more responsibility, but the manager provides a higher level of emotional support — high-relationship behavior. The manager encourages the employees and demonstrates greater trust and confidence in them.

The S3 leadership style is suitable when employees possess considerable task-relevant maturity. As employees become more experienced and skilled, as well as more achievement motivated and more willing to assume responsibility, the leader should reduce the amount of task behavior but continue the high level of emotional support and consideration. A continuation of a high level of relationship behavior is the manager's way of reinforcing the employees' responsible performance. Thus, S3 — high-relationship and low-task behavior — becomes the appropriate leadership style.

The S4 leadership style is for followers with the highest level of task maturity. At this stage, the employees are very skilled and experienced, possess high achievement motivation, and are capable of exercising self-control. The leadership style that is most appropriate for this situation is S4 — low relationship and low task. At this point the employees no longer need or expect a high level of supportive or task behavior from their leader.

Hersey and Blanchard argue that leadership style and effectiveness can be measured, and they have designed an instrument for this purpose — the Leader Effectiveness & Adaptability Description (LEAD). The LEAD provides feedback on leadership style and the effectiveness of the individual completing the instrument.[9]

You should not conclude from this discussion that it is easy to determine the appropriate leadership style. It can be difficult to diagnose the maturity level of followers, as well as the specific needs of a situation. A leader must have insight into the abilities, needs, demands, and expectations of the followers and be aware that these can and do change over time. Also, managers must recognize that they must adapt or change their style of leadership whenever the level of maturity of followers changes. Maturity levels can change for many reasons — for instance, change in jobs, personal or family problems, or switch in the present job to new technology. For example, a sales manager has been using an S4 leadership style in supervising John, who is normally a highly productive sales representative. But suppose that John's pending divorce has recently been adversely affecting his performance. In this situation, the sales manager might increase both the level of task and relationship behavior in order to provide John with the direction, support, and confidence he may need to cope with his personal problems and improve his sales performance.

In a recent review of contingency leadership theories, Graeff found that, for situational leadership to be effective, the leader must come to two conclusions: (1) the leader must be flexible in behavior; patterns of habit must be broken, and (2) the subordinate must be recognized as a major situational determinant. Drawing these conclusions involves not only careful observation of behavior, but the ability to interpret that behavior in a meaningful way.[10]

In summary, Hersey and Blanchard's theory provides a useful and understandable framework for situational leadership. In essence, their model suggests that there is no one best leadership style that meets the needs of all situations. Rather, a manager's leadership style must be adaptable and flexible enough to meet the changing needs of employees and situations. The effective manager is one who can change styles as employees develop and change or as required by the situation.

Vroom and Yetton's Leadership Decision-Making Model

Vroom and Yetton's **leadership decision-making model** is based on the idea that a leader must decide how much participation subordinates should be allowed when making decisions.[11] Such participation can

---

MANAGEMENT IN PRACTICE

Employee Maturity

Andrew Grove is president of Intel Corporation, one of North America's premier high-technology companies. He notes that there is no single style of leadership which works best in all situations. Rather, a subordinate's task-relevant maturity (TRM) determines the style a leader should adopt in order to be effective. Task-relevant maturity is a combination of a person's achievement orientation and readiness to take responsibility, as well as his or her education, training, and experience. A person could have high maturity in one task and low maturity in another.

Grove says that managers should strive to increase the TRM of their subordinates because they need to spend less time with a high TRM subordinate. As well, high TRM subordinates are internally motivated and work more effectively for the company.

SOURCE Andrew S. Grove, "What Kind of Boss Works Best?" *Canadian Business* (March 1984): 82–86.

range widely. At one extreme, the manager might allow no participation and simply make the decision: an autocratic style. At the other extreme, the manager might stress group problem solving and allow subordinates total freedom to make the decision: a participative style.

Vroom and Yetton suggested that each of these leadership styles can be effective, depending on the answers to 5 work-related questions that the leader answers:

1. Do I [the leader] have sufficient information to make a good decision?
2. Is there a quality requirement in the decision?
3. Is the decision problem structured?
4. Is subordinate acceptance of the decision important?
5. Do subordinates share the organization's goals?

Vroom and Yetton have developed a detailed model to guide managers through this process. To give you a general idea of how their model works, consider this case. A leader of a group of clerks in an insurance company is dissatisfied with the present filing system and wants to introduce a new one.The leader doesn't really know much about alternative filing systems, but she does know that the clerks must be comfortable with any new system or their productivity will decline. Her relations with the clerks are good and the clerks identify with the company, but they are consistently quite vocal about the routine procedures in their department.

What style of leadership should be used in this situation? Before the leader decides, she must ask herself the questions Vroom and Yetton posed. In this case, the answers would probably be:

MANAGEMENT IN PRACTICE

Participative Management at Algoma Steel

Since the mid-1970s, Algoma Steel has increasingly used participative management to make decisions in several important areas of the company's operations. For example, the company was dissatisfied with its safety record, so it instituted joint safety committees. Both union and management people sit on these committees, whose primary goal is to make the work place healthier and safer to work in.

Another area of participation concerns compensation plans. The company formerly had many different plans; this meant that workers in one department might earn a higher bonus than workers in another department. These inequities across departments made workers unhappy. Now, one incentive plan has been cooperatively developed for the entire plant, and all workers in the plant are paid a bonus based on the tonnage shipped from the plant.

Attitude surveys taken by the company suggest that there is a definite improvement in the workers' perceptions of the company, and a better cooperative spirit between workers and management.

SOURCE Dean Walker, "Flexibility Means Profitability," Executive (February 1982): 61–62.

1. No, she does not have sufficient information to make the decision alone.
2. Yes, there is a quality requirement because the leader wants to have a good system.
3. No; the decision is not problem structured — how to go about introducing a new filing system is not obvious.
4. Yes, because subordinates want a say in how the department operates.
5. Yes; subordinates identify readily with the goals of the organization.

Based on this series of answers, Vroom and Yetton would say that the leader should exhibit a highly participative style of leadership and should let subordinates actually make the decision. In the context of this situation, their suggestion seems to make good practical sense.

What happens if one of the situational features changes? Suppose subordinates did not identify with the goals of the organization. The best leadership style then would still be a participative style, but the leader must make the final decision based on the organization's goals. Allowing the subordinates to make the decision would be unreasonable.

Vroom and Yetton's theory is that several leadership styles may be effective or feasible for certain problems, but for other problems only one style will work. Their theory is clearly situational because the leader cannot decide on the appropriate leadership style until the specific situation has been analyzed through the answers to Vroom and Yetton's leadership questions.

AN INTEGRATED APPROACH TO LEADERSHIP

The notion that there is one best leadership style has been criticized as being unrealistic and simplistic. It is illogical to assume that the same leadership style would be equally effective in managing such diverse groups as auto assemblers, research scientists, clerk-typists, college professors, lawyers, or construction workers. The most effective leadership style is one that meets the needs of each particular situation. This requires a careful consideration of characteristics of the leader, the followers, and the specific situation.

The development of an integrated approach to effective leadership requires consideration of several important situational factors. As shown in Exhibit 11-9, characteristics of the leader, the followers, and the situation all interrelate to determine the most effective leadership style. Although the situational factors are presented in a different format, the importance of giving careful consideration to these factors remains. The management approach is associated with the leader. The followers represent the personnel. The situation includes the structure, the technology, objectives, and the external environment. Each of these elements is discussed in its context as a determinant of an effective leadership style.

Leader

Everyone has a different combination of abilities, personalities, experiences, and expectations. Because of these factors each person develops different patterns of doing work. If you discover that a certain behavioral pattern has worked successfully in the past, you will likely continue that pattern in the future. A person who has found that being an autocratic manager will get the job done will likely continue this pattern unless something happens to show that this style is no longer appropriate. A participative style may also continue to be used until it is no longer effective.

With the integrated approach to leadership, managers must be aware of the leadership style they are currently using. Then they must evaluate what managerial approach will be most effective based on a careful consideration of the nature of the followers and each situation. The leader adapts his or her style to meet the needs of the followers and the situation. This flexibility does not mean that the manager's basic beliefs must change. However, it does mean that for the time a manager is in a particular leadership role, his or her leadership style must be adapted to the followers and each situation.

Followers

Like the leader, followers have varying abilities, personalities, experiences, and expectations. With the integrated approach to leadership, managers must recognize that followers may not necessarily obey a leader's order. If the followers consider that it is in their best interest to abide by the wishes of the leader, they will accomplish the task.

Thus, followers are a major factor for consideration in the integrated approach to leadership. If the followers are inexperienced, lack the necessary education or skills, and do not seek more individual responsibility for their job, the most effective leadership style will likely be more directive or autocratic. If personnel are highly educated, experienced, and seek responsibility for decision making, a more participative style of leadership may be more appropriate. At times, any manager may need to emphasize task accomplishment strongly, and a statement like "Let's get the job done" may be necessary to accomplish the work. At other times a much more participative style suggested by a comment such as "I need your help and advice if this job is going to be done" will provide the most effective leadership. Managers must take into consideration the needs, goals, capabilities, and experiences of the followers if they are to be effective.

**EXHIBIT 11-9
An integrated
approach to
leadership**

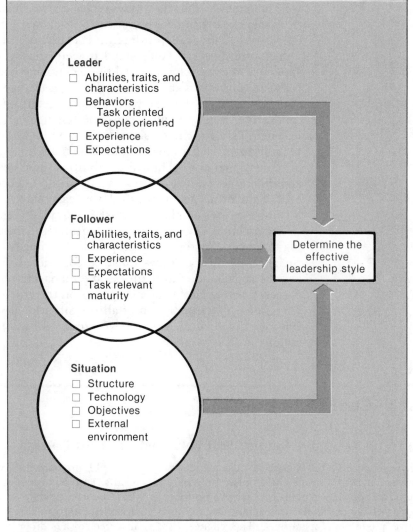

Situation

The four factors of structure, technology, objectives, and the external environment comprise the situation. (Refer to Exhibit 11-9.) Each must be considered if leaders are to determine their most effective style.

The organizational structure and the environment in which the manager operates affect the leadership style. In a highly structured environment, like a mass production factory, a more autocratic style may be more appropriate, whereas in a loosely structured environment, like a research lab, a more participative style may be more appropriate.

Technology is another major factor that affects the selection of the most appropriate leadership style. Technology has an impact on the design of work, which may in turn determine the most appropriate leadership style. For example, if the technology the firm is using is well understood and the workers have a great deal of experience with it, managers will probably not have to exercise close supervision of employees. Conversely, if the firm is experimenting with a new technology and does not understand it well, management may have to supervise workers closely until the technology becomes familiar.

As the objectives of the firm change, a change in leadership style may be necessary. For example, if a firm determines that it should be innovative, it may require personnel changes and a modification of leadership styles. The personnel who are hired to make the transition to an innovative firm may not accept an autocratic style. As the level of professional and technical capabilities increases, the style of leadership may lean toward a more relationship-oriented leadership style. Still, if the firm's goal is survival, the leadership style may again move toward a greater emphasis on task accomplishment.

The external environment has considerable influence on determining the most effective leadership style. Obviously economic, political, social, and cultural forces must be considered. For example, during periods of economic difficulty, some managers tend to become more autocratic and place greater emphasis on the efficiency of task accomplishment. The interaction of all the situational variables must be a consideration by managers who wish to use the most effective leadership style.

MANAGEMENT IN PRACTICE

Employee Involvement at Ford Canada

There has been a big change in management's attitude at Ford Motor's engine plant at Windsor, Ontario. Management has discovered that workers have excellent ideas about how to improve production operations. The change in thinking is called Employee Involvement (EI), and means that supervisors and employees work as a team to come up with better ways to make automobile engines.

Employee involvement is a change from the adversarial system (labor vs management) that existed at Ford for so many years. Changing to the EI system has involved training people to change their old views of the company. So far, Ford has spent more than $1 million on training. For example, hourly workers get 20 hours of training in problem solving and 20 hours of statistical process control. Managers are also being trained to deal with the newly involved employees.

The EI program has yielded very positive results. Ford has experienced a 59 percent improvement in quality (as measured by a reduction in customer warranty claims), and absenteeism has dropped sharply at the plants that use EI. For example, in November 1982 (before the EI program was introduced), 400 workers were absent from work at the Windsor plant; by November 1983, only 144 workers were absent during the month. The program has also had an impact on workers' compensation claims. During November 1983, Windsor's 5 plants had only 37 people on workers' compensation, while the Oakville plant (which has far fewer workers) had 125.

SOURCE Daniel Stoffman, "Blue-Collar Turnaround Artists," *Canadian Business* (February 1984): 38.

During the past three decades, there has been a significant increase in the educational level of the people entering the work force. There have also been changes in social and cultural values, which require that leaders adapt to this situation. These trends support the conclusion that there is no one best style of leadership that will meet the needs of all followers or the demands of every situation.

One final aspect of the situation that may have an impact on leadership is the possibility that there are "substitutes for leadership." Leadership may not be crucial if certain other characteristics of the work place help employees get their work done properly even without much guidance. Clearly defined jobs, a strong informal organization, and a professional orientation on the part of employees are examples of substitutes for leadership. They can help employees to know what to do even though the leader may not give them much guidance. These substitutes for leadership may be very important in some situations or unimportant in others. For example, in mass-production, jobs on the production line may be rigidly defined and leadership may not have a dramatic impact on employees. In an unstructured work atmosphere, however, the leader should have a major impact on employee job satisfaction and output.

OPENING INCIDENT REVISITED

Mission Chapel

At the Mission Chapel, Carolyn Barnes was concerned about whether her leadership style was appropriate for the chapel choir. What do the leadership theories discussed in this chapter suggest?

The situational leadership theory says that subordinate maturity levels are the key to determining effective leader behavior. Ten members of the choir are mature (they know what to do technically) while 35 are in various stages of immaturity. The theory suggests that different styles are appropriate for these two groups. Unfortunately, it is not feasible for Barnes to treat the high and low maturity people differently because the choir must perform as a group. Perhaps the maturity level of the inexperienced members will improve as time passes and they become technically more capable. Barnes can then use a more participative style. For the moment, however, the theory suggests that an autocratic style is most appropriate.

Using Fiedler's contingency model to analyze Barnes's situation, the following criteria can be established. Leader-member relations are good,

task structure is high (music is very structured), and leader position power is low (the choir members are volunteers). Given this combination, an autocratic style is most appropriate.

The path-goal model says that the leader should help subordinates get to their goals. The choir members have good performance as one of their goals; the nonprofessional singers would probably welcome guidance from a professional. As their leader, Barnes should probably adopt an autocratic style. Presumably, the professional members of the choir will be less satisfied with this style as they know what to do, but, as noted above, the trained and untrained members cannot be treated differently because of the nature of the task.

On balance, the analysis of the situation using these contingency leadership theories suggests that Barnes continue with her present directive style. The absenteeism may simply be an effect of the volunteer nature of the choir, while the talking and joking may indicate the interest and enthusiasm of the members. In neither case is Barnes's leadership style causing problems.

TALKING TO MANAGERS

Edwin Mirvish

Edwin ("Honest Ed") Mirvish may be the last of an unusual brand of entrepreneurs. He owns and runs an apparently eclectic clutch of Toronto retail and real estate operations, restaurants, and theatres which employs 1000. Yet, at age 69, as always, he's directly and personally involved in almost everything. It's management by personality. Mirvish himself is the glue which binds together the businesses. As a manager, Mirvish has a thing or two to teach the whiz kids from our business schools. He has no secretary. He doesn't need one to devise his systems for him. He's figured out his own and they work: keep in touch by talking to the right people and reading the right reports; make decisions today; trust the people you hire and encourage them to carry out their ideas (he once told an employee that it was all right to make mistakes — at least they told him she was working); gamble only when you can afford to lose.

As an entrepreneur, though, Mirvish is a classic. He started with nothing but a formula for retailing that worked (sell for cash, buy for credit) that led him to create what's said to be North America's first discount store in 1948. He knows his customers — whether they're the patrons of his classy theatre, the Royal Alexander Theatre, or customers in Honest Ed's, which does about $50 million in sales a year. Devotees of Honest Ed's can pick up such bargains as toothpaste for $0.99 or a set of glass utility tables for $4.99. Decisions are made by "feel." There are no long-term plans, no decision trees. Perhaps there will be a meeting or two among the small group which helps Mirvish run the empire, where ideas will be shouted across the table. Definitely, no management consultants. Mirvish has no partners — that would mean explaining his decisions. It would also mean sharing financial details — something Mirvish, like many, is loath to discuss.

Q: Honest Ed's sales volume is about $50 million a year. How does that compare with conventional department stores?

Mirvish: I'm not sure how it compares now; but for many years we were doing more dollars per square metre than most retail businesses. One reason is we've never branched out; we have just one location. And we do not have stock problems. Stock comes in every day and is held beneath or above the counter. We don't have stockrooms because I've always had the fear we'll forget what's sitting out there.

Each of our 14 buyers manages his own department. So it's all very tight and our gross per square metre and our turnover are both very high. The whole store turns over 24 times a year. That may not be unusual in drugs or groceries but, in our case, it also includes shoes and clothing and furniture.

Q: There have been a lot of changes in the world in the 35 years Honest Ed's been in business. How has your approach changed to keep abreast?

Mirvish: I try to keep in touch with what's happening. I'm at the store every day from eight until noon. And those 14 buyers must keep in touch too. I don't like them sitting in their offices too much. I want my buyers out on the floor so that, when we have a hundred-degree day, they will send the truck down and pick up a few hundred electric fans and sell them that day. We were the last to go into computer cash registers because, by the time a computer tape is fed into an office and the office digests it, it may be snowing outside. Our whole business is based on simplicity. Perhaps that's because I had little formal education.

Q: How do you stay in touch with the tastes and needs of your customers out there?
Mirvish: Every Tuesday and Friday we have a meeting with the 14 buyers. We go over everything, thrash it out, and resolve what's to be done. I don't feel that much out of touch. I feel the same as I ever did because I still walk in that door, I see and talk to the customers. It's up to my buyers to be up to the minute. They have to know this changing world's markets. They have a lot of freedom and unlimited money, but once every 4 weeks they have to answer for their turnover.

Q: Retailers tend to have high staff turnovers, yet you keep your people for years. Do you pay better than most stores?
Mirvish: Keeping help has to do with more things than pay. Because we have only one location, and I am involved, I get to know our people. We try to be interested in them as people. That has a lot to do with it. We used to have a retirement plan so that people would retire at 65. When I got to be 64, I changed the plan because I didn't want to be out of work. So now we have people here who are 75 and they still do a good day's work. The main thing is to find the time to be involved. There are people here who started when I only had 3 or 4 employees. Now the store must have nearly 400. Many of them grew and developed with me. Because we didn't go according to the book but by trial and error, they understand my way of thinking and I understand them.

Q: What do you look for when you hire?
Mirvish: We never hire at the top. Anyone who works for us starts as a young person. We look for stability. If someone has been out of school 3 years and has had 10 jobs, we don't take another look at that application.

Q: Have you a long-term plan?
Mirvish: No. Everything I've done has really been a development, an evolvement. The important thing always is to fulfill the needs that are there today. It's too hard to know what they'll be 5, 10 years down the road.

Q: Although you've had no long-term plans, there are things that you deliberately did not do. You could have taken Honest Ed's national, for example.
Mirvish: I never did that because I'd find it boring. It's not something I want to be involved in. Once you are making a living, you're making a living. I don't want to sit and look at a bunch of charts. I want to be out where the action is. If your goal is just to make money, you're going in a different direction. My goal is for the work I'm doing to be enjoyable and rewarding.

Q: How do you keep all these things going and continue to put your personal stamp on everything?
Mirvish: I've never had a secretary. I'm in the store every morning from eight to noon. I get a report on the day-before's business. It tells how many customers went through the store, how much each department did. If there's a trend, I can catch it. I'm in direct touch with each of the 14 department buyers. At noon I'm at the restaurant. From two-thirty to six, I'm at the theatre. Then I go home. I don't work evenings.

I have good managers. My people look after the housekeeping. One of the most important things in any business is the housekeeping. You won't have good turnover if your housekeeping isn't good. There are people responsible for the housekeeping at Honest Ed's, and the housekeeping in Mirvish Village, in the theatre and the restaurants.

If they change a menu they discuss it with me; but our menus are not big, they're simple. We take counts of everything. If something's not popular, it's out. It is not really that complicated. We have a thousand employees in Toronto but, over the years, I've surrounded myself with people who feel comfortable with me and I feel comfortable with them.

SOURCE Excerpted from Dean Walker, "From Discounts to Show Biz, Ed Mirvish Does It His Way", *Executive* (November 1983): 34–38. Reprinted by permission.

SUMMARY

Effective leadership is essential to the survival and growth of every organization. Leadership guides the process of motivating and directing others toward the accomplishment of goals. The requirements for being an effective manager and the definition of the most effective leadership style have been of concern to managers for generations and have been the subject of thousands of research studies. However, no simple list of traits or behaviors has been identified that is consistently related to effective leadership. In fact, the basic conclusion of these studies is that there is no one most effective leadership style.

The early studies of leadership attempted to identify universal traits and characteristics of effective leaders. Traits relating to physical characteristics, personality, or intelligence were studied to determine if they were related to effective leadership. For the most part, research has not shown that traits alone can distinguish effective from ineffective leaders. Despite these findings, the trait approach to the study of leadership has continued. Ghiselli has identified traits/characteristics that his extensive research indicates are related to effective leadership. These include supervisory ability, need for occupational achievement, intelligence, decisiveness, self-assurance, and initiative.

Dissatisfaction with the trait approach to the study of leadership caused the research emphasis to concentrate on the behavior and actions of leaders. The behavioral theories identified 2 basic dimensions of leadership behavior. Although these behaviors have been referred to by several different names, they are the leader's behavior and concern for (1) the accomplishment of tasks (task behavior) and (2) the relationship with people (relationship behavior). One of the most widely known leadership theories is Blake and Mouton's managerial grid. The 2 dimensions of leadership behavior identified in the 9×9 managerial grid are "concern for people" and "concern for production." Five basic styles of leadership on the grid were: do nothing (1,1), task centered (9,1), country club (1,9), organization man (5,5) and team builder (9,9). Blake and Mouton suggest that the 9,9 style of leadership is the most effective and achieves the best results in performance.

In recent years, considerable attention has been given to the situational approach to the study of leadership. The basic conclusion of this approach is that the most effective leaders are neither task centered nor people centered. Rather, effective leaders must be flexible enough to adopt a leadership style that fits their needs as well as the needs of their subordinates and the situation.

The theories of Fiedler, Hersey and Blanchard, House, and Vroom and Yetton suggest there is no one most effective style of leadership that is appropriate to every situation. In Fiedler's theory, the degree of favorableness or unfavorableness of the situation determine the style of leadership that is most effective. Hersey and Blanchard's theory is based on the notion that the most effective leadership style varies according to the level of maturity of the followers and the demands of the situation. Their theory offers 4 basic styles or combinations of task and relationship behavior of the leader. For instance, if the leader is dealing with "highly mature followers" the appropriate leadership style might be low emphasis on both relationships and task behavior. House's path-goal theory says that the role of the leader is to clarify the subordinates' performance goals and how these goals can be achieved. Vroom and Yetton's decision-making model requires managers to answer several work-related questions before they decide which leadership style to use.

Perhaps the most realistic approach to leadership is an integrated one that carefully considers the forces in the leader, the followers, and the situation. To be truly effective in achieving goals, the leader must recognize that no one approach will be equally effective for all circumstances.

REVIEW QUESTIONS

1. What is meant by the term *leadership*? Why is it important to management?
2. What is the distinction between management and leadership? How is it possible to be a good leader but an ineffective manager?
3. In the chapter, how did leadership cause the bankruptcy of the mobile home company?
4. Briefly describe and contrast the types of power a leader may possess to influence the behavior of others.
5. What is the trait approach to the study of leadership? To what extent are universal traits related to effective leadership?
6. List several significant traits identified by the research of Edwin Ghiselli as important for effective leadership.
7. What are the 4 basic styles or systems of management identified by Rensis Likert? Explain each.
8. Describe the 5 leadership styles presented in the managerial grid. Which style is recommended as most effective by Blake and Mouton?
9. What were the Ohio State leadership studies? What basic dimensions of leadership behavior were identified? What were some of the factors that determined the most effective style of leadership?
10. What basic conclusion can be derived from the Tannenbaum and Schmidt leadership continuum? What factors should be considered before choosing a given style of leadership?
11. What is the basic contention of Fiedler's theory of leadership? In what situations are task-centered leaders most effective? people-centered leaders?
12. Briefly explain Hersey and Blanchard's situational leadership theory. What is the key concept of their theory?
13. Briefly explain Vroom and Yetton's leadership decision making idea. How does their approach contrast and compare with Hersey and Blanchard's theory?
14. Describe what is meant by an integrated approach to leadership.

EXERCISES

1. Assume you have just been promoted to the position of office manager in charge of 12 clerical personnel — 8 typists and 4 general clerks. The previous manager was removed from the position because the office staff members were not able to complete their work on schedule. In addition, the office experienced excessive turnover of employees, and several of the employees had expressed concern about poor quality of work and attitudes of the clerical staff. Under the previous manager, the employees showed little interest in their jobs and generally viewed the office manager as a "soft touch."
   a. What style of leadership would you utilize as you assume the position of office manager?
   b. Explain, in terms of situational leadership theory presented in this chapter, how your leadership style might change, should output improve and employee turnover decrease.
2. Go to the library and make a copy of the article "So You Want To Know Your Leadership Style?" by Paul Hersey and Kenneth Blanchard, *Training and Development Journal* (February 1974): 22–32. Complete the Leader Adaptability and Style Inventory (LASI) instrument contained in the article. Then read the article. What is your leadership style as per the LASI? Discuss in class.

CASE STUDY

Choosing an Appropriate Leadership Style

Russell Allen was chosen 6 months ago to be manager of the research and development department for Western Engineering, after the existing manager left the firm. The senior vice-president who hired Allen reasoned that the R & D department could use a person who had experience in production problems. Allen had been a line foreman and had an excellent reputation for getting the job done. He was well organized and was credited with being able to solve problems prior to their reaching top management. The primary emphasis of Western's R & D department was to conduct practical research for the purpose of developing marketable products. Thus, top management believed Allen would do well in this assignment because of his knowledge of production operations.

When Allen arrived at his new job he could not believe how disorganized the researchers were. They might come to work at 10:00 and leave at 15:00. (Allen was not told that many of them worked late at night.) The employees were all dedicated researchers and considered themselves professionals. They did not feel that a task had to be lined out in detail for the job to be done. Allen believed that these conditions were not conducive to maximum productivity. He had been taught on the production line that efficiency is a direct result of the organization and structure of tasks. If it worked in one situation, it should work in another.

The first decision that Allen made was to install a time clock. He reasoned that, if the department members were to be productive, they must be at the plant during certain hours of the day. The researchers in Allen's department expressed disbelief of this decision. Before Allen became supervisor, most of the researchers were working an average of 12 hours a day. Although they might not be at the plant during normal hours, they were recognized as very productive. Many of the researchers actually liked to work Saturday morning because the activity level of the plant was lower and they could concentrate better. Without realizing it, Allen was actually telling the department members to reduce their work time by one-third.

When Allen arrived at work at 08:00 on Monday, he was pleased to see that all of the researchers clocked in at the proper time. They remained at the plant the entire day and left promptly at 17:00. He assumed that the employees had accepted him as their superior. This euphoria, however, did not last long. People throughout the plant began calling him to ask why their particular project was not finished. When he checked with the researchers responsible for each project, he found that each had been working on the project but had not had time to complete it. In virtually every instance this was the case.

Allen came to the conclusion that the researchers were goofing off, and he issued numerous memos of reprimand. Soon afterward,

several key researchers resigned to take other positions. The situation continued to deteriorate until virtually no useful work was conducted in the department. When the vice-president finally asked Allen what was causing this inefficiency, he responded: "They're a bunch of super-egos, but I can get them in shape." The vice-president is not so sure that this is the problem and asks for your advice.

QUESTIONS

1. What assumptions did management make with regard to making Russell Allen the research and development department manager?
2. How would you describe the leadership style of Allen? How appropriate was this style to the management of the R & D department?
3. What style of leadership would likely be most effective in managing this group of researchers?
4. Assume that you are the vice-president of Western (Allen's boss). What action would you take to improve the situation?

CASE STUDY

The Unhappy Salesman

Art Cranston was a regional sales manager for a major computer manufacturer. In this position he supervised 22 industrial salespeople who sold computers, word processors, and other office equipment to business and educational organizations. Supervising the sales force involved setting sales quotas and targets after discussion with the salespeople, checking on performance levels, developing and monitoring compensation programs, allocating salespeople to different territories, as well as the usual duties performed by sales managers. Salespeople were paid on a salary-plus-commission basis, with the salary portion being small enough that it did not provide an adequate standard of living. Cranston assumed that the commission component would motivate the salespeople to sell more aggressively.

On balance, the performance of the sales force was quite good, although 2 problems surfaced. One of these was turnover, which was averaging

23 percent per year. Cranston was concerned about this, but he also knew that high turnover was a common problem in selling occupations where incentive compensation schemes were used. His major concern about turnover was the time and money he had to spend looking for new salespeople and then training them to do the job the right way.

The other problem concerned 2 salespeople who chronically failed to reach their objectives. In an attempt to overcome this problem, Cranston had instituted a Management by Objectives system. He felt that, if goals were mutually decided on by the salesperson and the boss, the salesperson would be more committed to the goals and would work harder to achieve them. This system improved the performance of salespeople who were already satisfactory, but it had no effect on the 2 low performers. Over a period of several years Cranston had developed a detailed system that all salespeople used when they called on prospects. The feedback he received from salespeople was that the system was helpful in improving their sales. Cranston also heard comments such as: "Art, you're very task-oriented, but we're happy because what you're doing puts more money in our pockets." These views were widely held by the sales staff but not by the 2 problem employees.

At a sales convention in Banff during October, Cranston happened to overhear Jim Brewer (a top salesman) arguing loudly with Mike O'Donnell (one of the poor performers) about the nature of incentive schemes:

Brewer: I think our compensation scheme is really good. It forces a guy to keep moving. If he does that, he makes a lot of money and the company also benefits.

O'Donnell: That's easy for you to say! What about me? I can't make big money with the compensation scheme we're using.

Brewer: That's because you're not working hard enough.

O'Donnell: What do you know about how hard I work? We hardly ever see each other except at these conventions!

Brewer: You must not be working hard enough if you aren't making much money.

O'Donnell: I'm working very hard! The problem is that Cranston doesn't have any feeling for people. All he thinks about is sales volume. This incentive scheme just won't work for everyone, because each person is unique.

Brewer: Are you saying Cranston should develop a unique incentive scheme for each salesperson?

O'Donnell: Yes.

Brewer: That's ridiculous. Then everyone would be running around worrying about whether their deal was better or worse than someone else's. Besides, the paperwork would be outrageous.

O'Donnell: Well, the present system isn't working!

Brewer: That's not what most of the people here would say. You're out in left field on this one!

After hearing this conversation, Cranston was both pleased and disturbed. He felt that most of the salespeople would agree with Brewer, but he also knew that O'Donnell firmly believed what he was saying. He wondered what all this meant for his leadership of the salesforce.

QUESTIONS

1. Should Cranston try to use different leadership styles with different salespeople? Is this feasible?
2. Will O'Donnell's idea of a unique incentive scheme for each salesperson work? What are the benefits? What are the drawbacks?
3. What can Cranston do to improve the performance of O'Donnell and other low performers?
4. Use the leadership theories in this chapter to draw some conclusions about the most appropriate style of leadership for Cranston. What are the shortcomings of these schemes?

NOTES

[1] Edwin Ghiselli, *Explorations in Managerial Talent* (Pacific Palisades, Cal., Goodyear, 1971).

[2] Rensis Likert, *The Human Organization* (New York: McGraw-Hill, 1967).

[3] Used with permission of Robert R. Blake and Jane S. Mouton, *The New Managerial Grid* (Houston: Gulf Publishing, 1978): 11.

[4] Blake and Mouton.

[5] Robert House, "A Path-Goal Theory of Leadership Effectiveness," *Administrative Science Quarterly* 16 (September 1971): 321–338.

[6] Alan C. Filley, Robert House, and Steven Kerr, *Managerial Process and Organizational Behavior* (Glenview, Ill.: Scott, Foresman, 1976): 256–260.

[7] Fred E. Fiedler, *A Theory of Leadership Effectiveness* (New York: McGraw-Hill, 1967).

[8] Paul Hersey and Kenneth Blanchard, *Management of Organizational Behavior: Utilizing Human Resources*, 3d ed. (Englewood Cliffs, N.J.: Prentice-Hall, 1977): 94–95.

[9] See Paul Hersey and Kenneth Blanchard, "So You Want to Know Your Leadership Style?" *Training and Development Journal* (February 1974): 22–32. This article contains the Leader Adaptability and Style Inventory (LASI), an instrument that can be used to examine your leadership behavior, style adaptability, and effectiveness. Since this article, the LASI has become the Leader Effectiveness and Adaptability Description (LEAD). Information, LEAD inventories and training materials may be obtained from the Center for Leadership Studies, 17253 Caminito Canasto, Rancho Bernardo, San Diego, CA 92127.

[10] C. L. Graeff, "The Situational Leadership Theory: A Critical View," *Academy of Management Review* (April 1983): 290.

[11] V. Vroom and P. Yetton, *The Leadership Decision Making Model* (Pittsburgh: University of Pittsburgh Press, 1973).

REFERENCES

Adams, Jerome; Rice, Robert W.; and Instone, Debra. "Follower Attitudes Toward Women and Judgements concerning Performance by Female and Male Leaders." *Academy of Management Journal* 27, no. 3 (September 1984): 636–643.

Burke, W. W. "Leadership: Is There One Best Approach?" *Management Review* 69 (November 1980): 54–56.

Butler, Mark C., and Jones, Allan P. "Perceived Leader Behavior, Individual Characteristics, and Injury Occurrence in Hazardous Work Environments." *Journal of Applied Psychology* 64, no. 3 (June 1979): 299–304.

Carbone, T. C. "Theory X and Theory Y Revisited." *Managerial Planning* 29 (May-June 1981): 24–27.

Fiedler, F. E. "Job Engineering for Effective Leadership: A New Approach." *Management Review* 66 (September 1977): 29–31.

Fiedler, F. E. and Mahar, Linda. "The Effectiveness of Contingency Model Training: A Review of the Validation of Leader Match." *Personnel Psychology* 32, no. 1 (Spring 1979): 45–62.

Fox, W. M. "Limits to the Use of Consultative-Participative Management." *California Management Review* 20 (Winter 1977): 17–22.

Green, S. G., and Nebeker, D. M. "Effects of Situational Factors and Leadership Style on Leader Behavior." *Organizational Behavior and Human Performance* 19 (August 1977): 368–377.

Greene, Charles N. "Questions of Causation in the Path-Goal Theory of Leadership." *Academy of Management Journal* 22, no. 1 (March 1979): 22–41.

Griffin, R. W. "Relationships among Individual, Task Design and Leader Behavior Variables." *Academy of Management Journal* 23 (December 1980): 665–683.

Grove, Andrew S. "What Kind of Boss are You?" *Canadian Business* 57, no. 3 (March 1984): 82.

Himes, G. K. "Management Leadership Styles." *Supervision* 42 (November 1980): 9–11.

Katz, R. "Influence of Group Conflict on Leadership Effectiveness." *Organizational Behavior and Human Performance* 20 (December 1977): 265–286.

Klimoski, R. J., and Hayes, N. J. "Leadership Behavior and Subordinate Motivation." *Personnel Psychology* 33 (Autumn 1980): 543–545.

Leister, A., et al. "Validation of Contingency Model Leadership Training: Leader Match." *Academy of Management Journal* 20 (September 1977): 464–470.

Likert, R. "Management Styles and the Human Component." *Management Review* 66 (October 1977): 23–28.

Miner, Frederick C. Jr. "A Comparative Analysis of Three Diverse Group Decision Making Approaches." *Academy of Management Journal* 22, no. 1 (March 1979): 81–93.

Peters, Thomas J. "Leadership: Sad Facts and Silver Linings." *Harvard Business Review* 57, no. 6 (November-December 1979): 164–172.

Schriesheim, C. A., and Schriesheim, J. F. "Test of the Path-Goal Theory of Leadership and Some Suggested Direction for Future Research." *Personnel Psychology* 33 (Summer 1980): 368–370.

Sheridan, John E.; Vredenburgh, Donald J., and Abelson, Michael A. "Contextual Model of Leadership Influence in Hospital Units." *Academy of Management Journal* 27, no. 1 (March 1984): 57–78.

Sinetar, M. "Developing Leadership Potential." *Personnel Journal* 60 (March 1981): 193–196.

Stoffman, Daniel. "Blue Collar Turnaround Artists." *Canadian Business* 57, no. 2 (February 1984): 38.

Vroom, V., and Yetton, P. *The Leadership Decision Making Model.* Pittsburgh: University of Pittsburgh Press, 1973.

Yukl, Gary A. *Leadership in Organizations.* Englewood Cliffs, N.J.: Prentice-Hall, 1981.

Zaleznik, A. "Managers and Leaders: Are They Different?" *Harvard Business Review* 55 (May 1977): 67–68.

Zierden, William E. "Leading Through the Follower's Point of View." *Organizational Dynamics* 8, no. 4 (Spring 1980): 27–46.

Communication
and Conflict

The Business School

Vincent Carletti was the associate dean of the business school at a large western Canadian university. In addition to his regular duties as associate dean, he was required to inform in person students whose grades were so low that they must withdraw from the business school. Late one afternoon Carletti's secretary informed him that Randall Lane, a fourth-year student, had arrived for his interview. Carletti had mixed feelings about Lane. Through the student grapevine, he had learned that Lane was the only member of his family ever to attend university and that Lane was very impressed with this fact. In addition, Lane was pleasant, hard working,

and enthusiastic. Unfortunately, his grades had deteriorated to the point where he could not be allowed to graduate. Carletti therefore had the unpleasant task of informing Lane that, although he had reached fourth year, he was now required to withdraw.

Carletti asked Lane to step into his office, and the following conversation took place:

Carletti: Mr. Lane, I have been examining your scholastic records in some detail during the last few days. I regret to inform you that your grade point average has dropped too low for you to be allowed to graduate from the business school.

Lane (calmly): I admit I've been having grade trouble lately, but I believe I can raise them in time to graduate.

Carletti: I'm afraid you didn't understand me. You see, your grade point has dropped to a level where you must withdraw from the business school. It will be impossible for you to graduate with a business degree.

Lane (still calmly): But I only have four courses left before I graduate. Just let me complete those four courses and then I'll be able to graduate.

Carletti (getting slightly annoyed): Even if you do complete those four courses, you can't graduate because your grade point average is too low. Just forget the four courses; you're going to have to withdraw.

Lane (remaining calm): But once I complete the four courses, I will have satisfied all the requirements for graduation. That will solve the problem, won't it?

Carletti (getting angry): No, it won't solve the problem! Forget about those four courses! We have a requirement here that you must maintain a certain grade point average to graduate. You've known about it for three years. You haven't maintained it, so you won't be allowed to graduate. It's very simple. Can't you see that?

Lane (remaining very calm): But I only have four courses left before I graduate. I don't feel that it's reasonable to require me to withdraw when I'm so close to graduation.

Carletti (totally exasperated): I give up! You can sit there all day pretending everything is fine and you only have "four courses to complete and then you'll graduate," but that won't change reality. You'll get your ejection notice from the registrar and that will be that! Goodbye!

KEY TERMS

communication	barriers to	transactional analysis
source (sender)	communication	Parent ego state
encoding	timing	Child ego state
channel	communication	Adult ego state
decoding	overload	teleconferencing
feedback	filtering	conflict
noise	perception set	conflict management
lateral	differences	arbitration
communication	empathy	mediator
diagonal	listening	
communication	body language	

LEARNING OBJECTIVES

After completing this chapter you should be able to

1. Describe the basic components of the communication process and state what should be communicated to workers.
2. Explain the basic forms of organizational channels of communication.
3. Identify the barriers that can cause breakdowns in communication.

4. Describe the facilitators that are available to improve communication.
5. Explain why conflict develops and identify various means of managing it.

The exchange between Vincent Carletti and Randall Lane is an example of an unfortunate communication breakdown. Breakdowns in communication occur frequently in all types of organizations, and they have a negative effect on both interpersonal relationships and overall effectiveness. Even in organizations with a participative management attitude, with good leadership, and high employee motivation — poor communication can have a negative effect on production. Good communication and the ability to handle conflict effectively are essential to positive managerial influence. Given these facts, it is important that practicing managers and students aspiring to management positions understand how good communication skills can enhance their own careers and the performance of the organizations for which they work.

Managers spend a large portion of their time communicating with others — as much as 75 percent by some estimates. Accordingly, one of the worst criticisms that a manager can receive from peers, superiors, and subordinates is that he or she cannot communicate effectively. In a previous chapter, we defined management as the accomplishment of objectives through the efforts of other people. In order for an employee to achieve the goals of the manager, he or she must know what the supervisor wants to accomplish. When the goals of the manager do not match what has actually been completed, a breakdown in communication is often found to be the source of the difficulty. When a frustrated manager says: "You did what you thought I meant very effectively; unfortunately, that was not what I wanted you to do" — clearly communication did not take place.

Communication is the transfer of meaning and understanding between people through verbal and nonverbal means in order to affect behavior and achieve desired results. In an organization, communication has two primary purposes. First, it provides the means by which the objectives of the firm may be accomplished. The manner in which plans are to be implemented and actions coordinated to achieve a particular goal must be communicated to the individuals who must accomplish the task. Second, communication provides the means by which members of the firm may be stimulated to accomplish organization plans willingly and enthusiastically.

The inability to communicate effectively can severely hamper a manager in the accomplishment of his or her duties. In fact, a person cannot be effective as a manager unless he or she possesses good communication skills. Consider the manager who performs tasks that a subordinate should be doing and who says that he or she is doing the job because the worker is incapable of doing the assigned job. This is not really the case; the manager may actually be incapable of communicating his or her goals effectively. Rather than risk this occurring, the manager decides to do the work of the subordinate. In this instance, the failure to communicate has caused the efficiency of the unit to deteriorate because both the subordinate and the manager are not doing the work for which they were hired.

A crucial aspect of communication is that it is a learned quality. A person who truly wants to improve his or her ability to communicate can do so. In this chapter we first address the issue of communication through the communication process. Once each phase of the process is understood, existing problem areas and weaknesses in your own or other people's communications can be identified and corrected. Second, we note what should be communicated to employees to enhance their motivation and productivity. Third, we discuss the main organizational channels of communication. Fourth, barriers and facilitators to communication are examined in some detail to help managers to avoid poor communication practices.

The chapter concludes with a discussion of conflict because it is so often the result of poor communications. We define conflict, note its causes, indicate when it is constructive and when it is destructive, and make suggestions for managing it effectively.

THE COMMUNICATION PROCESS

Communication takes place only when two or more people are involved. Shouting for help on a desert island is not communication; similarly, if a professor lectures and no one listens or understands, there is no communication. The basic elements in the communication process are shown in Exhibit 12-1. Each step in the sequence is critical to the ultimate success of the process.

The **source**, or sender, is the person who has an idea or message to communicate to another person or group. The credibility of the source's communication depends on the characteristics of the source. A communicator can use a number of tactics to convince the receiver to accept the communication. These include playing on the emotions of the receiver, using logical arguments, or asking the receiver to accept what is being said because the source is trustworthy.

Once the source has decided what message is to be conveyed, the message must be put in a form that the receiver can understand. The message emerges as a result of **encoding**. Senders must encode their messages or ideas into symbols that their receivers will understand. Words on a page are symbols to readers. The sound of a siren on a busy highway may mean that there is traffic trouble ahead.

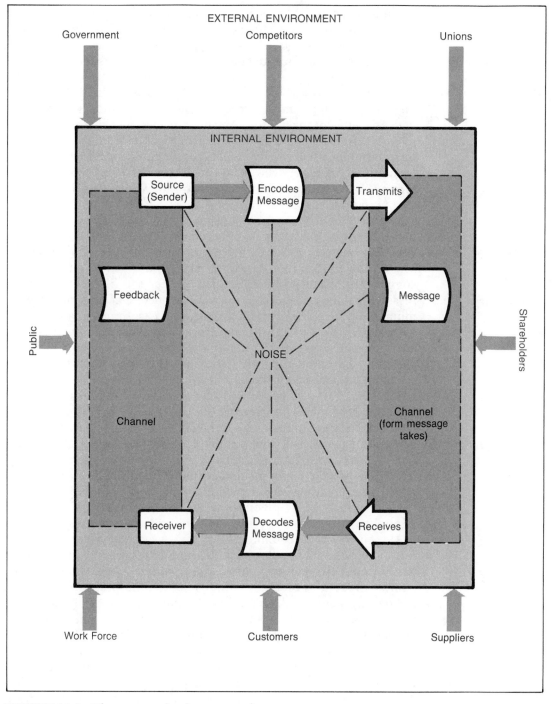

EXHIBIT 12-1 The communication process

SOURCE Adapted from H. Joseph Reitz, *Behavior in Organization* (Homewood, Ill.: Irwin, 1977: 342. Reprinted by permission of author and publisher.

The actual means by which the message is transmitted to the receiver is the communications **channel**. A number of channels may be used to transmit a message. The spoken word can be used through such channels as face-to-face, telephone, radio, and television. Books, articles, memos, and letters can serve as the channel for the written word. The senses of sight, sound, touch, smell, and taste also assist in communication. Senders must select the appropriate channel to avoid problems that may occur in either the understanding or the retention of a message. To explain a complex mathematical problem to students, an instructor may use a variety of methods: lecture, graphs, and formulas. Similarly, a manager who wants to increase the probability that a message will be retained by subordinates may follow a verbal instruction with a written memorandum.

The receiver of the message must convert the encoded symbols into meaning through the process of **decoding**. How accurately decoding is done depends very much on how similar the receiver is to the sender. The greater the similarity in the background or status factors of the communicator and the receiver, the greater the likelihood that the message will be understood as it was intended. One reason why communication between organizational levels is so often misinterpreted is that many background differences exist among the individuals who are communicating. For example, the company president may have difficulty communicating with first-line supervisors because of decoding problems caused by status differences.

The sender of a message will observe one of three reactions to a message: agreement, disagreement, or apathy. These various forms of **feedback** tell the sender whether the message was accurately received and whether proper action was taken. The speed at which feedback occurs varies with each situation. In face-to-face conversation, feedback may be practically instantaneous, whereas in the case of mass advertising, many weeks or months may pass before the source (the advertiser) knows how effective the communication was. Feedback can also take many forms — verbal, written, or facial expressions.

At each step in the communication process, both senders and receivers must cope with **noise**. Although the term noise may be taken literally (for example, two factory workers trying to talk over the noise of machines), the term is generally used to refer to conceptual noise — those personality, perceptual, and attitudinal differences in individuals that reduce their ability to communicate effectively. Noise can be powerful enough to block communication between senders and receivers. A manager is doing a performance appraisal of an employee whom the manager thinks is lazy. The manager makes the criticisms in a threatening manner; the employee reacts defensively to these words. They do not actually discuss the problem area. These two people will probably never reach the point of deciding how to resolve whatever problem exists between them because of their communication noise.

WHAT SHOULD BE COMMUNICATED?

In the past, managers often communicated only enough information to give subordinates clear orders. With the increasing educational levels of the work force, and the increased expectations that go along with increased education, managers are finding that employees often want to know far more than simply what to do. They also want to know why they should do a certain task, if there are better ways of doing it, and other information that will make them feel better about their job. Behavioral science research has demonstrated that when job-related information is provided, it often increases employee motivation to do the job well. This research also points out the importance of subordinates feeling that their managers hear, understand, and value their ideas.

The 1980s are likely to see continued organizational budget-tightening. Conflict over scarce resources can be expected at all levels in organizations. The responsibility to maintain a supportive and productive communication climate falls on managers.[1]

Determining what specific topics are to be communicated is often very difficult. The manager who believes that everything is suitable for transmission will not only clog the channels with trivia but may harm operations by releasing information that should be retained. The National Association of Manufacturers has suggested that the following should be communicated to employees:

- Information about the company — its operations, products, and prospects
- Information about company policies and practices related to personnel and their jobs, such as vacations, seniority, and pay systems
- Information about specific situations that arise in the company, such as a change in management or a change in plant layout
- Information about the general economic system in which a company and its employees operate.

Within these broad areas, many specific details must be considered. For example, management should inform its employees of the company's products, believing that their understanding will inspire interest, loyalty, and cooperation. But, disclosure of future product plans may jeopardize the company's future in a highly competitive industry. In matters more closely related to the employee's interests, such as seniority and pay, the tendency is toward providing all information that could possibly be desired. The two best guides for determining what information to provide are the responses to these questions: (1) What must personnel know in order to relate effectively to others and to the organization as a whole? and (2) What do employees want to know before they cooperate willingly and enthusiastically? The typical employee usually wants to know:

- His or her standing in relation to the official, formal authority structure
- His or her standing in relation to the informal organization (individual status, power, and acceptance)
- Events that have bearing on future economic security
- Operational information that will enable him or her to develop pride in the job.

ORGANIZATIONAL CHANNELS OF COMMUNICATION

A material component of the communication process is the channel through which the signals flow between sender and receiver. If only superiors and subordinates are considered, these channels follow the formal organizational structure in two main ways: downward and upward. However, as discussed in Chapter 8, the informal organization also has communications channels.

Formal Downward Channels

The traditional manager is likely to emphasize the importance of the downward channels of communication. Managers are aware of the necessity for conveying top management's orders and viewpoints to subordinates. They believe that the logic of these orders will stimulate desired action. Some of the various channels available to carry the information downward are indicated in the table below. Many other channels are used every day by management to communicate with subordinates. Middle- and lower-level managers are usually contacted personally by written memos, policy manuals, and authorized schedules. External means, such as radio, television, and the press, can be used to communicate with employees as well as the general public.

Downward Channels of Communication

The chain of command	Orders and information can be given face-to-face or in written fashion and transmitted from one level to another. The most frequently used channel, this one is appropriate on either an individual or a group basis.
Posters and bulletin boards	Many employees do not read such boards; this channel is useful only as a supplementary device.
Company periodicals	A great deal of information about the company, its products, and policies can be disseminated in this manner. To

(table cont'd.: Downward Communication Channels)

	attract readership, a certain percentage of space must be devoted to items about employees; thus, the periodical plays a part in developing the social life of the organization.
Letters and pay inserts	This form of direct mail contact is ordinarily used when the president of the organization wishes to present something of special interest. Letters are usually directed to the employee's home address. The use of pay inserts ensures exposure to every employee.
Employee handbooks and pamphlets	Handbooks are frequently used during the hiring and orientation process as an introduction to the organization. Too often, however, they are unread even when the firm demands a signed statement that the employee is acquainted with their content. When special systems are being introduced, such as a pension plan or a job evaluation system, concise, highly illustrated pamphlets are often prepared to facilitate understanding and stimulate acceptance.
Information racks	In a relatively small number of organizations, racks containing free paperback literature of all types are provided. Mixed in with books on hobbies and sports are pamphlets on the profit system, the company, or management techniques.
Loudspeaker system	The loudspeaker system is used not only for paging purposes but also to make announcements while they're hot. Such systems can also be misused, as in the case when the president of a company sent his summer vacation greetings from his cool place in the mountains to the sweating workers on the production floor.
Annual reports	A review of typical annual reports would indicate that they are increasingly being written for the benefit of the employee and the union

(table con'td.: Downward Communication Channels)

	as well as for the shareholder. It is a channel that appears to be designed for one group, the owners, to which others tap in, hoping to obtain information not intended for them.
The labor union	The union can be helpful in communicating certain philosophies to company employees. The union voice, added to the management voice, can be highly persuasive.

Formal Upward Channels

Advocates of participative management and leadership have emphasized the stimulation of upward communication from subordinate to supervisor. This channel is necessary not only to determine if subordinates have understood the information that was sent downward, but also to meet certain needs of people. A communication effectiveness survey of thousands of employees showed that only half believed that significant upward communication was present. The others saw little chance of discussion or dialogue with top management.[2] An upward flow of information is also necessary if management is to coordinate the various activities of the organization. As shown in the following table, there are several upward channels of communication to choose from.

Upward Channels of Communication

The chain of command	Theoretically, the flow of communications is two-way between superior and subordinate. The superior should have an open-door attitude as well as some of the skills of a counselor. If one has more courage, group meetings can be held in which expression of gripes and attitudes is encouraged.
The grievance procedure	A systematic grievance procedure is one of the most fundamental devices for upward communication. The subordinate knows that there is a mechanism for appeal beyond the authority of the immediate supervisor. If this grievance procedure is backed up by the presence of a labor union, one is even more encouraged to voice true feelings.

(table cont'd.: Upward Communication Channels)

The complaint system	In addition to grievance procedures, some firms encourage all types of upward communication by establishing means of preserving the identity of the complainant. Gripe boxes may be established, into which an employee can place a written complaint or rumor, that management will investigate. In one firm, a blackboard was divided into halves, one side being for employee complaints or rumors, the other for management's replies. An answer of some sort was guaranteed within a 24-hour period.
Counseling	Though all supervisors have a counseling obligation, the authority barrier makes true communication difficult. For this reason, special staff counselors may be provided to allow employees to discuss matters with them in privacy and confidence.
Morale questionnaires	This channel also preserves the identity of the employee when answering specific questions about the firm and its management.
An open-door policy	An open-door attitude on the part of each supervisor toward immediate subordinates is to be highly commended. Higher management seldom use it because the employee is usually reluctant to bypass his or her immediate supervisor.
Exit interview	If the employee leaves the organization, there is one last chance in the exit interview to discover feelings and views about the firm in general and reasons for quitting in particular. Follow-up questionnaires are also used at times, because employees are reluctant to give full and truthful information at the time of departure.
Labor union	A prime purpose of the labor union is to convey to management the feelings and demands of employees. Collective

(table cont'd.: Upward Communication Channels)

	bargaining sessions constitute a legal channel of communication for any aspect of employer/employee relations.
Special meetings	Special employee meetings to discuss particular company policies or procedures are sometimes scheduled by management to obtain employee feedback. The keystone of teamwork in the Pitney Bowes Company is monthly meetings in all departments involving all employees. In addition, a central employee council of 13 employee representatives meets with top executives on a monthly basis. Employees on this main council are elected for two-year terms and devote full time to investigating problems and improving communication processes.
The ombudsman	Though little used in North America, the ombudsman's role is to ensure corporate justice in nonunionized firms. In essence, the ombudsman acts as a complaint officer to whom employees may go when they feel they have exhausted the typical avenues of receiving an acceptable hearing. An ombudsman has only the rights of acceptance or rejection of complaints, investigation, and recommendation of action to the top organizational official. Most complaints center around salary, performance appraisal, layoff, and fringe benefits. In many instances, lower-level managers make voluntary adjustments precluding specific recommendations from the ombudsman. Though the position has existed for about 150 years, only recently have some North American business firms adopted the concept. Xerox Corporation inaugurated the position in 1972 and reports that: 40 percent of the final decisions clearly favored the employee, 30 percent were against the employee, and 30 percent represented some type of compromise.[a]

[a]   Information on Xerox Corporation from "Where Ombudsmen Work Out," *Business Week* (May 3, 1976): 114–116.

Informal Communication Channels

Informal communication channels are not included in the formal organizational structure. If a manager has a problem that is affected by another department, the two managers may get together informally. When managers are at the same organizational level, this channel is **lateral communication**; it results from established personal relationships. Mutual trust, which often takes time to evolve, must first develop. But effective lateral communication can improve the productivity of both departments. Some companies even provide for lateral communication as a part of the formal organizational structure.

Another type of informal channel is diagonal communication, which also bypasses the formal chain of command. In **diagonal communication**, communication channels are established with people whose levels are higher or lower in the organization but not directly in the formal chain of command. Again, this process is not automatic. Trust must first develop. Care must be taken in using diagonal communication because immediate superiors might take offense. However, used carefully, diagonal communication can be an important information source for the manager.

As noted in Chapter 8, the grapevine is the system of personal relationships and contacts that does not follow the firm's formal communication channels. The grapevine does not respect formal lines of authority and often extends throughout an organization. However, it does get much of its information from the formal organization. It usually transmits this information more rapidly than the formal system, although sometimes not as accurately. Employees generally rate the grapevine as one of the primary sources of current information.[3]

The grapevine has 4 basic characteristics. First, it transmits information in every direction throughout the organization. Information on the grapevine can go down, up, laterally, and diagonally, all at the same time. It can connect organization units that have distant or indirect formal relationships. Second, the grapevine transmits information rapidly because it is not restricted by any formal policies and procedures. The chain of command does not have to be followed. Once a message gets into the grapevine, it can be moved instantaneously to any point in the organization. Third, the grapevine is selective about who receives information. Some people are tuned in to it and others are not. Some people regard grapevine information as gossip and, therefore, disregard or disapprove of it. Consequently, some managers are not even aware of the grapevine. Finally, the grapevine extends beyond the formal organization. Considerable communication about the firm occurs off the job. Employees who are friends may talk shop among themselves, or workers at a party may pass on or receive information about the company to people who don't work for it.

Managers should not ignore the grapevine: it can be useful and cannot be eliminated. Wise managers attempt to remain tuned in to the grapevine. Not only will they obtain useful information, but they will be able to replace incorrect messages with accurate information. The grapevine is a prominent channel in the communication process.

BARRIERS TO COMMUNICATION

Effective communication means that the receiver correctly interprets the message of the sender. Often this does not happen because various breakdowns can occur in communication. If a manager tells an employee to "produce a few more parts," and the employee makes 2 but the manager wanted 200, communications certainly broke down. If a manager is to develop his or her communication ability, the reasons communication breaks down must be fully understood.

As seen in Exhibit 12-2, successful management decisions must pass through the bottleneck or **barriers to communication** if the organization's goals are to be achieved. If the barriers are excessive, communication may be reduced to the point where the firm's objectives cannot be achieved. Barriers may be classified as technical, language, or psychological. Knowledge of these possible communication barriers helps managers avoid them or minimize their impact.

Technical Barriers

Barriers to communication that derive from the work place are referred to as **technical barriers**. Some of these include timing, communication overload, and cultural differences.

Timing

Timing is determining when a message should be communicated. Managers need to determine the most appropriate time to transmit a message. For instance, a manager who must reprimand a worker for excessive tardiness must speak with the worker as soon as possible after the event happened. As another example, a firm might want to announce to the general public that it has a new product only when economic factors are most favorable.

Communication Overload

Communication overload occurs when the sender attempts to present too much information to the receiver at one time. A person can absorb only so many facts and figures at a particular time. When excessive information is provided, a major breakdown in communication can occur. In any organization, the number of channels of communication is likely to be profuse; the demands on employees can become excessive. One professor experienced overload while teaching statistics in a 4-hour class. For the first hour, students were eager and alert. By the fourth hour, however, few students were able to grasp what was taught.

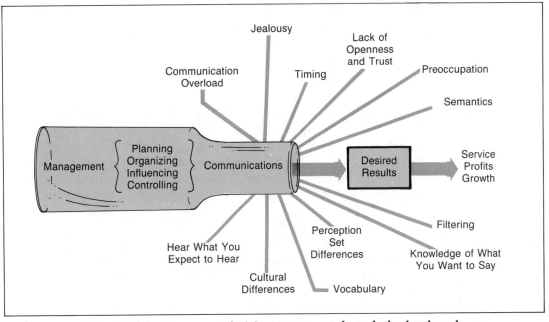

EXHIBIT 12-2   **Successful management decisions must pass through the bottleneck—or barriers to communications—prior to achieving desired results**

Cultural Differences

In North America time is usually a highly valuable commodity and a deadline suggests urgency. In the Middle East, however, giving a deadline to a person is considered to be rude; the deadline is likely to be ignored. If a client is kept waiting for 30 minutes in Canada, it may mean that he or she has low status. In Latin America, a 30-minute wait means nothing. If a contract offer has not been acted on in North America over a period of several months or a year, the conclusion is that the party has lost interest. In Japan, long delays mean no slackening of interest; delay is often a highly effective negotiation tactic when used on impatient North Americans.

Canadians and Americans conduct most face-to-face business at an interpersonal space of about 1.5 m to 2.5 m; an interpersonal space under a meter suggests more personal or intimate undertakings. The normal business distance for Latin Americans is closer to the personal distance of North Americans. Some highly interesting communication difficulties arise as North Americans back-pedal and their Latin American counterparts press ever closer. Regarding status symbols, a Canadian manager's office that is spacious, well furnished, and located on the top floor conveys high prestige. In the Middle East, size and decor of office mean little or nothing and, in France, the manager is likely to be located in the midst of subordinates in order to control them.

Language Barriers

Barriers to communication can occur when language problems result from vocabulary or from different meanings being applied to the same word (semantic differences).

Vocabulary

Managers must understand the audience being addressed if they are to be effective communicators. In one business organization, a market researcher, a supervisor, and a janitor will likely have different vocabulary sets. Words that the market researcher understands may have little meaning for the janitor, and vice versa, even though they both work in the same organization. Breakdowns in communication often occur when the sender does not tailor the message to match the knowledge base of the receiver.

All of us have a common level of vocabulary. (See Exhibit 12-3 for an illustration.) If we speak using level 4 words, both the market researcher and the janitor will understand. As we speak or write above this base level, more and more people will not be able to comprehend the message. If the market researcher uses words above the scale of 6, communication with the supervisor is lost. It will cease at level 4 with the janitor. Naturally, there will be times when higher-level words must be used to communicate a technical concept but, if managers can concentrate their messages in the common vocabulary base, they have a much better chance of being understood.

Two systems for measurement of reading ease are the fog index developed by the late Robert Gunning and the Flesch system developed by Rudolph Flesch. The purpose of the fog index is to determine the reading level of writing. A fog index of 10 would mean that tenth

EXHIBIT 12-3
Common
vocabulary base

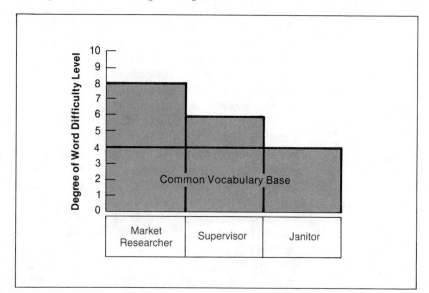

graders can understand what you write.[4] The Flesch system helps you determine whether your writing is interesting to read. The means by which both systems are used may be seen in the adjacent "Management in Practice" on fog indexes.

MANAGEMENT IN PRACTICE

Measure your Fog Index

Is your writing hard to understand? Do eyeballs glaze after a glance at your prose? Experts have devised measurements of reading ease, and you can rate your own performance.

One of the simplest and most consistent tests is the "fog index" developed by the late Robert Gunning. Here's how it works: Choose at random a medium-length paragraph of your own writing. A paragraph of about 120 words is ideal, says Douglas Mueller, president of the Gunning-Mueller Clear Writing Institute in Santa Barbara, Calif. Dates and other number combinations are single words. Count the number of words in your sample, then the number of sentences. Divide the word total by the sentence total to obtain the average number of words per sentence.

Step two is slightly more complex. Skim your sample and note each word of three or more syllables. Don't count words that are made by combining common short words, such as butterfly. And don't count verbs that acquire their extra syllable from tense endings — es or ed. Don't count words that begin with capital letters — place names, for example. And exclude the first word of any sentence. "I don't know why, but it works," says Mueller. "If you start a sentence with a polysyllable, it lowers the fog index. Magazines such as *The New Yorker* do it constantly."

Saying it simply. Once you have your polysyllable count, add it to the word average and multiply the total by 0.4. The product will be a number corresponding to a reading comprehension grade level. A nine means that a ninth-grader can understand what you write. If you score 17 or more, than your prose is so densely wrapped in fog that only a graduate student will

be able to grope through it. The Gettysburg Address has a fog index of 10. Most news magazines manage 11 (*Business Week* averages 10). The article that you are now reading scores eight.

If you want to know whether your prose is interesting to read, Rudolph Flesch, one of the most eminent of reading and writing specialists, has devised a human-interest score. Using a sample of 100 words, count the personal words, which Flesch defines as pronouns — I, you, he, she, them, but not it or a plural pronoun referring to a thing. Count all words with gender, such as father or sister, actress, businessman, and proper names. And count collective nouns such as people and folks.

Attracting the reader. Next, count up your sample's personal sentences: any sentence containing speech, set off by quotation marks or by references such as "she said"; sentences addressed directly to the reader as a question, a command, a suggestion; a sentence cast as an exclamation; any incomplete sentence of a conversational nature (Flesch's examples: "Doesn't know a word of English. Handsome though." Those are two incomplete but comprehensible sentences.).

Once you have done all this, the arithmetic is a little complicated. Multiply the number of personal words in your 100-word sample by 3.635. Multiply the number of personal sentences by 0.314, and add the two products. The total is your human interest score, which runs from dull at 5, through interesting at 30, to dramatic at 80. What you have been reading, by the way, scores about 21: mildly interesting.

SOURCE Reprinted from the July 6, 1981 issue of *Business Week* by special permission, © 1981 by McGraw-Hill, Inc., New York, NY 10020. All rights reserved.

The objective of both of these systems is to reduce the amount of pompous jargon and inflated prose. Of course, there is more to communication than can be revealed by counting syllables and sentence lengths. Each communicator must have a clear and coherent grasp of the idea he or she hopes to transmit. The Flesch and Gunning indexes help the writer to keep the reader in mind.

Semantics

When a sender sends words to which a receiver attaches different meaning from the one intended by the sender, a semantic — or meaning of words — communication breakdown has occurred. A major difficulty with the English language is that multiple meanings may be attached to a word, for instance, the word *charge*. A manager may place an employee *in charge* of a section. The company *charges* for its services. A person gets a *charge* out of a humorous event. When two individuals attach different meanings to a word, a breakdown in communication can occur.

The use of jargon can also create a barrier to communication. Virtually every industry develops certain jargon that is used in everyday business. The statistician, computer programmer, typist, or ditch digger likely develops expressions peculiar to his or her specific profession. When speaking to an individual not associated with the trade, a breakdown in communication may occur. For this reason, many firms provide new personnel with a list and definition of terms associated with the particular industry.

Psychological Barriers

Although technical factors and semantic differences are credited with causing breakdowns in communication, psychological barriers tend to be the major reasons for miscommunication and communication breakdowns. These include various forms of distortion and problems involving interpersonal relationships.

Knowledge of What You Want To Say

The expression "The mouth was in gear before the mind was operating" provides one form of breakdown in communication. Directives, orders, and even comments that are not well thought out can convey a message that the sender did not intend. A manager who asks for one thing but expects another has caused a breakdown in communication.

Filtering

An attempt to alter and color information to present a more favorable image to the manager is referred to as **filtering**. Managers often discover that information given to them by subordinates has been filtered. As subordinates contribute information to superiors, they know that it will be used for at least two purposes: (1) to aid management in controlling and directing the firm (and therefore the worker), and (2) to evaluate the worth of their performance. Managers at all levels are tempted to filter information as it progresses up the chain of command. Even the president may filter information before it goes to the board of directors.

Because the data have been filtered, an incorrect impression of the true situation may occur. There have been many managerial attempts to reduce both the number and thickness of the authority filters that clog organization communication channels. It should be apparent that decentralization reduces the number of managerial levels, with a consequent speeding up of the communication process. Such reorganizations are drastic and require considerable efforts in the area of retraining and establishing realistic control standards.

A consultant can serve as a means of reducing communication filters. One company noticed a steady decrease in productivity for no reason that could be identified by management. A consultant systematically interviewed all employees over a 6-month period. The results of these interviews indicated strong feelings on the part of many employees that work standards were too high, that older employees resented the high wage scales of the new employees, and that temporary transfers to new jobs to avoid layoff were widely resented. In each case, management had felt that it had communicated effectively its intent to the employees.

MANAGEMENT IN PRACTICE

Information and the Company President

Information is crucial to the president of a corporation. The president must use information to decide what changes are necessary in the way the organization is operating. Without accurate information, the president is in big trouble. Yet, corporate presidents are often isolated from important information because subordinates are fearful of being the bearers of bad news. However, subordinates are eager to communicate good news, so the president may get, from them, a very distorted view of how the company is actually faring in the marketplace.

Even presidents who consciously try to avoid this problem may have difficulty. Jim McDonald, president of National Silicates in Toronto, found that out. He had first worked for the company 30 years ago as a student, then returned and eventually became president. He found that the people who knew him previously think of him as "Jim," while the people who didn't know him earlier think of him as "Mr. McDonald." In an attempt to overcome this distinction, he holds periodic meetings with senior management as a group to get their views. He feels that this is less threatening than one-on-one confrontations, and that people will communicate more openly if they have peer support.

SOURCE Andrew Weiner, "Stay in Control by Mastering the Art of Listening Well," *Executive* (September 1983): 14–18.

Lack of Trust and Openness

Openness and trust on the part of managers and employees must exist if orderly changes in the organization are to occur. When employees feel that openness and trust do not exist, barriers to communication are present.

As was illustrated in Exhibit 12-1, the sender needs feedback to know whether communication has occurred. If employees perceive the manager is open and receptive to their ideas, communication is encouraged. Should managers give the impression that feedback is not desired and that their statements should never be questioned, communication tends to be stifled.

One of the major factors in the success of Japanese businesses is that managers trust not only their workers but also their peers and superiors. As a result, a simpler organizational structure evolves. For instance, Ford Motor company has 11 layers of management between the factory worker and the chairman, while Toyota Motor Company has only 6. These many layers cause high overhead and much red tape. Japanese firms assume that personnel at all levels are trustworthy, and they do not have to employ highly paid executives to review the work of other highly paid executives.[5]

Jealousy

It is perhaps difficult for managers to accept, but everyone, especially peers and subordinates, may not be pleased to see them perform successfully. Competence and effective performance may actually be viewed as a threat to the security of peers and subordinates. Individuals may attempt to diminish the accomplishments of another person because they are jealous. If jealous people are able to gain the attention of the supervisor, there is a possibility that when their peers attempt to communicate, they may find a less receptive ear. Because of jealousy, the effectiveness of communication may be reduced.

Perception Set Differences

Another major barrier to communication is **perception set differences** between individuals attempting to communicate with each other. Differences in past experiences, educational background, emotions, values, and beliefs — to name just a few — affect each person's perception of a message or of words. The word *management*, for example, may be defined by two individuals as planning, organizing, influencing, and controlling the activities of others. If one person's parents were managers and the second's parents were labor union organizers, the word *management* will evoke drastically different meanings. It is difficult enough if words are representative of tangible objects such as *chair*, *pencil*, or *hat*. But imagine the increased difficulties in using such terms as *liberal*, *conservative*, *philosophy*, *group dynamics*, or *communication*.

AIDS TO COMMUNICATION

Once managers recognize that communication can break down, they can then work toward improving communication ability. As previously mentioned, the major factor to remember is that communication is learned. If persons truly want to improve their communication ability, they can find the means available to assist in this undertaking. Empathy, listening, reading skill improvement, observation, word choice, body language, actions, and transactional analysis are discussed as aids to communication in the following sections.

Empathy

You have likely heard the expression "'I hear you," by which one person expresses empathy for what has been said. **Empathy** is the ability to identify with the various feelings and thoughts of another person. It does not mean that you necessarily agree with the other person but, while you are with the individual, you can appreciate why that person speaks and acts as he or she does. If a person is bitter, you are able to relate to this bitterness; if he or she is scared, you understand this fear.

Taken in its broadest meaning, an empathetic person is communicating. It is for this reason that managers should take the time to understand as much as possible about the people with whom they must work daily. With this information, the manager is in a much better position to understand why people act as they do. The manager may not agree with the individual but, if he or she takes the time to understand the reason for certain action, problems may be easier to resolve.

Listening

One of the most effective tools a manager has at his or her disposal to facilitate communication is the ability to listen. A person who is constantly talking is not listening or learning. Listening assists a manager in discovering problems and determining solutions to problems.

Communication cannot take place unless messages are received and understood by the other party. The average speaking speed is 120 words per minute, yet people are able to listen at the rate of 480 words per minute. What does the listener do with the excess time that results from this difference in speeds?

At least three types of **listening** have been identified: marginal, evaluative, and projective. The speed of listening provides the opportunity for marginal listening, a dangerous type that can lead to misunderstanding of and even insult to the speaker. For instance, most people have been speaking to a person but knew that the listener's mind was elsewhere. The individual may occasionally have heard some words, but the majority of the message was not understood.

Evaluative listening requires the listener to allocate full attention to the speaker. The excess time is devoted to evaluating and judging the nature of the remarks heard. Often, a listener is forming rebuttal remarks while the sender is still speaking, thus moving into a type of marginal listening. As soon as the sender says something that is not accepted, communication ceases and the receiver begins to develop a response mentally. Such thoughts as "this person does not know what he is talking about" can significantly reduce, or even eliminate, the communication process. Instead of one idea being transmitted and held by two people, the result may be two ideas, neither of which is really communicated to the other. If the listener allocated too much time to disapproving or approving of what is heard, it is doubtful whether he or she has the time to understand fully. This is particularly true when the remarks are loaded with emotion or concern over the security and status of the receiver.

Projective or nonevaluative listening holds the greatest potential for effective communication. Listeners attempt to project themselves into the position of the speaker and understand what is being said from the speaker's viewpoint. We should first listen without evaluation. After feeling that we understand what has been said, we can then evaluate what we have heard. Rogers suggested a rule to be followed to ensure some degree of projective listening: "Each person can speak for himself only *after* he has related the ideas and feelings of the previous speaker accurately and to that speaker's satisfaction."[6] There is no need to agree with the statements, but there is a need to understand them as the speaker intended. Only in this way is it possible to frame a reply that will actually respond to the speaker's remarks. Effective listening is empathic listening. It requires an ability to listen for feeling as well as for words. The person attempts to place himself or herself in the shoes of the other person.

Improved Reading Skills

Reading skills have received great attention in our society. The amount of written material a manager must cover has increased significantly, and some attempt should first be made to consolidate and reduce it. However, the ability to read rapidly and with understanding is an essential communication skill, particularly in larger organizations. It has been found that reading speeds can be doubled and tripled with little or no loss in comprehension.

Observation

As in the case of listening, managers make too few attempts to increase skill in observation, outside of training for law enforcement. Most people have heard reports where there were many witnesses to a traffic accident. When the police arrive and question the witnesses, there are many different versions about what actually occurred. "The blue car went through the stop light," says one witness. "No, that's not correct," says another, "the light was green." Most people miss a great deal by not carefully observing important elements in their surroundings. Some managers are very adept at assessing the general atmosphere of an organization by merely strolling through its work places. Observation of furnishings, housekeeping, dress of personnel, and activities can convey much information. Using our powers of observation to supplement listening and reading will add immeasurably to an understanding of what is actually transpiring.

Word Choice

As mentioned previously, virtually everyone can understand a certain threshold of words. If a manager wants to communicate effectively, he or she must make certain that the choice of the words transmitted by the sender is in the vocabulary set of the receiver. Generally, simple or common words provide the best means through which communication is accomplished. However, readers tend to be impressed with complex words. Studies have shown that hard-to-read journals are more highly rated than those containing the same information written in simpler language.[7]

Body Language

Most subordinates do not have to be told when their manager is displeased with them. A frown, arms crossed, and not smiling may communicate this message clearly. **Body language** is defined as a nonverbal method of communication in which physical actions, such as motions, gestures, and facial expressions, convey thoughts and emotions.

Appreciation of the significance of understanding body language in the communication process is also quite important for a manager. All people — managers, superiors, and subordinates — give off unintentional signals that can provide insight into the exact meaning that a person is attempting to communicate. The manager particularly must be constantly aware of the signals that he or she is presenting. Employees grasp at these small symbols to determine what the "boss" means. A frown, even though the words were positive in nature, may result in the words being taken wrong. A sarcastic smile when "you did a good job" was mentioned will likely be interpreted to mean that the worker actually did not do a good job. A blank stare in a conversation may mean to the employee that the manager is not interested.

A manager must also be aware of the signals that a subordinate may be giving off. Sweaty hands or nail biting in the presence of the supervisor may mean that the worker feels ill at ease. Managers need to recognize these signs and be prepared to adjust their behavior accordingly.

Actions

The manager must also recognize that people communicate by what they do or do not do. If a person comes to work one day and finds her or his desk moved from a location in a private office to one in an open area, communication of a sort has taken place. If no verbal explanation accompanies the action, people will interpret it their own way; the missing symbol or signal will be supplied by the observer. And despite any verbal statement to the contrary, such a move will likely be interpreted as a demotion for the person.

In one company, management introduced a change in procedure for a small crew of employees. The new method was timed and piece rates were established. None of the personnel produced more than half of the standard amount and were therefore on a time-wage basis rather than piece rates. They all filed grievances protesting the unfairness of the standard. Management tried everything it could think of to correct the problem, from all-day time studies to providing each employee with a private instructor in the new method. A check on similar jobs in other companies revealed that the standard was in line. Thus, management concluded that a concerted work restriction conspiracy was taking place.

The next move was one of communication by action. An engineer was sent to the production department, and he proceeded to measure various angles and spaces on the floor. He volunteered no information to the group. Finally, one man's curiosity got the best of him and he asked the engineer what he was doing. The engineer indicated that management wanted to see if there was sufficient room to locate certain machinery that could do the work of this crew. He continued about his business of measuring. The next day, all work crew members were producing amounts well above the established standard.

Transactional Analysis

One recently proposed system for facilitating communication involves analyzing transactions among people. **Transactional analysis** (TA) proposes that there are three ego states constantly present and at work within each individual: the Parent, the Adult, and the Child.[8] The manner in which these individual ego states interact can have a significant effect on interpersonal communication.

Parent

The **Parent ego state** may take on the characteristic of either the Nurturing or the Negative Parent. When the Nurturing Parent dominates, the person gives praise and recognition, comfort in time of distress, and reassurance in time of need. Statements such as "you have done a good job" or "I am certain the problem will work out all right" might be associated with the Nurturing Parent. Conversely, the Negative Parent is overcontrolling, suffocating, critical, and oppressive. Comments such as "children should be seen and not heard" or "be careful, you can hurt yourself with the knife" might be associated with the

Negative Parent. When the Negative Parent dominates, the person tends to lecture, believes that his or his moral standard is best for everyone, and often will not accept other ideas.

Child

The **Child ego state** may take on the characteristics of either the Natural Child, the Little Professor, or the Adaptive Child. The Natural Child is spontaneous, impulsive, untrained, expressive, self-centered, affectionate, and curious. The Little Professor tends to be intuitive, manipulative, and creative. The Adaptive Child tends to react in a way determined by parental figures.

Adult

A person who tends to evaluate the situation and attempts to make decisions based on information and facts is in the **Adult ego state**. No emotions are involved, and the individual tends to function like a computer, with all decisions based on logic.

The interaction of ego states can have a significant impact on communication behavior in organizations. The manager must recognize that a person will not always be in the Adult state and therefore will not always make decisions based entirely on logic. In fact, the greatest amount of creativity is associated with the Child state. Also, the manager will be able to recognize when communication is impossible. For instance, the manager who is in the Adult state may attempt to speak to the Adult state of the employee. The Child state of the employee returns the conversation to the Parent state of the manager. The following dialogue illustrates such a communication problem:

Manager: This task needs to be completed today.
Employee: Why are you always pushing me to work harder?

Communication has broken down because the employee is not addressing the problem that the manager was attempting to communicate.

Managers should also be aware of the ego state that they themselves are speaking from. If the state is properly interpreted, managers can recognize and possibly change their actions. Should you recognize that you are in one state and an employee is in a state that precludes effective communication, it may be best to postpone discussion. For instance, if the manager is in the Child state and the employee is in the Adult state, communication perhaps should be postponed. The employee who is in the Adult state is serious about his or her work at this time and may misinterpret, for instance, joking remarks.

Applying TA concepts on a broad basis may prove valuable in producing desired organizational change. As individuals in a firm learn to analyze their own social interactions, better communication and greater overall effectiveness can occur.

TALKING TO MANAGERS

**Michael Cowpland
Mitel Corp.**

Mitel Corp., a manufacturer of telecommunications equipment and semiconductors, is growing at the exponential velocity exclusive to high-tech organizations. Launched on $12,000 capital in the basement of an Ottawa home in 1975, it was ringing up annual sales of $1.5 million the following year, $11.5 million by 1978, $43.4 million by 1980, and $204 million in 1982. In a recent American study of 2400 publicly listed companies, Mitel was ranked third-equal among the North American corporations predicted to grow fastest between now and 1986. Creators of this startling success story are two English-born engineers, Terry Matthews and Michael Cowpland, both now in their late 30s. When they started in Cowpland's basement they vowed they'd be the world's best at whatever they did, and they seem to have kept that promise.

Q: Is there something in this industry that makes it not only possible but also necessary to grow so fast?

Cowpland: To a certain extent there is. We're looking at the world market and, if we don't grab whatever markets are available, somebody else will. After that they would be building on the strength of their position. We would be at a competitive disadvantage.

Q: Don't you now have to translate the company from entrepreneurial type management into something that will work for a large stable "corporate giant"?

Cowpland: I think that change has been underway almost continuously. Our management approach has changed almost every 6 or 12 months. One of the good things is that we're used to changing. There are thresholds at $1 million in sales; $10 million; $50 million; $100 million. It's a process almost of continuous change.

Q: Although you have grown so fast, Northern Telecom, for example, is a heck of a lot bigger. Does its size give it a considerable advantage? Or do you gain by having flexibility?

Cowpland: All things being equal it's a disadvantage to be big. Our biggest challenge now is to avoid accumulating the disadvantages that we could pick up. Fortunately, having been small so recently, we know how good it is to be small. Therefore we try to organize the company so that we stay responsive and fast-moving.

Q: Every company wants to cut red tape, and keep things informal. Yet they don't manage to do so.

Cowpland: One of the things we've done pretty successfully is keep an open-door policy. You'll notice when you're walking around here that things are open, there are no secrets. That's a policy I push very strongly throughout the company. We don't have a "need-to-know" policy — yet a lot of companies do, even small high-tech companies. They say: "You have no need to know this, therefore I'm not going to give this piece of information to you."

We have the attitude, on the other hand, that if you want to know something you *can* know it. There are only about two or three things that are confidential — they're mainly salaries and maybe the odd pricing deal on special marketing contracts. Apart from that everything is wide open. We flow the information as broadly as possible throughout the company for two reasons. One is that people want to know what's going on from a satisfaction point of view. Nobody wants to be a mushroom. Secondly it's a good training tool because the more that people can see the big picture the better decisions they're going to make in terms of what's good for the whole company.

Q: You can only share information like that if you're enormously self-confident. Traditional corporation people hang on to knowledge as a source of power.
Cowpland: That's right. A lot of people do that just for that purpose. Their knowledge base is their security blanket. The more people share their knowledge base, the less security they have because then they're dispensable. We push very hard to avoid letting that attitude creep in, because it's a real danger. When people are hiding information it can cause real problems. That's why we purposely promote and select people who have a lot of self-confidence. We try to avoid office politics. We try to continue to think about what's best for the company, not what's best for an individual. And we move people around and give them more or less power according to whether they feel that way.

Q: Does your engineering background help you handle the management job? Do these things link?
Cowpland: Not necessarily. But the open, team approach we've taken from Day One is very healthy because we all automatically learn from each other. Even though we have an organizational chart, we all look at each other's areas. There's very little sense of empire because everybody feels free to discuss and even criticize an area that's not his or her own, freely looking over the fence, as it were. Everybody worries about everybody else's area and that's good because it gives people peripheral vision and they don't get tunnel vision. The finance people thus know a lot about our engineering and our marketing guys know a lot about finance. We tend to make people more generalists than specialists, even though they're coming from a pretty specialized knowledge base.

Q: There's periodic talk in Canada about the need for an industrial strategy. Do you think we really need such a thing? Or might that just lead us into all the traps that usually go with central planning?
Cowpland: An industrial strategy as such is a waste of time. What we should have is an encouraging environment. "Strategy" sounds too detailed. If they would just recognize what's obvious to almost everybody, that high tech is going to be a tremendous thing for the future, then they could simply help create an environment which encourages that, recognizing the United States as the standard against which you're going to measure yourself. We have to have an environment which is better than the one in the States. We must have a better environment for raising money for these industries by virtue of better tax arrangements or whatever. We must have a better environment for education. Those are the main things.

Q: Is there a chance of Canada developing its own robotics industry?
Cowpland: We could; but I'm not convinced it's the area we should concentrate on. We now lead in the communications area. Robotics to me sound inherently quite mechanical and the Japanese are so good at mechanical stuff that they'd be tough to compete with. Where the Japanese have been so successful is mainly mechanical — the cars, the cameras, the motorbikes, the videotape recorders. Take one of those apart and you see mechanical wizardry more than anything else. The electronics involved are pretty straightforward. It's a big mistake to try to compete with the mechanical wizardry of the Japanese.

On the other hand, communications technology is almost all electronics and software and it's a much more natural fit for us. In Canada you can't get good craftsmen; they all get imported from eastern Europe and there's only a limited supply. There's no apprentice scheme here to train people who can lathe and machine beautiful parts. That's one reason why robotics would never be a big industry for Canada.

SOURCE Excerpted from Dean Walker, "Michael Cowpland of Mitel", *Executive* (April 1983): 26–32. Reprinted by permission.

EFFECTS OF NEW TECHNOLOGIES

As a consequence of the electronic revolution, communication methods in today's organizations are rapidly changing. Information processing is becoming increasingly automated, with word processors, micro-, mini-, and mainframe computers, as well as new developments in telecommunication and video technology. One reason for the electronics explosion is the tumbling cost of the technology.

Company video, or private television, has had its ups and downs since the late 1960s. Now, though, the problems caused by lack of standardization and compatibility between components have largely been overcome. With the advent of the video-cassette in 1972, video has become an inexpensive alternative for communication. Increasing numbers of managers are turning to this medium for information dissemination.[9] Since many persons are accustomed to, and even prefer, getting information through television, more emphasis is being placed on using video for transmitting corporate information. This medium "puts the face behind the memo."[10] Private television breaks through communication barriers and delivers the message straight, with no filtering by intermediate managers and less chance of misunderstanding through inappropriate prose.

Converging technologies in data and word processing, voice and data communications, networking, electronic mail and computer graphics have made communications more effective and efficient. Large data bases within management information systems (MIS) have speeded up data processing and information flows.[11] Communication networks connect various office machines together, making possible instantaneous electronic transfers of messages, images and data. Contrasted with traditional communication processes, these devices are fast, are convenient, and integrate a variety of communication tasks. "Information democracy" — equal access to information by all organization members — is arriving, as larger numbers of online terminals are installed in corporations.[12]

A new development, combining video, computer, and telecommunication technologies, is **teleconferencing**. Uses of teleconferencing run from the simple speaker phone to full-blown satellite transmitted video.[13] The middle part of this spectrum, audiographics, combines graphics-oriented visual displays with vocal teleconferencing facilities to provide the opportunity for enhanced multisite dialogues.[14] As computer hardware and software become more sophisticated, the machines are becoming more cost effective and user friendly. Fewer skills are required to use the latest systems, facilitating their adoption.

A new technology on the horizon is artificial intelligence (AI). AI computers have been developed to think and learn somewhat as human beings do. Expert systems are computers which can draw highly specialized conclusions from huge stores of data, much as the human brain does. Scientists predict their increasing use in routine management tasks.[15]

The new technologies have, in effect, changed the methods used in organization communications. Many of these devices decrease the effects of barriers to communications. However, they have their built-in limitations. Used ingeniously, they hold immense potential to enhance communication capabilities.

ORGANIZATION CONFLICT

As we noted earlier in this chapter, conflict often occurs as a result of poor communication practices. **Conflict** is behavior by a person or group that is purposely designed to inhibit the attainment of goals by another person or group. This purposeful inhibition may be active or passive. For example, in a sequential production line, if one group does not do its job and its output is the input for another department, the other department will be blocked from reaching its goal of, say, producing at standard. Alternatively, the blocking behavior may be active, like two fighters trying to knock each other out. The key issue in defining conflict is that of incompatible goals. When one person or group deliberately interferes with another person or group with the purpose of denying the other goal achievement, conflict exists.[16]

Two Views of Conflict

Looking back over this century, it becomes obvious that assumptions about whether conflict is good or bad for organizations have changed substantially. There are two distinct phases of thinking about conflict: the traditional view and the current view.

The Traditional View

This view of conflict, which was popular until the early 1940s, assumed that conflict was bad for organizations. In the view of the traditionalists, organization conflict was proof that there was something wrong with the organization. The Hawthorne studies (discussed in Chapter 1) were probably important in shaping the traditional view because in those studies the dysfunctional consequences of conflict were noted. Another likely factor in the traditional view was the development of labor unions and the often violent conflict between labor and management. During the early twentieth century, labor unions were struggling for the legal right to bargain collectively. It was not until the 1930s that this goal was reached. Along the way, many confrontations occurred between labor and management. These were almost always viewed as bad for both the organization and the individual, and it is therefore not surprising that the traditionalists viewed conflict as undesirable. Overall, the traditional view assumed that organization performance declined steadily as conflict increased.

Because conflict was viewed as bad, considerable attention was given to reducing or eliminating it. Perhaps the most general reaction was to suppress it. This was done in an obvious way by simply demanding that people in conflicting situations change their behavior for the good of the company. It was also done indirectly by rigidly prescribing the limits of authority of each job so that individuals would be less likely to be in conflict. While these tactics sometimes worked, they were largely ineffective because: (1) they did not get at the exact cause of the conflict, and (2) suppressing the conflict did not allow any of the positive aspects of conflict to come out.

The traditional view of conflict appears to be losing ground as time passes, yet it still describes the views of many people. Why should this view be so widespread, given that some conflict has been shown to be beneficial? One researcher answers this question by saying that the important institutions in our society — the home, church, and school — are founded on the traditional view of conflict, and these institutions have a powerful influence on society.[17] Since these institutions are very influential when we are young, we are subtly influenced to have a particular view of conflict. In the home, for example, parents suppress conflict by telling their children to stop fighting. In schools, teachers are assumed to have the correct answers, and exams are a check to see whether students are deviating from these. Most churches stress brotherhood and peace, not conflict. If this argument is correct, the change in the view of conflict from traditional to current will take many years.

The Current View

The view which prevails among researchers at present (and is gaining ground in the rest of society) is that organization conflict is neither good nor bad but inevitable. Thus, conflict will occur even if organizations have taken great pains to prevent it. Recall the informal organization, discussed in Chapter 8, where we noted that the informal organization will emerge and be active irrespective of management's attempts to suppress it. Thus, organizations will experience conflict even if they have carefully defined employee jobs and their managers are reasonable people who treat employees well. There are even some instances in which conflict is purposely created, such as the project management structure discussed in Chapter 7.

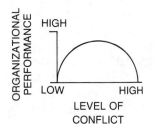

**EXHIBIT 12-4
The current view
of conflict**

The current view of conflict is shown in Exhibit 12-4. When the amount of conflict (low to high) is related to organization performance (low to high), there is an optimum level of conflict which maximizes organization performance. This optimum level is neither low nor high. In an organization where there is too little conflict, little impetus for innovation and creativity exists. Employees are comfortable and not concerned about improving performance. As a result, things which might improve performance get very little attention. At the other extreme, organization conflict is so disruptive that employees cannot give proper attention to performance goals because interpersonal or intergroup conflict saps employee energy. Here again, performance suffers. At moderate levels of conflict, however, employees are motivated to resolve conflicts, but these conflicts do not disrupt the normal work activities.

There are two crucial implications of the current view. First, much of the conflict in organizations may be good because it stimulates people to find new ways of doing things. If two employees are in conflict about the best way to do a job, the manager might be advised to encourage the conflict to see which individual is correct. The best technique can then be used in doing the job in the future. This approach should be used sparingly because it usually results in a winner and a loser and this has implications for the organization. As another example, consider two departments that are in conflict. Each department tries to get its own way and engages in whatever blocking behavior it thinks is necessary to prevent the other department from attaining its goals. Top management may see this as dysfunctional; but, instead of trying to suppress the conflict (the traditional approach), management might try to induce the departments to find a solution which allows each to get its way.

Second, management of conflict, not suppression, becomes a key activity. If conflict can be good or bad, constructive conflict should be encouraged and destructive conflict should be resolved. But what criterion should be used to make this decision? Robbins suggests that the most practical and important criterion is group performance.[18] Organizations exist to achieve goals, and high performance by groups in the organization increases the likelihood that organization goals will be reached. Thus, if the criterion of group performance is used, managers must view conflict in terms of its effect on group performance before they move to resolve it or encourage it. Specific methods for encouraging and discouraging conflict are discussed later.

Sources of Conflict

The sources of conflict within organizations are numerous. Conflict is caused by limited resources — each person or group wants more resources than are available; interdependent work activities — people interfere with each other's work; the formal organizational structure — people in different departments see the world differently; and communication difficulties — people don't say what they mean or they are not understood. These factors motivate people to block the goal attainment of others and open conflict is the result. (See Exhibit 12-5.) Once open conflict has occurred, some decisions must be made about how it will be resolved (see box 5). These resolution techniques may be functional or dysfunctional and, depending on the outcome of the conflict, it may be truly resolved or it may simply reappear later in a different form. These resolution techniques are most important in managing conflict in a functional manner.

Since conflict can be either positive or negative, managers should not simply suppress it but should manage it. **Conflict management** involves dealing with conflict in such a way that the organization and the individuals working in it will benefit from it. It also involves knowing when to stimulate conflict and when to resolve it quickly. Communication is a prominent aspect of conflict management because so many misunderstandings occur when individuals or groups are in conflict. The two basic approaches to the management of conflict are: (1) managing the human (interpersonal) aspects of conflict, and (2) managing the structural aspects of conflict. Several methods that are used in each of these approaches are discussed below.

Interpersonal Conflict Management

The techniques of dealing with interpersonal conflict are numerous. They range from the use of force by a superior over a subordinate to the problem-solving approach. Possible ways of managing interpersonal conflict are discussed below.

Force

When force is used in the resolution of conflict, official authority may compel one party to accept a solution. The expression "he may not be right but he's still the boss" applies in this instance. The party for which the decision was directed may not agree with the results, but if he or she wants to stay within the organization, the directive must be accepted.

Withdrawal

A solution that some individuals use in resolving conflict is to withdraw or avoid the person with whom the conflict exists. Conflict is reduced, but the reason that originated the conflict remains. It would be the same as seeing a person you do not want to speak to approaching you on the street, and you walk around the block to keep from having to speak to the individual.

Smoothing

When smoothing is used, a manager attempts to provide a semblance of peaceful cooperation by presenting an image that they're one big happy family. With this approach, problems are rarely permitted to come to the surface, but the potential for conflict remains.

Compromise

Neither party gets all it wants when compromise is used. This is the most typical way of dealing with labor/management conflict. For ex-

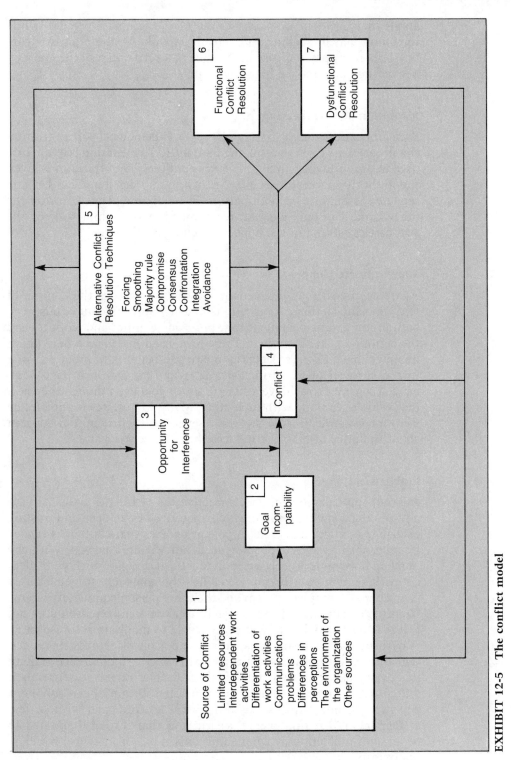

EXHIBIT 12-5   The conflict model

ample, management may offer to increase wages by 8 percent, while the union may be seeking a 12 percent pay hike. A compromise figure of a 10 percent pay increase may result in a settlement of the conflict, but neither side may be happy with it.

Mediation and Arbitration

Both arbitration and mediation call for outside neutral parties to enter the situation to assist in resolving the conflict. **Arbitration** is frequently used in union/management grievance conflicts. The arbitrator is given the authority to act as a judge in making a decision. The decision rendered is binding on both parties. In **mediation**, a mediator on the other hand, can only suggest, recommend, and attempt to keep the two parties talking in the hope of reaching a solution.

Superordinate Goals

At times, a goal may be encountered that supersedes the conflict of two opposing factions. If the firm is in danger of going out of business, both union and management may put aside conflict and work toward the common goal of survival. There have been instances where union members have taken a decrease in pay and benefits in order to assist in the survival of the firm. On a broader level, nations have often banded together to achieve a superordinate goal even though they normally don't get along with each other. Many Arab states in the Middle East, for example, do not see eye-to-eye, but their common concern about the price of oil often induces them to work together.

Problem Solving

Another approach to conflict management is problem solving. As usually practiced, problem solving is characterized by an open and trusting exchange of views and facts. A person realizes that conflict is caused by relationships among people and is not within a person. With the problem-solving approach, an individual can disagree with your ideas and still remain your friend. It is a healthy approach in which rarely is one person completely right and the other person completely wrong. Granting a concession is not a sign of weakness and a person does not feel that he or she has to win every battle to maintain self-respect.

With the problem-solving approach, a person recognizes that a certain amount of conflict is healthy. For instance, if a difference of opinion exists between two individuals and they openly discuss their difficulties, a superior solution often results. With problem solving, a person is encouraged to bring difficulties into the open without fear of reprisal. When this occurs, a situation that initially appeared to be a major problem may evolve into only a minor instance, which is easily resolved.

Structural Conflict Management

Conflict can also be managed by changing procedures, organizational structure, physical layout, or expanding resources. These methods for resolving conflict are discussed next.

Procedural Changes

There are times when conflict can occur because a procedure is illogically sequenced. When a credit manager and a sales manager were both about to be fired because of an irreconcilable personality conflict, it was discovered that the processing of credit applications too late in the procedure was the cause of the difficulty. The credit manager was forced to cancel too many deals already made. When the credit check was placed earlier in the procedure, most of the conflict disappeared. In another instance, the personnel director and the production manager were in continuous disagreement. At times the conflict actually came to blows. Then it was discovered that the production manager was not being permitted to review the applicants at an early stage of the hiring sequence and provide input regarding an applicant. When the procedure was changed, many of the difficulties were resolved.

Organizational Changes

The organization can be changed to either promote or reduce conflict. There are times when a department becomes too complacent and, although there is little conflict, very little is accomplished. To reduce undesired conflict within an organization, transfers of incompatible personnel can be made. Often this procedure is quite acceptable, but a manager must be careful that the workers are transferred for the proper reason. To transfer a worker who is incompetent merely because a manager is afraid to deal with the individual does an injustice to the overall goals of the organization. Some managers begin to suspect an employee who is transferred to their department with too glowing a recommendation. The issue for them is, if the employee is that good why is he moving? If transfers are handled on a professional basis, both the company and the employee benefit.

When the conflict is between two units of the organization, special liaison personnel can be assigned. A traditional problem exists between production and marketing. Production personnel have been taught to cut costs, and the technique to accomplish this goal is to produce as few variations of a product as possible. Marketing personnel want products of different colors, styles, and shapes. A person who understands and appreciates the problems of both departments can greatly assist in resolving conflict.

Physical Layout Changes

Changes in the design of the physical work place have been used effectively to reduce or eliminate conflict. Office space can be designed to either force interaction or to make it difficult. Personnel can use desks as barriers and buffers. Some offices have dividers to separate workers. However, if a manager desires to stimulate a problem-solving atmosphere, a more open office arrangement may be permitted. When known antagonists are seated in conference directly across from each other, the amount of conflict increases. When they are seated side by side, the conflict tends to decrease.

A detrimental conflict involving physical layout existed between two groups of workers in a truck assembly plant. Working at different phases on the assembly line, the two groups came into conflict because both had to obtain parts from the same shelving unit. Each group would deliberately rearrange the other group's supply of parts, which sometimes resulted in fights. The conflict was resolved by moving the shelving unit between the two groups so as to set up a barrier between them. Thus, each group had its own supply area or territory. As a result of this change, mistakes were reduced by 50 percent within two days.[19]

Expand Resources

A source of conflict caused by incompatibility of goals can be reduced if resources can be expanded. Thus, in a growing organization everything seems to run smoothly. When hard times come, competition among employees for a possibly diminishing job supply can cause conflict. As enrollment goes down in some colleges and universities, the battle for graduate assistants begins. Should everyone get a graduate assistant? Should the senior faculty members get one? Or should the most productive (but junior) member get the assistant? The same question must be asked when summer teaching assignments are made. Under these conditions, skills in conflict management of the highest order are demanded. Whatever the situation, the effective use of conflict management will have a major impact on overall organization effectiveness.

OPENING INCIDENT REVISITED

The Business School

After Lane had left his office, Carletti felt remorseful at having lost his temper and began to think of ways that he could make it up to Lane. However, the more he thought about it, the more he realized that he was completely constrained by university regulations and, in fact, could do nothing about Lane's withdrawal. Carletti reasoned that he could apologize for losing his temper but that would probably be little consolation to Lane. The more he thought about it, the more he became convinced that Lane understood him perfectly well but was simply feigning ignorance. Carletti therefore decided to do nothing.

One week later, Carletti received formal notification from the registrar that Lane had been required to withdraw. Carletti was later told by another student that Lane had transferred into liberal arts. He wondered why Lane had so readily accepted the brief written notice from the registrar but had refused to accept his detailed verbal communication in the interview.

This incident is typical of situations where one of the parties in the interview (Lane) simply does not allow understanding to develop. Lane's behavior is not surprising since he has a lot to lose if he is required to withdraw. How should Carletti have dealt with Lane's behavior? First, he should not have attempted to ram the required withdrawal idea down Lane's throat. Rather, he should have explained it clearly and, if Lane did not seem to understand, he should then have asked him to explain the policy on withdrawals.

By listening to what Lane was saying, Carletti could have developed a strategy for overcoming Lane's objections and communicating this unpleasant news to Lane without becoming exasperated.

Second, Carletti should have remained calm throughout the interview. After all, he knew that, in the final analysis, the registrar would deny Lane the right to register for courses in the business school; so, he need not have got excited about it at that stage. If he had remained calm, Carletti may have been able to get through to Lane.

SUMMARY

Communication is defined as the achievement of meaning and understanding between people through verbal and nonverbal means in order to affect behavior and achieve desired results. The source (sender) is the person who has an idea or message to communicate to another person or persons. Encoded messages are transmitted through such means as speaking, writing, acting, and drawing. A number of channels may be used to transmit the message. The receiver of the message must decode it by converting the symbols into meaning. Communication effectiveness is determined to the extent that the receiver's interpretation matches the sender's intention.

There are numerous channels of communication through which a manager transmits information. Downward channels provide means through which management's orders and viewpoints are transmitted to subordinates. Upward channels provide means through which subordinates can communicate with their superiors.

Effective communication is often not achieved because of various breakdowns that can affect the communication process. Barriers may cause communication to be reduced to the point that the firm's objectives cannot be achieved. Barriers may be classified as technical, language, or psychological. Technical barriers include improper timing, communication overload, and cultural differences. Language barriers result when different meanings are applied to the same word or when inappropriate vocabulary is used. Psychological barriers include various forms of distortion and problems involving interpersonal relationships.

Although there are many barriers to communication, there are means available to eliminate or reduce these breakdowns. The use of empathy and the development of good listening skills can facilitate good communication. In addition, improved reading and observation skills, as well as choice of words can aid the manager in better communication with employees. Studying transactional analysis and developing the ability to read body language have also been used to improve a manager's ability to communicate.

Management of conflict is important within an organization because there are so many different backgrounds, experiences, aspirations, and personalities among employees. In its broadest interpretation, conflict management can be used to overcome communication problems by resolving disagreements among individuals within the organization. Conflict management may be classified as interpersonal or structural. Interpersonal conflict management deals with conflict between two or more individuals. Structural conflict management is concerned with changing the structures and processes that can cause conflict.

REVIEW QUESTIONS

1. Define communication. Describe the basic communication process.
2. Distinguish by definition between downward and upward communication. What are examples of both types of channels of communication?
3. What is meant by the phrase "barriers to communication"? Distinguish among technical, language, and psychological barriers.
4. List the aids to communication discussed in this chapter. Briefly define each.
5. Explain how empathy may be used to assist a person to become a better listener.
6. What is transactional analysis? How can it be used as an aid to communication?
7. Describe how conflict management can be used as an aid to communication.

EXERCISES

1. Over a 24-hour period, identify factors and situations that created barriers to communication. Attempt to secure at least one example of each of the barriers to communication identified in the chapter. What aids to communication could have been used to reduce these barriers to effective communication?
2. Visit a business of your choice. Attempt to identify the various means of both downward and upward communication.
3. Try this exercise regarding observation skills. With one of your classmates, go to the window and observe what is occurring on the outside for 10 seconds. Each of you then write down what you saw. After completing the list, compare your list with your partner's list. Compare the differences.

CASE STUDY

The Promise

Philip Watase was in the top 10 percent of his graduating class and was extremely active in social activities. On graduating, Watase had many job opportunities. He took the time to study the firms and the type of positions that were available. He ultimately decided to take a position with Bedford International, a large conglomerate.

Watase and 20 other recent community college graduates were hired as management trainees. All of the management trainees were to start as first-line supervisors. There were no formalized training sessions, just on-the-job training. But, after one year, the individual trainees were all promised advancement to higher-level positions. Watase was considered to possess excellent management potential. During the quarterly progress reviews, he was told that his performance was exceptional in all areas. His employees showed less turnover, lower absenteeism, and higher performance than other similar groups.

Because of the large number of trainees hired and the low turnover rate of managers at Bedford, few openings for the next managerial positions were available. Watase felt that rec-

ognition was nearly impossible. At the end of one year, no new positions were available, yet many promises had been made regarding his advancement opportunities. At the end of 18 months, there were still no new positions available.

A few weeks later, Watase was approached by a professional recruiter and, after several interviews, he received an offer from another company. The offer Watase received included a 20 percent increase in salary and an increase in managerial responsibilities. Watase felt obliged to talk to his supervisor prior to accepting any offers. In his conversation with the supervisor, Watase reminded his supervisor of the promises that had been made but not fulfilled.

QUESTIONS

1. What do you believe Philip Watase should do with regard to the job offer?
2. How do you believe Watase's supervisor should answer the questions that he asked?
3. What problems in communication are evident in this case?

CASE STUDY

The Management Trainee

Lois Atkins, a recent graduate, had just joined Bellingham Electric Company as a management trainee. Bellingham was a manufacturer of electric light bulbs, transformers, and generators. Bellingham had been successful over a period of many years in recruiting management trainees through university and community college placement offices. In a typical year, the company would hire 200 management trainees from their recruiting efforts.

The company had a well-established management training program, lasting one year, during which time the trainee was assigned to a branch location to learn various phases of company operations. The program, designed to prepare

individuals for branch management, included training in: shipping and receiving, inventory control, purchasing, personnel, production, order service, and outside sales. In addition to this on-the-job experience, the trainee returned to headquarters 4 times during the year for one week of classroom-type instruction and to compare notes and review individual progress with members of upper management.

Atkins was assigned to a branch operation in Hamilton and was under direct supervision of Clayton Thomas, the branch manager. Thomas, 55, had been with Bellingham for 35 years. He had not attended college but had worked his way up and believed this way of making it into management provided better training than the company's one-year rotation program. Atkins was assigned to perform various jobs in the branch but not according to the planned program. Atkins was asked to fill in as needed: she became concerned about not receiving the type of training required to prepare her for her first management position.

During her second trip to headquarters for a one-week training session, Atkins discussed her problem with the coordinator of management training and development, John Wilson. Wilson assured Atkins that he would look into the matter. On her return to the branch, Atkins was reprimanded by Thomas for discussing the problem with Wilson. The conversation proceeded as follows:

Thomas: Lois, why did you discuss your problems with John Wilson? You work for me, at least as long as you're at this branch.

Atkins: I don't know — I guess I was just frustrated with the training I've received.

Thomas: You're just like a lot of young college graduates. You think your degree should entitle you to special treatment. Well, I'm sorry, but in my book it doesn't mean a thing.

Atkins: What should I do now?

Thomas: Go back to work and don't cause any more trouble.

QUESTIONS

1. What action do you think Lois Atkins should take?
2. To what extent should John Wilson have discussed Atkins's problem with the local branch manager, Clayton Thomas?
3. What evidence is there of a breakdown in communication between the branch office and the intentions of headquarters? Discuss.

NOTES

1 M. L. Fahs, "Communication Strategies for Anticipating and Managing Conflict," *Personnel Administrator* (October 1982): 28–34.
2 R. Foltz and R. D'Aprix, "Survey Shows Communication Problems," *Personnel Administrator* (February 1983): 8.
3 Foltz and D'Aprix.
4 Robert Gunning, "How to Improve Your Writing," *Factory Management and Maintenance* 110 (June 1952): 134.
5 "Trust: The New Ingredient in Management," *Business Week* (July 6, 1981): 104.
6 Carl R. Rogers and F. J. Roethlisberger, "Barriers and Gateways to Communication," *Harvard Business Review* 30 (July-August 1952): 48.
7 D. K. Denton, "Protecting Against Communication Fallout," *Management World* (April 1983): 28–30.
8 For an expanded coverage of transactional analysis, see Thomas A. Harris, *I'm O.K.–You're O.K.* (New York: Harper, 1969).
9 J. M. Brush and D. P. Brush, "Companies Tune in to Video," *Management World* (January 1984): 25.
10 Brush, 25.
11 P. F. Calise and M. Locke, "Office Automation: Who's in Control?" *Management World* (March 1984): 17.
12 Z. K. Quible, and R. A. Ankerman, "Office Connections," *Management World* (December 1983): 31.
13 Quible, 31.

14 L.G.A. Graham, "Audiographics for Sound Teleconferencing," *Computer World* 17:394 (September 28, 1983): 63.

15 "Artificial Intelligence Is Here," *Business Week* (July 9, 1984): 54.

16 This view of conflict was proposed in S. Schmidt and T. Kochan, "Conflict: Toward Conceptual Clarity," *Administrative Science Quarterly* 17 (1972): 359–370.

17 S. Robbins, *Organizational Behavior* (Englewood Cliffs, N.J.: Prentice-Hall, 1979): 289.

18 Robbins, 288.

19 H. Kenneth Bobele and Peter J. Buchanan, "Building a More Productive Environment," *Management World* 8 (January 1979): 8.

REFERENCES

Allen, T. H. "Communication Networks: The Hidden Organizational Chart." *Personnel Administrator* 21 (September 1976): 31–35.

Axley, Stephen R. "Managerial and Organizational Communication in Terms of the Conduit Metaphor." *Academy of Management Review* 9, no. 3 (July 1984): 428–437.

Davis, Keith, "Cut Those Rumors Down to Size." *Supervisory Management* 20 (June 1975): 2–6.

Deutsch, A. R. "Does Your Company Practice Affirmative Action in Its Communication?" *Harvard Business Review* 54 (November-December 1976): 16.

Donath, Bob. "Corporate Communications." *Industrial Marketing* 65 (July 1980): 52–53.

Ewing, David W., and Banks, Pamela M. "Listening and Responding to Employees' Concerns." *Harvard Business Review* 58 (January-February 1980): 101–114.

Foltz, Roy G. "Internal Communications, Give Them Facts." *Public Relations Journal* 36 (October 1980): 35.

Gildea, Joyce A., and Emanuel, Myron. "Internal Communications: The Impact on Productivity." *Public Relations Journal* 36 (February 1980): 8–12.

Hargreaves, J. "Six Keys to Good Communications." *International Management* 31 (December 1976): 54–56.

Huseman, R. C. "Managing Change Through Communication." *Personnel Journal* 57 (January 1978): 20–25.

Kikoski, John F. "Communication: Understanding It, Improving It." *Personnel Journal* 59 (February 1980): 126.

Laing, G. J. "Communication and Its Constraints on the Structure of Organizations." *Omega* 8 (1980): 287–301.

Leavitt, Harold J. *Managerial Psychology.* 2d ed. Chicago: University of Chicago Press, 1964.

Levine, Edward. "Let's Talk: Breaking Down Barriers to Effective Communication." *Supervisory Management* 25 (August 1980): 3–12.

Lewis, Carl B. "How to Make Internal Communications Work." *Public Relations Journal* 36 (February 1980): 14–17.

McMaster, J. B. "Getting the Word to the Top." *Management Review* 68 (February 1979): 62–65.

Miles, James M. "How to Establish a Good Industrial Relations Climate." *Management Review* 67 (August 1980): 42–44.

Muchinsky, P. M. "Organizational Communication: Relationships to Organizational Climate and Job Satisfaction." *Academy of Management Journal* 20 (December 1977): 592–607.

Roberts, Karlene H., and O'Reilly, Charles A. III. "Failures in Upward Communication in Organizations: Three Possible Culprits." *Academy of Management Journal* 17 (June 1974): 205–215.

Schuler, Randall S. "Effective Use of Communication to Minimize Employee Stress." *Personnel Administrator* 24 (June 1979): 40–44.

Tavernier, Gerard. "Improving Managerial Productivity: The Key Ingredient Is One-on-One Communication." *Management Review* 70 (February 1981): 13–16.

Weiner, Andrew. "Stay in Control by Mastering the Art of Listening Well." *Executive* (September 1983): 14.

13

Organization Culture, Change, and Development

Craig Ltd.

Lorna Kasian was the assistant to the president of Craig Ltd., a manufacturing firm located in Halifax. Her job occasionally included overseeing special projects that were given to her by the president. Recently, he had asked her to draw up plans for renovations to the company's administrative offices, and to see that the renovations proceeded efficiently and on time. Kasian was looking forward to this project because one of the outcomes would be a new office for her.

Because Kasian wanted to make a good impression on the president, she immediately put the project at the top of her priority list. She gave considerable thought to what should be included in the renovations; then she contacted a local architect and had him draw up renovation plans. When the blueprints were ready, Kasian circulated a memo to all those who would be affected by the renovation and invited them to a meeting to announce the changes that would be made.

At the meeting, everything went wrong. Several secretaries who were going to have to move their work stations as a result of the renovation were very upset. After they had received Kasian's memo, they had got together on their own time and drawn up an alternate plan, which Kasian could immediately see was better than hers. They argued that the renovations should be delayed until everyone had a chance to comment on them.

Several other groups were also upset. The drafting department members, for instance, complained that their proposed new quarters were unacceptable and that no one had consulted them about the specialized type of space they needed.

The marketing people complained that there was no area where sales meetings could be held. They reminded Kasian that the president had promised that, when renovations were made, a large meeting room would be included.

Kasian was exhausted by the time the meeting ended. She was concerned that the president would hear about the negative tone of the meeting, and that it would reflect badly on her. She also felt obliged to consult with several of the more vocal groups at the meeting. She realized that she would need more time and that the renovations project could not possibly be completed by the time the president wanted. Kasian thought to herself: "If only I had talked to some of these people before I had the renovation plans drawn up!"

KEY TERMS

corporate culture	survey feedback	management
participative culture	team building	development
organization	process consultation	programs
development	sensitivity training	stress
change agent		executive burnout

LEARNING OBJECTIVES

After completing this chapter you should be able to

1. Explain the concept of corporate culture and describe the factors that determine it.
2. Describe a participative culture and identify the values and limitations of participation.
3. Identify and describe the change sequence and relate sources of resistance to change and the approaches that can be used in reducing resistance to change.
4. Describe the organization development techniques that are available to implement change.
5. Explain the causes of stress management and executive burnout.

The basic management function of influencing can be performed by individual managers through motivation, leadership, and communication. The management of an entire organization, however, can influence all employees as well as factors in its external environment. In this chapter we examine three distinct, but closely related organization-wide topics regarding influencing.

We begin by looking at the concept of corporate culture (also often called organizational climate). The term is defined, the factors that influence culture are identified, and the various types of cultures that employees may experience are noted. The second major section of the chapter deals with organization change. We describe the change sequence and note some reasons why people resist change. We also offer suggestions on how to reduce people's resistance to change. The third section of the chapter explains what overall organization development is and the various techniques of organization development that are available to managers. We make the distinction between management development and organization development. The chapter concludes with a discussion of management stress and executive burnout and how companies can cope with these problems.

CORPORATE CULTURE DEFINED

The psychological atmosphere of the firm is described as its **corporate culture**. It is composed of such factors as friendliness, supportiveness, and flexibility. The culture of an organization may be characterized as, for instance, open and supportive. The perception of culture is gradually formed over time as a person performs an assigned activity under the general guidance of a superior and a set of organizational rules. The culture existing within a firm has an impact on employee satisfaction and performance. The assessment of the quality of the organization's culture is a subjective one made by the employee. One person may perceive a corporate culture as negative, while another may perceive the same culture in positive terms. An employee may actually leave an organization in the hope of finding a better culture.

In the early 1980s, several best-selling books were written on the topic of corporate culture. Books like *In Search of Excellence*[1] and *Corporate Cultures*[2] show how the atmosphere of an organization can have an enormous effect on employee satisfaction, employee productivity, and corporate profitability.

Factors that Determine Corporate Culture

The previous three chapters concentrated on the topics of motivation, leadership, and communication. These topics were presented prior to a discussion of corporate culture because of the impact they can have on a firm's psychological atmosphere. Several factors affect corporate culture: work groups, organization characteristics, supervision, and administration.[3] These factors are shown in Exhibit 13-1. As you can see, it would be difficult to discuss these topics without a good understanding of the concepts of motivation, leadership, and communication.

The nature of the immediate work group will affect a person's perception of the corporate culture. The factor "commitment" refers to whether or not this group is just going through the motions associated with a job. If so, it would be difficult for a particular individual to derive high levels of output and satisfaction. The factor "hindrance" is concerned with the degree to which a great deal of busywork of doubtful value is given to the group. Morale and friendliness within the group are factors with which you should be familiar.

The leadership style of the immediate supervisor will have a noticeable impact on the culture of the group. If the manager is aloof and distant in dealing with subordinates, the atmosphere will tend toward coolness. If the supervisor is always pushing for more output, this pressure will also influence the culture. Thrust refers to supervisory behavior characterized by personally working hard and setting an example. Consideration is a leadership characteristic.

Organizational characteristics may also affect a firm's corporate culture. Organizations vary on such attributes as size and complexity. Large organizations tend toward higher degrees of specialization and greater impersonalization. Labor unions often find that large firms are easier to organize than smaller ones because employees in smaller firms tend to be closer and have more informal relationships with management. Complex organizations tend to employ a greater number of professionals and specialists, who formalize the general approach to problem solving. Organizations also vary in the degree to which they write memos and attempt to program behavior through rules, procedures, and regulations. They can also be distinguished on the basis of the degree of decentralization of decision-making authority, which affects the degree of autonomy and freedom of personnel within the organization.

Corporate culture is also affected by administrative processes. Firms that can develop a direct link between performance and rewards tend to create climates conducive to achievement. Communication systems that are open and free-flowing tend to promote participation and creativity. General attitudes toward the handling of risk and the tolerance of conflict will, in turn, have considerable impact on the type of teamwork effected. They also affect the amount of innovation and creativity exhibited by the organization.

From the 16 factors in Exhibit 13-1, organization members will develop a subjective impression of the kind of place they work in. This general impression will have some impact on performance, satisfaction, creativity, and commitment to the organization.

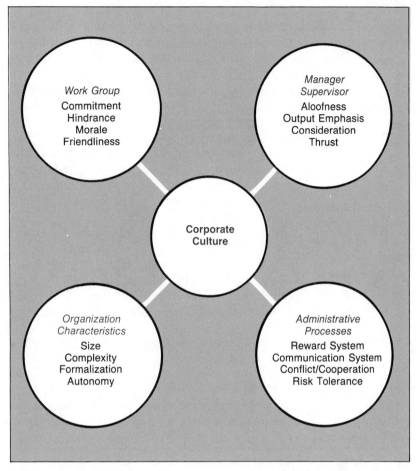

EXHIBIT 13-1
Factors that determine corporate culture

Types of Culture

At times an organization must alter its culture in order to survive. What are the types of corporate culture a firm might wish to emulate, and why should one particular culture prove superior to another? The one advocated by most behavioralists, such as Rensis Likert and Robert Blake, is the open and/or **participative culture**, characterized by such attributes as:

- Trust in subordinates
- Openness in communications
- Considerate and supportive leadership
- Group problem solving
- Worker autonomy
- Information sharing
- Establishment of high output goals.

Some behavioralists contend that this is the only viable culture for all organizations.

The opposite of this open and supportive culture is a closed and threatening one. It, too, is characterized by high output goals. But such goals are more likely to be declared and imposed on the organization by autocratic leaders through threats. There is greater rigidity in this culture, which results from strict adherence to the formal chain of command, narrower spans of management, and stricter individual accountability. The emphasis is on individual work rather than on teamwork. Employee reactions are often characterized by going through the motions and following orders.

Despite support by behavioralists, a more participative philosophy may not work on all occasions. In one instance involving the packaging of inexpensively priced china, low productivity of the work group was caused by excessive and unnecessary interaction among employees during working hours. Management found that the threat of termination did not prevent the unproductive talking because these low-skilled and low-paid employees were eligible for government subsidy programs. In this situation space allocated to the china packaging process was redesigned by building cubicles for each worker. These cubicles, constructed of sound-proofing material, virtually eliminated the unproductive conversation between workers. As a result, productivity increased substantially and employee turnover was reduced. The total cost was $3,200 — recovered during the first 3 weeks.[4]

The Participative Culture

The prevailing managerial approach in most organizations is to impose considerable structure on the work performance. Consequently, most

MANAGEMENT IN PRACTICE

A Change of Culture at Ford Canada

For the past several decades, an adversarial corporate culture has existed at Ford Motor Company. The adversaries are the union and company management. At several points during its history, Ford has had very bad labor relations, but that may be starting to change. The company is trying to dismantle the adversary system, and one of the techniques it is using to achieve this is Employee Involvement (EI). This system involves teams of workers and management cooperating to make the company more competitive.

John Chick, an EI team member who works on the motor mount line, says that, when he started work at Ford, things were done through fear and the best foremen were those whose subordinates were scared of them. Now, the EI program has changed the work atmosphere and management actively pursues worker suggestions on how to improve operations.

There is some fear that the new culture will disappear when the economic downturn is over. Japanese competition and the recession caused management to implement the program in an attempt to improve productivity and quality. If economic good times return, will the program be abandoned?

SOURCE Daniel Stoffman, "Blue-Collar Turnaround Artists," *Canadian Business* (February 1984): 41.

of the attempts to alter corporate culture have been directed toward creating a more open, flexible, and participative culture. The theme of participation developed by individuals such as McGregor, Herzberg, and Maslow relates primarily to self-actualization, motivation factors, consultative and democratic leadership, job enrichment, and management by objectives.

Values of Participation

The possible values of involving more people in the decision-making process within a firm relate primarily to productivity and morale. Increased productivity can result from the stimulation of ideas and from the encouragement of greater effort and cooperation. If employees are psychologically involved, they will often respond to shared problems with innovative suggestions and extra effort. Open and participative cultures are often used to improve the levels of morale and satisfaction. Specific goals in this area include:

• Increased acceptability of management's ideas
• Increased cooperation with members of management
• Reduced turnover
• Reduced absenteeism
• Reduced complaints and grievances
• Greater acceptance of changes
• Improved attitudes toward the job and the organization.

In general, the development of greater employee participation appears to have a direct and immediate effect on employee morale. Employees take a greater interest in the job and the organization. They tend to accept, and sometimes initiate, changes not only because of their understanding of the necessity for change but also because their fear of insecurity has been reduced by knowing more about the change. Unfortunately, there is little evidence that suggests a positive relationship between job satisfaction and productivity. If productivity is not harmed by participation, it would appear that merely improving morale would make a program worthwhile. If productivity decreases, then management will have to make some tough decisions about the use of participation.

Limit of Participation

There are certain prerequisites and limits to greater employee participation in decision making. The requirements for greater participation in decision making are: (1) sufficient time; (2) adequate ability and interest on the part of the participants; and (3) restrictions generated by the current structure and system.

If immediate decisions are required, time cannot be spared for group participation. The manager decides what to do and issues the order accordingly. Should management decide to switch from a practice of

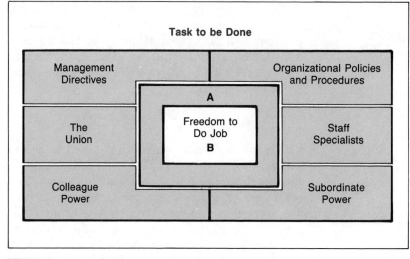

EXHIBIT 13-2 Limits to participative freedom

SOURCE   Edwin B. Flippo and Gary M. Munsinger, *Management*, 5th ed. (Boston: Allyn and Bacon, 1982): 360. Reprinted by permission.

autocracy to one of increased participation, some time for adjustment on the part of both parties will be required. Participation calls for employees to gain some measure of ability to govern themselves instead of leaning on others. In addition, time is required for subordinates to learn to handle this new-found freedom and for supervisors to learn to trust subordinates.

Whether greater involvement in decision making can be developed largely depends on the ability and interest of the participants, both subordinates and managers. This concept is not easy to implement. Obviously, if the subordinate has neither knowledge of nor interest in a subject, there is little need to consult. As organizations and technology become increasingly complex and as management becomes more professionalized, it is likely that employee participation will become more characterized by cooperation seeking or information gathering. We should also note that not all employees are equally interested in participation. Managers must face the fact that some workers do not seek more responsibility and greater involvement in their jobs.

Finally, as indicated in Exhibit 13-2, some restrictions to participative culture are caused by the organization's structure. An individual employee's task may be governed by management directives, organization policies and procedures, the union contract, relations with the union steward, staff specialists, and the degree to which the manager can obtain the cooperation of subordinates. The greater the area in the Freedom To Do Job section of Exhibit 13-2, the greater the degree of participative freedom available. In the illustration, *A* would have more freedom to accomplish the job than *B*.

ORGANIZATION CHANGE

The topic of managing change is one that comes closest to describing the totality of a manager's job. Practically everything a manager does is in some way concerned with implementing change. Hiring a new employee (changing the work group), purchasing a new piece of equipment (changing work methods), and rearranging work stations (changing work flows) all require knowledge of how to manage change effectively. Virtually every time a manager makes a decision some type of change occurs.

Change is a fact of life in all organizations. One study showed that most companies or divisions of major corporations find that they must undertake moderate organization changes at least once a year and major changes every 4 or 5 years. There are different levels of change, which range from a minor change in a work procedure all the way to a major revamping of the organization structure.

Recognizing that change occurs frequently should not imply that change should be introduced for change's sake. Managers should ask themselves: "Is this change really necessary?" There are some who unwisely believe that changes should be made for the sake of change. Managers who do so may create a disruptive effect on their section. When one of the authors was working as a consultant for a manufacturing firm, he inadvertently noticed a note on the desk of a new vice-president who had been brought in from the outside to attempt to improve the performance of a division that was doing poorly. The note said: "Do not make any major changes for 3 months." The new executive obviously wanted to be aware of the total situation before changes were made. If he began to make changes immediately, inappropriate changes could be made and an entire division could be further damaged. Organizations and people desire some degree of stability in order to accomplish their assigned tasks. But there are times when changes are necessary and failure to make them effectively can have a disastrous effect.

The Change Sequence

The sequence of events needed to bring about change in an organization is shown in Exhibit 13-3. Management must first recognize that there is a need for change. Then the specific change method(s) must be chosen. The actual change process cannot begin until these stages are completed.

Recognition of the Need for Change

Managers must train themselves constantly to seek improvement activities (areas for change). This is not always easy because of the tendency to permit existing conditions to continue; this attitude says basically that, if something was successful in the past, it will likely continue to be successful in the future. Managers and employees who view their ongoing performance as successful often resist any changes because the old way is comfortable. If their system is modified, people fear for their job, status, power, or whatever is meaningful to them. There are three basic conditions — curiosity and discontent, open-mindedness, and respect for oneself — a manager must develop in order to recognize that change is needed and to have the courage to implement the change.[5]

Curiosity and discontent are two terms that form perhaps a strange combination with regard to establishing a condition to recognize that change is desirable. A person should have sufficient curiosity to ask searching questions regarding why a task is being performed in a certain manner; it is vital in recognizing where change for improvement is needed. Discontent, on the other hand, has the implication that a person should fight the system. He or she is not satisfied merely to let things go along in their established pattern and concede that the old way is the best way. Through curiosity and discontent, managers place themselves in a position to recognize when a change may be needed.

Managers who believe that their way is always the best will recognize that a change is needed only if they personally make the discovery. Subordinates' opinions are not considered. Managers who are open-minded recognize and permit subordinates to make suggestions. They believe that, many times, two heads are better than one and that useful ideas can evolve from lower-level personnel if they are provided the opportunity.

Managers understand that any change is likely to be met with some resistance. However, managers who have respect for themselves do not fear to attempt a modification that may draw initial resistance but will eventually result in a better operation. These individuals believe in their ability.

Identifying the Change Method

Management has at its disposal numerous techniques that can be used to implement organization change. Specific techniques, discussed later, include survey feedback, team building, process consultation, management by objectives, job enrichment, and sensitivity training. The technique chosen should meet the needs of the organization in reacting to its external environment; it should also identify the type of culture that will provide for the greatest productivity in the organization.

The Process of Change

The steps involved in the change process are easier to describe than they are to implement. Simply stated, the change process as outlined by Lewin, involves 3 fundamental stages: (1) unfreeze the status quo,

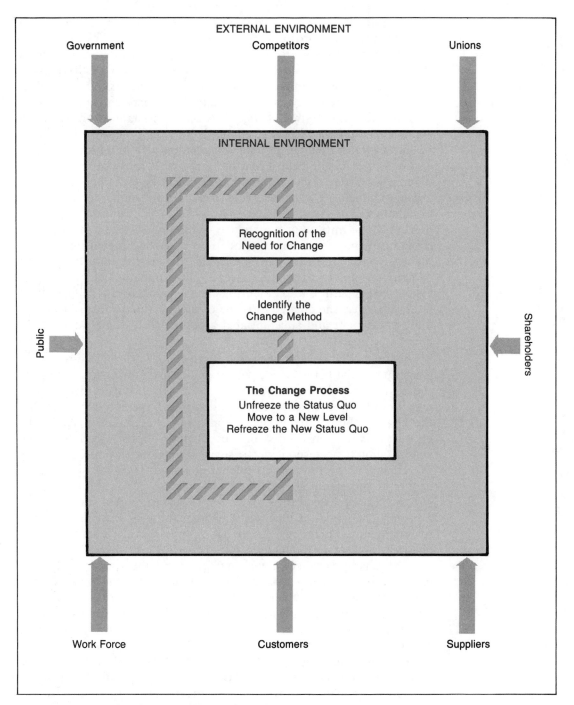

EXHIBIT 13-3   The change sequence

(2) move to the new level, and (3) refreeze at the new level, which becomes the new status quo.[6]

First, if individuals are to change their present attitudes, current beliefs must be altered; the status quo must be unfrozen. Resistance to change must be eliminated or reduced if a change is to be effective. Once resistance to change has been reduced, the manager is in a position to implement the desired change. Sources of resistance to change and approaches to reduce it are discussed later.

Unfreezing in the change process generates self-doubt and provides a means of remedying the situation. Employees must be made to feel that ineffectiveness is undesirable but it can be remedied. If organization members are to be receptive to change, they must feel that they can change.

Second, the initiation of a change — moving to a new level — can come from an order, a recommendation, or a self-directed impetus. A manager with authority can command that a change be made and enforce its implementation by threats, punishments, and close supervision. If this path of implementing change is taken, the manager will likely find that the change must be constantly monitored. Change is more permanent and substantial if a person truly wants and feels a need to change.

The most effective approach to initiate change is for a two-way relationship to exist between the person who is attempting to implement the change and the person who will be changed. Rather than a one-way flow of commands or recommendations, the person implementing the change should make suggestions, and the changees should be encouraged to contribute and participate. Those initiating the change should be responsive to suggestion, either by reformulating the change or by providing explanations as to why the suggestions cannot be incorporated.

Third, the new level must be frozen to become a new status quo; if a person changes to a new set of work habits for a week and then reverts to former practices, the change has not been effective. Too often changes that are introduced do not stick. If the change is to be permanent, changees must be convinced that it is in their own and the organization's best interest. One of the best ways to accomplish this is to collect objective evidence of the success of the change. A manager who sees production increase because of a change in leadership style has obtained excellent evidence of the success of the change. People should have feelings of competence and pleasure in using the new behavior. But the change will be completely accepted only if the reward system of the organization is geared to the new form of behavior. If a university states that all their faculty must publish more articles but no reward is attached to publishing, few faculty members will likely be motivated to make this change. An employee's job may be substantially enriched in terms of content and self-supervision but, if the change is not accomplished by properly enriched pay and status symbols, dissatisfaction is likely to result.

Sources of Resistance to Change

A change may involve some loss to the person who is affected by it. Attachments to familiar habits, places, and people must be given up. In major and unexpected changes, there is often daze, shock, recoil, and turmoil.[7] Some of the many sources of resistance to change are described next.

Insecurity

Once people have operated in a particular atmosphere for a long time, they begin to feel comfortable. Change often brings with it uncertainty; workers do not know exactly what to expect. For example, many students experience insecurity as they made the transition from high school to college. A similar sense of insecurity is felt by individuals who move from one job to another or from one city to another. Perhaps because of this feeling of insecurity so many people resist change, both in their personal and professional lives.

Possible Social Loss

A change has the potential to bring about social losses. As we discussed in Chapter 8, the informal work group may be extremely powerful. If change causes individuals in the group to be transferred, the power of the group is likely diminished. A change may cause established status symbols to be destroyed or an individual of lower status may even be awarded a high-status symbol.

The impact a change can have on social atmosphere was illustrated to one of the authors who was doing a consulting job for a small hospital that had decided to expand from 100 to 300 beds. In one department, all personnel reported directly to the department head, and a close rapport had developed among the members. On a rotating shift, staff members would have to work the evening and night shift, but they still maintained close contact with the other department members. Because of the great increase in work load the work force was expanded; a decision was made to have 3 shifts with a shift supervisor for each shift. The department head now had only 3 people reporting directly to him, and it was believed that the work could be performed much more efficiently. But the social loss was drastic. Subordinates no longer had a close relationship with the department head; some, because they were on a different shift, rarely saw the department head. This created a tremendous social loss to several long-term employees and resulted in over 50 percent of the personnel quitting within 6 months.

Economic Losses

Technology may be introduced that can produce the same amount of output with fewer personnel. While most companies make an honest attempt to transfer or retain employees who have been affected by technological change, the fear remains. When the computer was first introduced into a firm, the number of clerical personnel needed was often drastically reduced. The computer firms attempted to lessen this fear by claiming that the number of jobs had actually increased through the use of the computer. This claim was not very convincing to clerical employees, many of whom resisted the retraining necessary. To them, the new computer technology was a major threat. Use of robots on production lines has caused similar concern for assembly-line workers.

Inconvenience

Even if there is no social or economic loss associated with a change, it may still be resisted simply because it represents a new way of doing things. New procedures and techniques may have to be learned. This means that physical and mental energy must be expended — for some people this is not an enjoyable task. When a new phone system is installed in an organization, there initially can be many complaints. The new system means that time and effort must be expended in learning how a previously easy instrument now has to be used. It can take months for the system to be accepted by a majority of the firm's personnel at all levels of the structure.

Resentment of Control

Taken as a whole, Canadians are rather independent. When employees are told that a change must take place, they realize that they do not have control over their destiny. Even though the change may be for the better, a certain amount of resentment may develop. For instance, one government agency decided to implement a management by objectives (MBO) system. While management pointed out the many benefits of the new MBO system, many employees resented the new approach to planning and goal setting because they perceived it as a threat to their way of life in the organization.

Unanticipated Repercussions

Because the organization is a system, a change in one part is likely to have unforeseen repercussions in another portion. For example, a newly enriched job is likely to demand a change in supervisory behavior. The supervisor may resist this change in behavior even though he or she initially supported the concept of job enrichment.

Union Opposition

Labor union representatives in an adversarial atmosphere are inclined to oppose on principle any change suggested by management. Employees are often more comfortable with a fighting union than they are with one that cooperates with management on changes designed to promote organizational interest.

MANAGEMENT IN PRACTICE

Introducing Change at Cardinal

In 1982, Cardinal Meat Specialists Ltd. of Mississauga, Ontario wanted to introduce a change involving the way its employees were paid. The change involved introduction of a major productivity gain-sharing program that was designed to improve employee productivity and to satisfy employee requests for higher income.

The change was introduced in 4 phases. First, consultants did a feasibility study to determine whether the work the company did would allow the setting of quantitative standards which could be used to measure productivity accurately. Second, a plan was developed to implement the new system. All employees who were affected by the change were consulted and their views listened to. Third, both employees and management of the company got involved in implementing the change. All actions were explained to employees in small group sessions and in regular written communications. Finally, follow-up discussions were conducted with both employees and management to determine if the program was operating to the company's satisfaction.

SOURCE Sandra Bernstein, "Morale Booster: Productivity Gain-Sharing Helps You Get More From Your Workers," *Canadian Business* (April 1984): 122.

Reducing Resistance to Change

One of the authors, while working as a personnel administrator for a large insurance company, observed that an anticipated introduction of computers brought about considerable employee resistance. Management of the company had announced that a new computer system with greatly increased capacity would be installed in about 6 months. The new computer would bring substantial changes in many of the clerical jobs performed by office personnel. Uncertain as to what to expect from the change in computer systems, numerous employees began expressing fear and concern about the impact of the change.

Before management took any action, the employees caused a severe slowdown in work flow in the office. Customer and agent complaints rose substantially during the 6-week period after the announced change. Management therefore took action to correct the situation by holding a series of small group meetings to explain the new computer system and how it would affect each job and each work group. While there would be several major changes in job functions affecting some individuals and work groups, management made a commitment to all employees that no one would be dismissed as a result of the installation of the new computer. The company would provide retraining programs to increase the affected employees' skills, thereby improving their adaptability to the new system.

This incident demonstrates the importance of having a change strategy worked out before any change announcements are made. In the insurance company, management had not anticipated employee uncertainty; it had to scramble around on short notice to come up with a program that would reduce employees' fears and would get them to concentrate on their normal work. Fortunately, everything worked out all right, but the change was not planned very well.

When developing the change strategy, several principles should be kept in mind to reduce resistance. These are discussed below.

Make Only Necessary Changes

Changes should be made only when the situation demands, not because of a whim on the part of a manager. A manager who gains a reputation for making change for the sake of change will discover that the support for any change, whether beneficial or not, will be minimal.

Attempt To Maintain Useful Informal Relationships

We noted in Chapter 8 that the informal work group is a powerful force in organizations. Therefore, when introducing change, every effort must be made to ensure that crucial informal relationships, status hierarchies, or group norms are not disrupted. When safety shoes were first introduced, for example, few workers would wear them willingly because of their appearance. When they were redesigned to resemble dress shoes, resistance faded. The granting of fictional rank to civilian consultants who are to work with military personnel makes their integration into ongoing operations more understandable and acceptable. A staff expert who wants a change introduced may find it advisable to have the announcement made by a line executive with some sharing of the credit. Changes that go against established customs and informal norms will likely cause resistance and reduce the chance of acceptance.

Build Trust

If a manager has obtained a reputation for providing reliable and timely information to employees in the past, the explanation as to why a change is to be made will likely be more believable. The change may still be resisted but, if the manager is trusted by the employees, problems will be minimized. On the other hand, managers who have gained a reputation for providing incomplete or inaccurate information will experience considerable resistance as they attempt to institute change.

Provide Information in Advance

Whenever possible, the manager should provide in advance the reasons for the change, its nature, planned timing, and the possible impact on the organization and its personnel. Withholding information that could seriously affect the lives and futures of particular individuals, such as keeping secret the planned closure of a plant in order to preserve the work-force level until the last possible moment, should be avoided. The firm that gains a reputation for such actions will have a difficult time making future changes. There are occasions when competitive survival requires that information be closely held until shortly before introduction. In these cases, the information should be provided on an as required basis.

Encourage Participation

When possible, subordinate participation should be encouraged in establishing the change. A person who is involved in implementing change procedures will likely be more supportive of the change. Recall from Chapter 10 that Theory Y assumes that abilities are widespread in the population. Thus, many valuable ideas may be gained by permitting employees a degree of participation in implementing the change.

Guarantee against Loss

To promote acceptance of technological changes, some organizations guarantee no layoffs as a result of such changes. In cases of a change in methods and output standards, employees are often guaranteed retention of their present level of earnings during the learning period.

Provide Counseling

At times some form of nonthreatening discussion and counseling may be required. Nondirective counseling has been used effectively in many change situations. The approach rests on a fundamental belief that people have the ability to solve their problems with the aid of a sympathetic listener. The role of a counselor is one of understanding rather than of passing judgment. This requires a permissive, friendly atmosphere, with actions and statements that exhibit continuing interest but not judgment. In most instances, managers with authority are unable to establish this type of atmosphere. Successful nondirective counseling must usually be undertaken by staff psychologists. What the manager can do is to permit some subordinate ventilation of feelings, particularly those of frustration and anger. Discovering that others have similar feelings and doubts will often make the transition less painful.

ORGANIZATION DEVELOPMENT

Change that involves the entire organization is called organization development (OD). Although the term *organization development* has come into use only recently, practicing managers have been trying to improve organizations for many decades. OD is thus not a new activity but rather an extension of efforts that have been made during the long history of organizations. In the most general sense, OD is the attempt to improve the overall effectiveness of an organization. Since it is such a broad concept in practice, many different definitions have been proposed. However, we think the following definition conveys its important features: **organization development** is the systematic effort to improve the overall, long-term functioning of the organization, with emphasis usually placed on participative decision making and the development of a collaborative culture. The person who is responsible for assuring that the planned change in OD is properly implemented is referred to as a **change agent**. This individual may be either an external or an internal consultant. Change agents are knowledgeable about OD techniques and they use this knowledge to assist organization change.

When an organization first attempts to change, outside consultants are often used. An outside expert may bring more objectivity to a situation and be better able to obtain acceptance by and trust from organization members. With time, internal consultants may move into the role of a change agent.

Organization Development Techniques

Among the many organization development techniques available to management are: survey feedback, team building, process consultation, sensitivity training, management by objectives, job enrichment, and use of Blake and Mouton's managerial grid.

Survey Feedback

The systematic collection and measurement of subordinate attitudes by anonymous questionnaires is **survey feedback**. Three basic steps are involved in the process. First, data are collected from members of the organization by a consultant. Surveys are typically either the objective multiple-choice type (see Exhibit 13-4) or a scaled answer to suggest agreement or disagreement to a particular question (see Exhibit 13-5). Normally, anonymous questionnaires are used. If management wants to obtain truthful information concerning attitudes, care must be taken to ensure that employees feel comfortable, secure, and confident in responding.

In the second step, the results of the study are presented to concerned organizational units. In the final step, the data are analyzed and decisions are made. Some means by which the data may be compared and analyzed include:

- Scores for the entire organization now and in the past
- Scores for each department now and in the past
- Scores by organizational level
- Scores by seniority
- Relative scores on each question
- Scores for each question for each category of personnel.

The decisions are directed at improving relationships in the organization. This is accomplished by revealing problem areas and dealing with them through straightforward discussions.

Team Building

One of the major techniques of the organization development consultant is **team building**, a conscious effort to develop effective work groups throughout the organization.[8] The focus of team building is the development of effective management teams. These work groups focus on solving actual problems in building efficient management teams. The team-building process begins when the team leader defines a problem that requires organization change. Next, the group analyzes the problem to determine the underlying causes of the problems. These factors may be related to such areas as communication, role clarifications, leadership styles, organizational structure, and interpersonal frictions. The next step involves proposing alternative solutions and then selecting the most appropriate one. Through this process, the

EXHIBIT 13-4
Examples of multiple-choice response to survey questions

Why did you decide to do what you are now doing?

a. Desire to aid or assist others

b. Influenced by another person or situation

c. Always wanted to be in this vocation

d. Lack of opportunity or interest in other vocational fields

e. Opportunities provided by this vocation

f. Personal satisfaction from doing this work

What do you like least about your job?

a. Nothing

b. Pay

c. Supervisor relations

d. Problems with fellow workers

e. Facilities

f. Paper work and reports

SOURCE   R. Wayne Mondy and Robert M. Noe, III, *Personnel: The Management of Human Resources* (Boston: Allyn and Bacon, 1981): 493.

Considering all aspects of your job, evaluate your compensation with regard to your contributions to the needs of the organization. Circle the number that best describes how you feel.

Pay too Low		Pay Low		Pay Average		Pay Above Average		Pay Too High	
1	2	3	4	5	6	7	8	9	10

What are your feelings about overtime work requirements? Circle the number that best indicates how you feel.

Unnecessary			Necessary on Occasion			Necessary			
1	2	3	4	5	6	7	8	9	10

EXHIBIT 13-5   Examples of scaled responses to survey questions

SOURCE   R. Wayne Mondy and Robert M. Noe, III, *Personnel: The Management of Human Resources* (Boston: Allyn and Bacon, 1981): 493.

participants are likely to be committed to the solution. Interpersonal support and trust develops. The overall improvement in the interpersonal support and trust of group members enhances the implementation of the change.[9]

Process Consultation

Edgar Schein defines **process consultation** as "a set of activities on the part of the consultant which help the client to perceive, understand, and act upon process events which occur in the client's [culture]."[10] As the definition suggests, this particular OD program starts from the assumption that the outside consultant does not merely conduct an analysis of the organization and then suggest a remedy for the problem that is identified. Rather, the consultant and management jointly discuss and diagnose organizational processes (both structural and human) and decide what problems need to be solved. According to Schein, this approach to problem solving is based on the following assumptions:

- Management often has difficulty deciding what is wrong with the organization. Special diagnostic help is therefore needed.
- While most managers honestly wish to improve organization effectiveness, they may need help in deciding how to achieve it.
- When organizations learn to diagnose their own strengths and weaknesses, they can be more effective.
- The outside consultant cannot hope to get a clear understanding of the organization's culture in a short period of time; therefore, joint consultation with management, which does know the culture, is necessary.
- The client, not the consultant, must come to a conclusion regarding the problem, its causes, and its remedy. Decision-making authority about organization changes remains with the client.

Process consultation differs from two other typical OD models: the "purchase" model and the "doctor/patient" model. When the purchase model is used, the organization defines its problems without outside help and then hires an expert to solve them — for example, how to design a new plant, how to improve employee morale, or how to determine if consumers are satisfied with company products. This approach is often not optimal because the organization may have incorrectly defined its needs or because the consultant chosen is not technically competent. When the doctor/patient model is used, the consultant (doctor) diagnoses the organization (the patient) and then suggests a cure for the problem. The major difficulties here are that the unit that is diagnosed as having problems may reject the diagnosis and/or may resist implementing the solutions proposed by the consultant.

The limitations of these two OD models are overcome by the use of process consultation, since the consultant's main role is not to suggest solutions but instead to help management understand its organizational problem as clearly as possible. Once understood, the problem can be tackled properly by management. Solutions generated from within the organization are less likely to meet resistance.

Sensitivity Training

A controversial OD approach, **sensitivity training**, is designed to increase the awareness of individuals about their own motivations and behavior patterns as well as those of others.[11] This is accomplished through the use of training groups (T-groups). In the extreme, the technique uses the group confrontation method to achieve its fundamental goal of increased awareness. To achieve its objectives, the T-group operates as follows. Individuals who volunteer for, or are sent to, the T-group meet at a predetermined location away from the normal place of work. These individuals may be complete strangers coming from many different organizations (stranger groups) or they may all come from the same organization (family groups). The groups, usually composed of 10 to 15 individuals, meet for approximately 7 to 10 days. There is no set agenda or required material to cover as there is in a structured seminar. Instead, the members are faced with a very unstructured atmosphere in which the decision as to what direction to take must be made by the group. The sessions are moderated by a trainer, whose function is to clarify the basic goal of the session and to assist the group in its function. The trainer generally assumes no leadership role, although this can vary.

In an atmosphere like this, it is not surprising that high anxiety levels develop in the group as some members attempt to impose structure on the others. Conflicts of this sort are ideal for increasing members' awareness of their own feelings and behaviors during conflict or consensus situations. Although the actual conduct of a T-group varies considerably because of the lack of structure, it generally involves group discussions of individual behavior patterns as they relate to particular problems. For example, a group of executives who work together may decide to engage in a T-group session to improve their effectiveness as a team. Each individual might describe how he or she sees the behavior of others, and the group might suggest possible improvements. Afterward, group members diagnose their own feelings and pursue ways of changing interpersonal relationships.

Sensitivity training is not as widely used in business today as it formerly was. It has been labeled "psychotherapy" rather than proper business training. Leaders of T-groups have been criticized for having an insufficient background in psychology. It has been suggested that individual defense mechanisms built up to preserve the personality over a period of years may be destroyed without replacing them with more satisfactory behavioral patterns.

In business organizations, managers frequently must make unpleasant decisions that work to the detriment of particular individuals and groups. Excessive empathy and sympathy will not necessarily lead to a reversal of the decision, but may exact an excessively high emotional cost for the decision maker. Many business organizations have an internal atmosphere characterized by competition and autocratic leadership. The power structure may not be compatible with openness and trust. In some instances, an effective manager must practice diplomacy by telling only part of the truth, or perhaps even telling different stories to two different persons or groups. Truth is not always most conducive to effective interpersonal and group relations. Sensitivity training tends to ignore organizational values that are derived from aggressiveness, initiative, and the charismatic appeals of a particular leader.

Management by Objectives

In Chapter 4, we described management by objectives as a systematic approach that facilitates achievement of results by directing efforts toward attainable goals. MBO is a philosophy of management that encourages managers to plan for the future. Because MBO emphasizes participative management approaches, it has been called a philosophy of management. Within this broader context, MBO becomes an important method of organization development. The participation of individuals in setting goals and the emphasis on self-control promote not only individual development but also development for the entire organization.

Job Enrichment

The deliberate restructuring of a job to make it more challenging, meaningful, and interesting is referred to as job enrichment. As we suggested in Chapter 10, the individual is provided with an opportunity to derive greater achievement, recognition, responsibility, and personal growth in performing the job.

The Managerial Grid

One of the best known OD programs is the managerial grid of Blake and Mouton. As we discussed in Chapter 11, they suggest that the most effective leadership style is that which stresses maximum concern for both output and people. The managerial grid provides a systematic approach for analyzing managerial styles and assisting the organization in moving to the best style.

Management Development

Organization development techniques are designed to change the entire organization. **Management development programs** (MDP) are specifically tailored to enhance the development of management.[12] Managers learn more effective approaches to managing people and other resources. With MDP, specific areas that have been identified as possible organization weaknesses are included in the program. Some of these areas might relate to leadership style, motivation approaches, or communication effectiveness.

The training programs may be administered by either company personnel or external consultants. A typical management development program is illustrated in the following table. The intent of MDPs is not only to teach managers new methods and techniques, but also to develop in them an inquisitive thought process. Too often personnel within a firm become so accustomed to performing the same task day after day that they forget to think. A properly designed management development program places a person in a frame of mind to analyze problems and is often used to provide the foundation for a change to occur.

Course Content for a Management Development Program

   I. *Management Development Program Title*:
      "Improving Group Effectiveness and Team Building"
  II. *Objectives*:
      (1) To identify the reasons for group formation
      (2) To understand the types of groups and their attributes
      (3) To discover the implications of research on group dynamics
      (4) To acquire an understanding as to forces in intra- and inter-group processes
      (5) To learn the characteristics of teamwork and ways to achieve it
      (6) To provide experience in analyzing and diagnosing work group dimensions
      (7) To acquire an appreciation for various team-building techniques
 III. *Description and Evaluation*:
      The course is designed to provide greater understanding of, and ability to work with and through, groups. Special emphasis is given to understanding the various need levels of groups and what can be done to appeal more effectively to those levels. Actual practice in team-building techniques is given, as well as experience in analyzing work groups. Evaluation is made of the major contingencies affecting groups. Observing group behavior through various media is a portion of the course content.
  IV. *Size of Class*:
      The class should have a maximum enrollment of 20 participants so as to allow the group process to be seen in action in the group itself, yet small enough to allow for active participation.
   V. *Assignment of Instructor*:
      The instructor allocates an equal amount of time to lecture and active class discussion with approximately one-third of the time devoted to various media presentations and group involvement. The course is designed for a two- or three-day session.
  VI. *Enrollment Requirements*:
      Middle- and upper-level managerial experience desired.

TALKING TO MANAGERS

Judith Jossa
Personnel Administration Office

Judith Jossa is the Director of the Organization Development Division of the Alberta Personnel Administration Office. The division, which contains 21 full-time employees, provides management and organization development (OD) services to various individuals and departments in the Alberta public service. These services include specialized training for women and native people employed in the public service, management and executive officer training, and OD consulting services to departments on a request basis.

Q: Talk a little bit about how your division deals with other public service organizations that want OD work done.
Jossa: Our clients come from departments, boards, or commissions in the Alberta government. We are a centralized staff department sup-

plying a specialized service in the field of human resource and organization development. Our services are not based on forced compliance but, rather, are offered on request from user departments. Credibility is an important factor in that we must demonstrate that what we do is useful before other departments or divisions will request our services. We are involved in both custom designing of OD interventions and in the delivery of standardized management development programs. In 1974, over 10 000 employees — one third of the public service — were offered a "training event." A training event can range from a short workshop to a one-week management course.

Q: Can you give an example of a custom-designed OD program that was developed for a client?
Jossa: A couple of months ago, I received a call from an executive director in another government department. He felt that some substantial changes needed to be made in his division before it could really be effective in what it was attempting to do. He thought that it was important to get employees more involved in planning the department's activities; then they would be more enthusiastic and creative when making decisions about the day-to-day operations of the department. This was important, because the department dealt regularly with the private-sector business community and was really trying to serve it instead of being seen as an unresponsive, rules- and regulations-oriented government agency. Our first step was to do a needs survey to determine what employees really thought about their individual jobs and about the goals and objectives of the department. A summary of employee views was then analyzed and reviewed by management. At that point, it became clear that employees wanted some things that management hadn't thought of — for example, training in report writing and public speaking. After the data from the needs survey had been analyzed, the managers heading the department decided that our division should conduct a major "team building" exercise and put on several other educational programs that would deal specifically with employee needs as noted in the survey. Because of the success of this OD program, it was later provided on a department-wide basis.

Q: Can you give an example of services that are not custom designed but are repeated frequently with a different client each time?

Jossa: We offer 30 standardized management/supervisory development programs — such as Situational Leadership or Management, Leadership and Motivation — plus a supervisory development program for technical people who are ready to move into the first line of the management ranks. We have 21 supervisory modules that start off with theory and then bridge the gap to the job. These modules will be offered on a regular basis from the central agency; however, departments are encouraged to deliver these modules in-house. Modularized training programs offer choices, and each is based on an individual topic, such as discipline, motivation, or performance appraisal. Employees can take a particular module or all 21. In terms of pure OD services, on a regular basis, we provide mediation and process consultant services where techniques in needs surveys to team building are offered.

Q: Do you charge clients for the services you provide?

Jossa: We do not charge for the development of custom-designed OD programs because we want to encourage the various government departments to learn about OD and how it can be helpful to them. But we do charge for our standardized programs.

Q: How do you ensure that people attending either custom-designed or standardized seminars actually get something that they can use when they return to their job?

Jossa: Our division is very concerned about precisely that point; as a result we require each person who attends a training course to sign a "learning contract." This contract indicates the practical skills or knowledge employees need to learn in the course and how these skills will be applied once they return to their regular job. Both employees and their supervisors sign the learning contract before any employee goes to the seminar. We have found that this contract really focuses attention on the course objectives and increases the chance that people will actually use the new skills or knowledge once they return to the job.

Q: Is there ever a shortage of demand for the services your division provides?

Jossa: We have more business than we can comfortably handle. In fact, we sometimes have to turn down requests because we do not have enough staff to deliver all the programs requested. When demand exceeds our ability to supply it, we usually refer and/or contract the work to private consultants. This is particularly true for the standardized seminars.

Q: Suppose a line manager from a government department approaches you about doing some OD work and you don't agree with what the line manager wants. Since you are a staff division and don't have authority over line managers, how do you resolve disagreements like this when they arise?

Jossa: We don't usually have disagreements like that, because, after we do a needs analysis, it is pretty clear what employees need by way of training and what management needs to accomplish. Our emphasis is on total integration of organization and employee needs. If a manager originally felt that "X" should be done and then the needs analysis suggests that "Y" is necessary instead, most managers are very interested in doing what will maximize productivity for the benefit of all.

Q: Do you practice OD actively within your own division?

Jossa: Definitely. I feel that our division should continually be looking for new and creative ways to manage. This will help employees in this division to enrich their own job and to enhance their overall career prospect. Originally, the division focus was directed at providing centralized training and development programs. Today, the focus is on decentralized services and moving away from packaged programming to meeting the needs of the client. Flexibility and responsiveness are necessary in delivering tailored programs. As an example of this type of thinking, several consultants in this division who formerly taught management development programs on a regular basis are now managing those programs. In order to do that, they had to develop such new skills as process consulting, administration, program management, or consulting skills as a change agent.

STRESS MANAGEMENT

A by-product of some change is the stress that can develop in workers. **Stress** is the nonspecific response of the body to any demands made on it. Over a period of time or under intense conditions, stress can take its toll on the body. A vast array of ailments ranging from lower back pains to headaches to coronary problems and cancer are considered to be by-products of stress. If stress is strong enough and lasts long enough, it can damage both mental and physical health. Unmanaged coping with stress can create anxiety, depression, paranoia, and other mental difficulties for the individual. The cost and pain of stress are enormous. Although costs are difficult to state exactly, stress-related absenteeism, illness, and premature death cost Canadian companies millions of dollars each year.

Fortunately, managers are now beginning to realize that effective stress management is important to them, to their employees, and to the organization. Job-related stress can be as disruptive, and as costly, to the corporation as any accident that occurs to an employee. In fact, many employee accidents are considered to be stress related. Managers must recognize employee behavior patterns that may indicate excessive stress.

• Working late more than usual, or increased tardiness or absenteeism
• Difficulty in making decisions
• Increases in the number of careless mistakes
• Missing deadlines or forgetting appointments
• Problems interacting and getting along with others
• Focusing on mistakes and personal failure.[13]

Naturally, all behavioral change is not stress related, but astute managers can be made alert to changes in employee patterns. A normally productive worker becomes sloppy and productivity decreases. Or a normally friendly worker becomes irritable and short-tempered.

Management can anticipate or try to reduce stress for employees through preventive attitudes. For example, if management recognizes that the corporate culture is causing problems, a conscious effort can be made to change it. Perhaps it should be made more open and less threatening so that workers can do their jobs without stress. Another way to reduce stress is to redesign jobs so that workers feel that they are doing something exciting and worthwhile rather than boring and unimportant. Changes can also be made to the physical layout by reducing excessive noise, heat, or other poor working conditions. Some companies have introduced physical fitness programs for their employees, which help improve their physical condition and, in turn, allow them to cope more effectively with the stress that is unavoidable on the job.

MANAGEMENT IN PRACTICE

Fitness and Health Programs

Recently, the province of Ontario conducted a study of the health and safety activities supported by business firms. The researchers found the following:

Program	Companies Involved
Stop smoking	18%
Alcohol/drug abuse	59%
Stress reduction	23%
Weight control	28%
Physical fitness	13%

The majority of the companies pay all or part of the cost of these programs, but many of them do not have adequate facilities to conduct the program at an optimum level.

A concern has been expressed by Bob Dooner of Health and Wealfare Canada that major programs within corporations are few and far between. He feels that there is considerable apathy evident in many firms (particularly small ones), and the recession of 1981–1983 certainly didn't help, because firms were more worried about fundamental business activities than they were about employee fitness.

SOURCE   Robert Perry, "Fitness Programs Need Shaping Up," *The Financial Post* (April 14, 1984): 27.

EXECUTIVE BURNOUT

Although related to stress, executive burnout is a distinct concept. **Executive burnout** has been defined as "a state of fatigue or frustration brought about by devotion to a cause, way of life, or relationship that failed to produce the expected reward."[14] Burnout may affect as many as 1 in 10 managers. A major problem with burnout is that it is contagious. If one executive is a burnout victim, he or she may influence others to become cynical, negative, and pessimistic. The result is an entire group which is unhappy, unproductive, and resistant to improvements.[15]

Some of the symptoms of burnout include: (1) chronic fatigue, (2) anger at those making demands, (3) self-criticism for putting up with the demands, (4) cynicism, negativism, and irritability, (5) a sense of being besieged, and (6) a hair-trigger display of emotions.[16] Other symptoms might include recurring health problems, such as ulcers, back pain, and frequent headaches. The burnout victim is often emotionally changeable; unwarranted hostility may occur in completely inappropriate situations.

Burnout often occurs among talented, achievement-oriented workers. Many of these people are business executives. Perhaps they have set their standards too high and then refuse to admit that they cannot be achieved. Sometimes the organization itself designs situations that are capable of causing burnout. Giving a manager a job to do and then making it virtually impossible for the person to do the job is an example. Burnout is the "consequence of a work situation in which the person gets the feeling he's butting his head against the wall day after day, year after year."[17]

The problem can be corrected. Some firms are arranging for full-time staff counselors to help employees who are experiencing burnout. Seminars can be given to help managers help their workers overcome the problem. Some firms are granting disability leaves until the worker recovers.

Firms can also take measures to prevent burnout among their employees. For example, workers should not be permitted to work too much overtime, even on critical problems. It is often the best person who is always called on in times of crisis. These are the very people who are likely to burn out. Another method might be to rotate employees who are working on stressful jobs. Moving people to a new project may help. Some firms are starting physical exercise programs and counseling programs. Breaks in the business routines are helpful.[18] The job at hand should not be allowed to overshadow all other aspects of living.

OPENING INCIDENT REVISITED

Craig Ltd.

Lorna Kasian had run into a hornet's nest when she tried to implement a major renovation at Craig Ltd. Now that you have been exposed to some material on organization change, it is rather easy to see why this problem arose and what should have been done to implement the change properly.

Why have these groups objected so vigorously to the change? In the chapter, several reasons were given and one or more of them may apply here. The people may be insecure about their new work stations, how the proposed renovations will affect their informal social relationships, or how much inconvenience the renovation will cause.

How could this vocal opposition have been avoided? Again, the chapter makes several suggestions. Generally speaking, Kasian would have to demonstrate first that the change was necessary and, second, that it recognized and maintained important informal relationships. If Kasian hoped to gain general acceptance for the project from the other employees, she should have provided information in advance and encouraged participation in the plans along the way. Any concerns people may have had about social or status losses would have been dealt with; technical requirements for groups like the drafting department and promises made to marketing would have been noted earlier in the process. More specifically, Kasian should have consulted with each group before trying to have a renovation plan drawn up by an architect. Consultations would undoubtedly reveal good ideas for the renovation plan. Recall that the secretaries came up with a good idea that Kasian hadn't thought of.

What about the president's unhappiness at Kasian's inability to complete the renovations on time? If Kasian had consulted with various people right at the start, she would have known that renovations could not possibly be finished when the president wanted. Kasian could therefore have told him that he had two options: impose renovations without consultation and face the consequences, or proceed with consultations so that the renovations are enthusiastically accepted. The president could then decide what he wanted, but Kasian would not be to blame if he chose the first alternative. More than likely, he would have seen the wisdom of consultation and would have increased the time allotment for the renovations.

SUMMARY

The psychological atmosphere of a firm is described as its corporate culture. The culture existing within a firm has an impact on the employees' degree of satisfaction with the job, as well as on the level and quality of their performance. Typical factors that affect corporate culture are: work group, organizational characteristics, supervisor, and administrative processes. The culture advocated by most behavioralists is the open and/or participative culture, which is characterized by such attributes as trust in subordinates, openness in communication, considerate and supportive leadership, group problem solving, worker autonomy, information sharing, and the establishment of high output goals.

The sequence of events that are needed to bring about change in an organization begins with management's recognizing a true need for change. Next, the change method to be used is identified. The change process consists of unfreezing the status quo, moving to a new level, and freezing the new status quo.

A change may involve some loss to the person who is affected by it and thus generate resistance. Some of the possible sources of resistance to change include: insecurity, possible social loss, economic losses, inconvenience, resentment of control, unanticipated repercussions, and union opposition. Approaches that may be used to reduce resistance to change are: make only necessary changes, attempt to maintain useful informal relationships, build trust, provide information in advance, encourage participation, guarantee against loss, and provide counseling.

Change efforts that involve the entire organization are referred to as organization development (OD). OD is a planned and calculated attempt to change the organization, typically to a more open and participative culture. Some of the OD techniques available include survey feedback, team building, process consultation, sensitivity training, management by objectives, job enrichment, and the managerial grid approach. The person who is responsible for ensuring that the planned change in OD is properly implemented is referred to as a change agent.

Whereas organization development techniques are designed to improve the entire organization, management development programs are specifically tailored to benefit managers. Some of the areas for development include leadership style, motivation approaches, and communication effectiveness.

Stress management and executive burnout are of increasing concern to modern managers. Stress is the response of the body to excessive demands made on it. A person experiencing executive burnout is someone in a state of fatigue or frustration brought about by devotion to a cause, way of life, or relationship that failed to produce the desired reward. There are numerous ways to identify and treat both stress and executive burnout.

REVIEW QUESTIONS

1. Define *corporate culture*. What are the factors that interact to determine the type of culture that exists in a firm?
2. Identify the values and limits of a participative culture.
3. What is the primary reason for introducing a change in a business? Relate the situational factors in making a decision to change.
4. List and describe the elements in the change sequence.
5. What are the sources of resistance to organization change?
6. Describe the approaches that may be used in reducing resistance to change.
7. Define each of the following terms:
   a. *Organization development*
   b. *Team building*
   c. *Process consultation*.
8. Define and distinguish between *stress* and *executive burnout*.

EXERCISES

1. Identify the major changes that have occurred in your life during the past year. How did you react to these changes?
2. Visit 3 businesses. Attempt to assess the type of culture that exists in each of the firms and identify your reasons for reaching this assessment.
3. Assume that you are the president of a community college or a university and you would like to make the following changes:
   a. Students must be professionally attired at all times.
   b. Faculty members must be at their office daily by 09:00.
   c. All single students must live on campus.

Assuming that all these changes are made for a logical reason, what type of resistance to these changes could you expect? How could you overcome some of the resistance to these changes?

CASE STUDY

A Change of Culture

Until one year ago Wayne daCosta, Don Pio, and Roberta Vine were supervisors with a chain of 39 grocery stores. Each supervisor had responsibility for 13 stores and reported directly to the company president. All 3 supervisors worked well together, and there was a constant exchange of information, which was useful in coordinating the activities of the stores. Each supervisor had specific strengths that were useful in helping the others. DaCosta coordinated the deployment of the part-time help at all 39 stores. Pio monitored the inventories, and Vine interviewed prospective new employees prior to sending them to daCosta and Pio for review. It was a complete team effort directed toward getting the job done.

One year later, the chain had undergone some changes. The president, wishing to relieve himself of many daily details, decided to promote Vine to vice-president. Another supervisor, Phillips, was hired for Vine's position. Vine had a completely different idea of how the activities of the supervisors should be conducted. Under

Vine's leadership each supervisor was now responsible for the activities at only his or her 13 stores. If a problem occurred, the supervisor was to discuss it with Vine, who would provide the solution. When any of the 3 supervisors attempted to solve problems on their own, they were reprimanded by Vine. After a few reprimands, daCosta, Pio and Phillips decided not to fight the system and did as Vine wanted; they rarely saw each other any more. If Pio had a problem at his stores that caused him to work all night that was not any concern of daCosta or Phillips.

The main problem with the new system was that efficiency dropped drastically. For instance, daCosta was a good coordinator of part-time help. He had the type of personality that could talk a person into coming to work at 17:00 on Saturday evening when the individual had a date at 18:00. DaCosta's stores remained well staffed with part-time help, but the others suffered. Many times the part-time help did not show up, and either Pio or Phillips had to act as the replacement if the store manager could not be convinced to work overtime. On the other hand, daCosta's inventory control suffered because Pio was best qualified in this area.

Vine accused the 3 supervisors of working against her and threatened them with dismissal if operations did not get better. DaCosta, Pio, and Phillips thought that they could not be productive in this atmosphere and found other positions. When the president discovered what had occurred, Vine was fired. It took the president 2 years to get operations back to the level of efficiency that had existed previously.

QUESTIONS

1. What different corporate culture was created as a result of promoting Vine to vice-president?
2. How do you think that this situation could have been avoided?

CASE STUDY

Rumors at Duncan Electric

Donna Pichet is a supervisor for Duncan Electric Corporation, a manufacturer of high-quality electrical parts. Pichet had been with the firm for 5 years and had a reputation for having one of the best teams in the plant. Pichet had picked the majority of these employees and was proud of the reputation they had achieved. But a problem was now brewing that had the potential of destroying her department.

For weeks, rumors of a substantial reduction in personnel at Duncan Electric have been circulating. Pichet has not received any confirmation from the corporate office regarding the reduction. The rumors, all claiming to be from reliable sources, range from minor reductions to a large-scale reduction in personnel. Every day someone claims to have the inside story, and every day the story changes. Pichet, who has a reputation for leveling with her people, successfully discounted the rumors for awhile. But, as the doubts grew, work output began to suffer. Her employees were now spending time trying to verify the latest rumor. Speculation increased to the point where the best-qualified employees were starting to shop around.

The action by these employees did not make sense unless there was to be a very large-scale layoff. Pichet was convinced that a minor layoff was the worst that could possibly happen and she was demoralized to see her department falling apart for no good reason.

On Friday, two of the most skilled employees in the department told Pichet that they had taken a job with a competitor. This situation was what she had feared most; the best qualified workers would leave and the least qualified workers would remain. Instead of having one of the best departments at Duncan Electric, she may now have one of the worst.

QUESTIONS

1. Why have the rumors damaged the morale of the employees in Donna Pichet's department?
2. What should management do to reduce the fear of the anticipated change?
3. What should Pichet do in a situation like this?

NOTES

1 T. J. Peters and R. H. Waterman, *In Search of Excellence* (New York: Harper and Row Publishers, 1982).

2 Terrence E. Deal and Allan A. Kennedy, *Corporate Cultures* (Reading, Mass.: Addison-Wesley, 1982).

3 Many of the factors were taken from the Organizational Climate Description Questionnaire generated by Halpin and Croft as described in Andrew W. Halpin, *Theory and Research in Administration* (New York: Macmillan, 1966), ch. 4. Another widely used measure is that of Litwin and Stringer found in G. Litwin and R. Stringer, *Motivation and Organizational Climate* (Cambridge: Harvard University Press, 1968).

4 H. Kenneth Bobele and Peter J. Buchanan, "Building a More Productive Environment," *Management World* 1 (January 1979): 8.

5 Addison C. Bennet, "The Manager's Responsibility for Work Improvement," in *Improving the Effectiveness of Hospital Management* (New York: Preston, 1972): 161–162.

6 Kurt Lewin, *Field Theory and Social Science* (New York: Harper, 1964), chs. 9, 10.

7 Ralph G. Huschowitz, "The Human Aspects of Managing Transition," *Personnel* 51 (May-June 1974): 13.

8 Edgar F. Huse, *Organization Development and Change* (St. Paul, Minn.: West, 1975): 230.

9 Michael A. Hitt, R. Dennis Middlemist, and Robert Q. Mathis, *Effective Management* (St. Paul, Minn.: West, 1979): 462–464.

10 Edgar Schein, *Process Consultation: Its Role in Organization Development* (Reading, Mass.: Addison-Wesley, 1969): 9.

11 For a detailed review of 100 research studies on sensitivity training, see P. B. Smith, "Control Studies on the Outcome of Sensitivity Training," *Psychological Bulletin* (July 1975): 597–622.

12 Jon English and Anthony R. Marchione, "Nine Steps in Management Development," *Business Horizons* 6 (June 1977): 88–94.

13 John M. Ivancevich and Michael T. Matteson, *Stress and Work: A Managerial Perspective* (Glenview, Ill.: Scott, Foresman, 1980): 208.

14 Herbert J. Freudenberger, *Burnout: The High Cost of High Achievement* (Garden City, N.Y.: Anchor Press, Doubleday, 1980): 13.

15 Cary Cherniss, "Job Burnout: Growing Worry for Workers, Bosses," *U.S. News and World Report* 88 (February 27, 1980): 72.

16 Harry Levinson, "When Executives Burn Out," *Harvard Business Review* 59 (May-June 1981): 76.

17 Freudenberger, 17–18.

18 Levinson, 78–81.

REFERENCES

Allen, R. F., and Silverzweig, S. "Changing Community and Organizational Cultures." *Training and Development Journal* 31 (July 1977): 28–34.

Baird, John E. Jr. "Supervisory and Managerial Training through Communication by Objectives." *Personnel Administrator* 26 (July 1981): 28–32.

Baysinger, Rebecca T., and Woodman, Richard W. "The Use of Management by Objectives in Management Training Programs." *Personnel Administrator* 26 (February 1981): 83–86.

Bensahel, J. G. "How to Overcome Resistance to Change." *International Management* 32 (September 1977): 66–67.

Bhagat, Rabi S. "Effects of Stressful Life Events on Individuals Performance Efforts and Work Adjustment Processes with Organizational Settings: A Research Model." *Academy of Management Review* 8, no. 4 (October 1983): 660–671.

Biggart, N. W. "Creative-Destructive Process of Organizational Change: The Case of the Post Office." *Administrative Science Quarterly* 22 (September 1977): 410–426.

Carlson, H. C. "Organizational Research and Organizational Change." *Personnel* 54 (July 1977): 11–22.

Cosier, Richard A. "Equity Theory and Time: A Reformulation." *Academy of Management Review* 8, no. 2 (April 1983): 311–319.

Davis, L. E. "Individuals and the Organization." *California Management Review* 22 (Spring 1980): 5–14.

Fennell, Mary L. "Synergy, Influence and Information in the Adoption of Administrative Innovations." *Academy of Management Journal* 27, no. 1 (March 1984): 113–129.

Gaertner, Gregory H.; Gaertner, Karen N., and Akinnusi, David M. "Environment, Strategy and the Implementation of Administrative Change: The Case of Civil Service Reform." *Academy of Management Journal* 27, no. 3 (September 1984): 525–543.

Gordon, G. G., and Goldberg, B. E. "Is There a Climate for Success?" *Management Review* 66 (May 1977): 37–44.

Greiner, Larry E. "Evolution and Revolution as Organizations Grow." *Harvard Business Review* 50 (July 1971): 37–46.

Hellriegel, Don, and Slocum, John W. Jr. "Organizational Climate: Measures, Research, and Contingencies." *Academy of Management Journal* 17 (June 1974): 255–280.

Howe, R. J., et al. "Introducing Innovation Through Organizational Development." *Management Review* 67 (Februay 1978): 52–56.

Huse, E. F. *Organization Development and Change.* St. Paul, Minn.: West, 1980.

Jennings, Eugene E. "How to Develop Your Management Talent Internally." *Personnel Administrator* 26 (July 1981): 20–23.

Kelly, Joe, and Khozan, Kamiran. "Participative Management: Can It Work?" *Business Horizons* (August 1980): 74–79.

Margerison, Charles, and New, Colin. "Management Development by Intercompany Consortiums." *Personnel Management* 12 (November 1980): 42–45.

Miles, James M. "How to Establish a Good Industrial Relations Climate." *Management Review* 67 (August 1980): 42–44.

Miller, Danny, and Friesen, Peter H. "Momentum and Revaluations in Organizational Adaptation." *Academy of Management Journal* 23 (December 1980): 591–614.

Mintzberg, Henry. "Organizational Design: Fashion or Fit?" *Harvard Business Review* 59 (January-February 1981): 103–116.

Monat, Jonathan S. "A Perspective on the Evaluation of Training and Development Programs." *Personnel Administrator* 26 (July 1981): 47–52.

Olivas, Louis. "Using Assessment Centers for Individual and Organizational Development." *Personnel* 57 (May-June 1980): 63–67.

Oriorne, George S. "The Change Registers." *Personnel Administrator* 26 (January 1981): 57–63.

Peters, James W., and Mabry, Edward A. "The Personnel Officer as Internal Consultant." *Personnel Administrator* 26 (April 1981): 29–32.

Scott, Walter B. "Participative Management at Motorola — The Results." *Management Review* 70 (July 1981): 26–28.

Seers, Anson; McGee, Gail W.; Serey, Timothy T.; and Graen, George B. "The Interaction of Job Stress and Social Support: A Strong Inference Investigation." *Academy of Management Journal* 26, no. 2 (June 1983): 273–284.

Stoffman, Daniel. "Blue Collar Turnaround Artists." *Canadian Business* 57, no. 2 (February 1984): 38.

Tichy, Noel M. *Managing Strategic Change: Technical, Political and Cultural Dynamics.* New York: Wiley, 1983.

V

Controlling

14

The Controlling Process

Can-Mark Manufacturing

Henry Friesen was a foreman at Can-Mark Manufacturing, which manufactured a wide array of consumer products. Recently Friesen had been put in charge of a group of 9 people who were to produce the company's latest addition to its product line. The production process for the new product required use of state-of-the-art equipment, and the company's industrial engineers had just completed a lengthy series of tests to determine reasonable production standards for the new machines.

The production line experienced trouble right from the start. The workers had considerable difficulty getting the machines to work properly, and rejects were running substantially above the level that was considered acceptable. One afternoon, as Friesen was sitting in his office wondering how to resolve this problem, the plant superintendent, Peter Jansen, appeared at his door. Friesen invited him in and the following conversation took place:

Jansen: Henry, what's the problem with our new line? You know this product is high profile; I'm already getting pressure from the vice-president. He says the new product is crucial to our company and he wants these production problems resolved immediately. There's a lot of demand out there for this product and we've got to get your production volume up.

Friesen: After talking to the workers, I'm convinced those production standards are way out of line. My people are very motivated and experienced but they can't meet the standards the engineering people have set.

Jansen: Now, Henry, you know our engineers have a very good reputation for setting realistic job standards.

Friesen: I know that, but in this case they have made a big mistake. This state-of-the-art equipment we're using is more difficult to work with than they could have imagined.

Jansen: We've got to get output on this line up to standard or we'll both be in trouble with top management.

At this point one of Friesen's workers entered his office and told him of another problem with the new equipment, so Friesen had to cut the meeting short. For the rest of the day his discussion with Jansen weighed heavily on his mind.

KEY TERMS

control	obsolescence	critical path method
controlling process	just-in-time	(CPM)
standards	inventory system	event
time standards	overseeing controls	activity
productivity	comparison controls	optimistic time
standards	quotas	most likely time
cost standards	quality	pessimistic time
quality standards	statistical quality	expected time
behavioral standards	control	critical path
control tolerances	network controls	strategic control
disciplinary action	performance	points
progressive discipline	evaluation and	
initial controls	review technique	
inventory	(PERT)	

LEARNING OBJECTIVES

After completing this chapter, you should be able to
1. Define controls and describe the control process.
2. Explain the specific types of controls that are available to management.
3. Explain the importance of disciplinary action and describe what is meant by the concept of progressive discipline.
4. Explain the concept of statistical quality control.
5. Understand the advantages and disadvantages of a traditional and a just-in-time inventory system.
6. Draw a PERT network.
7. Describe and identify the characteristics of strategic control points.
8. Relate the reasons for negative reactions to controls and describe ways of overcoming negative reactions to controls.

The incident at Can-Mark Manufacturing portrays an all-too-common occurrence in organizations: a manager and a subordinate disagree about whether or not the employee's performance is up to standard. The incident reveals how sensitive managers and workers are when it comes to making conclusions about employee performance. Given this sensitivity, organizations need to have a reasonable control system that will make objective performance assessment possible.

A properly designed control system alerts managers to the existence of potential problems and permits them to take corrective actions when necessary. The control function, therefore, is a valuable part of the management process. Controlling is concerned with ensuring that results are achieved according to plan. Stated another way, controls provide management with the means of finding out if tasks have been performed properly.

Some managers believe that, if the functions of planning, organizing, and influencing are performed satisfactorily, they have little need for the control function. This belief is not wisely held for two reasons. First, unexpected events often occur that make the best of plans inoperable. Second, people do not always do what management expects them to do; that is, they don't work the way the plan says they should work. Therefore, managers must perform the control function to ensure that plans become reality.

In this chapter, we first describe the control function and the control process. Second, we examine the basic types of controls that are applied as organizations convert inputs to output. Third, we note the importance of establishing strategic control points, and analyze the nature of control at different management levels. The fourth section examines the reasons why employees in organizations so often resist control measures, and the fifth section offers suggestions on how to reduce this resistance.

THE NATURE OF CONTROL

Control is the process of comparing actual performance with established standards for the purpose of taking action to correct deviations. If a keypunch supervisor had decided that the error rate should not exceed 3 percent and, that on the last batch of work the rate was 6 percent, he or she would immediately know that a control problem existed. To have effective control, an organization must have clear standards. Thus, effective control requires comparing actual performance with preestablished goals. If results differ from established standards, corrective action may need to be taken.

Effective control depends on sound planning by management. As we discussed in Chapter 3, objectives and plans provide the basis for the control process. The purpose of the control function is to ensure that the objectives of the organization are achieved. As such, the planning and control functions are highly interdependent. Plans must be properly prepared and in agreement with the objectives of the firm. Controls ensure that actions taken by management to implement plans are appropriate.

Before standards can be established, objectives and plans must be developed. These objectives serve as the desired results. Plans are created to specify how objectives are to be reached. Appropriate policies and procedures are created to state, in greater detail, the manner in which the goals will be achieved.

THE CONTROLLING PROCESS

The **controlling process** involves 4 critical steps: (1) set standards and control tolerances, (2) observe or measure, (3) compare actual performance to standard, and (4) take corrective action if necessary. This process is shown in Exhibit 14-1. A discussion of each phase follows.

Set Standards and Control Tolerances

Managers must know what is expected before the controls can be implemented. **Standards** are established levels of quality or quantity used to guide performance. For example, if a shaft has a standard diameter, the machinist must try to cut it to that specific size. Standards are sometimes viewed as goals. The most frequently used types of standards are described below. Wherever possible, standards should be expressed numerically to reduce subjectivity and depersonalize the control process.

- **Time Standards**:   Time standards may state the length of time it should take to make a certain product or perform a certain service. An airline pilot has a standard time span in which to make a certain trip. Most organizations have a standard lunch time and a standard work week.
- **Productivity Standards**:   These standards are based on the amount of product or service produced during a set time period. For instance, a productivity standard might be to produce 10 units per hour or to serve 150 customers per hour in a fast-food restaurant.
- **Cost Standards**:   These standards are based on the cost associated with producing the goods or service. For example, the material cost might be $10 per unit. Cost standards are usually set in the expense budget for the supervisor's unit.
- **Quality Standards**:   These are based on the level of perfection desired. For instance, no more than a certain percentage of impurities may be allowed in a chemical, or a valve may have to hold pressure for 10 minutes in order to pass inspection. Some quality standards have legal minimum requirements.

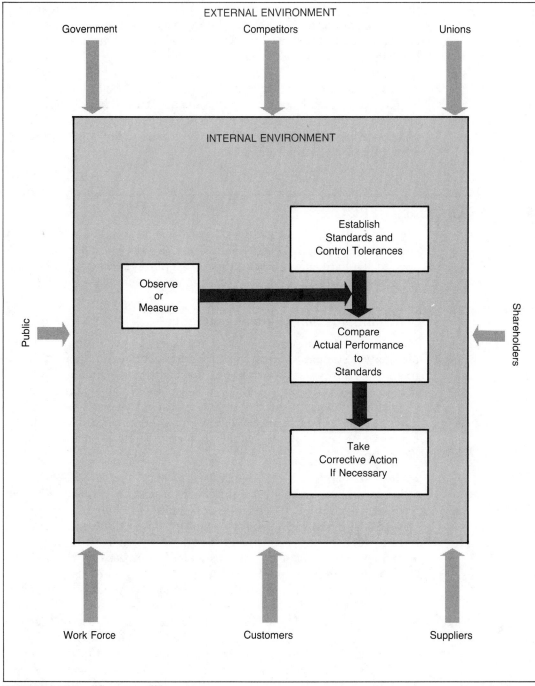

EXHIBIT 14-1   The controlling process

- **Behavioral Standards**: These are based on the type of behavior desired of workers in the organization. It is sometimes difficult to express these standards precisely. For instance, workers may be asked not to curse in front of customers, some workers may have to follow a strict dress code, or workers may be expected to maintain a level of cheerfulness or pleasantness toward customers.

Standards must be related closely to an organization's objectives. Suppose a clothing manufacturer has an objective of getting 10 percent of the Canadian market for men's suits. If industry sales across the country are forecast at $200 million, then the sales objective of this one company is $20 million. This $20 million then becomes the overall standard used to measure performance; this overall standard must be further subdivided into more manageable units for employees to know their individual goals.

To do this, specific standards might be developed for the company's regional sales managers, perhaps as follows: Atlantic region — $2 million, Quebec — $5 million, Ontario — $6 million, prairie provinces — $2 million, and British Columbia — $5 million. Each sales manager will then take his or her standard and develop a quota for each sales representative. For example, Brian Howe, a sales representative in British Columbia, might be given a sales quota of $500,000. By stating progressively more specific standards, the company is able systematically to plan its objectives.

Even when standards are clear, control tolerances also need to be established. **Control tolerances** are specifications of how much deviation will be permitted before the control system will actually go into effect. For instance, a standard of quality for the shaft diameter of a particular part may be 7.9 cm. (See Exhibit 14-2.) However, a tolerance of ±0.13 cm may be permitted. If a part is produced with a shaft diameter within the ranges of 7.77 cm and 8.03 cm, it is acceptable. If the shaft diameter falls outside this range, the part is rejected. As another example, a company might allow only 2 unexcused absences per month. A standard work day might be 8 hours, but most managers have a certain tolerance, perhaps 5 minutes later than starting time, that they will permit. Whether the standard relates to a product, a service, or to behavior, both the standard and the control tolerances should be communicated to workers. If managers make standards and tolerances clear, most workers will control themselves accordingly.

EXHIBIT 14-2   Standard and Control Tolerances

Standard	Tolerance
7.9 cm Shaft diameter	±0.13 cm Difference
0 Absences	2 Unexcused absences per month
08:00 Starting time	08:05 Starting time
1 min Waiting time	1 min 15 sec Waiting time
Clear polished surface	2 Visible defects
130 over 80 Blood pressure	±20 points for either pressure

Observe or Measure

The next phase in the controlling process, observation or measurement, is an important one. Managers need to determine what has actually taken place. In some work places, this phase may require only visual observation. In other situations, more precise determinations are needed. For example, a quality control inspector may use a micrometer or other instrument to take physical measurements in order to assess performance.

Managers should be careful to observe and measure accurately. For instance, a supervisor may believe that a worker has missed too many days from work. A check of attendance records may show that the worker has only averaged missing one day a month. One of the authors, as a young Navy personnel officer, reprimanded a clerk for working too slowly. The leading chief petty officer showed the young officer that, although the clerk appeared to be working slowly, he was actually doing more than his share. The manager should be careful to measure accurately before taking corrective action.

Compare Performance with Standards

If the first two phases have been done well, the third phase of the controlling process — comparing performance with standards — should be straightforward. For example, quality control inspectors keep in mind the standards and control tolerances as they make measurements. Often a quality control checklist, such as the one shown in Exhibit 14-3, is used. As another example, telephone operator supervisors keep strict count of calls handled and length of time per call; the manager knows immediately if an operator is working within time standards.

Behavioral standards are usually not as exact as other standards. Therefore, it is more difficult to make the required comparisons. Because of this problem some managers prefer to keep their subordinates guessing; for instance, they will not tell employees that being 5 minutes late is all right. However, since workers like to know where they stand, this may not be the best procedure.

Correct Deviations if Necessary

The final phase of the controlling process occurs when managers must decide what action to take to correct performance when deviations occur. Often the real cause of the deviation must be found before corrective action can be taken. For instance, if the number of allowable defects has exceeded standard, the cause may be a defective machine or a careless operator. Each cause requires a different corrective action.

Not all deviations from standard justify corrective action. Suppose that a usually dependable worker is 15 minutes late for work (a deviation from the standard), but the manager realizes the lateness was unavoidable. The manager may decide to take no action, even though a deviation occurred. The standard is to be on time, but some flexibility is allowable in this case.

EXHIBIT 14-3   Quality Control Tire Tread Checklist

	Minimum	*Maximum*	*Actual*
Width	56.0 cm	57.0 cm	56.2 cm
Length	183.0 cm	184.0 cm	183.2 cm
Thickness	2.08 cm	2.21 cm	2.16 cm
Mass	3.90 kg	3.99 kg	3.94 kg
Number of Visible Defects	0	2	0

There are two general types of corrective action — immediate and permanent. The type most frequently recognized is the immediate; something must be done now to correct the situation and get back on track. For example, a particular project is a week behind schedule and, if not corrected, will seriously affect other projects. The first problem is not to worry about who caused the difficulty but rather to get the project back on schedule. Depending on the authority of the manager, the following corrective actions may be ordered: (1) overtime hours may be authorized, (2) additional workers and equipment may be assigned, (3) a full-time director may be assigned to push the project through personally, (4) an extra effort may be requested of all employees, or (5) if all these fail, the schedule may have to be readjusted, thereby requiring changes all along the line.

After the degree of stress has lessened through any of the above measures, attention can then be devoted to the second type of corrective action. Just how and why did events stray from their planned course? What can be done to prevent a recurrence of this difficulty? Many managers fail at this phase. Too often they find themselves putting out daily fires but not discovering the actual cause of the problem. For instance, managers may find themselves constantly having to interview and hire new people to replace those who are leaving the firm. A manager may be working 12 hours a day attempting to locate new employees, but he or she must recognize that high turnover is not solved merely by employing new workers. Managers must take some type of corrective action after they have determined what has actually caused the high turnover. A supervisor may be extremely difficult to work with, or the pay scale may not be competitive for the area. Whatever the problem, it must be identified and corrected or the high turnover problem is likely to continue. The dull work of permanent corrective action must be done for the sake of future economical and effective operations.

The Role of Discipline in Corrective Action

In extreme cases, taking corrective action will involve disciplinary action against an employee. **Disciplinary action** is the process of invoking a penalty against an employee who fails to adhere to some work-related standard, for instance, production requirements, rules, or policies. Managers regularly deal with disciplinary actions. Many of the grievance cases appealed to arbitrators by labor unions involve disciplinary action, and management decisions are often overturned. Evidently, some managers do not apply disciplinary action in an acceptable manner.

Disciplinary action begins with a clear understanding of organization objectives. Standards should be created to facilitate accomplishment of these objectives, and they should be clearly communicated to employees. Performance is then observed and compared to standards. No difficulty exists if performance is in line with standards. However, disciplinary action may be needed when excessive performance deviations exist. Once disciplinary action has been taken, it serves to reinforce the importance of the standard to other employees.

At all times, the penalty must be appropriate to the violation or accumulated violations. This process is known as **progressive discipline** and its sequence is shown in Exhibit 14-4.

Once a manager observes improper behavior, he or she asks a series of questions about it. Moving down the list of questions, the discipline gets progressively more severe. Notice that the mere fact of a violation does not mean that disciplinary action must be taken. The manager may use discretion and decide that no action should be taken in one case but must be taken in another. Certain violations (for example, fighting on the job) may result in automatic suspension, while others (for example, failing once to inspect a product properly) may not.

Discipline Principles

There are several useful principles that managers should use when disciplining employees:

- The manager should exhibit the attitude of assuming that all employees want to conform to reasonable organizational requirements.
- The act, rather than the person, should be condemned.
- Although the act may be the basis for penalty, a model of future acceptable behavior should be communicated to employees.
- Promptness is important so that the employee can connect the penalty to the violation.
- A managerial listening role is highly recommended to: (a) effect greater understanding of the reasons for the act, and (b) prevent hasty decisions that may lead to unjustified penalties.
- Negative disciplinary action should be administered in private so that an employee can save face among colleagues.
- Definite, but tactful, follow-up should occur to determine the degree of success of the conditioning effort.
- Consistency and flexibility, though apparently contradictory, are both desirable elements of a superior's style of disciplining.

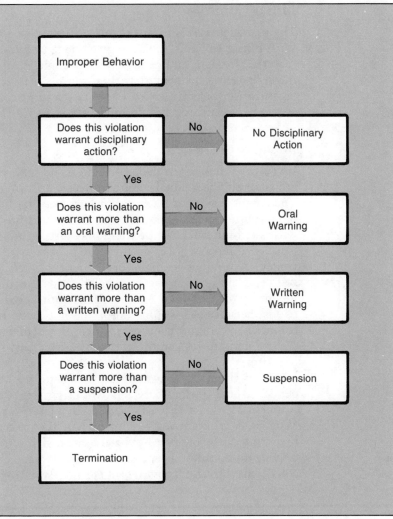

EXHIBIT 14-4
Progressive
discipline

SOURCE R. Wayne Mondy and Robert M. Noe, III, *Personnel: The Management of Human Resources* (Boston: Allyn and Bacon, 1981): 493.

SPECIFIC TYPES OF CONTROL

The control function can be divided into 3 basic types. Initial controls take place as resources enter the organization. Overseeing controls are used during the process when the products and services are being produced. Comparison controls are used after the final product or service has been produced.

Initial Controls

The manager uses initial controls primarily as a preventive measure. With **initial controls**, an attempt is made to monitor the resources — material, human, and capital — that come into the organization for the purpose of ensuring that they can be used effectively to achieve organization objectives. An effort is made to control resources that enter the organization in order to monitor these inputs.

Inventory Control

Inventory refers to the goods or materials that are available for use by a business. The general public is exposed to inventory almost daily. You might hear that a car dealer has excessive inventory and it will offer you a special deal to buy a car. A furniture dealer provides you with a similar offer. While there may also be a bit of sales promotion in these offerings, inventory does represent a cost that must be controlled. A product in inventory constitutes an idle but valuable resource. Suppose that the car dealer keeps a million dollars in extra inventory for one year. At a 10 percent interest rate, $100,000 would be lost because items in inventory do not draw interest. Much of the resources of some major companies are in inventory, yet failure to control inventories can mean the difference between a profit or a loss to a firm.

One of the major advantages of inventory is that it permits independence of operations between two activities. For instance, if Machine A makes a product that will be used in a later stage by Machine B and Machine A breaks down, Machine B will have to cease operation unless inventory of the product has been previously built up. Inventories also provide for continuous operations when demand for the product is not consistent. Electric razors are sold primarily during the Christmas buy-

MANAGEMENT IN PRACTICE

Inventory Control at Phillips Cables

Phillips Cables' construction division manufactures low-voltage electrical wires for the household and construction market. The division has improved customer service by 20 percent and cut inventory in half by introducing a Computerized Inventory Management System (CIMS) and a Transportation Service Plan (TSP). CIMS forecasts product demand and centralizes inventory control, while TSP ensures the timely delivery of products to the company's regional warehouses. These 2 systems now link the 8 regional and 2 central warehouses and factories together through a central computer.

With a centralized inventory, the amount of safety stock that needs to be held can be reduced. The risk of accumulating back orders is also decreased. CIMS and TSP have resulted in an increase in customer satisfaction.

SOURCE Adapted from David Wong, "High Inventory Headache — How Phillips Relieved It," *Canadian Transportation and Distribution Management* (August 1983): 22–23.

ing season, but manufacturers of electric razors typically keep production going through the entire year. Stability is assured, in that a skilled work force can be maintained and equipment usage can be kept at an optimum level. Another advantage of inventory is that it allows the company to fill orders when they are received, thereby maintaining customer satisfaction. If orders arrived on a constant basis, there would be no need to maintain inventory. But if 5 orders come in this month and 100 next month, a company might be hard pressed to fill the 100 requests unless an inventory had been maintained.

There are some equally good reasons for keeping inventories low, however. First, inventories require an investment of funds. A factory which operates with a lower inventory is operating more efficiently — that is, it is producing profits with a smaller investment than a factory with large inventories. Second, inventories take up scarce space. Third, goods in inventory may decrease in value because of deterioration, theft, or damage. Inventory goods also may be subject to **obsolescence**: this is what happens when something is out of date or not as efficient as newer products. New inputs or new finished goods may be invented or found which would make inventories obsolete. Many firms keep as little inventory as possible.

The Just-in-Time Inventory System

During the last few years, a completely new concept of inventory management, which was started in Japan, has begun to gain ground in North America. It is called the **just-in-time inventory system**, or JIT. When the JIT system is used, inventory is scheduled to arrive just in time to be used in the production process. This system is based on the idea that very little inventory is necessary if it is scheduled to arrive at precisely the right time. If it is properly managed, the JIT system saves

---

MANAGEMENT IN PRACTICE

The Just-in-Time Inventory System at Omark Canada

Omark Canada Ltd., a manufacturer of chain saw bars and sprockets, began using JIT in 1982. In the past, Omark's American supplier took 3 or 4 days to make deliveries, partly because drivers had to be changed at the border. As well, loads were often over- or underweight. The company solved both these problems by leasing a truck. Its driver picks up the steel needed to make the saw bars and sprockets and delivers it on the same day. He also synchronizes his arrival with the time the load is required at the plant. The new method has meant savings of $30,000 per year. The company is also planning to ship finished goods on the return trip, in order to save even more money.

SOURCE Adapted from Shelley Boyes and Michelle Ramsay, "Just-In-Time — The New Eastern Philosophy," *Canadian Transportation & Distribution Management* (June 1984): 33.

the company considerable money because inventory levels can be drastically reduced. All the risks associated with inventory — such as obsolescence, theft, or destruction by fire — can therefore be avoided.

The JIT system requires a major change in the way managers think about inventory. It requires great precision in the scheduling of production and in the delivery of inventory. Some companies that use it have found that they are able to schedule arriving inventory almost to the minute if they are very careful in their planning. Drastic inventory reductions are therefore possible, but only if control of the system is tight.

Substantial changes are also necessary outside the company. For example, the JIT system requires suppliers to time deliveries with much greater precision than formerly. Achieving this precision requires a very close working relationship between suppliers and manufacturers, perhaps by having a manufacturer purchase a given raw material from only one supplier. This motivates the supplier to be more careful when scheduling deliveries because the supplier knows how much business is at stake. In the past, many manufacturers purchased a certain part from several different suppliers. This kept competition up among suppliers, but it also meant that the business available to a given supplier was small. Under this system, manufacturers often experienced difficulties with uniformity of parts because they came from 3 or 4 different suppliers. If a manufacturer uses the JIT system and purchases from only one supplier, both of these problems are solved.

Some managers feel very uncomfortable about the JIT system because they are used to carrying inventory and feel good about having buffer stocks in case anything goes wrong. During the strike against General Motors of Canada in October 1984, thousands of American workers were laid off because their plants were using the JIT system. Their plants ran out of parts very quickly when the Canadian strike occurred, so management laid off the workers. But with increasing numbers of companies adopting the JIT system and gaining the financial benefits from it, other companies may have no alternative but to follow suit.

Personnel Selection Controls

If a firm is to maintain its present level of operations, there must continue to be an infusion of new workers into the company. This constant search for new employees is necessary because of such factors as deaths, retirements, loss of employees to other organizations, and any growth that the firm is experiencing. In order to obtain new people who are capable of sustaining the organization, certain controls must be established regarding the selection of individuals employed by the firm. Skill requirements of each job must be determined, and new employees should meet or exceed these skills before being employed. These activities were discussed in Chapter 9.

MANAGEMENT IN PRACTICE

Just-in-Time Inventory Management at Chrysler Canada

The JIT inventory system is highly refined at Chrysler Canada's Windsor, Ontario plant. Since the plant receives up to 300 truckloads a day of raw materials, much care must be taken to ensure that shipments arrive on a precise timetable.

At present, 120 of the 300 arriving shipments are made just in time. Suppliers must work to a strict schedule. For example, Chrysler might tell a supplier to deliver 260 units of a certain raw material to delivery dock "A" at 09:00, and another 340 units at 14:00. Chrysler expects a call from the supplier 30 minutes before the load is scheduled to leave the supplier's dock. If Chrysler doesn't get the load, it calls the supplier and asks what is wrong.

It took some suppliers time to accept that Chrysler meant business. One shipment arrived 12 hours ahead of schedule because the truck driver hadn't stopped to sleep. He had to wait 12 hours to unload. Overall, however, suppliers are responding positively to the system because it also makes them more efficient. Since they know exactly what is expected of them, they are able to schedule their own people more efficiently.

SOURCE   Adapted from Shelley Boyes and Michelle Ramsay, "Just-In-Time — The New Eastern Philosophy," *Canadian Transportation & Distribution Management* (June 1984): 33–34.

Capital Controls

The firm must have sufficient capital available to achieve its objectives. Equipment and people must be obtained and financed. However, when funds are expended on capital goods, the firm exchanges today's dollars in the anticipation of future profits. A firm wants to purchase capital equipment and pay people in such a way that the greatest benefit will accrue to the company — no easy matter because the future contains much uncertainty. However, there are techniques available to assess the value of various capital outlays. One of the most useful approaches — the net present value method — takes into account the fact that a dollar today is worth more than a dollar not to be received until next year. The procedure for using net present value described is in Chapter 15.

Overseeing Controls

Overseeing controls are used to monitor the actual creation of products or services, largely by observation and by interactions between supervisors and subordinates. Overseeing controls occur as the actual work activities are being performed. A large portion of the operating manager's time is devoted to this function.

The greatest opportunity for the discovery and correction of undesirable deviations takes place while the work is being performed. If an entire lot of 50 units is completed by a worker, and inspection reveals that all 50 have the same defect, the overseeing controls have failed. If someone had at least done a spot check while the first few units were being produced, the error would have been found and much time, energy, and raw materials would have been saved. The amount of overseeing necessary depends on such factors as the skill and attitudes of the workers, the confidence the manager has in the workers, the past work record of the employees, and the extent to which the job is carefully specified to reduce the chance of errors.

Comparison Controls

Comparisons determine the degree of agreement between performance results and performance standards. They can take place at or away from the work site. They can be applied to the cumulative performance results of departments or of the entire organization. The objective of **comparison controls** is to determine whether deviations from plans have taken place and, if necessary, to bring the deviations to the attention of the managers who are responsible.

There are several differences between the overseeing and comparison phases of control, even though both involve relating what is going on to what should be going on. First, overseeing occurs while the work is in progress, while comparison comes later and relies on information received after a step in a project is completed or on the results of an entire project.

A second difference between the two controls occurs as a result of the timing. Overseeing must be done by the immediate supervisor. Comparison, however, can be done not only by the supervisor but also by higher line managers or various staff officials. Because it relies on reporting, it can be separated physically from the place where the actual work was done.

Finally, overseeing requires face-to-face contact and personal observation as the method of obtaining information. The manager must evaluate work in both qualitative and quantitative terms and must be adept in human relation skills. Comparison, however, is usually concerned with only a quantitative and statistical evaluation of actions that have reached some state of completion. A monthly production report comparing the quality of all parts for 3 shifts is provided in Exhibit 14-5. Shifts I and II are above the 90 percent standard, while Shift III is slightly below standard. Though observation can be used to gain such information, it more frequently involves written reports, charts, graphs, and similar forms of communication. There are several types of comparison controls. Each one is briefly described below.

Evaluation of Employee Performance

Given a particular task to be accomplished, several people would likely perform at different levels of efficiency. One manager may be quite proficient in planning techniques and another in communication skills. But if each is to improve, each must know his or her specific deficiencies and determine what can be done to overcome them. An effective employee performance system is a means of control whereby individuals learn of their strengths and weaknesses and are told what they should do to overcome them. Employee performance evaluation systems that give each worker the same ratings do not benefit the individual who is a superior performer nor do they assist the substandard worker who wants to improve.

Quotas

Much of comparison control relates to **quotas** that have been established for individuals, units, departments, or divisions. Sales quotas specify the amount of sales an individual, district, or region is expected to meet. Production quotas specify the number of units of each item that must be produced. Control of quotas at every level is important if the organization is to achieve its objectives.

Quality Control

Since the Japanese have developed such a reputation for producing high-quality goods, they have set standards for all competitors. The issue of quality in manufactured goods has become very salient for most Canadians. Anyone who hears a buyer state that he or she got a "lemon" understands that the product was of inferior quality. But what exactly is meant when the term *quality* is mentioned? **Quality** is the degree of conformity to a certain predetermined standard. Standards result ultimately from the establishment of objectives. If the company has an objective of gaining a reputation for manufacturing a high-quality product, standards will have to be high. In order to meet these high standards, there would have to be a very rigid quality control program.

EXHIBIT 14-5
Monthly quality comparison report, by shifts

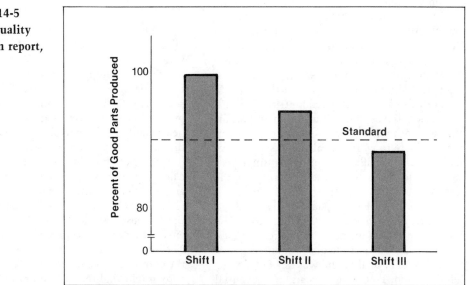

TALKING TO MANAGERS

Sharon Matthias
Alberta Occupational Health & Safety

Sharon Matthias is manager of the Standards and Projects Section in the Occupational Hygiene Branch, Alberta Occupational Health and Safety Division. In the province of Alberta, the division is the government agency responsible for matters concerning health and safety in the work place, including administration of the Occupational Health and Safety Act and its regulations. Matthias believes controlling is an important function both externally — ensuring that companies adhere to worker health and safety standards — and internally — ensuring that employees reporting to her achieve the objectives of the section.

Matthias has a BSc in pharmacy, an MSc in pharmaceutical chemistry, and an MBA. She worked for 8 years in the Crime Detection Laboratory of the Royal Canadian Mounted Police as an alcohol specialist and was head of the Alcohol Section. Following 2 years in residential real estate, she joined the Occupational Health and Safety Division as an occupational hygienist. Matthias has been promoted through several positions of increasing responsibility to her present position.

Q: What activities does your section perform?
Matthias: There are 5 basic areas of activity. First, we review the plans for major new plants in the province; "major" is anything exceeding $100,000,000 in capital costs. We examine these plans at the design stage to be sure that proper health and safety controls are scheduled to be built into the plant. Second, we develop worker health regulations; for example, there are about 750 substances, such as asbestos, coal dust, and chemicals, for which we have specific standards. When working on new regulations, we first develop a draft proposal for public comment by workers and employers. Third, we have a Chemical Hazards Information Program which disseminates information on chemicals and trade name products and their potential hazards. Fourth, our major projects program evaluates workplace hazards on an industry-wide basis; for example, we might research the status of health-hazard controls in welding shops in Alberta. Finally, we administer the Work Site Internal Responsibility Systems program, which ensures that employers develop and maintain a systematic approach to the protection of workers. These 5 programs are all external control programs, since they deal with ensuring compliance with provincial health and safety legislation.

Q: What is the province's view of the most effective way to be certain that health and safety standards are met?
Matthias: The position is currently in transition. Historically, regulations have been prescriptive. They have primarily regulated the process by which the objectives of workplace health and safety are to be achieved. We are now moving toward a more performance-oriented approach where the objective is clearly stated, but exactly how it is to be achieved is not. For example, whereas formerly a regulation might have read "a guard rail must be at least 58 cm high," the regulation would now say "an employer must ensure that workers are protected from falling." The key is to identify the objective and then let the companies decide how to achieve it. A company might find that a guard rail is not the best

way to achieve a particular safety objective. Under the former system, when accidents occurred, the government took the blame for not imposing the proper safety standards. Under the new system, the company is given the freedom to institute programs that will reduce accidents. Since they control the process, they also take the responsibility for the outcome of their safety programs. Also, since work places vary, one single approach may not be best. Some prescriptive-type regulations actually create more of a hazard on some work sites.

Q: What about the internal controlling function? What are your thoughts on the most effective way to carry out your controlling responsibilities, so that your subordinates perform at a high level?

Matthias: Actually, I have a strong philosophical interest in the controlling aspect of management. I am particularly interested in control systems — what works and what doesn't. The work we do on external control has influenced my behavior in performing my internal control responsibilities. I've learned that improper control systems can actually subvert good planning. I've learned that I cannot control without an objective or a sense of direction; otherwise, people focus on busy work.

Q: Do the characteristics of subordinates affect the type of control you use?

Matthias: Yes, to some extent. The people who work for me are professionals; they have a lot of technical training and considerable experience. Many managers set objectives for workers and also tell the workers how to get to those objectives, but I don't feel that approach works very well — especially with professionals. When I have professionals or competent people working for me, I'm concerned about making sure our objectives are achieved but I do not overcontrol the process. So, I set the objectives with the people who work for me, but they can achieve those objectives in a variety of ways. I find that this approach makes them more motivated, and they often find creative ways of doing their work that I wouldn't have thought of.

Q: Can you give us an example of your "control the result but not the process" philosophy?

Matthias: One of the outputs of this section is information brochures. When we are making up a new brochure, I set out the specific message we want to get across and the target audience. The person responsible for the brochure then writes a first draft and discusses it with me. To be consistent with my philosophy, I suppress the urge simply to tell the person how to fix it; instead, I try to tell the writer conceptually what is missing and then allow him or her to fill in the specifics. For example, instead of saying "add this sentence on respiratory equipment in the third paragraph," I say "we need to say something to identify clearly to the worker why it's important to wear respiratory equipment."

Staff control systems are another example. I work much harder, more effectively, and more creatively if I operate with a control system that says "achieve the objectives of the year plan within these dollar and person/year restrictions" than I do under a system which controls specifically each individual position I can recruit.

Q: What is the effect on the control process if the manager has the same technical training as his or her subordinates?

Matthias: If a manager knows the technical aspects of a subordinate's job, there is a tendency for the manager to tell the subordinate not only what the objective is but also how to achieve it. I have technical training in the same areas as some of my subordinates and I have to watch out that I don't overcontrol them. This reduces their decision-making discretion, their authority, and their motivation.

Q: Are you really saying that management by exception is the way to go?

Matthias: I think management by exception has some advantages; but, in practice, it too often leads to emphasis on negative outcomes because the only time the worker hears from management is when something goes wrong. We need a more positive approach to the controlling function of management. I agree that the manager should not get involved in the details of subordinates' work, but a manager shouldn't have dealings with workers only when work isn't going well. There must be positive feedback. I know that many managers think of a control system as a dirty word, but it's essential. Properly designed and properly administered, it can really make a difference in how people view their jobs and how they carry out their work.

MANAGEMENT IN PRACTICE

Quality Control at McDonald's

McDonald's has 7500 restaurants worldwide and had sales of almost $8 billion in 1983. In Canada, there are 425 restaurants and sales were $650 million. McDonald's sells the equivalent of one meal every 3 weeks to each Canadian.

Quality control plays a crucial role at McDonald's. In a Canadian franchise operation, quality control is important because consistency must be maintained in 425 diverse locations. Take meat, for example. It is purchased from independent suppliers that McDonald's doesn't own or control. McDonald's specifies the quality of meat that it wants, and the independent supplier makes sure that quality control at the meat plant is up to McDonald's standards. People from McDonald's purchasing department visit these plants on a regular basis to en-

sure that standards are being maintained. These activities are in addition to the inspection process that is required by the government.

McDonald's is a loyal buyer. If a relationship with a supplier has been going on for a long time, McDonald's will not suddenly curtail it without a very good reason. McDonald's has found that suppliers come up with innovative ways of doing things that benefits both the supplier and McDonald's. The Canadian president, George Cohon, says that the company would never sacrifice quality just to save a fraction of a cent on an item.

SOURCE Dean Walker, "Conversation With George Cohon of McDonald's," *Canadian Business* (June 1983): 32–36.

On the other hand, another firm may not have as its objective such a high-quality product. Increased quality generally results in higher prices; therefore, some firms may target their appeal to a market that desires lower prices and will accept lower quality. Certain standards remain, but they are not as rigid as with the high-quality product.

The Good Time Corporation makes children's outdoor play products. It produces a backyard slide selling for $19.95. The production manager has specified an inexpensive rust-resistant galvanized nut-and-bolt unit for fastening the slide's major parts. These nut-and-bolt units sell for $0.01 apiece in large quantities. The manager could have specified chrome-plated nut-and-bolt units costing $0.08 apiece and still have been able to guarantee against rust. But customers paying $19.95 for a backyard slide just don't expect chrome-plated parts, so the added cost is unjustified. This does not mean, however, that the production manager would accept even cheaper, lower-quality units than the ones selected just to reduce costs by a fraction of a cent. They might cause the slide to fall apart, and the firm would lose its reputation as a maker of good, low-priced play equipment.

What constitutes an acceptable range of quality standards? The range is narrow for firms in the pharmaceutical, nuclear, aircraft, and genetic engineering industries, but it is much broader for firms that make nails, garbage cans, and household furniture. Determining the proper quality levels in service firms can be quite difficult. How does a customer know whether a lawyer, doctor, accountant, or architect has rendered a service where the quality is equal to the price? While there are professional groups in each province that deal with issues like this, many consumers have the perception that these groups simply protect their members, not consumers.

Some firms traditionally insist on buying the highest quality materials available and telling about it in their advertising. For example, some firms advertise that they could reduce their costs by using cheaper ingredients but say that that would hurt their reputation for quality. There is little doubt that a lot of the success of Japanese car makers is a result of the image they have created for using strict quality control standards.

Quality standards may also vary within a firm. A manufacturer of canned foods is likely to exercise great care to ensure the highest quality for products it sells under its own brand. For those it sells as unbranded or generic products, meeting the minimum government standards for quality may be enough. Kitchenaid sets higher standards for its top-of-the-line dishwasher than for its bottom-of-the-line model.

There are numerous ways to maintain quality of a product. A company could make the decision to inspect 100 percent of the items manufactured but, even with a total inspection program, some defects will not be discovered. When you insert the human element into quality control, mistakes will occasionally be made. Some items that are good may be rejected and other items that are defective will be accepted.

In many instances, it is impossible to have a 100 percent inspection. For instance, if the standard for the life of a light bulb were 200 hours, you would have to burn the light for the assigned number of hours to determine if it met standards. Naturally, you would have no product to sell in this situation. Tire manufacturing companies set standards for their tires in order that they can be driven a certain number of

---

MANAGEMENT IN PRACTICE

Quality Control at Moldcraft Plastics

If a company hopes to be successful in the custom molding business it needs high-precision molding skills and strict quality control. One of the handful of Canadian firms that has made the grade is Moldcraft Plastics Ltd., which sold over $6 million worth of components to the telecommunications industry in 1984.

The company's president, Frank Zotter, notes that the products Moldcraft supplies to companies like IBM, Northern Telecom, Mitel, and NCR must have reliability levels that were unheard of a few years ago. A 2 percent rejection rate used to be acceptable, but even that is no longer good enough. Now, almost any rejection rate is unacceptable.

The only way to meet this kind of demand from buyers is to stress quality control from the factory floor up. Top management exhortations to produce high quality will not work. The Moldcraft system is as follows: When an order is received, a sheet listing the critical specifications of the mold is posted so that all workers can see what needs to be done. As the job progresses, both workers and management keep track of how well the specifications are being met. The result has been a slight increase in paperwork, but a very low rejection rate.

SOURCE   Adapted from Judith Nancekivell, "The Pursuit of Excellence," *Canadian Plastics* (June 1984): 24–25.

kilometres. If each tire were placed on a machine and run the assigned number of kilometres to determine if it met standards, there would be no product to market. In still other instances, the cost to inspect each item to determine if it conforms to standard is prohibitive. If each nail in a keg were inspected separately, the cost to inspect might be higher than the price of the nails.

The technique that is available to overcome the above problems is known as **statistical quality control**, in which a portion of the total number of items is inspected. For instance, 5 out of 100 items may be selected and an estimate made as to the characteristics of the other 95. Naturally, some degree of error exists. For instance, if there are 5 defective items in a batch of 100, and the 5 defective ones just happened to be chosen, the entire batch would be rejected. Likewise, if there were only 5 good items in a batch of 100, these 5 might all be chosen and the quality control inspector would erroneously conclude that all items in the batch were good. However, both these situations are very unlikely, so the benefits of sampling far outweigh the costs.

Network Controls

Techniques which monitor the progress of a particular project are referred to as **network controls**. With network controls, critical areas of a project can be identified and carefully monitored to assure a successful completion time. Two of the best-known means of network controls are **program evaluation and review technique** (PERT) and **critical path method** (CPM). PERT was developed to assist in the rapid development of the United States Polaris submarine program. At approximately the same time, researchers at DuPont and computer specialists at Remington Rand's Univac division combined their talents to develop a method to schedule and control all activities involved in constructing chemical plants. The result of their effort was a network model termed the critical path method.

Both PERT and CPM have received widespread acceptance since their introduction in the late 1950s. They are used primarily in construction projects, but some firms use the technique to assist in the development of new products. Network analysis is common to both PERT and CPM. Because of their similarity, only PERT will be discussed in its entirety. Two definitions are first needed: an event and an activity.

An **event** in a PERT network is a meaningful, specified accomplishment (physical or intellectual) in the program plan, recognizable at a particular instance of time. It does not consume time or resources. A circle or node is used to denote an event in a PERT diagram.

An **activity** in a PERT network is the time-consuming element of the program. It is represented by an arrow in a PERT diagram.

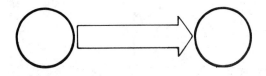

In order to demonstrate how PERT works, we consider the case of a company which is trying to get a government contract to build a certain type of aircraft. The main steps that must be taken by a project manager are as follows:

1. Define the objective of the project and specify the factors (time, cost) that must be considered as the variables to be controlled — for instance, how quickly the project must be completed or how much money is allocated for completion of the project.
2. List all of the significant activities that must be performed for the project objectives to be achieved:
   Preparing specifications
   Establishing quantity requirements
   Negotiating contract
   Preparing test facilities
   Developing airframe
   Developing engine
   Assembling airframe
   Installing engine
   Preparing test
   Testing
   Obtaining headquarters approval
   Evaluating by contractor
   Negotiating contract.
3. Develop a statement of the relationship among project activities. The order in which each task is to be accomplished is also specified. A PERT network is then developed through this information. (See Exhibit 14-6.)
   As may be seen, the prototype airframe and the prototype engine must be completed before the test model is completed.
4. Determine the expected times that will be required to complete each activity. PERT requires that 3 time estimates be provided:
   Optimistic time: If everything goes right and nothing goes wrong, the project can be completed in this amount of time.
   Most likely time: The most realistic completion time for the activity.
   Pessimistic time: If everything goes wrong and nothing goes right, the project will be completed in this amount of time.
   The expected time for the completion of each activity may be seen in Exhibit 14-7. For instance, the optimistic time for the

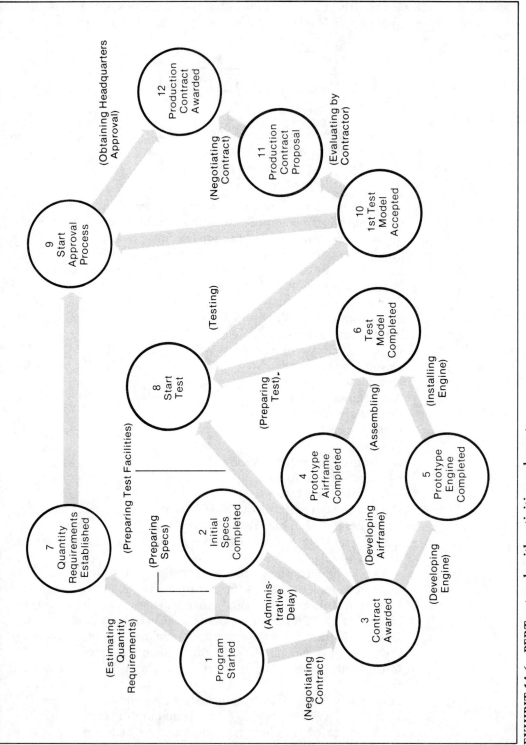

EXHIBIT 14-6 PERT network with activities and events

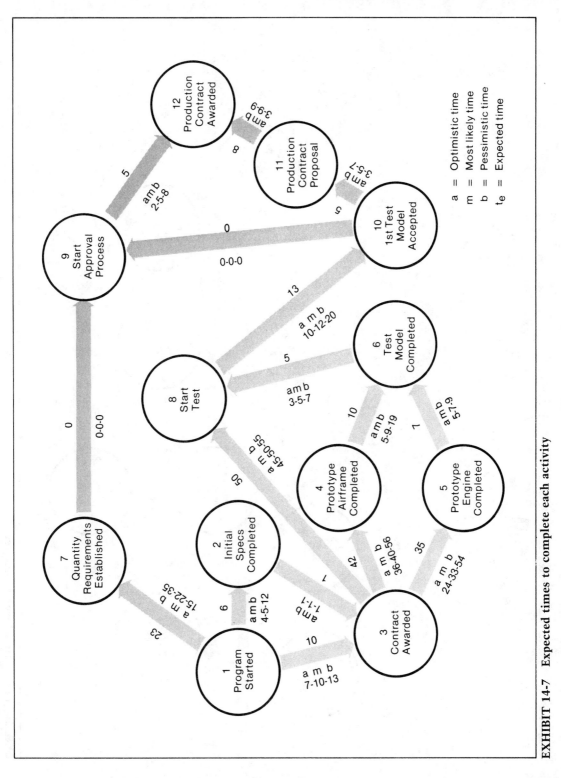

EXHIBIT 14-7   Expected times to complete each activity

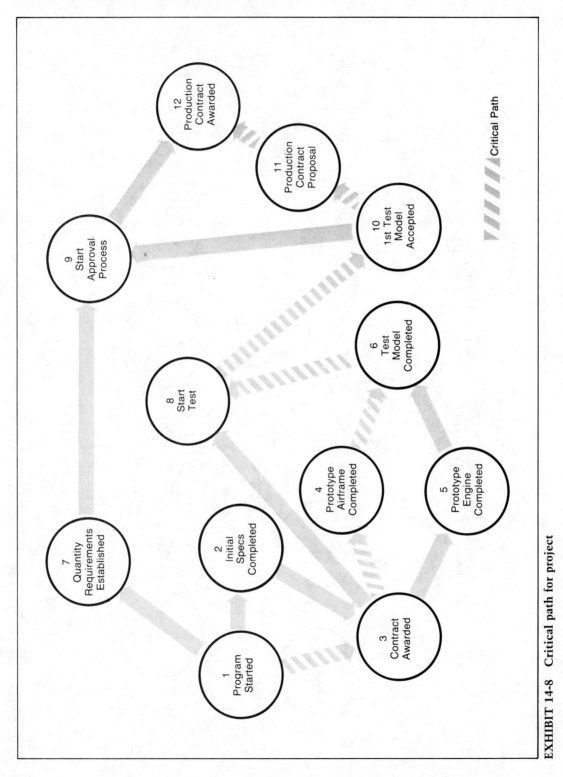

EXHIBIT 14-8   Critical path for project

activity "developing airframe" is 36 weeks, the pessimistic time is 56 weeks, and the most likely time is 40 weeks. Inserting these figures into the expected time formula below, we determine that 42 weeks is the expected time to complete the activity. **Expected time** is then computed by applying the 3 time estimates to the following formula:

$$\text{Expected time (te)} = \frac{\text{Optimistic time} + 4 \text{ (most likely time)} + \text{pessimistic time}}{6}.$$

5. Determine the **critical path**, that is, the longest path from start to finish of the project. (The actual work of the manager terminates once the 3 time estimates have been obtained.) There are numerous computer programs that are available to perform the mechanics of this task. The critical path for this project is represented by the broken line seen in Exhibit 14-8. If any activity along the critical path is a week late, the entire project will be delayed an additional week.

6. Determine the probability of completing the entire project or a particular activity on time. This in itself is a major feature of PERT. Because of the 3 estimates, the manager is able to obtain an estimate of whether the project will be completed on schedule. The optimistic and pessimistic times have been determined to assist in this operation. If there were but one time estimate — the most likely time — probabilities could not be computed.

   A manager usually finds it beneficial to compare the optimistic and pessimistic times to the most likely time. For instance, the activity "developing engine" would likely cause greater concern to the manager than the activity "developing airframe." The difference between the optimistic time and pessimistic time for "developing engine" is 30 weeks (54 − 24), while the difference for the activity "developing airframe" is but 20 weeks (56 − 36). A manager will likely monitor the activities that have the greatest difference between optimistic and pessimistic time because they provide the greatest potential for not meeting the completion date.

Once the critical path has been identified, the manager is able to determine quickly what activities must be carefully monitored. If an activity along the critical path slips one day, the entire project will be delayed one day. Activities that are not on the critical path may not have to be monitored as carefully as those on the critical path. The manager is also in a position to determine which activities are not likely to be completed on time and to monitor them carefully.

PERT may serve both as a planning and a control function. It forces a manager to think thoroughly through a project and identify the tasks that must be accomplished and how they interrelate in the completion of the project. It serves as a control function in that a critical path (the longest path from start to finish of the project) is identified. Thus, a manager is able to work with extremely complex projects and still to maintain control over the project.

Controls through Financial Analysis

The financial statement provides valuable information with regard to whether a company, department, or unit is effectively utilizing its financial resources. Intelligent interpretation of financial data provides an excellent means through which management can control its financial welfare. In order to analyze the financial position, a firm would likely begin with ratio analysis. Financial ratio analysis provides management with a basis for comparing current to past performance. In addition, financial ratios can be compared not only to past trends within the company but also to other divisions within the company and to other firms in the industry. If the ratios are not in line with what is considered acceptable, the manager is in a position to make corrections. These analyses are discussed in more detail in Chapter 15.

ESTABLISHING STRATEGIC CONTROL POINTS

Management through controls is concerned with monitoring a system comprised of resources, processes, activities, and outputs. Management may have difficulty deciding which phases of the system should be monitored. Theoretically, every resource, processing activity, and output should be measured, reported, and compared to some predetermined standard. This can be extremely costly and time-consuming since all activities are not equally significant. A manager must decide what to measure and when to measure it. These critical areas are **strategic control points**, areas that must be monitored if the organization's objectives are to be achieved.

A strategic control point has a number of basic characteristics. First, it is a point established to regulate key operations or events. If a difficulty occurs at a strategic control point, the entire operation may grind to a halt. For instance, if the manager of the word-processing center for Sun Life Insurance Company does not have control of the type and quality of equipment purchased, inaccurate and untimely information may be sent to policyholders. The problem created by poor-quality equipment may have a detrimental impact on the sales of the company even though the word-processing personnel and sales force are of exceptional quality.

A second major characteristic of a strategic control point is that it must be set up so that problems can be identified before serious damage occurs. If the control point is properly located, action can be taken to stop or alter a defective process before major harm is done. It does little good to discover after the fact that a million defective parts have been produced. The control point should be located so deviations can be quickly identified and corrections made.

One of the authors had the opportunity to observe how the improper selection of strategic control points almost caused a major tire manufacturer to cease operations. In the manufacture of a tire, 4 basic phases were required. (See Exhibit 14-9.) The mixing department had to obtain the proper blend of rubber for the type of tire that was being produced. The tread was then shaped with specific attention given to length, width, and thickness. The next phase, building, required placing the various components such as the tread, steel belting, and whitewalls together. In the molding department, the tires were heated and shaped into final form.

A major problem occurred that forced the tire company to reevaluate its entire control procedure. The former system of control consisted only of inspecting tires after they had been molded. Because there was already a large investment in a tire at this stage, a tire would have to have a major defect before it would be rejected. Recognition of the deficiency in the control process occurred when the tire manufacturing firm received an order for several million dollars from a company that purchased tires and sold them at retail outlets under a different brand name. The retail chain, after careful inspection of the tires, rejected the order and demanded that the entire batch be redone. The tire manufacturing firm nearly went out of business because of this decision.

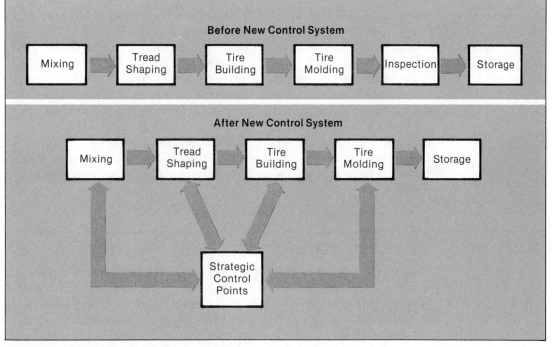

EXHIBIT 14-9   Example of placement of strategic control points

Because of the large investment tied up in rejected inventory, the firm had to go heavily into debt to remake the order.

After this experience, major changes were made in the tire manufacturer's control process. A separate quality control department, reporting directly to the president, was established. Quality control inspectors were hired and given authority to stop operations, even over the advice of the production superintendent, if they felt it was necessary to maintain high quality. Strategic control points were located in the 4 major departments. (See Exhibit 14-9.) If a problem occurred in the mixing department, it would be discovered before the tire progressed through the other stages. Because of this intensive effort to improve quality, the firm was able to survive and prosper.

A third consideration in the choice of strategic control points should be an indication of the level of performance for a broad spectrum of key events. At times, this comprehensiveness conflicts with the need for proper timing. Net profit, for example, is a comprehensive strategic control point, indicating the progress of the entire enterprise. Yet if a manager waits until the regular accounting period to obtain this figure, he or she loses control of the immediate future. It does little good to recognize that the firm is now bankrupt; managers need to have some accounting figures ahead of time so that corrective action may be taken.

Economy is the fourth consideration in the choice of proper control points. With computer and management information systems available, managers may be tempted to demand every conceivable bit of information. But there is a limited amount of information that any executive can effectively use. If every bit of information is available, critical information may be lost in the mass of data.

Finally, the selection of various strategic control points should be balanced. If only credit losses are watched and controlled, for example, sales may suffer because of an overly stringent policy in accepting credit risks. If sales are emphasized, then credit losses may mount. There is a tendency to place tight control over tangible functions, such as production and sales, while maintaining limited control over the intangible functions, such as personnel development and other staff services. This often leads to an imbalance where production line executives are held to exact standards and staff executives are apparently given blank cheques.

CONTROL AND LEVELS OF MANAGEMENT

Managers, unless they are the top officers in the firm, link two levels of organization. As illustrated in Exhibit 14-10, each management level plans for, organizes and influences the level below it. Lower levels of management require more specific planning, organizing, and influencing. Higher-level managers issue orders to lower-level supervisors to accomplish tasks generally planned by top management. As tasks are

MANAGEMENT IN PRACTICE

Control at Mirvish's Restaurants

Edwin ("Honest Ed") Mirvish is an entrepreneur who owns and runs retails stores, restaurants, real estate operations, and theatres which employ over 1000 people. He has a very hands-on style of management and has strong views about what a company must do to be successful. One reason for his success is his concern for the customer.

Mirvish's 4 restaurants serve more than one million meals a year. In the restaurant business, tight controls are necessary since there are so many things to look after. One of his control strategies was to serve only roast beef, even though other restaurateurs said you couldn't have only one item on the menu. The key control element in a restaurant is the chef, who is often a very individualistic person and doesn't like anyone meddling in his kitchen — Mirvish says

chefs have chased him out of the kitchen with a knife. Mirvish now has one chef controlling all the kitchens; the control strategy involves making the food consistent across locations.

Mirvish visits his restaurants regularly and talks to people to see if they have any complaints. He feels that, if he is visible, people will talk to him or send him letters saying what they really think of the restaurant. He responds quickly to any complaints that he receives. He also talks to the employees of the restaurant to get their views of the operation. In this way, the performance of individuals in the restaurants is kept up to his standard.

SOURCE   Dean Walker, "From Discounts to Show Biz, Ed Mirvish Does It His Way," *Executive* (November 1983): 34–38. Reprinted by permission.

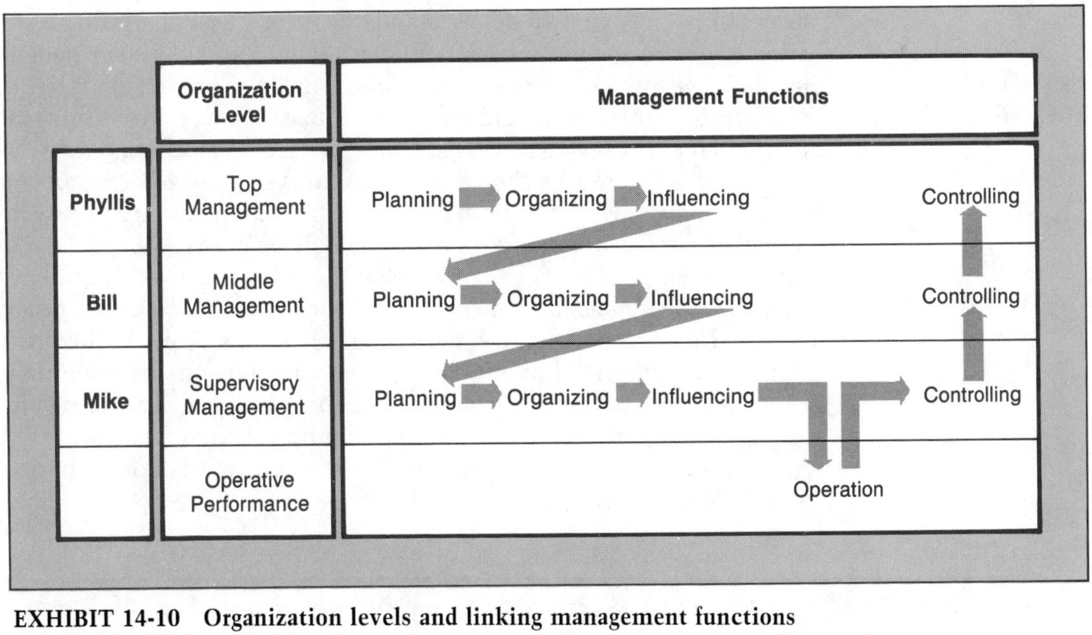

EXHIBIT 14-10   Organization levels and linking management functions

SOURCE   Adapted from Edwin B. Flippo and Gary M. Munsinger, *Management*, 5th ed. (Boston: Allyn and Bacon, 1982): 384. Reprinted by permission.

accomplished, results are communicated to both the immediate supervisor and other levels of management. This enables immediate supervisors to operate within the limits of their specific plan. The immediate supervisor must then provide the information to higher management to ensure that higher-level plans are being fulfilled. This information enables each level of management to determine if the actions of the lower levels are conforming to general plans and objectives and if corrective measures need to be taken.

Consider the types of controls a person would confront as he or she moved from a supervisory management position to a top management position. Mike Miller is a shift foreman for a firm that manufactures aluminum window and door frames. Each Monday, he is given a schedule of items that must be produced each day for that week. With this schedule, Miller plans, organizes, and directs the activities that must be accomplished that week. He knows the standards that have been established for each piece of equipment and monitors each of his employees to ensure that the correct number of frames are being manufactured. If an employee is deficient in any task, Miller must take immediate corrective action to ensure that the daily and weekly schedules are achieved. Each day, Miller sends a report of activities to the general manager, Bill Alexis.

Bill Alexis supervises the activities of 10 shift foremen within a division. He must plan, organize, and influence their efforts. He works in a much longer timeframe and views his task as coordinating the work of the foremen; he studies the daily reports of each of the foremen and determines if they need help to solve particular problems. If a foreman is consistently below standard, Alexis will analyze the situation to determine what action must be taken. Rarely will any decision be made entirely on one day's performance of one of the shifts, but the general overall trend is studied. Alexis submits a weekly performance report of his sections to Phyllis Towne, the vice-president of operations.

Towne also performs the various functions of management but from a different perspective. She has 5 divisions reporting directly to her. She uses control to ensure that the overall objectives of the firm are achieved. She attempts to ensure that a consistent level of quality is maintained, but she must also consider the cost of reaching the quality standard. Her view is even longer than Bill Alexis's. She sees controls as assisting her in solving problems that the divisions may be unable to handle. For instance, if quality is declining because of an aging piece of equipment, she has the authority to purchase new machinery. She monitors the day-to-day operations of the plants but is not as involved as Bill Alexis or Mike Miller.

REASONS FOR NEGATIVE REACTIONS TO CONTROLS

Although strategic control points and the various types of control that we have discussed are important in effective management, controls are often viewed in a negative way by employees. When the term *controls* is mentioned, it makes some workers realize that other people have the power to regulate their activities. There is a natural resistance to controls because a certain amount of individual freedom has been taken away. Employees may not like to be controlled, but they will likely accept the fact that some controls are necessary if the organization is to function successfully. When controls are inappropriate, unattainable, unpredictable, uncontrolled, or contradictory, major resistance is encountered.[1]

Inappropriate Controls

Controls that do not conform to the needs of the situation are inappropriate. In many instances, workers recognize better than management where controls need to be placed if efficiency is to be increased. Inappropriate controls can inhibit the accomplishment of the goals of a department or unit within the organization. For example, in one firm, because of an immediate need for more highly trained machine operators, the control system was changed from a measurement of skill level to one that measured numbers of machine operators who were trained. Many more workers completed the training program, but there was considerable grumbling among the production foremen because the skill level of the machine operators had actually declined. True, more people were available to run the machines, but performance had dropped to the point that the quality level could not be maintained. The controls that had been established were inappropriate to meet the needs of the situation.

Unattainable Standards

Employees realize when a standard is unrealistic. When unattainable controls are established, it may actually cause some employees to work below their capabilities. For instance, suppose that a machine operator has been producing effectively at a standard of 20 units an hour. If management arbitrarily increases the standard to 40 units, the operator may feel that the standard is unattainable, and output may decline to less than 20 units per hour.

Unpredictable Standards

When the control system is unpredictable and is constantly changed, much frustration and resentment can result. For instance, if a production manager is told that he or she should strive to achieve maximum output and, once this high output level has been achieved, is then told that quality is more important, resentment toward the control process can result. The production manager could not predict what standard he or she was to be evaluated on.

No Control of the Situation

All workers find it frustrating to be reprimanded for something they cannot control. Suppose that a manager is told that he will be evaluated on the profit performance of his division, but he is not given the right to determine his employees' compensation or the right to hire and fire people. This manager will rightfully feel that the control process is unfair because he is given no authority over what influences how profitable his division can be. This may lead the manager to resent other kinds of controls, even those which are reasonable and necessary.

Contradictory Standards

At times, various controls may be established that do not complement each other. It may appear to the manager that, if one standard is achieved, it will be impossible to accomplish the other. For instance, it might appear to some managers that high quality and maximum output are contradictory in nature. To a marketing manager, a control system that stresses both increased sales and reduced advertising expenditures may appear contradictory.

OVERCOMING NEGATIVE REACTIONS TO CONTROLS

While the reasons why people resist controls are numerous, managers can find ways to reduce this resistance. A good control system should be justifiable, understandable, realistic, timely, and accurate. If controls have these characteristics, adverse reaction by employees will be minimal.

Justifiable

If employees believe that there is a need for a particular control system, compliance is much easier to obtain. For instance, the firm may have to increase the quality of its product in order to obtain future contracts. These contracts will mean not only profit for the firm but job stability for the employees. A control system will have higher acceptability if the reason for the control appears justifiable to those who must comply.

Understandable

Employees who know exactly what is expected of them with regard to a control system tend to exhibit less resistance. For instance, a statement by a manager that quality should increase does not clearly convey what is expected. A requirement that the number of defects should decrease by 10 percent is precise and understandable. When workers do not understand what is expected of them, frustration and resentment can occur.

Realistic

A realistic control system is one that permits the organization to achieve its goals without straining employee output. At times it may appear that controls are established merely to harass workers. Excessive standards that are higher than needed to accomplish the purpose of the organization are not only expensive but are likely to be resisted by employees.

Timely

For a control system to be effective, information regarding deviations needs to be communicated to employees as quickly as practical. It does little good to tell workers that their performance was below standard 3 weeks ago. If a problem is to be corrected, it must receive immediate attention.

Accurate

A control system must provide accurate feedback to employees. If information feedback has been incorrect in the past, it may be difficult to convince individuals that their effort is below standard. If workers consistently find errors made by supervisors, belief in their ideas may be questioned. An employee who receives a low performance evaluation under such circumstances may have reason to suspect the evaluation is inaccurate even if it is not.

To attain organization objectives, managers perform their basic functions of planning, organizing, and influencing. To be effective with the fourth basic function — controlling — managers should always bear in mind two points: (1) that the controlling process is vital to organizational success, and (2) that workers will often resist controls if they are poorly designed or improperly implemented. A successful manager is the one who can perform all four basic functions well.

OPENING INCIDENT REVISITED

Can-Mark Manufacturing

Production foreman Henry Friesen was under pressure to get production levels up to standard on a new product using state-of-the-art equipment. The new product is crucial to the company. The production workers were complaining that the output standards were not reasonable, even though they had been set by engineering experts.

This situation portrays one of the classic con-trolling problems that management faces. Are the standards really unreasonable? Are the workers trying to take advantage of the uncertainty associated with a new production process to get lower standards established? Why are the workers objecting to the standards that were set by the industrial engineering department?

In the chapter, several causes of negative reactions to standards were noted. At Can-Mark, apparently, the workers genuinely believe that the standard is unattainable. They may also feel that they do not have sufficient control over the situation because they have to work with state-of-the-art machinery.

What can be done to reduce these negative reactions and get production back on track? The chapter notes that standards should be justifiable, understandable, and realistic. Can-Mark's management has a perception problem here because the standards for this new product are not perceived as either justifiable or realistic by the production workers who have good past records with the company. As a show of good faith, management will probably have to retime the jobs — taking into account the newness of the pro-

cess — to see if any unreasonable assumptions were originally made by the industrial engineers. Management will also have to deal with the quality issue. Perhaps quality standards were not clear enough to workers who may be worrying excessively about quality and not enough about volume. This imbalance would make the standards seem unreasonably high to them.

Overall, management personnel need to show the workers that they are concerned about the problem and want to cooperate with the workers to resolve it. If the workers who actually use the machines are encouraged to analyze the problem and work with management, they will undoubtedly come up with some suggestions for increasing output.

SUMMARY

Control is the process of comparing actual performance with established standards for the purpose of taking corrective action. However, before standards can be established, objectives and plans must be developed. Thus, standards serve as the link between planning and control.

The controlling process involves 4 critical activities: establishing standards and control tolerances, observing and measuring, comparing performance to standards, and taking corrective action. In an organization, the most important means by which performance can be compared to standards relate to quantity, quality, time, and costs. Corrective action is needed to straighten out deviations from planned performance or to alter the plan to allow for obstacles that cannot be removed. A natural byproduct of corrective action is discipline, the process of invoking a penalty against an employee who fails to adhere to standards.

The control function can be divided into 3 basic types: initial, overseeing, and comparison controls. Initial controls take place as resources enter the organization. Initial controls include inventory systems. High costs can be incurred by keeping large inventories on hand, especially in manufacturing firms; service businesses often have to maintain high inventories to serve customers well. Many manufacturers in North America have started using the Japanese "just-in-time" inventory system; this involves having suppliers deliver resources just at the point they are needed in the manufacturing process, cutting the costs of storing inventory drastically. Overseeing controls are used during the process when the products and services are being produced. Comparison controls are used after the final product or service has been produced. Comparison controls include quality control; certain products and services require very high quality, with little margin for defects, while others can be sold at lower quality and cost. Very few products can be manufactured with total quality inspection. Most firms use statistical quality control, inspecting a specified sample of products. Many manufacturers also use network controls; two of the best known are program evaluation and review technique (PERT) and critical path method (CPM). Both involve plotting diagrammatically the events and activities of a project in order to determine costs and time schedules. However, at all times, a manager must determine what to measure and when to measure an activity. These critical areas are referred to as strategic control points.

Managers must realize that there will be a certain amount of negative reactions to controls. Some of these negative reactions are caused by inappropriate controls, unattainable standards, unpredictable standards, or contradictory standards. However, there are means by which negative reactions to controls may be overcome. If controls are justifiable, understandable, realistic, timely, and accurate, they will likely cause little resistance.

REVIEW QUESTIONS

1. Define *control* as a process for assisting managers to accomplish their objectives.
2. Explain in your own words why the functions of planning and controlling are so closely related.
3. What are the phases involved in the controlling process?
4. What are the 4 means by which actual performance may be compared to standards? Briefly discuss each.
5. What are some guidelines that a manager should follow when disciplinary action must be used?
6. Distinguish initial controls, overseeing controls, and comparison controls. When would each type be used?
7. What are some advantages and disadvantages of the traditional North American inventory system and the Japanese just-in-time inventory system?
8. What is statistical quality control? Give 3 examples of statistical quality control and explain why a 100 percent inspection could not be used instead.
9. What kind of businesses use PERT or CPM network controls? Explain how PERT helps to control a complicated project.
10. What factors should a manager consider in establishing strategic control points?
11. What effect does the level of management have on the control process?
12. What characteristics should a control system have in order to overcome employee resistance?

EXERCISES

1. Develop objective(s), plans, and standards for obtaining an A in this course. What type of control measures must be developed for you to accomplish this goal?
2. Consider the following types of businesses and managers. What types of controls do you believe they must have to ensure that they accomplish their objectives?
   a. A small convenience store
   b. A community college or university
   c. A firm that manufactures a high-quality hand calculator
   d. An insurance agency
   e. An automobile repair shop.

CASE STUDY

A Problem of Inventory Control

As supervisor of 10 stores in a convenience store chain, Martha Young is responsible for their general operation. Each of these small stores has a day manager and 2 assistant managers who work the evening and midnight shifts. These personnel are not really managers because they have no subordinates reporting directly to them. The day manager is typically the senior person who has chosen the day shift.

Mark McCall is the day manager of one of the stores that Young supervises. McCall has been at the store for 3 months and sales have been increasing steadily. McCall maintains his store in good order, and the first 2 monthly inventory checks have been satisfactory. But as Young reads the inventory report for this month, she becomes quite disturbed. Inventory is $1,000 short for the previous month. (Anything over $200 is considered out of the ordinary.)

Young realizes that this report is extremely serious. Other personnel have been terminated for inventory shortages of this amount. She likes McCall but she must do something to keep this situation from occurring in the future.

Young reviews the situation regarding the store. The following points come to mind:

- The store is located close to a school. When McCall took control of the store, school was not in session. Some shoplifting might be occurring.
- One of the assistant managers has been with the store for only one month. There could possibly be internal theft.
- The other assistant manager broke up with his girlfriend last month. Perhaps he has not been paying close attention to his job.

QUESTIONS

1. What type of controls, if any, should Martha Young instigate?
2. If the inventory is short next month, what do you think Young should do?

CASE STUDY

A Question of Standards

Steven Dowling was a regional sales manager for McGavin-Shane Ltd., a firm that manufactured and sold hydraulic and pumping equipment for industrial uses. Dowling supervised 7 salespeople in Southern Ontario.

To ensure good performance from the salespeople, Dowling met with each one twice a year to set sales goals for his or her territory. At the end of each month, he received sales reports from each salesperson. After each 6-month period, he met with each salesperson and discussed the reports, then set goals for the next 6-month period. Whenever a salesperson fell short of a 6-month goal, Dowling tried to be positive and to give encouragement to do better during the next 6-month period.

Recently he had become quite concerned about Mike Litvin's sales performance. Litvin had worked for another firm in the same business for 17 years, but he had been with McGavin-Shane for only 5 months and Dowling didn't yet know him very well. For the last 3 months, Litvin had failed to reach his targeted sales; worse, the shortfall in each succeeding month had increased. In Dowling's mind, a trend had developed that he ought to investigate; once he found out what was wrong, he could help Litvin. At the regular 6-month meeting with Litvin, Dowling raised the issue of the shortfall during the last 3 months. The following conversation took place:

Dowling: Mike, I'm concerned about your sales volume during the last few months. You haven't been up to standard for 3 months now, and you know I can't let that continue.

Litvin: I've been meaning to speak to you about my sales territory and some of the things that are going on there. You know, you're very fortunate that I'm in that territory and have ex-

perience in this business. There has been a big drop in demand for our equipment, but I'm getting at the sales that are out there.

Dowling: I'm very surprised to hear you say that, Mike. The other salespeople aren't reporting any problems.

Litvin: Well, maybe they just don't want to worry you. I've never experienced so much difficulty in getting sales as I have during the last 3 months.

Dowling: But Mike, the sales figures of the other people are right up to standard. Yours aren't.

Litvin: Steve, if anybody else was in my territory, they wouldn't have sold nearly as much as I have.

Dowling: Mike, aren't you missing the point? Your performance has fallen below our standard.

Litvin: That's one way of looking at it. Another way is to say that my performance is very good given the tough sales atmosphere out there.

At this point, Dowling terminated the interview. He was astonished that Litvin would not even admit the obvious fact that his sales were not up to standard.

QUESTIONS

1. What is Litvin really saying about the sales standard that has been set for him?
2. What should Dowling do to resolve this problem?

NOTE

[1] Robert N. Anthony and Regina E. Herzlinger, *Management Control in Non-Profit Organizations* (Homewood, Ill.: Irwin, 1975): 222–226.

REFERENCES

Boyes, Shelley, and Ramsay, Michelle. "Just-In-Time — The New Eastern Philosophy." *Canadian Transportation and Distribution Management* (June 1984): 33.

Brennan, J. M. "Up Your Inventory Control." *Journal of Systems Management* 28 (January 1977): 39–45.

Buffa, Elwood S. *Modern Production-Operations Management*. 6th ed. New York: Wiley, 1980.

Camillus, John C. "Six Approaches to Preventive Management Control." *Financial Executive* 48 (December 1980): 28–31.

Chase, Richard B., and Aquilano, Nicholas J. *Production and Operations Management: A Life Cycle Approach*. Homewood, Ill.: Irwin, 1981.

Dalton, Dan R., and Todor, William D. "Win, Lose, Draw: The Grievance Process in Practice." *Personnel Administrator* 26 (March 1981): 25–29.

DeWelt, R. L. "Control: Key to Making Financial Strategy Work." *Management Review* 66 (March 1977): 18–25.

Flamholtz, Eric. "Organizational Control Systems as a Managerial Tool." *California Management Review* 22 (Winter 1979): 50–59.

Gitman, Lawrence J. *Principles of Managerial Finance*. 2d ed. New York: Harper, 1979.

Hayhurst, B. "Proposal for a Corporate Control System." *Management International Review* 16 (1976): 93–103.

Hostage, G. M. "Quality Control in a Service Business." *Harvard Business Review* 53 (July-August 1975): 98–106.

Horovitz, J. H. "Strategic Control: A New Task for Top Management." *Long Range Planning* 12 (June 1979): 2–7.

Lissy, William E. "Necessity of Proof to Support Disciplinary Action." *Supervision* 40 (June 1978): 13.

Machin, John L., and Wilson, Lynn S. "Closing the Gap between Planning and Control." *Long Range Planning* 12 (April 1979): 16–32.

Mittelstaedt, Arthur H., and Berger, Henny A. "The Critical Path Method: A Management Tool for Recreation." *Parks and Recreation* 7 (July 1972): 14–16.

Mondy, R. Wayne, and Noe, Robert M. III. *Personnel: The Management of Human Resources*. Boston: Allyn and Bacon, 1981.

Nelson, E. G., and Machin, J. L. "Management Control: Systems Thinking Applied to Development of a Framework for Empirical Studies." *Journal of Management Studies* (October 1976): 274–287.

Ouchi, W. G. "Relationship between Organizational Structure and Organizational Control." *Administrative Science Quarterly* 22, no. 1 (March 1981): 95–113.

Pingpank, Jeffery C., and Mooney, Thomas B. "Wrongful Discharge: A New Danger for Employers." *Personnel Administrator* 26 (March 1981): 31–35.

Plossl, G. W., and Welch, W. Evert. *The Role of Top Management in the Control of Inventory*. Reston, Va.: Reston Publishing, 1979.

Schroeder, Roger G. *Operations Management: Decision Making in the Operations Function*. New York: McGraw-Hill, 1981.

Solomon, Ezra, and Pringle, John J. *An Introduction to Financial Management*. Santa Monica, Cal.: Goodyear, 1980.

Smith, Martin R. "A 10-point Guide to Making Quality Control Management Effective." *Management Review* 64 (April 1975): 52–54.

Swann, James P. Jr. "Formal Grievance Procedures in Non-Union Plants." *Personnel Administrator* 26 (August 1981): 66–70.

Control Techniques

Cam's Corner

Cameron McIntyre opened a variety store called Cam's Corner in Charlottetown, PEI in 1970. During the first few years of operations, business was very good and McIntyre continually found himself having to expand to meet customer demand. He began adding more product lines and salespeople in the early 1970s and this continued through 1979. By that time he had opened 2 new stores and employed 22 people.

In 1979, interest rates began increasing substantially, and demand for the products he sold began to decline. Like most business people, McIntyre responded by tightening up operations in obvious areas like inventory control or employee overtime. This strategy did reduce costs somewhat, but not enough to make up for substantially declining sales. By 1981, his net profit after taxes was virtually zero; McIntyre was deeply concerned because he knew he couldn't carry on much longer without an improvement in sales and profits. He wanted to continue in business, but he didn't know what else to do.

In an attempt to resolve his problems, McIntyre asked his business acquaintances in Charlottetown how they were coping with the recession, and they were able to give him some additional ideas on better ways to control his business. By early 1984, the general Canadian economy was recovering and McIntyre's profits began to increase once again. McIntyre became very busy with the day-to-day operations of his 3 stores and didn't have much time to think about his earlier problems. However, in his quiet moments at home in the evening, he still had nagging doubts about the effectiveness of the control devices he was using in his business. He wondered what would happen if another economic downturn occurred.

KEY TERMS

socialization
management
  hierarchy
management audits
management by
  exception
exception principle
budget
operating budget
financial budget

cash budget
capital budget
Planning-
  Programming
  Budgeting System
  (PPBS)
zero base budgeting
  (ZBB)
break-even analysis
variable costs
fixed costs

net present value
profit center
ratio analysis
balance sheet
income statement
liquidity ratios
leverage ratios
activity ratios
profitability ratios
audit

LEARNING OBJECTIVES

After completing this chapter you should be able to
1. Explain the difference between financial and nonfinancial control techniques.
2. Identify 6 nonfinancial and 6 financial control techniques.
3. Describe how budgets are used to facilitate the controlling function.
4. Do a break-even analysis.
5. Explain how ratio analysis helps managers determine how effective an organization is.
6. Explain the difference between financial audits and management audits.
7. Indicate the manager's responsibility in choosing appropriate control techniques.

In the last chapter we analyzed the control process and the importance of the controlling function to management. In this chapter, we present several of the most commonly used control techniques. Some of these very diverse techniques require formalized management activity, while others do not. Some focus on the total organization, while others focus on individuals or small groups. Some of them require quantitative data, while others do not.

In order to simplify the discussion of the numerous control techniques that companies actually use, we divide them into 2 categories: nonfinancial and financial. As the names imply, nonfinancial techniques are used to control employee behavior without specific reference to corporate financial data. Financial control techniques can be used only when financial data like costs, profit, or sales revenue are available. Neither category of techniques should be considered more important than the other; rather, they complement each other. In total, they give management a good idea of what is going on in an organization.

NONFINANCIAL CONTROL TECHNIQUES

The most widely used nonfinancial control techniques are: rewards and punishments, selection procedures, socialization and training, the management hierarchy, management audits, management by exception, and PERT (discussed in Chapter 14). These control techniques can be used in any area of the firm, but corporate policy and the personality of the managers in the organization will determine how vigorously they are pursued. We discuss each of these techniques next.

Rewards and Punishments

Every organization has some systems for rewarding behavior that is desirable and punishing behavior that is undesirable. The systems may be formal or informal, but their purpose is to convey to employees how management prefers them to behave. Individual managers usually administer these systems, so, typically, they are not used consistently across all departments or divisions of a company.

The effectiveness of rewards and punishments as a control device depends heavily on the individual manager. The manager must: (1) identify what employees find rewarding and punishing, (2) be consistent in the application of rewards and punishments, and (3) be able to measure employee performance accurately in order for the system to work. If these criteria are not satisfied, managers may experience difficulty trying to control employee behavior with rewards and punishments. For example, in one company, management thought they were doing workers a favor by not making them work overtime, but they later found out that workers wanted to work overtime to earn extra money. Thus, management thought they were rewarding workers when in fact they were punishing them.

Rewards and punishments can have a powerful influence on employee behavior, so they are a potentially useful control device. However, they must be applied carefully or significant problems may arise. The role of rewards and punishments in motivation was discussed in some detail in Chapter 10.

Selection Procedures

Organizations also control employees by controlling the type of employee that is hired in the first place. When the personnel department recruits people for various jobs in the organization, it stipulates certain characteristics that applicants must have. The net effect is to control the type of people that comes into the organization. For example, if a company is hiring electrical engineers, it might require applicants to have a degree in electrical engineering. When newly hired electrical engineers begin working, they will find that they have something in common with other electrical engineers at the company because of their educational background.

This kind of control can, of course, have a negative effect on a company. Over time, individuals with a similar perspective may narrow their views; without infusion of new perspectives, they may come to dominate the firm, and it may have difficulty being innovative or creative. Further, if this stagnation happens, the company may find itself unable to respond to changes in its markets; the firm may experience these difficulties precisely because it is efficient in controlling the type of people it hires.

Socialization and Training

When a new employee comes into a company, he or she is given information about both the formal and informal activities of the firm. One of the subtle, but powerful, control techniques that new employees experience is **socialization** — the gradual change of attitudes and behavior of individuals so that they fit into the organization.

The influence of socialization is evident in the public school system in Canada. Graduates often don't realize that the way they view the business and social aspects of their lives is partially a result of how they were taught in school. Over the period of years in grade school and high school, students are socialized to fit into the Canadian economic and social systems. A similar process of socialization happens in organizations. Each organization has certain attitudes and procedures it wants employees to accept and, over a period of time, employees are socialized into accepting that these attitudes and procedures are good. Socialization can be a very powerful form of control over employees.

Training is also used to change employee attitudes and behavior so that they are in line with overall goals of an organization. For instance, if a company has quality as a top priority, it may require all production-line employees to take a course in quality control. Or, if a company is a leader in technological innovation, it may systematically train its employees to be effective in that area. Whatever the company's strategic goal is, it may want to control its employees through training. An employee who resists being trained will probably experience considerable difficulty.

The Management Hierarchy

One of the most fundamental and obvious control techniques is the **management hierarchy**. Employees in all organizations know that they are responsible to the manager above them in the chain of command. That manager, in turn, knows that he or she is responsible to the next manager up in the formal structure. In some companies the hierarchy is rigidly defined, while in others it is not. In either case, the hierarchy is a control device because each person must account for personal performance and behavior to the next person up the line.

Organizations have developed various control techniques, which are an integral part of the management hierarchy. Rules, policies, procedures, and objectives (discussed in Chapter 3) are examples of control techniques embedded in the management hierarchy. Each controls employee behavior in some way. Rules, for example, limit employee behavior with respect to specific activities, while policies allow considerable flexibility. Objectives may have a restrictive connotation, in that individuals are responsible for reaching certain objectives, but they also can motivate employees toward positive achievements — for example, higher wages if objectives are exceeded. All of these hierarchical controls allow management to predict what employees might do and how they might be motivated to do better while they are working for the company.

Management Audits

Management audits are designed to analyze systematically the strengths and weaknesses of the managerial talent in a company. The goal is to improve the organization by making sure that weaknesses in management can be identified and corrected. Some areas of the firm that might be subject to a management audit are economic performance, the state of research and development, production efficiency, sales effectiveness, and earnings growth. All these areas can reflect how well top management has been doing its job of strategic planning, organizing, staffing, and controlling the activities of the organization.

The audit is usually done by an outside consulting firm because the areas to be assessed are politically very sensitive. They may also be difficult to measure objectively, so an organization with no vested interest in the results should be used. The management audit is a control device because it measures how well the managers in a firm have been able to get actual corporate performance up to the desired level. This level may be an industry standard, or it may have been set by the company's own top management. In either case, the management audit compares actual performance against some standard.

Management by Exception

Perhaps the most fundamental of all control techniques is **management by exception** (MBE). The basic idea of MBE is that a manager should exercise general management of an area of responsibility, not daily detailed supervision of each worker. Management by exception is a control technique because it requires the manager to watch overall trends and take action when certain aspects of the operation become exceptions.

TALKING TO MANAGERS

Stephen B. Butler
Miles Laboratories, Ltd.

Stephen B. Butler has a BA from University of Toronto and an MBA from York University. Now, he is manager of operations, logistics, for Miles Laboratories, Ltd., a pharmaceutical manufacturer and distributor, situated in Rexdale, Ontario, a suburb of Toronto. The Canadian company is a subsidiary [see Chapter 17] of Miles Laboratories, Inc. of the United States, which in turn is owned by Bayer ag, a German multinational pharmaceutical company.

Q: How do you handle materials management at Miles Laboratories?

Butler: Our manufacturing process actually begins with a sales forecast generated by the marketing department. We translate that sales forecast into production requirements needed to replenish inventories to the level that will be required. The goal of materials management is to have the right product in the right place at the right time, but we need to do this in a cost-efficient manner. We must decide how to translate the forecast demand for all our products into a plan for using our production facilities — equipment, labor force, etc. — to the best advantage. We don't want to try for perfect customer service at the cost of supporting huge inventories. On the other hand, we don't want to produce something on Monday, change over the production line, and then change back to produce it again on Thursday. We have to try to find that optimal blend of investment, efficiency, and customer service standards that will allow us to be effective as a business.

One of the most difficult things that we must establish, then, is an acceptable level of customer service. There are conflicting objectives on this matter. Marketing and sales want to have enough stock in inventory to fill all orders as they come in. That level of service is unachievable; we would need cities of warehouses. On the other side, finance people want to minimize the amount of money we have tied up in inventory. What our customers really expect is consistency. They want to know that, if they order from Company X, they can expect delivery in 3 days — not in 2 days the first time, 10 days the second time, 5 days the third time.

Q: Once you establish standards, how do you control the process to get the results you want?

Butler: There are so many variables involved in the whole process that efficient control is extremely difficult. One thing we know about market forecasts is that they are always wrong. What we have to do is continuously monitor how wrong they are. We then establish a guideline that we can expect a given forecast to be wrong by a variation of, say, 20 percent. So instead of continually adjusting our production plans to meet changing market forecasts, we establish a safety margin that allows for likely inaccuracy. If you are dealing with only one product, the variables become fairly easy to handle in determining appropriate reactions; and, unfortunately, what we usually do is react rather than pro act. As a company grows and develops more products, the combinations of possibilities become so numerous that it is impossible to evaluate them all using traditional methods in time to take meaningful action. Only the computer can do that job, and that fact has led to the universal acceptance of the computer as *the* control device.

Computerized manufacturing resource planning systems are designed specifically to provide timely control of the execution of the production plan. Once you have established your basic guidelines, the computer can turn them into a detailed plan of action in a very short time. For each product we manufacture, the computer contains a bill of material; this is a list of all the components or ingredients required to make 1 unit of the product. If we know we need 10 000 units to replenish inventory, the computer can quickly compare what we need to produce to our existing supplies in inventory, and generate a list of products we need to order. An additional power of the system is that it has a lead time built into each item so that it can generate a master schedule for reordering supplies from outside or from our production floor, if we produce it ourselves. Production control managers don't need to spend all their time pushing a pencil against a piece of paper to make the plan; they can devote their time to making the plan happen.

Q: How do you react to the antagonism some managers feel toward computers?
Butler: When looking at computer control systems, managers must remember that a computer does not erase the need for human interface. A computer should be used as a mechanism for getting rid of the drudgery of number tumbling and number crunching, so that people can use their intelligence and skills to analyze situations and make decisions. So many times, I've seen people struggle to make a decision, because they didn't have all the data available to them. After a while, they may develop intuition, gut reactions, that give them appropriate answers. I prefer to have the relevant data available when making decisions. To me, the essence of a good system is that it not be person-specific. If a company is relying on the decisions of a manager who happens to have an exceptional intuitive feel for the products and the marketplace, then that company is extremely vulnerable should that person leave. The company is safer with a system that allows anybody with particular analytical skills to handle the situation.

Q: Can you discuss the other aspect of your job, controlling people?
Butler: People are so diverse that in my experience I need a variety of management styles in controlling people. About 25 people report to me, production and inventory control, purchasing, warehousing, and distribution staff. I regard people as my most important resource in managing my functional area. It is easy for managers to assume they have a system that works and to leave it static, but I prefer to challenge people to create improvements. There are people out there who are not motivated solely by money. They need challenge; they need standards of quality; they need to feel they are part of the thinking process, not just scribes.

Q: Computers can make it tempting to apply very tight controls to the productivity of individual workers; for instance, a manager can use a word processor to track the keystrokes of each operator and can push slower operators to meet the standards set by the fastest ones. How do you feel about that?
Butler: I think that monitoring results is an important task for a manager, but the attitude in which this is done is also important. I could quantify the efforts of my purchasing manager and use my information as a whip to beat him with — a Theory X approach; but, I would rather take the data to him and say there must be something in the system that we can change to improve this. I would encourage the employee to make suggestions. The whole range of activity associated with Management by Objectives must be endorsed. I have found that to be a very useful method of providing people that extra opportunity to improve themselves and their worth to the company.

We can learn a lesson from the Japanese and try to reduce the number of tiers of management so that a manager is closer to the workers. This improves the opportunities for communication. The Japanese have had success in using quality circles to generate ideas from employees. We can learn from the Japanese to change in an evolutionary rather than revolutionary manner. Sometimes we develop control systems that are more complex than the original problems. The Japanese approach is to stand back from the problem and to try to understand it in simple terms so they can find simple solutions.

The **exception principle**, that employees should handle routine matters and the supervisor should handle exceptional matters, is the basis for MBE. For example, a manager might require that employees inform him or her when quality checks on products are below standard more than 10 percent of the time. Otherwise, employees would have the right to continue production without consulting the supervisor. In a service organization, a manager might want to know about customer complaints only when they exceed a certain percentage of customers handled.

The use of MBE results in two advantages for organizations. First, it means a better use of the manager's time. We saw in Chapter 1 that some managers fail to confine themselves to managerial work; instead, they involve themselves in the same kinds of activities as their subordinates. This behavior is not appropriate for management, and use of MBE increases the likelihood that a manager will perform managerial duties, not operative duties. Second, MBE encourages workers to exercise judgment when doing their work. They need not continually consult the manager to check that their work performance is appropriate. As long as they are within the guidelines that have been established, they can continue working as they see fit.

Management by exception is both a motivational and a control technique. Generally speaking, when workers operate under an MBE system, they feel that management has a higher opinion of them and this feeling is motivating. At the same time, control is exercised by management, but only when unusual circumstances merit it.

FINANCIAL CONTROL TECHNIQUES

The most widely used financial control techniques are: budgets, breakeven analysis, net present value, profit centers, ratio analysis, and accounting audits.

Budgets

Though there are many devices that managers can use in controlling costs or expenditures, the most widely known and used is the budget. A **budget** is a formal statement — in dollar-and-cents terms — of the firm's planned expenditures in a future time period, usually one year. Budgetary control requires comparison of actual and planned expenditures.

Types of Budgets

Budgets are important documents used by managers in planning and controlling operations. There are 2 broad categories of budgets: financial budgets, and operating budgets. An overview of the components of these two types of budgets is provided in Exhibit 15-1.

- **Operating budgets** indicate the revenues and expenses the business expects from producing goods and services during a given year. As illustrated in Exhibit 15-1, these budgets consist of action plans, cost budgets, and a profit plan.
- **Financial budgets** indicate the amount of capital the organization will need and where it will obtain the capital. Two financial budgets are usually developed: the cash budget and the capital budget. The **cash budget** summarizes planned cash receipts and disbursements, while the **capital budget** indicates planned capital acquisition, usually for the purpose of purchasing additional facilities or equipment.

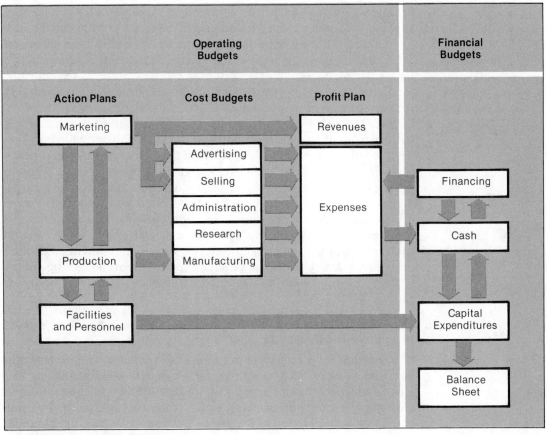

EXHIBIT 15-1 Types of budgets

SOURCE Gordon Shillinglaw, *Managerial Cost Accounting*, 4th ed. (Homewood, Ill.: Irwin, 1977): 137. Reprinted by permission of author and publisher.

BUDGET KEYPUNCH DEPARTMENT January 131				
Item	Budget	Actual	Over	Under
Director labor	$10,000	$10,800	$800	
Indirect labor	1,800	1,800		
Operating supplies	1,250	1,500	$250	
Maintenance	1,800	1,400		$400
Misc. expense (telephone)	190	150		40
Total	$15,040	$15,650	Over $610	

EXHIBIT 15-2
Department operating budget

An Illustration of Budgetary Control

The use of a budget as a control device is relatively simple. Exhibit 15-2 shows the monthly budget for a keypunch department. The major expense items include direct labor (wages for the unit's keypunch operators), indirect labor (the department manager's salary), operating supplies (keypunch cards), maintenance expenses (repair of machines), and miscellaneous expenses. As shown in Exhibit 15-2, actual expenditures are compared with budgeted or planned expenditures. In this department, actual expenditures exceeded budgeted expenditures for direct labor and operating supplies by $800 and $250, respectively. Actual spending for maintenance and miscellaneous was under the budgeted amount by $440. Budgetary control enables the manager of the department to identify significant deviations in actual versus budgeted or planned expenses and to take corrective action when necessary. For example, the $800 over budgeted expenses for the wages of keypunch operators may have been caused by the necessity to pay overtime wages. This cost may have resulted from ineffective work scheduling or the sudden appearance of a rush job. This situation, if it occurred in several successive periods, may cause the manager to take such actions as requesting additional personnel or improving the scheduling of work to correct the problem. In any event, budgeting control is a very useful tool of managers at virtually every level of an organization.

Benefits of the Budgeting Process

The fact that most profit and not-for-profit organizations operate within the framework of budgets attests to their benefits. Budgeting is a very significant part of both the planning and controlling processes. Budgets are widely used by managers to plan, monitor, and control various activities and operations at every level of an organization. There are several important advantages for preparing and using budgets. Some of the benefits of the budgeting process are that it:

• Provides standards against which actual performance can be measured. Budgets are quantified plans that allow management to measure and control performance more objectively. If, for instance, a department manager knows that the budgeted expenditure for supplies is $1,000 per month, the manager is then in a position to monitor and control the expenses for supplies.

- Provides managers with additional insight into actual organization goals. Monetary allocation of funds as opposed to lip-service more often than not is the true test of a firm's dedication to a particular goal. For instance, suppose that 2 firms of relatively similar size had a stated policy of hiring minority personnel. Firm A allocates $100,000 and Firm B provides $10,000. A personnel agent will realize that a much stronger commitment to minority hiring is expressed by Firm A than by Firm B.

- Tends to be a positive influence on the motivation of personnel. People typically like to know what is expected of them, and budgets clarify specific performance standards.

- Causes managers to divert some of their attention from current to future operations. To some extent, a budget forces managers to anticipate and forecast changes in the external environment. For example, an increase in transportation costs created by higher-priced petroleum might force the firm to seek an alternative transportation or distribution system.

- Improves top management's ability to coordinate the overall operation of the organization. Budgets are blueprints of the company's plans for the coming year and greatly aid top management in coordinating the operations/activities of each division or department.

- Enables management to recognize and/or anticipate problems in time to take the necessary corrective action. For example, if production costs are substantially ahead of the budgeted amount, management will be alerted to make changes that may realign actual costs with the budget.

- Facilitates communications throughout the organization. The budget significantly improves management's ability to communicate the objectives, plans, and standards of performance, which are important to the organization. Budgets are especially helpful to lower-level managers by letting them know how their operations relate to other units or departments within the organization. Also, budgets help pinpoint managers' responsibility and improve their understanding of the goals of the organization. This process usually results in increased morale and commitment on the part of managers.

- Helps managers recognize when change is needed. The budgeting process requires managers to review carefully and critically the company's operations to determine if the firm's resources are being allocated to the right activities and programs. The budgeting process causes management to focus on such questions as: What products appear to have the greatest demand? What markets appear to offer the best potential? What business are we in? Which business(es) should we be in?[1]

Limitations of the Budgeting Process

Although numerous benefits can be attributed to the use of budgets, potential problems may also arise. If the budgetary process is to achieve its maximum effectiveness, these difficulties must be recognized and an attempt made to reduce the potential damaging side-effects associated with the use of budgets. Some of the major problems are:

- The attitude by some managers that all funds allocated in a budget must be spent may actually work against the intent of the budgetary process. Some managers have learned from experience that, if they do not spend the funds that have been budgeted, their budget will be reduced the following year. Managers have found that they can actually hurt their department because of their conscientious cost-effectiveness approach. A manager who operates in this type of budget atmosphere may make an extraordinary effort to spend extra funds for reasons that may be marginal at best.
- A budget may be so restrictive that supervisors are permitted little discretion in managing their resources. The actual amount that can be spent for each item may be specified, and funds cannot be transferred from one account to another. This inflexibility may result in, for instance, funds being available for word processor paper, but not for word processor repairs.
- Budgets may be used to evaluate the performance of a manager as opposed to evaluating the actual results accomplished. If this philosophy is prevalent within the firm, a poor manager may gain recognition because he or she met the budget, but a good manager may be reprimanded for failure to follow exact budgetary guidelines. With this corporate philosophy, the amount of risk a manager will be willing to take may be severely reduced. Managers may spend a majority of their time ensuring that they are in compliance with the budget when their time might be better spent in developing new or innovative ideas.

Planning-Programming Budgeting System and Zero Base Budgeting

In recent years, two specific budgeting systems have received considerable attention: planning-programming budgeting system (PPBS) and zero base budgeting (ZBB). To date, these two techniques have been used more frequently in public-sector firms than they have in private-sector firms.[2]

The **planning-programming budgeting system** (PPBS) was designed to aid management in identifying and eliminating costly programs that were duplicates of other programs and to provide a means for the careful analysis of the benefits and costs of each program or activity. The essential elements of PPBS include:

1. Careful analysis and specification of basic objectives in each major program area. A vital starting point for PPBS is to answer such questions as: "What is the firm's basic purpose or mission?" or "What, specifically, is it trying to accomplish?"
2. Analysis of the output of each program in terms of the specific objectives. In other words, how effectively is the firm achieving its goals?
3. Measurement and analysis of the total costs of the program over several years. For example, in budgeting for additional buildings, management would need to consider not only the initial costs of construction but also costs of operating and maintaining the facilities in future years.
4. Determination of which alternatives are the most effective in achieving the basic objectives at the least cost.
5. Implementation of PPBS in an organized and systematic manner so that, over time, most budgetary decisions are subject to rigorous analysis.

The approach of **zero base budgeting** (ZBB) requires management to take a fresh look at all programs and activities each year, rather than merely building on last year's budget. In other words, last year's budget allocations are not considered as a basis for this year's budget. Each program, or decision package, must be justified on the basis of a cost-benefit analysis. The 3 main features of zero base budgeting are:

1. The activities of individual departments are divided into decision packages. Each decision package provides information so that management can compare costs and benefits of the program or activity.
2. Each decision package is evaluated and ranked in the order of decreasing importance to the organization. Priorities are established for all programs and activities. Each of these is evaluated by top management to arrive at a final ranking.
3. Resources are allocated according to the final rankings of the programs by top management. As a rule, decisions to allocate resources for high-priority items will be made rather quickly, whereas greater analysis or scrutiny will be given lower-priority programs or activities.[3]

ZBB is not a panacea for solving all problems associated with the budgeting process. Organizations may experience problems in implementing ZBB, as most managers are reluctant to admit that all of their activities are not of the highest priority or to submit their programs to close scrutiny. However, ZBB does establish a system whereby an organization's resources can be allocated to the higher-priority programs. Under this system, programs of lower priority are reduced or eliminated. Thus, the benefits of zero base budgeting appear to outweigh the costs.[4]

Break-Even Analysis

The technique used to determine the amount of a particular product that must be sold if the firm is to generate enough revenue to cover costs is **break-even analysis**. In order to do a break-even analysis, the manager must know: (1) the fixed cost, (2) the variable cost, and (3) the selling price of the product.

Fixed costs are costs that do not change with the level of output. Items that normally are considered fixed are the salaries of top management, rent, property taxes, and similar expenses. **Variable costs** are those costs that are directly related to changes in output. Items included as variable costs are direct materials and labor expenses needed in making a product or completing a service. As production output increases, these costs increase.

To demonstrate how break-even analysis works, consider the following problem. Suppose a product is priced at $15, the variable cost is $10 per unit, and total fixed costs are $1,000. The following formula can be used to determine the break-even point (in units of output):

$$\text{Break-even point} = \frac{\text{Total fixed costs}}{\text{Price} - \text{Variable cost}} = \frac{\$1,000}{\$15 - \$10} = 200.$$

Thus, according to break-even analysis, 200 units would have to be sold before profit can be registered.

The break-even point can also be illustrated graphically. (See Exhibit 15-3.) The vertical axis shows costs and revenues, while the horizontal axis shows the units of output. Since the $1,000 fixed costs do not change, they are represented as a straight line. The $10 variable costs change with the level of production, so the total cost line (fixed plus variable cost) slopes upward accordingly. The variable cost line is drawn starting at the point where fixed costs intercept the vertical axis. Next, the total revenue line is drawn showing the total amount of revenue (price multiplied by the number of units sold) at all possible combinations of production. When the total revenue line intersects the total cost line, the break-even point has been reached at 200 units.

How reliable is this one point in space? Would you risk your firm's survival on its accuracy? Not likely, because there are some uncertainties associated with fixed and variable costs. However, break-even analysis is an effective technique because it forces a manager to plan. An individual who plans is in a position to make better decisions than a nonplanner.

Net Present Value

As noted in Chapter 14, the **net present value** approach assesses the value of goods in order to help managers when purchasing capital equipment. A dollar earned today does not have the same value as a dollar to be received one year from today because it can be invested today

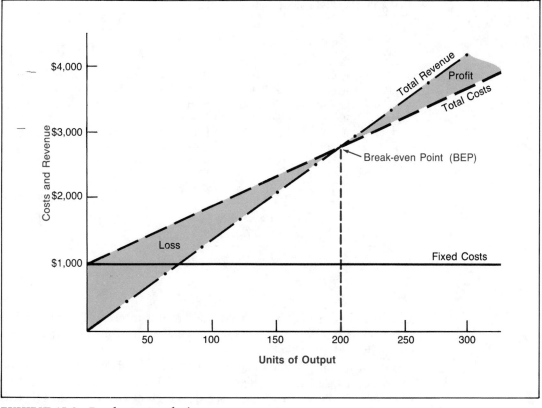

EXHIBIT 15-3   Break-even analysis

MANAGEMENT IN PRACTICE

Control Difficulties at Ontario Hydro

For the past several years, Ontario Hydro has been experiencing trouble controlling certain aspects of its operations. The first problem area is an inability to predict demand for electricity. Until 1976, demand for electricity grew at an annual rate of 7 percent, but, since the formation of OPEC and rising energy costs, consumers have been conserving with a vengeance. In 1982, electricity demand was actually down 0.8 percent from the previous year. To make matters worse, Hydro's generating capacity in 1983 was 42 percent above the highest expected peak load.

A second major problem is Hydro's inability to control costs. In 1983, Hydro's total debt was $18 billion, and the debt-service bill alone is $2 billion. For 3 years in a row, Hydro has paid out

more interest to foreign bondholders than all the foreign-controlled oil companies combined have paid out in dividends. Cost-plus contracts are also a problem. In 1978, Hydro signed contracts to buy uranium from the high-cost operations of Denison and Rio Algom. If Hydro goes through with its part of the bargain, it could end up paying $1.2 billion more than if it got its uranium from Saskatchewan's lower priced mines. The biggest embarrassment, however, is the Darlington Nuclear Generating Station. Originally estimated to cost $3.5 billion, it is now expected that $11.4 billion will be necessary.

SOURCE   Adapted from Robert Bott, "Power Failure," *Canadian Business* (January 1984): 96–101.

EXHIBIT 15-4   Slater's Purchase Decision

Year	Savings per Year Machine A	Savings per Year Machine B	Present Value of $1	Machine A	Machine B
1	$50,000	$60,000	0.870	$ 43,500	$ 52,200
2	$50,000	$60,000	0.756	$ 37,800	$ 52,200
3	$50,000	$60,000	0.658	$ 32,900	$ 45,360
4	$50,000	$60,000	0.572	$ 28,600	$ 39,480
5	$50,000		0.497	$ 24,850	$ 34,320
6	$50,000		0.432	$ 21,600	
7	$50,000		0.376	$ 18,800	
				208,050	171,360
	Less cost of equipment			200,000	150,000
	Net discounted cash flow			8,050	21,360
	Difference in cash flow			$13,310	

NOTE   Machine A costs $200,000; Machine B costs $150,000.

and a year later it will be worth the dollar plus interest. The time value of money is important in planning and controlling business activity in all businesses.

This idea is used when capital investment decisions are made in a manufacturing firm. Consider the case of Brian Slater, vice-president of production, who is trying to decide which of two machines to purchase for his factory. One piece of equipment costs $200,000 and is capable of providing a savings of $50,000 a year over the next 7 years. The other machine costs $150,000 and will generate $60,000 in savings each year for the next year 4 years. (Assume Slater has to pay an interest rate of 15 percent.) Referring to Exhibit 15-4, you can see that, based on the discounted cash flow method, Slater should purchase Machine B because cash savings would be $21,360 as compared to Machine A's savings of only $8,050. This illustration demonstrates the importance of the time value of money and the need for managers to evaluate carefully the various alternatives facing them.

Profit Centers

A **profit center** exists when a department or division in an organization is given the responsibility of making a profit, of making sure that its revenues exceed its costs. A profit center is both a motivational and a control technique. It is motivational because the people in the unit know that their unit's profitability, or lack of it, can be identified; they will therefore work to ensure that revenues exceed costs. It is also a control device because, at the end of the fiscal year, both top management and the unit in question can tell whether the established objectives have been achieved.

Top management personnel must ensure that the profit center concept makes sense before they implement it. For example, in a functional organization (refer to Exhibit 7-4 in Chapter 7), a profit center would cause great difficulty because none of the functional areas — production, marketing, or finance — can make a profit by itself. Rather, they must coordinate their efforts so that the total company can make a profit.

A profit center would, however, be very appropriate for a company with a divisional structure. (Refer to Exhibit 7-5 in Chapter 7.) Each of the divisions — consumer products, government products, and industrial products — can be held accountable for its profit picture because each is operating as separate divisions. Each has the resources it needs to conduct business independently.

Ratio Analysis

When a company wants to assess how effective its performance has been, it may use **ratio analysis**. This analysis involves taking 2 financial figures from the company's balance sheet or income statement and dividing one figure by the other. The resulting ratio is then assessed to see if it is indicative of good management. Since the figures used for ratio analysis come largely from the firm's income statement and/or balance sheet, we describe these two documents briefly.

The **balance sheet** is a key financial document that describes the company's financial position with respect to assets, liabilities, and owners' (or shareholders') equity at a particular point in time. It is therefore a snapshot of the company's financial position at that time. The balance sheet is divided into 3 main sections. (See Exhibit 15-5.) The first section contains information about the company's assets. These are subdivided into current assets (for example, cash, inventory, and accounts receivable) and fixed assets (for example, plant and equipment). The second section shows the company's liabilities, or debts. These are divided into short- and long-term liabilities; the former must be paid within one year, while the latter do not come due for at least one year. The final category is shareholders' equity, which is the residual value of the corporation after liabilities have been subtracted from assets.

The **income statement**, in contrast to the balance sheet, shows the company's financial performance over a period of time (usually one year). Income statements contain 2 parts: a revenue section and a costs section. (See Exhibit 15-6.) Although income statements can be very complex for large organizations, they basically show the revenue the organization had and the expenses which were incurred to obtain that revenue. The difference between revenue and expenses is profit.

The balance sheet and income statement provide valuable information with regard to whether a company, department, or unit is effectively utilizing its financial resources. Intelligent interpretation of financial data provides an excellent way for management to control its financial welfare. Financial ratio analysis provides management with a basis for comparing current to past performance. In addition, current financial ratios can be compared not only to past trends within

NORCAN LTD.
Balance Sheet
as of December 31, 198X

Current Assets:		Current Liabilities:	
Cash	$ 60,000	Accounts Payable	$100,000
Accounts Receivable	180,000	Accrued Expenses Payable	10,000
Inventory	100,000	Estimated Tax Liability	70,000
Prepaid Expenses	20,000		
Total Current Assets	$360,000	Total Current Liabilities	$180,000
Fixed Assets:		Long-Term Liabilities:	
Land	$ 40,000	Bond Payable	$100,000
Building	80,000		
Less Depreciation	40,000	Shareholders' Equity:	
		Common Stock (25 000 shares)	250,000
Other Assets:		Retained Earnings	10,000
Goodwill	100,000		
Total Assets	$540,000	Total Liabilities and Equity	$540,000

EXHIBIT 15-5   A balance sheet

NORCAN LTD.
Income Statement
Year Ending December 31, 198X

Sales		$2,670,000
Less Cost of Goods Sold		1,520,000
Gross Profit		$1,150,000
Less Expenses:		
Wages Paid	$682,000	
Administrative Expenses	380,000	
Interest Expenses	15,000	
Operating Profit		$1,077,000
Net Profit before Taxes		$ 73,000
Taxes		20,000
Net Profit after Taxes		$ 53,000
Less Dividends		40,000
Added to Retained Earnings		$ 13,000

EXHIBIT 15-6   An income statement

the company but also to other divisions within the company and to other firms in the industry. If the ratios are not in line with what is considered acceptable, the manager is in a position to make corrections. There are 4 basic types of ratios:

- **Liquidity ratios** measure a firm's ability to meet its current obligations.
- **Leverage ratios** measure whether a firm has effectively used outside financing.
- **Activity ratios** measure how efficiently the firm is utilizing its resources.
- **Profitability ratios** measure the overall operating efficiency and profitability of the firm.

Names of ratios, the formula for their calculation, and the meaning and definition of the ratios are shown in Exhibit 15-7.

EXHIBIT 15-7 Summary of Financial Ratio Analysis

Type of Ratio	Name of Ratio	Formula for Calculation	Meaning and Definition of Ratio
Liquidity	Current ratio	$\dfrac{\text{current assets}}{\text{current liabilities}}$	Measures ability to meet debts when due — short-term liquidity
	Quick ratio	$\dfrac{\text{current assets} - \text{inventory}}{\text{current liabilities}}$	Measures ability to meet debts when due — very short-term liquidity
Leverage	Debt to total assets	$\dfrac{\text{total debt}}{\text{total assets}}$	Measures percentage of total funds that have been provided by creditors (debt = total assets − equity)
	Times interest earned	$\dfrac{\text{profit before tax} + \text{interest charges}}{\text{interest charges}}$	Measures the extent to which interest charges are covered by gross income
Profitability	Return on sales (net profit margin)	$\dfrac{\text{net income}}{\text{sales revenue}}$	Measures percent of profit earned on each dollar of sales
	Return on total assets	$\dfrac{\text{net income (after tax)}}{\text{total assets}}$	Measures the return on total investment of a firm
	Return on equity	$\dfrac{\text{net income (after tax)}}{\text{shareholder equity}}$	Measures rate of return on shareholders' investment
	Earnings per share	$\dfrac{\text{net income (after tax)}}{\text{number of common shares outstanding}}$	Measures profit earned for each share of common stock
Activity	Total asset turnover	$\dfrac{\text{revenues}}{\text{total assets}}$	Measures effectiveness of assets in generating revenues
	Collection period	$\dfrac{\text{receivables}}{\text{revenues per day}}$	Measures amount of credit extended to customers
	Inventory turnover	$\dfrac{\text{sales}}{\text{inventory}}$	Measures number of times inventory is used to generate sales

Auditing

Corporations in Canada are required by law to conduct an **audit**, an independent analysis of their financial statements. Auditing is done by chartered accountancy firms. They analyze a corporation's financial statements and give an opinion on whether or not a company has followed generally accepted practices in developing its financial statements. A chartered accountancy firm does not develop a firm's financial statements; rather, it assesses them after they have been prepared by the corporation's internal accounting staff.

The audit is one of the most well known control techniques used by organizations. Even though it looks back on the financial transactions of a firm for the last year, it influences the day-to-day operations of the firm because managers know that the books will be examined. This acts as a deterrent against fraud. The audit is also a good control device as far as investors and the general public are concerned. They can examine the company's audited statements in order to make reasonable decisions about where to invest their money.

THE USE OF CONTROL TECHNIQUES BY MANAGERS

The control techniques discussed in this chapter are widely used by Canadian companies. There are, of course, numerous other controls that organizations might use. This profusion creates the problem for management to decide which technique should be used for a given situation. Since managers are always looking for ways to simplify their options, they may be tempted to ask which of these control techniques is best or most suitable.

There is no simple answer to either of these issues because no single technique can solve the multitude of control problems that managers face in their work. Rather, each of the control techniques is intended for a different purpose. For example, the profit center is designed to identify costs and revenues for a division, while ratio analysis retrospectively shows how well the organization as a whole has performed. Both these control techniques focus on financial data, but neither is sufficient by itself to fulfill the demands of the controlling function. Likewise, rewards and punishments are designed to motivate employees to perform in certain ways, while selection controls are designed to recruit certain types of individuals into a firm. Both of these nonfinancial controls are necessary; management cannot choose only one of them and hope it will do an adequate job of controlling behavior.

The major job of management, therefore, is to decide which control technique is appropriate for which job. When making this decision, the manager must balance the need for control against the potential employee resistance to controls. Generally speaking, controls should not convey to employees that they are not trusted; rather, they should

MANAGEMENT IN PRACTICE

Financial Control at the Pattison Group

James Pattison is the president of the largest solely owned Canadian company with 1983 revenues of $772 million. He controls a diverse set of companies in areas such as real estate, communications, food and beverages, and financial services. Because these are such diverse businesses, he has adopted certain financial controls to assess their performance.

The measure which he believes best pinpoints short-term performance in using assets wisely is Return On Invested Capital (ROIC). To calculate ROIC, he takes the value of company assets less accounts receivable and divides the figure by pretax profit added to the cost of financing. This percentage is called the "hurdle rate." Each company he controls is assigned a hurdle rate annually and managers are assessed on their ability to meet or exceed this goal.

A company in a stable industry is expected to achieve a rate of 16 or 17 percent, while a company in an extremely volatile industry and with a small asset base might be expected to achieve as much as 35 or 40 percent.

SOURCE   Adapted from David Cruise and Alison Griffiths, "Japanese-Style Tactics Work for the Shogun from the West," *Executive* (April 1984): 28–32.

indicate that certain fundamental checks on the work system exist so that the organization can continue to function and provide employment opportunities.

In order to make rational choices about which control techniques to implement, managers must understand what a given control technique can and cannot do. Unfortunately, there is often misunderstanding about controls. For instance, consider corporate financial statements. When certain profit figures are reported in the newspaper, some reporters may comment about "windfall profits," intimating that the company made an "excessive" amount of profit. But how do they measure what is excessive? The profit figures reported on the company's income statement are arrived at only after many judgments have been made about which costs are associated with the revenue the company generated. The amount of profit reported therefore depends to a considerable degree on the assumptions that are made when the income statement is prepared. It is beyond the scope of this chapter to get into a detailed analysis of this issue but, as a general comment, we can say that the dollar figures shown on company balance sheets and income statements are often not as clear cut as they appear. If people inside and outside the company make unreasonable assumptions about what the profit figure means, this particular control device will not have served a useful purpose.

The problem of misunderstanding control techniques is not restricted to financial statements. Take budgets, for example. Some managers assume that once the budget is set, everything is under control. But they fail to realize that people may overexpend their budgets, even though safeguards are supposed to prevent this from happening. Once an overexpenditure has occurred, what should be done? Since the money has probably already left the company, there is not much that can be done except to try to make sure that it doesn't happen again. A similar general problem is evident with other controls like policies, rules, and procedures. These are frequently violated in organizations, yet some managers seem to assume that, because these controls exist, all the potential problems have been dealt with. Managers must recognize that simply having controls in place does not guarantee that everyone will abide by them.

Managers must also deal with negative reactions to controls on the part of employees. As we noted in Chapter 14, there are a variety of reasons why employees resist controls. The manager must therefore: (1) spend some time thinking about what controls are necessary, and (2) explain these necessary controls and how they work to employees. If the manager and the employees can come to a consensus about what kind of controls are required for the work they are doing, the possible resistance to controls can be minimized. Obviously, the kinds of controls that are necessary at the Canadian Mint are different from the controls needed at a restaurant that serves tacos. Yet, for both organizations, controls are necessary.

Managers must assess the kind of work that is being performed and then choose control systems that are appropriate for that work. Managers must also recognize that, while one specific control technique may be necessary to control certain activities, a variety of controls may be required for the entire function of controlling. In the typical private-sector firm, for instance, all of the control techniques discussed in this chapter would be used. This demonstrates the diversity of activities of most firms and the need to use a variety of controlling techniques.

OPENING INCIDENT REVISITED

Cam's Corner

Cameron McIntyre experienced severe problems in controlling his variety store business during the 1979–1983 recession. Afterward, he wondered what he could do to ensure that he would not have similar problems if another recession occurred.

We purposely did not give much detail in the opening incident so that we can talk generally about the appropriateness of the control techniques presented in the chapter. In keeping with the organization of the chapter, we suggest that Cameron McIntyre systematically look at the controlling function in his organization from both the nonfinancial and the financial perspective.

Several illustrative questions McIntyre should ask himself regarding nonfinancial controls are:

- What kinds of rewards and punishments are being given to salespeople, and do these rewards and punishments motivate them to exercise self-control and behavior that is in the best interest of the company?
- What kind of controls is McIntyre using to ensure that the people he hires for his stores are appropriate?
- What kind of training is he giving employees?
- Is the reporting function clear to employees?

• Is he doing any auditing of management activities to see if they are effective?
• Is he trying to do all the work, or is he delegating a significant amount of day-to-day work so that he can concentrate on strategic planning for the business?

Questions like these deal with the nonfinancial aspects of the business — although what management does in these areas certainly shows up on the income statement and balance sheet. If McIntyre answers these questions honestly, he will see where improvements in nonfinancial controls are necessary.

Some illustrative questions in the financial area that McIntyre should ask himself are:

• Does he have an adequate budgeting system that gives him timely information on cost control?
• Are each of his stores profit centers, or is all activity in the 3 stores considered together?
• Does he know if all 3 stores are profitable, or is one store a problem?
• What do his liquidity, leverage, activity, and profitability ratios look like? Would these ratios give some clue regarding where potential problems exist?

As suggested in the chapter, McIntyre must consider the activity performed by employees and then adopt appropriate control techniques. These illustrative questions should help him get started on this task.

SUMMARY

Managers can choose from a wide variety of control techniques to increase the probability that planned objectives can be achieved. These control techniques can be divided into two main categories: financial and nonfinancial. Nonfinancial control techniques, used in the absence of any financial data, include rewards and punishments, selection procedures, socialization and training of employees, the management hierarchy, management audits, and management by exception. Generally, nonfinancial techniques help managers to control the behavior of employees. Financial control techniques require some form of financial data, such as profits, costs, or revenues, in order to be used. The most widely known and rigorously developed financial control techniques are: budgets, break-even analysis, net present value, profit centers, ratio analysis, and accounting audits.

A budget is a formal statement — in dollar-and-cents terms — of the firm's planned expenditures for a future time period. There are 2 broad categories of budgets: financial and operating. The former indicates the amount of capital the firm will need and where it will get it, while the latter indicates the revenues and expenses the firm will experience during a given year. Budgets are control devices because they tell people how much money is available for expenditures in a given time period. Budgets help in making planned activities actually occur. They may, however, make some people feel unduly restrained in their activity.

Break-even analysis allows a firm to determine the level of operations that will have to be achieved if it hopes to make a profit. Break-even analysis is a control technique because it shows management where actions need to be taken to improve the efficiency of the firm's operations. In order to do a break-even analysis, management must have a knowledge of fixed costs, variable costs, and the selling price of the product. The break-even point in units can be determined by dividing total fixed costs by the selling price minus the variable costs.

A profit center exists when a division of an organization is given the responsibility of ensuring that its revenues exceed its costs. It is a control technique because it allows management to determine if the goals that were set have been reached.

Ratio analysis helps managers to determine if their actions have led to an effective operation of the firm. A ratio can be computed by taking any 2 figures from the balance sheet or income statement and dividing one by the other. The most commonly used ratios are liquidity, leverage, activity, and profitability ratios.

An accounting audit involves analysis by a chartered accountancy firm of an organization's financial statements. The chartered accountancy firm gives an opinion on whether the firm has followed generally accepted accounting principles in the preparation of its annual financial statements. Because the firm's managers know an audit will be conducted, they must control the day-to-day finances.

Because there are so many control techniques available to managers, they must decide which ones are appropriate for each function that must be controlled. Managers must also try to use the techniques in such a way that employees do not feel threatened by it and, therefore, resist the controls. Most large organizations use all the control techniques presented in this chapter, but they use each of them in situations that demand the particular strength that the specific control technique has.

REVIEW QUESTIONS

1. What is the difference between financial and nonfinancial control techniques?
2. What determines how effective rewards and punishments will be in controlling behavior of employees?
3. What are the benefits and costs of personnel selection procedures as a control device?
4. Why are socialization and training considered to be control techniques?
5. The management hierarchy acts as a controlling mechanism. What other organizational controlling devices are embedded in the management hierarchy?
6. How is a management audit different from an accounting audit?
7. Explain the concept of management by exception as a control technique.
8. How does an operating budget differ from a financial budget?

9. What are some benefits and limitations of budgets?
10. What potential problem exists in using break-even analysis?
11. In what situations are profit centers appropriate? inappropriate?
12. Describe what each of the basic types of ratios — liquidity, leverage, activity, and profitability — are designed to measure. (See Exhibit 15-7.) Give an example of each kind of ratio.
13. What is management's responsibility when choosing control techniques?

EXERCISES

1. Examine the financial statements of several different kinds of companies and compute the profitability, leverage, activity, and liquidity ratios for each of them. What differences do you see across these companies?
2. Interview 3 managers in different types of organizations. What kinds of control techniques does each one use? Why do they use the control techniques? What problems do they have when using the techniques?
3. Discuss the uncertainties associated with an accounting audit with a chartered accountant. How much confidence can investors put in the opinion of chartered accountants?
4. What specific control techniques would be most obvious in a convenience store? a community college? an insurance company? an automobile repair shop?

CASE STUDY

A New Product Decision

Carolyn Loewen is the vice-president of marketing for Novelties Ltd., a small firm that manufactures and sells promotional material, such as buttons, decals, and book covers. She recently came up with the idea of producing miniature Canadian flag decals that could be sold to companies for conventions or sales meetings.

Loewen is familiar with break-even analysis, so she developed some cost figures for producing the flags. She estimates that the fixed cost for the project will be $2,000; the variable cost will be $0.50 per flag, and the company should be able to sell them for $1 each.

QUESTIONS

1. How many flags must Novelties Ltd. sell in order to break even?
2. How many flags must the company sell to make a profit of $1,000?
3. If Carolyn Loewen thinks that the maximum number of flags the company can sell is 5000, do you think that Novelties Ltd. should begin manufacturing the flags?
4. What uncertainties exist in this situation?

CASE STUDY

Ratio Analysis at Norcan Ltd.

Norcan Ltd. is a Saskatoon-based manufacturing firm that produces oil field equipment. At the last meeting of the board of directors, one of the outside board members expressed some concern about the company's financial condition. Several long-standing board members expressed surprise and said that they believed the company was doing very well. The outside member persisted in his questions, however, and a lengthy discussion took place regarding the company's activities over the last year.

After approximately 45 minutes of listening to various opinions and very few facts, the chairman appointed a subcommittee to analyze Norcan's financial statements and report back to the board regarding the firm's financial condition. As part of this responsibility, the subcommittee was asked to do a thorough ratio analysis.

QUESTIONS

1. Assume that you are the chairperson of the subcommittee. Use the balance sheet and income statement shown in exhibits 15-5 and 15-6 to compute the liquidity, leverage, profitability, and activity ratios for Norcan. (Refer to Exhibit 15-7 for ratios; for collection period ratio, assume revenues are collected 365 days a year.)
2. Based on this ratio analysis, what can you say about the company's financial condition?
3. What additional information do you need to make an overall judgment of the financial condition of the company?

NOTES

[1] Robert N. Anthony and Regina E. Herzlinger, *Management Control in Non-Profit Organizations*, (Homewood, Ill.: Irwin, 1975): 222–226.

[2] Anthony and Herzlinger.

[3] James A. F. Stoner, *Management* (Englewood Cliffs, N.J.: Prentice-Hall, 1978): 600–677.

[4] Gordon Shillinglaw, *Managerial Cost Accounting: Analysis and Control*, 4th ed. (Homewood, Ill.: Irwin, 1977): 142–143.

REFERENCES

Adam, N., and Surkis, J. "Comparison of Capacity Planning Techniques in a Job Shop Control System." *Management Science* 23 (May 1977): 1011–1015.

Bott, Robert. "Power Failure." *Canadian Business* 57, no. 1 (January 1984): 96.

Buffa, Elwood S. *Modern Production-Operations Management.* 6th ed. New York: Wiley, 1980.

Chase, Richard B., and Aquilano, Nicholas J. *Production and Operations Management: A Life Cycle Approach.* Homewood, Ill.: Irwin, 1981.

Clay, M. J. "Evaluating the Production Function." *Journal of Accountancy* 148 (May 1977): 82.

Cummings, L. L. "Needed Research in Production/Operations Management: A Behavioral Perspective." *Academy of Management Review* (July 1977): 500–504.

Green, T. B. "Why Are Organizations Reluctant to Use Management Science/Operations Research? An Empirical Approach." *Interfaces* 7 (August 1976): 69–62.

Harwood, G. G., and Hermanson, R. H. "Lease or Buy Decisions." *Journal of Accountancy* 147 (September 1976): 83–87.

Morey, R. "Operations Management in Selected Non-manufacturing Organizations." *Academy of Management Journal* 19 (March 1976): 120–124.

Petry, Glenn H. "Effective Use of Capital Budgeting Tools." *Business Horizons* 18 (October 1975): 57–65.

Remick, Carl. "Robots: New Faces on the Production Line." *Management Review* 68 (May 1979): 27.

Schmenner, Roger W. *Production/Operations Management: Concepts and Situations.* Chicago: Science Research Associates, 1981.

Solomon, Eyra, and Pringle, John J. *An Introduction to Financial Management.* Santa Monica, Cal.: Goodyear, 1980.

VI

Situational
Applications

16

Managing Small Businesses

Kent Computers

Evan Kent always had an entrepreneurial streak. After graduating from a British Columbia business school, he decided to go into business for himself. Kent considered several possibilities and decided to open a retail outlet which sold home computers. He reasoned that the rapid growth in the use of computers by both business and consumers would almost guarantee high demand for his products.

Kent opened his store, Kent Computers, in New Westminster. Right from the start customer interest was high. At once, Kent noticed that each customer required a very long time because everyone had many questions about the computers and what they could do. Kent was particularly discouraged when, after he had spent a lot of time with a customer, the customer would decide not to buy anything.

Competition astonished Kent. Apparently, a lot of other people had the same idea as Kent because he noticed more and more home computer stores springing up. Price competition was severe, and he was continually faced with customers pressuring him to give them a price deal that he couldn't afford. He also experienced irritation from customers who wanted to buy software that he didn't have in stock. Everyone seemed to want everything immediately. Kent was trying to keep his inventory to a minimum, but he was discovering that customers would go elsewhere when he didn't have a particular item in stock.

Kent found himself working extremely long hours both at the store and at home. In his non-store hours, he tried to keep up with the new developments in the computer field so that he could talk knowledgeably to customers. He also found he had to do all sorts of work that he hadn't anticipated. One evening after a particularly hectic day, he looked at the floor and saw what a mess it was. As he picked up a broom and began sweeping, he realized that he was mentally and physically exhausted. Somehow, running his own business wasn't the excitement or challenge he'd expected. Kent wondered whether it was worth the effort, particularly since he had yet to make his first dollar of profit.

KEY TERMS

small business
entrepreneur
franchising

nepotism
financial assistance
programs

Counselling
Assistance to Small
Enterprises (CASE)

LEARNING OBJECTIVES

After completing this chapter you should be able to
1. Describe what is meant by a small business and identify why some people want to have their own business.
2. Describe franchising and some of its advantages to franchisees and franchisers.
3. Describe some of the factors affecting the management of small business.
4. Identify some of the pitfalls to starting a small business.
5. Describe the types of assistance available to small businesses from the federal and provincial governments.
6. Identify some of the inconveniences caused for managers of small businesses by government regulations.

Every year, thousands of individuals motivated to be their own boss and to earn a better income launch a new business venture. These individuals, often called entrepreneurs, are essential to the growth and vitality of the Canadian economic system. Entrepreneurs develop or recognize new products or business opportunities, secure the necessary capital, and organize and operate various kinds of businesses. Most people who start their own business get a great deal of satisfaction from owning and managing their own firm.

Even with assistance provided by various government agencies, the failure rate of small businesses is extremely high. As we noted in Chapter 1, approximately half of all new businesses fail within the first 4 years of operation, and over 60 percent fail within 6 years. In spite of this high failure rate, people continue to challenge the odds. The entrepreneurial spirit is alive and well in Canada.

In this chapter we examine the important role that small business plays in the Canadian economy. We first define small business. The role of the entrepreneur is described and the advantages and disadvantages of owning a small business are noted. We also discuss the impact of franchising on small business. Second, we present the key factors affecting the management of small business. These factors include the external environment peculiar to small businesses as well as internal factors; the small business owner/manager must carefully manage each one of them if he or she hopes to be successful. Third, the pitfalls of owning a small business are described in some detail. Since the failure rate for small businesses is so high, the potential small business owner must be aware of them. We discuss the role government plays in assisting and regulating small business. We conclude the chapter with a lengthy checklist for individuals considering starting a small business.

At times, in our discussion of small business, we may appear quite negative. Do not think that the authors are trying to dissuade people from starting their own business. This is definitely not the case; we are simply trying to paint a realistic picture of small business in Canada and how successful management of small business takes a special type of person. If you are fully aware of the difficulties you might encounter if you start your own business, you are more likely to avoid the classic problems small business owners face. It is not very difficult to start a small business, but to operate one at a profit over a period of years requires knowledge and application of the fundamentals of business and management. This chapter is designed to give you realistic expectations about small business management.

SMALL BUSINESS IN CANADA

Although most of the media attention in Canada is directed at large business enterprises, the fact is that small businesses are thriving and are making a significant contribution to the economic well-being of Canada. A small business may be a corporation, sole proprietorship, or a partnership. Small businesses include those operated by professionals, such as doctors, lawyers, and accountants, and self-employed owners, such as mechanics, television repairs, and restaurateurs. Small businesses are found in virtually every industry; they are particularly prominent in the retail trade.

In terms of numbers, small business is the dominant type of business in Canada. Assuming for the moment that a firm is "small" if its sales are less than $2 million per year, over 90 percent of all business firms in Canada are small businesses. These small businesses account for approximately 30 percent of the total sales of Canadian business firms and approximately 40 percent of employment.

What Is a Small Business?

There is no simple definition of the term *small business*. Different groups have developed definitions of small business largely for administrative convenience. For instance, Industry, Trade, and Commerce Canada defines small business as manufacturing firms with less than 100 employees and firms in other sectors with less than 50 employees. For purposes of the Small Business Loans Act, a small business is one whose gross revenue for the year does not exceed $1.5 million dollars. For purposes of management consulting assistance from the government, a firm cannot have more than 75 employees if it is to be classified as a small business.

Note that all of these definitions use different criteria, so no single definition can be deduced. For our purposes, we define a **small business** as one with the following characteristics:

• The owner is actively involved in the day-to-day management of the business.
• The company is localized in its operation.
• The company is not a dominant force in the industry.

The Role of the Entrepreneur

The key individual in most small businesses is the owner. Because of the nature of the factors in establishing small businesses, the small business owner is often referred to as an entrepreneur. In fact, the small business is a natural haven for the entrepreneur. The **entrepreneur** is a unique person whose major characteristic is the ability to create an ongoing enterprise where none existed before. He or she performs the act of bringing ideas, skills, money, equipment, and markets together into a profitable combination. It has been suggested that this type of person strongly feels that security cannot be found in working for others in a well-structured situation. Rather, security is found only in working for oneself with minimum external restraints.

Entrepreneurs desire to control their own destiny and have a tremendous need for independence. They possess a constant drive to remove all restrictions and threatening persons. Any other person in the small firm who appears to bid for power will be quickly removed. For this reason, some small businesses fail when their owners die or retire; no one has been developed to take their place.

This yearning for security through independence demands a great deal of self-confidence. An entrepreneur finds it exceedingly difficult to accept leadership from others. Such a person often makes a poor

MANAGEMENT IN PRACTICE

Houseboating in Alberta

It seems unlikely that a houseboat manufacturing company would have much success in arid and landlocked Alberta, but Dave Steele and Phil Carroll are doing just fine. In the first 18 months of their business, they grossed $800,000 in sales.

The two men got the idea for the company when they saw all the houseboats in Sicamous, BC and thought that it was a great recreational idea. They tried to get one for the summer, but they were all booked up. Upon seeing this demand, they decided to get into the manufacturing end of the business. They set up shop in Airdrie, Alberta and hired 15 craftsmen to build

the boats, which sell for approximately $55,000. Currently, the plant produces about one houseboat per week at a cost of $30,000 to $40,000 per boat.

Steele and Carroll expect to have an active market for some time to come because older houseboats that other companies are renting to customers will have to be replaced. Sales to these organizations should keep demand high.

SOURCE Adapted from Alister Thomas, "Holiday Houseboating Gives Two Albertans a Place in the Sun," *Canadian Business* (July 1983): 147.

---

member of a large enterprise. In addition, entrepreneurs have little fear of failure; they seek risks eagerly. Venturesomeness is almost an obsession; their level of activity is steadily high. Entrepreneurs are ardent believers in a truly competitive system and take great joy in winning.

The management style of the entrepreneur is generally not one that fits well into structured and orderly organizations. Entrepreneurs often show great reluctance to formalize structure and processes. Leadership is primarily based on their charismatic attraction. Entrepreneurs are organization starters rather than organization builders. As a consequence, their level of mobility is great; they move from one deal to another, all of which are rationalized in the name of profit. They may have few qualms about severing relationships with people or with organizations. They would rather leave intolerable situations than stay and resolve problems. Because of these characteristics, many people become annoyed with entrepreneurs. However, they provide a dynamic and innovative element in the Canadian economic system.

There are both benefits and costs of entrepreneurship. On the positive side, entrepreneurs get a tremendous sense of satisfaction from being their own boss. They also derive ego satisfaction from successfully bringing together the factors of production (land, labor, and capital) and making a profit. Perhaps the greatest benefit, however, is the fact that entrepreneurs can make a fortune if they have carefully planned what the business will do and how it will operate.

On the negative side, entrepreneurs can go bankrupt if their business fails. Customers can demand all sorts of services or inventory that small businesses cannot profitably supply. Entrepreneurs must work long hours and often get little in return during the first few years their business is in operation. Each entrepreneur may find that he or she is very good at one particular aspect of the business — for example, marketing — but that he or she knows little about managing the overall business. This imbalance can cause serious problems; in fact, poor management is the main reason small businesses fail.

Becoming a Small Business Owner

Most people become involved in a small business in one of three ways: (1) taking over the family business, (2) buying out an existing firm, or (3) starting their own firm. Taking over the family business was very common in Canada until recently; it still happens, of course, but not as often as in the past, when it was often assumed that the eldest son would take over a business from his father. This trend was especially true for family farms.

Buying out an existing firm has become more common during the twentieth century. Entrepreneurs often keep a sharp eye out for business firms that are poorly run but that have good profit potential. They believe that if they buy them out, they can make the firms profitable using their entrepreneurial expertise.

Starting your own small business is becoming increasingly common. When you do so, you do not have to cope with any problems that an existing firm might have, but you must build up the business from scratch. Building a business can take many years, but, managed properly, it can produce large profits.

Why Some People Want their own Business

Many thousands of Canadians start their own business each year. Why? While there are probably dozens of reasons, some of the more common ones, seen in Exhibit 16-1, are discussed below.

- A strong desire to be one's own boss — to be independent, able to set one's own direction, relying on one's own talents, skills, and hard work.
- The opportunity to work at something enjoyable instead of settling for a possibly more secure job in a large organization.
- Achieving a goal of financial success and desire for and expectations of future profits and wealth. Earning a profit is a primary motivator for wanting to own a business.
- An ego identification with their business. Most small business owners have a close identification with their business and demonstrate a pride of ownership. The business often represents an extension of themselves and their ideals and values. Or a business may allow a family to maintain a historic tradition of ownership of a particular business firm.
- A strong motivation for recognition and prestige. Business owners may gain considerable prestige or status from owning and operating

a small business. A small business gives owners a base of power in the community and an opportunity for political and economic influence.

- A feeling they are controlling their own destiny. To many individuals, controlling their own firm is tremendously rewarding.
- A desire for achievement. One of the most prevalent characteristics of the entrepreneur is a strong drive for achievement. Most studies of the motives of individuals who own their own firm indicate that they are achievers — they prefer to set their own goals and like to try to control their future.

Franchising and Small Business

Franchising became popular during the 1960s and has continued to increase in economic importance. **Franchising** involves drawing up a contract between a manufacturer and a dealer that stipulates how the manufacturer's product or service will be sold. The dealer, called a franchisee, agrees to sell the product or service of the manufacturer, called the franchisor, in return for royalties. Franchising organizations that are well known in Canada include Holiday Inn, McDonald's, Weight Watchers, Kentucky Fried Chicken, Midas Muffler, and Canadian Tire.

The franchising arrangement can be beneficial to both the franchisee and the franchisor. For the franchisee, the following benefits are evident:

- Recognition — the franchise name gives the franchisee instant recognition with the public.
- Standardized appearance of the franchise — customers know that consistency exists from one outlet to another.
- Management assistance — the franchisee can obtain advice on how to run the franchise effectively.
- Economies of scale in buying — the head office of the franchise buys in large volume and resells to the franchisee at lower prices than he or she could get buying personally.
- Promotional assistance — the head office of the franchise provides the franchisee with prepared advertising and other promotional material.

The franchisee is not the only party who benefits in franchising. The following benefits are available to the franchisor:

- Recognition — the franchisor is able to expand its area of operation by signing agreements with dealers in widely dispersed places.
- Promotion savings — the various franchisees can decide on local advertising efforts; this saves the franchisor money on wasted coverage in areas where it has no franchise.
- Franchisee payments — the franchisees pay the franchisor for the right to operate their franchises.
- Attention to detail — since franchisees own their franchises, they are motivated to do a good job and to sell the franchisor's product or service aggressively.

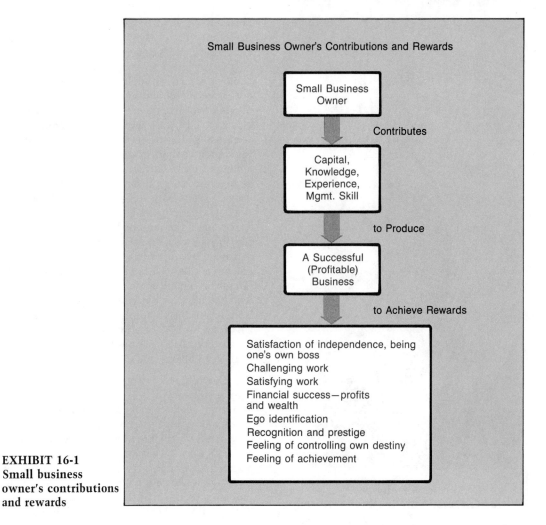

**EXHIBIT 16-1
Small business
owner's contributions
and rewards**

Franchising has facilitated the growth of small business in Canada. The financial and management assistance franchisees can receive from the franchisor removes many of the risks that typically face small business owners. For example, few McDonald's outlets have ever closed for lack of business. However, many entrepreneurs are not interested in becoming franchisees because their behavior will be too closely regulated by the franchisor. They would rather start their own business and take whatever risks are necessary in return for freedom to do what they want.

TALKING TO MANAGERS

Vic Smeelen
Astley-Gilbert Reproductions Limited

Vic Smeelen is the president of Astley-Gilbert Reproductions Limited. The company primarily supplies architects and engineers with reproductions of architectural, structural, mechanical, and electrical drawings, formerly called "blueprints" and now referred to as "white prints." These reproductions are used for tender, bid, construction, and record purposes and can be as large as 1 m by 1.2 m. A large building may have as many as 300 such drawings and may need 100 or more copies of them bound in book form. Astley-Gilbert is the largest volume white printer in Toronto.

Q: Can you tell me about your own background?

Smeelen: I went to Central Technical School in Toronto, majored in machine-design drafting, and spent 7 years as a tool-design draftsman for T & D Designs Ltd. While working at that job, I happened to be the draftsman who was sending out some reproduction work — the same type of work I receive now. I asked for the invoice to be extended by the reproduction company we were using, and when it came back it said $78. I said to my employers: "$78? Why don't we buy a blueprint machine and rent a Volkswagen and go into the blueprint business?" Later, they did decide to start Astley-Gilbert Reproductions, and they asked me to be the new company's manager. One of the reasons I was approached to do the job was that I looked pretty dependable. Within a 7-year period I was never late once and had never missed a day's work. A year and a half later I was offered some shares and, over the next 3 or 4 years, I kept buying more shares. In 1976, I offered to buy them out and I made the final payment in 1982. Astley-Gilbert started from absolutely nothing; now we're doing about $2 million in business a year.

Q: Did you ever formulate a goal to own your own business?

Smeelen: No. I had no intention of ever owning my own business. I just worked. My employers saw some potential in me, for which I'm grateful. After a year and a half, I got hooked. I became more or less trapped — I had to get bigger, I had to get more. But I never sat down and said to myself: "I want to be the president of Astley-Gilbert Reproductions." It's like a marriage; it's love; it grows from day to day. It sounds corny, but that's the way it sums up. Sometimes I've got 3 phone lines going at the same time, and someone says: "You're nuts. How can you?" I love it — slam the phone down, swear at the customer, rub my hands, and say: "Who's next? Let's see what's over on the other side." But you have to watch one thing in a small business: you can't do all the jobs yourself. My company was sort of stagnant, not growing, at one point. One major reason was that I was doing too many jobs; you can't run a company from behind a blueprint machine. You have to do it from behind a desk, over lunch with customers or over their desk. Otherwise, you're too tense and you're forever radiating irritability to your customers, when actually you should be thanking them for sending you the work. It's wild.

Q: How did you develop the drive you obviously have?

Smeelen: I came from Holland in 1951; I was 7 years old and I didn't speak any English. My family and I landed on a Friday, and Monday morning I went to school. I knew a couple of swear words in English — that was all. I was the classroom idiot, always getting Cs, Ds and Es from grade 2 all the way up to grade 8. I kept being promoted on trial, until I failed grade 8; I was shocked, but I went back to grade 8. The teacher started asking the same questions; I remembered the answers from the previous year and gave those answers. By the end of the first week, it was established that I was the smartest kid in the class. It was only because I remembered the questions from the year before but, I decided, if I'm going to get attention, I might as well do it by being the classroom smart kid rather than being the classroom idiot. The incident has stayed with me for the rest of my life. In my business, I know the product and I know what I'm doing — I hope people respect me for that.

Q: How would you say your style of management compares to the style of a chief executive officer of a large, established corporation?

Smeelen: I don't have people that I can pass the buck to. My job is hands-on management. One day I'm talking to my top customers doing sales; the next day I may be in jeans running a job from 9 o'clock Tuesday morning to 9 o'clock Wednesday night, through the night. It's not at all a GM-type operation, where all you do is sit at your desk and push buttons and dictate to people what you want to do. If you want it done, you have to follow it up.

Q: What major difficulties do you see from your position?

Smeelen: One is hiring competent help. The desirable people are not always available, and the available people are not always the desirable. The other area is being able to train people. There's no government program to support training white printers, although there are programs for other trades.

Q: Can you describe your ownership structure?

Smeelen: Originally, I worked for 3 partners who had been in business together for a long time. They owned T & D Designs Ltd., then started this reproduction business. Now I'm the sole owner. However, I do have a rather unique arrangement, in which I'm very fortunate. I have 2 advisors who meet regularly with me. One of these gentlemen, Jim Jones, is a certified industrial accountant whom I stumbled across in 1980 through the Federal Business Development Bank, when I was in financial hot water. He was instrumental in getting me through my toughest period and has worked for me ever since as a salaried employee, aside from providing invaluable advice. The other gentleman is one of the original owners of the company, Tom Fox. The three of us form what you might call an informal board, although these 2 gentlemen have no financial interest in the business. Sometimes I can't see the forest through the trees; with these 2 older, wiser men, I'm very fortunate, because they provide me with crucial guidance and direction.

Q: On a day-to-day basis, how much do you operate according to strategies and plans you've worked out, and how much do you operate on gut feeling?

Smeelen: There's an overall plan we try to follow to stay on top of technological changes. We get literature and we go to reproduction/reprographic shows to see what's coming down the road in that area and then try to plan toward that. In the day-to-day operations, I will deviate from the plan if I see something worthwhile. I'll present it to the board, which will either shoot it down or say "Yeah, let's pursue it." If I've got a gut feel for something, I'll pursue it. As an example, I bought some equipment which wasn't in the plan. I presented the idea to my advisors and, at first, they shot me down. I said: "I can see that. That's worth just too much money. But if I don't buy it, and my competition does, I'll lose existing business to them." So their reply was: "Well, you have a gut feel on that, and you're the only one who can tell that. If that's what you feel, then okay, we'll back you up 100 percent. Go for it." It turned out to be one of the best moves we ever made; that equipment earned over $250,000 in sales during the last two and a half years.

FACTORS AFFECTING THE MANAGEMENT OF SMALL BUSINESSES

The small business offers challenge, opportunities, and difficulties that are different from those encountered in larger businesses. To be successful, the small business owner/manager must cope with a variety of factors internal and external to the firm. These factors include the economic, political/legal, and social factors in its external environment, the firm's objectives, its technology, its organizational structure, and the personnel working in the firm. We next discuss each of these important factors.

Economic Factors

Unlike the large corporation, the small business can concentrate on a restricted economic market in one locale or in one segment of an industry. But this condition is a double-edged sword. If economic conditions become depressed in one portion of the industry, the small business may suffer severely, whereas the large, diversified firm may be capable of relying on other segments of the firm to offset the adverse conditions. However, in some situations the small business may be able to choose more favorable economic conditions in which to operate.

In numerous instances a small business may find itself in competition with a large enterprise. When it does, it often will seek to protect itself by serving a particular market segment. Microcomputer and minicomputer manufacturers competing against IBM often decide not to go head-to-head against IBM's strength. Rather, they might direct their effort at a market segment IBM hasn't pursued. The same situation exists for a small grocery store competing for sales against the major chains such as Safeway or Dominion. Because of the volume sales of the chains, the small stores may find it difficult to engage in strong price competition. Factors such as staying open late, offering shorter service lines, selling unusual products, and allowing customers to charge their purchases frequently provide the means for the small business to survive.

The flexibility of being small is somewhat offset by the weaker power resulting from limited resources. On occasion a major customer can take advantage of the small company by insisting on excessively favorable terms in price, quality, or delivery. A small business owner may feel he or she cannot withstand pressure from a supplier larger than the small firm itself. Small businesses often find it more difficult to secure adequate financing from institutional lenders because of their size. Lenders are aware of the fact that the small business has less depth in management. They are also aware of the statistics with respect to small business failure. However, many small businesses are able to secure a loan simply on the basis of personal reputation of the owner.

Unlike many large enterprises, the small business is typically unable to exert a major influence on the economic market. Whereas some suggest that large enterprises are engaged in closed enterprise, there is usually little doubt that the small firm is involved in a highly competitive free enterprise system. In this atmosphere, the small business that is able to maintain lower operational costs will be the most profitable and have the greatest chances of remaining in business.

The Political/Legal Factors

Both large and small businesses in Canada must adhere to provincial and federal laws that regulate business firms. For the small firm, however, adherence may be difficult because it does not have a staff of experts to make sure that government regulations are being properly followed. The small business owner may find that a certain action — like paying a young relative less than the minimum wage is against the law, even though it makes sense for the business. Because the small business owner/manager is totally occupied with running the business, he or she may not be well versed on the myriad laws that have been passed in the last decade.

Three major areas have become prominent for small business firms in the last few years: personnel practices, ecology, and paper burden. With regard to personnel practices, many small business owners may be unaware of provincial workplace health and safety regulations. When visited by a safety inspector, owners may be distressed to find that they must spend money to bring the workplace up to provincial or municipal standards, for instance, installing fire alarms and extinguishers or improving electrical wiring.

Ecological considerations can cause small business owners to pay huge costs to meet legal requirements or to pay fines for contravening them. Some small firms have been charged with excessively polluting sewer systems, waterways, and the air. Prevailing winds can carry animal and waste odors generated from hog and cattle feedlots as far as 3 km. Small laundries that bleach blue jeans have added blue water and sludge to municipal sewer systems. Most small businesses operate on thin margins and may be tempted to reduce their operating costs by pouring wastes into available streams, air, land, and sewers. This, combined with the lack of expert staff and alternative production facilities, makes coping with ecological demands a critical problem.

In a few instances, the owner/managers of small businesses have found ways to cope with ecological problems and to do so at a profit. For example, animal waste solids from feedlots have been collected, sterilized, and sold as organic fertilizer or converted to gas to be used to heat homes. Some laundry managers who were forced to buy a special tank truck to remove excessive sludge have expanded into the septic tank drainage business. The pressing necessity for ecological cleanup applies to both small and large enterprises.

Another political/legal factor in the external environment of small businesses is the variety of government reports that managers must fill out: forms for federal sales tax collection, workers' compensation, business licences, Statistics Canada surveys, and employee hiring procedures. Small business managers complain that this "paper burden" takes precious time away from the running of their businesses and reduces the chance that they will be successful.

Social Factors

The small business typically has fewer problems in coping with social factors in the external environment than does the large corporation. First, the small firm usually has only one community with which to deal. Also, the small firm's manager, being part of the local community, is better able to understand its customs than is the manager of a large corporation. Customers in the community may patronize the business because they know the owner. A small grocery store may find that some of its customers will pay a higher price for their groceries because they know and trust the owner.

Another positive social factor is the close relationship that usually exists between small business owners and their workers. While there is no guarantee that work will always go smoothly, generally speaking a closer working relationship exists between the owner and the workers because the business is small and everyone is on a first-name basis. Because the owner/manager knows each employee well and works closely with them, the employees are usually motivated to do a good job. Also, problems that turn up in daily work are likely to be worked out quickly and openly.

Objectives

The objectives of a small business are no different from those of a large enterprise, although the priorities that the owner places on them may be different. As we discussed in Chapter 3, the major objectives that a firm has are survival, profit, service, and growth.

For a small business, survival of the enterprise is the most crucial and difficult to attain. Since a significant percentage of new business ventures fail in the first year of existence, earning a profit is absolutely essential to long-term business survival. But a newly formed small business must be prepared financially and psychologically not to earn a profit during the early phases of operation. The profit objective provides incentive to assume business risks and, without the profit motive, few people would start their own businesses. But the survival objective constantly haunts the small business. A small business is limited in what it can do, being short on capital, being subject to competitive destruction, and often operating on a hand-to-mouth basis. With respect to the service objective, the typical small business is highly customer oriented. The large enterprise must also adapt to customer requirements, but such adaptation is not usually as specific or as rapid. Whereas the large enterprise can manipulate and control products and markets with its vast resources, the small firm must immediately be attuned to specific customer wishes and requirements. In this way, a unique market niche can be gained.

The small business has the advantage of specialization by concentrating on a limited number of services. Though real estate agents often concentrate on a particular type of property, such as residential or commercial, one particular agency carved out a niche by concentrating solely on providing faculty housing in a city that contained a major university. A retail supermarket may develop special excellence in providing unusually good meat products. One small pharmaceutical company prospered in competition with larger firms by concentrating on the needs of one type of medical specialty — the ophthalmologic surgeon.

Another basic objective of most small businesses is growth. However, certain limitations to growth must be considered. Unlimited growth cannot be an objective of the small business if:

• The owner/manager seeks to retain direct and personal control of the firm.
• The firm wishes to sell only selected products or services.
• Management wants the firm to remain highly flexible.
• The owner does not value growth.

The personal values and stage in life of the small business owner have a significant effect on the growth rate of the firm. If the owner is satisfied with the volume of the business and wants to spend more time with his or her family, growth will likely be slow. On the other hand, an ambitious entrepreneur with few commitments outside the business may work long hours trying to increase the growth rate of the business.

Technology

Technology exerts a significant impact on the types of products and services provided by small business firms. These products and services tend to possess characteristics that distinguish them from those of larger enterprises:

• The technology needed to create these products and services is characterized by shorter processing cycles. This enables promptness of service and does not require extensive investment in facilities.
• The demand for products and services of many small businesses tends to show greater seasonal variations.
• Small businesses are often in a better position to produce higher-quality products than are larger firms.
• The technology used to produce the products and services tends to be relatively stable. The small firm does not have the resources to be constantly bringing out new products as markets for old products disappear.

Because of these technological characteristics, there will always be a place for small business to provide products and services adapted to their particular capabilities. With the majority of small businesses in Canada being engaged in retailing, wholesaling, and services, the most commonly needed technology is that of dealing directly with customers. Because customers are not completely controllable, great flexibility and sensitivity is needed.

Many small businesses were started because of one technological innovation by its owner. Once the owner deals with the day-to-day operations of the business, he or she often does not have sufficient time to devote to continued research and development. The reason that caused the small business to be created may also be the cause of its failure. Should the competition develop a superior product, the small business may find itself in severe difficulties.

Organizational Structure

The major characteristics of small business organizational structure are: (1) an emphasis on informality, (2) the critical importance of the owner/manager, and (3) the necessity for increased departmentalization with growth. Small firms tend to operate in a somewhat informal manner. The small size permits it; the need for flexibility demands it. High degrees of formalization, in terms of organizational charts, job descriptions, and procedures, are not evident; this contrasts sharply with the large firm where much formalization exists. (Recall structural discussions in Chapter 7.)

Because of the size of the small business, its owner and/or operator is of critical importance. There has been a tendency for operators of successful small firms to remain in the position for long periods of time — sometimes as much as 20 to 40 years. In large enterprises, a president remains for a much shorter period, typically fewer than 10 years. Heads of small businesses almost always wear two or more hats; for instance, they must perform several important functions. Not only do they manage the total enterprise, but they almost always perform a second or third function, frequently the finance function. In some small manufacturing firms, owners personally handle the major sales, placing themselves in competition with subordinate sales representatives. If a labor union is present, the owner/manager often handles the negotiations personally. If the owner has an engineering degree, he or she may be the firm's only machine maintenance person; management problems may have to wait until a machine is back in operation.

As the small business grows, the variety, number, and complexity of functions and relationships increases. The typical span of control in the small firm ranges from 4 to 7 subordinates, whereas in the large company it ranges from 5 to over 11. Thus, in the small business, communication distances are short and personal contacts frequent.

Not only do the typical small business manager and virtually all personnel wear two or more hats, they are expected to perform many activities that would normally be handled by a staff of experts in a large organization. For example, consider a small business employing 6 people. One day all 6 may be sales personnel, the next day they may spend time seeking financing, and the next day they all may be on the production line. The limited number of different departments and specialization of personnel enables the small business to operate with speed and flexibility.

There also tend to be fewer rigid or formal rules to follow in small firms. Employees may leave assigned work places without permission, have more flexible starting and quitting times, and have a more flexible dress code. The culture of the organization is more personalized. Names are more important than time clock numbers. It is likely that there are neither time clocks nor codified rule books. When instances calling for disciplinary action do arise, there is more individualized handling of the case. The less-rigid scheduling of tasks permits greater degrees of interaction among employees.

The nature of the job assignment combined with the friendly culture that can be developed in a small business leads to greater employee identification with the enterprise. There is an excitement in being actively involved in daily operations, of having personal contact with managers and customers. Individuals' impact on the total organization is greater, and they can see what they have personally accomplished. Absence rates are often significantly lower in the small firm. There is also considerably less likelihood that a labor union will be present.

Personnel

There are many noneconomic reasons for a person to prefer to work in a small business. While work in a large organization is often highly specialized, the typical task assignments in the small firm offer variety, challenge, and a greater degree of self-control. This flexibility may explain why many recent graduates are beginning to seek jobs with small businesses. At times, an employee has an opportunity to carry a job through from the original idea to its introduction into the market. Experience is gained at an accelerated pace. Such opportunities provided by a small business are of great significance to many people.

Although there are exceptions, larger organizations usually pay their employees higher salaries than do small businesses. Most small firms tend to view salary as an expense rather than the employee as an asset. If the owner of a small business had to choose between a $25,000 accountant and one costing $35,000, the odds are heavily in favor of the former. If the owner were choosing between a $25,000 piece of machinery and one costing $35,000, however, considerably more deliberation would go into the decision. The owner may be aware that the more expensive machine might have certain advantages over the less expensive one, which would make the additional expenditure worthwhile.

A type of employee that is sometimes found in a small firm is a member of the owner/manager's family. The practice of hiring one's own relatives is **nepotism**. In the past this family member was often the son or son-in-law of the owner. More recently, a number of daughters of successful small business owners have gone to work in the family business. One writer states that the most lethal of all deadly triangles in small businesses is where all three — father, son, and son-in-law — are key people in the enterprise.[1]

Using family members has some advantages to the small business. Identification with "our business" should be great, thereby leading to increased effort and dedication. In addition, family members may constitute sources for funds to finance the enterprise. Bringing a son or daughter into the firm enables retention of control by the family in the years ahead. However, if a firm rigidly follows a policy of nepotism in its hiring or promotion practices, competent nonfamily personnel will leave the firm because they see little opportunity for advancement.

Employing family members can cause a number of interpersonal problems. Family quarrels can and do spill over into the everyday operations of the firm. In one instance, the introduction of the son initially caused few problems in a small hardware business. As the firm prospered, the standard of living of the son's family exceeded that of his sister and her husband. His sister brought pressure on their father to bring her husband into the firm. After this was done, head-on competition began to develop between the son and the son-in-law as the daughter used the firm to increase her family status. Ultimately the father was forced to dissolve the firm because of family warfare. In another company run by a father and his 4 sons, a disagreement about business procedures led to a fist fight between two of the brothers on the front steps of the business.

PITFALLS IN STARTING A SMALL BUSINESS

A person who wants to start a small business should be aware of a number of potential pitfalls.[2] These can be avoided; however, many small business owners fail to do so. Several of the most important pitfalls are discussed below.

Lack of Experience in the Business

A good rule of thumb for anyone thinking of starting a small business is: "You don't enter a business that you know nothing about." Much more experience is needed than merely a knowledge of the product or service that will be provided. Experience relates also to such areas as purchasing, marketing, and finance. It is because of lack of balanced experience that many small businesses fail. An engineer who has a tremendous idea for a new product will find that, before the product can be manufactured, capital must be available to secure parts required to produce the item. The engineer must also determine what quantities and quality levels are needed. Once the item has been manufactured, it must be marketed. A certain amount of personal selling is necessary. Thus, in order to go into business for oneself, a person should ask if he or she has the package of experience that is necessary to operate the business successfully.

Lack of Capital

A good idea does not guarantee the success of a small business. A person should also evaluate carefully the amount of capital that will be required both to start and to maintain a business. Often these calculations are much too optimistic, and a person can actually fail before the business has opened. For instance, an individual decided to take over the operation of a small convenience store. All expenses were carefully calculated: salaries, rent, utilities, and advertising. The only thing that was forgotten was that additional inventory had to be purchased for the successful operation of the business because the previous owner had reduced inventory to a very low level prior to selling the store. The new owner was not aware of this and did not have funds to purchase the inventory required. The store was never re-opened.

Poor Location

Since a large percentage of small businesses are retail store operations, a major factor that should be considered is the selection of the proper location. Low rent in the wrong location may be high; high rent in the right location may be low. Factors that should be considered might be:

- Population: What is the traffic volume surrounding the store? Are the types of customers who will potentially purchase the product located within the trading area? For instance, approximately 70 percent of all convenience store customers reside within 2 km of the store.
- Accessibility: Do cars have to cross traffic to get to the location? How fast is the traffic generally moving past the location? Are car parks nearby?
- Competition: Are there a large number of similar types of businesses in the marketing area? How will the competition affect the proposed location?
- Economic stability: The site must be considered not only for its current location but also for potential considerations. The anticipated move of a large supermarket across the street may have a detrimental effect on a new family-owned grocery.

Inadequate Inventory Management

Inventory represents a debt for a small business; it ties up funds that could be used for other purposes. Inventory management is crucial to successful operation. If a business attempts to get by on minimum inventory, its customers may begin shopping at other locations where all of the items they want are available. On the other hand, if excessive inventory is carried, funds cannot be used for other purposes. Also, if the items cannot be sold, they represent a complete loss for the business.

Another major factor related to inventory mismanagement is internal theft. Often the greatest number of thefts are committed by in-house personnel. A manager of a small business is often so closely involved with the personnel that he or she never believes that they would steal. There have been instances where an employee was making more than the owner because of internal theft. An inventory control system should be established to discover shortages before they become excessive.

Excessive Investment in Fixed Assets

Fixed assets, such as buildings and equipment, cannot be converted into cash easily, if at all. Sales may be increasing so the owner decides to purchase additional equipment. Additional personnel are then hired to use the equipment. If a decline in sales is experienced, payment on the equipment may prove difficult. Because of this, the business may be forced into bankruptcy even though at one time it had an excellent

---

MANAGEMENT IN PRACTICE

Success and Failure in Small Business

In the 1970s, Billy Hitzig started Pierre de Paris Fashions Ltd., a women's fashion manufacturing company. He expanded quickly and moved into the United States markets. He got the contract to produce clothes bearing the logo of the 1980 Moscow Olympics, and sales rose to $4 million by 1979. Then the United States announced that it was boycotting the Olympics, and the stores he had contracts with backed out. He was left with obsolete inventory valued at half a million dollars. The banks foreclosed on his business.

Mr. Hitzig has now started another business — Bohtogs Industries Ltd. and he is experiencing much more success on his second try. He accepts most of the blame for the failure of his first business and says that it was his poor management that caused it to fail. This time around, he is being much more cautious and trying to keep his operation manageable. For example, until recently, his line of credit was only $10,000.

When he decided he needed more, he paid for the services of a large accounting firm to draw up his application. This resulted in a more thorough financial analysis than if he had done it himself.

He is looking at the American market again, but this time much more carefully. He has decided simply to export to the United States rather than to set up operations there. He also has turned to the Ontario government's trade offices in the United States to help him explore that market more systematically.

Billy Hitzig isn't bitter about his initial failure in the garment business. He says that experience helped him to do a much better job of managing his business the second time around.

SOURCE   Adapted from "Chapter Two: The Resurrection of an Entrepreneur," *Canadian Business* (May 1984): 108.

chance for success. The small business owner must consider this factor much more carefully than do large, well-established firms.

Poor Credit Policies

One sure way to make a sale is to give credit. But small business owners have discovered that one of the fastest ways to go out of business is to give excessive credit. In many instances, credit is granted based on whether the owner likes a person. The owner has not determined if the individual is a poor credit risk. With this approach, an owner may find that sales are increasing but there is little cash inflow. Because the owner may feel uncomfortable about asking people to pay their debts, the debt owed by the customer may not be collected.

Taking Too Much Cash Out of the Business

Money that is spent by the owner cannot be used to make the business grow. When a small business is just starting to develop, it is likely that a major problem relates to securing sufficient capital. If the owner takes too much cash out of the business to maintain a high life-style, growth may be stymied. Sacrifices must be made at first to enjoy future success.

Unplanned Expansions

If one business location is doing fine, the owner may be tempted to add an additional location and do twice as well. Growth by acquisition has often caused major problems for owners of small businesses. When rapid expansions occur, difficulties are often experienced. The manager will discover that running two locations is much more difficult than one. He or she may not be accustomed to delegating authority, which must be done if there is more than one location. If the owner has been making all the decisions, efficiency may drop when additional locations are involved.

Having the Wrong Attitude

Let's face it; starting your own business is difficult. There is a good possibility it will fail. It is certainly not a structured job where you can leave the problems of the job behind at quitting time. If a business is to be successful, it will take a lot of hard work. The responsibilities of the business will likely mean that many outside interests will have to be reduced. Small business owners must assess the personal value of such outside interests, because the assessment is not merely in terms of money. Personal decisions may need to be made in light of how they will affect the business. If the owner decides to go on a holiday, this decision could reduce that time's business. Sacrifices will be necessary, but to see a business survive and grow is worth the effort. The business is yours and you are answerable to no one but yourself.

GOVERNMENT AND SMALL BUSINESS

Federal and provincial governments in Canada have a two-sided impact on small business. On the one hand, many government assistance programs are available for small businesses; on the other, small businesses must cope with many government regulations, some of which seem unnecessarily intrusive. We look at each of these issues in this section.

Government Assistance to Small Business

Unlike the United States, where the federal Small Business Administration coordinates the available aid to small business, in Canada a variety of federal and provincial programs exist. These programs show how strong the belief is in Canada that small business is something that should be encouraged at various levels of government. These aid programs are also an attempt to keep large firms from dominating markets. These government programs provide aid in two distinct areas: (1) financial assistance, and (2) management consulting assistance.

The **financial assistance programs** for small business are numerous, so only illustrative programs are presented here. One of the most well-known programs was established in 1978 with the passage of the federal Small Business Loans Act. Under this Act, small business owners can get loans up to $75,000 to purchase fixed and movable assets. The Federal Business Development Bank (FBDB) also encourages loans to small businesses; the interest rates it charges increase as the size of the loan increases. The Income Tax Act also assists small business because it allows Canadian-controlled private corporations to pay a low tax rate on the first $150,000 of income each year.

Financial assistance to small business is also prominent at the provincial level. The specific agencies and laws differ somewhat, but the aim in each province is to encourage small business activity. Examples are the Enterprise Development Group of Manitoba, the Alberta Opportunity Company, and the Industry Development Branch of Saskatchewan. These provincial agencies usually give financial aid to individuals wanting to establish a small business or to those wanting to improve an existing small business.

An important part of financial aid to small business is the incentive aspect of the aid. The federal Department of Regional Industrial Expansion (DRIE), for example, gives incentive grants to certain firms if they are located in such designated slow-growth areas as the Atlantic provinces, most of Quebec, northern Ontario, Manitoba, Saskatchewan, northern Alberta and BC, and the two territories. By giving incentive grants, the federal government hopes to influence entrepreneurial decision making. When considering these grants, the entrepreneur must ask whether the short term financial benefit of the grant more than offsets the potential negative effects of locating in a slow-growth area.

MANAGEMENT IN PRACTICE

Profiting from Garbage

Oonagh McNerney is president of Extrufix Inc., a Markham, Ontario firm that has Canadian sales of $5 million and export sales to the United States, Australia, Britain, and other countries totalling $1.25 million. The company manufactures and sells the "Roll and Rack", a device that dispenses small garbage bags for kitchen use.

The company started in 1970 with $20,000 from a remortgaged home and $50,000 from a venture capitalist. McNerney spent many hours demonstrating the product in Eaton's and Simpsons in the early years of the company. The marketing strategy was carried out in 3 phases: first, sell to stores like Eaton's to establish product credibility; second, sell to the large discount stores like Woolco; third, sell to grocery stores after the product's workability was established.

Sales doubled annually during the 1970s. The company eventually built a manufacturing facility on 2 ha of land in Pefferlaw, Ontario and hired 17 people with the help of a Federal Business Development Bank loan of $200,000. The company began selling in the American market some years ago, but the operation there became profitable only in 1983. The company now has a very bright future in both countries.

SOURCE   Adapted from Helen Kohl, "Mother Finds Marketing Gold in Patented Garbage Bag Gizmo," *Small Business* (November 1983): 6–7.

The owner/manager of a small business must give careful consideration to government aid. The role of an entrepreneur is to bring together land, labor, and capital to earn a profit. Government aid does not come without certain strings attached, and the entrepreneur must consider how much these strings will inhibit his or her ability to do what is necessary to run a profitable business. If the government aid requires setting up a business in a certain geographic area, the entrepreneur must ask hard questions about whether or not the area can support the business he or she has in mind. Or, if the aid requires a certain pay-back schedule, the entrepreneur must consider whether the business can meet the schedule.

Overall, government assistance to small business changes the payoffs to owner/managers. From the managerial perspective, the nature of these payoffs must be considered in relation to the performance the business would be capable of without the aid.

The other area of government assistance to small business involves low cost advice on how to manage a small business. The **Counselling Assistance to Small Enterprises** (CASE) program brings retired business executives into contact with entrepreneurs as consultants to small businesses. The small business owner can discuss problems in marketing, production, finance, and personnel with these consultants and also discuss the value of new ideas on how to improve productivity and the general effectiveness of the business. To be eligible for CASE, a firm must have less than 100 employees and sales less than $5 million per year.

Government Regulation of Small Business

We noted earlier in the chapter that often small business owners feel resentment toward government involvement. Governments must protect consumers and the ecology; it cannot allow even small businesses simply to do whatever they please. Entrepreneurs, conversely, often believe that government is unnecessarily strict in the regulation of small business.

As we discussed in Chapter 2, the federal, provincial, and municipal governments control business in several major areas. One involves the requirement that all businesses must procure certain licenses and permits before they are allowed to operate. For example, a restaurant must have a food and liquor license before the business can serve food and alcohol. Businesses must also — among other compliances with regulations — collect sales tax, carry workers' compensation insurance, and pay employer taxes. Most small business owners would agree that these kinds of things are necessary and desirable, but they do consume valuable time.

Small business owners must usually provide certain pertinent information to the municipal, provincial and federal governments. For example, small business owners might be required to fill out a questionnaire indicating how many employees the business has, how much they are paid, and other aspects of their operation. Many entrepreneurs feel that being required to provide information of this sort intrudes unreasonably into their activities. One survey by the Canadian Federation of Independent Businesses found that government-required paperwork was identified as the number one problem in 10 percent of the firms that responded; overall, it ranked fourth.

CHECKLIST FOR GOING INTO BUSINESS

A person considering starting a business should carefully and critically evaluate a number of factors. The Small Business Administration in the United States has developed a comprehensive checklist of questions that assist in this evaluation process. These questions are relevant for any small business owner. (See the table below.) As can be seen, these questions are organized under such topics as: "Before You Start," "Getting Started," and "Making It Go."

Once you have carefully answered the questions posed in the table, you have done some hard work and serious thinking. That's good! But you have probably found some things you still need to know more about or do something about.

Do all you can for yourself, but don't hesitate to ask for help from people who can tell you what you need to know. Remember, running

MANAGEMENT IN PRACTICE

Government and Small Business

John Brady is the owner of an ice cream parlor called "After All" on Mount Pleasant Road in uptown Toronto. From the time he conceived of the idea until he actually opened the store, he encountered a series of obstacles that had to be overcome. In addition to the usual managerial problems, he was faced with many government requirements. Consider the following:

- When he took his architectural drawings to City Hall for approval, he discovered that many building code requirements had not been considered by the architect who had drawn up the plans (a friend of his). He consulted the Building Code, added the changes he thought were necessary, and waited for approval. He received approval of his building plans, but had to make many changes that cost him a significant amount of money. For example, he had to add a sink on the main floor of the store so that employees could wash their hands.

- He could have got a loan from the Federal Business Development Bank, but it would have taken too much time to process; he wanted to get going immediately.

- As construction neared completion, a parade of public health, fire, electrical, and building inspectors toured the building. By and large, though, they were reasonable people.

- Other problems were not so easily solved. One concerned the sign he wanted to hang on his building. Since it extended 15 cm beyond his building, he was told he would have to pay a city tax on the sign. He also had much difficulty getting a permit to use a strip of land 1 m by 9 m next to his building for a patio. Thirteen different groups had to approve of the idea before he was allowed to set up his patio. That process took two months.

- Because he wanted to serve liquor, he had to get a liquor permit. When he went to the office of the chairman of the liquor commission, he was confronted by two people who were concerned about his having a liquor license. One was a tenant who lived over his store and was concerned about excessive noise, and the other was the Baptist church across the street. After several compromises, Brady got his license.

In spite of all this, John Brady says it was worth it. The freedom of owning your own business is, after all, better than working for someone else.

SOURCE Adapted from Tony Leighton, "The Emperor of Ice Cream," *Canadian Business* (March 1984): 32–38.

---

a business takes guts! You've got to be able to decide what you need and then go after it.

Good luck!

Checklist for Going into Business for Yourself

BEFORE YOU START

How about You?

- Are you the kind of person who can get a business started and make it go?
- Think about why you want to own your own business. Do you want it badly enough to keep working long hours without knowing how much money you'll end up with?

(table cont'd.: Small Business Checklist)

- Have you worked in a business like the one you want to start?
- Have you worked for someone else as a foreman or manager?
- Have you had any business training in school?
- Have you saved any money?

How about the Money?
- Do you know how much money you will need to get your business started?
- Have you counted up how much money of your own you can put into the business?
- Do you know how much credit you can get from your suppliers — the people you will buy from?
- Do you know where you can borrow the rest of the money you need to start your business?
- Have you figured out what net income per year you expect to get from the business? Count your salary and your profit on the money you put into the business.
- Can you live on less than this so that you can use some of it to help your business grow?
- Have you talked to a banker about your plans?

How about a Partner?
- If you need a partner with money or know-how that you don't have, do you know someone who will fit — someone you can get along with?
- Do you know the good and bad points about going it alone, having a partner, or incorporating your business?
- Have you talked to a lawyer about it?

How about Your Customers?
- Do most businesses in your community seem to be doing well?
- Have you tried to find out whether stores like the one you want to open are doing well in your community and in the rest of the country?
- Do you know what kind of people will want to buy what you plan to sell?
- Do those kinds of people live in the area where you want to open your store?
- Do they need a store like yours?
- If not, have you thought about opening a different kind of store or going to another neighborhood?

GETTING STARTED

Your Building
- Have you found a good building for your store?
- Will you have enough room when your business gets bigger?
- Can you fix the building the way you need to without spending too much money?

(table cont'd.: Small Business Checklist)

- Can people get to it easily from parking spaces, bus stops, or their homes?
- Have you had a lawyer check the lease and zoning?

Equipment and Supplies
- Do you know just what equipment and supplies you need and how much they will cost?
- Can you save some money by buying secondhand equipment?

Your Merchandise
- Have you decided what you will sell?
- Do you know how much or how many of each you will buy to open your store for business?
- Have you found suppliers who will sell you what you need at a good price?
- Have you compared the prices and credit terms of different suppliers?

Your Records
- Have you planned a system of records that will keep track of your income and expenses, what you owe other people, and what other people owe you?
- Have you worked out a way to keep track of your inventory so that you will always have enough on hand for your customers but not more than you can sell?
- Have you figured out how to keep your payroll records and take care of tax reports and payments?
- Do you know what financial statements you should prepare?
- Do you know how to use these financial statements?
- Do you know an accountant who will help you with your records and financial statements?

Your Store and the Law
- Do you know what licenses and permits you need?
- Do you know what business laws you have to obey?
- Do you know a lawyer you can go to for advice and for help with legal papers?

Protecting Your Store
- Have you made plans for protecting your store against thefts of all kinds — shoplifting, robbery, burglary, employee stealing?
- Have you talked with an insurance agent about what kinds of insurance you need?

Buying a Business Someone Else Has Started
- Have you made a list of what you like and don't like about buying a business someone else has started?
- Are you sure you know the real reason why the owner wants to sell the business?

(table cont'd.: Small Business Checklist)

- Have you compared the cost of buying the business with the cost of starting a new business?
- Is the stock up to date and in good condition?
- Is the building in good condition?
- Will the owner of the building transfer the lease to you?
- Have you talked with other business people in the area to see what they think of the business?
- Have you talked with the company's suppliers?
- Have you talked with a lawyer about it?

MAKING IT GO

Advertising
- Have you decided how you will advertise? (newspapers? posters? handbills? radio? by mail?)
- Do you know where to get help with your ads?
- Have you watched what other stores do to get people to buy?

The Prices You Charge
- Do you know how to figure what you should charge for each item you sell?
- Do you know what other stores like yours charge?

Buying
- Do you have a plan for finding out what your customers want?
- Will your plan for keeping track of your inventory tell you when it is time to order more and how much to order?
- Do you plan to buy most of your stock from a few suppliers rather than a little from many, so that those you buy from will want to help you succeed?

Selling
- Have you decided whether you will have salesclerks or be self-service?
- Do you know how to get customers to buy?
- Have you thought about why you like to buy from some sales representatives while others turn you off?

Your Employees
- If you need to hire someone to help you, do you know where to look?
- Do you know what kind of person you need?
- Do you know how much to pay?
- Do you have a plan for training your employees?

Credit for Your Customers
- Have you decided whether to let your customers buy on credit?
- Do you know the good and bad points about joining a credit-card plan?
- Can you tell a bad debt from a good credit customer?

(table cont'd.: Small Business Checklist)

A FEW EXTRA QUESTIONS

- Have you figured out whether you could make more money working for someone else?
- Does your family go along with your plan to start a business of your own?
- Do you know where to find out about new ideas and new products?

OPENING INCIDENT REVISITED

Kent Computers

In the opening incident, Evan Kent was having second thoughts about his decision to start his own small business. He was working extremely long hours, yet he had virtually nothing to show for all his efforts so far. The problems experienced by Kent are very typical in newly formed small businesses. In the chapter, we noted that a person starting a business from scratch would probably have to spend several years building up the business to the point where it was a viable entity. Kent has only been in business a few months, yet he is already thinking about quitting. His lack of a longer-run perspective could seriously damage his chances for success.

Since Kent is not involved in manufacturing, he does not have a key problem that some small businesses face — shortage of cash. He keeps as little inventory as possible and in this way is able to avoid cash problems. However, the kind of product he is selling requires intensive discussions with customers, so he is going to have to spend considerable time with customers if he hopes to make sales. He therefore has time problems, which can be just as serious as cash problems.

Kent's two major problems are: (1) no experience in the business, and (2) poor inventory management. His lack of experience can be overcome, but he is going to have to spend many hours becoming well-versed in the computer business. His inventory problems are probably going to cost him customers if he doesn't get a more complete line of products in the store. However, to do this will cost money. Kent seems to have successfully avoided most of the other pitfalls noted in the chapter, yet he still is wondering whether he made the right decision to go into business for himself.

Kent should have asked himself the kinds of questions contained in the checklist in the last section before he started a small business. Perhaps he is not suited to owning his own business, or at least not a business that sells this particular product.

SUMMARY

For thousands of Canadians, their dream is to own and manage their own business — to be their own boss. While the freedom to start and manage one's own business is available to everyone, each year thousands of new businesses fail. In fact, statistics reveal that, in Canada, half of all new businesses fail within the first 4 years of operation and over 60 percent fail within 6 years. Despite these grim statistics, virtually every large, successful business began as a small business. Also, it is important to note that small businesses make significant contributions to the health and vitality of the Canadian economy.

Franchising has facilitated the growth of small business in Canada. In franchising, a contract is drawn up between a manufacturer and a dealer stipulating how the manufacturer's product or service will be sold. The franchisee pays the franchisor a fee to get into the franchise; then the franchisee collects royalties based on sales revenue.

The small business enterprise offers challenges, opportunities, and considerable problems that differ from those encountered by large businesses. The large firm usually has the resources to withstand adverse circumstances. Limited resources may make it difficult for the small business to exert a major influence on the economic or political/legal aspects of their external environment. However, a small business may be more flexible and responsive to changing conditions. For example, a small firm may be able to offer more personalized service and maintain lower operational costs.

The high failure rates for small businesses are caused primarily by ineffective management. Some of the major pitfalls that small businesses encounter include the owner's lack of experience in the business, lack of capital, a poor location, inadequate inventory management, excessive capital investment in fixed assets, poor credit policies, the owner taking too much cash out of the business, unplanned expansions, and having the wrong attitude. Many small business owner/managers also spend much time and money complying with government regulations — coping with the paper burden or tailoring their business to meet legal requirements. However, to help prospective, new, and established small businesses avoid and/or overcome problems that might cause failure, federal and provincial assistance in the areas of finance and management is available.

REVIEW QUESTIONS

1. What is a small business? What is a franchise and how does it differ from small business ownership?
2. What is considered to be a small business in Canada in manufacturing? in other sectors?
3. What are the failure rates for small businesses in Canada? Why? Discuss briefly.
4. What external environment factors affect the management of small businesses? Do each of these factors affect small firms more than large companies?
5. What are the basic objectives of the typical small business? Is growth always an objective of a small business? Why or why not?
6. Products and services of small businesses tend to have characteristics that distinguish them from those of larger enterprises. Discuss any 3 of these characteristics.

7. What are the major characteristics of small business organizational structures?
8. What is meant by nepotism? Briefly discuss how the practice can affect a small business.
9. What is an entrepreneur? What are the major personality characteristics of entrepreneurs?
10. List and briefly discuss 5 of the more prominent pitfalls often encountered in starting a small business.
11. Briefly describe the various types of regulations that affect new small businesses and the types of assistance available to small businesses from the federal and provincial governments.
12. Review the Checklist for Going into Business for Yourself. What areas covered in the checklist are most significant?

EXERCISES

1. Using the Checklist for Going into Business for Yourself, evaluate the feasibility of starting your own restaurant specializing in steak and seafood entrées.
2. Visit 3 successful small businesses in your local area. Discuss with the owner/managers of each business the reasons for success of their business. Ask them if they would advise a person to begin his or her own small business.

CASE STUDY

The Lethbridge Inn

For many years, John Goodson had thought that Lethbridge, Alberta needed a first-class motel, restaurant, and private club. Although there was limited industry in the city, Lethbridge was a growing community. It was also the home of the University of Lethbridge. The building of a quality motel, restaurant, and club facility in Lethbridge had long been a dream of Goodson. He became particularly enthusiastic about the potential success of the motel facility after discussing his plans with local business people and university officials. The business and university leaders pledged their support and encouraged Goodson to continue with plans for the creation of the facility. Goodson, the president of a retail chain, was able to interest his brother-in-law,

Charles Jones, and two of Jones's business associates, Paula Prince and Bob Johnson, in the venture. Jones was a vice-president with an encyclopedia company and Prince and Johnson were highly successful sales managers. All 3 lived in Calgary.

After considerable discussion, the 4 people — Goodson, Jones, Prince, and Johnson — formed a partnership and began serious preparations for entering the motel business. While none of the partners had any previous experience in the motel, restaurant, or club business, each was considered a successful business person. The partners hired a nationally known consulting firm, specializing in hotel/motel operations, to conduct a study to determine the feasibility of the project. Prior to engaging the consulting firm, the 4 partners agreed on the location and size of the proposed facility. The consulting firm recommended the creation of the proposed motel, restaurant, and club facility on the location specified by the partners. The study was completed in 10 days at a cost of $5,000 to the partners. The consultants based their recommendation of the project on the following factors:

- Favorable general business conditions and projected growth of Lethbridge and the university.
- Supply of and demand for motel rooms seem to be favorable.
- There was a lack of quality motel and/or restaurant facilities in Lethbridge.
- Financial projections appeared excellent — a forecast of $50,000 net income during the first year of operation.
- The proposed site was excellent because of its location on a major highway and its proximity to the university.

Much of the consultants' study consisted of interviewing business and university leaders to obtain their estimate of the potential for such a venture.

After reviewing the feasibility study, the partners decided to proceed immediately with plans for the facility, which was to be named the Lethbridge Inn. An architectural firm completed plans for the facility and construction began in September; the inn opened for business the next September, with 60 rooms, a restaurant, and a private club. The total capital invested in the facility was $800,000 with $100,000 being contributed directly by the partners. A $700,000, 20-year loan at 14 percent annual interest provided the remainder of the capital.

Almost immediately on opening, the Lethbridge Inn began experiencing operational and financial difficulties. None of the partners was interested in managing the facility, so a professional manager was hired, as well as a staff of several full- and part-time personnel. During the first 2 years of operation, the inn had 5 managers and experienced losses totaling over $200,000. The occupancy rate was much lower than the level predicted by the feasibility study, and expenses for food and salaries were far out of line.

When questioned about the lack of success of the inn, Goodson stated: "Our poor results during the first 2 years of operation resulted from poor management — particularly in the areas of control of salaries and food expenses. Also, we haven't had the business we were promised from the university or from local towns people. We've also had a tough time finding competent managers."

QUESTIONS

1. What were the primary problems experienced by the Lethbridge Inn? What were the causes of these problems?
2. Do you think that Goodson and his partners should have entered the business? Discuss.
3. Do you spot any apparent weaknesses in the consultants' feasibility study? If so, what are they?
4. What do you predict in the future for the Lethbridge Inn?

CASE STUDY

The Photography Studio

The Clark Photography Studio located in Regina has an excellent reputation for high-quality photography. The studio specializes in bridal, family, and executive portraits. In addition, the studio is very active in photographing weddings. Raymond Clark is the owner and manager of the studio. He started the business in his garage 30 years ago, and it has since grown to become one of the leading photography studios in Regina with revenues in excess of $150,000 annually and 5 full-time employees. Clark has earned a reputation as a highly creative and innovative photographer.

Clark was the first portrait photographer to take outdoor garden color portraits some 15 years ago. Most of his bridal portraits and many of the individual and/or family portraits are taken in his outdoor garden studio. Because of the unique features of the studio's portraits, the studio has as much business as Clark believes he wants. He has never advertised in any form — depending on word-of-mouth to carry his message of quality photography. Throughout the history of the business, Clark's goal has been to be a high-quality photographer. In recent years, he has raised prices considerably, but has noticed no overall decrease in revenues.

The Clark Photography Studio has 5 key employees: Ray Clark; his wife, Joan, who handles customers and manages the office; Ray and Joan's son, Ken, who is also a professional photographer; Hilda, a professional spotter who does touch-up work on negatives and prints; and Cathy, who performs such duties as framing pictures and working with customers. Ken, 32 is one of 3 sons. He is interested in someday owning the business. Unfortunately, Ken has had a history of instability and unpredictability, especially with regard to work. He has either quit or been fired by his father several times and has not always been a very conscientious employee. Recently, however, he seems to have taken a more responsible attitude. Clark's other sons have never been interested in the photography business.

In recent years, Ray Clark has been spending less and less time in the business. Several years ago, he decided to close the studio on Mondays — which meant that the business was open from 9–5 Tuesday through Friday and from 9–noon on Saturday. Although the studio is currently operating on this schedule, Ray Clark, who is 60 and is interested in retiring from the business, has chosen to work a fewer number of days. His typical work week is as follows: Wednesday: 9–5; Thursday: plays golf; Friday: 9–5; and every other Saturday: 9–noon.

While not at the studio, Ray Clark spends most of his time at his ranch located about 145 km from Regina. Six years ago, he bought 60 ha of land and built a large, beautiful retirement home. He has 25 head of cattle on the ranch and enjoys having a garden. Ray Clark and his son-in-law, Bob Schroeder, have frequent discussions about the future of the Clark Photography Studio. One of their recent conversations was as follows:

Schroeder: Ray, how are your plans for retirement coming along? Do you think that Ken is ready to take over the business?

Clark: I'm ready to get out now, but I don't believe that Ken can handle the business on his own yet. He is doing a good job, but if Joan and I leave the studio, I'm not sure he could make it. Ken wants to buy the business but I think that he would have a difficult time making the payments. Just the other day I was offered $300,000 for the studio property by a group of investors who want to build condominiums on the land. That's an excellent price, don't you think?

Schroeder: The $300,000 offer sounds good to me, especially when you consider the interest income from that amount of money. However, your annual earnings from the business are more than the interest on the $300,000.

Clark: I want out of the city and the pressures of the business. However, I have been able to work 2 or 3 days a week now for 2 years and still earn almost what I earned when I was spending 5 days in the studio. Our business has declined some during the past year, but not drastically. Besides, I enjoy my golf day on Thursdays with the boys and Joan likes to come in to Regina to visit friends — so I'll probably continue the 2- or 3-day schedule for a while longer.

QUESTIONS

1. What are the present goals of Ray Clark as a small business person? Have they changed over time?

2. Why has the Clark Photography Studio been successful in the past? Do you believe its current goals ensure continued success in the future?

3. In view of what we discussed in this chapter, evaluate the effectiveness of Ray Clark as an owner/manager.

4. Since Clark wants to retire, would you advise that he accept the $300,000 offer for the studio property?

5. Why do you think Ray Clark does not have much confidence in his son Ken's ability to run the studio when he retires?

NOTES

¹ Howard J. Klein, *Stop! You're Killing the Business* (New York: Mason and Lipscomb, 1974).

² *Pitfalls of Starting a Small Business* (New York: Dun and Bradstreet, 1980).

REFERENCES

Black, Debra. "Strength in Numbers: The Joy of Franchising." *Canadian Business* 57, no. 5 (May 1984): 111.

————. "The Importance of Raising Money." *Canadian Business* 57, no. 5 (May 1984): 115.

Bruckman, J. C., and Iman, S. "Consulting with Small Business: A Process Model." *Journal of Small Business Management* 18 (April 1980): 41–47.

Carland, James W.; Hoy, Frank; Boulton, William R.; and Carland, JoAnn C. "Differentiating Entrepreneurs from Small Business Owners: A Conceptualization." *Academy of Management Review* 9, no. 2 (April 1984): 354–359.

Charan, Ram; Haber, Charles W.; and Mahan, John. "From Entrepreneur to Professional Manager: A Set of Guidelines." *Journal of Small Business Management* 18 (January 1980): 1–10.

Clute, R. C. "How Important is Accounting to Small Business Survival?" *Journal of Commercial Bank Lending* 62 (January 1980): 24–28.

Gilbreath, J. D., and Humphries, N. J. "Aggressive Contracting Strategies for Small Business Owners." *Journal of Small Business Management* 17 (October 1979): 30–36.

House, W. C. "Dynamic Planning for the Smaller Company — A Case History." *Long Range Plan* 12 (June 1979): 38–47.

"How to Start a Sideline Business." *Business Week* (August 6, 1979): 94–95.

McKenna, J. F., and Oritt, P. L. "Small Business Growth: Making a Conscious Decision." *Advance Management Journal* 45 (Spring 1980): 45–53.

Petrof, J. V. "Small Business and Economic Development: The Case for Government Intervention." *Journal of Small Business Management* 18 (January 1980): 51–56.

Robinson, R. "Forecasting and Small Business: A Study of the Strategic Planning Process." *Journal of Small Business Management* 17 (July 1979): 19–27.

"Small Business Process a Passport to Profits." *Nation's Business* 67 (April 1979): 48.

"Study Shows Companies in Trouble Invariably Lack Planning and Control." *Management Review* 70 (February 1981): 38–39.

Timmins, S. A. "Large-Firm Forecasting Techniques Can Improve Small Business Decision-Making." *Journal of Small Business Management* 17 (July 1979): 14–18.

Walker, Gene C. "Starting a New Business — Pitfalls to Avoid." *U.S. News & World Report* (July 13, 1981): 75–76.

17
Managing Multinationals

Canadian Implements Ltd.

Two years ago, Dan Shelton went to work for Canadian Implements Ltd., a firm with manufacturing and sales operations in several Far Eastern countries. Dan was originally hired to shape up the company's production facility at Hamilton. Management considered that the operation was not running nearly as efficiently as possible; Shelton was hired away from Braxton Manufacturing because he had a good track record there. In less than a year, Shelton successfully straightened out the Hamilton plant.

Late last year, Shelton was asked whether he would be interested in an overseas assignment. The situation was similar to what he had orig-

inally encountered at Hamilton; one of the company's Far Eastern manufacturing facilities was not operating as effectively as management had hoped. Shelton was chosen to go there and straighten production out. Shelton realized that, if he could be as successful there as he was in Hamilton, his reputation as a top-notch troubleshooter would be assured. This strategy would dramatically improve his long-run career prospects at Canadian Implements. Shelton accepted the assignment almost immediately, considering it a challenge.

Shelton was extremely busy during his first two months in the Far East, as he tried to learn all the important facts about why the production facility there was not functioning properly. Many of the key personnel spoke English well enough that he experienced few language misunderstandings. Once he felt comfortable with his new situation, Shelton planned what actions he believed were necessary to resolve the production problems. He decided to begin by firing one foreman who was notoriously incompetent. When he advised his assistant, a foreign national, to terminate the foreman in question, Shelton was told: "You can't fire that person. Our government will not permit the dismissal of a long-term employee unless the company agrees to continue paying his salary."

Shelton was amazed. Suddenly, he wondered how many other rules like this one would restrict him. Would he be able to turn the plant around and complete his new assignment?

KEY TERMS

multinational
  company (MNC)
parent country
host countries

less developed
  countries (LDC)
parent country
  nationals
host country
  nationals

third country
  nationals
repatriation plan

LEARNING OBJECTIVES

After completing this chapter you should be able to

1. Describe the characteristics of a multinational enterprise and briefly explain the history and development of multinationals.
2. Explain how the external environment, objectives, and technology affect managing international operations.
3. State how the organizational structure may change when firms are engaged in international operations.
4. Describe personnel requirements and management approaches for a multinational company.

Dan Shelton's experience illustrates just one of the many problems facing organizations conducting business in more than one country. In spite of significant problems, more and more organizations are getting involved in business activities on an international basis.

Many people believe that, with resources, technology, food, and trained personnel unevenly distributed throughout the world, international business activities have the potential for distributing goods and services more equitably and for improving standards of living for all people. A dissenting view is that international business activities will lead to exploitation of developing countries and will benefit only the companies who profit from international business. The one certain result is that international business activity has caused the countries of the world to become more closely interrelated; people in all countries are more aware of what is happening in other parts of the world.

In this chapter we examine the phenomenon of international business and the importance of effective management to the success of firms doing business in two or more countries. The chapter is divided into two main parts. First, we define the term *multinational company* and note the rapid development of multinational companies since World War II. Second, the actual management of multinational companies is examined in some detail. Included in this discussion is an assessment of the factors of the external environment the multinational company faces when it enters a foreign country. The management of objectives, technology, structure, and personnel in the multinational firm is also treated.

WHAT IS A MULTINATIONAL COMPANY?

A **multinational company** (MNC) is a firm engaged in business in two or more countries. These firms typically have sales offices and sometimes manufacturing plants in many different countries. MNCs are instrumental in improving the world economy and standards of living of many people; they can also significantly affect the technology, culture, and customs of the countries in which they operate. Peter Drucker refers to the multinational company as "the outstanding social innovation in the period since World War II."[1]

Technically speaking, any company conducting business in two or more countries is a multinational. However, this criterion is too simplistic because it does not give adequate recognition to the size and scope of operations of many such organizations. Some experts in the field of multinational business believe that organizations designated as multinationals should meet the following criteria:

- Operations are conducted in at least 6 different countries.
- At least 20 percent of the firm's assets and/or sales from business are in countries other than that where the parent company is located.
- Management has an integrated, global orientation.
- Resources are allocated without regard to national boundaries.
- National boundaries are viewed as merely a constraint that enters into the decision-making process.
- The firm's organizational structure cuts across national boundaries.
- Personnel are transferred throughout the world.
- Management takes on a broad, global perspective — it views the world as interrelated and interdependent.

A list of the largest 20 multinational companies is presented in Exhibit 17-1. To illustrate the impact of the multinational, one Massey-Ferguson executive states: "We combine French-made transmissions, British-made engines, Mexican-made axles, and United States-made sheet metal parts to produce in Detroit a tractor for sale in Canada."[2]

It is clear from Exhibit 17-1 that firms headquartered in the United States dominate the list of the world's significant MNCs. This dominance has caused considerable concern in Canada during the last 20 years since much of the industrial activity in certain Canadian industries is controlled by American MNCs. The issue is that American firms may not have any interest in the well-being of Canada other than to ensure that Canadian consumers continue to buy their products so that they can make a profit.

Several government inquiries have been conducted since 1950 and all have pointed out the potential problems of excessive foreign ownership of Canadian business. Recommendations have been made that the amount of foreign ownership be reduced, but how it is to be accomplished is not clear. Interestingly, recent statistics do show a

EXHIBIT 17-1   The Top Twenty Multinational Companies

Company	*Home Country*
Exxon	USA
Royal Dutch/Shell Group	Netherlands/GB
Mobil	USA
General Motors	USA
Texaco	USA
British Petroleum	GB
Standard Oil of California	USA
Ford Motor	USA
ENI	Italy
Gulf Oil	USA
IBM	USA
Standard Oil (Indiana)	USA
Fiat	Italy
General Electric	USA
Francoise des Petroles	France
Atlantic Richfield	USA
Unilever	GB/Netherlands
Shell Oil	USA
Renault	France
Petroleos de Venezuela	Venezuela

SOURCE   Adapted from "The Largest Industrial Companies in the World," *Fortune* (August 10, 1981): 205. Reprinted by permission.

decline in the dominance of American companies in certain sectors of the Canadian economy. Exhibit 17-2 shows the changes that occurred during the period 1977–1980. While most of the changes are not dramatic, if they continue, substantial reductions of foreign ownership in Canada may occur.

THE DEVELOPMENT OF MULTINATIONALS

Modern communications systems and jet travel have been a powerful incentive for the development of MNCs since World War II. With increasingly sophisticated technology and information about people in foreign lands, organizations began to think about the possibility of conducting business beyond the borders of their home countries.

The first MNC established with a global orientation grew out of a merger in 1929 between Margarine Unie, a Dutch firm, and Lever Brothers, a British company. The company became Unilever, and it has since become one of the largest companies in the world with approximately 500 subsidiaries operating in about 60 nations. Unilever even has two headquarters, one located in Rotterdam and the other in London.

Multinationals usually operate through subsidiary companies in countries outside their home nation. Some of the names of the largest multinationals have become household words; these include companies such as General Motors, Ford, IBM, General Electric, Gulf Oil, and Exxon. The worldwide impact of these companies is very significant. Their operations create interrelationships among countries and cultures, as well as among economic and political systems.

The economic output of MNCs contributes a major portion of the total economic output of the world. Some economists have estimated that by the year 2000, about 200 to 300 multinationals will account for half of the world's total output of goods and services. In recent years, there has been a rapid growth of direct investment by multinational firms averaging about 10 percent per year. MNCs based in the United States account for more than half of this worldwide investment.

FACTORS AFFECTING THE
MANAGEMENT OF MULTINATIONALS

Companies that conduct business in only one geographic region have relatively few problems understanding their external environment. However, the MNC, because it operates in many different countries, finds management of its activities is enormously complicated. MNCs face a staggering array of economic, cultural, and political issues. It is

EXHIBIT 17-2   Degree of Foreign Ownership by the United States and Others in Canada, as Measured by Assets, 1977–1980

Industry	Assets of Foreign-Controlled Corporations, as a Percentage of Total Industry Assets			
	1977	1978	1979	1980
Agriculture, forestry, and fishing	7.4	6.4	4.8	4.3
Mining:				
Metal mining	37.7	36.7	34.7	31.3
Mineral fuels	60.2	52.9	58.6	53.3
Other mining	55.0	48.1	48.3	40.4
Total mining	51.1	46.9	49.9	45.1
Manufacturing:				
Food	39.2	38.6	36.6	29.4
Beverages	31.1	31.2	31.4	31.7
Tobacco products	99.8	99.5	99.8	99.7
Rubber products	94.1	93.1	90.6	91.0
Leather products	20.3	19.1	23.6	22.8
Textile mills	58.1	57.6	55.2	54.1
Knitting mills	17.7	15.8	15.4	14.8
Clothing	16.2	15.3	13.9	14.1
Wood industries	21.0	21.2	20.5	19.0
Furniture industries	16.2	14.8	10.7	12.0
Paper and allied industries	41.5	39.5	38.3	35.3
Printing, publishing, and allied industries	11.2	11.3	11.8	11.5
Primary metals	14.0	13.9	14.4	13.4
Metal fabricating	40.1	39.6	36.6	34.5
Machinery	64.0	60.9	55.4	51.7
Transport equipment	76.9	74.7	73.2	70.7
Electrical products	69.0	66.2	58.5	53.9
Nonmetallic mineral products	70.0	71.8	71.9	70.4
Petroleum and coal products	92.3	83.9	69.2	69.8
Chemicals and chemical products	67.2	67.8	77.2	77.4
Miscellaneous manufacturing	48.0	47.8	44.4	42.9
Total manufacturing	53.8	52.0	49.4	47.6
Construction	11.7	10.4	11.1	10.0
Utilities:				
Transportation	12.2	8.2	7.8	7.3
Storage	6.4	4.7	5.8	5.2
Communication	14.3	13.2	13.2	13.0
Public utilities	2.1	2.0	2.2	0.3
Total utilities	7.3	5.8	5.8	4.5
Wholesale trade	26.1	26.7	25.8	24.0
Retail trade	15.6	15.2	13.0	13.0
Services	17.4	18.4	14.9	14.6
Total nonfinancial industries	30.4	29.0	28.9	27.3

SOURCE   Statistics Canada, Corporations and Labour Returns Act, *Annual Report* (1978): 147; (1980): 149. Reprinted by permission.

difficult for individuals or entire firms to be knowledgeable in all of these areas, but the external environment must be studied or the firm can find itself in major difficulties. During the past decade many stories have appeared in newspapers indicating how MNCs angered people in host countries by behaving in a way that was considered inappropriate or insulting to the people in the host country. North American business styles are not universal, as we noted in Chapter 12. On a more subtle level, managers in MNCs must know how to conduct themselves in their day-to-day business dealings or they will not be successful in a host country.

In this section we examine the important external and internal factors that influence the management of MNCs. Included are corporate objectives, technology, structure, and personnel practices of the MNC, as well as its external environment. The success or failure of the MNC is determined largely by how they respond to their external environment. As portrayed in Exhibit 17-3, the MNC must deal with the environment not only of the **parent country** (location of headquarters) but of all **host countries** (location of operational units) as well. As with small businesses, most of the external environment problems can be summarized as: (1) economic, (2) political/legal, and (3) social factors. As shown by Exhibit 17-3, an MNC's external environment is characterized by great complexity, variety, and uncertainty. Such a situation requires that managers develop sophisticated skills to deal effectively with this environment.

MANAGEMENT IN PRACTICE

Connaught Labs Goes Multinational

Connaught Laboratories at the University of Toronto is where insulin was first produced in quantity in 1923. The lab continues to be very active, and sales in 1983 were nearly $70 million. The goal is to boost sales to $200 million by 1989; this objective is to be met by expanding into the international market with several new products.

As part of its international expansion strategy, Connaught has entered into joint ventures with firms in Denmark and the United States. The international game is rough because the competitors in it are so big. All of them have sales in excess of $1 billion, and their research and development budgets are in the $100 million to $300 million per year category. No Canadian firm can match these figures.

With this kind of competition, Connaught Labs must carefully pick the niche where it can profitably operate. It must also get involved in joint ventures which will allow it to acquire the kind of technology needed to compete on an international basis.

SOURCE Adapted from Elizabeth Highstead, "Connaught Goes Multinational," *Financial Post* (April 14, 1984): 28.

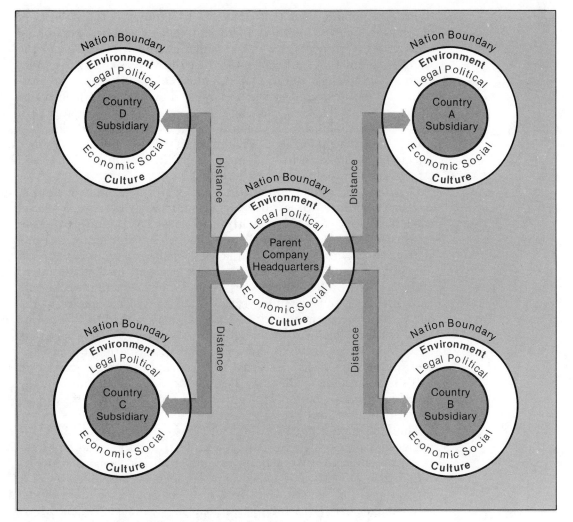

EXHIBIT 17-3 The multienvironments of MNCs

SOURCE Edwin B. Flippo and Gary M. Munsinger, *Management*, 4th ed. (Boston: Allyn and Bacon, 1978): 583. Reprinted by permission.

Economic Factors

The economic factors of the external environments of the various host countries is of prime importance to the management of multinational companies. A number of crucial questions must be answered:

• What are income levels, growth trends, inflation rates, balance of payments, gross national product, and the number and nature of economic institutions?

• Is there a local banking and financial resource that can be tapped?

• Are there organized labor unions, planning agencies, and the necessary service structures for power, water, housing, and communication?

• How politically stable is the country, and how stable is its currency?

A major economic issue that affects multinationals is the stability of the host country's currency. Many different events (for example, a change in governments, a war, or economic difficulties) can cause the currency to fluctuate and this may reduce the MNC's ability to extract profits from the host country. MNCs must constantly assess the prospects for the host country's currency or they may experience large losses as the currency is exchanged for that of the home country. In 1976, for example, the Canadian dollar was on a par with the U.S. dollar, but since that time it has dropped to U.S. $0.75. This difference affects both Canadian firms doing business in the United States and American firms doing business in Canada.

Generally speaking, the countries of the world are classified as either developed countries or **less developed countries** (LDC). An LDC lacks modern industry and the supporting services. The output per person is usually low. There is usually an unequal distribution of income, with a few very rich, a small middle class, and a great number of poor. The MNC provides an opportunity for a fast start in the building of an LDC economy. The objective is to reach a level where the economy can grow on a self-sustaining basis. A substantial percentage of the MNC's total investment is located in LDCs. Often, the LDC has strong feelings of nationalism. Although it needs the MNC to exploit its natural resources, it often perceives the MNCs as a threat to its sovereignty. When an LDC feels that it has effected sufficient transfer of skills in a particular technology, it might expropriate or confiscate the business organization. An MNC must consider this risk in making an investment decision.

The fact that so much of total foreign investments is in LDCs is evidence that possible returns are worth the risk. If the most important resources of a multinational are technological and managerial skills rather than property and goods, some companies can reduce the risk of expropriation or host country take-overs by one or more of the following means: (1) licensing agreements, (2) contracts to manage host country-owned installations, and (3) turnkey operations — constructing and developing the unit to the point where the key can be turned over to ownership by nationals of the host country. It is far more difficult to expropriate skills of persons than property. There are also far fewer conflicts of interest between this type of MNC and the various countries in which it operates.

Political/Legal Factors

MNCs operate in an environment with a variety of political factors. We have already noted host country nationalism. Perhaps the most important aspect that MNCs look for is political stability. Without it, the conduct of business becomes very risky. Since so many LDCs gained independence only in the 1960s and 1970s, there remains much concern about political stability in those areas.

Analyses of the political factors in the MNC's external environment increasingly take into account how competing political philosophies

MANAGEMENT IN PRACTICE

A Problem in International Fashions

Saul and Joseph Mimram own Monaco Group, Inc., a firm specializing in women's clothing. In 1978, Joseph Mimram met Alfred Sung, a designer. The Mimrams needed a designer, and Sung needed marketing expertise to sell his designs. So they combined their talents and went after a share of the big United States market.

They thought they had done their homework. They contacted all the key people, spent thousands of dollars preparing for the American market, and even got Saks Fifth Avenue to buy Sung's collection. Success seemed just around the corner. But they had forgotten one thing: American sizes are larger than Canadian sizes — for example, an American size 10 is a Canadian size 12. American women who had always bought a size 10 were unhappy when they had to buy a size 12. As a result, the merchandise had to be marked down a quarter of a million dollars in order to make it move.

The story has a happy ending, however. The owners quickly adjusted their sizes to fit the American market. The strategy paid off in Canada, too, because Canadian women like buying a size smaller. Everyone is happy. Sales for 1984 are expected to reach $45 million for Monaco Group, Inc., with 40 percent of that coming from the American market.

SOURCE   Adapted from Patrick Pardoe, "Selling Alfred Sung," *Canadian Business* (July 1984): 23–24.

or social unrest in a host country may affect the conduct of business. There have been numerous instances of terrorism and kidnapping of multinational executives in some parts of the world and these dramatically increase the stress levels on executives working in those areas. For example, a Goodyear Tire and Rubber executive was held hostage and then murdered in Guatemala. Some executives are reluctant to accept assignments in certain parts of the world because of these threats to their security.

Because there is no comprehensive system of international law or courts, the MNC must become acquainted in detail with the laws of each host-country. The United States, England, Canada, Australia, and New Zealand have developed their legal requirements by means of English common law; judges and courts are extremely important, for they are guided by principles declared in previous cases. In most of continental Europe, Asia, and Africa, the approach is the civil law; the judges play a lesser role because the legal requirements are codified. Civil servants or bureaucrats have greater power under the civil law than under the common law.

Regardless of their country of origin, MNC managers must take care to comply with legal requirements of the host country. And, if any laws should be contravened, the MNC must be prepared for the legal consequences. The costs of settling with victims of a lethal gas leak from an American pesticide plant in India may bankrupt the MNC involved. These costs will undoubtedly have an impact on future class action suits regarding MNCs, as well as on safety and ecological procedures in MNC work places. In addition, managers of MNCs must be knowledgeable about:

- Laws governing profit remission to the parent country
- Import and export restrictions and investment controls
- Degree of foreign ownership permitted.

Although Canada is a highly legalistic country and MNC executives tend to carry Canadian law with them, they must realize, for instance, that the Japanese dislike laws, lawyers, and litigation. In France, lawyers are prohibited from serving on boards of directors by codes of the legal profession. The vastness and sheer complexity of varying legal systems throughout the world demonstrate quite clearly the intricate and demanding political/legal factors in the external environment of the MNCs.

Social Factors

The culture of each nation in the world is unique. Managers of MNCs are not citizens of each country they do business in; rather, they are outsiders who are trying to mobilize resources effectively, so that a profit can be made. Managers of MNCs must be very careful not to superimpose their views of the world on the host country. If the MNC is to operate in many nations, it will of necessity be required to adapt some of its managerial practices to the specific and unique expectations and situations of each nation. Attitudes will differ concerning such subjects as work, risk taking, change introduction, time, authority, and material gain. It is unwise to assume that the attitudes within the parent country will be similar in all other countries.

In some nations, authority is viewed as a manager's natural right and is not questioned by subordinates. In other cultures, authority must be earned and is provided to those who have demonstrated their ability. David McClelland has discovered that the fundamental attitude toward achievement is somewhat correlated with rates of economic development. If a nation's citizens are willing to commit themselves to the accomplishment of tasks deemed worthwhile and difficult, a country will benefit economically. As previously discussed in Chapter 10, McClelland contends that the achievement motive can be taught.[3] Certainly, cultural beliefs concerning an individual's ability to influence the future will have an impact on the behavior of a country's work force. If the basic belief is one of fatalism — what will be, will be — then the importance of planning and organizing for the future is downgraded. Cultures also vary as to interclass mobility and sources of status. If there is little hope of moving up to higher classes in a society, then fatalism and an absence of a drive for achievement are likely.

In many instances, the MNC managers will have to adapt and conform to the requirements of the local culture. A multinational must introduce new technology and skills into a host nation's culture if economic development is to occur. Some changes proposed are revolutionary. There must be one common language and system of measurements when communicating between a subsidiary and its headquarters. English and French are currently the two most commonly chosen MNC languages. Despite the slowness of Canada and the United States to adapt, the metric system will be the common method of measurement.

This brief review of the differences in the economic, political/legal, and social factors of the external environments of MNCs serves to highlight the enormous complexity of the task of managing an MNC. It is apparent that sophisticated approaches to managing are necessary for survival and growth.

Objectives of the Multinational

At first thought, the objectives of multinational companies should not be any different from the objectives of businesses operating exclusively within Canada. The typical goals of survival, profit, and growth are indeed similar. An MNC seeks to produce and distribute products and services throughout the world in return for a satisfactory profit. It seeks to survive and grow by maintaining its technological advantages and minimizing risks. However, the MNC differs from the domestic firm because of the potential clash of its goals with the objectives of the economic and political systems of the host countries within which each operates. Some of the objectives of countries may coincide with the objectives of the MNC and some may not. Most countries want improved standards of living for their people, as well as, for instance, a trained labor force, full employment, reasonable price stability, a favorable balance of payments, and steady economic growth. Canadians, too, have had numerous debates about the advantages and disadvantages of MNCs operating in Canada.

In achieving some of these goals, there is an overlapping of interests between the MNC and the host country. (See Exhibit 17-4.) For example, a new MNC in a country will usually create new jobs, thereby

EXHIBIT 17-4
Overlapping interest of MNC and host countries

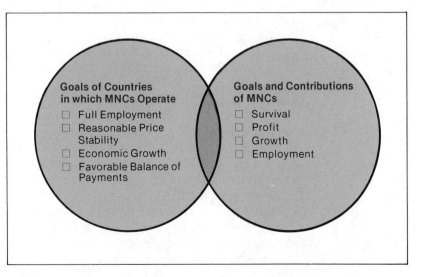

Goals of Countries
in which MNCs Operate

☐ Full Employment
☐ Reasonable Price
   Stability
☐ Economic Growth
☐ Favorable Balance of
   Payments

Goals and Contributions
of MNCs

☐ Survival
☐ Profit
☐ Growth
☐ Employment

contributing to a higher level of employment, increased income, and economic growth. While the company contributes to the accomplishment of these goals, it may not do so at the rate expected by the host country.

In some areas, there will be a conflict of interest. A multinational may close a plant in one country to streamline its worldwide production facilities. Considerable controversy can arise when an MNC increases its international activities, but decreases its activities in the home country of the company. For example, when Inco announced it would reduce the output of its Canadian operations and increase the output of its foreign mines, the company raised concern about unemployment for Inco's Canadian workers. Or, a company may subsidize a beginning assembly operation in Country A by underpricing component parts produced in Country B. Country B's economy in effect is required to make a sacrifice to enable the plant in Country A to get started.

If the MNC is to achieve its return-on-investment objective, some portion of subsidiary earnings must be returned to headquarters in the parent country. This arrangement could adversely affect the host country's balance of payments, particularly if the subsidiary unit does no exporting of its products. Funds may also be shuffled among various countries so that profits are maximized in countries having the most stable political systems and the lowest tax rates.

Some of the complaints various countries have regarding multinationals are that MNCs:

- Restrict or allocate markets among subsidiaries and do not allow manufacturing subsidiaries to develop export markets
- Extract excessive profits and fees because of their monopolistic advantages
- Enter the market by taking over existing local firms rather than developing new productive investments
- Finance their entry mainly through local debt and maintain a majority of the equity with the parent
- Divert local savings away from productive investments by nationals, hire away the most talented personnel, and exhaust resources of the host country
- Restrict access to modern technology by centralizing research facilities in the home country and by licensing subsidiaries to use only existing or even outmoded technologies
- Restrict the learning-by-doing process by staffing key technical and managerial positions with managers from the home country
- Fail to do enough in the way of training and development of host country personnel
- Ignore the host country's social customs or frustrate the objectives of the host country's economic planning
- Contribute to price inflation
- Dominate key industrial sectors

- Answer to a foreign government[4]
- Undermine the host country's culture by operating according to standards developed in other countries.

In response to such complaints as these, many countries have moved toward applying restrictions upon the operations of multinationals. For example, one of the guidelines in the Andean Common Market (Bolivia, Chile, Colombia, Ecuador, and Peru) is that 51 percent of the stock in manufacturing subsidiaries should be held by nationals of the host country within 15 to 20 years of start-up. When extremely discontented with the MNC or in response to a rising tide of nationalism, subsidiaries may be expropriated or confiscated by the host country. France gained control over its telephone system by purchasing a controlling interest from International Telephone & Telegraph Corporation of the United States and Sweden's L. M. Ericsson Group.[5] In other instances, the host country has seized the subsidiary unit without compensation.

Although the host country has power as a result of national sovereignty, the multinational is not helpless. Its power lies in its ability to grant or withhold needed economic resources and technological knowledge. Other MNCs will observe the kind of treatment given MNCs by the host country, and this treatment may influence whether or not they invest in that country. Should the host country have enterprises with investments in the parent country, retaliation can be threatened. If the parent country provides foreign economic aid, this can also be used as leverage in promoting equitable treatment for the MNC subsidiary.

MANAGEMENT IN PRACTICE

Doing Business in China

The People's Republic of China, with one-quarter of the world's population, is viewed with great enthusiasm by business firms wishing to tap that immense market. But there are monumental problems for Canadian firms wishing to do business in China.

In 1983, there were 10 Canadian business firms, 4 banks, and 3 media bureaus with business offices in China. Unfortunately, commercial transactions are few, bureaucratic red tape is excessive, prices are outrageous, and air pollution is bad. Patience is the main characteristic that a Canadian firm must possess to be successful. For example, if a company wants to set up a joint venture in oil exploration, it must deal with several different organizations, including the China National Oil Corporation, the Ministry of Petroleum Industry, the Ministry of Foreign Relations and Trade, and the Bank of China.

Identifying the individual in these organizations who actually makes the approval decision can be quite difficult.

Business expenses are also very high in China. Massey-Ferguson Ltd. pays $3,500 per month for a small, one-room office in the Peking Hotel. The Bank of Montreal pays $8,400 per month for a two-room office at the Jianguo Hotel. The changes Canadian managers must make to their personal lives also leave something to be desired. Executives know that in a police state they must be careful about what they say; for example, Jianguo Hotel residents are told that the hotel cannot guarantee that their rooms are not bugged.

SOURCE   Adapted from Gayle Herchak, "Behind the Bamboo Curtain: The Awful Truth about Doing Business in China," *Canadian Business* (August 1983): 15–16.

TALKING
TO
MANAGERS

Robert White
United Auto Workers, Canada

Robert White, who went to work as a wood-worker at the age of 15, has been the director of the United Auto Workers in Canada since 1978. From 1972 to 1978, he was the assistant director. The UAW has approximately 75 employees and has a membership of 125 000.

Q: What difficulties face a Canadian manager in a multinational corporation?
White: Having to pursue decisions that are made outside the country, which in many cases are not in the best interests of either the subsidiary or the employees who work there; having to carry out instructions just because the corporation has decided that such will be the policy for the whole corporation. Some multinational corporations don't act that way, but there are some that do, and many times Canadian managements are hamstrung in terms of dealing with the Canadian reality because of those kinds of policies and they don't have input into them. For example, I dealt with a large multinational corporation in collective bargaining where the labor relations person was instructed to put on the bargaining table a proposal which was totally unacceptable to us in Canada. The proposal had, in fact, been rejected in the United States as well, and he knew it was unacceptable and knew it would blow the negotiations up. Confidentially, he said to me: "I have no alternative. They've instructed me from Detroit to put this on the table." Such situations — where the company doesn't leave the freedom for input in Canadian situations — I think that's where multinational corporations make serious errors of judgment.

Q: How can the Canadian managers in multinationals deal with that?
White: I would advise them to lay out clearly the distinctions among the social, the economic, and the political structures in Canada, the attitudes of Canadians to certain things, such as health care, social services, foreign policy, and foreign investments; and point out the necessity for the branch plants of multinational corporations to be seen and to be dealing in the Canadian reality.

I think international corporations' headquarters have to give much more autonomy to the people in charge of the managing and the labor relations of the operations in Canada. On the question of trading relations for Canada, I know of situations where multinational corporations, before writing or sending a paper to the Canadian government, or before discussing the issue with the Canadian government, would check it with their headquarters in the United States. I think that's absolute nonsense.

Q: Do you see any positive aspects to multi-national management?

White: I think there are multinational corporations that have dealt with the Canadian reality and recognized the Canadians' right to do things differently, and also draw on some experiences that they've had in other countries. I think that the communications with employees and the communication between each other is sometimes just as bad in Canadian-based corporations as in multinationals. I've seen situations where multinational corporations are moving much more positively than they were, say, 10 years ago. It's an improving trend. I think the whole question of Canada coming of age, the Constitution, the debate on national energy, the role of the trade union movement, the different political and economic climate here. . . . I think a number of multinationals are gradually getting to understand the differences.

Q: What differences do you see between your role and that of someone in a profit-oriented business?

White: As an example, the head of General Motors in Canada takes complete direction from Detroit; the investment decisions for the corporation are made in Detroit. I'm not sure he's even on the board level in Detroit, where, even within the current international union, I'm also an officer of the union; I attend the international executive board. The decisions that we make in Canada in terms of the direction of our union in most cases are made by an elected body of about 300 people. And that's much different from managing a corporation.

Our organization mainly runs on the basis of people who understand what the rules are. They're self starters, and they go to work. It's not layered with the same kind of supervision,

for example, that a corporation is. It's really much different. In our organization, there is much more two-way interaction. For example, we never talk about employer/employee relationships. I consider myself to be leading a team here. The office staff know what the rules are. I have a person who's a sort of office manager who makes sure that we live within some guidelines, and people come to work and accept responsibilities. But again, I think you'd find the working conditions and the working environments in our offices much different from those in most corporations. There's nobody looking over our shoulders all the time, so to speak.

Our organization and profit-oriented businesses are different in terms of purpose and structure. The corporations' role in society is not like ours; theirs is to make a product and make a profit. Our role is that of a service organization, and it's to deal with the problems of our membership or play a role politically in society on some of the social issues. Therefore, we have a much different attitude. Our purpose is for a people; it's for an idea; it's for a broader section of society; it's for a particular issue. Maybe the feelings of a senior executive officer of a corporation toward his or her corporation may be very strong, but I think it's still a very different feeling from the one I have about our union.

Q: Can you see any positive aspects of management/employee relations in your situation being applied in a profit-making situation?

White: Well, it's a question of communication with employees. I think, yes, some aspects could be applied. I think more communication helps the relationship, but I don't think you're going to get a situation like ours — we're part of a social force in society. But, certainly, communication is a key factor.

In most instances, the economic power of the MNC and the political power of the host country will lead to accommodations whereby both parties can achieve some of their goals. Host country governments realize, for example, that the intense emotions of national sovereignty exhibited by some of their citizens do not always coincide with long-term national interests. For their part, MNCs will have to alter objectives to suit minimum requirements of the host countries if operations are to be conducted in that country. If such requirements do excessive damage to global objectives, the MNC may choose to conduct its business elsewhere in the world.

To head off an effort by some LDCs to establish, through the United Nations, a tough set of restrictions on MNCs, the governments of 24 developed, noncommunist nations have developed a proposed code of ethics. Important aspects of the code of ethics are:

1. MNCs are not to meddle in the political processes of the countries in which they operate.
2. No bribes are permissible under any conditions.
3. No donations to political parties are proper unless national laws allow them.
4. MNCs should make full disclosure of local sales and profits, number of employees, and expenditures for research and development for major regions of the world.
5. MNCs should refrain from participating in cartels and avoid "predatory behavior toward competitors."
6. The proper amount of taxes in the countries in which they are earned should be paid. One should not seek to avoid taxes by switching money from high-tax to low-tax countries.
7. MNCs should respect the right of their employees to organize into unions.[6]

Technology and Multinationals

Technological expertise is the primary advantage of the multinational enterprise. Many of the MNCs operate in such high-technology industries as oil, tires, pharmaceuticals, electronics, and motor vehicles. There are fewer MNCs in such fields as cotton, textiles, and cement. It is this technological gap in other nations that provides the opportunity for the MNC to transfer high technology from the parent country. The simpler industries are likely to be developed by each country for itself.

The more important the economies of scale to be derived from a particular technology, the greater the opportunity for an MNC to transfer knowledge to other countries. If the market size of a particular country is not such that it can absorb the output of an advanced economic unit, then many nations must be interlocked. MNCs in many small European countries started before those in Canada and the United States for just this reason. The development of the European Economic Community constitutes an attempt to develop a wide market area.

MANAGEMENT IN PRACTICE

International Business Activity at LeBlanc & Royle

George Patton is president of LeBlanc & Royle Communications Ltd., an Oakville, Ontario multinational company which builds communications towers. The company has an outstanding record for quickly reconstructing towers that have fallen down because of ice storms or vandalism. Since 1974, 49 towers have fallen in Canada alone, and LeBlanc & Royle has reconstructed 47 of them.

The company's success in the international market is based partly on the needs of Third World countries for microwave towers to intercept satellite transmissions. But there are many unexpected costs which are incurred when a Canadian company goes international. For example, distance can create big problems. When LeBlanc & Royle was constructing communications towers in Rwanda, Africa, a small engineering error was discovered that necessitated the shipment of reworked parts to the site. This would have presented no problem in Canada, but it took 3 weeks to get the parts to the site in Africa. While the workers were waiting for the parts, they ran up a bill of $25 per man per day for drinking water. That simple error ate up most of the profit on that job.

SOURCE   Adapted from Mike Macbeth, "Towering Triumph," *Canadian Business* (October 1983): 64–65.

The situation existing within a country will dictate the nature of the technology required to accomplish work. There are a wide range of external environment factors, objectives, and technologies that would preclude any significant general statements that would apply to all multinationals. It should be noted, however, that the strength of most MNCs lies in their ability to operate highly complex technologies.

Multinational Organizational Structures

The organizational structure of a multinational firm must be designed to meet its international needs. Normally the first effort of a firm to become a multinational is the creation of an export unit in the domestic marketing department. At some point, the firm may perceive the necessity of locating manufacturing units abroad. After a time, these various foreign units are grouped into an international division.

The international division then becomes a profit center with status equal to other major domestic divisions. It is typically headed by a vice-president and operates on a fairly autonomous basis from the domestic operations. The reasons for this approach are: (1) the necessity of obtaining managerial and technical expertise in the diverse external environments of many countries, and (2) the reduction of control from the often larger domestic divisions. Of course, this approach to organization has the disadvantage of decreased coordination and cohesion of the international division with the rest of the company.[7]

As the international division grows, it usually becomes organized on either a geographical or product base of specialization. In giant MNCs the international division is often a transitional stage in moving toward a worldwide structure that discounts the importance of national boundaries. As portrayed in Exhibits 17-5, 17-6, and 17-7, any such global structure requires a careful balance of 3 types of specialization: functional, geographical, and product. When the primary base is any one of the three, the other two must be present in the form of specialized staff experts or coordinators. A clear-cut decision that is heavily in favor of any one base is usually inappropriate.

Exhibit 17-5 illustrates a functional organizational structure for a multinational. The executive in charge of the production function has a worldwide responsibility. Together with the presidents and executives in charge of sales and finance, a small group of managers enables worldwide centralized control of the MNC to be maintained.

MNCs with widely diversified product lines requiring a sophisticated technology to produce and distribute tend to use the area base in their global structures. This form is shown in Exhibit 17-6. During the 1960s, General Electric adopted this structure. Four regional managers were established in Europe, Canada, Latin America, and the rest of the world. These executives were General Electric's eyes and ears in the countries assigned. They advised on the most suitable approach in each country for the product executives, identified potential partners, and aided in establishing locally oriented personnel programs. The area executive might be given line authority when a product division had not yet sufficient skill in the region or when a subsidiary unit reported to many product divisions. Although the basic emphasis is on product, the addition of the geographical concept produced a type of matrix organizational structure.

Finally, when the range of products is somewhat limited or when the product is highly standardized, MNCs tend to use the global product structure, as shown in Exhibit 17-7. Executives with true line authority are placed over major regions throughout the world. This type of structure is used by international oil companies (limited variety of products) and soft-drink producers (highly standardized product). As in the other instances, some supporting staff is necessary in the product and functional areas. In all forms of MNC structures, top management makes sure: (1) that the product is properly managed and coordinated throughout the world; (2) that the functional processes of production, sales, and finance are executed efficiently; and (3) that proper and efficient adaptations are made in response to the external environments in the host countries.

Personnel Management in Multinationals

Successful management of an MNC requires that the manager understand the needs, values, and problems of personnel in the countries where the company operates. Management must recognize that there is no one style of leadership that will be equally effective in all countries. People in the various countries will have widely divergent backgrounds, education, cultures, languages, and religions and live within a variety of social conditions and economic and political systems. All

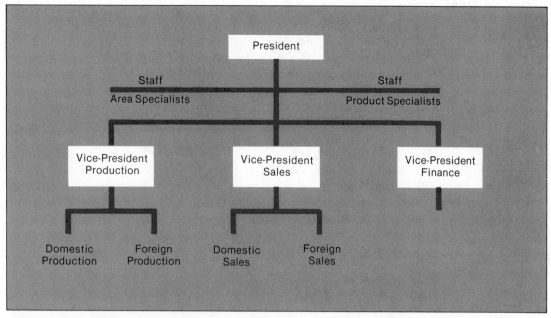

EXHIBIT 17-5 MNC: global-functional structure

SOURCE Edwin B. Flippo and Gary M. Munsinger, *Management*, 4th ed. (Boston: Allyn and Bacon, 1978): 588. Reprinted by permission.

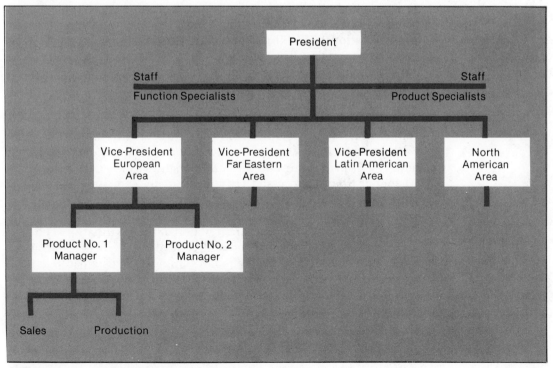

EXHIBIT 17-6 MNC: global-area structure

SOURCE Edwin B. Flippo and Gary M. Munsinger, *Management*, 4th ed. (Boston: Allyn and Bacon, 1978): 588. Reprinted by permission.

of these factors must be considered by managers because they can have a dramatic effect on the work atmosphere and performance.

The requirements for effective leadership of personnel in Canada, the United States, Great Britain, Australia, or many western European countries differ significantly from such countries as Turkey, Mexico, Malaysia, Taiwan, Thailand, or certain African, Asian, or Latin American countries. Research has shown that the needs and values of people vary from nation to nation. These often result from differences in economic living standards, cultural or religious influences.

As we discussed in Chapter 10, unsatisfied needs motivate behavior. In Canada and other developed countries, people's basic needs — physiological, security, and social — are fairly well satisfied. Research on the application of Maslow's hierarchy of needs theory of human behavior has shown considerable differences concerning the dominant needs of people in different countries. So, in some developed countries, managers must try to satisfy employee needs for esteem and self-actualization. However, in developing countries, appeals to physiological and safety needs may prove to be not only appropriate but the primary means for motivating desired behavior.

Types of MNC Employees

In filling key managerial, technical or professional positions abroad, multinationals can choose among 3 basic types of personnel: (1) **parent country nationals** (PCN), (2) **host country nationals** (HCN), and (3) **third country nationals** (TCN). Until the 1950s, it was very common for MNCs to fill their key foreign posts with trusted and experienced personnel from home (PCNs). Recently, stronger nationalistic feelings have led countries to alter their policies and require MNCs to employ more people from host countries (HCNs). Some firms have used personnel from countries other than the parent country or host country. Such personnel are known as third country nationals (TCNs); for example, a Canadian firm might build a highway in Saudi Arabia using personnel from Turkey and Italy. Still, many companies attempt to keep parent country personnel in at least half of the identified key positions, particularly in the financial function.

Using personnel from the parent nation of the multinational ensures a greater degree of consistency and control in the firm's operations around the world. This policy is not without its costs because these personnel may experience considerable difficulty with linguistic and cultural differences. In an attitude survey of personnel in 49 multinationals, personnel from the host country contended that parent country personnel tended not to question orders from headquarters even when appropriate to do so.[8] This enabled them to advance their own long-term interests in the firm by getting better headquarter evaluations and facilitating repatriation at the end of their tour of duty. In addition, the common practice of frequent rotation of key personnel intensified the problem of understanding and adapting to local cultures.

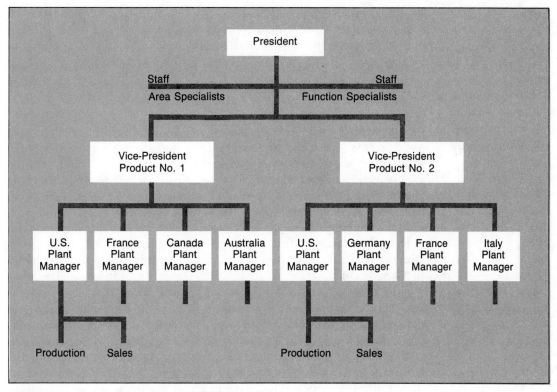

EXHIBIT 17-7 MNC: global-product structure

SOURCE Edwin B. Flippo and Gary M. Munsinger, *Management*, 4th ed. (Boston: Allyn and Bacon, 1978): 588. Reprinted by permission.

However, employing the PCN can facilitate communications with headquarters because both parties are likely of the same country and language.

Utilizing personnel from the host country in key positions will improve the MNC's relations with the host country government. It will also enable a quicker and more accurate adaptation to requirements of the local culture. Disadvantages include a lessened degree of central control and increased communication problems with headquarters. In addition, if the HCNs perceive that the opportunity for higher positions is blocked for ethnic reasons, they will use the MNC to gain experience so they may transfer to higher positions in local national firms.

Personnel Problems in MNCs

One of the most difficult personnel problems for the multinationals is that of selecting the appropriate people to be sent on foreign assignments. Careful plans should be made to assure that selectees possess certain basic characteristics, among them:

- A very real desire to work in a foreign country
- Spouses and families who have actively encouraged the person to work overseas or are willing to accompany him or her

- Cultural sensitivity and flexibility
- A high degree of technical competence
- A sense for politics.

Several surveys of overseas managers have revealed that the spouse's opinion and attitude should be considered the number one screening factor. Cultural sensitivity is also essential.

A second major problem that confronts MNCs is the establishment of equitable compensation systems for personnel given international assignments. Typically, personnel from the parent country receive a salary plus an overseas premium of up to 50 percent plus moving expense allowances and certain living allowances. Personnel from the parent country of the MNC receive a higher pay than personnel employed from the local country. This imbalance can create resentment and reduce cooperation. Many MNC managers have found their standard of living and social status to be considerably improved in foreign countries, so that they may experience some difficulties when they return to Canada. In addition to financial rewards, the foreign assignment usually provides career advancement opportunities.

Despite the company's intention to provide career advancement opportunities, there is still some danger that skilled personnel will come to feel that their career progress has suffered by leaving their home country. Some personnel have returned from foreign assignments to find no job available or a job that does not utilize skills obtained during the overseas service. To solve this problem, some companies develop a **repatriation plan** that includes a statement about the duration of the assignment and what job the appointee will do on his or her return. During the assignment, the individual is kept informed of major ongoing events occurring in the unit of future assignment. In this way, not only is there a logical career plan worked out, the person overseas does not feel lost in the vast international shuffle of the company.

The chief executive officer of each foreign subsidiary is confronted by the opposing flows of corporate uniformity and cultural fragmentation. If the officer is from the parent country, uniformity is likely to be emphasized. If the manager is from the host country, cultural adaptation may take precedence. Because of growing nationalistic tendencies of many countries, there is an increased chance that the top manager will be from the host country. Each of these host countries has a particular view of what constitutes a good chief executive officer. In Germany, for instance, the chief executive officer must have an engineering degree to be accepted and respected. In France, graduates of the Grandes Écoles are favored. If third country nationals are to be used as chief executive officers, varying mobilities must also be considered. A married Frenchman living in Paris is almost unmovable. However, German managers are often quite enthusiastic about working in other countries. The English and Scandinavians are typically willing to relocate, but they usually require assurance of return to their native lands.

Adaptation is not all one way. Local nationals will usually make an effort to understand and adapt to the culture of the MNC, which inevitably requires some understanding of the culture of the parent country of the MNC. This learning, too, will require considerable effort and time. In dealing with executives from headquarters of Canadian MNCs, the local national should learn to get to the point quickly because North Americans are notoriously impatient with lengthy and detailed explanations. Nationals must be positive in their approach, and they should avoid constant criticism. However, they must also learn to question Canadian executives, but know just how far they can go. For their part, Canadian managers should foster understanding and cooperation to help local nationals.

Effective managers of multinational operations must develop a style of leadership consistent with the needs of the situation existing in the host country. The appropriate style of leadership can be determined only after a careful assessment is made of the external environment of the host country, the type of personnel to be managed, the level of existing technology, and the specific goals and operational requirements of the company.

OPENING INCIDENT REVISITED

Canadian Implements Ltd.

In the opening incident, Dan Shelton had run into a problem when he tried to implement a troubleshooting plan by dismissing an incompetent employee. He suddenly realized that customs and rules he knew nothing about might prevent him from improving Canadian Implement's Far Eastern plant operations. Not completing this assignment will make him look less effective as a plant manager and may thwart Shelton's career aspirations.

Shelton's dilemma clearly demonstrates the kinds of difficulties Canadian managers can face when they go on a foreign assignment. These Canadian managers take with them a set of assumptions that may or may not be relevant in the country where they are assigned. The material in the chapter dealing with the economic, political, and social factors of another country's external environment demonstrates that managers must learn as much as possible about the country in which they will be working before their arrival.

In Dan Shelton's case, Canadian Implements should have provided him with information it must already have on the cultural and political/legal factors of the far Eastern country before he went there. However, since Shelton sees himself as a troubleshooter, he could have helped himself by finding out what kind of restrictions might affect his assignment. Failure to investigate the external environment meant that Shelton assumed that actions taken at the Hamilton plant could also be taken in the Far Eastern country.

What can Dan Shelton do now? First of all, he can rely far more heavily on his local national assistant for information that is critical to his troubleshooting plans. The assistant can tell him about any other customs, laws, rules, or regulations that will influence his plans to improve the Far Eastern facility. The assistant can also convey a sense of the culture of the country and how Shelton might proceed with his reorganization plans so that he has the greatest chance for success. Shelton is probably going to have to allow much more time to acclimatize himself and then solve this plant's problems than he had taken to help the Hamilton plant.

SUMMARY

Canada is now in the age of the multinational corporation (MNC). Few other developments have had the overall impact of multinationals, which have caused the countries of the world to become more closely related to each other. An MNC is a firm engaged in business in two or more countries. These firms typically have sales offices and sometimes manufacturing plants in many different countries. The MNCs are not only instrumental in improving the world economy and thereby standards of living of many people but also can significantly affect the technology, culture, and customs of the countries in which they operate.

The multinational corporation is the type of enterprise that provides a special challenge to managers. Effectiveness in managing an MNC requires the manager to give careful consideration to such factors as the external environment, objectives, technology, structure, and personnel. The external environment that confronts multinational enterprises consists primarily of the economic, political/legal, and social factors in the various countries in which the MNC operates. This external environment characterized by complexity, variety, and uncertainty requires that managers develop sophisticated skills to deal effectively with these conditions. Objectives of the MNC would not seem to be any different from the objectives of businesses operating exclusively within Canada. However, the MNC differs from domestic firms because of the potential clash of its goals with the objectives of the economic and political systems of the various countries within which it operates.

Technological expertise is the primary advantage of the MNC. Many MNCs operate in such high-technology industries as computers, oil, pharmaceuticals, electronics, and motor vehicles. Another major factor to be considered in managing the MNC is the organization of the firm. The organizational structure of an MNC must be designed to meet its international needs. Such a structure may differ significantly from that found in the company's domestic operations.

Successful management of an MNC requires that the manager understand the needs, values, and problems of personnel in the countries where the company operates. Management must recognize that there is no one style of leadership that will be equally effective in all countries. People in the various countries have widely divergent backgrounds, educations, languages, cultures, and religions and live in a variety of social conditions and economic and political systems.

Effective managers of MNCs must develop a style of leadership consistent with the needs of the situation existing in the host country. The appropriate style of leadership can be determined only after a careful assessment is made of the external environment of the host country, the type of personnel to be managed, the level of existing technology and the specific goals and operational requirements of the company.

REVIEW QUESTIONS

1. What is a multinational corporation? List 3 of the major criteria used to classify multinationals.
2. Name 4 of the largest multinational corporations (MNCs).
3. "The success or failure of the MNC is determined largely by how it responds to the external environment." Comment.
4. List the major factors affecting the management of multinationals.
5. Describe 2 major economic factors than often cause difficulty for multinationals.
6. Distinguish between developed and less developed countries from the perspective of top management of a Canadian MNC.
7. How does the political/legal factor affect an MNC?
8. What specific types of laws or local regulations must a multinational corporation be concerned with?
9. How may the objectives of the MNC differ from domestic firms?
10. Identify 5 of the more typical complaints host countries have against MNCs.
11. Is a code of ethics needed for MNCs? Why or why not? Give examples of what might be included.
12. "Technological expertise is the primary advantage of the multinational enterprise." Explain.
13. Describe the types of personnel used by MNCs and any potential problems with these personnel.

EXERCISES

1. Assume that you have agreed to accept a 2-year position in Helsinki, Finland effective in 60 days. You are married and have a 6-year-old daughter. What would you do to prepare yourself and your family (who are staying at home) for this assignment?
2. If you were selecting MNC personnel to be sent on international assignments, what qualities, experience, and characteristics would you look for in prospective personnel?
3. Review 2 current journal articles on the problems multinational companies have in recruiting and placing Canadian managers and/or technical personnel in assignments in foreign countries. Make a list of the problems and how the companies are able to overcome them.

CASE STUDY

The Overseas Transfer

In college, Pat Marek majored in industrial management and was considered by his teachers and peers to be a good all around student. Marek not only took the required courses in business, but he also learned French. After graduation, Marek took an entry-level management training position with Tuborg International, a multinational corporation with offices and factories in 30 countries, including Canada. Marek's first assignment was in a plant in Toronto. His supervisors quickly identified Marek for his ability to get the job done and still maintain good rapport with subordinates, peers, and superiors. In only 3 years, Marek had advanced from a manager trainee to the position of assistant plant superintendent.

After 2 years in this position, Marek was called into the superintendent's office one day and told that he had been identified as ready for a foreign assignment. The move would mean a promotion. The assignment was for a plant in France; but Marek wasn't worried about living and working there. Marek was excited and wasted no time in making the necessary preparations for the new assignment.

Prior to arriving at the plant in France, Marek took considerable time to review his French textbook exercises. He was surprised by how quickly the language came back to him. He thought that there wouldn't be any major difficulties in making the transition from Canada to France. However, Marek found, on arrival, that the community where the Tuborg plant was located did not speak the pure French that Marek had learned. There were many expressions that meant one thing to Marek but had an entirely different meaning to the employees of the plant.

While meeting with several of the employees a week after arriving, one of the workers said something to Marek that Marek interpreted as uncomplimentary; in actuality, the employee had greeted him with a rather risqué expression but in a different tone than Marek had heard before. All of the other employees interpreted the expression to be merely a friendly greeting. Marek's disgust registered in his face.

As the days went by, this type of misunderstanding occurred a few more times, until the employees began to limit their conversation with Marek. In only one month, Marek managed virtually to isolate himself from the workers within the plant. He became disillusioned and thought about asking to be relieved from the assignment.

QUESTIONS

1. What problems had Pat Marek not anticipated when he took the assignment?
2. How could the company have assisted Marek to reduce the difficulties that he confronted?
3. Do you believe the situation that Marek confronted is typical of a Canadian going to a foreign assignment? Discuss.

CASE STUDY

International Expansion

James Cartwright is the marketing manager for communications products for National Systems Limited, a Canadian company based in Halifax with sales in all 10 provinces. Sales revenues are in the area of $210 million annually. National Systems had indicated its intention to expand its marketing efforts to countries other than Canada.

In Canada, the communications products division has a 28 percent market share. Its product competes against products imported from other countries. It is regarded as having one of the better products for the Canadian market.

Issues that Cartwright is considering, in determining whether to enter international markets and how to enter them, include the product he offers, what markets he should attempt to sell in, what personnel he can utilize to develop these market opportunities, and what arrangements if any he should make with organizations in potential foreign markets.

Regarding the product, Cartwright knew that the National Systems product competed well in Canada. He wondered whether the same product features and characteristics would be equally well accepted in various foreign markets. He also wondered whether it was necessary to develop new products for each foreign market or whether he should follow an approach of testing and proving his products in Canada and not offering them for sale in other countries until they were proven successful in Canada.

Regarding the market, Cartwright was concerned whether he should initially attempt to penetrate the United States market, or whether he should focus on developing the market for his product in developing countries. His major concern about the United States was that competition was fierce. Offsetting this concern was the fact that this very large market was geographically and culturally the most similar to the Canadian market with which he was most familiar. Regarding markets in developing countries, he felt that the Canadian reputation and the quality of his products were particularly strong points. He would be able to use products that had been tried, tested, and proven in the Canadian market, some of them for a number of years. Cartwright had reports indicating certain cultural and market development problems associated with the sophistication of product use in many of the developing countries.

Another issue was the personnel he had available to develop these markets. He had what he considered to be 5 key senior marketing management people in Canada, along with 15 other people at the level immediately below them. They were all fully engaged in their present jobs and none had any international marketing experience. Cartwright himself had no international marketing expertise other than a 2-week seminar he attended on international marketing. One option was to recruit a new graduate from a university program in business administration. His concern in this instance was that the individual would not have sufficient experience to be able to handle the area. Another option was to recruit someone from a major consulting firm which specialized in international marketing. However, this approach would not lead to long-run development of an international marketing team.

Another issue was to decide how to enter different foreign markets. Should they export from plants in Canada? Should they license people to manufacture the product in foreign markets? Should they enter into a joint venture agreement to market the product in these other countries?

There was also the general issue, raised by the board of directors of National Systems Limited, of whether or not expansion from the Canadian market was wise. Some of the attractions for international expansion included increases in sales and potential for profit, the experience and learning that would take place in working in other countries, the fact that many of their domestic competitors were from other countries, and international experience would make it easier for National Systems to compete in the Canadian market. Some of the disadvantages to international expansion were the investment that would be required to develop these markets, the fact that other companies had a considerable lead on National Systems in the international market, and the fact that they were already doing well and were profitable in serving only the Canadian market.

QUESTIONS

1. Are there other considerations that James Cartwright should take into account in formulating his recommendation about whether to advise National Systems to go into foreign markets?

2. Are there other issues that are important to Cartwright if they do decide to enter foreign markets?

3. Considering the issues he faces of products, markets, personnel, and business arrangements, what are the options available and what are the pros and cons of each option? Where can Cartwright look for information that will be useful to him in addressing these issues?

NOTES

[1] Peter F. Drucker, *Management* (New York: Harper, 1973): 729.
[2] Robert W. Stevens, "Scanning the Multinational Firm," *Business Horizons* 14 (June 1971): 53.
[3] David C. McClelland, *The Achieving Society* (Princeton, N.J.: Van Nostrand, 1961).
[4] R. Hal Mason, "Conflicts between Host Countries and Multinational Enterprise," *California Management Review* 17, no. 1 (1974): 6 and 7, by permission of the Regents of the University of California.
[5] "France Seizing Control of Technical Industries," *Business Week* (May 17, 1976): 47.
[6] United Nations information.
[7] L. Drake Rodman and Lee M. Caudill, "Management of Large Multinationals: Trends and Future Challenges," *Business Horizons*.
[8] Yoram Zeira, "Overlooked Personnel Problems of Multinational Corporations," *Columbia Journal of World Business* 10 (Summer 1975): 96–103.

REFERENCES

Alpander, Guvenc G. "Multinational Corporations: Home-based Affiliate Relations." *California Management Review* 20, no. 3 (Spring 1978): 47–56.

Capstick, R. "The Perils of Manufacturing Abroad." *International Management* 33 (March 1978): 43–46.

Davis, S. M. "Trends in the Organization of Multinational Corporations." *Columbia Journal of World Business* 11 (Summer 1976): 54–71.

Davis, Stanley M., and Lawrence, Paul R. "Problems of Matrix Organizations." *Harvard Business Review* 56, no. 3 (May-June 1978): 131–142.

Davidson, Frame J. *International Business and Global Technology.* Lexington, Mass.: D. C. Heath and Co., 1983.

Duncan, Robert. "What is the Right Organization Structure?" *Organizational Dynamics* 7, no. 3 (Winter 1979): 59–80.

Evans, William A. *Management Ethics: An Intercultural Perspective.* Hingham, Mass.: Martinus Nyhoff Publishing, 1981.

Fitzpatrick, Mark. "The Definition and Assessment of Political Risk in International Business: A Review of the Literature." *Academy of Management Review* 8, no. 2 (April 1983): 249–254.

Galbraith, J. K. "The Defense of the Multinational Company." *Harvard Business Review* 56 (March 1978): 83–93.

Galbraith, J. K., and Edstrom, A. "International Transfer of Managers: Some Important Policy Considerations." *Columbia Journal of World Business* 11 (Summer 1976): 100–112.

Ghymn, K. I., and Bates, T. H. "Consequences of MNC Strategic Planning: An Empirical Case Study." *Management International Review* 17 (1977): 83–91.

Gladwin, Thomas N., and Walter, Ingo. *Multinationals Under Fire: Lessons in the Management of Conflict.* New York: John Wiley and Sons, 1980.

Harbron, John D. "How International Executives Have Responded to the New Challenges of World Recession." *Business Quarterly* 48, no. 4 (Winter 1983): 77–79.

Lawrence, Paul R.; Kolodny, Harvey F.; and Davis, Stanley M. "The Human Side of the Matrix." *Organizational Dynamics* 6, no. 1 (Summer 1977): 43–61.

May, W. F. "Between Ideology and Interdependence." *California Management Review* 19 (Summer 1977): 88–90.

Mitchell, J., and Shawn, A. "All Multinationals Aren't the Same." *Financial World* (January 1977): 36.

Morris, James H.; Steers, Richard M.; and Koch, James L. "Influence of Organization Structure on Role Conflict and Ambiguity for Three Occupational Groupings." *Academy of Management Journal* 22, no. 1 (March 1979): 58–70.

Paulson, Steven K. "Organizational Size, Technology, and Structure: Replication of a Study of Social Service Agencies among Small Retail Firms." *Academy of Management Journal* 23, no. 2 (June 1980): 341–346.

Pazy, Asya, and Zeira, Yoram. "Training Parent Country Professionals in Host Country Organizations." *Academy of Management Review* 8, no. 2 (April 1983): 262–272.

Pohlman, R. A. "Policies of Multinational Firms: A Survey." *Business Horizons* 19 (December 1976): 14–18.

Prahalad, C. K. "Strategic Choices in Diversified MNCs." *Harvard Business Review* 54 (July 1976): 67–78.

Sparkman, J. "Economic Interdependence and the International Corporation." *California Management Review* 20 (Fall 1977): 88–92.

Vernon, R. "Multinational Enterprises and National Governments: An Uneasy Relationship." *Columbia Journal of World Business* 11 (Summer 1976): 9–16.

Zeira, Yoram. "Management Development in Ethnocentric Multinational Corporations." *California Management Review* 18 (Summer 1976): 34–42.

Zeira, Y., and Harari, E. "Managing Third Country Nationals in Multinational Corporations." *Business Horizons* 18 (October 1977): 83–88.

18

Social Responsibility and Business Ethics

OPENING INCIDENT

Papeterie Boulanger

Adrian Kulik is the plant superintendent of a paper mill, Papeterie Boulanger, located in a northern Quebec town. During the 1970s the mill received a great deal of negative publicity because it was polluting the air and water. The mill has been fined regularly for violating air and water quality standards. Until recently, opinion among local townspeople was mixed. Most didn't like the pollution, but they didn't complain much because the mill provided most of the jobs in town. Over the past year, however, people have become increasingly critical of the company's refusal to install air and water pollution control devices.

Kulik has lived in the town for 14 years and has a good reputation. He is very involved in local volunteer and civic activities. He knows most of the workers at the mill personally, and he coaches a local minor league hockey team. During the past few years, he has grown depressed about the pollution issue, partly because he has some doubts about what his company is doing, but also because complaints about pollution are getting more obvious. He is aware of the health threats and wonders if his work might be a potential danger to his children.

Two years ago, he had made a presentation to the company's head office requesting that pollution control equipment be installed at the plant. Kulik made this request based on the fact that the mill should be able to operate at its present site for many years to come, allowing the company time to recoup their pollution control costs. Head office is now considering 3 alternatives: (1) install the pollution control equipment, (2) continue to pay the regular (but affordable) fines the company incurs for air and water quality violations, or (3) close the plant. Despite repeated applications, head office can get no help from governments in Ottawa or Quebec City to defray costs of the needed equipment.

Kulik has been assured that, if the plant is closed, he will have a good job elsewhere in the company. He knows that, from a strictly financial perspective, doing nothing and continuing to pay the fines is the best alternative because it avoids both a plant closure and a costly bill for installing pollution control equipment. But that doesn't make Kulik feel any better about the situation.

KEY TERMS

economic function
corporate social
 responsibility
social audit

iron law of
 responsibility
Friedman's view of
 social responsibility

ethics
ethical dilemmas
managerial code of
 ethics

LEARNING OBJECTIVES

After completing this chapter you should be able to
1. Describe corporate social responsibility.
2. Explain the role of business in society.
3. Identify the arguments both for and against social responsibility of business.
4. State some of the current corporate practices regarding social responsibility and explain what is meant by a social audit.
5. Define business ethics and describe why it is important for an industry and/or company to establish codes of ethical behavior.

The opening incident demonstrates what is perhaps the most fundamental dilemma facing Canadian business firms: should they pursue profit to the exclusion of all else, or should they consider what they perceive as their social responsibilities when they make business decisions? There are no easy answers to this question, as we shall see in this chapter. In the areas of social responsibility and business ethics, management often has to agonize over which course of action is best. In many situations, managers find themselves doing a juggling act as they try simultaneously to adhere to government regulations, to pursue their profit objectives, and to meet the competing demands of employees, customers, shareholders, and suppliers.

Because there are no easy resolutions to many of the issues that arise with regard to corporate social responsibility and business ethics, our goal in this chapter is to sharpen your awareness of the issues; with this knowledge, you will be better prepared to deal with these issues from a business perspective when you work as a manager. The chapter is divided into two main parts. The first part examines corporate social responsibility. We note how the role of business has changed in Canadian society during the twentieth century and what the concept of corporate social responsibility means. We also examine the arguments for and against corporate social responsibility. The second part of the chapter deals with business ethics. We describe some typical ethical dilemmas facing managers and note the factors which determine the level of ethical behavior of managers. Overall, this chapter demonstrates some of the difficult decisions that managers must make in their day-to-day work. The fact that there are no straightforward formulas for handling such matters further reinforces the dynamic nature of the manager's job that we have tried to convey throughout the first 17 chapters of this book.

THE CHANGING ROLE OF BUSINESS IN SOCIETY

Traditionally, the responsibility of the business firm in Canada has been to produce and distribute goods and services in return for a profit. Businesses have performed this function effectively. Largely as the result of the North American economic system and the important contributions of business firms, Canada enjoys one of the highest overall standards of living in the world. Rising standards of living in Canada have enabled a high percentage of the population to have their basic needs for food, clothing, shelter, health, and education reasonably well satisfied. Businesses can take pride in these accomplishments.

Business has been able to make these significant contributions to the rising living standards primarily because of the way the free enterprise economic system operates. The profit motive provides incentive to business to produce products and services as efficiently as possible. Business firms try to improve the quality of their products and services, reduce costs and prices and, thereby, attract more customers to buy from the firm. By earning profits, the successful firm pays taxes to government and makes donations to provide financial support for charitable causes. Because of the efficient operations of business firms, an ever increasing number of people have the means and the leisure time to enjoy the good life.

But businesses operate by public consent with the basic purpose of satisfying the needs of society. People in North America have begun

MANAGEMENT IN PRACTICE

Corporate Support for the Arts

American Express, Toronto, recently launched an unusual marketing effort. Each time a customer uses an American Express card, the company will donate $0.01 to the National Ballet School, the National Theatre School, and the National Youth Orchestra. Each time a customer purchases American Express Travellers Cheques, the company will donate $0.05 to the 3 Canadian arts organizations. For each new card member signed, the company will contribute $2.

The company openly states that it is benefiting from the program through increased sales, but it points out that the 3 arts groups are also benefiting, both by the money they receive and by the exposure the campaign is generating. The company introduced the campaign in Canada after successfully using it in the United States.

SOURCE   Adapted from "American Express Tries an Arts Tack," *Marketing* (March 15, 1982): 7.

---

expecting — even demanding — more of all of its institutions, particularly large business firms, to take more responsibility for the quality of life. Goals, values, and attitudes in society are changing to reflect a greater concern for the quality and quantity of life. These concerns include such goals as:

- Elimination of poverty and provision of quality health care
- Protection of the environment by reducing the levels of pollution
- Provision of equal employment and educational opportunities regardless of race, color, creed, or gender
- Provision of a sufficient number of jobs and career opportunities for all members of society
- Improvement of the quality of working life of employees
- Provision of safe, livable communities with good housing and efficient transportation.[1]

Society's expectations of North American business have broadened considerably in recent years to encompass more than the traditional economic function. This is illustrated in Exhibit 18-1. Inner circle I represents the traditional economic functions of business. The **economic function** is the primary responsibility of businesses to society; in performing the economic function, businesses produce needed goods and services, provide employment, contribute to economic growth, and earn a profit. Level II represents the responsibility of business to perform the economic functions with an awareness of changing social goals, values, and demands. Management must be aware of such concerns as: the efficient utilization of resources, reducing pollution, employing and developing skills of minorities and females, providing safe products, and providing a safe work place. Level III is concerned with the corporation's responsibility for assisting society in achieving such broad goals as the elimination of poverty and urban decay through a partnership of business, government agencies, and other private institutions. While the responsibilities in Level III are not primary obligations of businesses, there is increasing interest by business in voluntary social action programs.

CORPORATE SOCIAL RESPONSIBILITY

Modern corporations need to develop an opinion about what each considers right or wrong on particular issues. Many companies develop patterns of concern for moral issues, through policy statements, through practices over time, and through the leadership of morally strong individuals. Some companies have programs of community involvement for their employees and managers. Many cooperate with fund drives such as the United Way. Open-door policies, grievance procedures, and employee benefit programs often stem as much from a desire to do what is right as from a concern for productivity and avoidance of strife. Managers have great influence over whether corporate behavior includes conscientiousness or not because they are the ones who establish policies, develop the company's mission statement, and listen to employees' concerns.

A Definition of Social Responsibility

Social responsibility is concerned with how organizations deal with the issues and problems confronting society. **Corporate social responsibility** has been defined as: "a firm's obligation to constituent groups in society other than stockholders and beyond that prescribed by law or union contract."[2] Acceptance of the social responsibility concept means that a primary obligation of an organization is to ensure that its decisions and operations meet the needs and interests of society.

If a business firm contributes large amounts of money to charity, institutes a training program for the chronically unemployed, is actively involved in civic affairs, or gives scholarship money to a university or community college, it is behaving voluntarily in a socially responsible fashion because these activities are not required by law. Whenever an organization behaves in this way, it usually does so without regard for the effect of this action on its profit. However, if the general public thinks the organization is involved in these activities because they will increase profits, the public may still think highly of the firm, but technically the organization is not adhering to the spirit of social responsibility.

If the definition of social responsibility quoted above is accepted, then clearly most business firms have historically not behaved in a socially responsible way. The general nature of business — perfectly legal — was to mobilize the factors of production efficiently in the hope of making a profit. The general public seems to be increasingly

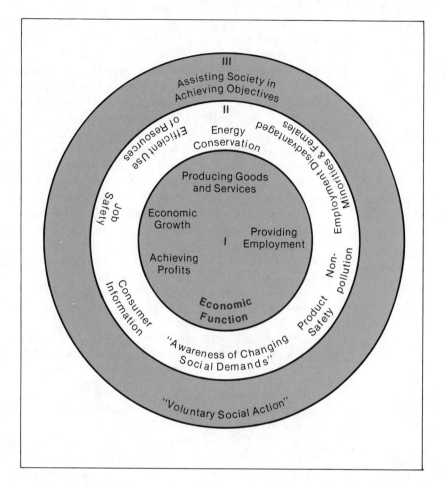

EXHIBIT 18-1
Primary roles
of business

suspicious of businesses that follow the historical pattern. Surveys conducted during the 1960s and 1970s show a substantial decline in the public's confidence in business. However, these same surveys also show a decline in the public's confidence in various other groups — for example, doctors.

Managers in modern corporations should be very concerned about misperceptions that the general public may have about business. The most prominent misperception deals with consumer beliefs about business profits. As we noted in an earlier chapter, if you ask the typical consumer how much profit a business firm earns on each dollar of sales, they will generally say between $0.25 and $0.30 cents. If he or she is then asked how much is a reasonable amount, the answer will usually be about $0.10. The actual profit that business makes on each dollar of sales is only about $0.05. Unless misconceptions like this one are corrected, business will continue to get very little sympathy from the general public.

Another major problem regarding consumer misconceptions of business is how they perceive ethical behavior demonstrated (or not) by top management of businesses. Various surveys show that the public has a relatively low opinion of the calibre of the business executive's ethical behavior. Typically, such surveys show that, while a majority of the public believes business firms have an obligation to help society even if it means making less profit, fewer than half of those surveyed accept the notion that executives actually have a social conscience.

These two public perceptions — excessive concern for profits on the part of businesses and a low level of ethical behavior on the part of business managers — constitute a major image problem for business. If the general public has serious reservations about the role of business and the people who carry it out, Canadian society cannot function as effectively as it should. In Japan, for example, this kind of problem seems almost nonexistent; employees and management have worked together to become a formidable economic force in the world. Studying the Matsushita company, the largest manufacturer of electrical appliances in the world,[3] two American scholars attributed part of Matsushita's success to the basic business principles of the company's founder. Commitment to the following principles are expected from every Matsushita employee:

> To recognize our responsibilities as industrialists, to foster progress, to promote the general welfare of society, to devote ourselves to the further development of world culture.[4]

One way to increase the effectiveness of the Canadian economic system is to create proper expectations of the role of business in the mind of the average Canadian.

Socially responsible decision makers within corporations consider both the economic and social impact of their decisions and the firm's operations on affected groups in society. Keith Davis, a professor who has written extensively about the concept of corporate social responsibility, believes that, in meeting its responsibilities to society, a firm must be concerned with more than the narrow technical and legal requirements.[5] It should recognize that an obligation exists to protect and enhance the interests and welfare of not only the corporation but also those of society.

Modern business organizations are often expected to assume broader and more diverse responsibilities to the various groups within society. There is little doubt that an increasing amount of attention is being directed to social responsibility by business firms. However, critics argue that there is more lip-service than real action, more public relations programs than concrete activities. Nevertheless, social responsibility is an area in which the modern business firm must develop a stance, accompanied by appropriate policies and activities.

The factors that affect corporate social responsibility are illustrated in Exhibit 18-2, which depicts the relationship of a business firm to its external environment. How business conducts itself with regard to each of these groups will greatly affect its opportunities for survival,

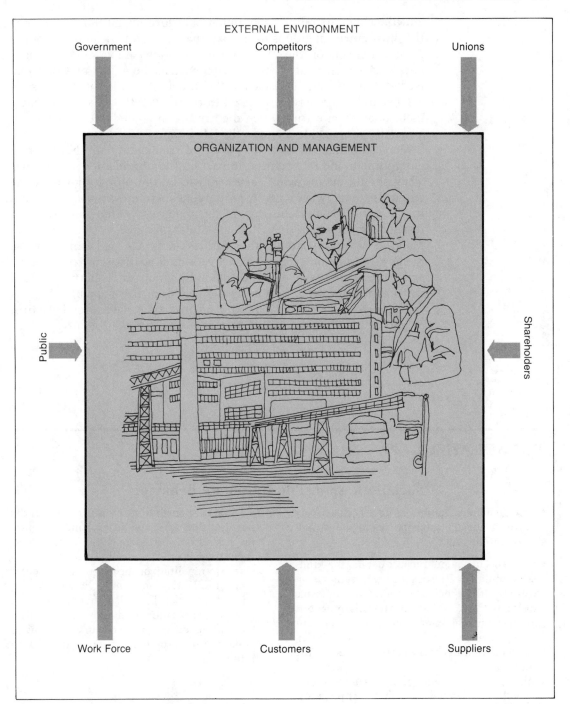

EXHIBIT 18-2 Relationship of the firm to groups in society

growth, and profitability. Labor unions and government units are among the most powerful groups in the external environment in terms of the potential effects on the firm. Consumer groups are gaining increased power, as have special interest groups, such as the Acid Rain Coalition, Nader's Raiders, and the Canadian Consumers' Association. On occasion, even shareholders have organized to try to alter the existing management of an organization when the firm has not conducted business in a socially responsible manner. (Recall Chapter 2.)

Managers must assess the power of each group in the external environment and its potential impact on the organization's activities. They should pursue what they deem to be the primary goals of the enterprise, but always with an eye out for constraints imposed by forces in the external environment. When managers go too long without responding or when they fundamentally disagree with actions demanded by various groups, they can risk boycotts, picketing, adverse media attention, new legislation, government hearings, proxy contests, and strikes. However, demands made by groups in society will keep the organization from becoming too selfish or irresponsible. Actions by these groups, rather than profits or conscience, have often led a firm to pursue socially responsible actions.

MANAGEMENT IN PRACTICE

Socially Responsible Corporate Behavior

Many Canadian corporations have been actively involved in social responsibility programs. Consider the following:

- Imperial Oil's annual report details the kinds of community activities the organization is involved in; these include the formation of teams to deal with the problem of oil spills, programs for upgrading job safety and reducing accident rates, continued support for higher education, and reduction in energy costs incurred by the company.
- John Labatt Ltd. spends hundreds of thousands of dollars each year on such social programs as community recreational facilities where Labatt's has production plants; creating summer jobs for students; the establishment of

a Social Responsibility Committee within the board of directors; and an exchange program for children of Labatt's employees, which allows them to visit other areas of Canada.

- Gaz Metropolitan opened a training center where firefighters were taught how to contain natural gas leaks. They also offer employees a free medical examination and, for those who are nearing retirement, free courses on how to make the important transition from work to retirement.

SOURCE Adapted from Louis Demers and Donald Wayland, "Corporate Social Responsibility," *CA magazine* (February 1982): 59–60.

MANAGEMENT IN PRACTICE

A Problem at Key Lake

Key Lake Mining Corporation operates a uranium mine at Key Lake, Saskatchewan, 600 km north of Saskatoon. In January 1984, 100 million L of radium-contaminated water escaped from a reservoir into the lake. The open-pit mining operation had been in operation only 3 months before the accident. It was later learned that 8 smaller spills had preceded the big accident, and 2 smaller spills followed it.

Company officials concede that these accidents have not created an image of competence about the operations of the mine. Neal Hardy, the Environment Minister for Saskatchewan, called the company's president and bluntly asked him what the province could expect from the company in the future. If operations are not improved, the province could close the mine.

It appears that the company wasn't prepared for the spill or for the publicity surrounding it.

After the incident occurred, the company hired a public relations specialist to help deal with the publicity problem. Because the site is so isolated, reporters had a hard time getting to the mine. At one point, the company denied landing permission to two reporters who had flown in to investigate the spill. This incident created further concerns about the company. The bad publicity has also caused the union, the United Steelworkers of America, to question safety at the mine.

After the incident became well known, the company's president offered the opinion that the media had sensationalized the incident. This comment brought forth further criticism of the company.

SOURCE Adapted from Edward Greenspan, "Key Lake Spills Will Mean Some Public Relations Repairs," *Financial Post* (January 28, 1984): 23–24.

The Social Audit

A **social audit** is a commitment to systematic assessment of and reporting on some meaningful, definable domain of a company's activities that have social impact. Some firms have demonstrated their concern for the area of social responsibility by periodically surveying and assessing their activities through social auditing. Systematic social auditing is only in its infancy, and relatively few firms do periodic appraisals. However, a social audit does provide information to management that contributes toward decision making; it also provides information to the general public in response to pressures on the enterprise.

Four possible types of audits are currently being used: (1) a simple inventory of activities, (2) compilation of socially relevant expenditures, (3) specific program management, and (4) determination of social impact. The inventory, generally a social audit's starting point, consists of a simple listing of activities undertaken by the firm over and above what is required. For example, firms have itemized the following types of activities: (1) minority employment and training, (2) support of minority enterprises, (3) pollution control, (4) corporate giving to charities and educational institutions, (5) involvement in selected community projects by firm executives, and (6) programs for the chronically unemployed. The ideal social audit would help determine the benefits to society of socially oriented business activity.

TALKING TO MANAGERS

Kelly M. James
ERCO Industries Limited

ERCO Industries Limited, a Canadian-based chemical company, is one of our top 300 manufacturers. The company has 1200 employees, with 8 plants in Canada, in British Columbia, Ontario, Quebec, and Newfoundland. ERCO is a part of Albright and Wilson Ltd. (the second largest chemical company in the United Kingdom), part of Tenneco Inc., one of the largest industrial companies in the United States, with business interests ranging from natural gas to ship building and auto parts, to insurance and land management. ERCO is a major producer of phosphorous, phosphoric acid, industrial and food grade phosphate. Kelly James, ERCO's Manager, Corporate Affairs, has been with the company for 25 years. James, whose education includes courses in psychology and philosophy, has a degree in commerce.

Q: What are ERCO's policies regarding social responsibility?

James: We've been in Canada for about 90 years, and we have moved from being a more paternalistic company to being a less paternalistic one. In the old days, we even went so far as to go around to all the pubs and tell the pub keepers not to sell liquor to certain members of our staff because we felt they had a problem. We moved away from that in the 1900s to a more sophisticated, modern operation, but we have kept our links with the community. Our policy is to spend most of our attention, efforts, donations and grants within the communities in which we work. We match the efforts of our people; for instance, if one of our people decides to sponsor or manage a baseball team or a little league hockey team, we will match his or her efforts in the same activity. If our employees decide to help the old folks build an addition on one of their homes, again, the same kind of attention is given. In the area where we don't have requests from our employees, for instance, the United Way, our contributions are based on a formula of donating $30 for every employee, plus an adjustment based on the current rate of inflation. The emphasis on what the company does stays within the community in which it works, which means that most of the money is spent in the plant communities.

Q: What is the volume of donations made?

James: As a guideline, we allow 0.2 percent of corporate profits before tax. However, it's a variable expenditure, because in some years there will be more need in Newfoundland and less need in BC, so our attention is spent that way. In other years, our profit position is extremely low, so all of these are balanced; the figure I've given you is simply a guideline, not a mandate. That figure is broken into groups: the national charities, like the Parkinson Foundation or the National Heart Fund; the arts, like the National Ballet; and education. In the field of education, we try not to compete with government grant programs. For instance, we contribute to scholarships put out by the Canadian Manufacturers' Association, in the geographical areas in which we operate, and we participate in the Chemical Institute of Canada's programs.

Q: What happens if there is a concern about safety in the communities where ERCO operates?
James: The time when that is likely to happen is when there has been a chemical spill or accident somewhere else — it could be anywhere in the world. In one such situation, through the Chemical Producers' Association, we gathered information on the emergency that had occurred and produced an analysis of the situation's affect on us. We circulated this to all of our plant managers and we requested them to remind their people of all the procedures and policies we had in place, and to go out and speak to the community leaders; we communicate with the mayor or reeve or MLA to let them know that we had in place good policies and good procedures, and that this kind of accident wouldn't happen at any of our plants.

We have a commitment that we have made to the industry and a statement of guiding principles as a responsible chemical producer in Canada. We have in place transportation emergency response procedures, which incorporate the training of our people in conjunction with the training of emergency measures people in the community, including such people as the fire chief. We are part of the Canadian Chemical Producers' Transportation Emergency Assistance Program, which has response centers from the east to the west coast operated by the chemical industry. And because of our uniqueness in phosphorous production, we're part of a Phosphorous Emergency Response Team program that can send highly skilled specialists wherever there's a phosphorous spill in North America. We also conduct safety and hazard training programs with our people and with our customers' employees; we have a policy that no carrier — be it truck, rail, or ship — can handle our products unless it is trained by our people. On the plant side, we have a control program which specifies safety and audits into design; it looks after insurance audits, hazards and operational studies, and so on. We make sure that we have analyzed each one of the conditions that might come up if an accident occurred in any of the plants.

Q: How have fluctuating profits and budgets affected your involvement in community activities?
James: I don't think they've really had any ef-

fect at all. Our social commitment and our commitment to the community, if anything, is constantly rising. We can go back to the 1900s when we built a golf course at Buckingham, Quebec and, as of 1985, we're putting more effort into that golf course because the new generation who are working on it have come to us and said, "We're prepared to raise this kind of money. Can you help us match it or develop it or raise it with us?" And we've certainly participated in that. I think it's also fair to say that, if our people continue to work hard in the community, we will continue to do everything we can to help them.

We also work with the community in bad times, such as when layoffs occur. We often use the community when that happens. We'll work with community leaders in the town and some of the senior people, our union, our management people, and they'll all sit down and say "How can we survive the layoffs?" And there's been payback on that sort of thing. For example, there will be opportunities for laid-off employees to pick up in another industry on a short term. The thing is that you're making the community aware, so it doesn't come as a great shock.

Q: Is there a written code of ethics for your employees?
James: Yes, there's a written code of ethics put out by Tenneco Inc., in French and English. When an employee signs on, we make sure that the individual understands the code, has a copy of it, and follows it.

Q: Have you run into any situations where the demands of your employer created a difficult situation for you in terms of your own personal integrity?
James: No, I haven't. Certainly I have never experienced that within this company. I work closely with the public affairs group in the chemical industry, and I also know of no situation. Here, of course, the media often get on these things and run many circles in many directions, without really getting down and trying to have everyone understand what's truly out there and what is truly happening. I suspect that, if you were to do a hard-nosed analysis of the chemical industry in Canada, you'd probably get the same answer out of every single one of them . . . there's very little conflict at all.

THE DEBATE ABOUT SOCIAL RESPONSIBILITY

To this point, we have noted that: (1) the general public perceives that the role of business has changed during the twentieth century, and (2) the majority of Canadians think that business firms should behave in a socially responsible fashion. Corporate social responsibility has some forceful opposition. Its critics argue that forcing business into a socially responsible role will not benefit society and will, in fact, harm it. The debate that has arisen during the last decade disputes the role business should play in North American society. In this section we examine the major arguments from both sides of this debate.

Arguments Favoring Social Responsibility

Various groups and individuals have argued that business should be involved in socially responsible activities. Proponents of corporate social responsibility stress such areas as provision for better jobs and promotion opportunities for minorities and women, financial support for education, charitable donations to civic organizations, financial and managerial support for improving health and medical care, a safer work place, leadership and financial support for urban renewal, and means to reduce ecological pollution. The major arguments for the acceptance of social responsibility by business are:

- People expect businesses and other institutions to be socially responsible.
- It is in the best interest of business to pursue socially responsible programs; consumers are likely to continue buying from businesses with good reputations.
- Socially responsible activities improve the image of the firm.
- Business should be involved in socially useful projects because it has the resources to see that they succeed.
- Corporations must be concerned about society's interests and needs because society sanctions business operations.
- If business is not responsive to society's needs, the general public will press for more government regulation requiring more socially responsible behavior.
- Socially responsible actions may increase profits in the long run.
- Business firms have a great deal of power; with this power goes the responsibility to exercise it in a socially responsible fashion.

Davis summarizes these arguments with what he terms the **iron law of responsibility**: "in the long-run, those who do not use power in a manner in which society considers responsible will tend to lose it."[6] Thus, if business firms are to retain their social power, they must be responsive to society's needs.

Arguments against Social Responsibility

There are numerous arguments against businesses assuming an active role of social responsibility. A leading opponent is Dr. Milton Friedman, a Nobel Prize–winning economist. **Friedman's view of social responsibility** is:

> There is one and only one social responsibility of business — to use its resources and engage in activities designed to increase its profits so long as it stays within the rules of the game, which is to say, engages in open and free competition without deception and fraud. . . . Few trends could so thoroughly undermine the very foundations of our free society as the acceptance by corporate officials of a social responsibility other than to make as much money for their stockholders as possible.[7]

Friedman goes on to assert that social responsibility is a "fundamentally subversive doctrine." He argues that managers are agents of the owners of an enterprise and that for them to engage in any activities not related to earning profits may be illegal. Diverting funds to social projects without shareholder approval is, in effect, "taxation without representation." He says that business performance is economic, not social.

Concentrating resources in the social area could lead to less economic efficiency and therefore actually be detrimental to society. Friedman and others who argue against the assumption of social responsibility by business believe that government should deal with the social demands of society. The major arguments against social responsibility are:

- Concern for social responsibility violates sound business decision making and diverts the attention of managers from the pursuit of profit.
- Social responsibility might be illegal, in that executives do not have the legal right to use corporate resources (the property of the shareholders) to pursue activities like giving to charity.
- The cost of socially responsible behavior exceeds the benefits; the net result is higher prices to consumers.
- Managers aren't trained, nor do they possess the skills or resources, to determine which socially responsible projects to pursue.
- Too much power is concentrated in the hands of business executives, none of whom is elected by the public.
- An emphasis on social responsibility leads to a deterioration in the free enterprise system.

An Evaluation of the Debate

Both the positions for and against corporate social responsibility make logical arguments to support their case. Often, business executives themselves are proponents of corporate social responsibility when profits are high or social conditions unfavorable, and are opponents when the economy is under great pressure, when the company is in financial difficulty, or when social conditions do not warrant a great deal of concern.

Friedman's arguments against the assumption of social responsibility by business firms have been criticized on a number of grounds. First, Friedman implies that business should engage in open and free competition as part of its basic operations. However, open and free competition does not exist in most sectors of the North American economy. A second and more fundamental point is that business firms, particularly large ones, cannot avoid making decisions that influence society. Almost every major decision made in a corporation affects various groups in and outside the organization. Problems confronting society — employment discrimination, pollution, unsafe products, corporate bribery, illegal political contributions, price fixing — are all past practices of some companies that are not in the best interest of society.

Because of the social undesirability of such acts, there has been an increasing amount of government regulation. Some managers have concluded that "if it's legal, it's ethical" — if it is not in violation of the law, one is free to act as one wishes. This managerial philosophy will invite more and more outside regulation and may be self-defeating in the long run. Being socially responsible means more than just following the law. It means considering the consequences of actions and asking if such actions are socially responsible. Social responsibility starts where the law ends. Keith Davis stresses this point:

> A firm is not being socially responsible if it merely complies with the minimum requirements of the law, because this is what any good citizen would do. A profit maximizing firm under the rules of classical economics would do as much. Social responsibility goes one step further. It is a firm's acceptance of a social obligation beyond the requirements of the law.[8]

BUSINESS ETHICS

Our previous discussion was concerned with the issue of corporate social responsibility as it relates to the decisions made by managers within organizations. Whereas social responsibility is primarily concerned with how the total corporation conducts itself, **ethics** deal with the contemporary standards or principles of conduct that govern the actions and behavior of individuals within the organization. They provide a basis for determining what is right or wrong in terms of a given situation. Getting agreement on what is ethical or unethical is often complicated because: (1) social values tend to change over time, and (2) different groups within society have divergent views of acceptable conduct at one point in time.

As illustrated in Exhibit 18-3, ethical norms are established by society and govern the development of ethical standards for an industry, a business firm, or an individual manager. Each industry develops its own ethical standards, and the firms and individual managers in the industry are expected to adhere to these codes of behavior.

The ethical norms provided by society in general are not so specific and long lasting that they always give clearly defined guidelines for everyone to follow. The difference between conduct that is barely tolerated and conduct that is clearly indefensible is sometimes blurred. Elected representatives have been known to take foreign trips on taxpayers' money to attend conferences that seem little more than paid holidays. Highly respected business people hire professional accountants and lawyers to identify loopholes in tax laws. Business executives engage in a variety of practices that are often viewed with suspicion by the general public. Yet there is seldom agreement in public opinion that these and similar activities are unconditionally unethical.

EXHIBIT 18-3
Frames of reference for ethical standards for managers

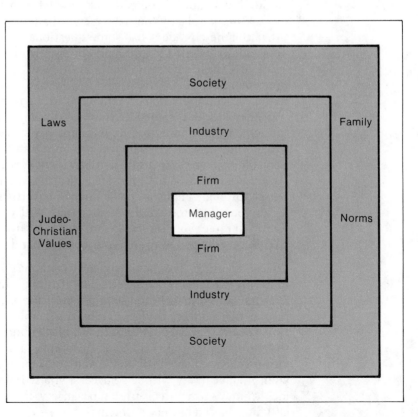

Ethical Dilemmas Facing Managers

Today's managers are continually confronted with situations where difficult ethical choices must be made. An **ethical dilemma** exists when a manager has difficulty making a decision because he or she feels uncomfortable about the morality of one of the alternatives. Very often the alternative that makes the manager feel uncomfortable is weighted with financial or career-advancement benefits offered to the manager. Consider these examples of ethical dilemmas:

- Suppose you are a sales manager attending a regular meeting of your sales staff. Three senior salespeople report that salespeople employed by two major competitors are paying customers under the table to accept their contracts. The meeting breaks into a chaotic debate over what should be done. Several salespeople state without hesitation that your company should follow the competitors' example. You argue that your company has never used such tactics. What decision do you make? What do you tell your sales staff to do? Will you suspect some of your salespeople will act contrary to a recommendation not to pay kickbacks?

- Suppose you are the vice-president of marketing for a consumer products company and you've been with the company for 27 years. You've worked all your life for the presidency of the company; you've been assured it's yours if you can make the latest new product successful in the marketplace. You have received a letter from a parent noting that this new product has some questionable features that make it potentially unsafe for the small children who will use it. Would you suppress these safety problems in order to assure your selection as president?

- Suppose you are a department head in a government agency and a vacancy has just opened in your department. Your boss asks you to lunch one day and makes an extraordinary suggestion. He notes how tight your department's budget has been for the past couple of years and offers to increase it substantially for next year. In return, he wants a female friend of his promoted into the vacant position, without going through the usual procedures of advertising and interviewing. Can you afford to turn down the offer? Will your boss be willing or able to protect you from awkward questions from other departments? What do you decide to tell your boss? What do you actually do?

Ethical dilemmas like these frequently confront managers in their work. In trying to resolve these ethical dilemmas, managers would like simultaneously to feel good about the decision and to have the decision further their career. Unfortunately, this combination is often impossible because the decision that they consider unethical may be the one that will further their career. For example, if you are the marketing vice-president mentioned above and you ignore the safety warnings, your product likely will be a success; you will probably become president, but you may feel uneasy because you promoted a product for children that had safety problems.

We do not mean to imply by these examples that managers can never feel that, by making ethical decisions, they may be restrained in pursuit of their careers. But it is true that managers continually face ethical dilemmas that create mental anguish for them. Unfortunately, we cannot provide easy answers for students aspiring to be managers. We can, however, warn you that these kinds of circumstances will arise and that you will often feel you are in an untenable position.

Illegal versus Unethical Behavior

It is important to make the distinction between illegal behavior and unethical behavior. If there is a law prohibiting an action, it is illegal; most people will also consider such actions to be unethical. For example, most people would say that murder is not only illegal but also unethical. However, some people argue that some conduct that is illegal is not automatically to be considered unethical. They argue that some laws — like abortion or marijuana possession — should not be on the books. The classic example of this dichotomy is the law that was passed prohibiting the consumption of alcohol in the United States in the 1920s. Many people, forced to recognize that the consumption of alcohol was illegal, did not consider it unethical.

As we noted earlier, different people may view one issue with differing ideas about its degree of properness. Assessing whether or not behavior is unethical is therefore a difficult task. Is the behavior portrayed in the following examples unethical or not?

- A manager has objective evidence that he is underpaid. He consistently pads his expense account to make up for some of the shortfall in his regular salary.
- A broker quietly hints to a relative about a major stock deal involving the company where the relative works as a manager. The manager quickly sells his own shares and tips off one or two of his close friends in the company.
- A manager creates doubts about the competence of some of her peers in order to enhance her chances for a promotion. She does so without ever lying about her peers; rather, she selectively passes on unfavorable information about them.
- A purchasing agent takes a gift from a supplier in return for purchasing some of the supplier's products. The purchasing agent is not sure in his own mind whether or not the gift influenced his purchasing decision.
- A manager discovers a computer programmer has been using the company computer to program harassing telephone calls in a personal vendetta. The programmer has saved the company money and works well, so the manager decides to ignore the discovery.
- An employee gives industrial secrets to a competitor of the company she works for. She was induced to divulge the secrets after being encouraged to work for the competitor at a large increase in salary.

If a list of examples like these were given to a sample of practicing managers, it is likely that there would be considerable disagreement about which practices are unethical and which ones are acceptable. This is sometimes the difficulty with business ethics — each individual considers the facts of the situation and makes a judgment about whether the behavior in question is unethical. If a firm has no policy statements or has shown no strict intolerance of certain conduct, individual managers must depend on their personal perspective to reach a consensus on what constitutes ethical behavior.

Factors Affecting Managerial Ethics

Although we cannot predict what decision an individual manager will make when confronted with an ethical dilemma, we can identify what influences the levels of managerial ethics. These factors are discussed below.

Government Regulation

Laws may be viewed as the results of a trend of what society expects in terms of acceptable behavior. Behavior can be made illegal if society views it as excessive or unethical. The law defines and clarifies acceptable standards or practices in a given area. For example, if contributions to political candidates from corporations are illegal, then firms either obey the law or violate it. However, in either case the guidelines or standards are clear, and a violator may be punished for engaging in the illegal activity. Laws regarding corporate behavior are often passed as a result of long-standing low ethical standards or the failure of corporations to recognize their social responsibilities.

Beyond explicit laws, governments also form regulations to define acceptable and unacceptable practices. For example, the areas of minimum product safety, fire precautions, acceptable levels for auto emissions, safe working conditions, and nondiscriminatory employment practices are all supported by government regulation. The interpretation of the laws by the courts and the development of guidelines by government agencies assist managers in understanding what constitute acceptable practices in the work place.

Codes of Ethical Behavior

Many industries and individual companies have formal, written codes of ethics that provide specific guidelines for managers and other employees to follow. The key issue in this regard is whether individuals within organizations are truly governed by the code of ethics or simply give lip-service to it. Another issue is whether the company or industry enforces the code if individuals or companies violate it. In any event, these codes of ethics define or clarify the ethical issues and allow the individual to make the final decision. An example of a code of ethics is presented in the adjacent insert.

There are advantages in having each industry form industry associations which develop their own codes of ethics. It is difficult for a single firm to follow ethical practices if its competitors undercut them by taking advantage of unethical shortcuts. But if an entire industry agrees that certain behavior will not be tolerated, there is a much greater chance for an improvement in the level of ethical conduct in that industry.

A particularly difficult ethical problem currently exists in international trade. Several highly publicized cases have appeared in recent years where business executives or "middlemen" companies paid bribes to foreign government officials in return for major sales contracts. In Canada, bribery is considered to be highly unethical, but in some other parts of the world it is viewed by people in authoritative government posts as acceptable business practice. If Canadian multinational companies cannot get some agreement from other multinationals that this practice should be stopped, they may find themselves at a disadvantage when they try to get business in some foreign countries.

MANAGEMENT IN PRACTICE

Guiding Principles — Great-West Life Assurance Company

1. Great-West Life's management recognizes that, to prosper, the company must serve its customers, staff members and sales representatives, shareholders, and the community at large to the best of its ability. Moreover, this is based on a conviction that those elements which make Great-West Life an outstanding company for its customers are beneficial to all its constituencies.

2. We will maintain an environment of confidence in, and respect for, the dignity of the individual. We will strive to select superior people. We will build and maintain a dynamic organization through an open and participative style of management. We will give staff members and sales personnel every opportunity to make the most of their abilities and reward them according to their contribution to meeting our objectives.

3. We will distribute our products and services in the best interests of our customers through distribution systems that are contemporary, innovative, and socially responsible.

4. Our investment program will carefully balance the quality, terms, and rate of return on our investments. We will strive to achieve a consistently superior rate of return to meet our overall financial objectives and obligations to our customers.

5. We will find new and better ways to serve our customers by offering products and services that are both contemporary and innovative to satisfy their changing needs and desires. We will maintain their goodwill by meeting our commitments to them both in spirit and letter with particular emphasis upon the financial management and security of their funds.

6. We will work to increase the long-term value of shareholders' investment to maintain our reputation as a sound and growing financial institution.

SOURCE Guiding Principles of Great-West Life Assurance Company, Winnipeg. Reprinted by permission.

Social Pressures

Social forces and pressure groups have considerable impact on ethics or acceptable standards of behavior. Examples of pressure groups seeking to make organizations more responsive to the needs and desires of society are numerous. Removal of lead paint from baby furniture, the banning of urea formaldehyde home insulation, and stopping of fraudulent practices by transmission dealerships are all results of action by pressure groups. They have also actively promoted more employment of women and minorities, some have boycotted products, and others have tried to prevent the construction of nuclear arms devices. Such actions by pressure groups may, in fact, cause management to alter certain decisions by taking a broader view of ecological and consumer needs.

At the same time, however, there may be strong social pressures within the firm urging managers to band together to ward off the pressures from external groups, particularly if these external pressures are seen as unreasonable or too costly. Most managers are more susceptible to pressure from their peers than they are to pressures from outsiders; thus, even desirable change may be very slow to occur. For example, reducing air pollution is certainly a desirable objective, but installation of control devices may be an excessive cost for management to consider as a quick solution.

Individual Ethics
versus Corporate Demands

The needs and goals of the firm may conflict with the values and ethical standards of a manager. This dilemma between organizational goals and personal ethics or values greatly complicates the life of the typical manager. There is often considerable pressure on managers to increase performance and generate higher profits. At times, this objective may create pressures to compromise personal ethics to meet the goals of the company. For example, a manager in an autocratic firm may be given what he or she considers to be in impossibly high sales goal; that manager, unable to persuade superiors to change the goal and unable to quit, may feel forced to engage in practices like getting together with managers from other firms and fixing prices so that they can all make their profit goals. This practice is, of course, illegal and unethical. It reduces competition and harms the consumer, but it can happen when individual managers in a nonparticipative corporation become desperate enough or are driven far enough by a conflict between individual and organizational goals.

One study found that managers can feel a great deal of pressure to compromise their personal ethical standards in order to achieve organizational goals. A. B. Carroll's study, representing the response of 258 American managers, revealed that 50 percent of top-level managers, 65 percent of middle-level managers and 84 percent of lower-level managers felt "under pressure to compromise personal standards to achieve company goals."[9]

A Managerial Code of Ethics

The medical and legal professions have established codes of ethics that provide guidelines and standards for conduct. These codes are known to everyone in the profession but may or may not be practiced to the letter. Managers do not have an established code of ethics, but in recent years there have been numerous attempts to develop and promote one. The following list provides an example of such an attempt to formulate what might be included in a **managerial code of ethics**:

- I will recognize that management is a call to service with responsibilities to my subordinates, associates, supervisors, employer, community, nation, and world.
- I will be guided in all my activities by truth, accuracy, fair dealings, and good taste.
- I will earn and carefully guard my reputation for good moral character and citizenship.
- I will recognize that, as a leader, my own pattern of work and life will exert more influence on my subordinates than what I say or write.
- I will give the same consideration to the rights and interests of others that I ask for myself.
- I will maintain a broad and balanced outlook and will look for value in the ideas and opinions of others.
- I will regard my role as a manager as an obligation to help subordinates and associates achieve personal and professional fulfillment.
- I will keep informed on the latest developments in the techniques, equipment, and processes associated with the practice of management and the industry in which I am employed.
- I will search for, recommend, and initiate methods to increase productivity and efficiency.
- I will respect the professional competence of my colleagues and will work with them to support and promote the goals and programs of the industry.
- I will support efforts to strengthen professional management through example, education, training, and a lifelong pursuit of excellence.[10]

To be realistic, we must admit that such a code of ethics will have very little effect on some managers, and a substantial effect on others. The statements contained in the code are general, allowing each individual to interpret the statements according to his or her own view of the world. For example, in the first statement, the word "responsibility" would undoubtedly be interpreted in many different ways; given that, any manager could probably say in good conscience that he or she was acting responsibly toward subordinates.

A final comment on the difficult subject of ethics: remember that human beings are capable of infinite amounts of self-delusion. This means that if a certain manager does something that 99.9 percent of his or her peers think is unethical, we should not be surprised if that manager remains convinced that what he or she did was perfectly all right. If students aspiring to management positions expect this kind of behavior, they will be able to recognize it and deal more effectively with it.

OPENING INCIDENT REVISITED

Papeterie Boulanger

Adrian Kulik, the plant superintendent of Papeterie Boulanger, was very concerned about the water and air pollution his paper mill was creating in the northern Quebec town where it operated. He was not sure what should be done to resolve the problem. Like most managers, Kulik believes he is a reasonable person. Yet he finds himself at the center of a major controversy and he is experiencing considerable anxiety because of it. What alternatives are open to him? At one extreme, he could demand that the company do something to protect the people of the town, many of whom are its own employees, or he will quit the company. If he is truly a top-notch plant superintendent, the company may give serious consideration to his request. At the other extreme, he could continue to do his job and not make waves. He'll probably never be blamed personally for the air and water pollution and, even if someone challenges him, Kulik can point to the request he sent to head office. Kulik can say that he did all he could, even if he isn't persuaded of it himself.

The positions that the supporters and opponents of social responsibility will take on this issue are fairly clear. The supporters will say that the pollution control equipment should be installed immediately, while the opponents will point out that, if the company is forced to install the equipment, it may have to close the plant and many jobs will be lost.

What should Kulik do? We're not sure.

If you are uncomfortable with our answer, perhaps you should ask yourself what you would do in Kulik's position. Be honest with yourself when you think about this issue and try to imagine what Kulik is going through. You have worked for this company for many years; are you going to demand that they do something about this problem or you will quit? Is it realistic to think that a company will spend millions of dollars on pollution control equipment just to keep one valued employee? Are you going to throw away your career over an issue like this? On another level of thought, can you live with yourself if you don't do something? If you truly want to act, you might petition your MNA and MP to help the company. Only you can answer these questions. When you realize that tough decisions like this one are made by managers every day, you begin to realize why the occupation of management is so important to our society.

Perhaps it is appropriate to end this text with a problem that creates much uncertainty in your mind. In the first 17 chapters we have tried to give answers to a wide range of important questions facing managers. But we must recognize that the practice of management is filled with uncertainties and that clear-cut answers are simply not possible in all cases. If you can accept that, and if you can make a decision on a tough issue and live with the consequences, perhaps you have what it takes to be a good manager.

SUMMARY

Managers in today's organizations have the difficult job of trying to meet the demands of employees, shareholders, government, customers, the public, and other groups in their external environment. Social responsibility is concerned with how organizations and managers deal with the issues and problems confronting society.

Although a universally acceptable definition of corporate social responsibility has not been developed, we define it as the basic obligation of an organization to constituent groups in society other than shareholders and beyond that prescribed by law or contract. Full acceptance of this definition means that a firm ensures that its decisions and operations meet the needs and interests of society. While business firms have contributed greatly to the high standards of living enjoyed in Canada, they are being expected by many people to do more. But how much responsibility for society's problems should business assume? Those favoring increased corporate social responsibility advance arguments that: (1) it is in the best interest of the firm to pursue socially responsible programs, (2) they have the resources to do so, (3) society expects business to be socially responsible, (4) long-run profits for the business may increase, and (5) if business is not responsive to society's needs, the public may press for more government regulation.

There are several arguments against business assuming social responsibility. Dr. Milton Friedman, a leading opponent of business assumption of social responsibility, asserts that there is one and only one social responsibility of business: to generate profits within the rules of the game by engaging in open and free competition without deception and fraud. The major arguments against social responsibility include: (1) it misdirects resources and violates sound business decision making that should concentrate on making profits, (2) costs are excessive relative to benefits and therefore may cause prices to increase, (3) managers do not have the resources or skills to engage in social projects, (4) it concentrates too much power in the hands of business executives, and (5) it may lead to the deterioration of the free enterprise system. What has been the response of business? Many large corporations are engaged in numerous socially responsible programs such as minority employment and training, pollution control, job and product safety programs, energy conservation, quality of life, and the elimination of poverty.

While social responsibility is primarily concerned with the overall operation of the corporation, ethics are contemporary standards or principles of conduct that govern the actions and behavior of individuals within the organization. Ethics provide a basis for determining what is right or wrong. What is ethical or unethical is complicated because societal values and moral concepts tend to change over time. Acceptable practices are established by society and govern the ethical standards for an industry, a business firm, or an individual manager. Laws, government regulations, industry codes of ethics, social pressures, and conflicts between the manager's personal standards and the needs of the firm all affect decisions made by managers involving ethical dilemmas.

REVIEW QUESTIONS

1. In general, how is North American business viewed by the general public? Provide examples. Do you think the perception is accurate? Why or why not?

2. What is meant by corporate social responsibility? Define and describe the relationships a firm has with groups in its external environment.
3. What traditionally has been the primary role of business in society? Explain. Should this role change? Why or why not?
4. Compare and contrast two opposing views of corporate social responsibility. Which, in your view, is more correct or appropriate?
5. Can corporate social responsibility be legislated? If so, give examples of such laws.
6. What are some examples of current practices of companies engaging in social responsibilities? Be specific. Are there others you are aware of from your own experience or reading?
7. What is a social audit?
8. What is meant by the term *ethics*? What determines ethical norms for managers?
9. Briefly discuss several examples of unethical practices by business managers. What factors affect managerial ethics?
10. What are some examples of ethical dilemmas faced by managers? How can they cope with these dilemmas?
11. What is the difference between illegal behavior and unethical behavior?

EXERCISES

1. Visit two local companies that have formal codes of ethics. Evaluate the code of ethics, bearing our discussion of ethics in this chapter in mind.
2. Select what you consider to be a local social or ecological problem — such as water or air pollution. Make a list of the groups or businesses within the community that are concerned about the problem. Analyze the impact of the problem on the various segments of the community. Develop a proposal for solving the problem, giving consideration to the benefits and costs of your solution.
3. Interview a manager about an ethical dilemma that he or she has faced. How did the manager resolve it?

CASE STUDY

Dilemma at Can-Roc Ltd.

Sandi Bentley is the chairman of the board of Can-Roc Ltd., a manufacturing firm with headquarters in a large Canadian city. During the past few years the company has been under considerable but polite pressure from the business school at the local university to contribute to a scholarship fund for promising students. The dean of the business school argues that, since business firms like Can-Roc are one of the prime beneficiaries of university business schools, they should help with the cost of training students.

The university is not the only organization applying pressure for funds. The symphony and the ballet are also asking for charitable donations so that they can continue to contribute to the cultural richness of the city. Their representatives suggest that business firms like Can-Roc should contribute to the arts — like patrons in past eras — because they have a responsibility for the cultural development of the city where they carry on business activities.

After several years of this pressure, the board of directors agreed to establish a $10,000 university scholarship and to contribute $5,000 each to the ballet and the symphony on a one-year trial basis. The board hoped that these donations would demonstrate the firm's good citizenship. Sandi Bentley has pointed out that Can-Roc would get considerable free publicity from these philanthropic actions.

At the annual meeting at the close of the fiscal year, these contributions were mentioned by Bentley. At that point, Peter Illych stood up and, noting that he represented a group of 40 shareholders, said that they were unhappy with the donations. Illych claimed that the board had no right to give $20,000 to scholarships and cultural activities; he argued that the board was supposed to run the business well and see that it made a good profit. By giving to charity, the board was taking money out of the shareholders' pockets because less money could be distributed as dividends. Illych stated that shareholders had bought Can-Roc shares to get good dividend payments; with this kind of behavior, the board was preventing them from achieving their financial goals. Illych also questioned the board's competence to make decisions on charitable donations.

At the conclusion of this negative speech, several other shareholders stood up to say that they disagreed with the sentiments Illych expressed. While they agreed that the board's action meant a slight reduction in dividends, they felt that the decisions were reasonable. These shareholders agreed with the university and the arts groups that Can-Roc could not ignore important organizations in the city that were in real need of funds and that the corporation had a responsibility to consider requests for charitable donations.

The meeting ended with a promise by Bentley that the board would examine the issue of corporate charity and would report to the shareholders at the next annual meeting.

QUESTIONS

1. What kinds of arguments can you pose in favor of and opposed to corporate charitable donations?
2. What should the board of directors do about this issue? How should they defend their decision to the shareholders represented by Illych? to the shareholders not opposed to charitable donations?

CASE STUDY

The Hiring of a Friend's Daughter

Petra Underys recently graduated from university with a degree in general business. Petra was quite bright, although her grades might lead a person to think otherwise; her education had been funded by her parents and she'd felt no pressure to excel. When she graduated from university, Petra did not find a job immediately. When he discovered this, Petra's father, Stan Underys, took it on himself to see that Petra became employed. Underys was executive vice-president of a medium-sized manufacturing firm. One of the people he contacted in seeking employment for his daughter was Bill Garbo, the president of another firm in the area. Underys's firm purchased many of its supplies from Garbo's company. On telling Garbo his problem, Underys was told to send Petra to his office for an interview. Petra duly presented herself and was surprised that, before she left Garbo's firm that day, she had a job. Petra may have been lazy but she certainly was not stupid. She realized that this job was obtained because of the hope of future business from her father's company.

It did not take long for the employees in the department to discover the reason she had been hired — Petra told them. When a difficult job was assigned to her, Petra normally got one of the other employees to do it, inferring that Garbo would be pleased with them by helping her out. She developed a pattern of coming in late, taking long lunch breaks, and leaving early. When her department manager attempted to reprimand her for these unorthodox activities, Petra would bring up the close relationship that her father had with Garbo. The department manager was at his limits when he asked for your help.

QUESTIONS

1. From an ethical standpoint, how would you evaluate the merits of Garbo employing Petra Underys? Discuss.
2. Now that she is employed and not behaving well on the job, Petra presents a problem to her department manager. How can the manager handle her in order to get her to work more productively?
3. Do you believe that a firm should have policies regarding such hiring practices? Discuss.

NOTES

[1] Adapted from the Committee for Economic Development and from Sandra L. Holmes, "Corporate Social Performance and Present Areas of Commitment," *Academy of Management Journal* 20 (1977): 435.
[2] Thomas M. Jones, "Corporate Social Responsibility, Revisited, Redefined," *California Management Review* 22, no. 2 (Spring, 1980): 59, 60.
[3] Matsushita Electric Annual Report, 1979.
[4] Richard Tanner Pascale and Anthony G. Athos, *The Art of Japanese Management* (New York: Simon and Schuster, 1981): 51.
[5] Keith Davis, "The Case for and against Business Assumption of Social Responsibilities," *Academy of Management Journal* (June, 1973). Reprinted in Archie B. Carroll, *Managing Corporate Social Responsibility* (Boston: Little, Brown, 1977) p. 35.
[6] Davis, 36.
[7] Milton Friedman, "The Social Responsibility of Business Is To Increase Its Profits," *New York Times Magazine* (September 1970): 33, 122–126.
[8] Davis, 36.
[9] Archie B. Carroll, "Managerial Ethics: A Post Watergate View," *Business Horizons* (April, 1975): 77. See also Archie B. Carroll, "A Survey of Managerial Ethics: Is Business Morality Watergate Morality?" *Business and Society Review* (1976): 58–63.
[10] Code of Ethics of the Institute of Certified Professional Managers.

REFERENCES

Alvarez, Rodolfo; Lutterman, Kenneth G.; et al. *Discrimination in Organizations: Using Social Indicators to Manage Social Change.* San Francisco: Jossey-Bass, 1982.

Armandi, B. R., and Tuzzolino, F. "Need Hierarchy Framework for Assessing Corporation Social Responsibility." *Academy of Management Review* 6 (January 1981): 21–28.

Behrman, Jack N. *Discourses on Ethics and Business.* Cambridge Mass.: Oelegschlager, Gunn and Hain, 1981.

Carroll, Archie B. "A Three-Dimensional Conceptual Model of Corporate Performance." *Academy of Management Review* 4, no. 4 (October 1979): 497–505.

Clutterbuck, D. "Blowing the Whistle on Corporate Misconduct." *International Management* 35 (January 1980): 14–16.

Drory, Amos, and Gluskinos, Uri M. "Machiavellianism and Leadership." *Journal of Applied Psychology* 64, no. 1 (February 1980): 81–86.

Ford, Robert, and McLaughlin, Frank. "Perceptions of Socially Responsible Acts and Attitudes: A Comparison of Business School Deans and Corporate Chief Executives." *Academy of Management Journal* 27, no. 3 (September 1984): 666–674.

Greenough, William Croan. "Keeping Corporate Governance in the Private Sector." *Business Horizons* 23, no. 1 (February 1980): 71–81.

Grunig, James E. "A New Measure of Public Opinions on Corporate Social Responsibility." *Academy of Management Journal* 22, no. 4 (December 1979): 738–764.

Henderson, H. "Changing Corporate-Social Contract in the 1980s: Creative Opportunities for Consumer Affairs Professionals." *Public Relations Quarterly* 24 (Winter 1979): 7–14.

Hipp, H. "Business Ethics and Society's Future." *National Underwriter* 3 (property ed.) (September 14, 1979): 7–14.

"How Business Treats Its Environment." *Business and Society Review* 33 (Spring 1980): 56–65.

Jones, T. M. "Corporate Social Responsibility Revisited, Redefined." *California Management Review* 22 (Spring 1980): 59–67.

Lippin, P. "When Business and the Community Cooperate." *Administrative Management* 42 (February 1981): 34–35.

Marusi, A. R. "Balancing Power Through Public Accountability." *Public Relations Journal* 35 (May 1979): 24–26.

"Privacy Issue Arouses Concern about Ethics in Marketing Research." *Sales and Marketing Management* (December 8, 1980): 88–89.

Rosen, G. R. "Can the Corporation Survive?" *Dun's Review* 114 (August 1979): 40–42.

Shapiro, I. S. "Accountability and Power: Whither Corporate Governance in a Free Society?" *Management Review* 69 (February 1980): 29–31.

Sonnenfeld, Jeffrey, and Lawrence, Paul R. "Why Do Companies Succumb to Price Fixing?" *Harvard Business Review* 56, no. 4 (July-August 1978): 145–156.

Waters, James A. "Catch 20.5: Corporate Morality as an Organizational Phenomenon." *Organizational Dynamics* 6, no. 4 (Spring 1978): 3–19.

White, B. J., and Montgomery, B. R. "Corporate Codes of Conduct." *California Management Review* 22 (Winter 1980): 80–87.

White, Louis P., and Wooten, Kevin C. "Ethical Dilemmas in Various Stages of Organizational Development." *Academy of Management Review* 8, no. 4 (October 1983): 690–697.

Comprehensive Management Case Studies

HOW TO ANALYZE COMPREHENSIVE CASES

This section of the text contains 9 comprehensive management cases, which are considerably longer than those at the end of each chapter. In these comprehensive cases, you are given a great deal of information about a real company that has certain management problems. Your task is to analyze the information and then make suggestions that will resolve the management problems facing the company.

There are two basic approaches that can be used with case studies. Your instructor may ask you to answer the questions found at the end of each case. These questions focus on specific topics that have been covered in the text, such as leadership, communication, conflict, or change. To answer the questions, reread the relevant section in the text and then decide how it can be applied to the practical problems that are evident in the case. Using the text material to answer the case questions will help you bridge the gap from management theory to management practice.

The second approach to case analysis is a more general one and involves using a four-step problem solving process. Your instructor may suggest that you ignore the questions provided for you. Rather, you are required to:

1. Define the problem or opportunity: In each case you will be able to observe either a problem that needs to be solved or an opportunity that can be exploited. When defining problems, don't be sidetracked by symptoms of the problem. For example, if a company's employees have low productivity, this is not the problem but a symptom of the problem. What you must do is discover specifically what is causing low employee productivity. Be careful about the assumptions you make. For example, don't automatically assume that something is wrong with the employees just because their productivity is low; management may not have designed the work system properly, and employees therefore might not be able to be productive even if they are highly motivated.

2. Develop plausible alternative solutions: Once you have defined the problem or opportunity, you must develop several plausible alternatives that might solve the problem or help management exploit the opportunity. Make sure that your alternatives will actually improve the situation; a "do nothing" suggestion is generally not worthwhile. Creative thinking is also important when you are developing alternatives. Try to think of unconventional ways to solve the problem or exploit the opportunity. Some of the most successful managers are those who are able to see alternatives that other, more traditional, managers cannot see.

3. Evaluate the alternatives: Each alternative that you develop must be evaluated. This is probably the most difficult part of case analysis. Do not start this step with an opinion about which alternative is best and then try to find information to support that opinion. Rather, develop a list of pros and cons for each alternative through a systematic assessment of the material in the case. This takes time but, when you have completed this step, you will be able to decide which alternative(s) should be chosen.

4. Choose the best alternative(s): Select the alternative which, considering all the pros and cons, promises to do the best job of resolving the problem or exploiting the opportunity you have defined. More specifically, pick the alternative which best satisfies the specific criterion you think is important to the company — for example, profit, employee satisfaction, or product quality. In some situations, there will be multiple and conflicting criteria that should be satisfied. In these situations, the decision will be much tougher. Be aware that, no matter which alternative you choose, some individuals or groups in the case are going to be unhappy. From a management perspective, your job is to decide what will benefit the organization as a whole.

Keep in mind that, while there is no simple answer to a case study, some solutions are better than others. Therefore, the emphasis should be on working through the 4 steps to reach a workable solution to a problem or a workable strategy for exploiting an opportunity. If the process, rather than the outcome, of decision making is stressed, you will become adept at analyzing any management problem with which you are confronted. Developing the ability to solve management problems is one of the key elements in the manager's job.

CASE STUDY 1

Sun Life Assurance Company of Canada

Corporate History

Sun Life Assurance Company of Canada was incorporated on March 18, 1865 by an Act of parliament which authorized the establishment of the Sun Insurance Company of Montreal. Its founder, Matthew Hamilton Gault, a Scottish immigrant, was one of Montreal's foremost businessmen. The company's sponsors were headed by George Stephen, one of the builders of the CPR and then president of the Bank of Montreal, and A. W. Ogilvy, a flour mill manager and, like Gault, a member of parliament. Sun Life was conceived because, at the time, the Canadian insurance industry was dominated by foreign interests. In 1871, the firm was joined by Canada Life and, together, they comprised the sole native Canadian presence in the business.

Sun Life was soon noted for its leadership in life insurance practice and service. In 1880, the company took what was then regarded as a bold step by adopting, for the first time in the history of life insurance, a worldwide "unconditional" policy. The generous provisions created much adverse criticism from competitors. Subsequent experience, however, established proof of the soundness of this liberalization. Operations were extended across Canada. The West Indies was selected as the site for Sun Life's first overseas agency. In the 1890s, Sun Life representation was established in the more important cities of Asia, Africa, Europe, South and Central America, and the United Kingdom. Offices in the United States followed.

Since the company's first policy was written in 1871, Sun Life has grown into a successful and dynamic enterprise. In 1872, net income was reported as $48,210, assets were valued at $96,461, and the life insurance in force amounted to $1,064,350; in 1925, net income totalled $69 million, assets approached $300 million, and life insurance in force exceeded $1 billion. In 1976, the net income was $1.14 billion and asset valuation $5.04 billion; life insurance in force totalled $31.79 billion worldwide.

In the late 1970s, Sun Life was the largest Canadian life insurance company and the twelfth largest in North America. The company employed 1150 salespersons stationed at its 77 branches across Canada. It had 67 branches in the United States, with headquarters in Boston, Mass., and 41 in the United Kingdom. Throughout the world, the firm employed directly and indirectly some 7500 sales and administrative people. The network was centrally administered by the head office in Montreal, although some foreign offices operated relatively independently. In the Montreal home office, aside from the large proportion of clerical staff, there were a large number of specialty and professional personnel. The company occupied the Sun Life Building, a massive 26-floor structure of Corinthian architecture, completed just prior to the start of World War II. Montreal had been the site of Head Office since the firm's inception in 1865.

Industry Notes

A life insurance policy is a contract between its owner and the life insurance company. It is a legal document that sets out conditions of the transaction which will be in effect for years ahead.

The life insurance company promises the payment of a sum of money at some unknown future date when a specified event takes place, such as death or the surrender of the policy. The holder promises to pay the insurer a certain sum of money in specified installments. This payment is called the premium. The "savings" of Canadians through life insurance and annuities are channelled by the companies into investments to help minimize the cost of life insurance and to guarantee future benefits to policyholders and beneficiaries. These "savings" also provide capital funds for the growth of Canada's economy.

Insurance companies are members of an established industry, whose existence is secured by commercial need for security from risk on one hand and the crucial role of insurers as public trustees and financial intermediaries on the other.

For over 100 years, Canadian governments have supervised the life insurance business to ensure that commitments to policyholders are provided for and met. Every life insurance company doing business in Canada must, each year, obtain government certification of its right to continue to do business. The certificate or licence is evidence that a company has complied with Canadian laws designed for the protection of policyholders, is subject to regular periodic examination by the superintendents of insurance, has filed its annual financial report with the authorities, maintains required legal reserves, and has been judged as qualified to do business. Owing to the nature of the industry, the insurance company is highly vulnerable to its external environment and the general level of confidence of its investors. When the economic environment is in a state of insecurity, brought on by such factors as recession, inflation, a fluctuation in interest rates, legislation, or a change of government, investors may react by investing in ways that offer more security and financial stability.

Marketing and Sales

Sun Life relies heavily on personal sales representatives with respect to the marketing of its underwriting services. The high level of performance of its sales staff is a result, in part, of intensive in-house training programs. The sales force is considered to be one of the industry's finest. All agents in Quebec are members of the Provincial Association of Quebec Life Underwriters. The sales force in the Montreal region was composed almost entirely of anglophone personnel but, recently, recruiting has been conducted at francophone universities.

Of the firm's agents, 31 percent have had some university training, while 21 percent are university graduates. Successful applicants are trained by experienced field personnel and have extensive exposure to various audio-visual training media. Sun Life salespersons are equipped to offer many services to potential clients including personal financial planning and analysis, life insurance, health and accident coverage, and mutual funds. The company enjoys an excellent reputation among consumers. It offers, for example, a 10-day "free look" provision, whereby policyholders have a 10-day period within which they may examine the new policy. If, during this period, they decide to change their mind, they may return the policy and receive a full refund of their premium. This feature not only complies with the Quebec Consumer Protection Act, but gives the client a further 5 days during which to express a change of heart. The company also makes available additional policy cost information to account for accrual of interest. Sun Life has worked to speed up and streamline policy claim, cancellation and collection procedures, as well introducing a new, simplified policy form.

Mass advertising is not, in itself, considered to be an effective merchandising and promotional strategy at Sun Life. For this reason, the company has, as an adjunct to its personal sales programs, sponsored various sporting themes and events, such as the 1976 Montreal Summer Olympics and the annual Canadian cross-country ski touring marathon between Montreal and Ottawa. The emphasis has been to make Sun Life's name synonymous with physical health and fitness.

Operations

Sun Life's facilities have been constantly modernized in order to maintain operations at peak efficiency, while ensuring the provision of customer service of the highest level. Such a process is ongoing and is constantly under review.

Competition

During 1977, Canadians purchased $41.55 billion of life insurance, $3 billion more than the amount bought in 1976 and almost 3 times the 1970 total. At the end of 1977, Canadians owned $293.7 billion of life insurance. This figure represents an increase of $36.0 billion over the amount at the end of 1976 and, once again, is approximately 3 times the 1970 figure. Canadians buy their life insurance in a highly competitive, international marketplace, served not only by Canadian companies, but also by companies from the United States, Great Britain, and Europe. In turn, a number of Canadian companies, such as Sun Life, have been operating successfully on a worldwide basis for many years.

Of the $293.7 billion of life insurance owned in 1977 by Canadians, 77.1 percent was with Canadian-incorporated companies, 17.5 percent with American companies, and 5.2 percent with British and European-incorporated companies. There are 169 active life insurance companies in Canada: 82 Canadian-incorporated, 68 United States, 10 British, and 9 from continental Europe. Of these 169 firms, 145 are registered under federal laws and 24 hold provincial registration. Federally registered companies provided 94.6 percent of the total life insurance in force at the end of 1977.

Life insurance is one of Canada's most important exports. Over 2 million people in over 20 different countries own policies with Canadian companies in the amount of $76 billion. As Sun Life's operations expanded regionally, nationally, and internationally, the scope and magnitude of the firm's competitive threats grew proportionally. Aside from the formidable threat posed by life insurance companies, an additional threat is represented by the operations of trust companies and the Canadian chartered banks. These institutions generally offer tax-deductible Registered Retirement Savings Plans (RRSPs), a form of annuity. Sun Life's principal competitors are Mutual Life, London Life, Imperial Life, Assurances Desjardins, and its largest competitor, Manufacturers Life. Exhibit 1 presents selected industry average figures for the period 1971–1976.

Finances at Sun Life

An insurance company is highly sensitive to its financial and economic environment. The firm needs to invest its policyholders' premiums at the highest possible yield, consistent with the safety of capital; assure the safety of its investments to guarantee payments to policyholders; and earn a high yield on investments. The Sun Life Assurance Company of Canada is involved in the stewardship of the savings of its hundreds of thousands of policyholders in Canada and throughout the world.

Since the stock market disaster of 1929, insurance companies are restricted as regards their reinvestment opportunities, in that only a certain percentage of capital may be invested in stock. Sun Life's investment portfolio includes stock in Canada's metal, oil and gas, and paper industries, as well as holdings in government bonds, public utility bonds, mortgages, and real estate. The firm's main sources of revenue are premiums from life insurance/annuities and investment income from its own portfolios and those managed on behalf of others. Sun Life's primary uses of funds include: payments to policy-

EXHIBIT 1   Industry Average Figures for Selected Indicators (1971–1976)
(dollar figures in millions)

	1971	1972	1973	1974	1975	1976
Gross Industry Assets	16,771	18,385	20,046	21,656	24,097	26,759
Average Interest Rate Earned (%)	6.35	6.56	6.79	7.11	7.34	7.69
Gross Premium Income $	2,145	2,391	2,756	3,099	3,516	4,010

holders, investment portfolio additions, and operating expenses. Exhibit 2 presents income statements respectively for the years 1972–1977.

Sun Life in 1974 developed a sophisticated computerized model to simulate the liability side of the firm's business. As an insurance company, its business can be conceptualized by the following model:

better. The company philosophy statements acknowledge:

- the unique status of participating policyholders
- the need to maintain adequate financial strength to ensure continuity as a thriving entity
- the dictates of good corporate citizenship.

sales (liabilities)	$\dfrac{\text{\$ from sales support}}{\text{investments}}$	investment management (assets)
corporate model	$\dfrac{\text{\$ from investments}}{\text{support policy payout}}$	investment models

SOURCE   Robert White, *Utilization of Computerized Corporate Models for Strategic Decision Making in Canada* (MBA Thesis, Concordia University, 1980): 19.

Pursuant to powers granted by an Act of parliament (1957–1958), the company purchased, retired, and/or cancelled its entire share capital issue and became a mutual life insurance company. Accordingly, today profit sharing is on a policyholder basis as opposed to a shareholder basis. The policyholders are also the owners of the company and therefore have not only the right to participate in the selection of the board of directors, but also the rights of participation in profit distribution or its reinvestment on their behalf. Canadian legislation requires that a minimum of 97½ percent of distributable profits shall be paid to policyholders as dividends.

Senior Management

Sun Life prides itself on a philosophy of management based on unyielding principles, strong moral character, and a sense of purpose; it believes these influences have helped establish the firm as one of the world's great life insurance companies. The company endeavors to provide services and products which meet the actual and anticipated needs and desires of its present and future policyholders, and for the optimum utilization of its human, physical and financial resources in the quest to serve its constituency

Management of Sun Life is vested in a board of directors whose duties include the supervision and control of the affairs of the corporation. The ultra-conservatism of the upper echelons, and particularly the board of directors, is a tradition: 13 of the 21 directors belong to the exclusive Mount Royal Club of Montreal.

The chairman, Alistair M. Campbell, was the sixth president of Sun Life. Born in Strachur, Argyllshire in Scotland, educated at Inverness Royal Academy and the University of Aberdeen, he graduated in 1927, with an MA with first-class honors in mathematics. He commenced his career as a Sun Life student actuary in 1928. On returning from military leave in 1946, he assumed the post of actuary. While directing the battle against foreign control in 1962, Campbell was named president of the firm. In February of 1970, he was elected chairman of the executive committee of the board of directors, a position he retains.

The president, Thomas M. Galt, a Manitoban, was educated at Ashbury College and had completed 3 years' studies at Queen's University before entering the Royal Canadian Air Force in 1941. After 4 years of service and holding the rank of Flight Lieutenant, he returned to Kingston, Ontario to complete his degree. He graduated in 1948 (from the University of Manitoba) with a B.Comm. degree with honors in the ac-

EXHIBIT 2   Sun Life Assurance Company of Canada — Income Statements

	1977	1976	1975	1974	1973	1972
Revenues						
Premiums for insurances — life	416,001,863	406,865,611	378,645,374	352,205,968	341,837,385	332,101,721
— health	71,258,153	63,156,332	55,159,642	44,031,590	33,864,162	28,002,290
Sub-total	487,260,016	470,021,943	433,805,016	396,237,558	375,701,547	360,104,011
Premiums for annuities	151,929,523	146,664,085	95,934,789	61,254,959	42,342,948	37,316,973
Policy proceeds/amounts left at interest	60,833,731	58,110,885	51,940,386	49,283,574	50,779,419	50,344,882
Interest, dividends and rents	364,199,253	328,401,674	291,768,239	266,638,959	251,459,334	233,021,833
Net gain from the sale/ redemption of securities after adjustment of asset values	4,461,442	1,478,394	1,066,728	1,009,176	2,427,333	3,036,437
Variable accumulation and other segregated fund deposits and other income	103,281,685	135,707,283	138,023,119	77,356,019	87,597,332	122,148,593
Total revenue	1,171,965,650	1,140,384,264	1,012,538,277	851,780,245	810,307,913	805,972,729
Expenses						
Payment to policyholders & beneficiaries						
Death benefits	119,618,730	117,598,265	108,710,532	103,150,472	100,017,515	94,888,690
Disability benefits	3,509,515	3,411,484	3,251,638	3,265,219	2,910,013	3,237,606
Matured endowments	27,764,675	31,615,887	33,371,251	32,855,132	33,837,935	33,571,919
Annuity payments	54,812,200	46,307,125	37,954,326	32,636,200	23,625,372	22,252,485
Dividends	104,833,601	98,797,935	95,679,546	84,687,101	82,590,611	80,551,272
Surrender values	82,034,241	76,734,410	73,608,876	67,946,749	63,463,455	81,615,278
Health insurance benefits	67,397,750	58,147,263	48,852,206	40,833,014	30,283,369	24,892,283
Variable accumulation/ segregated fund pmts.	41,110,868	47,386,796	19,294,719	28,808,635	36,376,393	9,381,719
Sub-total	501,081,580	479,999,165	420,723,094	394,082,522	373,158,563	350,391,252
Payments of policy proceeds and other amounts previously left at interest	63,674,453	59,408,501	52,926,514	71,936,896	56,284,391	60,407,953
Additions to actuarial liabilities	306,588,821	305,647,250	220,762,034	153,470,995	168,123,472	142,627,888
Variable accumulation/segregated fund	62,170,817	88,320,487	118,728,400	48,544,241	51,301,379	112,602,714
Operating expenses including commissions	150,226,824	149,653,584	135,752,897	117,611,335	112,646,275	101,331,203
Government taxes	40,434,993	32,995,714	26,629,674	26,334,376	31,353,814	23,315,809
Addition to reserve for fluctuation in securities	16,300,000	5,000,000	9,000,000	25,000,000	3,000,000	3,000,000
Increase in surplus	31,488,162	19,359,563	28,015,664	14,799,880	14,440,019	12,295,883
Total Expenses:	1,171,965,650	1,140,384,264	1,012,538,277	851,780,245	810,307,913	805,972,729

tuarial sciences. He joined Sun Life as a clerk in the Mathematical Department, assuming the position of chief clerk in 1950. In 1951, he attained his Fellowship in the Society of Actuaries and was named Sun Life's assistant mathematician. By 1953, he had been elevated to the post of mathematician. In 1961, Galt was named actuary of the company. In 1963, he was named vice-president and chief actuary and, in 1968, he assumed the position of executive vice-president. Galt was elevated to the board in 1970 and was confirmed as president in early 1972.

Corporate Image and Social Responsibility

Sun Life's corporate image has a two-sided perspective. On one hand, the firm is seen to represent a shining example of how a large corporation should behave. The company's image has traditionally projected a sense of stability and prosperity. During the Depression, Sun Life continually hired personnel and gave them training of an exceptionally high quality. These otherwise destitute individuals were able to survive tragic times with a sense of worth and dignity. On leaving Sun Life, departing personnel were better able to market their services, as they had been trained to a very high standard.

Sun Life contributed heavily to the war effort — it only stopped buying war bonds at a point where more than half of the company's assets consisted of these low-return financial instruments. Sun Life encouraged its employees to fight for Canada during World War II, assured them of their jobs on return, and ensured that there was no monetary loss involved in joining the armed forces.

When Sun Life in India was nationalized, the company changeover was carried out without malice or ill-will.

In 1976, Sun Life sponsored the Olympic Games by providing physiotherapy equipment for use by the athletes. After the games, the equipment was offered to hospitals and rehabilitation centers across Canada. In 1977, in association with the Canadian personal fitness organization, ParticipAction, and the Kinsmen Club, Sun Life became involved in the construction of public parks and fitness trails across the country.

In collaboration with the Canadian Red Cross, Sun Life distributes a film on water safety and, in association with ParticipAction, a film dealing with cardiovascular health.

Sun Life's "Get Your Life In Shape" campaign in 1977 was selected as one of the four winning entries of the corporate "Social Responsibility Advertising Award." This campaign also won the coveted "Andy Award of Merit" from the Advertising Club of New York, as well as numerous other awards recognizing merit and responsibility in promotion.

The firm regularly makes monetary contributions to various local hospitals and the United Appeal. Senior management also encourages other corporate donations to charitable organizations from the insurance industry.

Socio-political Environment

Quebec society changed radically during the early 1960s in what was known as the "Quiet Revolution." This period saw sweeping social change; these times were marked by the increasing intervention of government into the private domain. Nationalization of the electric utilities serves as an example of the aggressive legislative course plotted by the provincial administration. One of the main proponents of these measures was René Lévesque, now premier of Quebec.

There was a general reawakening of Quebec nationalism which had long lain dormant. On November 15, 1976, the Parti Québecois, led by René Lévesque had swept into power in a provincial general election. The major tenet of the party's platform pledged to effect the separation of the province from Confederation.

The PQ government's first legislative priority was language. In August 1977, in the form of Bill 101, French became the official working language of Quebec. While the Bill did not specifically delineate regulations regarding head office regulations, the law was perceived as a formidable obstacle for large multinational firms headquartered in Montreal. The education provisions of Bill 101 created concern at Sun Life. Under the terms of the legislation, the children of immigrant parents were to be funnelled into the French school system. Sun Life stated that this requirement hindered the firm's ability to attract and retain qualified personnel from outside the province. Quite simply, the company believed its ability to secure sufficient personnel with necessary qualifications and fluency in English was being tested.

Other insurance companies voiced similar concerns. The president of Prudential Life Insurance, Ian Mair, stated that recruitment was a key factor contributing to the stability of his company. In response, René Lévesque stated as his opinion that large firms, such as Sun Life, had never shown any great interest in recruiting bilingual francophone graduates from Quebec business schools.

The impact of proposed Quebec sovereignty association in the late 1970s affected policyholders and investors in the insurance industry. Some policyholders or prospective policyholders refused to purchase from any life underwriters with head office operations in Quebec. Even though Sun Life holds a federal charter, it claimed

Employment at Sun Life 1977

Total Company Employees	3430
Quebec employees	2640
Employed in branches	220
Employed at head office	2420
Non-Quebec employees	790
Total Head Office Employees	2420
Unilingual English	1500
Bilingual with French mother tongue	230
Bilingual with English mother tongue	690

that it lost considerable business for this very reason. Proposed Quebec independence created concerns about requirements that a portion of investments should be made within the province. Sun Life viewed suggestions that the value of investments in Quebec should be equal to the value of policy premiums as interfering with its opportunities to maximize yield and control its own destiny. Also of great concern to the business community was the hint of government imposed restrictions on investment flows and deposits in response to the large outflows of capital noted since the 1976 election. Many head offices have abandoned Montreal. A few have moved all of their corporate operations outside Quebec. Often such moves were undertaken so as to arouse little public awareness. Other firms have retained the head office function in Quebec but have transferred sensitive operations elsewhere. Business reasons were often given as justification.

Sun Life's Response

On January 6, 1978, T. M. Galt, president of Sun Life, announced the decision of the company's board of directors to move corporate headquarters from Montreal to Toronto. The reasons given at the time of the announcement included what was termed the "disturbing effect of Bill 101" on the day-to-day operations of the company. Galt pointed out that Sun Life was no longer able to attract qualified anglophone personnel from outside Quebec. This feature was essential to operations, since 92 percent of the firm's business was generated outside the province. The firm had to retain the capability to transact business in English, as approximately 90 percent of its policyholders were English-speaking residents of Canada, the United States, the United Kingdom, and Ireland.

After more than a century of operations in Quebec, Sun Life had become a symbol of the anglophone Montreal business community. Politicians and individuals called the move socially irresponsible. A summary of the various reactions are contained in Appendix 1. Sun Life was branded by some people as a bad corporate citizen and a supporter of Canadian disunity. By July 1980, Sun Life's head office was operating in Toronto.

Appendices to Sun Life Case Study

Appendix 1   Reactions

Summary of media response to the proposed Sun Life move:

- A. Wilson, the *Montreal Star*: "It is the most striking and disturbing demonstration to date of investor uneasiness over the uncertainty inherent in the current Quebec political climate. This is a deeply disturbing period."
- John Meyer, the *Gazette*: "Business is adaptable, but only to the point where it is no longer profitable."

- Nick Auf de Maur, CJAD radio station, Montreal: "We've discovered that head offices are important and a good indicator of the city's economic health. And after years of smugly knowing we were the metropolis and financial capital of Canada (from about 1750 to the early 1970s), we have now discovered competition. Slowly we are discovering that we can no longer rely on good fortune and history (because of our geographic location), but that we actually have to work at it. Montreal, like other cities, has to go out and hustle."

Summary of business community response to the proposed Sun Life move:

- John Bulloch, president of the Federation of Industry and Business: "Montreal has become an economic sewer. Montreal's loss will be Toronto's gain."
- Louis Hébert, chairman, Banque Canadienne Nationale: "Sun Life's move will encourage other companies to move."
- Dominik Dlouhy, chairman, Montreal Stock Exchange: "The situation is tragic, and the shift could accelerate what has been a slow erosion of the financial community in this city."
- Hydro-Québec president Robert Boyd said the utility (which has about 20 000 Sun Life policyholders) will review its participation as Sun Life policyholder.
- The 180 000-member Public Service Alliance of Canada (PSAC) indicated that it may not renew its group insurance plan with Sun Life, which has handled the union's $103-million life and accidental death plan since 1963.
- January 11, 1978, Richard Holden, Montreal lawyer acting on behalf of several unnamed policyholders, brands votes by proxy on Sun Life's proposed move "morally wrong."
- Twenty-seven Toronto MPs urge Sun Life to negotiate a settlement with Quebec to remain in the province.

Summary of federal government response to the proposed Sun Life move:

- January 9, 1978, Finance Minister Jean Chrétien meets Sun Life's president, T. M. Galt and company chairman, Alistair Campbell, in Ottawa. He urges them to reconsider their decision.
- January 13, 1978, in Ottawa Chrétien announces Sun Life directors have agreed to call another meeting of the board to review their decision. "I have good reason to be optimistic that the damage to the city of Montreal and the province of Quebec will be minimized," Chrétien said.
- January 16, 1978, Sun Life agrees to delay meeting to seek approval of its planned move to Toronto for 3 months and promises that there will be no large-scale movement of employees for 2 years.

Summary of official Sun Life commentary on the proposed move:

- T. M. Galt, President: "We are losing considerable business because of the location of our head office. . . . Competition has an unfair advantage because the prospective policyholder is refusing to buy from any company with its head office in Quebec. . . . Sun Life is the custodian of savings central to our business as an insurer. Sun Life is the security of those savings."

Appendix 2
Socio-economic Consequences

- The physical move will cost Sun Life at least $10 million.
- With the transfer of Sun Life, some 1800 jobs will disappear from Montreal. The multiplier effect will put another 6300 jobs in jeopardy.
- Donald Armstrong, a professor of management at McGill University, stated that, "if a head office of 1000 employees leaves Montreal, a further 3000 jobs are lost in the city and another 500 elsewhere in the province."
- Approximately $1.6 million will be lost by the Quebec government in taxes.
- Wheatly and Wilson Ltd., a local office supplier, estimated a decrease in revenues from $150,000 to $200,000 annually.
- $1.5 million in advertising may be shifted to Toronto.
- The Gazette Canadian Printing Ltd. claims that it will lose approximately $140,000 yearly.
- A large share of the audit fees of more than $100,000 in 1975, equipment rentals exceeding $3 million (including an IBM computer system), and about $1 million spent in the company's cafeterias could be lost to Toronto.

Appendix 3   Montreal's Response

Can big firms be replaced?

Special Report by R. G. Gibbens *Montreal Star, May 26, 1979*

Montreal, Jan. 6, 1978 — The Sun Life Assurance Company of Canada is issuing a notice calling a special general meeting of qualified policy-holders . . . to consider: and if deemed advisable, to pass and approve a bylaw changing the head office of the company from Montreal to Toronto.

It came like a bolt from the blue. Word of the pull-out of the Sun Life Assurance Company of Canada, then with over $5 billion in assets and the largest life insurance firm in the country, two years older than Confederation, jolted anglophone Montreal from its post-New Year lethargy.

It jolted the new Parti Québécois government in Quebec City as well. Within hours, the kid gloves were off and an angry minister of finance, Jacques Parizeau, branded the Sun Life as "one of the worst corporate citizens Quebec has ever known."

The government accused the company of underinvesting in the province by $400 million, and a battle of figures then developed as a side-show. And Mr. Parizeau invited all other "bad corporate citizens of Quebec" to leave the province.

Other anglophone firms had moved head offices or departments out of Montreal already since the November, 1976, election. More had threatened to do so because of the climate created by the government. The Sun Life itself nearly a year earlier had warned that English would have to be the language of head office . . . but few were listening.

Symbolic case

But the Sun Life's decision was a landmark in the turbulent history of Montreal and Quebec in the Seventies. The impact left some deep scars in the anglophone and francophone communities, but moderated the attitude of Quebec City.

It was not only the numbers of people who would be leaving the city — 200 or so have already moved and ultimately the total will be around 1,800. Several years before, Sun Life had moved several hundred employees to Boston to man the head office operation for its U.S. business.

More it was the symbolic effect of the decision — the final and irrevocable sign of the steady decline of Montreal from its position as the metropolis of Canada, its commercial centre, its political power-base, and its cultural heart.

In the Parizeau budget which followed the decision of the Sun Life, it became clear that the restrictions on the language of education were not all. Average tax levels for managers in the $30,000 a year class and above emerged with a disadvantage to Quebec of about $2,500 a year. The government eventually softened its proposed rules for the language used in head office operations, but it became even more difficult to get people to transfer from other parts of Canada or from abroad to Quebec operations.

The government had gambled that by putting in the language-of-education restrictions on Canadians moving here from other provinces it would put the gun at the head of Ontario and force a reciprocity agreement to give francophones full educational rights there.

Early trendsetter

The gamble failed, and some members of the Quebec government sincerely regret now that the clause was inserted in Bill 101.

One of the first major companies to move its head office from Montreal with the election of the Parti Québécois government was the American-owned Combustion Engineering, with its main Canadian plant in Sherbrooke for many years. The move involved more than 300 people and the location chosen was Ottawa, then thought of as neutral ground.

The move was clearly announced, but no one took a great deal of notice. Yet for manufacturing industry, especially firms making engineering products for national and international markets and whose business connections are predominantly in English, it was a trendsetter.

Still, in terms of the numbers of people moving out and the spin-off effects on the city's economy, the exodus in the financial sector has been most serious.

The shift of departments of the two anglophone banks, the Royal and the Bank of Montreal, has gone on steadily, partly due directly to government policies, but also due to the growth of Toronto as the financial centre of Canada as well as being the base of the country's most progressive manufacturing industries and high technology firms. The bank moves will total perhaps 1,500.

The re-arrangement of the Royal Trust's assets, so that non-Quebec assets are managed from a new power-centre in Toronto, will mean the departure of nearly 300 head office people.

Technically the headquarters of the mighty Canadian Pacific group remains in Montreal, though its famous redevelopment project for the Windsor Station area is frozen indefinitely.

Grew up here

But the group's financial services and computer operations have largely been moved to Toronto, and the operations base of subsidiary Canadian Pacific Investments (holding company for the non-rail interests) is in Toronto.

In the manufacturing sector, an early mover was the head office of the CAE Industries group, one of Canada's most successful high-technology firms, and which had been built up to international prominence from this city. About 100 people were involved.

Montreal was once the chemical industry centre of Canada, surpassed now by Sarnia. The two best-known companies in this field, Du Pont Canada and CIL, both foreign subsidiaries but with significant autonomy for many years, have moved out engineering, sales and other departments in part, accounting for well over 500 people, though technically their head offices remain and their Quebec manufacturing operations have been in an expansion phase.

Lesser-known names such as Cyanamid Canada and Allied Chemical Canada are committed to move head offices — they are in the same general sector.

In general manufacturing, the Redpath group is now operated from Toronto, Cadbury-Schweppes, for a long time a prominent employer on Masson Street, Montreal, has shifted to Whitby, Ont.

Standard Brands Ltd., the highly successful Canadian arm of the big U.S.-based multinational food processing giant, decided to move from Montreal in late 1977. It was another trendsetter for manufacturing industry. About 200 people were involved.

At the time the company had annual volume running at over $325 million a year and its meteoric expansion in this country had been planned and executed from its long standing headquarters on Sherbrooke St.

The company is now part of the Toronto head office scene.

One of the oldest names in Quebec manufacturing, Canron Ltd., the manufacturer of steel and concrete products and one of the largest companies of its kind in Canada, is in the process of moving its head office operation to Toronto.

In pharmaceuticals, Smith, Kline & French Canada Ltd. decided to meet rising national demand on its manufacturing and research operations by building anew in Ontario. Its head office operations have moved to the sister province, and the old Montreal plant will become a Quebec satellite manufacturing and sales operation.

For warmer climes

In the transportation field, British Airways moved its Canadian head office to Toronto last year, and in real estate, Trizec Corp. is operated from Toronto and Calgary more than Montreal, and the executive power of Genstar, which is also very important in building materials and financial services, is on its way to warmer and more hospitable climes in San Francisco.

Several hundred people, from senior executives to lower managerial staff, either have or will be leaving Montreal because of these moves.

Appendix 4

SUN LIFE ASSURANCE COMPANY OF CANADA

Notice of a Special General Meeting of the Company

Notice is hereby given that a Special General Meeting of the Company will be held in the Canadian Room of the Royal York Hotel, 100 Front Street West, Toronto, Ontario, at 11:00 A.M. on Tuesday, the 25th day of April, 1978 for the following purposes, namely:

1. To consider and, if deemed advisable, to pass and approve the following by-law:

"By-law 1(a)

The Head Office of the Company is hereby changed from the City of Montreal in the Province of Quebec, Canada, to the Municipality of Metropolitan Toronto in the Province of Ontario, Canada."

2. To transact such further and other business as may properly come before the Meeting or any adjournment thereof.

DATED at Montreal

this   day of

1978

By order of the Board
P. R. MacGibbon
Vice-President and Secretary

Sun Life Building,
1155 Metcalfe Street,
Montreal, Que.

SUN LIFE ASSURANCE COMPANY OF CANADA
Head Office, Montreal

February 15, 1978

TO: PARTICIPATING POLICYHOLDERS OF THE SUN LIFE ASSURANCE COMPANY OF CANADA

Dear Member:

I am writing to you on a very important matter. The Board of Directors of the Company has decided to call a Special General Meeting of the members to be held on April 25, 1978, for the purpose of considering and if deemed advisable passing a by-law changing the Head Office of the Company from Montreal, Quebec to Toronto, Ontario, all as set out more fully in the accompanying Information Circular.

The Board of Directors considers that the proposed change of Head Office is in the best interests of the policyholders and of the Company. The Board accordingly recommends the change and solicits "For" votes of members of the Company in favour of passage and approval of the by-law.

We invite you to read the Information Circular carefully and urge you to support the change by signing the enclosed form of proxy and mailing it to the Company in the enclosed postage paid envelope as soon as you conveniently can.

Yours sincerely,

T. M. Galt
President

SOURCE T. Kubicek from Harold A. Gram, *Facts & Figures: Cases in Business Policy* (Toronto: Wiley, 1982): 152–170. Reprinted by permission of the author.

QUESTIONS

1. Was Sun Life's decision to move its head office from Montreal to Toronto socially irresponsible? Explain.

2. When there is a conflict between corporate profitability and the provision of jobs, how should a decision be made? Do you think this was the case for Sun Life?

3. To what extent is government responsible for creating an environment that facilitates business activity?

CASE STUDY 2

Maids, Maids, Maids Inc.

Following the sale of his small business, Corporate Janitorial Services, Desmond Kennedy decided to move to Edmonton. After 3 months of relative inactivity, he became itchy for an entrepreneurial challenge. Not long afterward he noticed an advertisement for Minit Maids, a franchised residential-cleaning operation. After a brief conversation with a Minit Maid representative, Kennedy determined that, if he wanted to enter this field, he would be better to strike out on his own.

A search through *The Entrepreneur* magazine revealed a May 1979 article entitled "Maid Service Mops Up Money." The article described high first-year profits, low start-up costs, and rapid growth. Experience indicated that teams of 2 to 4 maids could clean 7 to 10 apartments or houses in one day. The team-cleaning approach was found to be price-competitive with traditional single housecleaners and, with better training and technology, could result in a better job.

Kennedy decided that, before investing any more time or money on this opportunity, he should try to find out something about the competition. From the telephone directory he identified 12 firms currently serving the Greater Edmonton market. All of the competitors performed the same set of standard services:

- Washing and waxing floors
- Vacuuming rugs and furniture
- Cleaning fridges and stoves
- Cleaning appliances and countertops
- Cleaning bathroom and kitchen tiles and fixtures
- Cleaning kitchen sink and cupboard fronts
- Dusting and polishing wood furniture
- General tidying
- Changing bed linen
- Washing inside windows and window sills.

Of the 12 identified competitors, Desmond Kennedy was able to obtain information from 8. (See Exhibit 1.) One telephone number was no longer in service; at two companies no answer could be obtained after repeated calls; and one firm used an automatic answering device but did not respond to the message. Kennedy wondered what implications these data had for corporate life expectancy in this industry.

Although he was surprised by the number of competitors, he was not discouraged. He felt that there was a large opportunity in the residential-cleaning business. From his conversations with the various cleaning firms, he identified a number of different pricing schemes. None of the companies reported formal contracts with customers. Two firms bonded their employees and two said they were insured to cover security problems. Four of the eight firms contacted operated on a team basis, while the other four sent out individual cleaners. Three cleaning companies provided training, another one sent its people to a community college course, and a fifth firm had an on-the-job training program.

Kennedy was convinced that his background in the office-cleaning field gave him an advantage in terms of technology and selection and training of personnel. He believed the market would continue to grow. Kennedy cited the following factors:

- The increasing number of women in the workforce
- The growth in household incomes
- The decrease in family size (for instance, more singles and more childless couples)
- Changing values which place more emphasis on keeping fit, being creative, doing important things and give less importance to mundane household activities
- More people living in apartments
- The growing intensity of life with family members involved in a multitude of activities.

In evaluating the home-cleaning business, Desmond Kennedy concluded that there were a number of needs satisfied. First, and perhaps most important, is the natural need to be clean. This is perhaps magnified in Canada by the Protestant Ethic and by the concern that someone might see one's home is not tidy. Another important need satisfied by a maid service is the desire to have time free to satisfy other needs, such as recreation and creative activities. There is also a sense of social status which may be had by being able to say, or perhaps just to think, "I have someone do my house cleaning for me." In a household where both husband and wife are employed, having a cleaning service may reduce the friction among spouses and children related to keeping their home tidy. Kennedy was also made aware of a modern aspect of this problem, described by a young woman. Before hiring a maid service, this young working woman had shared the cleaning chores with her husband. If he didn't perform his share well, and they had guests arrive, she felt that the guests would see her as a poor homemaker, not thinking that the husband was at fault.

In considering a target market for his proposed operation, Kennedy wondered whether he would be best to target on particular geographic areas, particular types of residences, or particular types of people. These factors obviously intertwined. There were a number of areas in the city with large family homes occupied by high-income professional and managerial people. There were a few districts with concentrations of apartment buildings where, in many cases, both spouses worked. Most of these people were at the ex-

tremes of the family life cycle. In other areas, there were multitudes of average-sized homes within which resided households with a number of employed members. For example, it seemed to Kennedy that there were many families in which both the parents and one or more adult children were employed.

Should Maids, Maids, Maids — the first name which popped into Kennedy's head and which he was stuck on — go into geographic areas where there was competition or try to identify an area that was not now serviced heavily? Should Kennedy try to take customers away from current services or identify people who were not now using a cleaning company?

Kennedy envisioned his service taking the form of a number of two-person crews, carefully trained and motivated to work with efficiency. Each worker would be bonded. Teams would travel on a pre-set route in an economy car. They would be equipped with tote-boxes of cleaning materials and highly efficient vacuum cleaners. Each worker would wear a distinctive smock with large pockets to carry cleaning tools and chemicals. Arrangements would be made with customers to be admitted to their homes by means of a key, apartment manager, or neighbor. The cleaners would be trained to move through each room in a predetermined time and fashion. Teams would operate systematically; each member would specialize in certain rooms of the residence. One team member would be designated as lead hand and would be responsible for the team's performance. The prime orientation would be to do an extremely good cleaning job very quickly. This would be the major selling point for Maids, Maids, Maids, according to Kennedy.

To ensure quality control, Kennedy was considering an inspection form that the lead hand would complete for each customer's home. It would list the standard and extra services performed and have an area for comments. The team would leave a copy of this inspection form behind for the customer and turn a copy into the office. Unannounced spot checks would be made by Kennedy, who would also telephone a selected group of customers each week to ascertain whether they were satisfied.

Kennedy was also thinking about a set of extra functions which could be performed on a complimentary basis. Such things as polishing silverware, cleaning the oven, or washing a wall

EXHIBIT 1   Companies Competing in the Home Cleaning Market in Greater Edmonton

Company	Price	Contract	Bonding	Team/ Individuals	Training
Molly's Home Cleaning Service Ltd.	$10.00/1st hour $8.00/each add. hour per person	no	no—insured	teams of 3	on-the-job
Edmonton Personnel	$4.50–$5.00/h plus carfare	no	no	individuals (placement agency)	no
Classical Personnel	$6.00/h	yes, bring girls from overseas to work for 12 months	yes	individuals	no
Helping Hands Agency	$7.50/h minimum $30.00	no	no—unnecessary expense— checks refs., checks up new employees with customers	individuals, sometimes teams	community college fall, spring sessions
Broomhilda's Services	$17/wk. 1-bd. apt. $25/wk. 2-bd. apt. $30–$50 houses windows $15–$20 extra	no	insured	both individuals and teams	yes
OMO Maid Service	makes estimates for ea. job; 3 bdm. 2 bth. home $45/wk.	no	yes	teams of 2 or 3	yes
Ajax Home Services	quotation basis	no	no—checks refs.	individuals	yes
Mop Squad	$30/1st visit $24/subsequent visit	no	yes	not available	n.a.
Girl Tuesday	n.a.	n.a.	n.a.	n.a.	n.a.
Overseas Home Help	n.a.	n.a.	n.a.	n.a.	n.a.
Top Notch Services	n.a.	n.a.	n.a.	n.a.	n.a.
Exquisite	n.a.	n.a.	n.a.	n.a.	n.a.

Variable costs, calculated as follows:	Per hour	
Wages:		
Lead hand $5.00 + 5 percent for benefits	$5.25	
Cleaner $4.75 + 5 percent for benefits	4.99	
Total for crew		$10.24/h
Materials:		
Gas and oil	$0.40	
Cleaning materials	$0.60	1.00
Total variable costs		$11.24/h

Fixed costs, estimated to be:	Per month	
Fixed costs per crew:		
Leased vehicle	$130	
Insurance and handling	40	
Equipment depreciation	50	
	$220/month	
General fixed costs:		
Office rent	$150	
Telephone and answering service	105	
Leased vehicle	130	
Advertising	40	
Business license	30	
Miscellaneous	20	
	$475/month	

Assuming each crew would work 160 hours per month, fixed costs per crew per hour would be:

One crew	$4.34
Two crews	2.86
Three crews	2.36
Four crews	2.12
Five crews	1.97
Six crews	1.87

EXHIBIT 2   Kennedy's Variable and Fixed Costs

could be done at no charge every once in a while to surprise the customer. Kennedy felt that this would be valuable for retention of customers.

Determining what price to charge was difficult. Based on his analysis of the competition, and considering it would take about 1½ hours for a crew of 2 to clean a unit, the average competitive price might be between $25 and $30.

Competitive prices ranged between $17 for a one-bedroom apartment to $50 for a large house.

Kennedy assembled the information in Exhibit 2.

With an average cleaning job taking 3 person-hours and 30 minutes travelling between assignments (a lapsed time of 2 hours), the variable and fixed costs per job would be:

One crew   2 x $11.24 + 2 x $4.34 = $31.16
Two crews   2 x $11.24 + 2 x $2.86 = $28.20
Three crews   2 x $11.24 + 2 x $2.36 = $27.20
Four crews   2 x $11.24 + 2 x $2.12 = $26.72
Five crews   2 x $11.24 + 2 x $1.97 = $26.42
Six crews   2 x $11.24 + 2 x $1.87 = $26.22

If the operation was to generate a surplus of $10,000 to compensate Kennedy for his work and risk, the average price to customers would have to be:

One crew $31.16 + $10.42 = $41.58
Two crews $28.20 + $ 5.21 = $33.41
Three crews $27.20 + $ 3.47 = $30.67
Four crews $26.72 + $ 2.60 = $29.32
Five crews $26.42 + $ 2.08 = $28.50
Six crews $26.22 + $ 1.74 = $27.96

Clearly, Kennedy would have to have a number of crews operating to bring the price in line with the market. Attracting customers, he felt, would be based on an aggressive marketing campaign emphasizing superior cleaning, speed, efficiency, and trustworthiness. He considered that a direct mail campaign followed up by personal selling would be the best way to kick off his marketing program. He was convinced that, once the operation was off the ground, word of mouth would result in fast growth.

The personnel area was one which Kennedy considered to be key to the success of this venture. Should he recruit people experienced in cleaning or just try to attract willing and able individuals? Would it be best to advertise for employees, work through an employment agency, or contact Employment Canada? Kennedy knew that turnover would likely be high at first, and he wanted to reduce this as much as possible by careful selection, good training and supervision, and some form of incentive. Based on comments in the article in *The Entrepreneur*, Kennedy planned to use his own home as a training center for the first teams. Once a number of clients had been obtained, on-the-job training with lead hands would be possible.

Desmond Kennedy was not sure what success the Minit Maids organization had had in selling franchises, but he felt that this was a fast-developing opportunity. He believed he should decide right away whether to enter this market or not.

SOURCE Robert G. Wyckham from Beckman, Good and Wyckham, *Small Business Management: Concepts and Cases* (Toronto: Wiley, 1982). Reprinted by permission of the publisher.

QUESTIONS

1. What are the strong and weak points of Desmond Kennedy's idea?
2. What kinds of supervision and control problems might Kennedy encounter?
3. What will be involved in performing the four basic functions of management?
4. Should Kennedy start the proposed company? Indicate how you reached this decision.

CASE STUDY 3

City of Fasofurn, Ontario

Fasofurn is a mid-sized municipality located in southern Ontario. The Planning and Development Department is one of eight municipal government departments integrated into a well-defined hierarchy. This department is responsible for the administration of the majority of bylaws and actions which affect private property. The department is comprised of urban planning, land use control (zoning), building and plumbing inspection, and property mainte-nance. (See the area within the dotted line in Exhibit 1.) With the exception of municipal taxes which it does not handle, the enforcement of all municipal bylaws, the inspection of all building and property, and all short-term and long-range planning that affects private property is controlled by this department.

By the fall of 1976 the director of planning and development had become concerned that his department was not functioning as effectively as it should. He felt that increasing staff dissatisfaction represented an important symptom of this problem. The following is an initial report which the director submitted to a firm of management consultants who were retained by the city to study the municipal government.

Unlike all other city departments, which are directly responsible solely to the city administrator, some employees of my department are responsible not only to me, and thus to the city administrator, but also to boards and committees that may or may not be responsible to city council.

There are occasions when council opposes a committee decision and staff are requested to testify before the Ontario Municipal Board (OMB), the provincial government's body that regulates municipalities. Staff try to maintain their professionalism and testify in accordance with their prior decision. However, conflicts of interest may arise because council pays all staff wages. Over the years some staff planners have found themselves unemployed for some minor reason, after testifying too many times for the side opposing council. Our professional staff thus learned the hard way and now strive to reach a compromise when disputes arise. They are still left in an untenable position regarding some matters.

One recent case found planning board and department staff supporting an official plan amendment for a commercial development project which would have benefitted a neighborhood. The residents had been using the area as a private park and did not want the developer to build on his property. The ratepayers association raised such a commotion that council reversed the board's recommendation and the developer appealed to the OMB. The city solicitor requested council to hire an outside planner to support the city's negative decision, since staff had favored the proposal. Council gave instructions to the solicitor to discredit its own planning staff, which he did and won the case for council.

One cannot help but notice the ramifications of this type of situation, which occurs frequently. Despite these instances which impair relations between staff and council, the department generally operates more smoothly than other city departments and has far more real output.

Procedures

The rules and regulations within the city government are very rigid. All bylaws and amendments thereto which it enforces are prepared by solicitors. All procedures and terms of reference are to be updated regularly to ensure all aspects of any work are covered. There are very few gray areas. When one is discovered, it must be clarified through either a legal interpretation, a policy statement, or an amending bylaw.

The degree of discretion for municipal employees would appear limited or nil. However, depending upon council's attitude (which will be discussed below), the staff acquire a sense of where discretion may be used. In gray areas or where procedures are not spelled out, the staff use their own discretion, as long as decisions can be substantiated if called upon to do so at a later date. This department has, on occasion, told council not to enforce its bylaws and constantly recommends amendments to make these bylaws and documents more flexible. Although our bylaws and procedures have rigid time requirements for staff action spelled out, discretion regarding enforcement is left between the accused and the staff member, provided his or her action can be justified if required.

Flexibility and discretion is a dangerous thing for staff. When one works for 13 elected members, one soon learns that 13 interpretations of a single issue will arise. If it is black and white, staff can avoid trouble by a strict interpretation. But, when staff provide flexibility to better serve the public, their job positions or chances for promotion are placed in jeopardy if their discretionary decisions do not sit favorably with the elected. Staff can always make decisions which meet the approval of 90 percent of council. However the opposing 10 percent is not the same 10 percent for each case. It only takes 7 members of the 13-member council to remember some instance when staff did not support their view. They return the favor when staff are reviewed for promotion or for a salary increase. This is the one major reason government employees do not desire discretionary powers.

Recently, I was verbally attacked by an alderman for having a charge laid against a person for a zoning violation. The accused had cleaned up an abandoned eyesore building in an industrial zone and opened a commercial venture, which was not permitted. The alderman accused

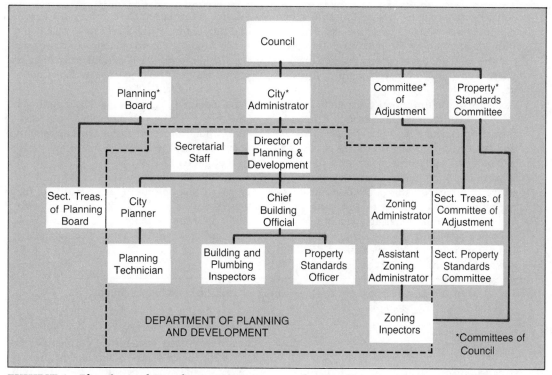

EXHIBIT 1 **Planning and Development Department showing liaison with city council boards and committees**

our department of being cold, inflexible, harassing, and forcing individuals onto the welfare roll. The following day the same alderman accused us of using no discretion when we legally issued a building permit for a house addition along his street, which he felt would devalue the streetscape. It is a perfect example of staff following the bylaws of their council and being accused on both occasions of using no discretion when the outcome did not agree with one member of council.

The degree of impersonality in administering the regulations could have been described as extreme at one time. However, our department is now trying to create a more positive city attitude. When proposals do not comply to regulations, we do not use the "that's it — like it or not" attitude. We say, "Sure you can do it if you get these extra approvals," such as in the Committee of Adjustment or council. We also explain how the system works, how long it will take, what the cost will be, what the chances are, and whether or not we will support the request. We attempt to treat members of the pub-

lic in the way we would want to be treated, if we were in their position.

Several months ago, a professional engineer visited our offices to obtain a building permit to renovate a house into offices for his staff. He was given a firm reply that he could not do that. Although the zone in which the house was located was zoned commercial, conversions from residential to commercial had to meet certain criteria, such as off-street parking and lot size, which his property could not do. He stormed out of the office only to advise by letter the following day that he was suing the municipality. I had the concerned staff member reply to his letter, stating that he had not said the engineer could not renovate the house but that Committee of Adjustment permission was needed before he could renovate. The gentleman returned to our office. We explained the procedure, supported his application, and we lost. But, he did go away happier, with an understanding of the system, and the feeling that he had received all the help and support that could be expected.

1. Advise council on the means of implementing its goals which affect this department through recommending bylaws, policy procedures, and related programs and setting department goals, objectives, and planned actions.
2. Achieve and maintain an open and mutual system of communication through which information can pass between this department and the general public. Members of council and other administrative staff are to create a climate of understanding and cooperation.
3. Strive to project an image of courteousness, friendliness, and sensitivity to members of the general public so as to overcome their apprehensions; provide the service in a similar manner we would expect if we were on the other side of the counter.
4. Provide information to members of the general public to expand their knowledge about the use and regulation of land; stimulate their input and interest in development in order to encourage their involvement in the future of the community.
5. Advise council, its boards, and the public on the management, development, conservation, and protection of our municipal resources of land, water, and air as they relate to the quality of life.
6. Keep abreast of improved techniques and concepts that pertain to the operation of this department to provide improved information, optimum efficiency, and a desirable standard of service, all at an acceptable cost.

EXHIBIT 2   Goals and objectives of the Department of Planning and Development

Goals and Objectives

The department established, for the first time, long-range goals during January of this year. (See Exhibit 2.) We did have policy established for our day-to-day procedures, but we had not previously formulated goals that our department could strive to realize. The goals were established by senior people and basically apply to our public image. These goals cover such items as achieving better communication with the public, being more sensitive to the public, encouraging more public input, and advising the public of the management of land, water, and air.

Although we realized it would take years of effort to change the public's thinking about municipal employees, the goals were established provisionally for one year. Many employees immediately noticed a change of attitude at the senior level and changed also. Some remained the way they were. All knew that goals existed, but many did not know how this would affect them, or even what the goals meant to the overall operation of the department. The senior staff failed to explain adequately the overall philosophy.

I am now in the process of explaining the reasons for our goals to each employee and am receiving startling feedback as a result. Although the younger, more aggressive intermediate staff agree with the goals, the older, longer-term employees do not want the public knowing more than absolutely necessary, in the event that the public might challenge an administrative decision. This same group also wants to discourage, instead of encourage public input. They appear to be afraid that they, the staff, will be proven wrong; instead of adopting the intended attitude that the public's feelings are a necessary consideration in every proposed change. At the other end of the scale, we have employees who are not in the least interested in goals. These are the younger ones, people who work in the department just because it is a job and who would move on for better money. There are also a few in this group who do not care about the department goals since only senior staff prepared them and they had no input. These differences in opinion seem defined by age group. The older, more established employees do not want change. The intermediate level, who are career oriented, strive to reach established goals. The younger, alienated employees do not care in the least what goals are established.

Policy had previously been established through tradition and authoritarian decree. Along with the municipality's general change in attitude to lessen the degree of bureaucracy and our department's internal goal setting, we are now beginning to review and revise policies to use wider staff participation. On one recent occasion, a task force was established. Although the task force created much strife at the senior level because I did not explain my motives clearly enough, it did facilitate the required communication links.

I had decided it was time to review our policy for accepting building permit applications, because the requirements set down by the Ontario government had changed and it had been years since the policy's last review. The chief official was appalled at the thought of changing a policy he had established earlier. He saw nothing wrong with it as it was. The head secretary, whose clerk was responsible for accepting the permits, was of the opinion that the policy did not reflect today's requirements, was difficult to follow, and created unnecessary paperwork and confusion for the public. The two were at loggerheads. I established a task force among the clerks in the secretarial staff receiving permits and the inspectors under the chief building official for whom the applications were received. I wanted fresh ideas from these people who were actually involved in the process. I thought both divisions would keep their superiors informed of what was happening, so I did not take time to explain my action to the division heads whose employees were involved in the task force.

Unforeseen problems occurred. The chief building official was infuriated that only clerks and inspectors were being allowed to establish policy. He ordered his inspectors to prepare the policy by themselves, submit it, and say the other division was involved. The inspectors then told the chief official that they were selected without him because I had lost my confidence in him as a leader. The head secretary was upset because she thought the policy had been established without her clerks' input, which was not what had been decided earlier when the task force was established. And the lonely clerk, who reported to the head secretary, was still anxiously awaiting the first task force meeting to put forward a collection of ideas.

After the task force staff were assembled and the motives explained, the task force quickly established the policy, implemented it without senior staff ratification, and established a communication link which had never existed before. The chief official, however, still will not recognize the new policy and continues to work with the old.

Communication

Our organization could be described as a typical hierarchy, and the chain of command attitude is enforced to show authority. We have always stressed two-way communication because upward communication keeps senior staff aware of what is happening at the lower levels and serves as a motivator for the worker. With our tall organization, supervisors are more accessible than with a flat organization, because fewer people report to each manager. It is not unusual to find the worker, senior staff, and department head sitting together to find a solution.

To encourage upward communication to our council, I attempt to call bimonthly meetings of the council committee I report to. Most departments object to such committee meetings. They do not appreciate the elected representatives dealing in matters over which they feel departments should have control. Our staff enjoy the meetings because they let the elected representatives know what we are thinking and vice versa. Whether or not they implement our recommendations is not as important as the continuing contact.

Lateral communication between departments has been encouraged to reduce senior staff's workload. Formerly, most communications were directed through the hierarchy, leaving most senior staff no time except to handle communications. With the present system, the communication travels laterally, and a copy of the letter or a verbal report is given to the supervisor to keep him or her informed. Some departments ask that their employees remain at the department for all business, but I encourage physical movement for face-to-face discussion if the other department is within easy reach. As a social builder it is great; for immediate feedback it is even better. It consumes more time, but usually more relevant information is volunteered, which may help in any decision.

Like most organizations, we have an unofficial network which can be of great benefit if department heads could tap into it. Usually, however, I never become involved unless a disgruntled employee complains about a circulating rumor. I found this system very informative prior to becoming part of the management but, since my promotion, I have been entirely cut out. Most of the information circulating within this network did have to do with management decisions. Because that information was so informative when I was working my way through the ranks, I now circulate minutes of senior staff meetings to my own employees, which in turn are fed into the unofficial network. The idea is not to control this system but to ensure undistorted information is received by it.

Downward authoritarian communication is avoided wherever possible because of the coldness and demoralizing effect of the order. However, I do have one long-term employee who can be moved in no other manner. He hates change and even verbal direction has no effect. Anything of any importance must be written to him giving full directions. I do not know whether this is a result of his having spent so much time in the navy, or whether it is a result of him wishing to cover himself for every move or decision he makes.

Our channels of communication are among divisions within the organization, among our department and other city departments, and between our department and the general public. At one time our means of transmission was by personal letter. Now, we stress telephone calls to the public or to other departments and personal contact within the department. We have found that this method has cut down on distortion as well as providing immediate feedback. We follow up any out-of-the-ordinary telephone conversation with a confirming letter. We have also attempted to hire qualified technical help, on a part-time basis, which costs a little more per week, but has drastically cut down on training time and errors caused by the misunderstanding of technical matters.

External Relationships

Since we are a department within a municipal body, we have dealings with city council, provincial government departments, programs and legislation, public wants and needs, other city departments, and the housing market and construction industry. Also important, though indirectly, are the influence of federal legislation on provincial policies; provincial legislation on municipal programs and policy; federal and provincial legislation and municipal policy regarding other city departments; market conditions and the construction industry; and the public's influence on municipal, provincial, and federal representatives.

To keep abreast of this complex external environment, we meet regularly with council, provincial departments, and other municipal departments to discover what types of legislation, policies, and programs are being proposed. We also monitor government newsletters, local papers, and opinion polls. We have even developed a system to provide this type of information to any external person or organization who requests it. Good communication links exist to our federal and provincial members of parliament, and we have a former provincial government employee on staff with numerous contacts within the provincial civil service.

Thus we were able to discover one funding program prior to its release by the federal government and quickly take the necessary steps to take full advantage of it. This will result in the city receiving close to $1.5 million in grants. Similarly, an Ontario program resulted in a $5.58 million noninterest loan to the city. During one of our regular meetings with the provincial government representatives, they had accidentally mentioned that the new program was forthcoming.

To keep the provincial and federal bureaucrats informed of our interests, we have established an arrangement with our mayor where we prepare a letter for his signature to our local MP or MPP. This has been very effective, since the elected representatives respond far better to other elected officials than they do to civil service staff.

Although committees of our council meet almost daily, council, the legislating body, meets only twice per month. Some member of the public might ask permission of council to do something for which council's permission is needed. Two weeks later they meet and refer it to staff for a recommendation. We respond and they adopt it one month after the original letter was received. If they need more information, there is a delay of another two weeks. The public are also very slow to respond. We publicize apartment rezonings on radio, on television, and in the newspaper. We mail notices to everyone within 122 m but few respond. After perhaps a 6- to 9-month period, the builder is ready to start construction and moves onto the site. The public then respond with complaints, but it is too late. The majority of politicians will stick with their original decision but are always sensitive to public pressure and critical of their own staff.

They quietly check to see if we carried out the proper procedures. It is hard on staff morale to have politicians asking demeaning questions of our personnel in front of the televised council sessions, with staff given little opportunity to respond in depth.

Because of the complexity of our work, 80 percent of our staff are professionals; but the strong lines of authority that would be required to force the adoption of current government ideology do not exist. Government bodies are typically slow to act, leaving their staff much time to prepare for any response to the elected. Municipal staff personnel have an advantage over those reporting to the higher levels of government. Our aldermen are elected every two years, and the average turnover is about 40 percent. This forces staff to adopt to a different government philosophy every other year, instead of becoming entrenched and stale as provincial and federal bureaucrats may. Yet this periodic change of bosses may also be a source of hostility and conflict.

One former council always viewed staff as working hand-in-hand with developers against council. A large apartment complex was being designed and a road widening was required as a final condition. A recent transportation study had called for a 3 m widening. The old official plan, which had never been updated, called instead for a grass strip about 1.5 m in width. Normally staff would recommend the result of the latest study. But because of constant criticism by council, the problem was referred to the elected representatives to make a decision. We quietly supported the 3 m widening. After two months, they chose the opposite for no apparent reason. They indicated staff was not telling them what to do. Had it been a cooperative council, staff would have made the decision and had council ratify it, thus saving two months of interest carrying charges for the builder.

SOURCE   Randy Hoffman, *Canadian Management Policy* (Toronto: McGraw-Hill Ryerson, 1981): 168–176. Reprinted by permission.

QUESTIONS

1. Comment on the goal-setting system used by this organization.
2. What are the important organizations in the external environment of the Planning and Development department? How can the department more effectively cope with city council?
3. What kind of leadership style is being exhibited by the Director of Planning and Development?

CASE STUDY 4

Electronics Unlimited

Mike Craig, an economics major from Laurentian University, was employed by Agriculture Canada for the last 3 years at the government offices for this department, in the downtown area of Hamilton, Ontario. His work was assessed as above average and his ability to organize and present work efficiently as noteworthy. His job involved preparing reports and statistics based on current trends and developments in farm management. Mike had a number of colleagues with whom he worked on a cooperative basis, each supplying the others with pertinent data for their studies. The organizational hierarchy under which he worked was a traditional bureaucratic structure; supervisors tend to be formal and impersonal and there is strict adherence to procedure. It was within this atmosphere that Mike performed his research and administrative activity.

Mike's role was very clearly defined: he was assigned a supervisor to whom he reported directly. His research work was submitted at various intervals, but current progress was frequently examined. While there was cooperative effort among the workers, there was very little enthusiasm for the work. The challenge seemed to be missing from the required task, for seldom were the results of his research implemented into a strategy for action. Instead much of the work was collated with other material for government reports and sent to Ottawa.

Mike had been dissatisfied with his job for

about 6 months. He felt he had nowhere to go in this government position and, since he was still single and without family responsibility, he thought it was time to look for a more challenging job. He, therefore, watched the newspapers for an interesting position and consulted a Toronto placement agency for opportunities. His interests, as he described them to an interviewer, were in joining a more growing and dynamic company, possibly a young company looking for people to train as managers in an expanding operation.

Eventually the placement agency in Toronto uncovered an opportunity for Mike in a Montreal firm with a new subsidiary company in northern Toronto, called Electronics Unlimited. The company was new and growing in the field of electronic equipment for the home and office. At present it has a growing sales and distribution network with production to follow in the near future. The product line the company distributes is broad and serves both the industrial and commercial markets. There are many new and innovative developments in this field and in this organization. For example, the Toronto plant is organizing for a more sophisticated warehousing and distribution operation, and plans are forthcoming for a fully integrated Marketing Department.

Frank Wilson, the personnel manager, interviewed Mike Craig for an opening at Electronics Unlimited. Mike was immediately impressed not only with the organization but by the personal style of Frank Wilson who, as a manager, appeared innovative and progressive. He was quite empathetic to Mike's predicament and understood the value of growth opportunities in any company; also the discussion on money and potential for moving up in the organization seemed very promising. Wilson further discussed the young company's need for energetic managers with ambitious goals for achievement. As he suggested: "We have outlets to develop, contacts to be made, people to recruit, and many more activities that will challenge a young college graduate."

Mike was very excited about his meeting with Frank Wilson and his application with the company. He felt sure that Wilson liked him and would offer him a job with the company. The situation, too, he thought would be a complete change from his current position and a welcome relief from the routine. For the first time in 3 years Mike was enthusiastic about his life and the prospects it held for him. The job offer came through 3 weeks later, and he accepted the position with a substantial increase in salary. He was due to begin in early September, and he proceeded to resign from his government position and to find an apartment in Toronto.

The first 2 months on his new job were a real learning experience as Mike Craig made himself acquainted with the people and the situation. Three other recent college graduates were hired from the area at about the same time. One of these was John Corrigon, a marketing major from the University of Western Ontario, a very aggressive, outgoing individual. The other 2 coworkers had degrees from McMaster in engineering and were studying for the MBA degree in the evening. The 4 new employees to the company all seemed to hit it off well at the start.

For the first 6 months the 4 young men were expected to get acquainted with the firm's operation and make themselves available to do reports and other tasks as required by the managers. (See the firm's organizational chart in Exhibit 1.) Mike Craig and John Corrigon became involved with the distribution and sales side of the organization. Their first task was to generate a report on potential users of electronic equipment in the area on a commercial basis. Their guidelines were to examine demographic trends, store openings, potential volumes, and customer needs. The existing group had made some contacts in this area but a thorough report and strategy were required. The managers of various departments indicated they would be available for consultation and enquiries. Craig felt very confident about this new assignment. His economics background provided him with all the knowledge to complete a thorough analysis of the area. Though he and Corrigon kept each other informed about their activities, they worked independently in different areas. Their plan was to meet before the date of submission and review their efforts.

Mike followed a steady pattern of work in the next week, confining much of his efforts to written material and research. Statistics Canada, *Financial Post* surveys of markets, and other books were among his sources of information. He gained confidence as the time passed. Corrigon, to avoid duplication, spent much of his time out of the office and in the field. He visited people and talked to them of their needs and requirements.

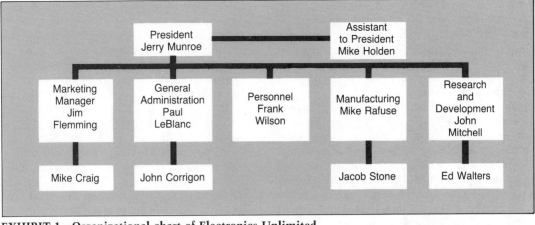

EXHIBIT 1 Organizational chart of Electronics Unlimited

When he was in the office, he frequently visited the executive offices to gather information and to learn about the operation. Mike, for his part, conversed with the managers only at lunch. He would also take work home with him at night and at weekends. Many of the avenues he was pursuing were of great interest to him, and he wanted to follow them through in what was now becoming a lengthy report.

Craig and Corrigon met at the end of the month just prior to their submission to management. It was a brief meeting, with Corrigon flipping through Craig's typed pages of report material. Then, behind closed doors on a Friday afternoon, 2 of the managers, Flemming and LeBlanc, discussed the research and activities with the 2 new employees. The meeting was expected to take most of the afternoon, a rather formal atmosphere prevailing throughout the early part of the encounter. Later, however, over coffee the meeting became more relaxed. Jerry Munroe, the president, came in for a moment and exchanged casual comments with the group. It seemed as though Corrigon had got to know Munroe, since they were on a first-name basis. Much of the discussion centered around Corrigon's ideas. He quoted names of people in key locations and presented an understanding of the needs and requirements of the area. Corrigon did not hesitate to initiate discussion and when necessary to focus the direction of the meeting. Craig, on the other hand, spoke infrequently and made vague references to his written report, his confidence dwindling as the time passed. Mike was continually forced to confirm by figures much of what Corrigon was expressing in his ideas and pro-

posals. At the conclusion of the meeting, a short summary was sketched out by Flemming and LeBlanc on a flip chart summarizing much of what Corrigon had suggested.

Mike Craig left the office that afternoon somewhat dismayed by the results of the meeting. He felt Corrigon had dominated the discussion and not contributed Mike's ideas as he had expressed them in their pre-meeting discussion. He thought over the way Corrigon was so much at ease with managers and of the way they responded to him. Ideas and action were clearly the bywords of this company.

In the next few weeks many of the major ideas of the meeting were broken down into smaller areas of focus; both Craig and Corrigon were left alone on their jobs without too much direction. The managers continued to hurry through one task then address another. Potential customers were given full details of the company aspirations and frequently Corrigon was asked to entertain customers and show them the operations. His aggressive and outgoing style seemed most suited to this task. Craig was given small reports to make and was generally left to muddle in the details. He would ask Corrigon for support from time to time on some of the matters, but seldom could he sit Corrigon down long enough for a meaningful exchange of ideas or plans. At the bimonthly meetings, Corrigon was never short of a comment or an idea for a particular project.

The manufacturing side of Electronics Unlimited was now coming on-line for full production. The 2 engineers who had been hired were working well under Rafuse and Mitchell in their departments. They had settled in their own offices and were very productive in their field developing changes and ideas for the product line. Both Rafuse and Mitchell were satisfied with the new employees, particularly since they provided current ideas for their work. They had already been invited to Montreal to visit the main plant and production operation.

Flemming and LeBlanc continued to make good use of Corrigon and Craig, who were busy on the marketing side of the operation. However, nothing was clearly defined in this company. John Mitchell, for example, frequently provided data and reports for Paul LeBlanc on distribution networks for the area. The organization was run on a flexible pattern of interactions and responsibilities. Corrigon continued his aggressive style and developed an excellent rapport with Jim Flemming. They were in the process of hiring salespeople for the field and Corrigon was given an opportunity to conduct the interviewing and initial screening. Craig, on the other hand seemed always to be preparing more reports and analyzing data, largely because he had not been asked to take other responsibility.

Mitchell and Rafuse had also begun to take advantage of Craig's report writing. By now, however, Craig had had enough and had become quite discouraged at these frequent requests. He began to wonder just what he was going to be expected to do on this "dynamic job." This uncertainty bothered him. At the same time, Corrigon was now beginning to annoy him with his abrasive style. He would ask for information and request of Craig routine jobs a secretary could do. Craig resented these requests but, in the interest of the company, would complete the tasks. Despite Craig's increased efforts at establishing rapport with the Marketing Manager, Flemming, he couldn't seem to produce results.

After 6 months on the job Craig had still not found it a satisfying experience. He was determined not to give up, however, and proceeded to present lengthy and detailed studies of market trends and other reports that would help the company. All the managers took advantage of his services to the point where Craig was frequently working on weekends.

Corrigon, well on his way to organizing a sales staff, also requested a lengthy analysis of sales potential for the company. Craig had worked himself into complete frustration. He refused Corrigon's request. He didn't feel he was there just to write reports but rather to become more involved with managing the company. He felt he was receiving little recognition for his contribution, while Corrigon and the 2 engineers were progressing much more rapidly. However, his refusal to write the report for Corrigon earned him a sharp rebuke from Flemming. This upset Craig and he felt he had to redeem himself.

Electronics Unlimited had been growing and stabilizing in the months that had passed. The retail outlets had been contacted and connections organized to complete the network of distribution. New products had been developed by the company and were marketed in an effective manner. The administrative staff had been growing to meet the requirements of the production and sales force. An incentive system for the sales force had been designed in the Toronto office and had received wide recognition from the Montreal company. Corrigon was instrumental in this effort and was appropriately rewarded for his contribution. A small achievement award was presented to Corrigon for his part in the design of the plan that had been implemented. The award was presented to him at an office get-together.

The event further deflated Craig's self-image in the growing company. What little spirit of camaraderie that had existed among the 4 employees who had arrived almost together had been lost by this time. Mike Craig had retreated into a gloomy silence, anticipating a difficult time in an upcoming evaluation that had been announced. The notice had come to the desks of the respective employees that they would be evaluated in the next month by the managers. It would be a formal evaluation, one that would take place in their offices over coffee. It would be verbal and based on discussion rather than a written document channelled through personnel.

Craig looked glum as he peered up from his desk after reading the memo, the first of its kind. Corrigon in his usual attitude and cockiness suggested that he would have to get the boss a bottle of good Scotch but that he really didn't have much to worry about.

Craig had less secure feelings about the whole procedure. He had this terrible feeling that he would handle himself poorly. In a brief discussion with Flemming one afternoon, he made enquiries about the method of evaluation pointing out the traditional function of personnel administration. Flemming laughed at this idea, responding that around here they worked to get things done and did not worry too much about who did the evaluations.

The evaluation day arrived and Craig was assigned to Rafuse, the person he felt was least involved with his work. The interview and discussion went smoothly and very cordially. There were many silent moments during the course of the interview, and he went away feeling that his work was regarded as less than satisfactory. Rafuse had hinted that the company's interest lay in more outgoing individuals. Craig was left with mixed feelings about the company and his future.

Indeed, Craig felt the time had come for a confrontation with the management of the company and he proceeded to make an appointment with the personnel officer for a lengthy discussion about his future. He felt he might be able

to get some straight answers from Frank Wilson, but he knew that he was taking a chance in finding out the worst. Some hard discussions would follow.

SOURCE   Peter McGrady, Thunder Bay, Ont.: Lakehead University, 1982. Reprinted by permission of the author.

QUESTIONS

1. What kinds of problems is Mike Craig having at Electronics Unlimited? Discuss in detail why you think Craig is having these problems.
2. What can Craig do to increase his job satisfaction? What can he do to make his performance look better to management?
3. What factors might limit Craig's ability to improve his situation?

CASE STUDY 5

Atlantic Store Furniture

Atlantic Store Furniture (ASF) is a manufacturing operation in Moncton, New Brunswick. The company located in an industrial park employs about 25 people with annual sales of about $2 million. Modern shelving systems are the main products and these units are distributed throughout the Maritimes. Metal library shelving, display cases, acoustical screens and work benches are a few of the products available at ASF. The products are classified by two distinct manufacturing procedures which form separate sections of the plant. (See Exhibit 1 for ASF's organizational chart.)

The Metalworking Operation

In the metalworking part of the plant, sheet metal is cut and formed into shelving for assembly. The procedure is quite simple and organized in an assembly-line method. Six or eight stations are used to cut the metal to the appropriate length, drill press, shape, spotweld, and paint the final ready-to-assemble product. The equipment used

in the operation is both modern and costly, but the technology is quite simple.

The metalworking operation employs on average about 8 or 10 workers located along the line of assembly. The men range in age between 22 and 54 and are typically francophone Canadians. Most have high school education or have graduated from a technical program. The men as metalworkers are united by their common identity in the plant and have formed 2 or 3 subgroups based on common interests. One group, for example, comprising the foreman and three other workers has seasons tickets to the New Brunswick Hawks home games. Another group bowls together in the winter and attends horse races in the summer months.

The foreman's group is the most influential among the workers. The men in this group joined the company at the same time and James Savoie, the foreman, was once a worker with the three other men in the group. The group characteristically gets to the lunch counter first, sits together in the most comfortable chairs, and punches the time clock first on the way out of work. Conrad LeBlanc, another group member, has a brother who plays professional hockey in the NHL and he frequently describes the success of the team and his brother's large home.

The metalworkers as a group operate on one side of the plant and work at a very steady pace. The demand for their products in this section is high and the production is usually constant. The group adjusts well to changes in the order requests and the occasional overtime pressures. The salespeople on the road provide a constant flow of orders, to the point where there is a small backlog of requisitions to be filled. The products vary in size and style but for the most part they are standardized items. A small amount of work is performed on a customized basis.

Woodworking Operations

The woodworking operation differs considerably from the metalworking operation. It is a new addition to the plant and has had some success. It is separated from the metal production unit by a wide sliding door.

The organization of the wood shop is haphazard because the majority of its work is customized. Some areas are organized to produce standard products like screening, but the majority of the woodworking section is organized around a particular project. Typically tools, equipment, and supplies are left in the area of the partially completed projects. Custom cabinets and display cases are made for large department and retail stores. A small line of products are produced as a regular

line while the rest of the products are custom designed. The flow of work is basically steady in the shop, but there are stages where the work orders become intermittent. Though the appearance of the woodworking shop is quite disorganized and messy, reflecting the nature of the work, the workers in this section of the plant see themselves as real craftsmen and take considerable pride in their work. Typically, 2 or 3 projects are in progress simultaneously along with the normal run of standard products. The metalworkers store some of their completed units in the woodworking area to the dislike of the woodworkers and to the disorganization of the section.

Unlike the metalworkers, there is a distinct hierarchy among the woodworkers based on seniority and ability. Sam Kirby is the quick-tempered but fiercely loyal foreman; most of the full-time woodworkers have come through apprenticeship programs or have similar backgrounds to the metalworkers'. Most are middle-aged anglophone Canadians and, beyond an occasional after-work beer at the local tavern, they do not spend time together. Through Kirby's persistence, an apprenticeship program within the company has produced a number of good carpenters. This section of the company, though still relatively young, has produced good work and has a reputation for quality craftsmanship.

The morning coffee break for the woodworkers follows that of the metalworkers. Lunch hour is staggered by 20 minutes as well. Only a minimal amount of interaction occurs between the woodworkers and metalworkers, as there tends to be rivalry and competition between the two groups.

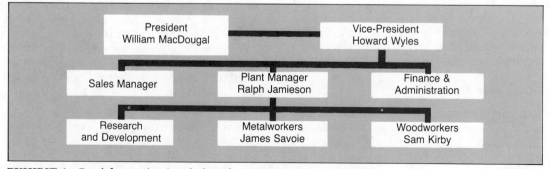

EXHIBIT 1   Partial organizational chart for Atlantic Store Furniture

Recent Events

The supervisor who oversees these 2 sections of the plant (plant manager) is Ralph Jamieson, a production engineer from a local university. As plant manager he reports to the vice-president. At the time of his hiring, ASF had not developed the woodworking section of the plant. Jamieson's work at the university became integrated into the production line when he discovered a method of galvanizing the metal product in final stages of production. He spends a good deal of his time in the metalworking operation planning and discussing problems in production with the foreman, James Savoie. Laboratory research is another occupation assigned to Jamieson, who enjoys experimentation with new methods and techniques in design and fabrication of metal products. Jamieson and Savoie are good friends and they spend a good deal of time together both on and off the job. James Savoie is quite happy with the way his operation is running. His boisterous, good-humored attitudes have created a very good rapport with his men and absenteeism is minimal.

A recent personnel change that has occurred within ASF is the addition of 2 new salesmen who are on the road in New Brunswick and Nova Scotia. Their contribution to the company is most notable in the metalwork area. They have placed many orders for the company. The new sales incentive program has motivated these people to produce and their efforts are being recognized.

Sam Kirby, the woodworking foreman, blew up at Jamieson the other day after some metalworkers had pushed open the sliding doors with an interest in storing more excess shelving units in the woodworking area without seeking Kirby's advice or permission. Sam is a hothead sometimes and has become quite annoyed with all the intergroup rivalry that has been going on between the metalworkers and the woodworkers. Storage space has been a sore point between the groups for the last 6 months or so, ever since the metalworkers became very busy. Jamieson and Howard Wyles, the vice-president, were asked to settle the problem between the two shops and decided that the metalworkers were only to enter the woodworking shop if absolutely necessary and with consent of the foreman.

This latest incident really upset the fellows in the woodworking shop. The woodworkers feel intimidated by the metalworkers who are taking space and interrupting their work. They grumble among themselves about the shouting and joking from the francophone assembly lines next door.

In a later conversation Kirby and Jamieson smoothed things over somewhat. It was explained to Kirby that it was the metalworkers who were really turning out the firm's work and that they need the extra space. The area that metalworkers want to use is not really needed by the woodworkers; rather it is simply an area around the perimeter of the room by the walls.

Kirby did not like Jamieson's response, knowing full well his commitment to the metalworking operations. With this decision, the metalworkers proceeded to use the area in the woodworking shop and never missed an opportunity to insult or criticize the woodworkers in French. The effect of the situation on the respective groups became quite obvious. The metalworkers became increasingly more jocular and irritating in their interactions with the woodworkers. The woodworkers grew resentful and their work pace slowed.

The infighting continued and became of concern to the president and vice-president. For example, the large sliding doors separating the shops were too hastily closed one afternoon on a metalworker who was retreating from a practical joke he was playing on a woodworker. The resulting injury was not serious but it did interrupt a long series of accident-free days the company had been building up. This incident further divided the 2 groups. Meetings and disciplinary threats by management were not enough to curtail the problems.

The woodworkers were now withdrawing all efforts to communicate. They ate lunch separately and took coffee breaks away from the regular room. Kirby became impatient to complete new products and to acquire new contracts. He urged management to hire personnel and to solicit new business. The work atmosphere changed considerably in the woodworking shop as the workers lost their satisfying work experience. Much of the previous friendly interaction had ceased. Kirby's temper flared more frequently as small incidents seemed to upset him more than before. After-work get-togethers at the tavern were no longer of much appeal to the men.

The metalworkers were feeling quite good about their jobs as the weeks passed. Their orders remained strong as demand continued to grow for their products. The metalworkers complained about the woodworkers and demanded more space for their inventory. The metalworkers were becoming more cohesive and constantly ridiculed the woodworkers. Their concern for the job decreased as back orders filled up and talk of expansion developed for the metalwork operation.

Just as the metal shop became more confident there were more difficulties with the woodworking shop. The woodworkers were completing the final stages of an elaborate cabinet system when information came regarding a shipping delay. The new store for which the product was being built was experiencing problems, causing a 2- or 3-month delay before it could accept the new cabinet system. Kirby was very disturbed by this news, as his woodworkers needed to see the completion of their project and the beginning of a new one. The predicament was compounded somewhat by the attitude of the metalworkers, who heard of the frustration of the woodworkers and added only more jeers and smart remarks. Morale at this stage was at an all time low. The chief carpenter, an integral member of the woodworkers, was looking for a new job. One or two of the casual workers were drifting into new work or not showing up for work they had. Contracts and orders for new products were arriving but in fewer numbers, and casual workers had to be laid off. Defective work was beginning to increase, to the embarrassment of the company.

Management was upset with the conditions of the two operations and threatened the foreman. Kirby was disturbed at the situation and was bitter about the deteriorating state of the woodworking shop. Despite many interviews he was unable to replace the head carpenter who had left the company attracted by a new job prospect. Efforts to reduce the intergroup conflict were tried but without success.

The president of ASF, William MacDougal, was alarmed with the situation. He recognized some of the problems with the different operations. One operation was more active and busy while the other section worked primarily on project work. The organization was designed, he thought, with the normal structure in mind. The men in the company, he thought to himself, were very much of the same background and what little diversity there was should not have accounted for this animosity. As president, he had not developed a culture of competition or pressure in the company.

The disorganization and chaos in the woodworking shop was alarming and there was very little that could be done about it. Kirby had been discussing the problem with the president trying to identify some of the alternatives. This had been the third meeting in as many days and each time the conversation drifted into a discussion about current developments in Jamieson's metalworking pursuits. James Savoie had told the president he felt that there was too much worrying going on "over there"! Plans for expanding the building at ASF were developing at a rapid pace. The president felt that more room might alleviate some of the problems particularly with respect to inventory, warehousing, and storage.

Kirby became enthusiastic about the prospects of some relief for his side of the operation. He was very much aware of the fact that the performance of his operation was quite low. The president of the company felt satisfied that the woodworking concern was going to improve its performance. One or two new contracts with large department stores inspired an effort to improve the operation.

The men in the woodworking section became relaxed. A few positive interactions between the woodworkers and metalworkers became evident. One afternoon about 2 weeks after the disclosure by the president of the new plant development, Kirby observed blueprints for the new expansion. The plans had been left on Jamieson's desk inadvertently and, to the surprise of Kirby, revealed full details of the expansion for the new building. Kirby sat down and examined the details more carefully and recognized that the woodworking area was not to be included in the expansion plans.

Kirby left the office in a rage and stormed into the president's office to demand an explanation. Kirby shouted that he had changed things around in the woodworking shop on the promise of more room and possibility of expansion. The president shook his head and apologized; he explained Kirby was going to be told but nothing could be done. The market demand was simply just not that great for wood products. Kirby left the office and went straight for his car and drove off.

SOURCE   Peter McGrady, Thunder Bay, Ont.: Lakehead University, 1979. Reprinted by permission of the author.

QUESTIONS

1. List and analyze the factors which have led to intergroup conflict between the woodworkers and the metalworkers.
2. What negative outcomes have occurred because of this conflict? Are any positive outcomes evident?
3. Assess management's handling of the intergroup conflict so far.
4. Develop an action plan for resolving the problems at Atlantic Store Furniture.

CASE STUDY 6

Scott Trucks

"Mr. McGowan will see you now, Mr. Sullivan," said the secretary. "Go right in."

Sullivan looked tired and tense as he opened the door and entered McGowan's office. He had prepared himself for a confrontation and was ready to take a firm approach. McGowan listened as Sullivan spoke of the problems and complaints in his department. He spoke of the department's high personnel turnover and the difficult time he had attracting and keeping engineers. McGowan questioned Sullivan as to the quality of his supervision and direction, emphasizing the need to monitor the work and control the men.

"You have got to let them know who is boss and keep tabs on them at all times," said McGowan.

"But, Mr. McGowan, that is precisely the point; my engineers resent surveillance tactics. They are well-educated, self-motivated people. They don't want to be treated like soldiers at an army camp."

McGowan's fist hit the table. "Listen, Sullivan, I brought you in here as a department manager reporting to me. I don't need your fancy textbook ideas about leading men. I have 15 years as a navy commander and I have run this plant from its inception. If you can't produce the kind of work I want and control your men, then I will find someone who can. I don't have complaints and holdups from my other managers. We have systems and procedures to be followed and so they shall, or I will know the reason they aren't."

"But that is just the point," continued Sullivan, "my men do good work and contribute good ideas and, in the face of job pressures, perform quite well. They don't need constant supervision and direction and least of all the numerous and unnecessary interruptions in their work."

"What do you mean by that?" demanded McGowan.

"Well, both Tobin and Michaels have stated openly and candidly that they like their work but find your frequent visits to the department very disconcerting. My engineers need only a minimal amount of control and our department has these controls already established. We have weekly group meetings to discuss project and routine work. This provides the kind of feedback that is meaningful to them. They don't need frequent interruptions and abrasive comments about their work and the need to follow procedures for change."

"This is my plant and I will run it the way I see fit," shouted McGowan. "No department manager or engineer is going to tell me otherwise. Now I suggest, Mr. Sullivan, that you go back to your department, have a meeting with your men, and spell out my expectations."

Sullivan was clearly intimidated by this time and very frustrated. He left the office hastily and visibly upset. McGowan's domineering style had prevailed and the meeting had been quite futile. No amount of pleading or confrontation would change McGowan's attitude.

Sullivan returned to his department and sat

at his desk quite disillusioned with the predicament. His frustration was difficult to control and he was plagued with self-doubt. He was astonished at McGowan's intractable position and stubbornness. He posted a notice and agenda for a meeting to be held the next day with his department. He left the plant early that day, worried about the direction he should take, and thought over the events that had led to this situation.

Background at Scott Trucks

The operation at Scott Trucks is housed in an old aircraft hangar in the Debert Industrial Park, near Truro, Nova Scotia. The government of Nova Scotia sold the building for a modest sum as it no longer had use for the hangar after the armed forces had abandoned it. The facility, together with the financial arrangements organized by McGowan, the president of Scott, made the enterprise feasible. (See the organizational chart in Exhibit 1.)

Inside the building, renovations have provided for an office area, a production operation, and an engineering department. The main offices are located at the front of the building, housing the sales team and the office clerks. The sales manager, Mike McDonald, and 2 assistants make up the sales team at the Debert location of Scott Trucks. Three or four field representatives work in southern Ontario and the United States. Mike is considered a good salesman and often assumes a role much broader than sales. Customer complaints, ordering, and replacement parts also fall into his domain. The production manager frequently makes reference to Mike's ability to talk on 2 phones at the same time!

Art Thompson has been production manager at Scott Trucks for 8 years. The area he manages is behind the sales office and takes up most of the space in the building. The engineering department comprising small offices is located behind the production department, which is divided into 2 areas by a long narrow corridor. The shop floor is divided into basic sections of assembly, with a paint, a welding, and a cab section as well as other areas used to assemble the large Scott trucks.

Owing to the limited capacity of the plant only 2 or 3 truck units are in production at any one time. Another constraint on capacity is the nature of the system used to produce the trucks. There are no pulleys, belts, or assembly lines used in the system; rather, the production takes place in large bays, where sections of the truck are individually completed in preparation for the final assembly.

The truck units are used for a variety of functions, particularly where a heavy truck requirement is in demand. Fire trucks, highway maintenance trucks, and long-distance hauling trucks are some of the units produced by Scott. To some extent the trucks are custom-made as each purchaser will request changes on the basic design. The engineers are also adapting the trucks to meet the various standards and specifications of the Canadian government and of the vigorous and changeable Canadian climates.

Tom Sullivan, who is a recent engineering graduate from Nova Scotia Technical Institute, is the newest of the managers at Scott. He shows good promise as an engineer but, as with his predecessor, Tom Sullivan is having adjustment problems as a manager. Tom also received an MBA from Dalhousie University and majored in management science and organizational behavior. He completed project work in participative management styles under the direction of a specialist in this area. He tries to practice this approach in his new position and enjoys the ideas and flow of discussion at the department meetings. Tom works in a department with men much his senior and is the youngest of the department managers at Scott Truck. He works hard and is well liked by his subordinates. Personal satisfaction, though infrequent, comes as a direct result of the open and participative management style he uses.

The Engineers

The composition of the group of engineers at Scott is unusual. One of the members is not an engineer by qualification but has many years of practical experience. He moved from Detroit to Truro having worked with Ford Trucks for 15 years. Since his recruitment by McGowan he has worked with Scott for 8 years. Retirement for this man is not far off, a fact he frequently makes known to the group. His work is good, and he seems to have many answers to difficult problems, a redeeming factor in the absence of an engineering degree. Don Jones, another member of the group, is a good engineer. His work day is solid; however, most evenings are spent at a local tavern. His wife was killed 6 months ago, and he does not seem to care any more about anything. The remainder of the group is a combination of senior and junior men who have been with the company for a number of years. Two engineers left the group for better jobs and for a "less confining atmosphere," as they put it. Tom Sullivan's efforts to lead the group are proving to be a difficult task.

The Production Workers

Work for the men in the production plant is reasonably stable. A good paying job in production in Truro is difficult to find, a situation of which the men are fully aware; many of them have experienced the monotony of unemployment and job hunting before this opening presented itself.

With the exception of a few francophone Canadian welders, the workers are Maritimers whose experience and skills range from those of a skilled tradesman to those of a casual laborer. The local trades school in Truro has provided the organization with a number of good machinists, welders, and painters that the foreman hired and began to develop.

The morale on the plant floor has been very good, particularly since the company has improved its sales position. The once frequent layoffs resulting from work shortage have ceased in the presence of higher demand for the trucks. The new field sales group contributes significantly to the situation with their efforts in southern Ontario and the northern United States.

The pay scale is above average for the area and there is a good rapport between the production manager and the workers.

Administrative Control

Administrative control in the plant has been accomplished by two methods: one in terms of the quality of the product and the other in terms of its cost. Attention has been paid to the quality control function through a quality control supervisor, whose task it is to examine the end product in a thorough manner using rigorous criteria. The other method of control is that implemented by the accounting office. Through the adoption of a standard cost program, material, labor, and overhead variances are accumulated and presented on data report sheets.

The production manager, Art Thompson, is responsible for collecting cost data and for sending it to the office on a weekly basis. Art is not an easy-going person; he frequently gets upset when problems occur on the shop floor. He is closely watched by McGowan, the president. Consequently, to Art, the monthly meetings of the managers are a real ordeal, since McGowan, as owner, tries to watch the costs very carefully and to make sure the plant is running as efficiently as possible.

McGowan uses 3 approaches to managing the operation at Scott Trucks: (1) a monthly meeting with the three managers, (2) a series of interdepartmental memos that interpret the results of cost figures presented to him throughout the month, and (3) frequent plant visits and observations.

None of these controls is favorably received by the managers as they feel they are being

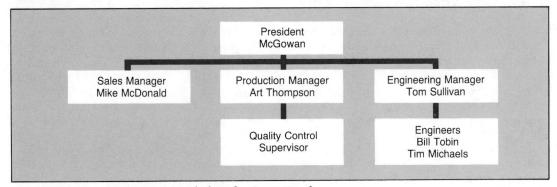

EXHIBIT 1   Partial organizational chart for Scott Trucks

watched too carefully. Interdepartmental memos may read as follows:

May 12, 198X
To: Mr. Art Thompson, Production Manager
From: Mr. McGowan, President, Scott Trucks
Re.: Materials Quantity Variance
I noticed a considerable amount of material quantity variance in your production reports for last week. The standard cost system has been implemented for 6 weeks now, and it no longer suffices to say that you are still "working the bugs out of the system." It is time you paid closer attention to the amount of materials going into the production process and to avoiding any spoilage.

Another example of an interdepartmental memo reads as follows:

May 20, 198X
To: Mr. Art Thompson, Production Manager
From: Mr. McGowan, President, Scott Trucks
Re.: Inaccurate Recording of Time and Use of Time Cards
I noticed last week on your labor cost submissions that a number of employees have been neglecting to punch time cards. Please see that this system is properly followed.

Art Thompson's reaction to these memos has been one of apprehension and concern. It is the practice of the foreman and himself to try to resolve the problems as quickly as possible and, together, they have been able to rectify these difficulties quite rapidly, as the men are eager to cooperate.

The plant visits to the production area made by McGowan are frequent and effective. He has been known to come out in shirt sleeves and literally assume the worker's job for a period of time. This is particularly true in the case of a new worker or a young worker, where McGowan will dig in and instruct the individual on how he should be doing his job. On such occasions, McGowan will give specific instructions as to how he wants things done and how things should be done.

It makes McGowan feel right at home when he is involved with the workers. He spent 15 years as a navy commander, and he often used to remark that there was only one way to deal with his subordinates. The reaction of the workers to this approach is mixed. Some of the production people dislike this "peering over the shoulders"; others do not seem to mind and appreciate McGowan's concern for a "job well done." The workers grumble at McGowan's approach but feel most of his criticisms to be constructive.

McGowan's management approach in the monthly meetings with his managers is not considerably different. As with the production workers, McGowan assumes a very authoritarian style in dealing with his managers. The monthly meetings are an integrative effort among engineering, sales, and production, with the purpose of ironing out difficulties both on a personality basis and on a work basis. The work load in the engineering department has been growing for the last 6 months at a considerable rate. This reflects the increase in production and the need for people in the area of engineering and design to provide a high quality of technical expertise.

The number of engineers currently working at Scott is eight. Relations with the engineering department have been less than satisfactory and a good deal of conflict has occurred over a number of issues. For example, the reports from quality control at Scott have been poor from time to time and, increasingly, the problem has been traced to unclear engineering specifications. Upset about these conditions, McGowan has expressed his feelings in his memos to the department.

Lately, the engineers have been bombarded with McGowan's memos, the results of more frequent complaints about the engineering department from the quality control supervisor and the production manager. Along with other factors, they have provided the ammunition McGowan needed to confront the engineering department. The engineers, however, have resisted, refusing to accept these memos in the same way that the production people have. As a result of these memos, complaints and misunderstandings have arisen. The engineers have responded by suggesting that the production people cannot interpret the blueprints and that they never bother to question them when a change is not understood or clear.

Disturbed by this situation, McGowan has made it a point to visit the engineering department at regular intervals and his tactics have been much the same as with the production people. Unfortunately, the engineering manager, Tom Sullivan, was feeling the pressure and could not seem to keep his department running smoothly. Being new to the job, he did not know how to handle McGowan. Two engineers had quit recently, apparently to leave the "confining atmosphere," going to better jobs elsewhere.

Tom Sullivan had reacted poorly to his new job situation and had been in a somber mood for about 2 months. His work and his adjustment had not been successful. The veterans in the department, though understanding his frustration, could not help Sullivan, who felt he was better off trying to accommodate McGowan than resisting him. To make matters worse, the 2 engineers who had recently quit had left a large backlog of work incomplete, and efforts to recruit new engineers had been a strain on Sullivan. The marketplace quickly absorbed all the engineers graduating from Nova Scotia Tech, and Debert had few attractions available to enable it to compete with larger centers.

Tom did get a big break, however, in his recruiting drive when he discovered, through a contact in Montreal, 2 engineers who wished to return to the Maritimes. Both men were young and had experience and good training in engineering. In their interview, they discussed their experiences and their ability to work independently. Moreover, both were looking for a quiet work atmosphere. Sullivan liked their credentials and hired the two men: Bill Tobin and Tim Michaels.

McGowan had been on vacation at the time and had not met the new engineers until a month after they had been on the job. His first encounter, however, was a cordial meeting with the 2 engineers and, although the atmosphere in the department was always unpredictable and changing, activities and relations were smooth for a month or two, much to the relief of Sullivan. McGowan maintained his surveillance of the plant, including the engineers. Tim Michaels and Bill Tobin, the new engineers, felt uncomfortable with McGowan around but just proceeded with their work and ignored the long stares and the continued presence of the boss.

One Friday afternoon McGowan walked into the engineering department with a smug look on his face. It was near the end of the month just prior to the monthly meeting. Sullivan looked up immediately as McGowan moved toward Tobin's drafting table. McGowan was irate. He began talking to Tobin in a loud voice. Shaking his fist, he threw down a report on a change proposed by Tobin for the interior of the cabs made at Scott.

"What gives you the right to implement such a change without first going to Sullivan, then to me?" shouted McGowan. "You have only been with this company for two and a half months and already you feel you can ignore the system."

"Well, Mr. McGowan, I thought it was a good idea, and I have seen it work before," responded Tobin, flustered by McGowan's attack.

Sullivan came out from his office to see what the problem was about. McGowan turned to him and asked him why he couldn't control his men, adding that the changes were totally unauthorized and unnecessary. Sullivan glanced at the blueprint and was taken by surprise as he examined it more carefully. In the meantime, McGowan raved on about Tobin's actions. Sullivan roused himself to reply.

"Oh, um, ah, yes, Mr. McGowan, you're right; this should have been cleared between, uh, you and me before production got it but, ah, I will see that it doesn't happen again."

McGowan stormed out, leaving Tobin and Sullivan standing by the desk. Tobin was upset by "this display of rudeness," as he put it. "Tom," he went on, "this was a damn good idea and you know it."

Sullivan shook his head, "Yes, you're right. I don't know how to deal with McGowan; he wears me down sometimes. But you and Bill have to channel your changes through the system."

Tobin turned back to his table and resumed his afternoon's work.

For the next six weeks the plant operated smoothly as production picked up and more people were hired. Work in the engineering department increased correspondingly as people wanted new and better parts on their trucks. New engine and cab designs were arriving and put an increased burden on the engineering department. In fact, it fell well behind in its efforts to change and adapt the truck specifications to meet the Canadian marketplace. The lengthy review process required to implement change put an added burden on the operations at Scott. Moreover, summer was approaching, which meant decreased personnel, owing to the holidays.

McGowan's frequent visits added to the difficult situation in the engineering department. Sullivan had taken to group meetings once a week with the engineers in an attempt to solve engineering problems and personal conflicts. At each meeting, Tobin and Michaels discussed their work with the group and showed signs of real progress and development. They were adjusting well and contributing above expectations. At these meetings, however, they both spoke openly and frankly about McGowan's frequent visits and his abrasive style. A month had passed since they first suggested to Sullivan that he talk to McGowan about the problems he presented to the engineers by his visits to the department. At first the rest of the group agreed passively to the idea that Sullivan confront McGowan on this issue but, by the fourth week, the entire group was very firm with Sullivan on this issue, insisting he have a talk with McGowan.

Tom Sullivan knew the time had come and that he had to face McGowan. Only that morning he had received a call from a local company inquiring about Bill Tobin and the quality of his work. Presumably Tobin had been looking for work elsewhere. This was the last straw. Sullivan had made and kept his appointment with McGowan.

SOURCE Peter McGrady, Thunder Bay, Ont.: Lakehead University, 1982. Reprinted by permission of the author.

QUESTIONS

1. Contrast in detail the leadership styles of Sullivan and McGowan.
2. Describe the communication processes at Scott Trucks. What areas are most effective? What areas are ineffective? What can be done to improve the ineffective areas?
3. What is the most effective leadership style for the engineering manager at Scott Trucks? Support your choice fully.
4. What should Sullivan do now? What limitations exist in the engineering department that might constrain Sullivan's alternatives?

CASE STUDY 7

Eastern Tel

Mary Jacobs has been with Eastern Tel in Amherst, Nova Scotia, for 10 years, ever since the opening day of the telephone unit assembly plant in 1974. She speaks highly of the company, which has always served her well, the management, and her friends. She is a member of an informal work group in the plant that has developed over the years. A native of Amherst, Mary Jacobs left her job at Margolians, a local department store, to join a better paying operation at Eastern Tel. The clerical job she left had little future for her, while the new position appeared more demanding and less confining. A new opportunity, more salary, and a fresh start prompted her move to the factory position.

Testing and Getting Acquainted

A routine testing procedure is part of the job application system at Eastern Tel, and Mary met the requirements well. Hand and finger dexterity are needed for the job of soldering small wires together in preparation for further assembly of the telephone units; Mary Jacobs demonstrated a good capacity in these job requirements. A short personality test is also administered as part of the application procedure, and Mary performed well in this too. Of the original group hired, Mary Jacobs showed the greatest ability on the job, reaching the hourly quota output in the early days of her new job. A pleasant personality is also one of her characteristics. Her supervisor was impressed with her and Mary quickly won the respect and the liking of the management. Her satisfaction with the job and the factory atmosphere is very gratifying to her, particularly the informal status afforded to her by management, who frequently ask for ideas and advice. Mary's energetic style is evident in the plant where she is often asked to introduce a new worker to the operation. Not only is her help very valuable to many of the new girls but, also, most of the Amherst girls follow Mary's direction on the job and in other activities.

Indeed, Eastern Tel is not faced with a large number of personnel problems. The company pays well and relations are kept favorable with a good basic salary and frequent increases. Moreover, the reputation of the company is good in the area and the personnel manager often boasts about how many applications he has on file and the numerous job interviews he carries out during the week.

Production is usually on schedule, and the product is in high demand. Currently, the production comprises partial assembly of telephone units. Work is done at independent tables that resemble large drafting boards. Material parts are brought to the tables by stock clerks, and the product is subsequently shipped to Montreal for completion.

Company Image

To foster good morale in the plant and a good image in the community of Amherst, the company sponsors bowling teams, baseball teams, and other sports teams. The Eastern Tel logo is frequently seen in the community on sports sweaters and jackets. Mary Jacobs, as convenor of the bowling league in town, participates actively in organizing and administering the league. A good deal of camaraderie is evident within the plant, centering around the bowling results or playoffs in the league. Someone on the plant floor is frequently congratulated or made fun of regarding the scores in a previous night's game. Thomas, one of the stock clerks, has just begun to bowl and takes a considerable amount of banter from the plant workers.

The company has taken the time to develop supervisors and managers in the plant who understand the value of worker satisfaction on the job. As a result, production quotas are not compromised and satisfaction is very high. (A partial organizational chart can be found in Exhibit 1.)

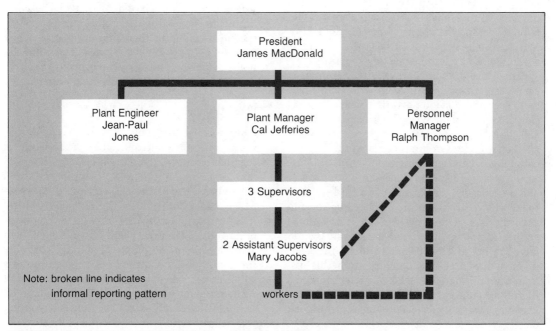

EXHIBIT 1   Partial organizational chart for Eastern Tel

Company and Workers' Background

Eastern Tel, which is associated with Bell Canada and Maritime Tel and Tel, has a steady supply of customers willing to purchase the products. The operation at Eastern Tel is one of subassembly, as mentioned, with the units completed at the Montreal plant. Costs and market structures make this approach viable.

Eastern Tel was attracted to Nova Scotia and the Amherst Industrial Park on the basis of location incentive and lower wage rates. There had been more promise for the industrial park than had materialized, but a number of reputable companies had come to town. Amherst is a small town on the border of Nova Scotia and New Brunswick with a population of about 10 000 people. It is well located in terms of direct accessibility to other parts of Nova Scotia, but the economy is not fast developing. Other nearby centers, such as Springhill and Oxford, have very few industries or manufacturing operations.

Eastern Tel has a number of workers from Springhill who travel in a large van to and from the plant each day. The workers who come from Springhill can typically be found playing cards with their group over lunch or chatting about a previous night's hockey game. This group is usually quite friendly with the other workers but is notorious for its lunch-hour gossip. Pam Walters is one woman who comes in to the plant from Springhill. She is best described as an excellent worker, who rarely misses a day's work.

Pam Walters, though an excellent worker, is easily excited when things go wrong. An incident occurred not long ago that upset Pam, as she got into a fight with the stock boy over a shortage which prevented her from doing what she preferred for her afternoon's work. Pam became upset when the stock clerk gave the last carton of parts to Karen Henderson, a new worker and a friend of Mary Jacobs. The clerk refused to recognize Pam's seniority in the situation and gave the box to the new worker. It was not a serious incident, but it did mean Pam would have to work at a less desirable job for the afternoon. A few problems emerged from this dispute, but nothing serious. Pam's group supported her in this conflict, and much of the talk on the way home was about the foolishness of the stock clerk.

The group from Springhill occasionally found itself being slighted by one incident or another, though their common transportation difficulties and hometown kept them together and looking out for one another. Moreover their success on the job kept them in good standing with most of the workers and management at Eastern Tel; one or two of the foremen were from the Springhill area, which added some support during the occasional conflict.

The culture in the plant at Eastern Tel could be described as relaxed and noncompetitive. The shop is clean and, though it is not tidy, a sense of organization and accomplishment exists. Country music is heard throughout the shop as the women work away at their large tables. An informal atmosphere prevails on the floor. Managers and workers speak freely, discussing and resolving problems. At one large table, 4 women sit facing one another, working on an output quota, soldering minute wires into an exact pattern to form the innards of a telephone unit.

The main composition of the work force at Eastern Tel is women. Many of these women support their families, as employment opportunities for men in the area are limited. While the productivity of the plant is usually quite high, the morale is likewise fairly good as the women have good opportunities to interact and socialize both on and off the job. The hourly wage is good, in relation to that of the community in general — the minimum rate being typical in many of the adjoining plants, while Eastern Tel pays higher salaries. The company holds barbecues and skating parties to keep people active and involved with the company.

Plant Changes at Eastern Tel

One morning the plant manager, Cal Jefferies, walked into the plant and called the supervisors together to inform them of a meeting that would take place in his office in 30 minutes. The 3 supervisors, the plant engineer, and the personnel manager collected in the manager's office. Jefferies introduced Mel Pardoe, the chief engineer from the Montreal plant, who informed them about an important proposed plan for changing the layout of the plant floor. The operation was going to be changed as head office wanted the Amherst plant to complete the telephone units to the full assembly stage. The Maritime market was beginning to grow and demand for the telephone units was increasing. The more complex process of shipping the partially completed units to Montreal would soon be ended. Pardoe elaborated very carefully on the new changes that would take place on the shop floor.

"You see, ladies and gentlemen, the new design is more efficient and it will reduce the time required to assemble each unit. Floor space will be utilized to a greater extent, and the system is designed to require fewer workers. This is the rationale behind the plan. Our operations in Montreal and California are much more efficient. Now you may be thinking that the operations are not comparable since we are just putting in the new plan, but my point is that overall the plants are more efficient with this line assembly. Allowing Amherst to complete the task from start to finish will fulfill this objective. The cost structures of production in the plant are forcing us to make this decision. We expect to produce 30 complete units an hour initially, then move to 50 units at full capacity. The line assembly you will see is quite efficient.

"The diagram on this chart," Pardoe continued, showing them Exhibit 2, "illustrates the changes we will make adding this new line and allowing us to complete the product here in Amherst. This method will eliminate the work tables altogether. The work tables are okay for the work in the early stages of assembly, when the product is small and the operation simple and precise. However, when the telephones reach more complete stages of assembly, moving them from table to table will become difficult and so the line method will be more efficient.

"We will eliminate the stock boys' moving partially completed units from table to table," the engineer explained. "The units will now move down the assembly line with each worker adding a part to the unit.

"Are there any questions, ladies and gentlemen? Do you understand the concepts? It is basically a simple rearrangement of the existing operation."

The personnel manager, Ralph Thompson, smoked his pipe as he examined the chart. "How many people are we going to need to work on this new line assembly?" he asked. "How many lines are we going to have? Do you think this is the best system? Our workers are not used to or may not adjust to this kind of a system. You know as well as I do the pace of the shop is not all that high."

"That is precisely the reason we need to increase the production output! Your workers will adjust," said the engineer. "The change is not all that great. If they don't adjust, get rid of them. Don't be soft."

The plant manager, Jefferies, interjected, "Now wait a minute. We don't deal with our workers that way. We've established good worker relations here in Amherst and we have loyal employees."

Questions and discussions followed, but the plans were in place. The changes were introduced over a long weekend in May by a team from Montreal. The work tables were replaced with a new line assembly system.

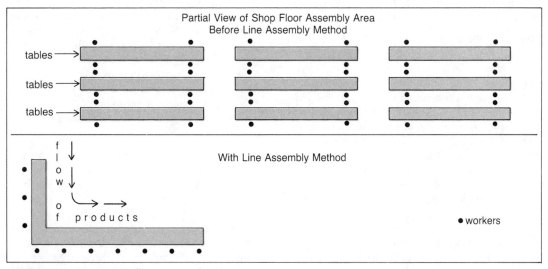

EXHIBIT 2   Eastern Tel's new production set-up

First Four Weeks of Production

The first 4 weeks of production proved to be very discouraging with the new line setup. The supervisors tried to appease higher management by saying the problems were all the result of learning and the workers still trying to get the bugs out of the new system.

Jefferies could not accept the excuses, as pressure was being put on him from Montreal head office to get production on stream. Jefferies recalled also the details of that promotion for Mary Jacobs. Thompson had pushed hard for it, emphasizing Mary's spark and enthusiasm on the job. It hadn't been part of the original plans for change, but Thompson felt that she deserved the position since she'd been so helpful and cooperative in the past. Jefferies had thought it might ease the change for the workers.

Jefferies tried to find the answer to the problems by interviewing the supervisors and the key people on the assembly line. Thompson followed up by approaching Mary Jacobs. Their findings were revealing.

Jefferies's Reaction

Jefferies was upset with the developments. A month had passed and the change was taking longer to implement than anticipated. Interpersonal conflicts had erupted throughout the plant. The once-present congeniality among the workers was decreasing noticeably. Rumors were rampant about layoffs that were forthcoming. In a conference one morning, Jefferies and one of the supervisors discussed the situation.

Jefferies: What's going on out there? The line is 50 percent below production levels. How do you explain it?

Supervisor: Well, I don't know. I'm used to the old system of the women working on individual tables and working at their own pace — enough to meet the quota. The workers seem so discontented. You kid with them now and they complain. The job seems the same but not as relaxed as before. One woman told me she feels pressured all the time and hates not being able to leave her position when she wants to get a cup of coffee. Others complain of having to wait until 12:30 to eat lunch. I don't know; I can handle the paperwork on this job but the damn complaints are driving me crazy. Mary Jacobs bickers a lot with those 2 girls from Springhill you hired for the line job. You should have heard the remarks the other day. Wow!! I guess we'll give it a few more weeks and see what happens. But the situation could blow up any time. The Springhill group is upset about Mary Jacobs and her new title and increase. Assistant supervisor might have been a hasty move. I mean she is good . . . but!

Jefferies: That was really more Thompson's decision than mine! But we have to live with it now.

Supervisor: I am telling you quite frankly, Mr. Jefferies, I feel the trouble is going to worsen. Pam Walters is a very capable and respected worker. Many feel she should have been promoted.

Ralph Thompson Reacts

Ralph Thompson, the personnel manager, walked back and forth in his office with signs of concern showing on his face. He too did not like the feel of the change that was in place. As usual in times of difficulty, he called Mary Jacobs into his office to talk over the situation. He tried to keep things on an informal basis and spoke in a light-hearted way about the problems with the change, but he was visibly concerned about the production figures and the discord he observed among the workers.

He felt Mary's experience would bring to the job a level of confidence, to establish this new system of telephone assembly. Thompson felt that by taking workers from the existing work force and training them on the system a stable situation would develop. These workers together with ten new workers made up the new group. A small pay differential was used to attract the workers from existing jobs in the plant. After a briefing and a number of trial runs, production had begun. There was going to be difficulty with the new layout, Thompson could feel it.

Thompson: Mary, I'm surprised things are not running more smoothly than they are. The boys in Montreal think we're asleep out here in Amherst, and the boss would like to get to the bottom of the problem pretty quickly. The line's organized to produce 50 units an hour and we're doing 20 units. What's the problem?

Mary: Mr. Thompson, nothing seems to be going very well. We get the telephones down the line, but the people at quality control constantly reject the units for one reason or another. I don't know! The women on the line are an odd bunch. They don't seem to want to listen and they do not like the pace of the line. They don't seem to be involved with their job and those two you hired from Springhill are hopeless. All the job requires them to do is add a small element to the unit as it comes down the line, and they get it wrong a lot of the time. I've told them to concentrate on the job rather than talking, but they don't seem to listen. The work is not that hard, just boring and tedious. And at lunch hour, no one talks or jokes any more. The idea of having to produce so many units an hour as a group is different from individual quotas. The women don't seem to like it much. I guess too, Mr. Thompson, it's the freedom we miss. It's so confining on the assembly line. Morale is really low and the complaints among the workers are tremendous. It's not the same as before the change. People are quitting now and those late to work are also on the increase. That van from Springhill is always 10 or 15 minutes late.

Thompson: Well, I don't know! You are one of our more experienced workers. I've given you more responsibility with this change hoping you could lead the group. Try to keep it together and reduce the number of defective units

the quality control turns back. The executives from head office are due to come down next month for a review.

The difficulties in the plant worsened in the next week. Production runs were behind schedule, bickering among the workers was very noticeable and quality control became backed up with rejects. The pressure continued with missing inventory, and flattened tires on employees' automobiles. The supervisors were at a loss to know what to do. Employees from Springhill were arriving late more frequently and some days not at all. Mary approached Thompson with her concerns, but he was too overworked with hiring new people to replace those who had left.

SOURCE   Peter McGrady, Thunder Bay, Ont.: Lakehead University, 1984. Reprinted by permission of the author.

QUESTIONS

1. What is the central problem at Eastern Tel? Why has it developed?
2. Assess in detail management's handling of the change in production methods.
3. List the steps that can be taken to improve the morale and productivity of the workers at Eastern.

CASE STUDY 8

Kryzowski and Sons Ltd.

Art Kryzowski, one of three sons of an immigrant tradesman, was in his final year of pre-law studies at University of Manitoba in 1941. In more ordinary times he would have looked forward to staying in school, working for admission to the bar, and an eventual comfortable living in a local general practice. His father, a sheet-metal worker by training, had built up a moonlight business repairing and reselling industrial salvage. By the early 1930s, it had grown into a full-time business, which brokered used machinery to small business owners, providing the

family with a stable and substantial income. Kryzowski senior was the personification of the work ethic, pouring countless hours, heart and soul, into running the family business. He dreamed, like so many of his generation, of a company which would become Kryzowski and Sons and allow his children and grandchildren to enjoy the advantages in life that he and his wife had missed.

By 1941, Kryzowski senior's dreams were well on the way to realization. All three sons had been exposed to the business through summer and part-time work. Carl, just finishing high school, was a dismal student and rather easy-going, but had a natural bent for mechanical objects. His good nature and empathic touch with lathes, pumps, and presses made him popular among the shop hands and an obvious candidate for running the production activities of the company. The oldest brother, Alfred, was tall, handsome, and outgoing; Alfred frequently accompanied his father on visits to customers. Persuasive and likeable, Alfred was visualized by all concerned as the future sales director of Kryzowski and Sons, although his interests clearly lay more in enjoying the good life than setting sales records. Nominally in his fourth year in business studies at McGill, Alfred was active in fraternity life, a dinnertime companion of young men whose fathers ran major corporations, but a "Gentleman's C" scholar only by dint of numerous purchased papers. Art was nearly the opposite of his older brother; short, stocky, intense, and introverted, Art inherited his father's tendency to be a workaholic. He was regarded by fellow students as a greasy grind, but one whose constant efforts were grudgingly respected. Art had comparatively little social life during those years, instead spending most of his spare time helping out in the company office.

1941 was a year of decision for the Kryzowski family. As the war effort moved into high gear, the family business prospered. With new components and virgin materials in short supply, new customers and orders were added. However, the war effort also made its demands on the company's staff. Early in the year, Alfred surprised the family with a dinnertime announcement that he had resigned from the university and enlisted in the RCAF. Three weeks later, Alfred reported for training as a pilot officer and, except for short home furloughs, he was absent until demobilization in July 1945. From his infrequent letters, it was evident that Alfred cut a dramatic circle in the RCAF. He flew Wellingtons and later Lancaster bombers on night operations over occupied Europe until late 1944, completing three tours of duty and accumulating several decorations before being posted to an operational training unit in the north of England. What came through less clearly in his letters was the taste Alfred had acquired for reinforcing his battered nerves with whisky, which accounted for his failure to advance beyond Flight Leader rank.

Late in 1941, against the protests of the entire family, Carl enlisted in the Navy. Carl's mechanical aptitude was quickly recognized, and he was assigned to a service school for machinists, fitters, and artificers after an initial tour in Corvettes, small anti-submarine crafts. Carl was retained as an instructor by the service school and passed the remainder of the war as a petty officer. He was able to take most of his furloughs at home, at the cost of many sleepless nights on the train between Halifax and Winnipeg, but was lost as a contributor to the firm for the duration of the conflict. By 1945, Carl was a chief instructor at the technical school and received superlative service evaluations. However, a few stints filling in for the director while the latter was on leave convinced both Carl and his superiors that he would never be an effective administrator.

1941 was also the year in which Kryzowski senior had his first heart attack. A bull of a man in his mid-50s, Kryzowski rebounded well, but it was a bad portent and forced him to reduce his activities drastically. The brunt of this fell directly on the shoulders of Art Kryzowski. The shop hands were typically older men who had been with the company for years and required little supervision. However, the onus of inspecting, estimating, and haggling on lots and prices, keeping fences mended with established customers, and running the financial side of the business fell increasingly on Art Kryzowski. Despite his ambitions for law school, and accompanied by sub rosa entreaties from Mrs. Kryzowski, Art began to spend mornings — then afternoons and weekends — making calls, visiting suppliers, and troubleshooting for client firms.

By the Christmas holidays, Art Kryzowski found himself hooked. Every day he spent at the office uncovered new problems and crises which only he had the stamina to unravel. He could count on his father's advice, but all of the footwork and a growing proportion of the key decisions had to be handled alone. In the process, Art also burned bridges behind him. The long hours at the office included many cut classes, late assignments, and a barely passing average for the semester despite dropping one course. When Kryzowski senior had his second heart attack in February 1942, Art, who was already hopelessly behind in his coursework at Manitoba, spoke with his faculty advisor and dropped out of school.

Art Kryzowski's youth was all that sustained him through the next 3 years. With Kryzowski senior now partially invalided, although mentally alert, Art not only took over the leadership of the firm, but assumed the equal burden of negotiating every minor change or decision past a suddenly conservative and reluctant Kryzowski senior. In the months before the end of the war and the return of his brothers, Art learned first-hand the folly of running a firm out of one's hip pocket. Records were disorganized or absent entirely. Scheduling was nonexistent. Every supplier and nearly every customer had been demanding and receiving special concessions, and much of the machinery had been jury-rigged so many times that repairs were a nightmare. Art managed. He managed, however, only by putting in still more hours, gradually learning all the peculiarities and wrinkles of the business on a case-by-case basis, and looking forward to the day his brothers would return and share the responsibility. Having learned the hard way how overextended and harassed one can become running a business as a one-man band, Art entered into a career which for the most part emulated his father's example.

This is not to say that Art did not make any changes, or that the firm did poorly in his hands. With Mrs. Kryzowski too occupied and distraught caring for her husband, Art found it necessary to hire a full-time bookkeeper and office assistant. He wondered at times if it was the right decision, but it did free him from a lot of routine activities and brought a semblance of order to the financial records. He also engaged a general accountant to handle tax matters and give him periodic financial advice. Art was frankly surprised when he examined the financial statements. The company, despite years of seat-of-the-pants management, was financially healthy. The building, machines, and trucks were owned outright, and there were no outstanding long-term debts. The short-term picture was equally good. The company was paying salaries to himself, both parents, his brothers in absentia at reduced scales, and 18 hourly employees, and was turning a surplus, which his father had been plowing back into inventory. The inventory, in turn, secured any credit necessary to fund new purchases. Nominally valued at $30,000 in 1944, the inventory was a mixed blessing, as many of the items stocked were obsolete and unlikely to sell except as scrap. Looking forward, although little could be done under war-time conditions, the entire physical plant and truck fleet would require replacement within a few years.

The return of Carl and Alfred was initially unremarkable. Alfred was furloughed on terminal leave in July 1945, and Carl in October of the same year. Carl slid unobtrusively into his old activities in the shop, where his knowledge and energy measurably improved output. His old Navy and seaport contacts were extremely useful in obtaining war surplus tools and equipment to modernize the shop and expand the inventory. The shop and warehouse became Carl's personal domain over the years, and on a day-to-day basis he ran them well. Although his title was a more grandiose "vice-president for production," Carl was in fact a glorified foreman, referring any unusual decisions directly to Art Kryzowski.

The Post-war Years

The decision to move away from the scrap and salvage business into the provision of new and used pumps and air compressors tended to change the nature of the business. Although the company continued to stock scrap and salvage, the emphasis was on pumps, pipe, and hoses. The company became known as the source for used specialized pipe (stainless steel, copper, natural gas, and for hoses for pumping chemicals and corrosive liquids). The pumps sold and remanufactured by the company were used in the pulp and paper industry, gas transmission, chemicals, and manufacturing. Air compressors provided power for equipment in construction, manufacturing, and assembly work. The importance of pumps and air compressors to the various firms meant that a breakdown required prompt repairs. Often plants or construction sites were shut down for lack of a pump or the failure of an air compressor.

Under the direction of Art Kryzowski, the firm responded to the needs of its customers. Air compressors and large pumps were not only sold and rebuilt, but rented. A 24-hour service department was added. The company prided itself on being able to deliver new or used pumps or air compressors anywhere in the province within 24 hours. The trucking fleet was expanded. As the industries which Kryzowski and Sons served grew after the war, the company prospered along with them.

Art, although he welcomed the reduced workload made possible by Carl's return, was still more hopeful about what Alfred could do for the firm. He looked to his outgoing and imaginative older brother as someone who would be a more active managing partner and who would help to redirect and expand the firm to exploit post-war opportunities. Alfred at least verbally concurred and agreed to work as rapidly as possible into the taking over the entire marketing and customer relations function.

In a business sense, the company did well indeed. The company's reputation for quality repairs and used machines carried over into the new enterprises, often with the same customers. The building was modernized and expanded to include a showroom and a second warehouse. Sales continually grew and the firm grew with them. Over the next 30 years, the Kryzowskis pursued a conservative and prudent course, building the firm into one of the dominant forces in the regional market. The general economic decline of the late 1970s saw sales peak and then slip, but business remained both comfortable and profitable.

The firm also did well by the Kryzowski family. With the business apparently well in hand, Mr. and Mrs. Kryzowski gradually relaxed their vigilance, slipping by 1950 into unofficial retirement on very healthy executive paycheques. The Kryzowski brothers, as they acquired family responsibilities and their own children grew into their teens, also did well. At the behest of their tax accountant, a real estate subsidiary was formed to rent the Kryzowskis' homes to them, and most of their families were put on the payroll in one or another capacity. It was only when one looked at the internal dynamics of the firm, that any cause for concern might have arisen.

In that initial period of reorganization and expansion after the war, everyone was on unusually good terms. There was so much work to be done that the Kryzowski brothers all worked horrendous hours to keep the growing business together. But Art Kryzowski gradually became aware of a sense of disengagement by Alfred. Alfred dutifully made calls on all of his regular customers and took over the supervision of the one, and then three, young men Alfred and he brought in to keep up with customer relations, direct sales, and running the showroom. However, his initiative in seeking out new clients

and trying to broaden offerings gradually trailed off. Alfred spent more and more time in sales lunches with old customers and commensurately less at the office. His conversations with Art increasingly centered on taking more out of the firm. He regularly suggested bringing in bright young professional managers so that he, Art, and Carl could have more time for their families, and seemed to be as concerned with how to set up tax sheltered benefits for family members as with making the company grow. As Art put the situation in a family argument in 1974, Alfred was acting more like a paid employee and less like one of the family team, leaving Art to work ever more hours and make all of the tough, important decisions virtually on his own.

Alfred's version of the story was substantially different. Like Art, he looked back fondly on the rush and bustle of the post-war period, when everyone was too busy to worry about family politics or titles or the like. And in his off-guard moments Alfred would occasionally admit to confidants that he was not going to "kill himself" for the company, like Art. However, Alfred's major objection was the behavior of Art Kryzowski. In Alfred's terms, Art was treating the company more and more as his personal property, which had to be protected at all costs from mistakes by Alfred or Carl. He insisted that they adopt his viewpoint on all significant decisions, intervened in their deliberations with major customers, and in general acted as though he were the father and they were his teenaged, impulsive offspring. So if Art wanted to run the show, let him. Alfred was making a good living, doing a fair share of the work for what he earned and, if he felt excluded from the corridors of power, he more than compensated by a fuller family and social life.

Carl was largely oblivious to all of this, although the issue occasionally arose in family arguments. He ran his shop and ran it well. And until Art started making mistakes which hurt his shop, he would stick by him.

This process continued for years, never emerging into open confrontation, but never existing far below the surface. Art became the man who dominated the firm, made the key contacts, and met with customers. Customers called Art almost any time of the day or night when a pump failed or an air compressor broke down. During the construction season, customers often demanded immediate service, and Art grew accustomed to staying at the office for extended periods of time.

On July 17, 1980, Art Kryzowski had a fatal heart attack. He was alone in his office and was not found until the next morning. He was 59 years old.

The death of Art Kryzowski was duly noted in the local obituary column, but it did not cause much of a stir. The company closed for the funeral, and all 30 employees attended the funeral. Everyone knew Art as an intense and likeable workaholic. It was only after the funeral that Carl and Alfred looked at one another helplessly and asked each other: "What do we do with the company?"

SOURCE   Ronald L. Crawford from Harold A. Gram, *Facts & Figures: Cases in Business Policy* (Toronto: Wiley, 1982): 193–197. Reprinted by permission of the author.

QUESTIONS

1. Describe the management problems that are evident in Kryzowski and Sons Ltd.
2. Create a plan that will allow Carl and Alfred Kryzowski to remedy these problems and put the company on a solid, long-term footing.
3. What role has organization and family politics played in this company?

CASE STUDY 9

Central Decal, Ltd.

Late in the evening of January 20, 1981, Roger McIntyre sat in his hotel room in Calgary thinking about one of the most significant business decisions he had ever faced. During the last several months, McIntyre and his business partner, John Altman, owners of Central Decal, Ltd., had been having difficulties with their business. McIntyre attributed some of these difficulties to Altman. At dinner earlier in the evening, McIntyre had told Altman that either Altman had to leave the firm or he would. Altman expressed shock and surprise at this comment and asked why McIntyre felt this way. McIntyre replied that Altman's work in the finance area of the firm was completely unsatisfactory and that unless this problem was resolved the company could not survive. As he sat in his hotel room, McIntyre wondered if he had been right to give Altman the ultimatum.

Company Background

In June 1978, Roger McIntyre and Bill Merrill formed Central Decal, Ltd., a private corporation with McIntyre and Merrill as the shareholders. Each man had put $15,000 into the business. As well, they had received a $40,000 federal grant after they promised to create 11 new jobs with the money. The company manufactured four products: decals, point-of-purchase displays for retailers, displays for trade shows, and plastic forming products. Most of the sales of the firm were to retailers and manufacturers in the prairie provinces, eastern Canada, and the upper midwest in the United States.

The company has $200,000 worth of machinery (book value) in the plant. The equipment is as modern as any in western Canada. In fact, there is only one other firm in Canada that can compete with the UVSP process used at Central.

Marketing. The basic marketing problem is to avoid getting into contracts that consume significant amounts of production time but don't give much financial return. Since screen printing can be done on almost any material, there is a temptation to accept a wide diversity of jobs. Specialization and high volume in a few areas are the key to both production and marketing success. McIntyre doesn't know what the total market potential is, but the company has never had any trouble generating sales.

The marketing strategy involves both personal and mass selling. The company employs 5 industrial salesmen, including McIntyre and Altman, who are paid a salary plus bonus. The company also spends approximately $600 per month on advertising in the Yellow Pages and

EXHIBIT 1

CENTRAL DECAL, LTD.
Balance Sheet as at April 30

ASSETS

	1981	1980	1979
CURRENT ASSETS			
Cash	$ 100	–	–
Accounts receivable	235,407	$160,943	$ 62,719
Inventories	134,032	81,239	25,057
Prepaid expenses	1	626	978
	$369,540	$242,808	$ 88,754
OTHER ASSETS			
Shareholder loans receivable	–	–	$ 6,015
Development incentives grant receivable	$ 5,352	$ 5,352	$ 5,352
Deposits	–	3,521	6,868
	$ 5,352	$ 8,873	$ 18,235
FIXED ASSETS			
Equipment and leasehold improvements	$210,070	$175,761	$ 88,874
Less accumulated depreciation & amortization	57,702	31,549	7,950
	$152,368	$144,212	$ 80,924
TOTAL ASSETS	$527,260	$395,893	$187,913

LIABILITIES

	1981	1980	1979
CURRENT LIABILITIES			
Bank advances, secured by demand debenture over all assets	$198,949	$155,440	$ 76,160
Bank loan	–	58,946	–
Accounts payable and accrued liabilities	135,514	119,276	67,409
Taxes payable	13,366	10,658	4,425
Principal due within one year on long-term debt	8,002	8,002	8,002
Cheques in excess of cash on hand	45,966	–	–
	$401,797	$352,322	$155,996
LONG-TERM DEBT			
GMAC loans, payable $867 monthly including principal, interest, secured by chattel mortgages	$ 17,194	$ 24,262	$ 31,598
Less principal included in current liabilities	8,002	8,002	8,002
	$ 9,192	$ 16,260	$ 23,596
SHAREHOLDERS' LOAN	151,334	108,484	–
DEFERRED DEVELOPMENT INCENTIVES GRANT	1,784	10,706	21,413
TOTAL LIABILITIES	$564,107	$487,772	$201,005

SHARE CAPITAL & DEFICIT

	1981	1980	1979
SHARE CAPITAL	$ 63,000	$ 31,000	$ 46,000
DEFICIT	(99,847)	(122,879)	(59,092)
Excess of deficit over share capital	(36,847)	(91,879)	(13,092)
	$527,260	$395,893	$187,913

EXHIBIT 2

CENTRAL DECAL, LTD.
Statement of Profit and Loss
Year Ending April 30

	1981	1980	1979
Sales	$855,653	$583,605	$192,992
Cost of goods sold	556,174	416,032	145,781
Gross profit	$299,479	$165,573	$ 47,211
Expenses	276,447	229,360	106,303
Net profit (loss)	$ 23,032	$(63,787)	$(59,092)

elsewhere. The company does extensive direct mail advertising and regularly attends trade shows. Sales are often made to other exhibitors at trade shows. The emphasis in all these areas is on what Central can do for the customer. To demonstrate this, the company is actively involved in making up samples of their work that are relevant to a potential customer. Sales contracts are often signed after the customer sees these samples.

Finance. The relevant financial information for the company is contained in exhibits 1 and 2.

Personnel. Employees are hired if they are experienced in screen printing and if their personal interview is successful. There is no union at the company. No formal personnel testing is done. Performance appraisal is also informal. Wage rates for production workers are based on their performance and aggressiveness as determined by Roger McIntyre. Thus, workers with more seniority may make less than workers with less seniority. McIntyre feels that there will be no need to hire any production or administrative staff (excluding replacement for resignations) for at least one year.

Recent Developments

In December 1979, Bill Merrill left the business for personal reasons. Roger McIntyre was left as the only shareholder, so he began looking for someone who wanted to join the firm and share the management responsibilities. After some searching, John Altman was brought into the firm as one of the shareholders because he was both a chartered accountant and a management consultant for small business.

Central was growing very rapidly, and McIntyre felt that some financial control was necessary. Altman came into the company on the understanding that he would produce the firm's financial statements, conduct financial dealings with the bank, and share management responsibilities with McIntyre. Shortly after Altman joined the firm, however, two problems arose. First, Altman had difficulty delegating authority. As a result, many jobs were not being completed on time because Altman would not delegate the work, nor could he do it all himself. There was also some uncertainty among the workers in the company as to who they reported to — McIntyre or Altman.

Second, it became clear that Altman was actually more interested in production and marketing than he was in finance and accounting. The cash flow projections and financial statements which Altman was supposed to produce rarely got done. Relations with the bank were also less than satisfactory. In May 1980, several of Central's cheques were returned because of insufficient funds. McIntyre felt certain that Altman knew a cash flow crunch was imminent, but Altman had made no plans to cope with it. Promises had been made to the bank that they would get monthly financial reports on the firm's condition but this had not been done either. When the crunch came, Altman put about $50,000 of his own money into the business to resolve the crisis; he was able to do this because he came from a wealthy family. After this incident, McIntyre and Altman had a meeting, when it was agreed that Altman would not let this happen again. However, after about two months it became clear that finances were returning to their former disorganized state. A second meeting was held, and McIntyre basically demanded that Altman either do the job properly or get someone who could.

When the second crunch came in September 1980, Altman put in another $50,000 to resolve the problem. McIntyre felt that this behavior on Altman's part merely hid the real financial problems the firm was facing. McIntyre discovered, for example, that Altman had not increased the firm's line of credit even though monthly sales volumes had nearly tripled. Altman had not pursued further grants either, even though these were likely to be approved because the company had more than fulfilled its obligation to create a certain number of jobs with its first grant. In addition, the bank had sent a very critical report to McIntyre detailing other shortcomings in the financial affairs of the company.

After the second incident, McIntyre had reached the end of his rope. He knew that Altman would be financially solvent even if the business folded, because he was wealthy; Altman also had a CA degree which was very marketable. McIntyre, on the other hand, had nothing to fall back on. He felt that he had several alternatives: (1) buy out Altman's shares, (2) drop out of the business and sell Altman his shares, or (3) start a new screen-printing company. With regard to the first alternative, McIntyre had approached several individuals about financing who had agreed to put up $250,000 in return for being made shareholders. McIntyre could then use this money to buy Altman's shares and to put the firm on a more solid financial footing. McIntyre felt this was a very desirable alternative except that Altman probably would resist selling his shares.

With regard to option 2, McIntyre felt that Altman could not keep the business going by himself, because during the last few months Altman had been showing signs of extreme anxiety and emotional stress; also, in spite of Altman's management consulting background, McIntyre felt Altman couldn't manage the firm. McIntyre felt uncomfortable about leaving the company because he felt he had a moral obligation to not put Altman in a position which would cause him even more stress than he had been experiencing.

With regard to option 3, McIntyre was confident that he could start a new business. He also felt that many of Central's customers would bring their work to his new firm once it got started. Once again, however, he felt something of a moral obligation to Altman; the increased competition of another screen-printing company would make it even harder for Altman alone to keep Central going.

As he considered these alternatives, McIntyre had great difficulty deciding what to do. He wondered if there were other alternatives to be considered or if he should make the decision and get it over with.

SOURCE Frederick A. Starke, from Beckman, Good, and Wyckham, *Small Business Management: Concepts and Cases* (Toronto: Wiley, 1982). Reprinted by permission.

QUESTIONS

1. Assess McIntyre and Altman as managers of Central Decal.
2. How are the functions of management operating at Central Decal? Debate the possibilities that:
   a. McIntyre and Altman could split the functions to perform more effectively.
   b. McIntyre or Altman could each run the company alone.
3. As a management consultant, what would you advise McIntyre to do now? What would you advise Altman to do?

Glossary

accountability Final responsibility for results that a manager cannot delegate to anyone else.

action planning Establishment of performance objectives and standards for individuals. Requires that challenging but attainable standards be developed for the purpose of improving individual or group performance.

activity In PERT, it is the time-consuming element of a network.

activity trap The state in which personnel are so enmeshed in performing assigned functions that they lose sight of the goal or reasons for their performance.

Adult The ego state of transactional analysis that identifies the person who tends to evaluate situations and attempts to make decisions based on information and facts.

analytical skills The ability of managers to use logical and scientific approaches or techniques in the analysis of problems and business opportunities.

aptitude tests Used to determine a person's probability for success in a selected job.

arbitration Calls for outside neutral parties to assist in resolving the conflict. The arbitrator is given the authority to act as a judge in making a decision.

assessment center Designed to provide systematic evaluation of the potential of individuals for future management positions.

audit An assessment of the financial condition of a company, conducted by an external group such as a chartered accountancy firm. *See also* management audit.

authority The right to decide, to direct others to take action, or to perform certain duties in achieving organization goals.

balance sheet A financial statement that describes the company's financial position with respect to assets, liabilities, and owners' equity at a particular point in time.

barriers to communication Factors that can reduce communication effectiveness between the sender and the receiver.

behavioral management science The approach to management evolved during the last few years, which stresses the development of techniques to use people more effectively in organizations.

behavioral school of management The management concept that people are an important part of organizations.

board of directors A group of people who are given the power to govern a corporation's affairs and to make general policy; they are elected by the corporation's shareholders.

break-even analysis Approach used to determine the amount of a particular product that must be sold if the firm is to generate enough revenues to cover costs; the point at which revenues and costs are equal.

budget Formal statement of financial resources — planned expenditures of money for personnel, time, space, or equipment.

budgetary standard The accepted norm or level to which actual and planned expenditures can be compared to determine whether a budget is being met or overspent.

business firm An entity that seeks to make a profit by gathering and allocating productive resources to satisfy consumer demand.

capital budget Indicates planned capital acquisition, usually for the purpose of purchasing additional facilities or equipment.

career objectives A determination of the specific type of career that an individual desires to pursue.

centralized The type of situation in which decision-making authority is concentrated at the upper levels of the organization.

chain of command Hierarchical means by which authority flows through the formal structure from top to bottom in the organization.

change agent The person who is responsible for ensuring that the planned change in organization development is properly implemented.

channel The means by which communications are transmitted from sender to receiver.

Child The ego state of transactional analysis that identifies the person who bases decisions primarily on personal satisfaction.

classical school of management School of management thought, evolved in the late nineteenth, early twentieth centuries, which attempted to provide a rational and scientific basis for the management of organizations.

cohesiveness The degree of attraction that the group has for each of its members.

common stock Those shares showing ownership in a corporation, the holder of which has voting rights.

communication The achievement of meaning and understanding between people through verbal and nonverbal means in order to affect behavior and achieve desired results.

communication overload Exists when a sender attempts to present too much information to the receiver at one time.

communication skills The ability of a manager to provide information in oral and written form to others in an organization for the purpose of achieving desired results.

comparison controls Used to determine whether deviations from plans have taken place and, if necessary, to bring them to the attention of the responsible managers.

compensation All rewards which individuals receive as a result of their employment.

conceptual skills The ability of the manager to understand the complexities of the overall organization and how each department or unit fits into it.

conflict Discord caused by behavior by a person or group that is purposely designed to inhibit the attainment of goals by another person or group.

conflict management As an aid to communication, has the ability to resolve disagreements between individuals within the organization that could have an adverse effect on attainment of organization goals.

consideration The extent to which leaders have

relationships with subordinates characterized by mutual trust, respect, and consideration of employees' ideas and feelings.

contact chart Identifies the informal connections that an individual has with other members of the organization.

control The established standard against which actual performance is compared for the purpose of taking action to correct deviations.

control charts Record or measure the progress of actual performance during operations.

controlling The basic management function that compares results achieved to planned goals.

controlling process Involves establishment of standards and tolerances, comparison of performance to standards, and taking of corrective action.

coordination The integration of the basic management functions of planning, organizing, influencing, and controlling.

corporate bylaws The rules by which the corporation is run.

corporate culture The psychological atmosphere of an organization.

corporation An artificial organization, existing only in contemplation of law, that is composed of shareholders, managers, employees, and a board of directors.

Counselling Assistance to Small Enterprises (CASE) Federal government program to aid small business, which uses retired business executives to give management consulting advice.

critical path In PERT and CPM, it is the longest path from start to finish of a project.

critical path method (CPM) A network control technique developed by industry. Only one time estimate is used, thereby making the network a deterministic model.

cyclical demand patterns Variations in market demand that fluctuate around the long-run trend line. A cycle typically is 2 to 3 years in duration. Used in forecasting.

decentralized The type of situation in which decision-making authority has been delegated to lower levels in the organization.

decision maker The person who has the responsibility for choosing the course of action that will solve a problem or take advantage of an opportunity within the area for which he or she is accountable.

decision making The process by which managers evaluate alternatives and make a choice among them to solve a problem or take advantage of an opportunity.

decision-making skill A manager's skill in selecting a course of action designed to solve a specific problem or take advantage of an unplanned opportunity.

decoding Converting communication symbols into a message; it requires a receiver to determine what the sender meant.

delegation The process of granting specific work assignments to individuals within the organization and providing them with the right or power to perform these functions.

demand forecasting An attempt to estimate the demand for a firm's products.

departmentation The structural grouping of related functions or major work activities into manageable units to achieve more effective and efficient overall coordination of organizational resources.

disciplinary action The process of invoking a penalty against an employee who fails to adhere to standards.

divisional structure An organizational structure composed of divisions, in which each division performs all the functions necessary for it to reach its objectives. Each division operates as a profit center.

economic function Businesses' production of needed goods and services, provision of employment, contribution to economic growth, and earning of profit.

economic objectives Goals of a firm associated with survival, profit, and growth.

empathy The ability to identify with the various feelings and thoughts of another person.

employment application Form that collects objective, biographical information about an applicant, such as education, work experience, special skills, general background, and references.

employment requisition Issued whenever a job becomes available, it is the result of an analysis of a company's personnel requirements.

encoding Putting a communications message in a form that the receiver can understand.

entrepreneur A person who has the ability to create an ongoing enterprise where none existed before.

E-R-G Theory Motivation theory developed by Alderfer that attempts to make Maslow's theory more consistent with knowledge of human needs. Alderfer's classification of needs is *E*xistence, *R*elatedness, and *G*rowth.

ethical dilemmas Situations involving questionable moral issues that confront managers and are often difficult to resolve or avoid.

ethics Contemporary standards or principles of conduct that govern the actions and behavior of individuals within the organization.

event In PERT, it is a meaningful specified accomplishment (physical or intellectual) in the program plan, recognizable at a particular instance of time.

executive burnout The state of a manager brought about by devotion to a cause, way of life, or relationships that failed to produce the expected reward, often characterized by exhaustion and frustration.

expectancy An individual's perception of the chances or probability that a particular outcome will occur as a result of certain behavior.

expectancy theory Attempts to explain behavior in terms of an individual's goals, choices, and the expectations of achieving those goals.

expected time In PERT, it is calculated by using a formula consisting of 3 time estimates: optimistic, most likely, and pessimistic.

exponential smoothing Technique using the forecast from the previous period, the actual demand that resulted from this forecast period, and a smoothing constant.

external environment Factors outside the organization (legal, social, political, and economic) that can affect the firm.

feedback Tells the sender of a communication message whether it was properly decoded and acted on by the receiver.

Fiedler's contingency model Suggests that there is no one most effective style that is appropriate to every situation.

filtering Attempts to alter or edit information to present a more favorable message.

financial assistance programs Various forms of financial assistance to small businesses, on a provincial or federal level.

financial budget Indicates the amount of capital the organization will need and where it will obtain the capital.

forecasting An attempt to project what will occur in the future of an organization.

franchising Establishment of a small business through a contract between a manufacturer and a dealer that stipulates how the manufacturer's products or services will be sold.

Friedman's view of corporate social responsibility Businesses have one and only one social responsibility: to earn maximum profits for their shareholders.

functional authority The authority derived from a staff position that has direct line authority over specialized functions or activities.

functionalization The structural process of splitting and differentiating functions as an organization expands.

functional similarity Work that is similar in content and activity is grouped together.

functional structure Departments are structured formally on the basis of the key functions an organization must perform in order to reach its objectives.

functions Work activities that can be identified and distinguished from other work, such as production, marketing, research, and finance.

grapevine The informal means by which information is transmitted in an organization.

group Two or more people who join together to accomplish a desired organization goal.

health An employee's physical and mental well being.

Hersey and Blanchard's situational leadership theory Theory based on the notion that the most effective leadership style varies according to the level of maturity of the followers and the demands of the situation.

hierarchy of needs Maslow's theory that human needs such as psychological, safety, social, esteem, and self-actualization are arranged in a hierarchy.

horizontal differentiation The creation of different departments at the same structural level in an organization.

host country Country where a multinational company is operating away from its home base.

host country nationals Personnel in an MNC from the host country.

hygiene factors According to Frederick Herzberg, the factors include pay, status, and working conditions.

hypothesis A tentative statement of the nature of existing relationships.

income statement A financial statement that shows the company's financial performance over a period of time — usually one year.

influencing The basic management function of motivating and leading personnel.

informal relationships Are created, not by officially designated managers but, by any and all organizational members.

informal work group A group of people who join together to accomplish mutually satisfying organization goals.

initial controls Monitor the resources — material, human, and capital — that come into the organization for the purpose of ensuring that they can be used effectively to achieve organization objectives.

initiating The extent to which leaders establish goals and define and structure their roles and the roles of subordinates toward the attainment of the goals.

innovative objectives Concerned with unique or special accomplishments, such as the development of new methods or procedures.

inputs Human (employees) or nonhuman resources, energies, supplies, and information, processed within an organization to create planned outputs.

interview Face-to-face method of assessing the qualifications of job applicants.

intuition Insight acquired through experience and accomplishment rather than through a formal decision-making process.

inventory Stored goods or materials available for use by a business.

iron law of responsibility States that, if business firms are to retain their social power and role, they must be responsive to society's needs.

job analysis Process of determining the responsibilities and operations of a job leading to the development of a job description.

job description Summarizes the purpose, principal duties, and responsibilities of a job.

job design The process of altering the nature and structure of a job for the purpose of increasing productivity.

job enlargement A horizontal expansion of duties that involves an increase in the number of tasks an employee is required to perform.

job enrichment Refers to basic changes in the content and level of responsibility of a job to provide additional satisfaction of the motivation needs of personnel.

job specification Statement of the minimum acceptable human qualities necessary to perform the job.

just-in-time inventory system Inventory system developed in Japan, in which supplies arrive just in time to be used in the production process. Cuts down on the need for inventory storage, but requires accurate delivery schedules.

leader-member relations According to Fiedler, the degree to which the leader feels accepted by the subordinates.

leadership The process of influencing the behavior and actions of others toward the accomplishment of goals.

leadership continuum As developed by Tannenbaum and Schmidt, suggests that choosing an effective leadership style depends on the demands of the situation. The continuum ranges from boss-centered, autocratic management to subordinate-centered, participative management.

leadership decision-making model Vroom and Yetton's model, based on the idea that a leader must decide how much participation subordinates should be allowed when making decisions.

Likert's system of management Universal theory of leadership consisting of a continuum of styles ranging from autocratic to participative.

line and staff organization Type of structure that makes provision for the use of staff specialists who provide advice to line managers.

line organization Structure that shows the direct, vertical relationships between different levels within the firm.

listening One of the most effective tools in communication, it entails active participation in hearing what type of communication the sender is attempting to transmit.

lower-level managers Usually referred to as supervisors or foremen, they are responsible for managing employees in the performance of daily operations.

management The process of planning, organizing, influencing, and controlling to accomplish organization goals through the coordinated use of human and material resources.

management audit Is used to assess systematically the strengths and weaknesses of the managerial talent in an organization.

management by exception The general management of an area of responsibility, not detailed supervision of each worker.

management by objectives (MBO) A systematic and organized approach that allows management to attain maximum results from available resources by focusing on achievable goals.

management development programs Techniques used to help managers learn more effective approaches to management.

management hierarchy The chain of command in an organization, which can be used as a control device.

management information system (MIS) A means by which managers obtain timely, accurate, and useful information.

managerial code of ethics Provides guidelines and standards for conduct of managers.

managerial grid Leadership theory developed by Blake and Mouton that depicts 5 primary styles of leadership described according to the leader's concern for people and production.

mathematical model An equation or set of equations that defines and represents the relationship among elements of a system.

matrix organization The structure created when a temporary project structure is continued on a more permanent basis; it is used when a firm must be responsive to rapidly changing external environment conditions.

mediation Assistance in resolving organization conflict from outside neutral parties.

microcomputer The smallest computers.

middle managers Between supervisors and top managers, they are concerned primarily with the coordination of programs and activities necessary to achieve the overall goals of the organization.

minicomputers Computers a step above microcomputers that are larger and more powerful.

model An abstraction of a real situation.

most likely time In PERT, it is the most realistic completion time for an activity.

motivation The process of influencing or stimulating a person to take action by creating a work atmosphere wherein the goals of the organization and the needs of the person are satisfied.

motivators According to Herzberg, these consist of factors intrinsic to the job, such as recognition, responsibility, achievement, and opportunities for growth and advancement.

motives Why people engage in certain behavior. They are the drives or impulses within an individual that cause behavior.

moving averages Forecasting technique for smoothing the effects of random variation.

multinational company A firm engaged in business in 2 or more countries.

need for achievement According to McClelland, the need for achievement is concerned with an individual's desire for excellence.

need for affiliation According to McClelland, this need is concerned with the desire for affection and establishing friendly relationships.

need for power According to McClelland, this need is concerned with an individual's desire for influence and control over others.

nepotism The practice of hiring relatives.

network A control approach through which the various interdependencies of a project may be studied. *See* critical path method *and* program evaluation and review technique.

noise Those personality, perceptual, and attitudinal differences in individuals which reduce their ability to communicate effectively.

nonroutine decisions Those decisions that are designed to deal with unusual problems or situations.

norms Standard of behavior that is expected from group members.

not-for-profit organizations Organizations that do not pursue profit as a goal; they generally have service goals instead.

objectives The results a person or organization wants to accomplish.

obsolescence The state of products or services that are no longer useful or as efficient as they once were.

Ohio state leadership studies Detailed studies of the behavior of leaders in a wide variety of organizations.

operations management The application of management functions to the inputs, processes, and outputs of business organizations, whether they are producing physical goods or intangible services.

optimistic time In PERT, the time in which a project can be completed, if everything goes right and nothing goes wrong.

organization Two or more people working together in a coordinated manner to achieve group results.

organizational structure Framework for providing a pattern for organizing the formal relationships of responsibility, authority, and accountability.

organization behavior modification Rests on the concepts that people act in ways they find most personally rewarding and, by controlling the rewards, organizations can shape and determine people's behavior.

organization development A planned and calculated attempt to move the organization as a unit from one state to another, typically to a more participative culture.

organizing The basic management function that uses allocation of resources and establishment of the means to accomplish plans.

orientation The process of introducing the new employee to the organization.

outputs The products and/or services that are the result of the conversion process in an organization.

overseeing controls Monitor the actual creation of products or services, these controls are accomplished largely by observation and by conference between supervisor and subordinate while the actual work activities are being performed.

Parent   The ego state in transactional analysis that identifies the person who bases decisions primarily on what the individual has heard or learned in the past.

parent country   Home base or headquarters for a multinational firm.

parent country nationals   Personnel in a multinational from the parent country.

participative culture   An open type of culture characterized by trust in subordinates, openness in communication, considerate and supportive leadership, group problem solving, worker autonomy, information sharing, and establishment of high output goals.

partnership   A form of business that comes into being when two or more individuals agree to combine their financial, managerial, and technical abilities for the purpose of earning a profit.

Path-Goal Leadership Theory   Developed by House, this theory stresses that managers can facilitate job performance by showing employees how their performance directly affects them in receiving rewards.

payoff relationships   Situations in which costs or profits of various courses of action and benefits that may be obtained can be measured.

people skills   The ability of a manager to work with and get along with other people.

perception sets   Differences in individuals' background and experience that may result in different meanings and interpretations being associated with various words or phrases.

performance appraisal   An evaluation of employees that determines how well they are performing their assigned tasks.

performance results standards   Standards that are straightforward to measure accurately used to specify what results are required.

personal development objectives   Goals that provide the opportunity for each individual to state his or her personal goals and action plans for self-improvement and for personal growth and development.

personal objectives   Goals of individuals who are employed by the firm.

personnel planning   Determination in advance of how many workers and what kinds of skills are needed to accomplish the firm's objectives.

pessimistic time   In PERT, it is the time in which a project can be completed if everything goes wrong and nothing goes right.

physical models   Models that look like the system they represent.

physical resources   Materials, equipment, and money required to accomplish the objectives of the organization.

planning   Determination of what is to be achieved.

planning process   Determination of the objectives and courses of action needed to achieve them.

planning-programming budgeting system (PPBS)   A budgetary aid to management in identifying and eliminating costly duplicative programs and in providing a means for the careful analysis of the benefits and costs of each program or activity.

plans   Specifications for the manner in which objectives are to be accomplished.

policies   The predetermined general guide established to provide direction in decision making.

politics   A network of interaction by which power is acquired, transferred, and exercised when dealing with others.

power   The ability of one person to influence the behavior of another person.

preferred stock   Those shares showing ownership in a corporation, holders of which generally do not have voting rights.

preliminary screening interview   Used to eliminate obviously unqualified applicants for such reasons as excessive salary requirements, inadequate education, or lack of job-related experience.

problem content   Includes the situation within which the problem exists, the decision maker's knowledge of that situation, as well as the situation that will exist after a choice is made.

problem-solving objectives   Goals that are established to deal with special projects or situations that need management attention.

procedure A series of steps established for the accomplishment of some specific project or endeavor.

process consultation A set of activities on the part of the consultant which help a client to perceive, understand, and act on process events that occur in the client's organization.

process standards Standards that attempt to evaluate a function for which accurate measurements are difficult or impossible to quantify.

production The conversion of inputs into outputs, which results in the creation of goods and services.

professional decision maker A person who uses the best features of both the intuitive and research approach in the decision-making process.

profit The difference between the costs of inputs and the revenue from outputs.

profit center A department or division in an organization that is given the responsibility of making a profit.

program evaluation and review technique (PERT) A network control technique developed by the U.S. Navy that is used to think through a project in its entirety. Three time estimates are used, which permit the user to develop probabilities of occurrences.

progressive discipline Efforts made to make the penalty appropriate to the violation(s).

project organization Temporary organizational structure designed to achieve specific results by using a team of specialists from different functional areas within the organization.

quality The degree of conformity to a certain predetermined standard.

quality circles Groups of employees who meet periodically to brainstorm ways to improve the quality and quantity of their work.

quality control Technique that measures the degree of conformity according to form, dimension, composition, and/or color.

quantity control An established standard in terms of volume or numbers.

random demand No pattern to consumer sales. Occurs for reasons managers cannot explain.

ratio analysis An assessment of a firm's performance made by taking two financial figures from the balance sheet or income statement and dividing one figure by the other.

reactive planning Flexibility of a planner to be able to respond to changing external and internal conditions.

receiver Individual who interprets the communication signals from a sender through such means as listening, observing, and reading.

recruiting Encouragement for individuals with the needed skills to make application for employment with a firm.

regression analysis A quantitative technique that is used to predict one item through knowledge of other variables.

reinforcement theory Concerned with the way in which behavior is learned — the result of either positive or negative consequences.

reinforcers Rewards used in organization behavior modification.

reliability Concerned with the degree of consistency of test results.

repatriation plan A statement about the length of an assignment a multinational executive will have in a foreign country and the kind of position that executive will have when he or she returns to Canada.

responsibility An obligation of personnel to perform certain work activities.

résumé A written description that a job applicant provides to a prospective employer with such information as career objectives, education, work experience, and other biographical data.

risk The probability that a particular decision will have an adverse effect on the company.

role The total pattern of expected behavior, interactions, and sentiments of an individual.

routine decisions Daily decisions made by managers that are governed by policies, procedures, and rules of the organization, as well as the personal habits of the manager.

routine objectives Goals that represent recurring day-to-day activities that are expected to be performed. They represent standards of performance.

rule A specific and detailed guide to action that is set up to direct or restrict action in a fairly narrow manner.

safety Protection of employees from injuries caused by work-related accidents.

schematic models Line drawings, flow charts, graphs, maps, organizational charts, and similar items that represent the major features of a particular system.

scientific approach Based on a systematic, formal approach to decision making.

scientific management The concept that management is a process in which the scientific method could be used.

seasonal demand Demand patterns in a shorter timeframe than cyclical, typically 12 months.

selection The process of identifying those recruited individuals who will best be able to assist the firm in achieving organization goals.

self-fulfilling prophecy What one expects to happen actually occurs. A manager's expectations often determine employee performance.

semantics Relating to different meanings for one word — often leading to misunderstandings between sender and receiver that cause communication breakdowns.

sender The source of a communication message.

sensitivity training Technique used to develop awareness of sensitivity to oneself and others.

service objectives The reason that a firm is in business as viewed by society.

Seven S model A model that attempts to identify what makes an enterprise successful or unsuccessful; factors include: strategy, structure, systems, staff, skills, style, and superordinate goals.

shareholders Persons who own the common and preferred shares of a corporation.

single accountability The concept that each person should be answerable to only one immediate supervisor — one boss to each employee.

situational approach The ability to adapt to meet particular circumstances and constraints that a firm may encounter.

small business A business that is independently owned and operated and is not dominant in its field.

social audit A commitment to systematic assessment of and reporting on some meaningful, definable domain of a company's activities that have social impact.

socialization The gradual change of attitudes and behavior of an individual so that he or she fits into a society or an organization.

social responsibility A firm's obligation to constituent groups in society other than shareholders, and beyond that prescribed by law or union contract.

sole proprietorship A business owned and managed by one person.

span of management The limit to the number of employees a manager can effectively supervise.

specialization of labor Division of functions into small work activities.

staffing process Involves planning for future personnel requirements, recruiting individuals, and selecting from those recruited individuals employees who fulfill the needs of the firm.

standard A norm, or criterion, to which something can be compared.

state of nature Refers to the various situations that could occur and the probability of each happening.

statistical quality control Technique that allows for a portion of the total number of items to be inspected.

status A person's rank or position in a group.

status symbol A visible, external sign of a person's position in society or in an organization.

strategic control points Critical areas that must be monitored if the organization's overall objectives are to be achieved.

strategic planning The determination of how

the organization objectives will be achieved. Primarily accomplished by top-level management.

stress The nonspecific response of the body to any demands made on it.

structure The manner in which the internal environment of the firm is organized or arranged formally.

survey feedback The systematic collection and measurement of subordinate attitudes through anonymous questionnaires.

synergism The whole is greater than the sum of its parts. When 2 or more people work together, they can often produce more than if each worked separately.

system An arrangement of interrelated parts designed to achieve objectives.

systems approach A concept that facilitates a manager's ability to perform the major functions of management and to respond effectively to external environment factors. Through the systems approach, a manager is better able to understand and work with the various units within the organization to interrelate and coordinate the accomplishment of the goals of the firm.

task behavior Behavior of the manager designed to provide direction and emphasis on getting the job done.

task structure The extent to which goals are clearly defined and solutions to problems are known.

team building A conscious effort to develop effective work groups throughout an organization.

team objectives Established in group meetings to provide overall direction and coordination of action of a group or division.

technical skill Ability of a manager to use specific knowledge, methods or techniques in performing work.

technology All of the skills, knowledge, methods, and equipment required to convert resources into desired products and services.

telecommuting Computer hookups in a home from an office.

testing Process of screening job applicants in terms of skills, abilities, aptitudes, interests, personality, and attitudes.

Theory X Traditional philosophy of human nature, suggests that motivation of employees requires managers to coerce, control, or threaten employees in order to achieve maximum results.

Theory Y A theory of human nature that provides an alternative to Theory X, Theory Y suggests that people are capable of being responsible and mature.

Theory Z Label for the type of company that creates a strong relationship between management and workers. The company demonstrates great responsibility toward its workers, and the workers in turn show great loyalty to the company.

third country nationals Personnel in multinationals from countries other than the parent or host countries.

time series analysis Mathematical approach in which the independent variable is expressed in units of time.

time standard Monitoring of the time required to complete the project.

timing Selecting the most appropriate time to transmit a message.

top management Referred to by such titles as president, chief executive officer, vice-president, or executive director, these managers are responsible for providing the overall direction of the firm.

training and developing Programs designed to assist individuals, groups, and the entire organization to become more efficient.

trait approach Study of leadership that focuses on leader's physical, intellectual, and personal characteristics.

transactional analysis (TA) A method that assists individuals in understanding both themselves and the people with whom they work. TA consists of three ego states that are constantly present and at work within each individual: the Parent, the Adult, and the Child.

trend line Used to project the long-run estimate of the demand for the product being evaluated.

union   A group of employees who have joined together for the purpose of presenting a united front in dealing with management.

valence   How much value an individual places on a specific goal or result he or she is seeking.

validity   Concerned with the relationship between the score on the test and performance on the job. Questions whether the test measures what it was intended to measure.

vertical differentiation   The creation of multiple levels of authority and activity in an organization. Work at one level may be managerial, while at another level may be operative.

work-force analysis   Process of identifying the skills of current personnel to determine if work loads can be accomplished by these employees.

work-load analysis   Process of estimating the type and volume of work that need to be performed if the organization is to achieve its objectives.

work simplification   Organizes jobs into small, highly specialized components.

zero base budgeting   (ZBB)   A budgetary system that requires management to take a fresh look at all programs and activities each year, rather than merely to build on last year's budget.

Index

Numbers in Italic type indicate that subject can be found in two-column text, for instance, in "Management in Practice" inserts.